T0113647

Praise for Ernest B. Furgurson's

FREEDOM RISING

"A beautiful book. Every sentence, every paragraph is rich with history and the detailed rush of events, peopled with the greatest leader we have ever had. . . . Add the spies, scoundrels, hookers, pussyfooters and the embryonic capital's ten-inch-deep mud and manure, and you have this nation's greatest drama, wonderfully woven by Pat Furgurson."   —Hugh Sidey, author of *John F. Kennedy, President* and
A Very Personal Presidency: Lyndon Johnson in the White House

"The excellence of *Reveille in Washington* served to intimidate historians for decades, but no longer. . . . Furgurson has written a book worthy to stand alongside [it]."   —*The Washington Times*

"A great story, admirably told. . . . A mighty good book."
—*St. Louis Post-Dispatch*

"Furgurson exposes the cutthroat politics of our nation's capital during America's darkest period. . . . [He] brings the people and places to life.   —*The Indianapolis Star*

"A remarkable story . . . recounted remarkably well. . . . Furgurson deftly ties Civil War locations to their modern sites. He offers a wealth of vignettes that move the narrative along. . . . A fine book . . . [and] an enjoyable read."   —*Civil War News*

"[Furgurson's] writing [is] as skillful as could be expected of a man who has devoted his life to the art. . . . A well-founded, well-told chronicle that is not likely to be challenged for many years to come."
—*The Roanoke Times*

"Fascinating. . . . Furgurson lives up to his reputation as a superb storyteller. . . . [A] beautifully written history."   —*Huntington News*

"Highly recommended. . . . [Furgurson] deserves great praise."
—*The Milford Daily News*

ALSO BY ERNEST B. FURGURSON

Not War But Murder: Cold Harbor 1864
Ashes of Glory: Richmond at War
Chancellorsville 1863: The Souls of the Brave
Hard Right: The Rise of Jesse Helms
Westmoreland: The Inevitable General

Ernest B. Furgurson

FREEDOM RISING

Ernest B. "Pat" Furgurson, formerly a correspondent and columnist for *The Baltimore Sun*, has spent most of his life in the nation's capital. A native of Virginia, he is also the author of *Chancellorsville 1863*, *Ashes of Glory*, and *Not War But Murder*. He lives in Washington, D.C.

FREEDOM RISING

*Washington in the
Civil War*

Ernest B. Furgurson

VINTAGE CIVIL WAR LIBRARY
Vintage Books
A Division of Random House, Inc.
New York

FIRST VINTAGE CIVIL WAR LIBRARY EDITION, NOVEMBER 2005

Copyright © 2004 by Ernest B. Furgurson

All rights reserved. Published in the United States by Vintage Books, a division of Random House, Inc., New York, and in Canada by Random House of Canada Limited, Toronto. Originally published in hardcover in the United States by Alfred A. Knopf, a division of Random House, Inc., New York, in 2004.

Vintage is a registered trademark and Vintage Civil War Library and colophon are trademarks of Random House, Inc.

The Library of Congress has cataloged the Knopf edition as follows:
Furgurson, Ernest B., 1929–
Freedom rising : Washington in the Civil War / Ernest B. Furgurson.—1st ed.
p. cm.
Includes bibliographical references (p.).
1. Washington (D.C.)—History—Civil War, 1861–1865.   2. Washington (D.C.)—Biography.
3. Lincoln, Abraham, 1809–1865.   4. Washington (D.C.)—History—Civil War,
1861–1865—Social aspects.   5. United States—History—Civil War, 1861–1865—
Social aspects.   I. Title.
E501.F87   2004
973.7′092′2753—dc22
2004040820

Vintage ISBN-10: 0-375-70409-4
Vintage ISBN-13: 978-0-375-70409-3

Author photograph © Thomas N. Bethell
Book design by Anthea Lingeman

www.vintagebooks.com

146122990

For my father,
who deeply loved his country

CONTENTS

Washington is full of ghosts, the looming spirits of giants and pygmies who have led, misled, betrayed and saved our country. For most of my life I have lived and worked surrounded by them, and I have never spent a day without sensing their presence.

My first assignment here was to cover the Senate. As I watched Paul Douglas and Barry Goldwater, Hubert Humphrey and Richard Russell debate civil rights and war, I could not help but hear echoes of Charles Sumner and Jefferson Davis, William Seward and Judah Benjamin in the days when those issues literally split the nation. In March 1965, looking down from the House gallery onto Lyndon Johnson as he made his memorable "We shall overcome" speech on voting rights, I could picture the uncompromising abolitionist Thaddeus Stevens listening and saying, "About time." Many times, sitting waiting for the president to appear in the East Room of the White House, I have envisioned Jim Lane's volunteer militia camping there in those nervous weeks when the Confederate army was expected to march in at any time.

The day I was married in St. John's Church on Lafayette Square, and in later years when attending too many funerals there, I have imagined beside me all the presidents, beginning with Madison, who worshiped in those pews, bowing in prayer for guidance. From the roof of the Hay-Adams Hotel, near the site where the society widow Rose O'Neal Greenhow lived, I have looked over the White House down the Potomac, the same line of sight along which Lincoln peered through his telescope at the secessionist flag flying over Alexandria. For years, my office was in the National Press Building—on the same stretch of Fourteenth Street that was once called Newspaper Row—overlooking the Willard Hotel, direct descendant of the Willard's that Nathaniel Hawthorne said was "the center of Washington and the Union" during the Civil War.

Ford's Theater on Tenth Street is properly a shrine, and every time I have stepped inside it, I have been moved. But that feeling caught me by surprise the night I saw the brassy musical *The Hot Mikado* performed on the stage to which John Wilkes Booth vaulted after murdering the president. Some might have been offended seeing such irreverent song and dance performed there beneath the presidential box, which is still draped with flags as it was that night in 1865. But I believe that if the Great Emancipator were looking on, he would have been pleased. A devoted theatergoer, Lincoln had applauded many a comedian and tragedian at Ford's, including the man who would later assassinate him. Perhaps the sight of black and white actors making bright music together, and a cosmopolitan audience from all over America so clearly captivated by the performance, would have been more proof to him that he had not died in vain.

However momentous the national crises of our own lifetime, the emergency the Union faced from 1860 to 1865 was graver than any other in the history of our country. Here in Washington, as on the battlefield, that mortal crisis was confronted and defeated. Over decades, my intention to write about the history surrounding me grew into a need and then a compulsion. For just as long, I and many other writers were scared off that effort by the fact that an excellent book about Washington at war had been done, seemingly leaving little else to say on the subject. That book was Margaret Leech's *Reveille in Washington,* justly praised in its time. But since that time, more than sixty years ago, thousands of letters and memoirs left by major and minor participants have come down from attics and been unearthed in repositories. From them we have learned more not only about grand political and military decisions, but also about hidden plots and the private lives of both heroes and villains. For this book, I have sought new material on the familiar figures of the Civil War and brought in other important but unfamiliar men and women, black and white—a supporting cast that enriches our understanding of the politicians and soldiers who dominate the history textbooks. They include architects and courtesans, detectives and embezzlers, feminists and fugitives, inventors and newly freed slaves, teenagers and octogenarians, spies for the Union and for the Confederacy—all of them necessary to the epic story of Washington at war.

Many of these documents illustrate the casual racism and religious prejudice of the nineteenth century, and this would not be a realistic account of the time if all such language were edited out. But I have omitted much more than I have included. Some readers of *Ashes of Glory,* my book about Richmond at war, have wondered whether I was disclosing a prejudice of my own by sometimes using the word "Yankees" to describe Union soldiers. If so, the bias was unconscious;

during my childhood in southside Virginia, everyone I knew referred to citizens from north of the Potomac as Yankees. No doubt there was resentment in the name when our Confederate great-grandparents used it, but most of that wore off with the years. For my generation, it was a slur only when accompanied by an adjective. Today, "Yankee" is probably less pejorative than "Rebel," when the latter is used as a synonym for Southerners. I employ both terms without intending insult in either direction. It is simply a way of avoiding repetition of Union vs. Confederate; furthermore, it reflects the way people talked at the time.

My appreciation goes to Robert E. L. Krick and Scott Hartwig at the Richmond and Gettysburg National Battlefield Parks, Michael Musick and Budge Weidman at the National Archives, William C. Allen, architectural historian of the Capitol, and the helpful staffs of the institutions mentioned in the source notes following the text. I am also thankful to Jim Lehrer, Nathan Miller and Richard Moe for much needed encouragement during a low point in this long-running project, and am deeply grateful to Thomas N. Bethell and Benjamin F. Cooling for their close reading of the manuscript, and the valuable advice they offered. Such friends are beyond price. This is the fourth book on which I have worked with Ashbel Green, my editor at Alfred A. Knopf, and, as always, it has been a pleasure. I appreciate the easy relationship I have enjoyed with him and his associates, including Luba Ostashevsky, Victoria Pearson, Anthea Lingeman, and Carol Carson, as well as with the superbly scrupulous copy editor, Fred Wiemer, and my literary agent, David Black. Finally, neither the first nor the last word of this book would have been written without the unwavering patience and support of Cassie Thompson Furgurson.

Ernest B. Furgurson
Washington, January 1, 2004

Balloonist's View of Washington in 1861

FREEDOM RISING

Freedom Triumphant

I n early 1856, the American sculptor Thomas Crawford sent from his studio in Rome his first drawings of a statue to be erected atop the planned new dome of the United States Capitol. An Irish-American New Yorker, Crawford had spent nearly half his forty-three years in Rome, deeply influenced by classical works as he perfected his art and carried out commissions from both sides of the Atlantic. His grandest project had been the towering horseback statue of George Washington for Virginia's Capitol Square in Richmond, a figure whose image would later become the official seal of the Confederate States of America. To crown the Capitol in Washington, he chose symbols that drew on deep reserves of patriotism. He was proud of his concept: "I have endeavored to represent Freedom triumphant—in Peace and War. In her left hand she holds the olive branch, while the right hand rests on a sword which sustains the Shield of the United States. These emblems are such as the mass of our people will easily understand."

That was all very well, said the secretary of war in Washington. However, on its head the proposed figure wore a liberty cap, a symbol handed down from Roman times that he understood too well. That cap is recognized everywhere as "the badge of the freed slave," he reminded Crawford—and thus "its history renders it inappropriate to a people who were born free and would not be enslaved. . . .

"Why should not armed Liberty wear a helmet?"

By order of President Franklin Pierce, the War Department was in charge of civil works in Washington, and the secretary of war at the time was once and future U.S. Senator Jefferson Davis of Mississippi. His objection to the liberty cap prevailed, foreshadowing his later deeds that would vastly enlarge upon mere dislike of anything that suggested freeing slaves. After unsuccessfully proposing a laurel wreath instead, the sculptor Crawford bowed to Davis. He changed the cap to a helmet, topped by an eagle's head crested with Indian feathers—which the Capitol's architect would later call "the buzzard."

In the months after he revised his drawing, Crawford created a full-scale plaster model of the Freedom figure. He urged that the statue be cast in bronze by German artisans rather than taking the chance of sending the fragile model across the Atlantic for casting in America. As this slow transoceanic exchange of messages with Washington went on, Crawford's vision was dimmed by a tumor growing behind one eye. After an exploratory operation, he went to Paris for treatment, and before the question of where to cast the statue was settled, he died in London. Six months later, in April 1858, his widow followed orders from Washington, had the plaster model crated in five sections, and dispatched it across the Atlantic.

From conception to eventual delivery, casting, erection and dedication, the course of that symbol of freedom sometimes seemed as bedeviled by politics, personalities and the elements as the birth of freedom itself. Between the time when Crawford offered his first drawing and the arrival of his model in the United States, James Buchanan had been elected president; Chief Justice Roger B. Taney had handed down the Supreme Court's Dred Scott decision, ruling essentially that slaves had no legal rights; Congress had struggled over whether to admit Kansas as a slave state; Abraham Lincoln and Stephen Douglas had debated slavery across Illinois; and the 1858 congressional elections had assured that deeper conflict was coming.

The bark *Emily Taylor,* with Crawford's model of Freedom carefully stowed below, sailed from Leghorn on April 19, 1858. On her third day at sea, she sprang a leak, and her captain decided to put into Gibraltar for repairs. On June 26, she departed Gibraltar for New York, but promptly struck heavy storms, and started leaking again on July 1. In another eleven days, she was taking on water at a frightful rate. Desperate to lighten her load, the crew jettisoned 117 bales of rags and four dozen cases of citron, and on the following day threw another 133 bales overboard. By July 27, the leak had increased, and two days later the *Emily Taylor* was forced to make an emergency stop at Bermuda. Surveys showed she was beyond repair; her cargo was brought ashore and stowed, and the vessel was condemned and sold.

The New York agents commissioned to bring the model to America chartered another ship, the bark *G. W. Horton,* especially for the purpose, and in December 1858 she reached Manhattan with some but not all of the plaster Freedom. The last sections did not arrive until March 1859, when they were shipped from New York to Washington by the schooner *Statesman,* arriving three weeks short of a year after the model had departed Italy.[1]

When the complete model finally reached Washington, all eighteen feet nine inches of it were assembled for temporary display in the Capitol's unused old House Chamber. From that resting place to Freedom's eventual perch atop the building's new dome was less than three hundred vertical feet, but reaching that height would take much longer than the adventurous voyage across the ocean. In fact, the majestic dome itself did not exist yet, and no one knew whether the nation would hold together until it was built. Month by month, the capital watched the erratic progress of its construction, until its stops and starts became a public barometer of the Union's determination to endure, and the prospect of seeing the statue of Freedom on high inspired hope that something grander than simple survival lay ahead.

CHAPTER ONE

God Alone Can Avert the Storm

B urn the building! Burn it down!"
Hiding on the roof of the ransacked Tremont House, three
blocks from the United States Capitol, a handful of scared
young Lincolnites peeked down at the shouting mob in the street, sure
that they were in mortal danger.

All that fall of 1860, boisterous Republicans who called themselves
"Wide-Awakes" had marched along the avenues of other northern
cities in black oilcloth capes and caps, waving torches and carrying
fence rails to show their enthusiasm for their candidate, the Great
Rail-Splitter. But in Washington, surrounded by Southern partisans,
they had kept quiet until the last weeks of the presidential campaign,
when Abraham Lincoln's victory seemed more and more likely. Then,
sure that history was with them, some 500 paraded openly, with a few
blacks tagging along behind. As they strode along Pennsylvania
Avenue, they defied showers of rocks and taunts from proslavery ruffians shouting "Damn niggers! They oughtn't to be allowed on the
streets." Late on November 6, the Wide-Awakes gathered to greet the
election returns at the Tremont House, at Second Street and Indiana
Avenue, the former office of the *National Era,* which had serialized
Harriet Beecher Stowe's *Uncle Tom's Cabin* eight years earlier. Now the
building was headquarters for local Republicans, who called it their
"wigwam," after the Chicago hall where Lincoln had been nominated
the previous May.[1]

Loud as some Washingtonians were, they had no legal voice in
what was coming; they could not vote for president, so all their excitement was focused on the returns from elsewhere. Pennsylvania

Avenue, Seventh Street and C Street were alive that night with people streaming from one hotel to another, one political club to another, looking for news and free whiskey. An anxious crowd surrounded the telegraph office on Fourteenth Street, awaiting the figures from crucial New York, and another watched results posted on the bulletin board outside the National Hotel. At the theater on E Street, in the city where he had made his stage debut at the age of four with a blackface comedian called Jim Crow, the wildly popular Joe Jefferson was playing to a full house. He repeatedly interrupted his performance to announce the latest election returns; the audience cheered each Democratic upswing and hissed at Republican successes. At the Democratic Jackson Association (derided by opponents as the "Dem. Jack. Ass."), misleading early bulletins encouraged officers to send for a brass band to lead a triumphant parade. But after tuning up, the musicians slumped away when the hard truth set in. Disappointed losers then milled around Brown's Hotel, the traditional base of Southern legislators, where one young gladiator dared anybody to admit being "a damned black Republican," thus setting off a mass scrimmage that left noses bloody. When police broke up the melee, the crowd surged toward the Republican wigwam.

By that time, half an hour after midnight, the news that Pennsylvania had gone Republican spread up and down the Avenue: Abe Lincoln would become the sixteenth president of the United States. The jubilant Wide-Awakes were celebrating with songs and speeches when one of their members rushed in shouting that the gang of frustrated Democratic toughs, many of them from the secessionist National Volunteers militia company, were on their way to tear down the Republican clubhouse. The Lincoln boosters quickly scattered, leaving behind only a handful of their officers, who turned out the gaslights and locked the doors.

When the fighting-drunk mob arrived, it let go three loud cheers, then started firing pistols and throwing rocks, smashing windows and breaking in doors. The few remaining Republicans retreated to the second floor, then the third, then the roof, where they armed themselves with bricks from the chimney to hold off the intruders. But the mob was busy wrecking the building's interior, pitching furniture out the windows, ripping up banners, ransacking club records, smashing statuettes of Lincoln and his vice presidential running mate, Hannibal Hamlin of Maine. When police arrived, rioters leaped down stairwells and out windows to escape, but once outside they re-formed and

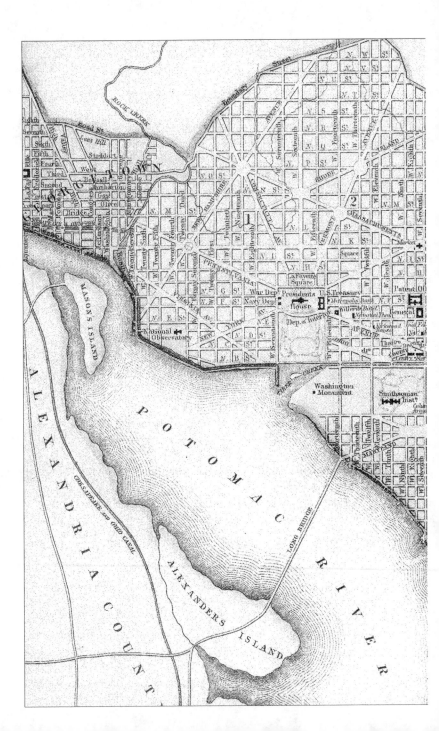

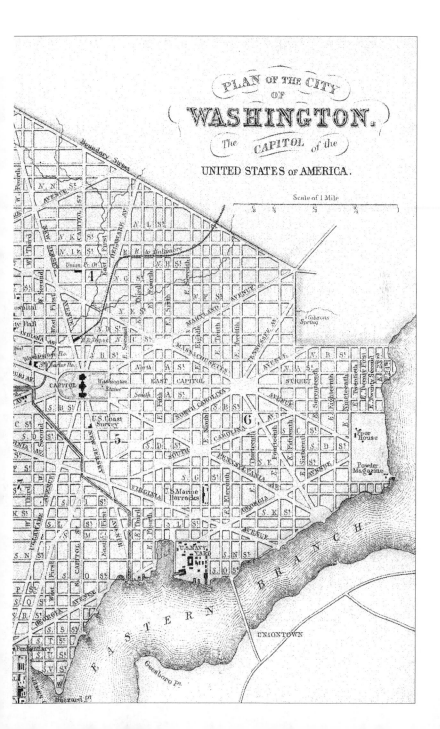

PLAN OF THE CITY
OF
WASHINGTON.

The CAPITOL of the

UNITED STATES OF AMERICA.

Scale of 1 Mile

began chanting "Burn the building! Burn it down!" The Wide-Awakes trapped on the roof were finally saved when the police arrested a batch of the wreckers and drove the rest away. Even then the mob marched off defiantly, filling the street from curb to curb, shouting allegiance to the National Volunteers, until at last its energy flickered out in the approaching dawn.[2]

In the most momentous election in the nation's history, Lincoln had won only 39.9 percent of the popular ballots but 59.4 percent of the electoral vote, against a divided field: the Northern Democrat, Senator Stephen A. Douglas of Illinois; the Southern Democrat, Vice President John C. Breckinridge of Kentucky; and the Constitutional Unionist, former Senator John Bell of Tennessee. The result inspired more political turbulence than celebration in a capital dominated by Marylanders, Virginians and the Southern Democrats who had held power for most of the previous decade. The day after the vote was confirmed, a North Carolinian in the capital wrote to friends back home that the election of the "Black Republican" Lincoln was "the greatest calamity that has ever befallen the United States. The sun that rose on Tuesday morning cast its bright rays upon a powerful & noble Republic, in the evening it went down on a ruined, tattered Union, for such I believe will be the result."[3]

Both Virginia and Maryland, the two states that enclose the capital on the Potomac, had rejected Lincoln by overwhelming margins. Hotheaded politicians farther south immediately started moves toward secession; some of the ultras among them had spoken secretly of mounting a coup to prevent the president-elect from taking office. The National Volunteers, whose rioting members had tried to burn down Republican headquarters, would be heard from again and again. Extremists on both sides took spirit from the emergency; the roar from Southern militants antagonized radical abolitionists up north. But Washingtonians, most of them, epitomized the millions of conservative Americans in between, who were more alarmed than exhilarated by the clamor.

At the Capitol, surrounded by construction sheds, scaffolding, iron girders and scattered columns of marble, Thomas Ustick Walter was near despair. "Our country is in the midst of a terrible partisan conflict," he told his son-in-law, "and we are in the vortex of it."

Walter was a tall, imposing Philadelphian, his German-American roots deep in the North. But he was torn. He had been appointed architect of the Capitol by a Whig president and kept in his prestigious job by two Democrats. As tension rose, he wrote that "the North looks to me to be insane. [It is] mere stinking pride of opinion that is this moment moving on to allow the country to be deluged in blood."[4]

"I have no idea that there will be any appropriation this winter for public works," he wrote—and so the climactic mission of his distinguished career, building the new dome that he had just redesigned, might stop before it was well started. Vendors could still hawk fruit, beer and souvenirs within the hallways of the Capitol, and members of Congress could still trade votes in their hideaway watering holes. But Walter feared that work on the new House and Senate wings would halt and the Capitol would stand as it was, seeming decapitated, leaking around the edges of new construction, some of its brick walls without their marble facings, its niches without their statues.

If war came, Walter wrote, he might even leave the country, to "try how it goes to live under an autocrat; Russia is the place." Perhaps he was remembering how the Italian architect Francesco Bartolomeo Rastrelli had conceived so many of the masterpieces of Peter the Great's capital. "If I knew the language, I believe I would make straight for St. Petersburg the moment our politicians 'break the machine.' . . .

"God alone can avert the storm," Walter wrote. "We must trust in *Him.*"[5]

But on the Senate floor, Benjamin Franklin Wade, an irrepressible antislavery senator from Ohio, backed up his confidence in the Almighty. Remembering how his abolitionist colleague Charles Sumner of Massachusetts was caned near to death a few desks away by the South Carolina Congressman Preston Brooks, he made known that any Southern fire-eater who threatened or insulted him would be invited to duel—with rifles, at twenty paces, with paper targets the size of silver dollars over each man's heart.[6]

For four weeks after the election, Southern voices in the capital were even more dominant than usual, because Congress was in recess. Until the legislature returned, most of the politicians on hand were Democratic bureaucrats and supplicants, whose party had controlled the White House and thus patronage through the Franklin Pierce and James Buchanan administrations. Between the election and Congress's return, Buchanan called two meetings of his ideologically split cabinet, and reached no consensus at all on how to deal with the situation. But in the cabinet, in the saloons and in Congress when it returned, the focus of debate had shifted from expansion of slavery to the right of secession, and the use of Federal force to prevent it.

The legalistic Buchanan, whom one fellow Democrat had called "that damned old wry-necked, squinty-eyed, white-livered scoundrel who disgraces the White House with his presence," was squeezed from both sides. He had come to the job with what seemed eminent qualifications: after service in the War of 1812, he had been elected to the Pennsylvania legislature in 1814, spent ten years as a congressman and ten years as a senator, then become minister to Russia, secretary of state, and minister to Great Britain, and was three times an unsuccessful contender for the Democratic presidential nomination before finally winning it and the election of 1856. But now, in a crisis potentially mortal to the Union, that matchless experience failed him. In his tensely awaited State of the Union message to Congress, the sixty-nine-year-old president infuriated Republicans by asserting that "the long-continued and intemperate interference of the Northern people with the question of slavery in the Southern States has at length produced its natural effects." But, still trying to have it both ways, he added that the election of any particular candidate was no just cause for dissolving the Union. Secession, he said, was unconstitutional—but the Federal government had no right to prevent it by force.

To South Carolina, this was a green light to proceed. All eyes turned to Columbia, where the state legislature had scheduled a secession convention to begin December 17. Far less attention was paid to Springfield, Illinois, where President-elect Lincoln carefully said little beyond warning against compromise on the extension of slavery, and making clear how unhappy he was that Buchanan had blamed the free states for the crisis.

W ashington, like the shaky president, was caught in the middle. In 1860, the District of Columbia had only 75,080 persons, 61,122 of them in Washington City, 8,733 in Georgetown and 5,225 in the rural remainder of the District. Of the total, 11,131 were free blacks and 3,185 slaves. Sixteen percent of the population was born in Virginia, 14 percent in Maryland, and most of the 47 percent born in the District was from families in those states. Slaves and ex-slaves were governed by the local "black code," which duplicated the laws of slaveholding Maryland when the District was created in 1791. It required free African-Americans to carry a residence permit, without which they risked being sold into slavery, and dictated the way blacks could assemble, worship, drive carriages, race horses, swim in the Potomac, or walk abroad after 10 P.M. Despite such restrictions, a few free blacks had prospered as restaurateurs and merchants. One of them, the caterer James T. Wormley, was General-in-Chief Winfield Scott's landlord.

The Virginia city of Alexandria, part of the original ten-mile-square District of Columbia laid out by George Washington, had been returned to state jurisdiction in 1846. But Georgetown, a former Maryland tobacco port half a century older than the capital city, was still a separate town within the District. Hemmed in by Rock Creek on the east, Georgetown College on the west, and Oak Hill Cemetery to the north, its population increased by only 400 in the 1850s, while Washington's grew by more than 23,000.* But while Georgetown's growth and commerce seemed stagnant, its role in society was undisturbed. There and downtown near the White House and Lafayette Square lived most of the local establishment—old-line families, ranking politicians, high military officers, and a diplomatic corps whose principals and staff together numbered just forty-four bodies. In this fashionable circle, etiquette followed the traditions of the slave-owning chivalry of nearby counties.

Politicians moving between White House and Congress, crinolined ladies moving from receptions to balls and recitals, ne'er-do-wells offering shady deals to visitors, all had to traverse streets deep with mud and muck in winter and clouded by dust in summer. Washington's unfinished Capitol stood above an unfinished city; less than seventy years before, the place had been woods, swamps and tobacco fields. Its few monumental government buildings and broad avenues were far out of scale with its scattered brick townhouses, rows of low-rise hotels and squalid slums of blacks and immigrants. Cattle, pigs and geese roamed free over broad empty stretches, including the acreage around the square stub of the Washington Monument, where indecision, vandalism and politics had halted construction at the 156-foot level. Close by, on what is now called the Ellipse, the Baltimore Excelsiors had defeated the Washington Potomacs 40 to 24 the previous June, in the first intercity baseball game played outside the New York area. Only Pennsylvania Avenue and the adjacent stretch of Seventh

*Pressed by property owners and businessmen, the Circuit Court of the District scheduled a vote for Georgetowners to decide on December 4, 1860, whether to merge their town with Washington. National events canceled that vote, and Georgetown eventually joined the capital when Congress decided to unify the entire District of Columbia in 1871.

Street were paved, with broken cobblestones. Along more than a mile of "the Avenue" between the Capitol and the White House, the conglomerate rest of Washington tested the credulity of innocent visitors and the wit of writers like Dr. George William Bagby.

The city "is the paradise of paradoxes," Bagby wrote—"a great, little, splendid, mean, extravagant, poverty-stricken barrack.... The one and only absolutely certain thing is the absence of everything that is at all permanent." In his cubbyhole office on newspaper row, across Fourteenth Street from Willard's Hotel, Bagby whipped out dispatches for the cosmopolitan readers of the *New Orleans Crescent* and the *Richmond Dispatch*. A Virginian, a physician by training, he preferred his incisive pen to the lancet, delighting in the ripple of his own words.

"Presidents, Senators, Honorables, Judges, Generals, Commodores, Governors, and the Exs of all these congregate here as thick as pickpockets at a horse race," Bagby wrote. "Add Ambassadors, Plenipotentiaries, Lords, Counts, Barons, Chevaliers, Captains, Lieutenants, Claim-Agents, Negroes, Perpetual-Motion Men, Fire-Eaters, Irishmen, Plug-Uglies, Hoosiers, Gamblers, Californians, Mexicans, Japanese, Indians and Organ-Grinders, together with females to match."[7]

This mix of transient opportunists was thickest in the hotels and rooming houses that lined both sides of the Avenue, from the sweetcake and ginger-pop stands at the foot of Capitol Hill to the columned Treasury, still abuilding at Fifteenth Street. Halfway along sprawled the Center Market, on the south side between Seventh and Ninth streets. Heaped in season with fruit, vegetables, oysters, shad and beef, it swarmed with flies from the canal behind it, a loathsome stone-walled gulch that ran alongside the Mall where Constitution Avenue would later lie, then cut across the foot of Capitol Hill. Wiser pedestrians avoided the blocks between the Avenue and the canal, a neighborhood called Murder Bay because of the cutthroats and cut-rate prostitutes who infested the slums there.

Along the Avenue itself, the stranger was likely to be welcomed by a better class of entrepreneur. Visitors were warned against oversolicitous gambling-house decoys, phony congressmen and others who claimed to be able to fix appointments or contracts for cash in advance. Checking into Willard's, Brown's, the National, or the Metropolitan Hotel, or stepping up to the bar at one of the fancy saloons on the north side, any newcomer showing signs of prosperity might be greeted by a sportily dressed, black-mustached bon vivant who styled himself "Colonel" Beau Hickman. Hickman was a local institution for decades, offering friendly advice at modest rates—a racing tip for a gambling chip, a helping of local lore for a leisurely meal—and had a remarkable variety of excuses for leaving without paying at restaurants and hotels. Yet even those who knew his tricks tolerated him because he carried them off with "such grace and *sang-froid*."[8]

But after Lincoln's election, tolerance and good humor faded along the Avenue. The long-simmering anger of partisans began to boil; George Bagby's usual light touch turned to heavy pessimism as the crisis deepened. "Blessed with the name of the purest of men, [the capital] has the reputation of Sodom," he wrote. "The seat of the law-making power, it is the centre of violence and disorder.... It has a Monument that will never be finished; a Capitol that is to have a dome; a Scientific Institute [the Smithsonian] which does nothing but report the rise and fall of the thermometer...."

Washington's "destiny is that of the Union," Bagby said. Quoting from the Bible's warning to ancient Jerusalem in Jeremiah 17, he concluded that "it will be the greatest capital the world ever saw, or it will be 'a parched place in the wilderness, in a salt land and not inhabited.' "[9]

Anna Ella Carroll was determined that Washington would neither dry up nor be surrounded and seized as the capital of a breakaway South. Strong-minded, self-educated in law and politics, she had grown up on an Eastern Shore plantation, daughter of a Maryland governor whose famous ancestors had owned part of the land laid out for the District of Columbia. At forty-five, Anna had written and published widely on national affairs, decrying "political Romanism" and urging western expansion and the transcontinental railroad. Now she had more devotion than property to offer to the cause; she was inspired by the election to free her household staff, her last remaining slaves. Promptly afterward, she moved into the Washington House, on the Avenue at Third Street, close by the St. Charles Hotel, which still had underground cells built before slave trading was outlawed in the District in 1850. From there, Carroll took the Baltimore & Ohio Rail Road at the station just north of the Capitol. Beyond Baltimore, she headed for New York on the Philadelphia, Wilmington & Baltimore, the single rail connection between the capital and the Northeast. The train crossed the broad Susquehanna by rolling on and off a rickety, seemingly top-heavy ferryboat.

In Manhattan, Carroll rallied editors and politicans behind the president-elect and warned of secessionist plots. If political confrontation led to secession, she said, the schemers intended to start an uprising to seal off Washington, take over the government, then petition for foreign recognition of a new proslavery administration. To those who doubted such a wild possibility, Carroll could point to the words of a Georgia editor who wrote, "Let the consequences be what they may—whether the Potomac is crimsoned in human gore, and Pennsylvania Avenue is paved ten fathoms deep with mangled bodies . . . the South will never submit to such humiliation and degradation as the inauguration of Abraham Lincoln." And to those who said this was madness, she and others quoted Thomas Carlyle's description of the French Revolution: "Madness rules the hour."[10]

From New York, Carroll returned south to buck up an old family friend, Governor Thomas Hicks, in Annapolis. Secessionists in Baltimore and Maryland's southern counties were sounding like red-hot South Carolinians as they raved against Lincoln's election. Fewer than 3 percent of Marylanders had voted for Lincoln, and if the General Assembly met in this mood, it might join the Deep South's rush toward secession. If Virginia left the Union, Washington's position as national capital would be shaky; if Maryland seceded, it would be impossible.

Gadding about the city, in and out of hotels and public receptions, secession-minded Southerners started wearing a blue cockade on their hats to show their solidarity with South Carolina. But many in Washington hoped the loud noises from that state were just another bluff like those heard repeatedly since the heyday of John C. Calhoun. They did not want to believe what they were reading in the *Evening Star* and the *National Intelligencer,* about the pellmell course of events at the state convention in Columbia. They grieved at what was happening around them: The Rev. C. H. Hall, an Episcopal minister, recalled how "men went mad with fear or rage. Old sores broke out, and cords of amity that seemed eternal were broken. Men were here loyal, and then suddenly and violently disloyal."[11]

Even before the crisis arose, devoted Southerners and Northerners in Washington had preferred to socialize with their own kind. This clannishness was most pronounced among the women; when protocol threw them together, as at presidential and diplomatic receptions, they still managed to uphold their regional loyalties with averted eyes and conspicuously upturned chins. Mrs. Clement Clay, wife of an Alabama senator, boasted of the twists and turns she went through to avoid meeting that shrewd but inelegant Republican leader, Senator William Henry Seward of New York. "Not even to save the Nation could I be induced to eat his bread, to drink his wine, to enter his domicile, to *speak* to him!" she declared. The one time Seward broke through her defenses was when both were masquerading as fictional characters at a fancy dress ball given by Mary Gwin, wife of the proslavery senator from California. Although caught off guard, Mrs. Clay recovered in time to make a slicing comment on Seward's earlier remarks about the "Slave Oligawky" of the South.[12]

When Congress returned after the election, Mrs. Clay acknowledged with sadness that the "very reckless gaiety" that had prevailed during the growing crisis was waning. Just before Christmas, many of those invited to the wedding of Congressman John E. Bouligny of Louisiana to Mary Parker, daughter of the capital's most prosperous grocer, realized that it might be the last social fling before disunion. Some of them hoped so.

The rosy-cheeked bachelor president himself was there, with his niece and White House hostess, the handsome Harriet Lane. So were Congressman Lawrence Keitt of South Carolina and Senator Thomas Clingman of North Carolina, who earlier had been rivals for Harriet's favor. After vows were spoken and Buchanan kissed the bride, the wedding guests crowded Parker's glistening dance floor and sipped champagne in high-ceilinged parlors and conservatories overflowing with fresh roses and lilies. The president, his wry neck tilting his head as if he awaited the answer to a witty question, sat at one end of the drawing room and shook hands with well-wishers, commiserating with them about the gathering political storm.

As guests began to leave, Sara Pryor, whose husband Roger was Virginia's most volatile congressman, stood listening to the president. Suddenly there were shouts outside, and voices rose in the entrance hall. "What is it?" asked Buchanan. Turning to Mrs. Pryor, he said, "Madam, do you suppose the house is on fire?"[13]

In the largest sense, it was.

Sara stepped into the hall to investigate. There was Keitt, who had declared weeks earlier that "South Carolina should shatter the accursed Union—and if she could not otherwise accomplish her designs, she should throw her arms around the pillars of the Constitution and involve all the States in a common ruin." Now he was leaping and shouting with joy, waving a telegram: "Thank God! Oh, thank God!"[14]

Mrs. Pryor pulled at his sleeve. "Mr. Keitt, are you crazy? The President hears you, and wants to know what's the matter."

"Oh!" cried Keitt. "South Carolina has seceded. Here's the telegram. I feel like a boy let out from school!"

Sara Pryor returned and whispered the news to the president. Buchanan fell back and gripped the arms of his chair as excitement swept the room around him. Some men cheered, others solemnly gathered up their ladies, hurried to thank the Parkers and departed.

Pale and trembling, the president turned to Mrs. Pryor: "Madam, might I beg you to have my carriage called?"

Harriet Lane took his elbow as he stepped out into the cold December rain and hurried home to the White House, wondering what to do.[15]

CHAPTER TWO

The Sword of Damocles

That Christmas morning dawned as peacefully as any in Washington's past. A steady snow covered the frozen mud streets, muffling the clop and rattle of the few carriages that tracked through the darkness to meet the 6 o'clock train at the Baltimore & Ohio station. As the sky paled behind the construction crane hanging over the Capitol, children and sleds appeared and the city came awake with a defiant gaiety, seemingly forgetful of politics. At the YMCA on Capitol Hill, well-to-do ladies spread a festive meal for the children of the poor. Beside the Anacostia River (then known as the Eastern Branch of the Potomac), what began as a happy party for Navy Yard workers turned into a boozy riot; when a policeman came to break it up, one Tib Mullins objected, was shot in the knee and taken to hospital, and there his leg was amputated. In the evening, about thirty young hellions paraded along the Avenue, through hotels and bars, blowing bugles and tin whistles and insuring themselves serious hangovers. The normal cast of overcelebrants was arrested and sentenced according to race at the Central Guard House, among them "Mason Harrington, cursing and obscenity, fined $4.17"; "Samuel Gassaway, colored, obscenity and profanity, whipped," and "Andrew Brown, colored, out after hours, workhouse 60 days."

Beyond Rock Creek in Georgetown, a bountiful feast of roast turkey, mince pie and accompaniments was set before the inmates of the poorhouse, courtesy of the banker W. W. Corcoran, "who has, with his accustomed liberality, given $25 for that purpose every Xmas day for some years past." Streets and alleys there were lively with men and boys racing ahead of policemen who had suddenly been ordered to enforce the widely ignored "Hog Law" that prohibited roaming swine. Occasionally an owner headed home toting a squealing shoat, distracting sedate Georgetowners from their holiday dinner.[1]

Elizabeth Lindsay Lomax, an old-family Virginian, descendant of one of Light-Horse Harry Lee's Revolutionary War cavalry captains and widow of Major Mann Page Lomax, had lived long enough to see beyond the glitter of the snow and the Christmas cheer. At her home on G Street near Lafayette Square, she wrote in her diary of her "terrible feeling of uncertainty—and fear. Fear of separation, fear of danger to those we love, fear for our beloved country. God grant us peace." She was torn, like so many caught between state and family loyalties on one hand and generations of service to the Union on the other. But she had decided, "after much thought and deliberation," that she was "definitely for the Union"—with "some amendments to the Constitution." Her fears centered on her twenty-five-year-old son, Lieutenant Lunsford Lindsay Lomax, who was four years out of West Point. With his closest friend and classmate, Fitzhugh Lee, he had crossed the river to Arlington Plantation on Christmas Eve to pay his respects to Lee's aunt, Mary Custis Lee, whose husband, Robert, was a colonel far away on the Texas frontier.

For Christmas, a magnificent wild turkey had arrived from Virginia for the Lomax family, and after dinner and presents the young folks danced far into the night. Elizabeth indulged them: "I do not think [they] realize as yet 'The sword of Damocles' hanging over our heads—perhaps it is just as well."[2]

Dozens of Washingtonians opened gift packages that morning to find photographs of loved ones that bore the label of Brady's National Portrait Gallery. In 1858, after fifteen successful years in New York, Mathew Brady had started his local studio at 352 Pennsylvania Avenue. At Christmas, he offered twenty-five full-length visiting cards for $5, as well as imperial portraits of every president from Jackson to Buchanan, every member of Congress and "nearly all our prominent Statesmen, Poets, Artists, Authors, Editors, Clergymen, Generals and Commodores," plus "the Prince of Wales and a large number of foreign personages."[3]

Among the distinguished couples who had posed for Brady were Senator Jefferson Davis of Mississippi and his wife, Varina. Just before midnight, Varina had been busy decorating the family Christmas tree when her husband appeared in the parlor, tired and drawn. As he complimented her on her handiwork, he realized someone was in the

next room. Turning, he saw the talented dressmaker Elizabeth Keckley, carefully sewing the final stitches into a silk dressing gown.

"That you, Lizzie?" said Jefferson Davis. "Why are you here so
late?"

Keckley did not let on that the handsome gown she was finishing
was to be Varina's gift to him. She explained that because Mrs. Davis
was so eager to have this piece done, she had volunteered to stay and
work on it.

"Well, well, the case must be urgent," Davis said. He stepped close
to inspect the silk in the dim light of the gas lamp. Then he smiled,
realizing that the robe was for him, but careful not to spoil his wife's
pleasure when she presented it to him the next morning.

Keckley was a Virginia-born former slave who had used her skill to
repay the $1,200 that she borrowed to buy freedom for herself and her
son. She was a stylish, tawny-skinned woman of dignity, with "a face
strong with intellect and heart, with enough of beauty left to tell you
that it was more beautiful still before wrong and grief had shadowed
it," wrote an admiring journalist. "Lizzie's father was a gentleman of
'the chivalry' and in her mother's veins ran some of the best blood of
the Old Dominion." She had come east from Missouri that spring, and
after trying for six weeks to make a living as a modiste in Baltimore,
she moved to Washington. In the capital, her artistic flair and attention
to detail attracted more business than she could handle. When Varina
wanted to hire her, Keckley offered to come at midday to the late-
rising Davis household, after working for others in the morning.
According to Keckley, she was soon so trustingly accepted in the family that "the prospects of war were freely discussed in my presence by
Mr. and Mrs. Davis and their friends."*

But much more went on than Keckley was allowed to hear. Live-in
servants told her of secret meetings that continued far into the night.
In homes and boardinghouses on all sides of the Davises, Southern
senators, congressmen, cabinet secretaries and bureaucrats stayed up

---

*When Keckley published her memoir, *Behind the Scenes,* in 1867, she spelled her last
name with two *e*'s. But her recent biographer, Jennifer Fleischner, has discovered letters
that were signed "Keckly." Since the quotations cited in the present book are from the
memoir, the author has retained the spelling that Keckley used there. When Keckley's
memoir appeared, many readers assumed that she had not written it alone. Some
believed the correspondent Jane Grey Swisshelm had helped her, but it is now considered more likely that she was aided by another journalist and abolitionist, James Redpath,
who was associated for many years with Horace Greeley's *New York Tribune.* (Jennifer
Fleischner, *Mrs. Lincoln and Mrs. Keckley: The Remarkable Story of the Friendship Between a
First Lady and a Former Slave* [New York: Broadway Books, 2003])

late to debate among themselves first whether, then when, to secede from the Union. The Davises lived on Fourteenth Street; near them in what is now the 1300 block of F Street were Senator Robert A. Toombs, who often had his Georgia colleague, Representative Alexander H. Stephens, as his boarder; Roger A. Pryor, the hotheaded congressman and editor from Virginia; Senator Judah P. Benjamin of Louisiana; and Thomas Miller, a Virginia-born physician who had attended Davis as well as Presidents Harrison, Tyler, Polk, Taylor, Fillmore, Pierce and Buchanan. Close by was young, vigorous Vice President John C. Breckinridge of Kentucky.[5]

Davis and some of the other Southerners involved in these tense midnight talks were members of the Senate Committee of Thirteen and the House Committee of Thirty-three, officially appointed earlier in December to find some way out of the crisis. In the daytime, they went through the motions of seeking legislated compromise. Later, in private, some of them crossed the line from debate to planning, and then to conspiracy.

On Christmas Day, Senator Louis T. Wigfall of Texas, a hard-drinking native South Carolinian who had "the eye of a man capable of anything," visited Secretary of War John B. Floyd to propose a radical step beyond politics. He asked Floyd to join a cabal already organized to kidnap Buchanan, a coup that would make Breckinridge acting president. Wigfall asserted that with the Kentuckian in the White House, the unhappy South would feel secure against being "trapped into a war" by presidential action. The scheme was fully planned, said Wigfall. All it needed was the secretary of war's cooperation in getting Buchanan and his captors safely out of Washington.[6]

Floyd, a former governor of Virginia, was a frank Southern sympathizer. But he rebuffed this proposal, infuriating Wigfall, and the plot went no further. The secretary was already in enough trouble, suspected of involvement in the "purloining" of $870,000 of Indian trust bonds in the Interior Department. And that very day, the president had found out that Floyd had ordered a shipment of artillery from Pittsburgh to Texas, where it could easily be seized by Rebels if war came—this in addition to more than 100,000 muskets sent south earlier. Buchanan, acting decisively for once, cancelled the order. Newly appointed Secretary of State Jeremiah Sullivan Black urged the president to fire Floyd when the cabinet next met. Although Buchanan confronted Floyd then, virtually accusing him of treason and provoking a shouting match, Floyd clung to his office for another three days.[7]

It was a time of choosing sides. To families like the Lomaxes and the Lees, who had served the nation for generations, making a decision was most painful. Nancy Macomb, daughter of an honored naval hero and wife of an army captain, feared that if her native Maryland seceded, her brother John Rodgers, another naval officer, would go with it. But she wrote to her brother-in-law, Captain Montgomery C. Meigs, that "we & you, I am sure, will stand by the Government as long as we continue to have [strength] & so long as we have a right to raise the U.S. Flag.... Our dear country, bought with the blood & patriotism of our own forefathers. May God avert from us the calamity of disunion. The Star Spangled Banner, Oh long may it wave.... If we should be plunged into crisis, I should believe that Almighty God had made these crazy Southern people the instrument for the destruction of their own peculiar institution ('Whom the Gods would destroy they first make mad'). I used to think I was a Southern woman, but I find now that I turn with disgust from the secessionists to the Northern Barbarians, preferring the least of two wrongs."[8]

To others, the decision came so easily that they could be flip about it. Although she loved life in Washington, Sara Pryor never had a moment's doubt about her own course. Eager to go south with her husband Roger, she urged Lieutenant David Dixon Porter to come along, to help create "a glorious monarchy." At age forty-seven, Porter had developed a sarcastic sense of humor during his thirty-one years in the U.S. Navy. He asked her: "And be made Duke of Benedict Arnold?"

"We will make you an admiral," Mrs. Pryor said.

"Certainly," he came back—"Admiral of the Blue. For I should feel blue enough to see everything turned upside down, and our boasted liberty and civilization whistled down the wind."

Porter, from an honored seafaring family that reached back into colonial times, had been twenty years a lieutenant in the slow-moving peacetime service. In wartime, he would become an admiral in Union blue. But he maintained later that if the hot-blooded Southerners who dominated the capital and plotted so busily had been entertained on a grander scale, the war that brought him fame might have been averted. "The Romans understood these things better than we," he wrote. "They omitted nothing to keep the people amused; they even had the street fountains at times run with wine, and the investment was worth the money spent." But no such diversion was likely, he said, with "a court presided over by an old bachelor [Buchanan] whose heart was dead to poetry and love; who sat at dinner with no flowers to grace the festive board, and never even had a boutonniere on his coat lapel."⁹

Other Unionists could not find even wry humor in the situation, or in the hapless president. Benjamin Brown French, who had been commissioner of public buildings in the Democratic administration of Franklin Pierce, had nimbly switched parties to become a leader of local Republicans. In his diary, he noted that though South Carolina had seceded, "the earth did not quake, the sun shone on, & Nature did not mark the event with any uncommon convulsion." To listen to the Southern orators, he wrote, "one would suppose that this act of secession of an insignificant, nigger-ridden state was really one of the greatest & most sublime events that the World ever witnessed! when in fact it has about the effect in regard to our great Union that the sailing of a jack o' lanthorn across a swamp has upon the solar system. . . ."¹⁰

According to French, the president himself was "generally believed to be in league with the treason that is working its way through the South." Determined Unionists could not believe that Buchanan might simply be frozen with fear of what might follow his moving in any direction. Senator Lafayette S. Foster of Connecticut, while sitting pretending to listen to others' speeches at the Capitol, wrote to his wife that "these are indeed perilous times for our country. . . . The saddest part of it is that everyone is powerless to mend matters except the *President* who alas! is too imbecile & treacherous to *do right.* . . ."¹¹

On the same day, the *Harrisburg Telegraph,* close by Buchanan's home town of Lancaster, Pennsylvania, got it about half right: "The miserable old man, responsible, to a great extent, for the dangers which now encompass the Union; selfish, unpatriotic, and seemingly without moral courage, dares not do his duty to his country, and shrinks from the responsibilities of his position. Evidently all he hopes to accomplish is to avert the calamity until after the close of the Administration, and then, for aught he may care, the Union can go to pieces. In fact, his policy makes him open to the suspicion that he is ambitious to be the last president of the United States, and will rejoice if the nation is divided at the close of his distressing Administration. . . ."¹²

Although some future historians would rank James Buchanan dead last among American presidents, he was not traitorous. Nor was he imbecilic, or selfish, or unpatriotic. But weak and miserable he surely was: "...the poor old Public Functionary looks wretchedly thin & pale," wrote Mrs. Macomb—"we hear that he weeps often!" He was the ultimate lame duck, unsure of his duty, hoping to hold the Union together for another few weeks, long enough to let Lincoln decide what to do.[13]

Of all Buchanan's long experience in Washington and abroad, his years in diplomacy and Congress best suited his character. In controversy, his reflex was to smooth things over, to split the difference, and it had served him well in situations less grave. A feminine admirer remembered the day when one of the many American Indian delegations who came to Washington on treaty business in those years met the president in the East Room of the White House. She told how the Indians, adorned in buckskin, paint and feathers, seemed ready to smoke the peace pipe with the president and his officials. All went calmly until one younger brave leaped up from the floor. His bare bronze torso gleamed as he gestured about him and spoke strange words that sent a thrill of danger through the ladies looking on. The interpreter passed them on to Buchanan: "These walls and these halls belong to the redmen!" he declared. "The very ground on which they stand is ours! You have stolen it from us and I am for war, that the wrongs of my people may be righted!"

As he spoke, the warrior chopped his arms about so threateningly that many of the ladies present rose, about to flee, until "our dear old Mr. Buchanan, with admirable diplomacy, replied in most kindly manner."

The White House did indeed belong to the "redmen," the president explained; it belonged to all the peoples of the Great Spirit together. He was merely the caretaker, looking after their interest. Thus he "welcomed his red brothers to their own on behalf of the country." He rambled on courteously, gradually pacifying the Indian delegation, and the ladies resumed their seats with a murmur of relief.[14]

B̲ut the fire-eaters of South Carolina were not to be pacified. The seceded state, acting as if it were a sovereign foreign power, sent a three-man commission–ex–Speaker of the House of Representatives James L. Orr, ex–U.S. Senator Robert W. Barnwell and ex–Governor James H. Adams—to negotiate relations with Washington, beginning with the surrender of the Federal forts in Charleston Harbor. Many Washingtonians looked on this mission as "a huge joke—as a harmless outcome of the vanity and pride of South Carolina," wrote a Massachusetts Republican, Henry L. Dawes. But it was no joke to Buchanan. It deepened his dilemma: if he received these three on their terms, he would be effectively recognizing South Carolina's claim of independence; if he "turned them out of doors, not to say arrested them for the treason they were committing," he would bring on the crisis he was trying to hold off until Lincoln's inauguration on March 4.[15]

When the commissioners left Charleston, there was a tacit understanding that South Carolina would not attack the forts as long as the U.S. government did not reinforce them or otherwise change their status, and vice versa. By the time they arrived, however, the Federal commander in Charleston Harbor, Major Robert Anderson, had further excited the Carolinians and their sympathizers by moving his defenders under cover of night from untenable Fort Moultrie to formidable Fort Sumter. Angry Southern leaders rushed to the White House to chastise the president; Jeff Davis told him that "you are surrounded with blood and dishonor on all sides." But Buchanan had no more foreknowledge of the move than Davis did. "My God," he moaned, "are calamities . . . never to come singly?"[16]

The emissaries from South Carolina established their "embassy" in a fine house on K Street and ran up their palmetto flag out front. Buchanan postponed seeing them for a day and received them "only as private gentlemen," not as official envoys. Then he passed the matter to Congress. When a select House committee summoned the delegates to the Capitol, they sent their "secretary of legation" to state that since they represented a sovereign power, they were not obliged to respond. Dawes, a member of the committee, made fun of the idea: "It was our first experience of this new-fledged eagle, and the bird had spread its wings for so lofty a flight at the first opportunity that we stood back in wonder and amazement."

The secretary, Dawes wrote, "was a very young man for one representing in his person the majesty of an independent government, seemingly having hardly attained his majority, with light hair, boyish face, and a mustache trained after the imperial order, rare in those days, which was a surprising success upon a face otherwise so downy. He wore patent-leather shoes and light-colored trousers in very large plaids, twirled on the tips of his fingers a cane with an apparently golden head turned over and finished in the hoof of a horse; in short, he was a dude of the dudes of that day. . . ."

When Dawes opened their interview by asking what brought him to Washington, the young man drew himself up and said: "You cannot be ignorant, sir, that the new sovereign state of South Carolina has sent ambassadors to negotiate a treaty of friendship and alliance with this neighboring government of the United States, with which she is desirous of living on the most liberal terms of amity and good fellowship. . . ." After a long disquisition on South Carolina's right to secede, he took offense at the committee's skeptical questions and, "gathering up [the delegation's] dignity and sovereignty as well as he might, took them both, with himself, out of such profane presence and back to the nursery on K Street. . . ."[17]

The South Carolina delegates may have seemed foolish to Yankees like Dawes, but the president had to deal or not deal with them seriously. He was wire-walking, trying to do nothing that would tip crisis into war. But when South Carolina troops followed Major Anderson's move to Fort Sumter by seizing the other forts at Charleston, Buchanan stiffened. Under those circumstances, he said, he "could not, and would not, withdraw the Federal troops from Sumter."[18]

Whatever slightest move the president made, it provoked more trouble in South or North, or both. In trying to push and pull him in opposite directions, his cabinet broke apart.

Howell Cobb of Georgia, secretary of the treasury, had urged his state's immediate secession after Lincoln's victory, then quit in early December, to be succeeded by Philip F. Thomas of Maryland, who would soon be succeeded by John A. Dix of New York. A few days later, the seventy-eight-year-old secretary of state, Lewis Cass, resigned in anger over Buchanan's failure to reinforce the forts at Charleston, as urged by Winfield Scott. Cass's replacement was the waspish Attorney General Jeremiah Sullivan Black, an antiabolitionist who nevertheless urged the president to fire Secretary of War Floyd for his pro-Southern sentiments. In a cabinet meeting, Floyd threw a fit of "mingled mortification and anguish and rage and panic" over Buchanan's refusal to abandon the forts after Major Anderson's move—a calculated display that supported his later claim that he had not been fired, but had quit in protest. Black accepted the State Department job only on condition that Buchanan name his protégé, Edwin McMasters Stanton, to replace him as attorney general. Postmaster General Joseph Holt of Kentucky succeeded Floyd at the War Department, and Horatio King succeeded Holt at the Post Office Department. Two more secretaries, Jacob Thompson of Mississippi at Interior and Isaac Toucey of Connecticut at Navy, soon took South Carolina's side in the showdown and departed.

The signal result of this wholesale shuffle was to bring into the cabinet one of the least understood players in the crisis months and years ahead. Edwin Stanton had started in politics as an antislavery Democrat, then switched to the Free-Soilers and then rejoined the Democrats under Buchanan. To one contemporary politician, he was "a great hero . . . a marvel of resolution and rigor, of industry and vigilance." To a later observer, he was "a man of oblique and sinuous character . . . impetuous ambition and unscrupulous methods. . . . Few men in American history have presented such divergences of behavior." Both assessments were correct.[19]

A brilliantly successful lawyer, Stanton was famous for defending then-Congressman, later General, Daniel E. Sickles in his 1859 trial for murder. In Lafayette Square across from the White House, Sickles had shot and killed Francis Scott Key's son, Philip, for carrying on an affair with Sickles's wife. For the first time in an American court, Stanton used the defense of temporary insanity, and won Sickles's acquittal. Before his appointment as attorney general, he was active behind the scenes at the White House, trying to stiffen the president's backbone. Then, promptly after being sworn in, he became a secret informant within the administration for congressional Republicans and Lincoln. Using a go-between and furtive postmidnight rendezvous, he kept key members of the opposition aware of "whatever occurred tending to endanger the country. . . ."[20]

By late December, "conspiracies were rife in the Cabinet, in Congress, in the departments, in the army, in the navy, and among the citizens of the capital, for the overthrow of the government and the dismemberment of the Union." So wrote Senator Henry Wilson of Massachusetts, who was echoed by his colleague, Henry Dawes: "The public mind at Washington had become greatly excited by the belief that a conspiracy had been formed to seize the Capitol and Treasury, to get possession of the archives of the government, and to prevent the counting of the electoral vote and the election of Lincoln; thereby creating chaos and anarchy, out of which might come the establishment of the Confederacy as the government *de facto* in the very halls of the national Capitol. Treason was known to be plotting to that end in the Cabinet itself, and Mr. Buchanan was bewildered and nerveless."[21]

Although overwrought, those conspiracy scenarios were not pure imagination. Wigfall's plot to kidnap Buchanan went nowhere, but

Virginia's former Governor Henry A. Wise and his son Jennings, editor of the *Richmond Enquirer,* were openly urging a coup d'état against the Federal government. In late December, the *Enquirer* asked, "How long will Maryland and Virginia delay before taking steps to protect their people and institutions from the powers of the Federal Government, prostituted to a reckless fanaticism? If the government of Maryland, influenced by timidity or actuated by treachery, shall longer delay to permit the people of that state to protect themselves, can there not be found men bold and brave enough to unite with Virginians in seizing the capitol at Washington and the Federal defences within the two States? . . . If Virginia and Maryland do not adopt measures to prevent Mr. Lincoln's inauguration at Washington, their discretion will be as much a subject of ridicule as their submission will be of contempt."[22]

To defend Washington, at year's end there were fewer than 500 regular Federal troops—between 300 and 400 Marines at their barracks at Eighth and I streets in southeast Washington, plus 50 or more ordnancemen at the Washington Arsenal at Greenleaf Point, later the site of Fort McNair, where the Anacostia River meets the Potomac. In theory, they were backed by four small volunteer militia companies, but these were more social and political organizations than they were companies of ready soldiers. The four together totaled perhaps 500 more men, whose loyalty to the Union was by no means certain. Buchanan was reluctant to summon more troops, lest that push the crisis to explosion—and besides, almost all of the 16,000-man regular army was thinly spread across the western frontier.

Seventy-four-year-old Winfield Scott, hero of the War of 1812 and the Mexican War, had been general-in-chief of the army for the past twenty years. He was now so heavy and decrepit that he could no longer mount a horse, but he was still respected for his experience and professionalism. On New Year's Day, the president called him in for another strategy talk. Hours later, at his quarters in Wormley's Hotel, Scott summoned his old friend Charles P. Stone and told him the policy of pure conciliation was over, that now it would be mixed with force. Stone, an 1845 graduate of the U.S. Military Academy who had served under Scott in Mexico, had resigned from the army in 1856 to seek his fortune in civilian life. Now, at Scott's request, the president appointed him colonel, and inspector general of the capital. Scott asked him how many Washingtonians he thought would stand by the Union. Stone estimated that two-thirds of the capital's "fighting stock" would be willing to defend the government if called on, but he said they had no rallying point. The massive, rheumatic Scott, a caricature of his former grandeur, groaned to his feet, thinking. Then, as he left to see Buchanan again, he turned, grabbed Stone's shoulder, looked him in the eye and told him, "Make yourself that rallying point!"[23]

While Buchanan was conferring with Scott, at the other end of Pennsylvania Avenue the scene in the Senate was "the most intensely exciting that was ever witnessed in that chamber." Southern sympathizers packed the Senate galleries and corridors, eager to hear Judah P. Benjamin of Louisiana deliver what was earlier expected to be a conciliatory speech. But Benjamin had let it be known that conciliation was now the last thing on his mind, and so had drawn an "immense audience."

Before he took the floor, the Senate's Committee of Thirteen had announced that it was unable to agree on "any general plan of adjustment." The House's Committee of Thirty-three had met, but the *New York Times* reported that it was "generally understood that the mission of this Committee was ended. It will probably now break up without accomplishing anything"—which it did, a few days later.

However inflammatory the subject, Benjamin was by habit a calm and lubricious speaker. On this day, he hardly raised his voice, but his words were as defiant as those of any red-hot orator in Charleston. "The day of adjustment has passed," he said. "If you propose to make one now, you are too late." Within a week, Mississippi, Alabama and Florida, and then Georgia, Louisiana and Arkansas, would follow South Carolina out of the Union. "We desire, we beseech you, to let this parting be in peace," he said.

"I conjure you to indulge in no vain delusion that duty, or conscience, or interest, or honor, impose upon you the necessity of invading our States, and shedding the blood of our people. You have no possible justification for it." But if that happens, "we must meet the issue you force upon us as best becomes freemen defending all that is dear to man. . . . you may carry desolation into our peaceful land, and with torch and firebrand may set our cities in flames . . . you may give the protection of your advancing armies to the furious fanatics who desire nothing more than to add the horrors of servile insurrection to civil war; you may do all this, and more, but you never can subjugate us; you never can subjugate the free sons of the soil into vassals, paying tribute to your power; you never can degrade them to a servile and inferior race. Never! Never! Never!"

That closing declaration set off "uproarious applause" in the galleries—"shouts and cheers and waving of handkerchiefs and hurrahs, and the greatest confusion and excitement prevailed all over the house." As soon as he could be heard above the chaos, James Mason of Virginia asked that the galleries be cleared. This provoked hisses and whistling, until at last the sergeant-at-arms succeeded in sweeping out the raucous onlookers and the Senate adjourned.[24]

Benjamin had eloquently stated the cotton South's position, and accurately anticipated some of its consequences. However, in the upper South, the tobacco South, a clear majority of public and politicians still clung to the Union. In Virginia, Henry Wise, the *Enquirer* and the *Examiner* angrily agitated for secession; the *Southern Literary Messenger* demanded that "there be no plastering over of the great political cancer . . . let us cut it off; for the time has fully come for us to do so." But Governor John Letcher held back, insisting that the Old Dominion must mediate between the extremes of "passion and recklessness." Against his wishes, Virginia's legislature voted for a state convention to consider secession. But Letcher also renewed his earlier call for an emergency national peace conference, and this time he prevailed; the conference was set to begin in Washington in early February.[25]

Just before midnight on New Year's Eve, the bells at Trinity Church, a triumph of Gothic Revivalism at Third and C streets, rang out "Hail Columbia" and "Yankee Doodle" over the streets at the western foot of Capitol Hill. James Ayliffe, who had played the bells on such occasions for years, must have decided on his own to add this patriotic flair to his usual repertoire of Scottish airs and "Home Sweet Home," for the church's minister was a stalwart Southerner who would hardly have chosen "Yankee Doodle" at that moment in history. As clocks tolled the hour, partygoers at scattered halls and hotels punctuated the evening's dancing and romancing with occasional political insults and fistfights.[26]

The first day of the year had always been a festive time in Washington, but to Elizabeth Lomax, this one was "oh, so different. No social calling, everyone looks harassed and anxious—the state of our beloved country the cause." Lieutenant George Washington Custis

Lee, eldest son of the Lees of Arlington, came with a friend to dinner, and that was as gay as things got at Mrs. Lomax's.[27]

At the White House, only a fraction of the traditional crowd turned out for the annual New Year's reception. Guests on both sides went through the motions of courtesy, though many flaunted their politics by wearing secession or Union cockades on their hats. As Buchanan took the hand of one Southern woman in the receiving line, she needled him: "Here I am, Mr. President, and my cook will be here in a few minutes! I left her dressing to come." Outside in the bright, frigid morning, some Washingtonians made a red, white and blue statement of their loyalty, delighting the editor of the *Star*, who noted "a beautiful American flag flung to the breeze from the residence of Capt. Lemuel Towers, of Company A, Washington Light Infantry. We believe that, with a single exception, every military company in Washington has, in some form or other, exhibited its love for the Union and its readiness to sustain law and order in this city. All praise to the patriotic citizen-soldiery of Washington!"[28]

The day after Charles Stone was appointed inspector general of the capital, he encountered Captain F. B. Schaeffer, of the National Rifles, at the door of the Metropolitan Hotel and complimented him on his company's reputation for precision drill.

"Yes, it is a good company," said Schaeffer, who had not heard of Stone's new commission. "I suppose I shall soon have to lead it to the banks of the Susquehanna!"

"Why so?" asked Stone.

"Why! To guard the frontier of Maryland and help keep the Yankees from coming down to coerce the South!"

Stone told him that he thought it was imprudent for a government employee and captain of volunteers to talk that way. But he still did not disclose his own assignment. Later, he admitted that "this was not a very cheerful beginning."[29]

Between Washington and the Mason-Dixon line, secessionists put Governor Hicks under increasing pressure to convene the Maryland General Assembly, hoping to take the state out of the Union. Questioned early in the year by the select congressional committee, Hicks said that would-be Rebels had come to him before Christmas, when "taunts were used, my personal safety was alluded to, and reference was made to the hazard I would run" unless he called the legislature into session. "One of them spoke of abolitionists coming through Maryland on or about the fourth of March [Lincoln's inauguration day], with arms and bands of martial music, as a cause leading to bloodshed." After more such threats, Hicks issued a public statement saying that "I have been repeatedly warned . . . that the secession leaders in Washington have resolved that the border States, and especially Maryland, shall be precipitated into secession with the cotton States before the 4th of March. . . . They have resolved to seize the federal Capitol and the public archives, so that they may be . . . acknowledged by foreign governments as the 'United States' . . . the assent of Maryland is necessary, as the District of Columbia would revert to her in case of a dissolution of the Union."

Hicks told the committee that agents had come and written from Alabama and Mississippi urging him to cooperate, and he had said to them what he said to the congressmen: "I was born and raised in Maryland; I am a slaveholder, and have been the owner of slaves since I was 21 years old; and my sympathies are with the south; that I say to the world. But I am a Union man, and would live and die in the Union."[30]

Hicks's words in Washington were stronger than his political position in Maryland. They were nearly identical to those uttered by many other public officials, army officers and plantation owners in the upper South during the early days of 1861, before the crisis dragged them with their states into the Confederacy.

Urged by his new cabinet, Buchanan ordered reinforcements sent to Fort Sumter. But on January 9 the Federal vessel *Star of the West* turned back when it was fired on by South Carolina coastal batteries; friends in the administration had warned state authorities that the ship was coming. Though shots had been fired, it was not war, not yet. Maybe that could still be headed off somehow, if reasonable voices could be heard above the bombast.

Those who prayed for reason turned their hopes to the most genial and influential of conservative Republicans, the senator from New York, William Henry Seward. They believed that the best chance of some settlement lay in his long-cultivated friendships on both sides. Indeed, Henry Clay had described Seward as "a man of no convictions," which was an insult in Clay's day but seemed just what was needed in this situation. A Southern sympathizer thought that

Seward's "inscrutable features, though sharp and angular, conceal more meaning than they enunciate; thought is written on their worn characters—it seems a face that scrutinizes all, while defying scrutiny itself." The journalist Benjamin Perley Poore wrote: "Political friends and political foes, the most conservative and the most ultra, the Abolitionist from Vermont and the fire-eater from Mississippi, all looked upon that pale, slight figure in a gray frock coat—so calm, so self-possessed, so good-natured—as the man who had but to speak the word and the country would be saved." Seward, now Lincoln's secretary of state–designate, encouraged such thinking.[31]

The *Evening Star* said it was "undeniably true that [Seward's] positions carry more popular weight with them than those of any other living man in America"—obviously including Lincoln. That held especially among "the class of citizens ... whose present hostility to a conciliatory and peaceful settlement of the national troubles is now the chief obstacle to that so desirable consummation." The paper asserted that Seward's heralded Senate address on January 12 would be "the most momentous one in its results ever delivered before that body," because he was considered "the Premier of the incoming government," so whatever he said would be taken as the authorized word from Lincoln in Springfield. "We believe that he is about to extend the olive branch," the paper said, "and pray that such may prove the fact. If he does, the union may yet escape destruction.... If not, disunion reigns triumphant, and the horrors of civil war bid fair to be its attendants."[32]

The *Star* and much of the nation were disappointed. At least outwardly, Seward had always been an incurable optimist, and in his speech he did indeed offer the olive branch. While declaring again his fealty to the Union, he called for a constitutional convention to settle differences, and broke with the Republican platform by suggesting yet another version of compromise. But, as Judah Benjamin had said in that chamber less than two weeks earlier, the day for compromise was gone. Seward did not come close to satisfying the radicals on either side. Senator John Hemphill of Texas shrugged: "It was a fine address for the Fourth of July, but we are going to secede."[33]

In barely three weeks after Seward's speech, Mississippi, Florida, Alabama, Georgia, Louisiana and Texas followed South Carolina by deciding to leave the Union. Hour by hour, tempers rose at the Capitol and rumors surged in the city. Day by day, telegraph keys clicked with news of cotton states confiscating Federal real estate, ships, supplies and weapons. Evening after evening, Colonel Stone and his officers went about inspecting the existing militia outfits and organizing new companies to defend the capital.

Stone could not count on unanimous Union loyalty even among the high officers of the rank-heavy district militia. Time had escalated two of them, R. C. Weightman and former mayor Peter Force, to major general, and though they were steadfast, they were long past their prime. Two of the three militia brigadiers, Edward C. Carrington and P. F. Bacon, were young and reliable, but the Southern sentiments of the third, District Attorney Robert Ould, were so well known that Stone cut him out of all confidences during the crisis.[34]

Cautioned by General Scott that "we are now in such a state that a dog-fight might cause the gutters of the capital to run in blood," Stone sent letters to forty prominent Washingtonians, inviting them to form loyal companies in their neighborhoods. Some ignored the request, while some declined courteously, and a few sarcastically. But within about six weeks, twenty-three new and old rifle companies and two cavalry troops were on the rolls, uniformed, equipped and drilling. Among them were the Washington Light Guards, the Crittenden Rifles, the Metropolitan Rifles, the Mechanics Union Rifles, the Constitutional Guards, the National Guards, Georgetown's Potomac Light Infantry, the Perseverance Fire Company, the Lafayette Hose Company, the Northern Liberties fire companies and units formed by masons, carpenters, painters and other craftsmen.[35]

Meanwhile, Stone slipped undercover agents into Captain Schaeffer's National Rifles and the National Volunteers, the latter a new force that had resolved to "stand by and defend the South" and, if Maryland and Virginia should secede, to resist "the evils of a foreign and hostile government within and near their borders." This company barred the press from its meeting on January 14 in "a darkey ballroom" at Fourteenth and D streets, but two nights later a *Star* reporter slipped into its gathering upstairs over Burch's livery stable. "The principal business in hand when we entered was cussing," he wrote. "There was considerable miscellaneous swearing, but the *Star* came in for the hottest of it." First Lieutenant Tyler Powell resigned, saying "I cannot lend my aid to, or countenance, any movement that casts reflections or imputations upon the Executive of the United States. I am also of the opinion that political military organizations are antagonistic to the principles of a true Republican Government." In that company, he was a misfit.[36]

Stone's agents reported regularly on what the two suspect companies were up to. The National Volunteers' captain was Cornelius Boyle, son of the chief clerk of the Navy Department. After arranging that any requests for arms from militia companies must pass through the inspector general, Stone demanded that the captain present him a list of all the members who would get those weapons. On receiving that roll of potentially disloyal citizens, he said thank you, dropped it into his desk drawer and bade Boyle goodbye.

When the blustery Schaeffer sought more weapons for his already fully armed company, Stone refused him, angering Schaeffer, who said that if necessary, his men could take what they wanted from the Armory by force. Stone turned him away with a bluff, asserting that if Schaeffer tried, 150 loyal soldiers would open fire when he came out—though in fact, only a few enlisted ordnancemen guarded the Armory. Later, Stone called Schaeffer in and informed him that he had been promoted to major but must first take an oath of loyalty. When Schaeffer hesitated, Stone quickly returned the commission to his drawer, saying that no one who was so uncertain should be a militia officer. With these strokes, he had effectively disarmed the National Volunteers, and under a new commanding officer, the National Rifles were purged of secessionists and reorganized into a loyal company.* Stone had shrewdly neutralized the two most visible, organized threats, but he had not quelled the rumors or quieted Scott's nerves— or his own.[37]

By mid-January, the midnight conversations among Deep South politicians were no longer about whether to leave, but when. Political spouses were packing to depart on short notice. Varina Davis, who had become a sophisticated hostess during nearly fifteen years in Washington society, was reluctant to leave that life behind. According to Elizabeth Keckley, she told a friend that "I would rather

---

*Schaeffer and a hard core of secessionists from the National Rifles later crossed the Potomac to Alexandria with other pro-Southern Washingtonians and formed a company of the First Virginia Infantry, under Schaeffer's command. (Benjamin F. Cooling, "Defending Washington During the Civil War," p. 317)

remain in Washington and be kicked about, than go South and be Mrs. President." The friend was surprised, but Varina insisted that she meant it.

Later, Varina told Keckley that she had been so useful as friend and seamstress that the Davises would like her to go south with them. War was coming, Varina said, and when the North realized that the South was in earnest, it would yield rather than go through a long and bloody conflict. If Keckley would leave with her, she would take good care of her, while in the North people would blame the colored people for the war and treat them harshly. And then, Varina said, her husband would become president of the South, his Southern army would march on Washington, and "I shall live in the White House." Keckley had long wanted to work in the White House and told Varina she would consider her offer. But the ex-slave had no intention of moving to Mississippi.[38]

On January 21, five senators, some with swagger, some with sadness, stood to make farewell speeches before leaving Washington for the South. As Clement Clay of Alabama spoke, his wife looked on from the gallery. "It seemed as if the blood within me congealed," she wrote. Women around her grew hysterical, waving their handkerchiefs and shouting encouragement as each departing senator took his turn. "Men wept and embraced each other mournfully. . . . Scarcely a member of that Senatorial body but was pale with the terrible significance of the hour. There was everywhere a feeling of suspense, as if, visibly, the pillars of the temple were being withdrawn and the great Government structure was tottering; nor was there a patriot on either side who did not deplore and whiten before the evil that brooded so low over the nation."[39]

The last of the five to stand was Jefferson Davis. Since entering West Point in 1824, he had served the nation as soldier, congressman, senator and secretary of war. He had been seriously wounded leading the Mississippi Rifles at Buena Vista in Mexico. In debate, Davis stood unswervingly for states' rights and slavery, but he had not been one of the young red hots, ignorant of war and eager for secession. The stress of making this decision had brought on an attack of facial neuralgia so disabling that he had to "rise from a bed of suffering with an aching head," an effort that he said heightened his "unutterable grief" over what was happening. Now the galleries were hushed as he summed up his case and said with quavering voice, "I am sure I feel no hostility to you, senators from the North. I am sure there is not one of you, whatever sharp discussion there may have been between us, to whom I cannot now say, in the presence of my God, I wish you well. . . . Mr. President, and senators, having made the announcement which the occasion seemed to me to require, it only remains for me to bid you a final adieu."[40]

To his wife, who had watched from the gallery, leaving Washington this way seemed "death in life." "Deeply depressed and supremely anxious," the Davises headed home to their Brierfield Plantation, near Natchez. They would not stay there long.[41]

In the last weeks of January, the procession of seceding states and the growing furor around Fort Sumter all but mooted the national peace conference promoted by Virginia's Governor Letcher. This last-gasp effort came to order at Willard's Hall on February 4, the same day the seceded states met in Montgomery to form their Confederate government. Before the Washington conference opened, Senator Solomon Foot of Vermont warned his state's arriving delegates that the whole thing was "a fraud, a trick, a deception—a device of traitors and conspirators again to cheat the North and gain time to ripen their conspiracy." If such an attitude among responsible Northerners did not doom the prospect of peaceful compromise, the first roll call did: There was no answer from any of the seven seceded states, or Arkansas, or from five states of the West. Only twenty-one of the thirty-four states were on hand.[42]

Seventy-year-old ex-President John Tyler of Virginia creaked up from Richmond to chair what Horace Greeley called "the old gentlemen's convention." It included six former cabinet members, nineteen former governors, fourteen former U.S. senators and fifty former congressmen, politicians thoroughly experienced in debate, negotiation and parliamentary wrangling. They put all these skills to work trying to agree on a way to appease the Confederate states and prevent the upper South from splitting away. Three days after convening, they paid a courtesy call on President Buchanan, whom one delegate found "advanced in years, shaken in body, and uncertain in mind . . . every symptom of an old man worn out by *worry*." Buchanan "threw his arms about one stranger after another, and, with streaming eyes, [begged] him to yield anything to save his country from 'bloody, fratricidal war.' " The president's performance echoed the arguments of Southern delegates so closely that some of the Northerners suspected collusion. Afterward, Republican participants met and agreed to block any action until their party caucus had cleared it. Back at Willard's, the delegates hung above their deliberations a portrait of George Washington, lent by Democratic Mayor James G. Berret, to remind them of the gravity of their business.

As they labored, General Scott mobilized his forces for another critical moment of transition on February 13, when the capital feared a coup attempt. Some Republicans, who did not know the upright Vice President Breckinridge personally, believed rumors that he would betray his duty to preside over counting the electoral votes that confirmed Lincoln's victory. If plotters had such a thing in mind, the traditional ceremony at the Capitol was their opportunity.

Since the election, the vice president had kept the official election certificates from the states in two boxes in his personal custody. On the appointed day, he and a messenger carrying those boxes would lead members of the Senate through the crowded corridors and rotunda of the Capitol to the House Chamber. There, in the Speaker's chair, Breckinridge would open and tally the votes, and announce the result. "The ease with which desperadoes, mingling with the crowd, might fall upon the messenger as he passed . . . and violently seize the boxes, or from the galleries of the House might break up the proceedings, was apparent," wrote Henry Dawes.[43]

But the old Virginian Winfield Scott had warned that "any man who attempted by force or unparliamentary disorder to obstruct or interfere with the lawful count of the electoral vote . . . should be lashed to the muzzle of a twelve-pounder and fired out of a window of the Capitol. I would manure the hills of Arlington with fragments of his body, were he a senator or chief magistrate of my native state!" He made clear his determination by lining up two batteries of cannon along First Street near the Capitol. To watch for trouble inside, he salted among the onlookers several hundred armed plainclothes policemen, recruited in Philadelphia, New York and other Northern cities.[44]

All was tense; the halls and galleries were packed, and the peace convention delegates jammed onto the House floor as guests. But there was no trouble. Breckinridge, runner-up to Lincoln in the electoral count, performed his ritual duty firmly, ruling down every attempt at interruption. Even dedicated Republicans admired his performance; one would write that "if he could be remembered only for his services on that day, Vice-President Breckinridge would fill a high place in the gallery of American statesman, and merit the permanent gratitude of the American people."[45]

Secessionist lawmakers vented their frustration when they realized that the act was irretrievably done, and for hours afterward angry crowds milled along the Avenue. The following week, on George Washington's birthday, Scott paraded all the troops he could muster, a show of force that helped calm the capital's jitters. But tension mounted again as the nation's attention turned briefly away from the capital, toward two presidents-elect making rail-stop speeches on their roundabout way toward triumph and tragedy.

CHAPTER THREE

We Must Not Be Enemies

A t 4 A.M. on Saturday, February 23, at Camden Station, a few blocks west of Baltimore's Inner Harbor, three men lay awake behind curtains in a darkened railway car. Now and then a trace of song drifted in from all-night saloons beyond the bustle of passengers and freight handlers.

One of the men stretched in his berth, smoking a cigar, alert and watchful. He was forty-one-year-old Allan Pinkerton, alias E. J. Allen, alias John H. Hutchison, who ran a Chicago private detective agency and earlier had helped slaves escape northward by the underground railroad. The youngest of the three was Ward Hill Lamon, thirty-three, a strapping, fresh-faced lawyer who had been born in Virginia, then moved to the free state of Illinois, but still despised abolitionists like Pinkerton. The oldest was Lamon's fifty-two-year-old friend and law partner, a lanky, rumpled figure who lay listening as a boozy celebrator somewhere varied his standard barroom medley with that popular new minstrel favorite, "Dixie."

"No doubt there will be a great time in Dixie by and by," he murmured.[1]

There was sadness in Abe Lincoln's voice, for he understood that what happened to Dixie and the nation in the weeks ahead depended as heavily on him as on any man.

Twelve days earlier, he had departed Springfield, bound for Washington, on the same day that Jefferson Davis left his plantation in Mississippi, bound for Montgomery to accept the presidency of the new Confederate States of America. Lincoln's journey had become a triumphal procession, greeted by serenades, torchlight parades and ever larger crowds at Indianapolis, Cincinnati, Columbus, Pittsburgh, Buffalo, Albany, New York City, Trenton, Philadelphia, Harrisburg and points between. Speaking to those crowds, he had repeatedly tried to calm the war fever that was rising in North and South. "In plain words, there is really no crisis, except an artificial one," he said at Pittsburgh. "Let it alone, and it will go down itself," he said at Cleveland. "The man does not live who is more devoted to peace than I am," he said at Trenton. In Philadelphia, "a countless multitude of people were shouting themselves hoarse, and jostling and crushing each other around his carriage-wheels" in their enthusiasm.[2]

And now all that glory had come to this: the president-elect of the United States hiding from his enemies, sneaking in the dark toward the national capital, in fear for his life.

Over and over, in the mail that poured into the president-elect's office at Springfield, there had been scrawled threats to murder him. Months earlier, S. M. Felton, president of the Philadelphia, Wilmington & Baltimore Railroad, had heard more credible rumors that secessionists were plotting to stop Lincoln's train and kill him on his way through Maryland. Concerned that this might happen on his railroad, Felton hired Pinkerton to investigate. Calling himself John Hutchison, the detective set up in Baltimore as a stockbroker, and sent his agent-provocateurs to draw out suspicious characters in the city and along the rail line from the Susquehanna. According to Pinkerton, Baltimore was full of plotters bragging of how they would do away with the president-elect.

To traverse the city, southbound cars had to be drawn slowly by horses from either the Calvert Street or the President Street Station west along Pratt Street to Camden Station, where they hooked up again to head for Washington on the Baltimore & Ohio. This gave Baltimore's infamous plug-uglies, the street ruffians who had earned the city the nickname of Mobtown, more than a mile in which to cause trouble. Pinkerton believed that Marshal George P. Kane, chief of police, was in on the assassination plan. It was allegedly led by a militia captain and former barber named Cipriano Ferrandini, who had trimmed mustaches at Barnum's Hotel, headquarters for local secessionists. Pinkerton quoted Ferrandini as saying, "If I alone must strike the blow, I shall not hesitate or shrink from the task. Lincoln certainly shall not depart from this city alive." (Lamon later scoffed at Pinkerton's account, but Lucius E. Chittenden, a Vermont delegate to the peace convention in Washington, told of being summoned secretly to Baltimore and hearing much the same version, except that his talkative ex-barber was named Ruscelli and used the alias of Orsini, after an Italian conspirator who had tried to assassinate Napoleon III.)[3]

On February 20, Pinkerton hurried to Philadelphia to head off the president-elect. He talked first to Felton and Norman B. Judd, a Chicago railroad lawyer who had become Lincoln's 1860 campaign manager and close adviser. The next day, the detective and Judd urged Lincoln to avoid trouble by hastening unannounced through Baltimore that night, but Lincoln insisted on going ahead with plans for speeches at Independence Hall and Harrisburg on February 22. Later, however, William Seward's son Frederick arrived in Philadelphia with a similar warning, sent from General Scott. In this version, New York detectives hired by Colonel Stone, the officer in charge of Washington's defenses, had reported "imminent" danger in Baltimore, beyond the control of local authorities. This set off debate in Lincoln's suite over what to do, with one old-army colonel declaring that anything evasive would be "a damned piece of cowardice." But after hearing the separate warning from such high-ranking sources, Lincoln gave in and agreed to go along with a scheme devised by Judd to slip secretly through Baltimore.[4]

After his appearance in Harrisburg, rather than going directly to Baltimore as expected, Lincoln would take a special train back to Philadelphia that evening. Felton would detain the regular 11 P.M. train from there to Baltimore, ostensibly to await important official documents. Lincoln, posing as the ailing brother of Kate Warne, the chief of Pinkerton's Female Detective Force, would travel on that train in the curtained rear section of a sleeping car. His wife Mary and most of his retinue would stay back and follow the original schedule. To keep these movements secret, telegraph officials shut down all lines out of Harrisburg.

All went well. Lincoln put on "a soft, light felt hat, drawn down over his face when it seemed necessary or convenient," instead of the high stovepipe that was his trademark before and after. He wore "a shawl thrown over his shoulders, and pulled up to assist in disguising his features." Thus attired, he returned to Philadelphia, where his little party boarded the Baltimore train without being noticed. He tried to stretch out in his berth, but it was too short for him. The "official documents," actually an elaborately sealed bundle of old railroad reports, were handed over to the conductor. As the train clacked into the night, Lincoln told a few droll stories that eased the tension. Occasionally, Pinkerton went onto the rear platform to watch for signals from his agents along the route.[5]

At about 3:30 A.M., they reached Baltimore's President Street Station, rather than Calvert Street where they would have arrived if they had come directly from Harrisburg. They were quiet as the sleeping car was hitched to horses and rumbled slowly through the streets past bay steamers and oyster boats crowded along the waterfront. Then they learned that the connecting train from the west was running late. Thus, for nearly two hours, Lincoln had to lie listening in the darkness, in the heart of the city where men were allegedly waiting to kill him.

Suddenly a loud pounding startled the party upright. It was not an attacker, but someone banging a club outside the office of the sleeping ticket agent, yelling over and over in an unmistakably Irish voice that it was past four o'clock, time to open for business. This went on for twenty minutes as the covert travelers behind their curtain began to laugh along with the rest of the passengers. Then the late train from the west finally arrived, coupled to the waiting car, and puffed away toward Washington.[6]

By the first rays of dawn, Lincoln could barely make out the skeleton of the Capitol dome from just north of the city. At about six o'clock, ten hours before he was expected, the train eased into the B&O Station at New Jersey Avenue and C Street. The president-elect towered above the crowd pushing along the platform, seemingly unrecognized until one man reached out and said to him, "Abe, you can't play that on me." Lamon clenched his big fist to drive the man away, but Lincoln caught his arm. "Don't strike him!" he said. "It's Washburne. Don't you know him?"[7]

It was his friend Elihu B. Washburne, Republican congressman from Galena, Illinois, who had been tipped off by young Seward. Pinkerton whispered, "No talking here," and the group quickly boarded a hack, making its way in the semidarkness to Willard's Hotel. There, Lincoln, Pinkerton and Washburne went in by the ladies' entrance on Fourteenth Street while Lamon took the carriage around the corner to the hotel's main entrance on the Avenue. The proprietor, Henry A. Willard, greeted the president-elect, and within minutes Seward senior was there to shake Lincoln's hand and say how wise he had been to make his "secret passage" through the dangers of Baltimore. He was eager to talk business.

But Lincoln, after twelve days of travel, at least fifty speeches, and finally a sleepless night of high anxiety, said he was "rather tired." He wanted to rest. Willard showed him to the best suite in the house, on the second floor corner overlooking the Avenue. Upstairs and ready to relax, the president-elect realized that in all the confusion of the past twenty-four hours, he had left his favorite slippers behind. This set off Willard's first test as host to the incoming president. His own slippers would not do for Lincoln; Abe's feet were too big. Nor could Willard think of any guest whose slippers might fit. Then he remembered that his wife's grandfather, seventy-eight-year-old former congressman William Czar Bradley, who was visiting at Willard's house across the street, had "a good, large foot." The old man was delighted to have the honor of lending his slippers to a Republican he greatly admired, and so Lincoln wore them for days, perhaps weeks, before returning them with a note of appreciation. With the note, the slippers became a Willard family heirloom.[8]

Lincoln was already familiar with Willard's. As a young congressman from 1847 to 1849, he had not been able to afford hotel life, and had lived most of the time at Ann Sprigg's boardinghouse on Capitol Hill, where the Library of Congress would later be built. But as his one term in Congress was ending, he had been among the organizers of fellow Whig Zachary Taylor's inaugural ball who met at the hotel, and likely had been there on other occasions in those two years. Now in 1861 he led a procession of famous and infamous guests who would soon make Willard's the country's most important hotel: Nathaniel Hawthorne wrote that it was "much more justly called the center of Washington and the Union than either the Capitol, the White House or the State Department."[9]

Since Lincoln had last been there, Willard's had become grander inside and out. When Henry Willard took over its management in 1847, it had been a row of six two-story wooden townhouses built in 1816, run together as a forty-room hotel. He had expanded it upward and along Fourteenth Street into a 150-room establishment before his brother, Joseph C. Willard, came back broke from the California gold rush and joined him in 1853 as an equal partner. Willard's major competition in the decade was the National Hotel on the Avenue at Sixth

Street, especially favored by Southern politicians. But the National had a setback during Buchanan's inauguration in 1857, a period when many of its guests, including the incoming Democrat, mysteriously fell ill, apparently from a sewer line leaking in the cellar where food was stored. (Some Confederate partisans later asserted that the victims were poisoned by arsenic, in a radical plot to eliminate Buchanan.) In 1858, the Willard brothers expanded their hotel all the way to F Street. The next year, they bought the adjacent F Street Presbyterian Church, an architecturally modest structure except for its imposing columned facade. They renamed the 600-seat church building Willard's Hall and turned it into a busy venue for lectures, poetry readings, young folks' hops, concerts by touring opera stars and political gatherings, including the peace convention that was still getting nowhere when Lincoln arrived.[10]

The affable Joseph Willard kept the firm's books and office, while Henry did the hands-on managing. At three o'clock any morning, Henry was likely to be on his way down the Avenue to the Center Market to buy fish, oysters, game and vegetables for the hotel's vast dining rooms, where ladies and gentlemen could sup separately. Mary Clemmer Ames, the acerbic correspondent of the *Springfield Republican,* explained to her readers that the better hotels kept separate facilities so men could "scrabble and bolt as many beefsteaks and sausages as men are supposed to be able to do," or they could join the ladies, where they "are supposed to be gentlemen; supposed to have time to masticate their food in a Christian manner; time to read the newspaper and to discuss the news with their lady friends over their coffee." At Willard's, men were catered in a room thirty by a hundred feet, with a fifteen-foot ceiling, a cubic footage that exceeded the ladies' bath, which was merely twenty-eight by sixty feet and had a nine-foot tub. The gaslit public and private rooms were opulently furnished, with rosewood, lace, velvet, damask and spittoons in all directions. Eighteen hundred guests had partied there in 1859 at the grand send-off for the British ambassador, Lord Napier, and when a fancily coiffed and costumed delegation of Japanese came to open diplomatic relations in 1860, the Willards redid sixty rooms to make them feel welcome.[11]

L incoln, arriving exhausted, did not demand special handling; all he needed then were big-enough slippers and a long-enough bed for his six-foot four-inch frame. But Mary Lincoln arrived that afternoon with their sons, after passing safely through a Baltimore crowd and reaching Washington in a driving rainstorm. Among the throng of wet welcomers were some Wide-Awakes who had gone to Baltimore on the morning train to greet the Lincolns there, and returned when they found out the president-elect was already safely in the capital. One of the disappointed many at the depot was a brave Virginian who had dared to vote for Lincoln across the Potomac in Fairfax County and been rolled in printer's ink and feathers by outraged neighbors. Mrs. Lincoln, who enjoyed luxury, gladly joined her husband in the Willard's Suite 6, a bedroom and parlor. Lincoln's young assistants, John G. Nicolay, John M. Hay and Elmer E. Ellsworth, were assigned less deluxe rooms close at hand.[12]

As Lincoln briefly rested, word of his clandestine arrival spread "consternation and amazement" through Washington and the country. "Never idol fell so suddenly or so far," wrote Henry Dawes. "His friends reproached him, his enemies taunted him," said Lamon. After the *New York Times* reported that Lincoln en route had worn a "Scotch plaid cap," cartoonists delightedly caricatured him attired in kilt and tam-o'-shanter. In the streets, men said that anyone afraid to come through Baltimore openly was unfit to be president. One seasoned well-wisher wrote that at any time such a thing would be "deplorable and scandalous," but at that tense moment, when so much depended on the public perception of Lincoln's strength and steadiness, it appeared "nothing less than calamitous." This old Washingtonian* happened into Attorney General Stanton outside Willard's and found him "bitter and malignant" about how Lincoln " 'crept into Washington'. . . . every word was a suppressed and a very ill-suppressed sneer." According to Lamon, Lincoln himself soon came to regret being misled and alarmed over "a danger purely imaginary." But within weeks, events would prove that the menace of mob violence in Baltimore was real.[13]

Lincoln was not yet aware of all this criticism when Seward returned to Willard's at 11 A.M. and escorted him to meet Buchanan at the White House, where the president graciously introduced him to the cabinet. After the two went to call on General Scott but found him

---

*The identity of this citizen, the author of *Diary of a Public Man*, published anonymously in 1879, is still not firmly established. Some have attributed it to the lobbyist Samuel Ward (1814–1884), who was active in Washington at the time. Others believe it was written by Amos Kendall (1789–1869), Andrew Jackson's postmaster general and a prominent player in Washington journalism, politics and municipal life for forty years.

not at home, they drove about the city for an hour, each taking the measure of the other as they discussed cabinet candidates. Before leaving Springfield, Lincoln had made up his mind about most of his key appointments, but he was still considering his final decisions on how to balance politics and geography in the cabinet. He also had written his inaugural address and had it privately set in type. But those close to him understood his "lifelong habit to listen patiently to counsel from all quarters," of "holding his convictions open to the latest moment, and of not irrevocably committing himself to specific acts until the instant of their execution." He made a particular point of asking advice on the wording of this speech, which could be the most important of his and the nation's life.[14]

As secretary of state–designate and as an experienced Washington operator, Seward had encouraged the belief that he would function as "premier" of the incoming government, backed by his patron, the Albany publisher and New York State political boss Thurlow Weed. Others distrusted him. There had even been a minor test of strength over Lincoln's housing arrangements: trying to protect him from over-exposure to Seward, allies of Seward's strongest rival, Salmon P. Chase, the uncompromising antislavery senator from Ohio, had arranged quarters for the president-elect at a private home in Washington. But Weed, asserting that Lincoln was now "public property," had a friend persuade the industrialist William E. Dodge, a New York delegate to the peace convention, to vacate Willard's Suite 6, which happened to be just down the hall from Chase's rooms.[15]

Lines of office-seekers and congratulators promptly filled the hotel's lobby and second-floor corridors—among them other contenders for power, like the old Free-Soiler Francis P. Blair, Sr., of Maryland (who had written earlier that Seward "has the most eager, restless and unscrupulous ambition of any man I ever knew & Weed has the greatest maw for the spoils of the Government"). Blair came that afternoon with his son Montgomery, eager to place the younger man in the cabinet. General Scott, when he learned that he had missed Lincoln's call, came lumbering to see him at Willard's in full regalia, with epaulets shining. Later, Stephen Douglas, who had been Lincoln's leading Democratic opponent in senatorial and presidential elections, came with Illinois's congressional delegation and made clear his firm backing, putting aside partisanship in support of preserving the Union. The other two defeated candidates of 1860, Southerners John Breckinridge and John Bell, would also come and be cordial if not supportive.

That evening, Lincoln and his ticket mate Hannibal Hamlin went to Seward's home for dinner, and at 9 P.M. delegates from the peace convention called on him at Willard's.[16]

News of Lincoln's early arrival in Washington had thrown the convention delegates into confusion that morning, bringing on angry argument over whether they should ask for an audience with the man some Southerners called "Ignoramus!" and "Vulgar clown!" Ex-President Tyler managed consensus by suggesting that they would be paying their respects to the office, not to the man. That evening, as they filed in to shake hands, Lincoln's friendliness and sincerity impressed those who had not met him before. They particularly appreciated the way he knew every man's name and something about him. But a few delegates, first predictable Southerners and then Dodge, Lincoln's benefactor at Willard's, could not pass up this chance to press him.

"It is for you, sir, to say whether the whole nation shall be plunged into bankruptcy; whether the grass shall grow in the streets of our commercial cities," said the wealthy New Yorker.

"Then I say it shall not," Lincoln replied. "If it depends on me, the grass will not grow anywhere except in the fields and the meadows."

When Dodge said that meant the president would "yield to the just demands of the South," Lincoln firmly disagreed. But when asked what he would do in specific situations, he fell back repeatedly on the Constitution. It must apply to every part of every state, said Lincoln. "It must be respected, obeyed, enforced, and defended, let the grass grow where it may.... In a choice of evils, war may not always be the worst. Still I would do all in my power to avert it, except to neglect a Constitutional duty."[17]

His first day in Washington ran on. After the convention delegates came a variety of welcoming citizens; after that he dropped in on ladies gathered to see him in all the hotel's public rooms, and finally at ten o'clock Buchanan's cabinet called to return his earlier visit.[18]

Despite their dismay at the way Lincoln had come to town, most Unionists who shook his hand were willing to agree with Chittenden, who thought that in a matter of hours the president-elect had created a favorable impression: "The Republican members of the Conference felt encouraged and strengthened," he wrote, while "the sympathizers with secession were correspondingly discouraged and depressed."[19]

On Sunday morning, accompanied by Seward, the president-elect walked five blocks to services at St. John's Church on Lafayette

Square. "Not a dozen persons" there, apparently not even the Reverend Smith Pyne, realized who Lincoln was as he slipped into Pew No. 1, directly facing the chancel.

One newspaper noted that with his neatly trimmed dark hair and whiskers, Lincoln seemed "a different man entirely from the hard-looking pictorial representations seen of him. Some of the ladies say in fact he is almost good looking." This was welcome comment after the "gorilla" treatment he had seen for months and was still enduring from cartoonists, editorialists and politicians below the Potomac.[20]

Like President Buchanan, the Thirty-sixth Congress was a lame duck, sitting through its final days. Thus when Lincoln decided to visit the legislators as an early order of business, he might have been merely following protocol, paying his respects to the institution of Congress, not to the senators and representatives themselves. But many of these men had been reelected, and he would have to deal with them individually as the crisis deepened. Some were from slave territory: though most legislators from the first Confederate states had made their farewell speeches and taken their leave, those from the upper South were still in Washington. To Lincoln, their states had become the most important of all; he hoped that if they remained loyal, the Confederacy would collapse without them. That is why he was stubbornly noncommittal when pressed for his reaction to various possible developments. The reporter Henry Villard wrote that the president-elect would say unequivocally that the Union must be saved, and "go into long arguments in support of the proposition, based upon the history of the republic, the homogeneity of the population, the natural features of the country, such as the common coast, the rivers and mountains, that compelled political and commercial unity." But when it came to specifics, he still generalized about his duty to the Constitution.[21]

In the course of the next four stressful years, Lincoln would work lasting changes in the balance between the executive and legislative branches. But no one could foresee how that ongoing struggle for power would develop; the one sure thing was that it would be a struggle, and at the beginning the new president would need all the good will he could win among the proud and contentious barons of the Hill.

That Monday, Lincoln headed down the Avenue from Willard's to shake hands with those lawmakers. The broad eastward vista was framed by three- and four-story hotels, shops and boardinghouses along both sides of the rough-paved street, converging in the distance on the looming Capitol. As Lincoln drew closer, he could see that the building he had known so well as a young congressman was now surrounded by a jumble of wooden sheds and building materials; stacks of bricks and marble clogged nearby streets. The Capitol, like the nation, was in a state of suspense. Its new wings were unfinished, and where its dome should be, an awkward construction crane stood silhouetted against the sky. The crisis of the states had brought a crisis in the Capitol's reconstruction, one more chapter in an ongoing rivalry between two brilliant Americans to whom the nation would long be indebted for the architectural dignity of official Washington.

When Thomas Walter came to Washington as architect of the Capitol in 1851, Congress was outgrowing the building whose cornerstone had been laid by George Washington in 1793, seven years before the government moved there from Philadelphia. William Thornton's original plan for the Capitol had been elaborated upon by a series of architects including Benjamin Latrobe, who worked on the building before and after British soldiers fired it in 1814. The Capitol and White House were so badly damaged then that some legislators wanted to move the seat of government elsewhere rather than pay to rebuild Washington. In 1817, after losing one of many arguments with the authorities, Latrobe quit, and President James Monroe hired Charles Bulfinch to succeed him. Over the next thirteen years, Bulfinch brought the redesigned Capitol to completion, thirty-seven years after construction had begun. During the 1830s and '40s, running water and gaslights were installed. But at the same time, new states were being admitted and government business was growing so fast that much more space was needed.[22]

Following a national design competition, President Millard Fillmore chose Walter as architect for the job. At forty-seven, the Philadelphian was widely known for his work on churches, banks and municipal buildings, especially his design for Girard College, said to be "the climax, and at the same time ... the death knell, of the Greek Revival in America." He was a devout Baptist and Whig, willing lobbyist for his projects, and attentive husband. His first wife, Mary Ann Hancock, had died at the birth of their eleventh child; with his second wife, Amanda Gardiner, he would have two more. The nine who were living when he arrived in Washington ranged from four to twenty-five years old.[23]

Walter's first task as Capitol architect was to design massive north and south wings for Senate and House, additions that would more than double the length of the existing building. Soon it became clear that the expanded building would be far out of proportion to Bulfinch's copper-covered wooden dome, which had become a leaky fire hazard. Thus in 1855, Walter was also charged with creating a new dome to crown the expanded Capitol. But before that, a persistent complication had arisen.

When Democrat Franklin Pierce became president in 1853, he moved the Capitol project from the Interior Department to the War Department, then headed by ex-Senator Jefferson Davis. In direct charge, overseeing Walter, Davis placed Montgomery C. Meigs, an engineer and rising star in the peacetime army. At first, Meigs and Walter worked smoothly together. The architect accepted the engineer's changes on his plans for the wings, and wrote that "he is one of the noblest of men and a faithful friend and coadjutor." But two such men were not meant to proceed amiably for long.[24]

When Meigs was only six years old, his mother had written that he was "high-tempered, unyielding, tyrannical toward his brothers, and very persevering in pursuit of anything he wishes." He had not changed. He was the son of a prominent Philadelphia obstetrician, and grandson of a Yale mathematics professor who became president of the University of Georgia at Athens, where Montgomery was born in 1816. His father, Charles Delucena Meigs, steeped his sons in family history and a rigid sense of duty to "do whatever might be in their power to promote its honorableness." By the time Montgomery Meigs finished fifth in the West Point class of 1836, his self-respect needed no reinforcement.[25]

In America, particularly in the War Department, engineers had long considered themselves superior to other professionals, including architects. After West Point, Meigs was appointed to the artillery but soon transferred to the engineers and won assignment to one major project after another. In 1841, he solidified his career prospects by marrying Louisa Rodgers, daughter of Commodore John Rodgers, hero of the Barbary Coast Wars and the War of 1812. Architecture was one among Meigs's collection of talents; he was a Renaissance man, an accomplished administrator, technician, artist, lobbyist and amateur scientist. In addition to the Capitol project and other smaller local works, in the 1850s he was given charge of expanding the General Post Office and, most notably, building the Washington Aqueduct, to bring fresh water more than ten miles from the Great Falls of the Potomac into the city. Assuming correctly that those works would endure, he had his name cast conspicuously on the bridges, pipes, girders, steps and hydrants of his projects, as well as on the aqueduct's Chesapeake & Ohio Canal boat and a steam-powered fire engine that used the water his project delivered.

As Meigs juggled these varied projects, he found time to meddle constantly in Walter's work, revising this, arguing about that, until in 1857 the architect found out that Meigs had been claiming credit for his design of the new Capitol wings and dome. Furious, Walter refused to speak to him for almost two years, communicating exclusively through the secretary of war.[26]

Though Meigs's arrogance brought on this break, Walter had a healthy ego, too, and placed a high value on his own accomplishments. He was a founder of the American Institute of Architects, and had done as much as anyone to raise the status of his profession in the United States. But he was not a domineering personality like Meigs; he tended to keep his accumulated grievances quiet until there was one too many. In 1858, he wrote to a friend that "I was so unfortunate as to have a man placed on my works of the most imperious, self-conceited, vain, arrogant and unscrupulous character of any human being I ever met." A year later, Meigs was still trying to take not only control of the Capitol project, but credit for its conception.[27]

Walter justifiably felt more pride in the design of the new dome than in anything else he had ever undertaken. In scale and construction, it was unlike anything ever attempted in America. For inspiration and technical guidance, he looked to examples he had studied in Europe in 1838, including St. Paul's in London, St. Peter's in Rome and the Panthéon in Paris, as well as a dome that he had never seen, on St. Isaac's Cathedral in St. Petersburg. But he faced challenges that did not exist for the builders of those architectural triumphs: he had to create his huge new dome atop an existing building, which presented special problems not only of esthetics, but of structural engineering.

To minimize the weight of his dome, Walter decided to make it of cast iron, strong but much lighter than stone. Within the outer shell would be a second dome, open at the top. Suspended between them, seen from below through this opening, would be an immense allegorical painting by Constantino Brumidi, an exiled Roman artist who had restored Raphael's frescoes in the Vatican and would spend thirty years on such works in the Capitol. To erect the dome, Meigs devised a steam-powered derrick mounted on a triangular tower that was anchored on the floor of the Rotunda, reaching up through a temporary wooden roof installed when the Bulfinch dome was dismantled. Over 2,500 tons of new masonry was added to support the 4,500 tons of iron to be hoisted above. All this was in progress when Walter realized that Thomas Crawford's statue of Freedom, which would crown the dome, was taller, and its base was broader, than originally intended. This called for serious revision of the dome, and for it Walter obviously drew heavily on St. Isaac's, created in 1818 by the French architect Auguste Montferrand. The proportions of Walter's 1859 redesign are almost identical to those of the monumental dome in St. Petersburg, and the only drawing of a European building that he left in his Capitol records was of St. Isaac's.[28]

Early that year, Meigs's Washington Aqueduct brought municipal water to parts of the city for the first time—not yet from Great Falls, but from the reservoir beyond Georgetown. To mark the moment, Meigs invited senators to watch as a fountain spurted on the Capitol grounds. Afterward, he wrote to his father that this great success was "for free use of the sick and well, rich and poor, gentle and simple, old and young for generation after generation, which will have come to rise up and call me blessed." He was full of himself then, in no mind to take orders from Secretary of War Floyd, who had replaced Meigs's patron, Jeff Davis, when Davis returned to the Senate. After an escalating series of insubordinations, Floyd fired Meigs in November 1859, and soon afterward ordered him to Fort Jefferson on the Dry Tortugas, sixty miles beyond Key West. But after Lincoln's election, when Floyd departed to the South, the staunch Unionist Joseph Holt became secretary, and in response to Meigs's congressional friends, he brought the engineer back in February to oversee completion of both the Capitol and the Aqueduct projects.[29]

How the personal politics of Meigs and Walter figured in these decisions is unclear. Though the Southern Democrat Davis had been his strongest congressional promoter, Meigs was sternly pro-Union. Walter, a Whig appointee who had stayed on through Democratic administrations, was antiabolitionist (he owned one slave, a house servant named John Keith). Sometimes the architect was strangely naïve about what was happening beyond the Capitol grounds. In early February 1861, he wrote of his "animosity against the black republicans who have brought these horrid evils upon us," and predicted sadly that there would be war for the next decade. Less than two weeks later, he said he expected that before the year was out the states would be united again: "Some hot heads say '*never, never, never,*' but ... their words are idle wind. I learn that even South Carolina is sound at heart for Union. ... Let them alone and they would put an end to slavery in 2 or 3 years; crush them out, and bring S. Carolina back into the traces and slavery will be perpetuated forever."[30]

Within days after returning to Washington from the Tortugas, Meigs tried to fire Walter, but Walter held on, insisting that only the president had authority to discharge him. Unaware of this struggle, Lincoln arrived at the Capitol on February 25 to visit first the Supreme Court, which sat in the old Senate chamber, and then the Senate and House, each in its new wing.

Congressman Dawes had never seen Lincoln before; he wrote that "in spite of all I had heard to the contrary, [I] was expecting to see a god. Never did god come tumbling down more suddenly and completely than did mine, as the unkempt, ill-formed, loose-jointed, and disproportioned figure of Mr. Lincoln appeared at the door." Yet Dawes soon witnessed how the president-elect's "kindly homeliness of manner" became an attractive part of his personality, and helped overcome the dislike remaining from Lincoln's surreptitious entry into Washington.[31]

On that same Monday, Horace Greeley, the fiery abolitionist editor of the *New York Tribune,* arrived in Washington. According to the *Star,* he came "to help kill off a settlement of the National troubles, and to secure, if possible, the election of an out and out anti-compromise cast of the new Cabinet." The *Star*'s proprietor, W. D. Wallach, was unshakably Unionist, but like Lincoln, he wanted to save the whole Union. He did not admire Greeley, either politically or personally. The New York editor "has grown quite fleshy," said the *Star.* "His face looks as plump and fat as the body of a plucked reed bird in the height of the shooting season."[32]

But Wallach's hopes for a settlement misled him when the peace convention at Willard's Hall made its final effort at compromise, proposing six constitutional amendments before it adjourned sine die. His *Star* rejoiced that "every border state has been saved to the Union by the Convention's work of today, and the return of the seceded states to the Union is now but a question of short time." In wishful enthusiasm, General Scott ordered a hundred-gun salute in honor of the "pacification" that the convention agreed on and recommended to Congress. In reality, there was no chance that any meaningful amendments would clear the legislature; they were soon buried, mainly by unyielding Northern radicals. But the peace convention had been an unstated success in one sense, by helping to hold Virginia and the border states within the Union as long as compromise was being discussed.[33]

The president-elect fully realized that although he had evaded Baltimore's mobs safely, he was still surrounded in Washington by thousands of arch-Southerners who wished he had stayed in Springfield. One Northern journalist would write that in fashionable circles, "It was sufficient to bring any man into contempt, and place him under social ban, to know of him that his conscience was tender upon the subject of slavery." Not all of the capital's ruling class were slaveowners, but most were pleased to leave things as they stood. Mayor Berret was one of them. The previous June, he had been reelected by a margin of 24 votes out of almost 7,000 cast; the principal loser, independent Richard Wallach, brother of the *Star*'s editor, was still alleging fraud. On Wednesday evening, Berret was friendly but far from effusive as he spoke for a delegation of city officials who came to Willard's to offer Lincoln a formal welcome.[34]

Lincoln would take office "under circumstances menacing the peace and prosperity of the Republic, which have no parallel in the history of our country," said Berret. Washingtonians hoped and had no doubt that the new president could "bring the old ship into a harbor of safety and prosperity," and "true to the instincts of constitutional liberty, [they] will ever be found faithful to all the obligations of patriotism. . . ." He did not spell out his version of constitutional liberty or patriotism, but everyone present understood the difference between Berret's and Lincoln's attitudes in the current crisis.

Responding, Lincoln was just as noncommittal. He noted that he was unused to speaking publicly in a place where slavery was legal, but he believed that "very much of the ill feeling that existed and still exists between the people in the section from whence I came and the people here is dependent upon a misunderstanding of one another." He assured his welcomers that he felt just as kindly toward them as to the people back home, and would treat them as he would his own neighbors. He said he was confident that "when we shall become better acquainted . . . we shall like each other better."[35]

Between such obligatory public events, Lincoln spent many more hours socializing, gauging local sentiment, talking to other politicians about appointments and his inaugural address. He had essentially formed the cabinet in his own mind the day after his election, but when he left Springfield he had offered only two positions, to Seward and to Missouri Congressman Edward Bates, who would become attorney general. For the trials ahead, he needed to solidify the Republican Party behind him, which meant trying to satisfy both its conservative and radical wings while also rewarding his major bases of voting strength. Thus he decided that the man who dominated Pennsylvania politics, Senator Simon Cameron, would have a place despite allegations that he was "reeking with the stench of a thousand political bargains." Cameron's backers wanted him at Treasury, the job desired by Salmon P. Chase, the hard-liner from Ohio. But after polling Republican senators, Lincoln settled on Chase for Treasury and Cameron for War.[36]

The conservative Seward was angry. He insisted that he had "irreconcilable differences" with Chase; he was so upset that he wrote Lincoln a note threatening to withdraw if the decision stood. At this, Lincoln stiffened despite his liking for the New Yorker. "I can't afford to let Seward take the first trick," he told John Nicolay. He pretended to ignore Seward's note, and when Seward's friends appealed on his behalf, Lincoln quieted them by suggesting that one alternative might be to make him minister to England rather than secretary of state. Then, on the night before inauguration, the president gave a dinner for all his cabinet choices. For the Navy Department, he had picked Gideon Welles, a bewhiskered Connecticut editor of progressive mind and deep conscience. For Interior, he chose Caleb B. Smith, an Indiana lawyer and railroad president who had campaigned hard for the Lincoln ticket. For postmaster general, he nominated Montgomery Blair of Missouri and Maryland, whom Buchanan had fired as a government lawyer because of his firm stand against slavery, demonstrated later when he served as counsel for Dred Scott in the historic case that decided slaves were noncitizens without legal standing. The four other nominees had all aspired to the presidential nomination won by Lincoln: Cameron at the War Department, Bates as attorney general, Seward at State, and Chase at Treasury. Only the morning after this dinner, shortly before his inauguration, did the president-elect send Seward a brief note asking him to reconsider his threat to withdraw, which Seward promptly did. As Lincoln would later say, the New Yorker was "a man without gall."[37]

Seward had tested Lincoln's firmness and tact, and found what the rest of the world would soon discover. And even as this issue momentarily strained their alliance, Lincoln was asking and welcoming Seward's advice on the wording of his inaugural address. Seward offered changes that he said were "of little importance severally, but in their general effect tending to soothe the public mind. Of course the concessions are, as they ought to be, if they are to be of avail, at the cost of the winning, the triumphant party" rather than "the defeated, irritated, angered, frenzied party." He feared that unnecessarily strong wording would push Virginia and Maryland toward secession. "You cannot lose the Republican party by practicing in your advent to office the magnanimity of a victor," he wrote. In that spirit, he suggested a gentle ending to the speech: "some words of affection—some of calm and cheerful confidence." Lincoln accepted this advice, taking Seward's proposed final lines and slightly reworking them into one of the most eloquent paragraphs in American history.[38]

Thousands of outsiders poured into Washington the weekend before the inauguration on Monday, March 4. Willard's was so overcrowded that the proprietors rounded up 475 mattresses and laid them in the corridors and public rooms, and still could not accommodate everyone who wanted a bed. It was the same story at Kirkwood's and Brown's hotels. Every billet was filled, and still the visitors came. "Swarms of dusty-looking chaps, bearing carpetbags, wandered forlornly about the town" looking for a place to sleep. Some bunked down on lumber piles, and some walked all night, then took a turn on someone else's bed during the day. Lines of the bathless did their ablutions at public pumps and horse troughs. The *Star* said the crowds were half again as great as any for past inaugurations, with a typical turnout of crazies, but fewer ladies than usual; ninety-nine faces out of a hundred were those of strangers, and two-thirds of those were obvious westerners. On Friday evening, a group of Wide-Awakes joined the throng outside Willard's, calling for Lincoln. He appeared at a window, but they wanted more, so he stepped onto the windowsill, hanging on to the blinds, and offered them brief greetings.[39]

For days, the newspapers had printed a detailed schedule of the inaugural program, with long lists of officials, marshals, state delegations, diplomats, brass bands and military units in the order of march.

(Among the politicians was John Bouligny of Louisiana, married to Miss Parker on the day South Carolina seceded, who would be the only congressman from the Confederate states who chose to remain in Washington.) A hundred street-sweepers did their best to tidy up the Avenue. On Sunday, Scott conferred with Colonel Stone and his staff on final plans for protecting the incoming president in the midst of all these crowds and the threats that had started soon after Lincoln was elected. Among the many hate letters arriving in Springfield had been this one from Washington:

> Dear Sir:
>
> Caesar had his Brutus, Charles the First his Cromwell. And the President may profit by their example. From one of a sworn band of 10, who have resolved to shoot you in the inaugural procession on the 4th of March, 1861.
>
> Vindex.[40]

Scott and Stone had arranged for special police with prominent badges, and others as inconspicuous as possible, to mingle with the crowds. Lincoln and Buchanan would ride in one carriage, between files of cavalry. A company of sappers and miners would march ahead of the carriage, with infantry following. Riflemen would be posted on the roofs of houses along the way, with orders to watch windows on the opposite side. Regular cavalry would guard each intersection, moving from one to the next as the procession passed. A battalion of District of Columbia troops would be stationed around the Capitol steps, with sharpshooters looking on from windows in the wings. Horse artillery would stand ready nearby.[41]

Inauguration Day dawned raw and damp, but a raspy wind blew the clouds away and stirred dust from the streets as the sun climbed. Before nine o'clock, horses and men began to form into parade order, and at eleven they moved toward the White House. At Willard's, Lincoln wanted to know how his speech would sound, so he asked his son Robert to read it aloud to him. Buchanan, busy until the last moment signing bills, joined the procession at twelve-thirty and called for Lincoln at the hotel. Together, the two stepped out to board an open barouche, sitting facing Senators Edward D. Baker of Oregon and James A. Pearce of Maryland. As they moved off, they were so densely surrounded by troops that they could hardly be seen from curbside, and any attacker at street level would have scant chance of getting through. Scott in his carriage moved along the streets north of the Avenue, personally checking security details at each block.

The presidents talked little on the way down the Avenue, perhaps remarking on the Republican float symbolizing Constitution and Union, which had thirty-four girls in white to represent all the states, including those already seceded. Now and then Lincoln stood and took a little bow to applause from onlookers. At the Capitol, the two men walked from carriage to building through a temporary passageway of heavy lumber. They were escorted first to the Senate chamber. There, John Breckinridge, elected again to the Senate, swore in Hannibal Hamlin, his successor as vice president. Then, just after one o'clock, Lincoln emerged onto the inaugural platform on the east front, looking "as grave and impassive as an Indian martyr." He faced a crowd of uncounted thousands spread across the grounds toward Mrs. Sprigg's boardinghouse, where he had lived as a raw one-term congressman.[42]

The rough-edged son of the frontier had not yet impressed all of those who would later admire him. Twenty-five-year-old Charles Francis Adams, Jr., proud grandson and great-grandson of New England presidents, looked down his nose at the proceedings. He thought Lincoln's "lank angular form and hirsute face," as well as his dress and bearing, fell short of the moment. Although the veteran correspondent L. A. Gobright of the Associated Press wrote that "never was there a more solemn spectacle," and estimated the crowd at 30,000, Adams made it closer to 4,000 or 5,000. To him, the unfinished Capitol and temporary inaugural structures contributed to an atmosphere less than heartening—"A tall, ungainly man addressing a motley gathering . . . with a voice elevated to its highest pitch. . . . a somewhat noticeable absence of pomp, state, ceremony. . . ." The French Minister Henri Mercier agreed with Adams, maintaining that Lincolnian simplicity was out of character with the "marble and gilt" of the Capitol— "It's as if one wanted to inaugurate a Quaker in a basilica." But Adams admitted later that he was unable to hear most of what Lincoln said, thus missing what made the occasion so memorable.[43]

After Senator Baker drew cheers with a simple introduction of the incoming president, Lincoln stood, bowed and looked about for a place to put his stovepipe hat. In a calculated gesture of solidarity, his old rival Stephen Douglas quickly took the hat and held it. Lincoln laid his printed text, with its many handwritten revisions, upon the rostrum and used his gold-headed cane to hold the pages down. He brought his steel-rimmed glasses from his pocket, placed them carefully on his nose, and began.

He laid out his case in a measured, lawyerly way. By his third sentence, he made clear that he was addressing the unhappy South, asserting that it had no cause for alarm. Though he would never recognize secession, he had no intention of interfering with slavery where it then existed. Near the midpoint of his address, there was a crash far back in the crowd, stirring momentary fear of trouble, but it was merely a tree branch falling beneath a young spectator who had climbed up for a better view. Lincoln insisted that the Union is perpetual, that no state on its own motion can get out of it. Thus, despite the formation of the Confederacy, he considered the Union still unbroken, and pledged to enforce its laws in all the states. He raised his voice slightly as he vowed to take and hold property belonging to the government, and emphasized that passage with a brief pause afterward. If some considered this a threat, he spoke to them as he concluded:

> In your hands, my dissatisfied fellow-countrymen, and not in mine, is the momentous issue of civil war. The government will not assail you. You can have no conflict without being yourselves the aggressors. You have no oath registered in heaven to destroy the government, while I shall have the most solemn one to "preserve, protect, and defend it."
>
> I am loath to close. We are not enemies, but friends. We must not be enemies. Though passion may have strained, it must not break our bonds of affection. The mystic chords of memory, stretching from every battlefield and patriot grave to every living heart and hearth-stone all over this broad land, will yet swell the chorus of the Union when again touched, as surely they will be, by the better angels of our nature.[44]

His voice faltered slightly as he spoke the last sentence, and one correspondent wrote that those final words "broke the watering pot" of many listeners. Then Lincoln faced eighty-three-year-old Chief Justice Taney, who looked at least his age; since 1836, he had sworn in six presidents. Lincoln placed one hand upon the Bible and repeated the oath of office, then bowed and kissed the book. A cacophony of brass bands and cannon marked the moment when he became the sixteenth president of the United States.[45]

Though troops and sharpshooters were still on guard, tension eased as the new president and his weary predecessor rode past the crowds, back up the Avenue to the White House. There, Lincoln registered his regard for the old Union in its entirety, by kissing each of the girls who stood for the thirty-four states. Then, as if this were any ordinary change of presidents, the departing Buchanan wished him a happy and prosperous administration.

CHAPTER FOUR

Why Don't They Come?

George William Bagby sat in his office on Newspaper Row, two blocks from the White House, and penned a farewell to Washington for his New Orleans and Richmond readers. He had stayed to hear what Lincoln would say on March 4, then briefly watched as the new president tried to decide what to do about Fort Sumter while besieged by job-seekers at the White House. But Bagby, even though he was a deep-dyed Virginian, was too angry to wait for the Old Dominion to make up its mind about secession. In the crisis, bitterness overrode the fluent humor that distinguished his work in calmer times.

"In lieu of deeds, we have gab, endless gab," he wrote. "Each day of the week is set apart by the delegations from the triumphant States for paying obsequious civilities to the various and sundry animals freshly caged in the Federal menagerie. Early in the morning some hotel vomits a dark stream of human forms, containing the souls of insects. Now, Willard's gapes its great jaws and lets out a thousand pismires from New York; now the Avenue House heaves on a couple of hundred ascarides from Indiana. These wind their way to the white den of the Imperial Gorilla; thence to the burrow of the preeminent weavel, Seward; thence to the coop of the plumed peacock and bustard-of-war, Scott; thence to the kennel of the incomparable hound, [Senator] Andy Johnson, and so on around the entire ring of royal beasts, princely nondescripts, and martial birds of prey."

Bagby raged on for 1,800 words, concluding that "the drama is but begun . . . . a new principal actor appears on the stage. By nature a low comedian, will he doff his grinning mask and don the hideous visage of high tragedy? We shall see. Meantime your critic in the pit retires to another part of the stage." And so he returned to Richmond, where he would hold forth for years to come.[1]

The wave of well-wishers who had come to celebrate the new president's ascendancy receded from the streets and roominghouses of Washington, leaving behind some of the ambitious many who had come hoping to stay. The *Providence Press* reported that hotel proprietors of the capital were holding more than four hundred carpetbags and valises left by unsuccessful job-seekers who departed unable to pay their bills. "As far as heard from there is only one valise that contains anything valuable," the paper said, "and in that one was found a well executed counterfeit twenty dollar bill on the State Bank of Ohio." As usual when one party takes power from another, the most prominent men on the losing side began packing. But there had never been and never would be a change of administrations as meaningful as this one, never departures so charged with emotion.[2]

Although the Texas convention had voted for secession weeks earlier, the determined Senator Wigfall, who had plotted at Christmas to kidnap Buchanan, hung on in Washington. Before Congress adjourned, he had told loyalists on the Senate floor, "We have dissolved the Union," and challenged them to "mend it if you can; cement it with blood." Yet for nineteen days after Lincoln's inauguration, he stayed, fighting off a Republican effort to expel him from the Senate, all the while busily socializing, gathering gossip about the new president's intentions and passing it along to the Confederate government in Montgomery. Such intercourse went on unchecked for weeks between the first wave of secession and the advent of war. Wigfall colluded with Colonel Ben McCulloch, who had led the takeover of Federal forts in Texas, when McCulloch came to Washington to buy pistols for his mounted regiment of Confederates. Wigfall and friends suggested that rather than conducting this business in the Federal capital, it would be more discreet for the rash Ranger to take a room across the river in Alexandria. Soon afterward, Wigfall voluntarily left Washington and then turned up in the drama at Charleston, as an aide to Confederate General Pierre G. T. Beauregard.[3]

Yet many of those who headed south were neither raging nor taking up arms. They were weeping.

Sara Pryor, whose congressman husband would soon join the angry chorus at Charleston, had bubbled with excitement at the first news of secession. But when it was time to leave Washington, that eagerness was gone. Just after beginning her trip on a steamboat down the Potomac, she came on deck from the dinner table to salute Mount Vernon as she passed, perhaps for the last time. She looked back: "My own pride in the federal city was such that my heart would swell within me at every glimpse of the Capitol: from the moment it rose like a white cloud above the smoke and mists . . . to the time when I was wont to watch from my window for the sunset, that I might catch the moment when a point on the unfinished dome glowed like a great blazing star after the sun had really gone down. No matter whether suns rose or set, there was the star of our country, the star of our hearts and hopes."[4]

Thousands of Southerners looked back as nostalgically as Sara Pryor had done when they left Washington that spring. Northerners flooded in behind them, some in the spirit of an occupying army, some dreaming of riches. A few of those newcomers recognized this as the adventure of a lifetime; among them were the smart young men who accompanied the Lincolns to Washington, where they would become as close as family members.

John G. Nicolay had immigrated with his family from Germany at the age of six, and turned twenty-nine years old shortly after arriving in Washington. His parents had died when he was a boy, and he rose from printer's devil to proprietor of a county-seat newspaper before becoming clerk to Illinois's secretary of state and then private secretary to presidential candidate Lincoln. For a decade, he had been friends with John M. Hay, before and after Hay left Illinois to attend Brown University and returned to Springfield to practice law next door to Lincoln. With Lincoln's approval, Nicolay brought on the smart, congenial Hay as assistant private secretary at the age of twenty-two. William O. Stoddard, twenty-five, had been a small-town antislavery editor, among the first to support Lincoln for president. As reward, Lincoln brought him to Washington to sign land patents, but soon reassigned him to sift presidential mail. Together, these three would handle virtually all of the new president's overwhelming clerical work. The fourth of the young Illinoisans, twenty-three-year-old Elmer Ellsworth, had hoped to go to West Point and become a soldier when he was a teenager in New York. Unable to do so, he moved to Chicago and won praise commanding a colorful militia drill team before entering Lincoln's law office and working in his presidential campaign.

When Lincoln moved into the White House, he was welcomed by the same burly, genial Irish doorman who had greeted visitors for six previous presidents, beginning with John Tyler. This was Edward McManus, valued by Lincoln as the first person he met in his new surroundings who could make him laugh. McManus called himself "the most ancient Institution in Washington," and liked to entertain those waiting to see the president with tales from Daniel Webster's day. Early one morning, soon after Stoddard came to work there, McManus presented to him what he said was the original front door key to the premises. Inside, the new second assistant secretary looked around.[5]

The throng of place-seekers and patriots who filled the mansion's portico, great rooms, corridors and stairs during office hours, insisting on making their appeals to Lincoln in person, was wearing things to a shabby state. As Stoddard looked westward toward the old War and Navy buildings, the word that occurred to him was "dingy." The East Room, scene of the grandest occasions in the building's history, was "faded, worn, untidy"—its paint and furniture needed renewal, and "so did almost everything else, within and without." Unhousebroken visitors among the "ill-bred, ravenous crowd" had actually clipped off pieces of damask drapery, satin curtains and expensive carpets as souvenirs.[6]

The family occupied the west end of both the main and second floors of the mansion; the east end, toward the State and Treasury departments, was the business section. The president's office was upstairs, with an adjacent room where he could work when applicants swarmed too thickly. Nicolay labored in the southeast corner of the second floor, and he and Hay slept in a bedroom on the north side. Stoddard, junior man of the clerical staff, was allotted merely a desk at the time, and slept elsewhere. From its private quarters upstairs, the family had a broad view of Virginia, from Arlington down the Potomac toward Alexandria.[7]

Although the White House was far more splendid and spacious than any place the Lincolns had ever lived, Mary Todd Lincoln was more offended than anyone else by the dwelling's sorry state of maintenance. She was, after all, one of the Todds of Kentucky, daughter of a well-to-do banker, manufacturer and merchant. She resented the crush of supplicants and visitors who thought they had a right to walk into the White House uninvited, to see the man they had elected in the mansion they had paid for. She took over the Red Room, on the first floor, as her own reception space. But within the first week, she also sought a refuge from the crowds that had surrounded the Lincolns at almost every waking hour since they left Springfield. Apparently at the suggestion of Buchanan, she persuaded her husband to inspect the Soldiers' Home, beyond Boundary Street (Florida Avenue) in the rural northern stretch of the District. Buchanan had sometimes spent the night in the stone structure, set among cool woods away from the muggy Potomac bottomland.[8]

But months would pass before the Lincolns could make the Soldiers' Home their country place. For the president, the flood of business was too great; for Mary, there were the demands of first ladyship, and she was eager to impress Washington society. It was a challenge. At forty-two, she had become a bit dumpy, and capable of being gracious at one moment, demanding at the next. Her first appearance in her new role, at the inaugural ball in a vast temporary shed behind City Hall, had been less than a shining success; many social and political Washingtonians stayed away, the exhausted president left early, and Mary, according to one old-timer, was "all in blue, a feather in her hair, and a highly flushed face . . . anything but an ornamental feature. . . ." She intended to make her at-home debut on March 8, when the Lincolns gave their first levee, the kind of reception that was expected of nineteenth-century presidents. For the occasion, Mrs. Lincoln wanted a gown that would be remembered, one that might compensate for her shortage of personal glamour. For it, she turned to Elizabeth Keckley, who only weeks earlier had been dressing Varina Davis, now the first lady of the Confederacy.[9]

Ever since coming to Washington, Keckley had wanted to work in the White House. When the wife of a distinguished soldier pleaded with her to do a rush job for a special dinner, Keckley said no until the woman offered to say a word on her behalf to Mrs. Lincoln. At that she changed her mind, and the result was another rush job, this one for Mary Lincoln, who had told her, "if you work cheap, you shall have plenty to do." Keckley barely completed it in time for the levee, but the first lady was able to descend the stairs proudly in rose-colored moire-antique, wearing a pearl necklace, pearl earrings, pearl bracelets, and red roses in her hair. According to Keckley, who had heard talk of Mary's western "ignorance and vulgarity," she seemed as calm and graceful as any queen. From that evening onward, the first lady and her free black seamstress would become the closest of friends.[10]

For the president, that levee was an endurance test. From eight-fifteen till ten-thirty, he stood shaking hands at an estimated rate of 25 per minute, or 3,375 in those two hours and fifteen minutes. When guests began to leave, they found that their hats and coats were all mixed up and some had apparently been stolen, so that "perhaps not one in ten of that large assemblage emerged with the same outer garments they wore on entering."[11]

Barely two weeks after moving into the White House, the Lincolns' ten-year-old son William Wallace "Willie" Lincoln, probably the smartest and most promising of their three surviving boys, came down with measles. So did their youngest, Thomas D. Lincoln, not quite eight years old, a "perfectly lawless" but loving little scamp called "Tad." The oldest son, the sober, businesslike seventeen-year-old Robert Todd Lincoln, named for his maternal grandfather, had entered Harvard in 1859 but came to Washington for his father's inauguration. Another boy, Edward Baker Lincoln, named for the president's boon friend who was now a senator from Oregon, had died in Springfield in 1850, at the age of three. Willie and Tad soon became pets of the White House staff and mischievous masters of the mansion, its closets, attics, grounds and stables; their "good-natured disobedience . . . kept the house in an uproar."[12]

Between urgent conferences on the Fort Sumter crisis and fending off job applicants who had once made a Republican speech or commanded a contingent of Wide-Awakes, the boys' doting father had few moments to indulge them in those first weeks in Washington. He had never held an administrative office before; his résumé was pathetically skimpy compared to that of Jefferson Davis, West Point graduate, colonel of volunteers, combat veteran, secretary of war and twice U.S. senator from Mississippi. As a lawyer and one-term congressman, Lincoln had never needed to delegate authority, and now was trying to do too much himself. He carried a little pocket memorandum book in which he kept a record of what patronage he had promised to whom during the campaign. His Republican backer Orville Browning had written to him in sympathy, "Surely no man ever assumed the reins of government beset by such complicated and oppressive difficulties as have surrounded you," yet in the beginning Lincoln busied himself with details that could have been carried out by third-level appointees.[13]

One of his easier problems was how to deal with the Confederate delegation sent by Davis in an attempt to negotiate peaceful secession: Lincoln simply refused to have anything to do with the three commissioners—former Congressman Martin J. Crawford of Georgia, John Forsyth of Alabama and former Governor Andre B. Roman of Louisiana. He instructed Seward not to see them, to prevent their claiming that the administration had thus recognized the Montgomery government. But Seward, still acting as if he were prime minister, communicated with them confidentially, suggesting that if the Confederates were patient, Sumter would be evacuated. He was playing for time, hoping that by staving off gunfire and avoiding the sore subject of slavery, he could keep Virginia and the border states within the Union, then put together a dominant new Union party of conservatives north and south. Young Charles Francis Adams would call this the secretary's "Southern-Unionist dreamland."[14]

The day after Lincoln's inauguration, Major Anderson at Sumter had changed his earlier confident stance and warned Washington that his supplies were running out. Now Scott, other generals and naval officers were advising the president that withdrawal was unavoidable, and newspapers were predicting that it would happen within days. But the president cast about for any solution other than backing down so promptly from his inaugural promises. When he polled his cabinet in mid-March, all but Chase and Blair came down on the side of withdrawal. And besides Sumter, there was the problem of Fort Pickens, at Pensacola, which the Confederates had cut off from resupply.

Using Supreme Court Justice John A. Campbell of Alabama as an intermediary, Seward told the Confederate commissioners that Sumter would be evacuated within five days—by March 20—and nothing would be done about Pickens. While the ever-optimistic Seward assumed that he was manipulating things in favor of himself and the Union, the Southern commissioners confided to officials in Montgomery that he was playing into Confederate hands. "It is well that he should indulge in dreams which we know are not to be realized," they wrote. Although Seward was seeing Lincoln daily, he told him nothing about these back-channel communications.[15]

March 20 came and went, and all that changed was the degree of tension in Washington and the number of Confederate coastal guns aimed at Fort Sumter. Facing near-unanimous pessimism among his closest advisers about the possibility of reinforcing Sumter, Lincoln sent his friend and bodyguard Ward Lamon to Charleston to bring back yet another assessment, untainted by politics. Lamon, like earlier emissaries, confirmed that pessimism. At the same time, angry Republican radicals held out against any compromise, some charging that the president was drifting just as indecisively as Buchanan had done. Lincoln was shocked in late March when Scott unexpectedly urged pacifying the Confederates by giving up both Sumter and Pickens. When he called his cabinet secretaries together following his first state dinner on March 28 and told them what Scott had said, they were jolted as well. The next day, Good Friday, he asked again for their thoughts. Chase, Bates, Welles and Blair criticized Seward's reluctance to do anything at Charleston that might offend the Confederates, but even Seward would not abandon Fort Pickens, which had not taken on the symbolic importance of Sumter.[16]

After that cabinet meeting, Lincoln ordered an expedition to be ready to sail for Fort Sumter by April 6. The same day, Seward brought Captain Montgomery Meigs, recently back from the Gulf of Mexico, to see the president. Meigs was still nominally in charge of the Aqueduct, the Capitol and his other projects. But the time he had spent at the Dry Tortugas for insubordination to Floyd had now qualified him for special assignment by Seward. Because he had become familiar with the Gulf forts, Seward had picked him to lead an expedition to reinforce Fort Pickens, off the Florida panhandle. The secretary of state intentionally excluded the secretaries of war and navy from his plans for this combined army-navy operation. He did so for security reasons, but also because he was still proceeding as if he were de facto president, with Lincoln in the ceremonial role of head of state.

On April 1, by sending the president a memorandum intended to spell out this relationship, Seward finally overasserted himself. He began by stating that after a month in office the administration had no policy, either foreign or domestic. Further delay would bring scandal and danger, Seward wrote. He urged that "*we must change the question before the public from one upon slavery, or about slavery,* for a question upon *union or disunion*." Since the Confederates seemed to consider Fort Sumter a slavery or party issue, it should be evacuated and removed from the agenda, he said. All other Union outposts in the South should be defended. Meanwhile the administration should demand explanations from France and Spain for their adventures in Haiti and Santo Domingo, and if their answers were not satisfactory, the United States should declare war on them.

Whatever the nation's policy, Seward wrote, "it must be somebody's business to pursue and direct it incessantly. Either the president must do it himself, and be all the while active in it, or devolve it on some member of his cabinet. Once adopted, debates on it must end, and all agree and abide."

"It is not my especial province," he said, but he made clear that he was eminently available: "I neither seek to evade nor assume responsibility." In other words, if Lincoln was not going to run the government, Seward would.

Nicolay and Hay wrote later that this "extraordinary state paper" was "unlike anything to be found in the political history of the United States." And Lincoln recognized it for what it was, for he wrote an immediate reply, calmly rejecting Seward's every contention. To the most pointed suggestion, that someone should take charge, the president said, "if this must be done, I must do it." He reminded Seward of his place by concluding: "I wish, and suppose I am entitled to have, the advice of all the Cabinet."[17]

Between two other forceful men, this exchange might have created mortal enemies. But in the long run, Lincoln would have no more sincere or devoted supporter than his secretary of state, whom he came to trust completely. And within days, the world would see who was chief executive of the United States government.

But Seward's usurpation of authority from the civilian heads of the army and navy, already set in motion, was still being played out. Although Lincoln gave orders to resupply both Sumter and Pickens, Seward arranged to divert the Sumter expedition's powerful flagship, *Powhatan,* to Meigs's Fort Pickens mission instead. He replaced her commander with David Dixon Porter, who was almost as brash and ambitious as Meigs himself. Seward, as he had promised the Confederate commissioners, also sent word indirectly to Charleston that the fleet was coming. Thus he undercut his own president but kept his secretly given pledge to the Confederates, virtually assuring the failure of the effort to resupply Sumter. When the navy secretary, Gideon Welles, found out about these and surrounding machinations, he was properly furious.[18]

Meigs returned to his home on H Street, two blocks from the White House, and told his wife, Louisa, to pack his trunk for New York. But he refused to tell her his real destination, or how long he would be gone. "This was hard and tantalizing as you can imagine," Mrs. Meigs wrote to her mother. "However there was nothing to be done, but to 'obey orders.' . . . I have been quietly learning the lesson of several years that my husband does not belong to me but to the country and at this time when she needs the service of her great and true hearted men, I should be wanting in patriotism to desire to keep him at my side. These are times to try one's courage." Louisa had grown up in a navy family, whose women had told loved ones goodbye many times without knowing when or whether they would return.[19]

Near midnight on April 5, Welles roused Seward, demanding an explanation for what was going on, and insisted that they take the matter to the president. When they woke Lincoln, he confirmed that he had signed the orders drawn up by Seward and Meigs, but said he had not carefully read them. Responding to Welles's complaints, he told Seward to return *Powhatan* to her original captain and her course to Fort Sumter. But before that order, signed by Seward, arrived in New York, Porter had sailed. When an officer caught up with *Powhatan* off Staten Island, Porter kept going, asserting that his earlier orders ruled because they were direct from the president.[20]

The Meigs-Porter expedition cleared New York four days late, and by the time it rounded the Florida Peninsula and reached the waters off Pensacola, two other reinforcing parties had already landed. Scott had ordered these operations within days after the inauguration, and Seward initiated the Meigs mission because they had not been heard from since. Thus the secret excursion to Fort Pickens ended less gloriously than Meigs and Porter had hoped. In history, it became a hardly noticed sideshow to what was happening at Charleston and Richmond in early April.

Save Virginia, and we will save the nation." So said Stephen Douglas, and Lincoln seemed to believe him. Virginia, so close across the river from the White House, was the most prestigious and populous of the slave states, with the South's biggest industrial complex in Richmond and the nation's best naval anchorage at Hampton Roads. She swung heavy influence in the other states of the upper South; if she remained loyal to the Union, the cotton-state Confederacy might shrivel and die. On April 4, as Confederate guns at Charleston boomed away, practicing and hoping to impress the garrison of Fort Sumter, the Virginia convention in Richmond took a test vote on secession and rejected it by a margin of two to one. Lincoln desperately wanted the convention to let that vote stand and go home. At Seward's urging, he invited the state's Unionists to discuss a deal.[21]

When the convention voted against seceding, Lincoln told Virginia loyalist John B. Baldwin that if the delegates adjourned without changing their stand, he would call off the resupply mission that was about to sail for Fort Sumter. According to John Minor Botts, the most outspoken Unionist in Richmond, the president told Baldwin, "If you will guarantee to me the state of Virginia I shall remove the troops. A state for a fort is no bad business." But Baldwin could make no such promise, and he unaccountably failed to rush the offer to the convention. Botts heard of it two days later, when he came to the White House. When he asked if he could take the same proposition to Richmond, Lincoln told him it was too late, the Sumter expedition had sailed.[22]

Lincoln had to negotiate this maze of overlapping cabinet feuds, secret expeditions, insubordinate officers and diplomatic maneuvers as he went ahead with the decisions that would determine war or peace. He sent word to Governor Francis W. Pickens of South Carolina that he was dispatching ships not to reinforce Fort Sumter with arms and men, but merely to resupply the garrison with food. If there was to be war, the Confederates would have to fire the first shot. Seward finally informed the commissioners from Montgomery that there would be no recognition of the Confederate government, and they headed huffily home. That night, April 8, entertaining the British correspondent William Howard Russell, the secretary of state was still predicting that within three months the seceded states would come to their senses and rejoin the Union.[23]

Within hours, Seward's months of optimism, maneuvering and duplicity were proven useless. From Montgomery, Davis sent orders for Beauregard to demand the fort's surrender and, if refused, to take the offensive. Anderson told Beauregard's emissaries that he would not surrender, but if the fort was not pounded to pieces, he would be starved out in a few days. Later they returned to ask him for a specific time when he would evacuate. Anderson said he would pull out by noon, April 15—if he did not receive other orders from Washington. This conditional answer did not satisfy Beauregard's officers. They handed Anderson a note saying their guns would open fire in an hour. After shaking hands with him, they rowed away, reaching the Confederate batteries at 4 A.M.[24]

Roger Pryor, the Virginia congressman whose wife wrote of her sad departure from Washington, was not so sentimental about leaving the Union. He had been speechifying in Charleston, declaring that

South Carolina must "strike a blow," and if she did, Virginia would be at her side "in less than an hour by Shrewsbury clock." This so pleased the Confederate gunners that now they offered Pryor the chance to fire the first cannonball at Fort Sumter. But after all that rhetoric, Pryor could not bring himself to do it. He passed the honor to another Virginian, the monomaniacal secessionist Edmund Ruffin, who had been so impatient with his home state's weeks of deliberation that he left and joined South Carolina's Palmetto Guards. At 4:30 A.M. on Friday, April 12, Ruffin proudly fired the opening gun of the Civil War.[25]

In the hours after that cannon boomed, no one in Washington, including the president, had an accurate picture of what was happening at Charleston. There was more hearsay than news: The firing had begun—no, negotiations were going on. There was a furious battle—no, the fort had surrendered. Crowds gathered at the telegraph offices and hotels, swapping rumors. In all the excitement, many secessionists who had hidden their true colors now cut loose, celebrating the start of war. Fistfights broke out. Southern sympathizers openly sought recruits for the Confederate army, a disloyal act that patriots briefly tolerated because they were glad to get rid of such men. When the truth arrived—that Major Anderson had been forced to surrender Fort Sumter after exchanging fire with Confederate guns for thirty-four hours—another rumor followed: the Rebels were about to march on Washington with an army of 20,000 men.

On April 14, Colonel Stone called into service five more Washington militia companies, making a total of some 2,500 local troops on active duty. He posted mounted soldiers at the approaches to the city. Twenty cavalrymen guarded the White House, with another 200 troops nearby, plus 300 at the Treasury, 200 at the Capitol and 150 at the post office. The cabinet approved the president's request for 75,000 troops to put down the rebellion, and for Congress to return in special session on July 4. The next day, Lincoln issued the nationwide call for troops, assigning each state a quota.[26]

Virginia's quota was only three regiments, proportionately far short of her share by population. But any was too many for Governor Letcher, who for nearly six months had held firm against increasingly angry pressure from the state's secessionists. Even now, as crowds in Richmond's Capitol Square celebrated the fall of Fort Sumter, he refused to respond until he had official word from Washington. When it came, the loyal John Botts said Lincoln's call for troops was "in many respects the most unfortunate state paper that ever issued from any executive since the establishment of the government." Letcher, saying the troops were summoned "to subjugate the Southern states," refused to meet the requisition. "You have chosen to inaugurate civil war," he told Secretary of War Cameron, "and having done so we will meet you, in a spirit as determined as the Administration has exhibited toward the South." In that spirit, on April 17 the Virginia convention reversed itself and voted 88 to 55 for secession—subject to approval by a public referendum to be held May 23. But once the dam of conservatism was broken, the referendum was moot.[27]

Hours before news of the convention's reversal reached Washington, a letter and a message arrived at Arlington Plantation, the home to which Robert E. Lee had returned from seceded Texas six weeks earlier. In early March, Lee had a long and solemn conversation with General Scott, his friend and mentor since the Mexican War. Soon after that, he was promoted to full colonel and given command of the First U.S. Cavalry. Now, on April 17, a letter from Scott and a message from Francis Blair, Sr., came to Lee, each asking him to call the next day. The following morning, he went first to Blair's home, diagonally across Pennsylvania Avenue from the White House. Blair told him that he was authorized by the president to ask if Lee would accept command of the entire United States Army. It was an offer of the highest position in American military life, at a time of mortal crisis for the nation that Lee and his family had served so long. He declined it, saying that though he opposed secession and hated war, he could not take part in an invasion of the Southern states.

From Blair's, Lee went to see Scott and told him what had just happened. "Lee," said the old general, "you have made the greatest mistake of your life, but I feared it would be so." For years, he had admired and promoted Lee, repeatedly telling others that he was the best soldier in the army; they had developed something close to a father-son relationship. Now he advised Lee to resign from the service to which he had devoted most of his life. In deep inner turmoil, Lee rode home to Arlington.[28]

As rumors escalated, loyal citizens and even travelers were signing up for emergency duty in Washington. At the National Hotel, New Yorker Francis Low was told to report to Willard's. There he found the rambunctious abolitionist Cassius M. Clay of Kentucky, recently appointed minister to Russia, surrounded by arms and ammunition and enrolling reliable "strangers" in the capital to defend the White House. When Clay offered his service to the secretary of war, Cameron had said, "Sir, this is the first instance I ever heard of where a foreign minister volunteered in the ranks," to which Clay replied, "Then let's make a little history." Clay's volunteers elected him captain and made lieutenants of several other worthies who were already or soon would be generals. John Hay told how Clay came to see the president ready for hand-to-hand combat, wearing "three pistols and an Arkansas toothpick [Bowie knife]." After drawing rifles and twelve rounds of ammunition each, his men were briefly put through the manual of arms, bypassing the esthetics of drill to concentrate on loading and firing.[29]

Senator James H. Lane, who had been a militia general in the border wars in "bleeding Kansas," went Clay one better by recruiting his own Frontier Guards at Willard's and marching them into the East Room of the White House, where "under the gorgeous gas chandeliers, they disposed themselves in picturesque bivouac on the brilliant-patterned velvet carpet." Lane was seen as "gaunt, tattered, uncombed and unshorn" when dining in polite company. But under arms, he was crisp and businesslike, "brandishing a sword of irreproachable brightness" as he inspected his Jayhawker colleague, Senator Samuel C. Pomeroy, and other dignitaries standing at attention as privates.[30]

With dozens of regular army and navy officers resigning to go south, these ad hoc companies of known loyalists were meant to hold the fort until trained militia companies arrived from the North. Reports came that Virginians had seized the Federal armory at Harpers Ferry and navy facilities at Norfolk, and 3,000 Marylanders were secretly organized to block the passage of troops through Baltimore on their way to Washington. All of this fit into a suspected Rebel master plan—to cut off reinforcements by rail or river, force Maryland to secede, capture Washington and make it the capital of the Confederacy. "The loyal states cannot act too promptly," said the *New York Times,* as the Sixth Massachusetts Regiment paraded through Manhattan. Lincoln's young friend Elmer Ellsworth went from Washington to New York to recruit a regiment from the city's rough and eager volunteer firemen, whom he labeled "soldiers ready made." Four companies from Pennsylvania reached Washington and told of how crowds had threatened them and stoned their rail cars as they moved through Baltimore. They set up camp inside the Capitol building, annoying Thomas Walter in his architect's office. "They are making noises that are more like a bedlam," wrote Walter. "Every hole and corner of Washington is filled with soldiers." He had no inkling of how many more soldiers and noises were coming.[31]

Every official in Washington understood that Baltimore boiled with Southern anger, threatening peaceful passage by Union soldiers, but few understood why. Although Maryland was a slave state and tobacco plantations dominated its southern counties, there were relatively few slaves in the important port city on the Patapsco River. The *New York Tribune*'s correspondent thought that "the intense pro-slaveryism of [Baltimore] cannot ... be traced to a deep interest in bipedal property, nor to any care about insurrections, nor to any sincere colorphobia. *It is simply the sign of a caste.* It is aristocratic to be pro-slavery.... those who are so unfortunate as not to be highborn—i.e., born at the South—are given to feel that they must eke out their shortcomings with an extra amount of Southern ardor and pro-slavery talk." That may have explained the political culture of Baltimore, but it was the history of violence by the city's street mobs that put Federal regiments on guard as they headed south to Washington.[32]

On the morning of April 19, as the Sixth Massachusetts left Philadelphia, its commander, Colonel Edward F. Jones, ordered ammunition issued to his troops. They reached Baltimore with weapons loaded, aware of the trouble the Pennsylvania soldiers had met as they shifted from station to station the day before. Jones told his men, "You will be insulted, abused, and perhaps assaulted, to which you must pay no attention whatever, but march with your faces square to the front ... if you are fired upon and any one of you is hit, your officers will order you to fire. . . ."[33]

Without public notice, the train carrying the Sixth Massachusetts rolled into Baltimore's President Street Station. Horses pulled cars carrying seven of the regiment's companies through the streets to Camden Station without serious interference. But word spread quickly; behind those cars, a street crowd, yelling "Yankee scum!" and "You Yankee dogs, you'll never go back!" tore up the track and blocked it with heavy anchors dragged from piers along Pratt Street. The remaining four companies had to fall out into the street to march across town. By then they were surrounded by a mob of several thousand men and boys, throwing bricks and paving stones. Dishes and bottles crashed down from windows above. One of the frightened soldiers told how "the multitude was constantly increasing, and rage, wild, terrible and venomous, was in their distorted faces." The mob broke into a gun shop, and soon pistol shots were heard. The city's mayor, George W. Brown, put himself in front of the troop column, hoping to discourage the attacks, and the soldiers pushed ahead at quick time until the mob blocked the street.

At that point the Massachusetts men opened fire, their attackers fell back, and the soldiers fought their way to the station. Some of the crowd ran ahead to rip up the track toward Washington, but workmen among the soldiers quickly repaired it. The eventual toll in this first bloodshed of the war was 4 soldiers and at least 9 civilians killed, plus several dozen wounded. Arriving in Washington, the Sixth presented a sorry and demoralizing sight. Some of its men were carried to hospital, and many wore bloody bandages and torn uniforms as they collapsed into the Senate Chamber of the Capitol.[34]

That evening, the editor of the *National Republican* entered the American Telegraph office to send reports to New York of what had happened to the Sixth Massachusetts in Baltimore, and the condition of its wounded brought to Washington. Stone was there, on orders from Scott. He stopped the editor and engaged in conversation long enough for a sergeant to arrive with a squad of the National Rifles. Stone ordered them to take charge of the office and not to allow any dispatches to be filed without permission from the secretary of war. Thus began the first telegraphic censorship of the press in the United States.[35]

Before midnight, Mayor Brown of Baltimore sent Lincoln a message endorsed by Governor Hicks, admitting that they could not restrain their citizens, who were "exasperated to the highest degree by the passage of troops." Asserting that "it is not possible for more soldiers to pass through Baltimore, unless they fight their way at every step," they asked that the government send no more through the city. If that should happen, Brown wrote, "the responsibility for the blood shed will not rest upon me." Shortly after dispatching this message, Brown heard that more government forces were on their way. He told Hicks that the only way to avert calamity was to burn the bridges north of Baltimore, a move that Hicks reluctantly approved. Within hours, the bridges were afire and a detail was reported en route to Havre de Grace to scuttle the ferry that crossed the Susquehanna.[36]

Lincoln was determined that Maryland would not block reinforcements from reaching the capital. With the railroads cut, the regiments

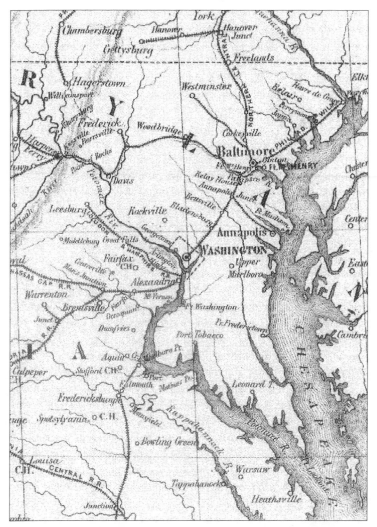

following would go around Baltimore instead of through it. At Philadelphia, Colonel Benjamin F. Butler, bringing two Massachusetts regiments, heard that the bridges were down and the Susquehanna ferry was sunk. He rushed his command to Perryville, on the northern side of the river, and found the ferryboat *Maryland* still afloat. Loading his men on board, he headed down the Chesapeake Bay for Annapolis, bypassing Baltimore. Colonel Marshall C. Lefferts, commanding the celebrated Seventh New York, chartered a ship in Philadelphia, and steamed down to the Virginia capes past Norfolk, where Union officers had burned the naval base and scuttled the ships in harbor rather than give them up to Virginia forces. Bearing up the Chesapeake, Lefferts heard that Rebel batteries were waiting along the Potomac, so kept on to Annapolis. But there, he and Butler found that the railroad to Annapolis Junction and the main line from Baltimore to Washington had been cut, and the locomotives left in Annapolis dismantled. Mechanics in Butler's regiment rebuilt the engines. They mounted a cannon on a flatcar and set out marching with a track repair crew bossed by a twenty-five-year-old Scottish railroad man named Andrew Carnegie, who had been hired by the War Department.[37]

It took time, and at the White House, Lincoln was in a state of gloom as rumor chased rumor about Confederates approaching by the thousands. "They are closing their coils around us," said General Scott. He was usually a mountain of calm confidence, or at least bluff, but he seemed shaken when he called in Colonel Stone for a status report. He noted that the Norfolk Navy Yard had been burned and that the Potomac bridges at Harpers Ferry and Point of Rocks and the railroad bridges north of Baltimore were down. Telegraph lines to the North had been cut. "How long can we hold out here?" asked the old general. Stone told him the capital could hold for ten days, after which help would arrive from the North through and around any roadblocks thrown up by the enemy.[38]

Stone described his three defensive centers: the Capitol, where two thousand barrels of flour and tons of other provisions were stored and local militia had barricaded entry points with sheets of cast iron meant for the dome above; City Hall, on Judiciary Square, with the Patent Office and General Post Office nearby, where another stock of flour was laid in; and the White House, with the War, Navy, State and Treasury departments. The Treasury Building, sandbagged and stocked with food and ammunition, would be the last stronghold, where the president would take cover if the worst should happen.[39]

Scott and the president did not know exactly how many Confederate troops were where, but the newspapers brought them daily threats from swashbucklers below the Potomac. The *Richmond Examiner* proclaimed it "desirable that Washington should be the capital of the Southern Confederacy." With that, "we should be looked upon by foreign nations as the victorious party—the real United States." The paper said that Washington's citizens were mostly Virginians and Marylanders, who had been temporarily diverted to the North because their economic interests lay in the capital. Now they must see that "Washington must be a Southern city—or a city of ruins, if she be not adopted as our capital. If we attack her we shall meet with little opposition and much aid from her citizens. Lincoln and his officials may well tremble in their seats, for they are surrounded by tens of thousands...." In response to such saber-rattling, Scott issued his General Orders No. 4, warning that attack could come at any time. It assigned specific officers to command each strongpoint and declared that all defenders must hold their posts until overrun.[40]

Rather than reassuring the city's civilians, the sight of all this military preparation sent many of them scurrying away. As one youth remembered it, "Panic seized the people and the previous emigration was child's play to the present hegira." Piling possessions on coaches, drays, wheelbarrows, pushcarts, even baby carriages, hundreds fled the city. "Property is valueless, business is dead," wrote Thomas Walter. To feed incoming troops, the government confiscated all the flour in mills at Georgetown and aboard schooners about to sail. Residents of Georgetown were awakened in early morning darkness by what they feared was cannon fire; it was 3,000 barrels of flour being rolled out of one of the town's thirty-three canalside warehouses, to supply ovens being built for the army in the basement of the Capitol. Within fifteen minutes after the confiscation order, the public price of a single barrel of flour more than doubled.[41]

But where were those hungry troops? "I don't believe there is any North," Lincoln said as he talked with men of the Sixth Massachusetts after their struggle through Baltimore. "The Seventh [New York] Regiment is a myth. Rhode Island is not known in our geography any longer. *You* are the only realities. The Seventh and Butlers are probably still at Annapolis." In the privacy of the White House, vainly watching the Potomac for reinforcements arriving by boat, he anguished: "Why don't they come? Why don't they come?"[42]

They were coming: Butler held his troops at Annapolis Junction for several hours expecting to fight off a mob of roughs reportedly coming from Baltimore, while the New Yorkers crowded aboard a train for the capital. Butler asked permission from Lincoln to "bag the whole nest of traitorous Maryland Legislators" about to convene in special session. The president, not wanting to excite the Maryland situation any further, said no.[43]

At noon on Thursday, April 25, six days after leaving New York, the Seventh Regiment arrived at Washington's B&O depot. Carnegie, streaked with blood from a gash suffered when a downed telegraph line snapped back in his face, rode the leading locomotive. The proud New Yorkers, greeted by cheers of relief from loyal citizens packed along the curbs, marched smartly down the Avenue and reported to the president. Then they settled into the House Chamber, and the next day, Butler's men arrived, taking over the Capitol Rotunda. They were followed by Rhode Island troops accompanied by their rich and boyish governor, William Sprague. For the moment, spirits lifted: Henry Villard, reporting for New York, Chicago and Cincinnati papers, wrote that "I cannot express the revival of hope and confidence, the exultation, that I felt and that filled all loyal hearts as that crack body of New York Volunteers, nearly a thousand strong, marched up Pennsylvania Avenue, preceded by a magnificent band."[44]

As more troops arrived from the North, the exodus of Southerners from Washington crested. Captain Franklin Buchanan, commandant of the Navy Yard, and Commander Matthew Fontaine Maury, the famed oceanographer and superintendent of the Naval Observatory, were among those who would be seriously missed. With them would go Samuel Cooper, adjutant general of the army, who knew more than even General Scott about which Union troops were where, and Joseph E. Johnston, quartermaster general, who knew more about what supplies were in hand and needed. Not only military officers and congressmen, but dozens and hundreds of departmental clerks, unwilling to retake the oath of loyalty to the government, headed south with their families.

None of those departures was watched more closely or agonized over more deeply than that of Robert E. Lee. The morning after his conversations with Blair and Scott, Lee rode into Alexandria, where he had grown up, and only then did he see newspapers confirming that the convention in Richmond had voted for secession. That night at Arlington, he paced and struggled over a decision that now seemed inevitable. In early morning, he sat and wrote a one-sentence resignation from the army, addressed to Secretary Cameron, and a personal letter to Scott, telling the old general that he would carry memories of his friendship to the grave. "Save in defense of my native State," he said, "I never desire again to draw my sword." Feeling the need to explain his decision to those dearest to him, he wrote to his sister and to his brother, Commander Sidney Smith Lee, a career naval officer who would also go south. "With all my devotion to the Union and the feeling of loyalty and duty of an American citizen," he said, "I have not been able to make up my mind to raise my hand against my relatives, my children, my home."

On Sunday evening, April 21, he got a message from Governor Letcher asking him to come to Richmond. The next morning, he left Arlington, where he and Mary Custis had been married thirty years earlier and their seven children had been born. He would never return.[45]

Lee's words expressed what many other Southerners felt as they wrestled with whether to stay or go from Washington and the Union. For them, it was not hot defiance, but all sadness. At least one resolved the trauma by committing suicide: the Reverend George Williamson Smith told of a "distinguished officer, a valued friend, who met me, chatted gaily for a few minutes, shook me warmly by the hand, went home and shot himself." Lieutenant Lunsford Lomax, son of an army officer, wrote to his 1856 West Point classmate, George Bayard, that "I cannot stand it any longer, and feel it my duty to resign. My State is out of the Union and when she calls for my services I feel that I must go. I regret it very much, realizing that the whole thing is suicidal. As long as I could believe in a war on the Union and the Flag I was willing to stay, but it is a war between sections—the North and the South—and I must go with my own people. I beg of you not to let my decision alter the friendship between us." Lomax left Washington on the same day that Lee left Arlington. In her diary, his mother, Elizabeth, wrote, "God only knows when I shall see him again."[46]

Though the Virginia referendum to approve secession was still a month away, on April 24 a convention committee approved a treaty with the Montgomery government, adopting the Confederate constitution and placing the state's military forces under Confederate control. This, too, was nominally subject to the popular vote, but already the First South Carolina Regiment was strutting into Richmond, ready to carry the fight to Washington. And on April 27, the Virginia convention invited the Confederate government to make Richmond its capital.

Lee accepted Governor Letcher's request that he take command of Virginia's troops, and thus cast himself in a leading role in what he called "the dire calamity of this fratricidal war." For him, there was no turning back. Yet his oldest son, George Washington Custis Lee, was still a U.S. Army lieutenant. He was an engineer restoring Fort Washington, on the Maryland side of the Potomac below Washington, to protect the capital against Confederate gunboats. From Richmond, the elder Lee wrote to Mary that Custis must make up his own mind about what to do. "I do not wish him to be guided by my wishes or example," he said. "If I have done wrong, let him do better. The present is a momentous question which every man must settle for himself and upon principle." Lee urged his wife to make quiet arrangements to leave Arlington for someplace safer, since fighting could break out at any time. She wrote later that "I was anxious to remain not fearing personal insult & believing I could protect a place dearer to me than my life, the scene of every memory of that life whether for joy or sorrow, the birthplace of my children, where I was wedded, & where I hoped to die & be laid under those noble oaks by the side of my parents...." Custis Lee stayed with the army and his mother until mid-May, when he resigned his commission and she said goodbye to her home with its priceless memorabilia from her step-grandfather, George Washington. She left Arlington in the trusted hands of her head housekeeper and friend, Selina Gray, who had been born in the slave quarters behind the mansion.[47]

Before the end of April, Lincoln suspended the right of habeas corpus along the line from Philadelphia to Washington, giving Scott the authority to order arrests without observing the niceties of law. By May, barely two weeks after the president's call for troops, volunteers were pouring in via Annapolis and soon started arriving by the restored line from Baltimore. A tentative sense of security had returned to the capital. The navy was rushing to blockade Confederate ports. Elmer Ellsworth's newly recruited Fire Zouaves arrived from New York on May Day, exciting comment on their fezzes and bright baggy trousers, splashy uniforms patterned on those worn by Algerian soldiers and adopted by many European outfits. The firefighters moved into the Capitol and were soon showing off for other regiments, some descending by ropes from the heights of the Rotunda. Soldiers of the Sixth Massachusetts complained of being ill fed, but their morale improved when the twenty gas-fired brick ovens built by Massachusetts masons in the Capitol cellar started turning out bread for the troops. Rhode Island's volunteers were better provisioned and equipped than the rest, because the wealthy Governor Sprague personally supplemented their supplies and pay. Regiments took turns and drew stylish crowds as they paraded with bands playing on the White House lawn.

Yet rumors still flew. Multitudes of Rebel cannon were said to be back of Arlington Heights, ready to roll up and open fire across the river. The first symptoms of spy fever were felt: At the Navy yard, several workmen were arrested for allegedly spoiling shells being readied for the fleet. All civilians, specifically including reporters, were barred from troop quarters in the city. Soldiers guarding the Capitol arrested several passersby because they looked suspicious. Experience would soon show that some of the most suspicious-looking citizens were innocent and some of the least suspicious were not.[48]

At the White House, Lincoln sometimes propped his feet on a windowsill and steadied a telescope between them to watch comings and goings on the Potomac and beyond. He could see up to Arlington and down to Alexandria, which had still been a part of the District of Columbia only fifteen years earlier but was as devoted to Virginia tradition as any place in the Old Dominion. One morning, Hay walked into Nicolay's office at the mansion's southeast corner and found Jim Lane and Carl Schurz, the Missouri German politician and future general, peering out the window. Lane was fuming as he squinted through the telescope at a bold secession flag, flying above rooftops six miles south in Alexandria.

"We have got to whip these scoundrels like hell," Lane growled. "They did a good thing stoning our men at Baltimore and shooting away the flag at Sumter. It has set the great North howling for blood, and they'll have it."[49]

CHAPTER FIVE

The Performance of a Sacred Duty

In his room at Willard's, Thomas Walter was startled awake at 3:30 A.M. on May 9 by cries that "The hotel's on fire!"

Walter got up, opened his door, smelled smoke, pulled on his clothes and ran downstairs. Joseph Willard told him a fire had started in the house next door, but assured him that he had put it out himself. Relieved, Walter went back to bed. Then, before he had fallen asleep, hotel employees came yelling down the corridors for all boarders to "get up and prepare for the worst!" Dressed again, Walter rushed out into the street. The adjoining house was a mass of fire from top to bottom, and flames were eating at the rear of the hotel. Guests started dragging trunks down the stairs, while the Willard brothers rescued cash and records from the hotel office. Total destruction seemed certain.[1]

But Walter was surprised to see swarms of Elmer Ellsworth's Zouaves, professional New York firefighters, come running to attack the roaring blaze. Ellsworth had ordered a hundred of them to answer the fire alarm, but hundreds more raced from the Capitol, where they were billeted, to show what they could do. Finding the city firehouses still locked, they broke in, took the engines and raced to Willard's before local firemen arrived. Without ladders, they formed human pyramids and climbed lightning rods to reach the upper floors. At least one of them hung upside down from the eaves, spraying water inside as two companions held him by the heels. For two hours, they fought and finally defeated the blaze, saving the hotel and earning the Willards' vocal gratitude.[2]

The New York firemen's bravery and acrobatics made them darlings of the capital despite their reputation for rowdiness between drills and emergencies. Less than a week after they came to town, John Hay had written that "One horrible [Zouave] story which has been terrifying all the maiden antiques of the city for several days, has the element of horror pretty well eliminated today by the injured fair [damsel], who proves a most yielding seductee, offering to settle the matter for 25 dollars." But Hay truly admired these jolly volunteers; to him, they were "utterly unapproachable in anything they attempt," and "their respectable demeanor to their Chief and his anxious solicitude for their comfort & safety are absolutely touching to behold."[3]

Walter was living at Willard's because he had taken his family home to Philadelphia to get away from the threat of war, and he felt under siege in his work at the Capitol. He and his wife, Amanda, and their six-year-old son, Gardiner, had made their way as far as Baltimore in late April, but with the railroad cut, he had to hire a hack to drive them from there to Philadelphia by way of York, which cost him $45 and took more than two days. Returning alone, he managed to get aboard a boat jammed with troops from Perryville to Annapolis. There he took another boat, full of families fleeing Washington, to reach Baltimore. But the railroad was still blocked, so he hired a horse and carriage for $40 plus tolls and feed, and drove the last forty miles to Washington. Since the family was giving up its house in the capital, he took a room at Willard's, where he had been in residence one miserable week when the fire broke out.[4]

The architect had a lot to be unhappy about, and was unhappier than most men would be about it. He still blamed Northern abolitionists for the crisis and was angry that his preacher at the E Street Baptist Church was so strong for the Union cause. "The little man is war mad," he wrote to his wife. "He has been very anxious to '*save*' souls' heretofore, and now he would hurl thousands of *southern* souls to the regions of unending despair because they have a proper, a scriptural, feeling in reference to the *nigger* question." Surrounded at work by some 4,000 troops camping in the Capitol, Walter said, "The smell is awful. The building is like one grand water closet. Every hole and corner is defiled. . . ." He admitted that "these are nasty things to talk to a lady about, but ladies ought to know to what vile uses the most elegant things are devoted in times of war." To his son-in-law, the Reverend Martin E. Harmstead, in Camden, he wrote that "this will never be a place again—Washington is done." He urged Harmstead not to go through with his intention of coming down as chaplain of a New Jersey regiment—not to have anything to do with this "unholy . . . fratricidal" war. He was having trouble chartering a steamer to take the family's household goods from Georgetown to Philadelphia. In the confusion, the family's only slave, John Keith, had slipped away, never to return. The food at Willard's was increasingly inedible: "Yesterday the tea tasted rank of cockroaches . . . I had, besides, 2 rotten eggs and a piece of fish rather stale, some indian cakes and rancid butter." Thus he was going to start taking meals at a boardinghouse.[5]

On top of all that, Montgomery Meigs was back from his expedition to Fort Pickens. The moment news came that Meigs had arrived in New York, Walter was on guard, telling his wife that "I suppose he will be here again soon, to commence anew his annoyances." Walter was so depressed that he wrote, "To be candid, I dont care much if the work is stopped." But he did care. Though Meigs's effort to fire him had been rebuffed by Secretary Cameron, Meigs was now replaced by his brother-in-law, Captain John N. Macomb, who ordered the architect to move his office into the building's attic. Walter had to wend through barrels of flour, salt beef, pork and hardtack stacked in the corridors and argue with sentries guarding each turn of the interior, but he obediently shifted his work upstairs. Once there, he was convinced that bedbugs had traveled up from the troops crowded below, and driven to distraction by soldiers drilling beneath his windows— "about 100 drummers all the time drumming, having a head drummer to teach them; they have been going over the same *toodle-de toodle-de toodle-de too* for the last 2 hours and that on at least 100 drums." Next he was asked for plans of the Capitol grounds so defensive works could be dug, a non-necessity that would destroy the west terrace and surrounding trees and shrubbery. "This is a great country," he grumbled.[6]

Meigs, as soon as he reached Washington, returned to assertive form in conferences with officials who nominally ranked far above him—Scott, Seward, Blair, the president. Eleven days after reporting to Lincoln, he was promoted from captain to colonel commanding the Eleventh U.S. Infantry. A day later, May 15, he was appointed brevet brigadier general and quartermaster of the whole United States Army, replacing Joseph Johnston, who had gone home to Virginia. That afternoon, as if to make clear that nothing could proceed at the Capitol without Meigs's full attention, Captain Macomb informed Walter that beginning immediately, all construction there would be suspended for the duration of the war. "Our work here is done for some time to come, if not longer," the architect wrote to his wife, and left the next day for Philadelphia. He could not stay away long.[7]

N ow troops were flooding into Washington. While those camping in the Capitol entertained themselves between drills and parades by making eloquent speeches in mock sessions of Congress, others were on the way. In early May, Lincoln called for another 43,000 volunteers plus more regulars for the army and navy. When the Nineteenth Massachusetts arrived at the receiving station called Soldiers' Rest, they marched into the mess hall before it had been cleaned up after a Pennsylvania regiment. Waiters climbed onto the tables to sweep them down with dirty brooms, but were soon forced into retreat by a barrage of bread, pork and tin dippers thrown by the angry newcomers. Once fed, the boys from Massachusetts had to bunk outside on the ground because the Pennsylvanians occupied the barracks. Exhausted, they slept peacefully until about 4 A.M., when they were prodded awake by a herd of wandering pigs. They rousted out and tried to chase down the fresh pork, but the pigs were too fast for them.[8]

The Sixty-ninth New York, flying its emerald green banners, moved into a dormitory at Georgetown College, where the usually ebullient Irish volunteers behaved themselves remarkably well under the eyes of the eighteen Jesuit fathers who taught and disciplined the school's 350 students. Three weeks later, the Catholic regiment departed and 800 less reverent Scots of the Seventy-ninth New York marched in with bagpipes skirling. When they had been there barely a week, the Reverend John Early, preceptor of the college, presented to the government a finely itemized bill for damages. The quartermaster general sympathized and sent the rowdy Highlanders elsewhere, but said that since the college paid no taxes and half of its students had left, another regiment would soon arrive.[9]

Ben Butler's command, including the blooded Sixth Massachusetts, occupied the critical Maryland rail junction at Relay and started artillery practice to discourage any opposition. Then on May 12, suddenly and without orders, Butler took a thousand of those men and swooped into Baltimore during a rainstorm, occupying Monument Square and siting cannon atop Federal Hill, which dominated downtown and the inner harbor.

General Scott was furious. He fired a telegram to Butler: "Your hazardous occupation of Baltimore was made without my knowledge, and of course without my approbation. It is a God-send that it was without conflict of arms. It is also reported that you have sent a detachment to Frederick, but this is impossible. Not a word have I received from you as to either movement. Let me hear from you."[10]

Butler had acted on his own as newly appointed commander of the army's Department of Annapolis, whose territory included Baltimore. He allowed the Sixth Massachusetts to enjoy a meager measure of revenge by moving into the city by rail with elements of the Eighth New York. They met no resistance. From atop Federal Hill, Butler issued a proclamation worthy of an emperor. To restore Union authority, he forbade all unofficial assembly. He ordered an end to transmission of arms to the South and decreed that any display of Confederate flags or symbols would be considered giving aid and comfort to the enemy. He closed by calling on "all good and Union-loving citizens" to help restore peace and quiet so Baltimore could resume its place as a major commercial city.[11]

Butler told Scott that "I should be deeply grieved if in any of my acts I should exceed propriety of action by going either too fast or too far." Scott was not satisfied; he promptly made Butler a major general but transferred him away from Maryland to command Fort Monroe, overlooking Hampton Roads. Considering this a rebuke despite the added star of rank, Butler stormed into Washington and had a loud row with Scott. For neither the first nor last time, he had aggravated his seniors but excited cheers across the North. Baltimore would remain a center of Confederate intrigues, but martial law brought peace to the streets, and for the moment fears of trouble from Maryland subsided. Because the political General Butler was one of the highest-ranking Democrats as well as one of the shrewdest and most ambitious men in Federal service, the president handled him carefully. Before Butler left for Fortress Monroe, Scott was congratulating him, telling him how lucky he was to be heading down the bay just when soft-shell crabs were at their seasonal peak. Official Washington breathed easier when he was gone, trailing the cloud of controversy that followed him all his days.[12]

After Elizabeth Lomax's son took his painful departure for the South, a young man who had been courting her daughter Victoria joined the Union army, after which the daughter refused to speak to him.

"Oh, the waste of devotion," Elizabeth wrote in her diary. "Real love is so rare and youth so blind."

Friends from the North were telling her that as a Southerner she would not be safe with so many Yankee troops on their way, and from the James River her son wrote urging her to come to Virginia. She was torn, but determined to stay as long as she could. Taken for a drive out to the Soldiers' Home, she stopped on the way back to watch the Seventh New York, which had moved from the House Chamber to Meridian Hill. She sensed no danger as she admired their band music and military precision—"but oh, to think they are drilling to kill—and to kill my own people."

A few days later, Mrs. Lomax made her sad decision to join relatives at Charlottesville. On her forty-first wedding anniversary, she wrote that "never in my life have I been so surrounded by such a complication of unfortunate circumstances. . . . The country riven with dissensions, obliged to forsake my home, to scatter my children, some here, some there, to know that my darling son is in constant danger, to endure poverty, to see armed men everywhere knowing that they are the enemies of my own people, and never knowing the outcome of this frightful war. I feel desolated." After friends came to tell her good-bye, she "retired with a sad heart at the thought of leaving our sweet home—perhaps forever." The next day, she and two daughters took a hack across the river to meet the train at Alexandria.[13]

On the April day when the Virginia convention voted to leave the Union, an innkeeper named James W. Jackson raised the first secession flag over the old town of Alexandria. Hoisting it above the Marshall House hotel, he announced that anyone who came to haul it down would have to step over his dead body.

In his enthusiasm for the Southern cause, the hotheaded Jackson was more conspicuous if not more devoted than other Alexandrians. During the 1860 presidential election, he had taken an ax to a Lincoln-Hamlin flagpole at Occoquan, a few miles down the river. In February, Alexandria had sent a Unionist delegate to the state convention—but then, after firing began at Fort Sumter, most of the city turned southward, along with most of Virginia. A crowd of townspeople came to cheer when Jackson flaunted his secessionist flag above the hotel he had leased from the slave-dealer A. S. Grigsby. To back up his defiance, Jackson mounted a four-pounder cannon in his back yard, aimed down the hall toward the front door. But in April, Union loyalists about the city had still been unafraid to answer his display by hanging U.S. flags from their windows.[14]

As Federal troops filled public buildings and set up tent camps in Washington, Virginia militia companies were drilling in Alexandria, and as Scott ordered guards posted at the bridges into the capital, Virginia pickets stood watch at the other end. They apparently did not recognize the individual Union engineers who rode across to scout high ground suitable for forts. Trans-Potomac business slumped, and food prices shot up. Some Virginia women held sewing circles to turn out clothes for soldiers, while others moved south, leaving their homes in the hands of servants. Federal gunboats hailed and inspected vessels coming up the river past the cannon at rearmed Fort Washington, and made sure that those heading downstream did not carry war matériel to the South. The much-feared USS *Pawnee* lay off Alexandria, its eight heavy guns discouraging such ideas.[15]

Despite their anxiety over the safety of Washington, Lincoln and Scott were careful not to disturb this status quo, even after the Confederate Congress voted on May 19 to move its capital from Montgomery to Richmond. They were waiting—first, to gather forces for the defense of Washington; then, for Virginians to vote in their referendum on May 23, the final formal step in secession. By then, the referendum had been overtaken by events, and there was no doubt about the outcome. Many Northern farmers, including Quakers, had settled in northern Virginia in recent years, so the pro-Union percentage in the counties around Alexandria was higher than in the state as a whole. But because the voting was viva voce rather than by secret ballot, and Southern passion was raging, many loyalist Virginians did not dare to register their opinion. The official count in Alexandria city was 983 for secession to 106 against; statewide, it was far more lopsidedly pro-secession than the true margin of sentiment in the commonwealth.

When the polling places closed, James Jackson led celebrators touring the town, serenading politicians and military officers, before having one last round at the Marshall House. They did not realize that, even as they partied, more than 10,000 Union soldiers were marching through the moonlit streets of Washington toward the Potomac River bridges. Winfield Scott had set in motion a plan for troops to cross that night in four coordinated thrusts from the capital into his native Virginia. Brigadier General Joseph K. F. Mansfield, commander of the District of Washington, was in direct control. The troops believed the real war was beginning.[16]

Soon after midnight, a squadron of Federal cavalry clattered across Chain Bridge, just below Little Falls. At 2 A.M., ten regiments of U.S. regulars and volunteers, plus the National Rifles of the District of Columbia militia, started over the Aqueduct Bridge from Georgetown and the Long Bridge from Fourteenth Street. As president, Lincoln was concerned about all of these moves into what was now enemy territory, but he had a personal interest in the fourth of the operations, because it was commanded by his beloved friend, Colonel Elmer Ellsworth.

"Brimming, running over with health, high spirits, ambition, hope, and all the exuberant life of a rarely vigorous nature," the twenty-four-year-old Ellsworth had had the run of the White House, as if his name were Lincoln. The night before he loaded out for Alexandria, he sat at Camp Lincoln and wrote a prescient letter to his parents. He said his New York Fire Zouaves expected their incursion into Virginia to be hotly contested:[17]

> Should this happen, my dear parents, it may be my lot to be injured in some manner. Whatever may happen, cherish the consolation that I was engaged in the performance of a sacred duty, and tonight, thinking over the probabilities of tomorrow, and the occurrences of the past, I am perfectly confident to accept whatever my fortune may be, and confident that He who noteth even the fall of a sparrow, will have some purpose even in the fate of one like me. My darling and ever-loved parents, good bye.[18]

Ellsworth had pleaded for his Zouaves to play a conspicuous role in this first Union offensive strike, and the generals could not turn him down. Other troops quickly occupied Arlington Plantation and the high ground overlooking the capital, then moved to take nearby road junctions and railways. Meanwhile the Zouaves marched to Giesboro Point, at the mouth of the Anacostia, loaded aboard the steamboats *Baltimore* and *Mount Vernon,* and headed for Alexandria.

When the troop transports appeared off the Virginia city in the dim light before dawn, Commander S. C. Rowan, aboard the *Pawnee,* gave away the intended secrecy and surprise of their mission. Without higher orders, Rowan sent Lieutenant R. B. Lowry ashore with a flag of truce to demand the surrender of Alexandria. Lowry told Confederate Major George H. Terrett, commanding a battalion of about 500 Virginia troops, that he faced overwhelming force, and had until 9 o'clock to evacuate the place or surrender. As Lowry was returning to the wharf, Rebel sentries fired a few shots at the approaching transports, and the Zouaves fired back, chasing them away before landing at the foot of King Street. Lowry met Ellsworth there and told him the Confederates had promised not to resist, because the town was full of women and children. "All right, sir," said Ellsworth. "I will harm no one."

When Lowry returned to the *Pawnee,* he was sent back to coordinate with the troops ashore. Well before the 9 A.M. deadline, most of the Confederate force had marched out Duke Street and left aboard a train waiting half a mile beyond the depot. The only Confederates captured were 35 troopers of a cavalry rearguard, caught and imprisoned at Price & Birch's slave pen. Lowry personally raised two U.S. flags, one of them over the Custom House. While the Zouaves moved into the city from the wharf, Michigan troops under Colonel Orlando B. Willcox had marched down from the Long Bridge and occupied the railroad depot. But Lowry could not find Ellsworth, who was not at the head of his regiment.[19]

Ellsworth had set out at quick time to capture the telegraph office, but his sense of drama drew him toward James Jackson's bold secession flag, still flying high. He knew what an eyesore that flag had been for those watching Alexandria through the telescope at the White House and knew they would be looking on that morning. With a handful of Zouaves, his regimental chaplain and a correspondent from the *New York Tribune,* he made his way to the Marshall House at King and Pitt streets. Striding upstairs to the roof, he ripped the banner down. As he brought it back down the stairs, Jackson appeared with a double-barreled shotgun and blasted him at point-blank range. Ellsworth gasped "My God!" as he fell. Before he struck the floor, a Zouave corporal named Francis E. Brownell killed Jackson with a musket round to the head. Jackson had kept his vow, that the flag would only be brought down over his dead body. At the foot of the stairs, for the first of thousands of times, the blood of Yankee and Rebel ran together. Within hours, soldiers had hacked away much of the stained staircase and floor covering as souvenirs.[20]

Lincoln was deeply grieved. The thrust into Virginia, though strategically defensive, was a complete success; one of his generals reported that in places "the movement was made so quietly, that the troops had stacked arms an hour before the inhabitants were aware that we had crossed the river." Union forces controlled the nearby hills, roads and railways, and were digging fortifications and artillery pits that made the capital far more secure than a day earlier. Michigan troops found one slave at the pen who had been overlooked; they told him he was free to go to his master, but he chose to stay with them as a cook. In the whole operation, there had been only one Union casualty. But that one had been like a son to the president.

Ellsworth's body was brought back to the Navy Yard, where thousands came to view it. Among them was the pugnacious adventurer, dime novelist and soldier E. Z. C. Judson, who wrote about his real and fictional escapades under the name of Ned Buntline. He laid a bouquet on the colonel's coffin and spoke for his comrades, saying, "We'll mourn him today, boys, and revenge him tomorrow." The body was moved to the East Room of the White House, where it lay in state, surrounded by flags and flowers, before the Reverend Mr. Pyne delivered the funeral sermon. Then Lincoln and most of Washington officialdom followed a solemn military cortege down the Avenue, where flags were at half-staff for Ellsworth and buildings were shrouded in mourning. Among the soldiers marching with reversed arms, Corporal Brownell carried the Confederate flag for which the young colonel had paid his life. It was a full-dress occasion, grander than the honors that would be rendered most fallen generals in the months ahead.[21]

As the procession neared the Capitol, a breathless courier, his horse foaming, dashed up beside the president's carriage. He handed Lincoln a message: a major Confederate counterattack was reported. Heavy booms came from across the Potomac, punctuating the band's mournful rendition of the Dead March. After the funeral procession ended at the B&O station, officers rode along the curbs ordering all soldiers to report to duty. Suddenly the streets were filled with flying artillery and troops crowded onto wagons and carriages. The Second U.S. Dragoons galloped down the Avenue, clearing all before them. General Meigs rushed across the river and offered his services to General Mansfield. But it was all a false alarm; the booms were from Union cannon adjusting the range from their newly dug positions on the heights.[22]

There were genuine though small clashes across the river. In the week after Union forces took Arlington and Alexandria, they not only dug forts, but sent scouts out every roadway, seeking and finding Confederate pickets, provoking brief skirmishes. Gunboats attacked Confederate batteries down the river at Aquia Creek, terminus of the Richmond, Fredericksburg & Potomac Railroad. A Union cavalry probe pushed all the way into Fairfax Court House, fourteen miles west of Alexandria, and had to dash through gunfire from Rebels in private homes to get out. The Confederates were reported concentrating farther in that direction, bringing regiments up the railroad to Centreville and the key junction at Manassas. As Union forces felt their way into Virginia, they captured a few soldiers here, arrested a suspectedly disloyal civilian there, and soon the number of prisoners rose to the hundreds.

These captives presented a puzzle to Lincoln and his cabinet, because the administration had not worked out a policy to deal with them. The Confederate cavalrymen caught in Alexandria were moved from the slave pen there to the brig at the Navy Yard and then into Washington's city jail, known as the "blue jug," on Fourth Street near G, north of Judiciary Square. But where to put them was not the problem, not yet. The government was worried over an issue that would drag on for months, of a kind that would recur in the centuries ahead: the nation was at war, but it did not want to recognize the enemy's government as legitimate. Not only were Federals capturing Confederates, but Confederates were catching Federals, and by the established protocols of war between nations, they could exchange prisoners. One journalist wrote: "Here is the embarrassment. If the government treats these men as rebels taken in arms against the government, they should be hung. This would not be deemed good policy, even did not humanity revolt against such a sacrifice of human life. On the other side, if the system of exchanges be adopted, there is in the act a recognition of the rebels as belligerents according to all the laws of nations. The Cabinet has discussed this point several times without coming to any result, but it is probable that in the end the minor rebels will be discharged on parole, and the leaders only hung."[23]

That correctly stated the problem, but not the eventual solution. The president had overridden civil rights when he told General Scott that his officers on the route through Maryland could ignore habeas corpus—the right of an arrested citizen to be brought before a judge, not to be held illegally. But that was a domestic matter; the treatment of prisoners of war, with its potential of seeming to recognize the Confederacy as a legitimate government, had serious international implications. If handled unskillfully, it could influence Britain and France, whose recognition was desperately sought by the Confederates. Thus, Lincoln and his advisers would chew on it as long as possible before committing themselves to the exchange of prisoners.

There was no such risk in handling civilian prisoners. In Baltimore, where soldiers had locked up a number of suspected anti-Unionists at Fort McHenry, Lincoln's suspension of habeas corpus was promptly challenged by the chief justice himself, Roger Taney. One of the prisoners was John Merryman, a prominent Marylander who had been a lieutenant in a secessionist cavalry company that had helped cut Washington off from the north in the tense days of April. His lawyer asked the Federal circuit court there for a writ of habeas corpus. Taney, acting as senior judge of the circuit, issued a writ ordering the commander of the fort to produce Merryman and show cause for his arrest. When the officer refused, Taney persisted, ruling that the president had no right to suspend habeas corpus. Lincoln based his action on the Constitution, which says the right can be suspended "when in cases of rebellion or invasion the public safety may require it." True, said Taney, but only Congress has that power, and besides, the Constitution does not allow soldiers to arrest civilians without permission from a civil court, and does not allow prisoners to be held indefinitely without trial.[24]

Constitutionally, Taney may have been right, and Lincoln wrong. But Lincoln had the army, and Taney did not. The president simply defied Taney's ruling, and nothing displayed the temper of the times more clearly than the vociferous support that came from the Republican press, lashing the chief justice as if he were Jefferson Davis in person. The *New York Times*'s man in Washington wrote that Taney "has finally subsided after for the third time endeavoring to destroy the Government. If he again attempts to impede the progress of the Administration, in its efforts to sustain the Constitution and the laws, he will certainly be impeached; but if he is content to be a law-abiding citizen, he will be permitted to enter into the grave without being officially branded as a traitor." So Lincoln got away with the first of many major steps that would expand the power of the presidency as the crisis stretched on.[25]

At the same time, what seemed then a less crucial question arose when officers across the Potomac wanted to know what to do with captured Rebel property. Arlington, for example, might be the most valuable plantation in Virginia, probably worth a quarter million dollars, not even counting the worth of its slaves. To confiscate and sell it would not only help finance the war, but make a mighty impression on other would-be secessionist planters in the Old Dominion. Doing that would take care of real property, but on many plantations, real estate was not the most valuable commodity. As the *Times*'s correspondent wrote: "Still another troublesome point to decide is what to do with the 'peculiar institution.'"[26]

CHAPTER SIX

Thirsting for Deliverance

Shortly after Union troops threw open the doors of Price & Birch's slave pen in Alexandria, New York Congressman Charles Henry Van Wyck poked about the building and brought back to Washington a set of iron shackles, a symbol of what he believed the war was about. But no one in the capital had to cross the Potomac to find souvenirs of what had long been called the South's "peculiar institution." In and around Washington, slaves and what to do with them had been an issue since early in the nineteenth century. Indeed, the model for Uncle Tom in Harriet Beecher Stowe's momentous novel was a slave named Josiah Henson, born in Charles County, Maryland, who lived for nearly thirty years just outside the District of Columbia in Montgomery County.*[1]

The Compromise of 1850 had ended legal slave trading, but not slavery, in Washington; at the same time, the Fugitive Slave Act threw the federal government on the side of slave-chasers. Before mid-century, the capital had been a busy slave market, in a class with Richmond, Charleston and New Orleans. An abolitionist broadside of those years asserted that:

> . . . Slave Factories, with *chains and grated cells,* are established at the Seat of Government, where slaves are constantly collecting from the neighboring States, and thence regularly shipped in cargoes, or sent, *literally manacled together, in droves,* to the more

---

*Henson spent most of those years as the slave of Isaac Riley, whose land lay between today's Rockville Pike and Seven Locks Road. He became an overseer on Riley's plantation before being sent away to Kentucky and later escaping to Canada, where he wrote

remote South.... **The District of Columbia is one of the greatest and most cruel slave markets in the world!**... When the
American people declare in a voice of thunder, that they will not
endure to have their own metropolis profaned with Slavery,
then, and not till then, will the legislation of Congress be the
echo of their voice. Speak then, fellow citizens! Overwhelm
Congress with petitions, and tell your representatives that Slavery and all traffic in human flesh at the Seat of Government must
be **totally, immediately, and forever abolished!**[2]

Congressmen could not have ignored this commerce in humanity.
They rode past Washington's slave pens every day; sales proceeded
within sight of the Capitol. The biggest pen, run by the interstate firm
of Franklin & Armfield, was seven blocks away; Williams's was on the
Mall at Eighth and B streets Southwest, adjacent to the Smithsonian
Institution, and Robey's was nearby at Seventh Street and Maryland
Avenue. A visitor in the 1830s described Robey's as "a wretched
hovel" surrounded by a wooden fence fourteen or fifteen feet high,
where "both sexes, and all ages, are confined exposed indiscriminately
to all the contaminations which may be expected in such society and
under such seclusion." Gannon's pen was near Market Square on the
Avenue. Other holding places and auction sites were in the cellar of
the St. Charles Hotel, on the Avenue at Third Street; in an alley just
north of Judiciary Square; in what became Potomac Park; in McCand-
less's Tavern in Georgetown; and even for a while at Decatur House,
facing Lafayette Park, within shouting distance of the White House.
Gangs of slaves en route to the South were often lodged for safekeeping in the city jail; sometimes free blacks without proper documents
were seized in the District and sold down the river. Legislators
offended and shamed by such outrages in the capital of "the land of
the free" tried many times to persuade Congress to abolish slavery in
Washington. They were invariably blocked by legislators from the
slaveholding states, who saw emancipation in the capital as a first step
toward emancipation nationwide.[3]

Among those who tried was Representative Abraham Lincoln,
Whig of Illinois, who disgustedly described Franklin & Armfield's as "a

---

the memoirs that inspired Stowe. The structure since called "Uncle Tom's cabin,"
attached to a larger house, still stood in 2003 near the intersection of Old Georgetown
Road and Tilden Lane, five miles beyond the District Line. (Mrs. Neal Fitzsimmons,
" 'Uncle Tom' in Montgomery County," pp. 3–6, 9–11; *Sunday Star,* 19 Oct. 1919)

sort of Negro livery-stable, where droves of negroes were collected, temporarily kept, and finally taken to southern markets, precisely like droves of horses." In 1848, he had drafted a legislative package that would have freed slaves in the District and paid their owners for their loss, but also assured Southerners that local authorities would help recover fugitive slaves—all subject to approval by a referendum of white male citizens. It was too much of a compromise: neither side was enthusiastic, and the effort got nowhere.[4]

But two years later, as part of the broader legislative package called the Compromise of 1850, the slave trade in Washington was at last banned. Much of the local business thus terminated merely shifted across the Potomac, boosting Alexandria's standing as a slave market. By the 1860 census, the ratio of free blacks to slaves in the District of Columbia was almost four to one, and in Washington City almost five to one. Many of the free black men and women were independent laborers and entrepreneurs—teamsters, barbers, seamstresses, washer-women, oystermen, gardeners, waiters, caterers, artisans of all kinds—while most of the slaves were house servants. In such numbers, free or slave, they were an essential part of Washington's workforce, coexisting in harmony with most whites. But within days after Scott's army crossed the Potomac, what had started as a trickle of blacks into Union lines and the capital was becoming a stream, a problem growing with each plantation, each mile of Virginia occupied by the Federals.[5]

"They are . . . in a measure the charge of the government," wrote a capital correspondent. "It will be readily understood that we cannot be long encumbered with such a charge, and as the masters are flying from the wrath to come, we are likely to have more chattels than it will be possible for us to take care of, if we still profess to hold them in bondage. The government has no desire to interfere with private property, and will not, but it cannot be expected that the government will take the place of owners, when owners abandon their property." With the kind of casual racism that was typical then even for New York journalists, he said "the negro has become a kind of Tartar, that the government can neither hold nor let go. The Cabinet adjourned without disposing of Sambo—not a surprising fact, considering that Sambo has been on hand so long."[6]

That may have been how Lincoln and his cabinet felt as they considered the problem in late May. But down at the tip of the Virginia Peninsula, where Ben Butler's troops were probing out of Fortress Monroe, slaves were slipping across the lines, having heard that once in Union hands, they were free. Butler characteristically made his own decision about how to handle this situation of "very serious magnitude." He declared those slaves contraband of war, as if they were cotton or cattle captured from the enemy. In a letter to Scott, he reported that some slaves who had helped build Confederate defenses at Sewell Point near Norfolk were coming with their families to Fortress Monroe. As a military question, he wrote, it would seem "a measure of necessity" to deprive the enemy of their labor and put them to work on the Union side. But, he asked, "can I receive the services of a father and mother and not take care of the children? Of the humanitarian aspect I have no doubt; of the political one I have no right to judge." Thus he referred the whole matter to Scott and Secretary Cameron. Meanwhile he was using those slaves at the fort, paying them day wages from which he deducted expenses for upkeep of their families. Butler also sent word to the Virginia colonel who had forced the issue by seeking return of his slaves, telling him that if he would take the oath of loyalty to the Union, he could have them back. That did not happen. Washington approved Butler's "contraband" approach, later officially limiting it to slaves who had actually labored for the Confederate army, a narrow definition usually ignored. Though the debate over confiscated slaves would run on, this would become basic Union policy in the months ahead.[7]

For decades, slave traffic in Washington had moved in two directions—south from the capital's notorious slave markets, but also north by way of the "underground railroad." Bondsmen escaping their local owners as well as those from surrounding Virginia and Maryland were secreted at certain locations in the city before moving onward. Few set foot aboard an actual railroad car. Instead they slipped onto coastwise vessels heading down the Potomac for Philadelphia or New England, or set out by land and dark of night, passed from one shelter to another by a network of friendly lawbreakers.

These black and white "conductors" on the underground railroad often hid escapees close to home until a small group was ready to dispatch to stationmasters above the Mason-Dixon line. The biggest such shipment ever sent out of Washington or any slave state was a whole shipload of slaves that sailed down the Potomac in April 1848 aboard the schooner *Pearl*. Her master was Daniel Drayton, a hard-luck captain who had lost vessel after vessel in storms along the Atlantic coast. After smuggling one slave family out of Washington, he was asked to charter a vessel for another run, ostensibly to take away a slave woman with her nine children and two grandchildren. When he brought the *Pearl* up near the Seventh Street wharf with the vessel's owner, Edward Sayres, he was told there might be more.

There were. Seventy-seven slaves belonging to forty-one owners were packed into the hold of the *Pearl,* and after midnight Drayton sailed away down the Potomac, intending to run up the Bay through the Chesapeake & Delaware Canal to New Jersey. But bad weather slowed the schooner, and she and her cargo were intercepted near Point Lookout at the mouth of the river. A disgruntled Washington hack driver named Judson Diggs, who had not been paid for bringing two escapees to the boat, had told what he saw, and a posse boarded a steamboat and caught up with the *Pearl* while she hid waiting for a favorable wind. Some of the captors wanted to lynch Drayton as the steamer towed the schooner back to Washington. They marched their prisoners through the streets, an angry mob ranting alongside. As they passed Gannon's slave pen, Gannon rushed out with a knife and slashed at Drayton. The crowd moved on the office of Gamaliel Bailey's *National Era,* threatening to burn it down because of rumors that it had encouraged the escapade. Drayton and Sayres were convicted and languished in the city jail for four years and four months before being freed by President Fillmore.[8]

Drayton had been recruited for his adventure on the *Pearl* by William L. Chaplin, Washington correspondent of the abolitionist *Albany Patriot.* Chaplin had replaced the Reverend Charles Torrey as Washington's chief white conductor on the underground railroad after Torrey, who claimed to have helped nearly 400 slaves to freedom, was arrested and died in a Baltimore prison in 1846. Torrey had worked closely with the free black Thomas Smallwood, an underground organizer in Washington, the city he called "that mock metropolis of freedom, and sink of iniquity." Smallwood fled to Canada in 1843 as authorities closed in on him. Chaplin himself was jailed in Rockville following a gun battle in 1850 as he tried to smuggle away two slaves owned by a Georgia congressman. After friends in New York raised his bail, he fled north.[9]

Although the law dealt harshly with such operatives, others followed and took the same chances. William Still, the African-American

secretary of the Philadelphia Vigilance Committee, who welcomed
and sent onward up to sixty escapees a month, often received "packages" from a retired Washington lawyer who signed his letters
"William Penn." This was the elderly Jacob Bigelow, a Massachusetts
native who lived on E Street. He and Ezra L. Stevens, an Interior
Department clerk, collaborated in sending the fifteen-year-old slave
Ann Marie Weems to Philadelphia disguised as a male carriage driver.
In 1856, "in a time of uncommon vigilance here," "Penn" wrote to Still
asking what had happened to fifteen or twenty men and women he
had sent that way. Two years later, Still wrote that "Penn" and friends
were doing a "marvellously large business," knowing where to find
"passengers who were daily thirsting for deliverance." Still recorded the
accounts of dozens of fugitives from in and around Washington as they
passed through Philadelphia. Most of those escapees did not fault their
owners for hard treatment; their main motivation for leaving was fear
of being sold south. George Johnson, for example, escaped from the
District, where he was hired out by his owner, Eleanor J. Conway. He
said he had fled, leaving behind his father, mother and two sisters,
because Conway had already sold two of his brothers. His traveling
companion was Thomas Smith, hired out to the National Hotel for $30
a month. Smith had made enough money of his own to offer to buy his
freedom for $800. When his owner insisted on $1,000, Smith departed
without saying goodbye.[10]

Even as war loomed, brave activists—free blacks, slaves and
whites—persisted in their dangerous business, concealing and shipping individuals and families north from the capital. Black Methodist
churches, like Bethel on South Capital Street and Mt. Zion on P Street
in Georgetown, seethed with underground intrigues. A burial vault in
the Mt. Zion Cemetery, at Twenty-seventh and Q, is said to have been
a hiding place for many transients. Over the years, at least four teachers in the city's schools for black children were prosecuted for helping
slaves escape. By 1860, though there were no public schools for black
children, about 1,100 were enrolled in private schools. They were
instructed by whites, as at the Union Seminary and the St. Vincent
de Paul Free Catholic Colored School, or by black teachers, as at the
girls' school run by Arabella Jones, who had once been a domestic servant for John Quincy Adams. Myrtilla Miner, a dedicated white
schoolmistress from upstate New York, educated black pupils with
support from Northern abolitionists for ten years until her health
failed soon after war began.[11]

As the flight of rural "contrabands" from occupied parts of Virginia into the capital grew, the influx of white soldiers, clerks and opportunists grew even faster. Under these strains, the relative harmony of prewar relations between the races began to break down. The black newcomers became a problem out of proportion to their numbers because most of them were illiterate, rural ex-slaves without skills to support themselves in the city. One response, after this situation had worsened for a year, became a landmark in the history of the capital: the opening of the first public schools for black children in the District of Columbia.

Sometime in early June of 1861, the first battle of the war was fought. The first shot had been fired at Fort Sumter, and the first blood had been shed when the Sixth Massachusetts marched through Baltimore. But exactly when and where the first battle was fought remains a matter of dispute. Union journals favored June 3, at Philippi in the mountains of western Virginia, where Federals under Major General George B. McClellan surprised a Confederate camp in the night and scattered it with few casualties. Rebels in Richmond scoffed at this minor embarrassment. They insisted that the first battle worthy of the name was on June 10 at Big Bethel, a church just above the town of Hampton. In a sharp encounter there, Confederates turned back 4,400 of Ben Butler's Union troops pushing up the Peninsula between the James and York rivers from Fortress Monroe. Washington newspapers minimizing this "unfortunate occurrence" were on Lincoln's desk the following evening, when he greeted the eminent scientist Joseph Henry, who brought a visitor to the White House.[12]

As the first director of the Smithsonian Institution, Henry was not enthusiastic about the war, wishing that his scholarly enterprise could somehow stay neutral, above it all. (William Howard Russell of the *Times* of London wrote that Henry "treated slavery as a geological question," while his assistant director, Spencer Baird, "connected it with climate and the Valley of the Mississippi.") But Henry was a leading physicist who had devised early versions of the telegraph and the electric motor, and was ready to promote any technology that might advance the cause of science. So he introduced the president to a tall, mustached former New Hampshire cobbler's apprentice named Thaddeus Sobieski Coulincourt Lowe. The ingenious Lowe, now styling himself "Professor," was a balloonist. Shortly after Fort Sumter, he had floated hundreds of miles from Ohio to South Carolina, almost getting himself arrested as a suspected Northern spy when he landed. Now he wanted to put his experience and his apparatus at the service of the Union army.[13]

Inventors with wild ideas for winning the war swarmed about Lincoln and the War Department. Fortunately for the few who brought practical innovations, this president "never assumed that an idea must be mad because madmen pursued it." He loved gadgets; sometimes when an inventor had been spurned at every other office, the only man who would listen and perhaps test his offering was the president himself. When Lowe arrived at the White House escorted by the internationally renowned Dr. Henry, Lincoln was eager to hear what he had to say.[14]

Lowe described to the president how he would make balloons practical for observation of the enemy. He had built portable equipment to produce hydrogen by combining sulfuric acid and iron filings, so his whole system could operate in the field, independent of municipal gas works like those he used to fill his bag in Washington. And he wanted to show Lincoln that direct telegraphic communication could zip down a wire from balloons in the air to commanders on the ground. Lincoln approved a test, and a week later got a message from Lowe saying, "I have pleasure in sending you this first dispatch ever telegraphed from an aerial station," and thanking him for encouraging "the science of aeronautics in the military service of the country."

Henry and a crowd of excited citizens watched as Lowe floated above the Armory on the Mall between Sixth and Seventh streets, where the National Air and Space Museum would later be built. From there, the aeronaut described for Lincoln the "superb scene" of the city and its encircling camps. Then the balloon was hauled down and towed along the streets, still inflated and bobbing above the rooftops, to the White House lawn, where it was tethered. As the papers said, the demonstration was a great success; a bugler ascended and heralded it across the capital. Lincoln sent Lowe with a letter of endorsement to Scott. But the general had no time for such newfangled foolishness. More than a month later, when the need for better intelligence about the enemy's movements had been proven painfully in the field, Lowe was still frustrated. Lincoln sent him back to Scott with another note; the general ignored him again. Lincoln, who liked to exercise his legs by delivering his own messages to subordinates in the complex of departments near the White House, then marched with Lowe to Scott's office in the Winder Building on Seventeenth Street. This got the general-in-chief's attention. Promptly afterward, Lowe was carrying out reconnaissance missions above the Arlington hills, watching the Rebels beyond—dispatching his findings downward not by telegraph, but by written messages attached to an iron ring that slid down a mooring line.[15]

Scott was not the only general skeptical of new inventions; arms and tactics that had been good enough to conquer Mexico in 1847 were still good enough for senior officers like sixty-six-year-old Lieutenant Colonel James W. Ripley, brought on to replace a still older chief of army ordnance. The irascible Ripley had impressed Scott by enforcing discipline at the Springfield Arsenal in Massachusetts, and would soon be made a brigadier general. He stepped into an office already enmeshed in red tape and staffed by slow-motion underlings, to be harassed by generals and governors demanding more and better weapons. He also inherited a vast supply of smooth-bore muskets. His immediate job was to move those arms from widely scattered U.S. arsenals to the volunteers responding to Lincoln's call. But however efficiently that was done, those muskets were not what the army needed in 1861. The age of smooth-bore muskets was past; though many soldiers would die before some generals realized it, rifled weapons of far superior range and accuracy were changing infantry tactics forever. Ripley was quoted as saying, "Men enough can be killed with the old smooth-bore and the old cartridges, a ball and three buckshot."

"Just so," Lincoln said. "But our folks are not getting near enough to the enemy to do any good with them just now. We've got to get guns that will carry further."[16]

Soon rifle-muskets would be in mass production, but this improvement still would not satisfy soldiers in the field because these most common weapons of the war were muzzleloaders. Recruits had to be taught no fewer than seventeen separate movements to load and fire each round, manipulations likely to expose the combat soldier to the enemy unless he was behind protective works. Breechloading weapons, eliminating this cumbersome procedure, had been invented decades earlier, but never adopted by the army. Now Ripley, fearing that faster-firing weapons would cause soldiers to waste ammunition, was resisting several new models.

But Lincoln, whose own military experience was limited to brief service as a militia captain in the Black Hawk War, sided with the troops against the bureaucrats. As a veteran of fairgrounds turkey shoots back home, he was fascinated by small arms, and if Ripley would not approve tests of some of these improved versions, the president would personally test them. William Stoddard recalled how Lincoln invited him to come in at six-thirty one morning to join in trying out some new weapons on the Mall—ignoring regulations forbidding the firing of guns within the capital. They set up a target against a pile of scrap wood. Lincoln was kneeling and plugging away when a guard sergeant came running with his squad, cursing at high volume. As they came close, Lincoln unfolded to his full six feet four inches. The sergeant stopped, gaped, spun about and raced back toward the Avenue.

"Well, they might have stayed to see the shooting," said the president.[17]

At about the same time Lincoln was enthusing over Professor Lowe's balloon, a trio of New Yorkers came offering a still more modern contrivance: the Union Repeating Gun, which had a hopper of cartridges on top, fed and fired by cranking a handle. Though the term "machine gun" had not yet come into use, that is what it was, crude but workable. Lincoln called it "the coffee-mill gun." He and a small crowd of military and political brass were impressed by a demonstration at the Arsenal grounds, but only a few were produced, against continuing resistance by Ripley.[18]

Willard's Hotel had become a "seething cauldron" of commercial intrigues, jammed with cigar-smoking salesmen and lobbyists touting materials of war, men who did not have to contend with curmudgeons as intractable as Ripley. Indeed, when properly massaged, military and civilian purchasing officers proved to be eminently receptive to deals proposed by salesmen of wartime necessities. And there was no more accommodating, skillful masseur among those salesmen than James Fisk, Jr., who was a star guest of the brothers Willard.[19]

Jim Fisk had been born in Vermont in 1831, son of a man who sold household goods from a peddler's cart. As a boy, he had sold tickets and cleaned animal cages in a traveling circus. Later he worked with his father and was such a natural salesman that he soon took over the business. When he sold it, he moved to Boston and joined the estimable firm of Jordan, Marsh & Company. In the carriage trade, the bonhomie that had been so successful for Fisk in New England villages did not work, and he was about to lose his job when war began. That launched him into bigger things. He immediately remembered the thousands of unsold blankets he had once seen moldering in the store's attic. Confident that the army would be needing blankets, he came to Washington and set up at Willard's. Stocking the best suite in the house with food, liquor and lighthearted ladies, he became a generous, cork-popping host. He casually let it be known that he knew where a supply of blankets could be had, and seemed to make fun of himself when he quoted the humorist Artemus Ward on a certain brand of pills: "For such people as like this kind of pills, these are just the pills they ought to take." He soon disposed of the moldy blankets for such an absurd profit that the firm was delighted for him to stay on.

As Fisk entertained more congressmen, quartermasters and bureaucrats, he signed bigger and bigger contracts for the firm's textile mill, for uniforms, underwear, socks and more blankets. One contemporary nonadmirer saw in him "a compound of contradictions," which was true enough, indeed was a great asset in his business. Fisk was capable of saying, in a confidential tone, "You can sell anything to the government at almost any price you've got the guts to ask"—and then, in a louder voice, "The man that will take the upper hand of a soldier in the field is worse than a thief." He was comfortable with the contradiction; after unloading those first mildewed blankets, he won a reputation for furnishing needed goods in a timely manner—at whatever price wartime traffic would bear. He was dispensing $1,000 a day, in drinks and treats and cash, but the resulting contracts were worth many times more. He urged the firm to buy more mills, which it did. When he heard that a certain Vermont mill was the only one turning out a kind of cloth soon to be in demand, he bought it, and Jordan, Marsh profited mightily from the monopoly. Cannily, he put some of the juiciest contracts in his own name, which gave him leverage to demand and get a partnership in the firm. But this did not come close to satisfying his jolly ambition. As the war proceeded, he turned his eye southward, to the thousands of bales of cotton piled in the warehouses and docks of the Confederate states. Soon the naval blockade ordered by Lincoln would cut commerce from Southern ports to a trickle, and the longer the mills of the world had to go without that cotton, the more it was worth.[20]

Fisk may have been the most successful salesman in town, but he was one among many who were making fast fortunes in Washington that summer. Of some $50 million in arms contracts let during the early months of the war, an estimated $17 million was later found to have been illegal overcharges. An investigating commission accused one senator of getting a $10,000 payoff on a deal for muskets. Many of these operators did indeed "take the upper hand of a soldier in the field" by delivering shoddy goods that fell apart in the rain, or by failing to deliver at all. Such malfeasance was inevitable in the chaotic first months when an unprepared nation was trying to arm, supply and train itself for war. Had there been diligent oversight, enforced from the top of the War Department, there might have been less of it. But Simon Cameron was there.[21]

"That, under Cameron, the War Department would degenerate into a political machine, abounding in graft and corruption, had been generally predicted, and this gloomy forecast Cameron, almost with malice prepense, immediately proceeded to vindicate." So wrote a later student of Lincoln's cabinet. But in Cameron's case, no passage of time was necessary to perceive what was happening.

The righteous Representative Thaddeus Stevens had warned the president about his fellow Pennsylvanian. Lincoln asked, "You don't mean to say you think Cameron would steal?"

"No," said Stevens, "I don't think he would steal a red-hot stove."

With a chuckle, the president repeated this to Cameron, thereby gently letting the secretary of war know that he was being watched. But Cameron did not think it was funny, and rebuked Stevens, who in turn chastised Lincoln for passing on his private remark. He told the president that Cameron had insisted that he retract his words.

"I will now do so," he said. "I believe I told you he would not steal a red-hot stove. I will now take that back."[22]

Cameron more than quintupled the number of Pennsylvanians in his department, and stuffed the commissioned ranks of the army with political allies. He appointed civilian speculators above army purchasing agents at scattered posts, and they raked off a percentage on nobid deals for broken-down horses and other such commodities. The department sold a stock of apparently worthless carbines for $2 each and then bought them back at $22. Cameron colluded blatantly with his and Seward's great friend Thurlow Weed, who allegedly got a commission of 5 percent on gunpowder sold to the army, and bought a decrepit vessel for $18,000, then promptly rented it to the army for

$10,000 a month. The evidence accumulating against the secretary of war and the legion of boodlers that had descended on Washington was immense, but in the hectic summer of 1861, no one ventured to expose them. There was too much confusion, too much excitement: the Rebels were too near.[23]

CHAPTER SEVEN

The Panick Is Great

Clark Mills's heroic statue of Andrew Jackson, waving his hat as his bronze steed balances miraculously on its hind legs, had marked the center of Lafayette Park for barely eight years, not yet long enough to acquire the dignified patina of age. The rectangle around the statue, called President's Square until the visit of the Marquis de Lafayette in 1824, turned from mud to dust as the seasons changed. But appearance was not all: Henry Adams, perhaps because he lived there, would write that those seven acres were the hub of American society—"beyond the Square the country began." This was an understandable exaggeration, for even before the Civil War, such memorable characters as Dolley Madison, Stephen Decatur, Daniel Webster, Henry Clay and Jackson himself had lived in homes about the unfinished park, which had once been the Pearce family's graveyard and apple orchard, a race course, a soldiers' campground, and pasture for Zachary Taylor's retired warhorse, Old Whitey.[1]

On a given evening in the early summer of 1861, toward midnight, no one stirred at William Seward's house on the east side of the square, where Lincoln often came to talk strategy and swap stories with the secretary of state. The windows were dark at Gideon Welles's home, looking south from H Street toward the White House. The entrance to St. John's Church, Benjamin Latrobe's little 1816 gem, where every president since Madison had worshiped, was shut against the night. But along Sixteenth Street, so close to all this quiescent power and anxiety, a portly senator rang the bell of a brick townhouse, and a hall lamp briefly lit his eager face as he was admitted to the presence of Rose O'Neal Greenhow.

Henry Wilson of Massachusetts often came visiting the widow Greenhow. One contemporary writer considered Wilson, who began adult life as a cobbler, to be a model of "New England frugality, thrift, shrewdness and industry, hale and hearty, gay as a lark and frank as a girl." He also was a dedicated abolitionist, who had replaced Jefferson Davis as chairman of the Senate Committee on Military Affairs, and he realized that Greenhow was the most brazen Rebel partisan left in Washington society. But that was part of her attraction. Born in neighboring Montgomery County, she was formidably intelligent, broadly educated, and probably knew more about what was happening in those critical weeks than most members of Congress. She was also beautiful in her way, slim, high-spirited and strong-featured, and frank to say that she used the assets God had given her. She was dangerous, and that danger gave Henry Wilson's passion for her a sharper edge.[2]

But Wilson, who had an ailing wife, was not the only man in Mrs. Greenhow's life. Her husband, Robert Greenhow, a Virginia-born physician, State Department linguist and historian, had died in California in 1854. Before that, she had returned to Washington with her three daughters and given birth to another as she retook her place as a hostess at the heart of national affairs. She may have been closest to Jefferson Davis and other Southerners she had met earlier, when she and her husband were intimate friends of John C. Calhoun. But she could be affectionate toward Democrat Buchanan and Republican Seward alike, indeed to all who were of sufficient political or military standing. As she flattered and flirted with them, some were desperate to know what those seductive eyes were promising, and in trying to find out, they talked too much.[3]

It is easy to believe that Wilson shared his thoughts with her that summer just as freely as he did with others outside his office. Breakfasting with Thurlow Weed, a couple of fellow senators, a West Point professor and the British correspondent William Howard Russell, he had openly disdained professional soldiers. "They don't understand a war of this kind," he said. "We want men of sense and courage who understand our political position." General Scott, said Wilson, was too old and did not know his business; he should already have taken Harpers Ferry and Manassas; cavalry was unnecessary. How much Wilson elaborated on such talk when he was with Greenhow is unknown, but men often talk more expansively with lady friends in late evening than they do around the breakfast table.[4]

Months earlier, a veteran captain on Scott's staff had seen how deeply Wilson was involved with Greenhow and realized how vulnerable that made the senator. He was Thomas Jordan, who had been the roommate of future Union General William Tecumseh Sherman in the West Point class of 1840. Jordan had stayed at his post in Washington for more than a month after most other officers from Virginia followed Lee's example and departed for the South. He was just as calculating and sophisticated as Greenhow, and after noting her dalliance with Wilson, he set out to win a share of her favors. But romance was not necessary to achieve his purpose, which was to use her as a spy for the Confederacy, an intelligence asset that would remain in place after he resigned and departed in late May. Greenhow was more than willing. Promptly after Jordan left for Virginia, to become adjutant of the Confederate force assembling around Manassas, she began sending him reports using a simple cipher that he had hastily devised for her.*[5]

By that summer, perhaps 400 municipal officials and ranking soldiers had left Washington for roles in the Confederate government. District Attorney Robert Ould became an assistant secretary of war in Richmond; Colonel Lloyd Beall of Georgetown became commandant of the Confederate Marine Corps; Charles Wallach, whose brothers were Richard, the former mayoral candidate, and W.D., proprietor of the *Evening Star,* went into the Confederate army's Quartermaster Department; Dr. Alexander Garnett became personal physician to Jeff Davis. The roles and sympathies of such men were well known, and their choices were clear. But dozens of others, whose conversation or connections made them suspect, remained in Washington, in positions high and low. They were the Washingtonians who worried Lincoln. William Towers, for example, chief clerk of the Printing Office and son of a former mayor, had one brother in the Union army and two in Virginia regiments. William H. Hickey, chief clerk of the Senate, had two sons in Maryland Confederate units. The chief clerk of the Quartermaster Department had a son in Confederate service. John F. Callan, clerk of Henry Wilson's Senate Military Affairs Committee, had two sons working for the Federal government, one of them in the

---

*We do not know whether Greenhow actually lifted her skirts for Wilson, or Jordan or other men said to have been infatuated with her. Some of the many love letters written to her survive, full of sighs, proving that passion existed, but how far it went is uncertain. The best known of these are feverish notes believed to have come from Henry Wilson, because they are on congressional stationery, mention legislation that concerned him, and are signed "H." Although some handwriting experts have questioned whether these messages came from him, they have not suggested who else among her suitors might fit those details. (John Bakeless, *Spies of the Confederacy,* pp. 9–10)

adjutant general's office, who would be fired later on grounds of disloyal conduct. Callan himself, yet another friend of Rose Greenhow, stayed longer in his critical job, with access to information of highest secrecy.[6]

Before the summer was past, a Select Committee on Loyalty of Clerks, headed by Representative John F. Potter of Wisconsin, would summon almost 450 witnesses and force out the most conspicuous of these suspect officeholders. But a sociable civilian could gather gossip just as well as a bureaucrat, and pass it on without attracting the attention that focused increasingly on officials of suspect loyalty. Soon a banker, a lawyer and a dentist would prove useful to Confederate intelligence; so would a cast of daring women, both prominent and little known, whose gender and elaborate clothing made messages hidden about their persons less likely to be discovered by sentries and detectives. Brigadier General Samuel P. Heintzelman, who would soon distinguish himself in battle, was dismayed by the casual way Lincoln and other high officials conducted what should have been highly confidential business, with doors and windows open to the ears of passersby. Heintzelman liked to say that every window curtain in Washington concealed two spies.[7]

Perhaps the general was thinking of Thomas Nelson Conrad, a devoted Virginian born at Fairfax Court House, who was headmaster of the Georgetown Institute, a boys' preparatory school on Dumbarton Street. Conrad was twenty-three years old, a lay Methodist preacher who had been graduated from Dickinson College in Pennsylvania in 1857. Although Methodists nationally preached against slavery, Conrad was frankly pro-Confederate. It is said that as soon as the guns opened on Fort Sumter, he devised an ingenious way of signaling to Virginia troops across the river by raising and lowering the window shades at his school. He imbued his students with secessionist fervor and quietly advised them how to go south, along with many other Georgetown youths, to join the Rebel army. At a time when some citizens were jailed for merely hinting publicly that they endorsed secession, the headmaster got away with his subversive teaching for months—perhaps because he was known to the community as the Reverend Conrad.[8]

Conrad's attitude was not unusual in his neighborhood, for while few in Georgetown were so daringly outspoken, statistically the town was even more Southern-oriented than Washington: only 142 of its 8,766 residents in 1860 originated north of the Mason-Dixon line. Of its other white residents, 669 were foreign-born, 2,080 were from Maryland, Virginia and other slave states, and the remainder were born in the District. Many of the Georgetown families who leaned toward Dixie were members of Christ Episcopal Church, at Thirty-first and O streets, while most at St. John's, just west of Wisconsin Avenue, were solid for the Union. But neither church ties nor place of birth nor parentage could determine where a Georgetowner's loyalty lay. The slave-owner Henry Cooksey Matthews of the 2900 block of P Street, for example, had left his Charles County tobacco plantation and taken the Federal post of collector of customs in Georgetown, only to resign when war started. Two of his sons left home to join the Confederate army, and after hoping they would recant, he cut them out of his will two weeks before he died in 1862.[9]

D ay after day, Horace Greeley's *New York Tribune* egged Union commanders on with the same headline: "FORWARD TO RICH-MOND!... The Rebel Congress Must Not Be Allowed to Meet There on the 20th of July. By That Date the Place Must Be Held By the National Army."[10]

Greeley's demand echoed in other papers across the North, and in both houses of Congress as they convened in special session on July 4. The recently malodorous Capitol building had been cleaned up after the troops temporarily housed there moved out, and now congressmen returning to work were saturated with the aroma of bread from the army's gas-fired bakeries still busy in the basement.* In his message to the legislators, Lincoln reviewed what had happened since they adjourned in early March. He asked for another $4 million and 400,000 men for the war, plus congressional approval of the emergency presidential powers he had already assumed. They gave him everything he wanted.

By then, soldiers seemed everywhere in Washington, in streets, trains, bars, restaurants and hotels. Roughly 50,000 had arrived, and

---

*The aroma was the least of the problems created by the twenty ovens running day and night in the Capitol basement to produce 58,000 loaves daily for the troops around Washington. Delivery wagons ruined walks and roadways, cursing teamsters disturbed congressional employees, and smoke vented into the heating system damaged books in the Library of Congress, located directly above the ovens. The army rejected efforts to close the bakeries until an executive order from the president finally moved them out of the Capitol in October 1861. (James Moore Goode, "Architecture, Politics and Conflict," pp. 271–273)

most of those who had camped in public buildings had moved into tent cities and forts in and around the city. With such a mass of man-power seemingly ready for combat, the great popular demand was to get the war over with, quickly, before the ninety-day volunteers went home. The capital's fear of invasion from across the Potomac had been replaced by impatience for Scott's army to invade Virginia and crush the rebellion. The ease with which Arlington and Alexandria had been occupied, the speed with which the sparse defenders there had withdrawn, made the task seem simple; one resounding battle should do it.

Cameron had brought Thomas A. Scott, vice president of the Pennsylvania Railroad, to be assistant secretary of war in charge of transportation and other matters, and Andrew Carnegie was working for him, supervising construction of a railroad trestle beside the Long Bridge across the Potomac. It would link Washington with the lines out of Alexandria, the most important of which led to Manassas, twenty-five miles west. There the Rebels were concentrated, covering the vital rail junction, waiting, as if daring the Union army and the clamoring editors and politicians of the North. Lincoln himself was pressing for action.

Winfield Scott was not so eager. He had laid out for the president and cabinet a long-range strategy that was derided as his "Anaconda plan" because it envisioned gradually strangling the Confederacy by controlling the Mississippi and blockading the coast. Old and wobbly he was, but he knew war, and he knew the troops parading and drilling about Washington were not ready for it. But he could not resist the press and political pressure for his army to move into Virginia without delay. Brigadier General Irvin McDowell, a career staff officer given command of Federal troops across the Potomac, had set up headquarters in the Lee mansion at Arlington. He admitted to visitors that he had no decent maps and no cavalry, but reluctantly, he prepared a short-range plan to do what Lincoln and especially the Radicals in Congress were demanding. He intended to outflank and defeat the approximately 20,000 Confederates at Manassas while another Rebel force blocking the Shenandoah Valley was held in place by Federals under sixty-nine-year-old Major General Robert Patterson.[11]

The Union army's broad objective was hardly a secret; newspapers across the North were reporting the names and locations of regiments, full of talk gathered in campgrounds and barrooms. Russell of the *Times* of London, recipient of just such gossip, could hardly affect events with his dispatches, which would not be read in America until they had crossed the ocean and returned from London printed in his newspaper. But he marveled at how other Washington correspondents collected "the florifications of the high-toned paymasters, gallant doctors, and subalterns" about town, causing the government "inconvenience" by chronicling the smallest movements for the perusal of the enemy.[12]

Northern newspapers, smuggled to Richmond within a day or two after publication, were the Confederate government's best source of wholesale intelligence, and Union generals resented it. Scott was heard to say that he would rather have a hundred spies in a friendly camp than a single reporter. After New York papers gave away a Union scheme to camouflage a tugboat's gun as crated cargo, Butler was so incensed that he told a Cincinnati correspondent "the Government would not accomplish much until it had hanged . . . half a dozen spies, and at least one newspaper reporter." He issued a general order that anyone who disclosed planned troop movements would be expelled from his department. On July 8, with major operations imminent, Scott summoned Washington correspondents of the New York papers and informed them that the War Department would censor any telegraphic reports of impending movements. By then, however, the public and the Rebel commanders were fully informed of what the Union army intended to do; yet unknown was exactly how and when they would go about it. The answers were not long in coming.[13]

On the morning of Thursday, July 18, Montgomery Meigs's nineteen-year-old son John, home from West Point, told his mother that he had volunteered to go to the front with an artillery battery. She was shaken, but not surprised. "It is not strange that the grandson of Commodore Rodgers and the son of General Meigs should be found ready when the country needs his service," she wrote to her mother. "But I felt a very motherly and womanly sinking of the heart nevertheless." That evening, the general helped his son buckle on his sword and pistol, reminding Mrs. Meigs of the time not long past when he had helped little John with his toy sword and tin trumpet. Then the eager cadet rode off to war.[14]

Unlike the serious young Meigs, a flood of other Washingtonians crossed the river in a holiday mood when the news spread that something was about to happen at Manassas. They wanted to be there, to see and cheer when McDowell and his mighty army whipped the Confederates and marched on toward Richmond. By Sunday morning, soldiers were followed by reporters, then by politicians in carriages, some with their ladies carrying parasols and picnic lunches, then by hundreds of ordinary citizens in hired hacks and on horseback, provisioned and eager for an exciting show. Henry Wilson was there, bringing a hamper of sandwiches for the troops, with some of his Radical colleagues. Along the slope of a hill at Centreville, this mélange of men, women and vehicles gathered, straining for a view of the armies as if they were spectators at a gala horse race.[15]

McDowell had started his command from Washington and Alexandria on July 16, and two days later he drew up with some 32,000 troops near Centreville. Across the creek called Bull Run, he faced Brigadier General Pierre G. T. Beauregard, who was waiting with about 22,000 Confederates along an eight-mile front. McDowell tried to turn the enemy's flank, but changed his mind after the Rebels repelled a reconnaissance in force. News of this opening contact reached Washington in fragments: General Mansfield, commanding the Department of Washington, told Russell "we are whipped," but shortly afterward, Senator Sumner informed the correspondent of "a great success . . . General Scott tells me we ought to be in Richmond by Saturday!"[16]

The battle had barely begun. McDowell spent another day testing Beauregard's line before deciding where to make his main attack. This delay gave the Confederate force in the Shenandoah Valley, commanded by Joseph E. Johnston, time to cross the Blue Ridge and reinforce Beauregard at Manassas. Johnston's column got orders to move at midnight on July 17. Led by a Virginia brigade under Thomas J. Jackson, it boarded rail cars at Piedmont (since renamed Delaplane) to cover the last miles of its journey, the first time in the history of warfare that railroads had been used for strategic mobility. By midday Sunday, July 21, the Confederates had brought about 10,000 more troops onto the field.

The onlookers at Centreville could not tell what was happening, but they could see smoke and hear gunfire. At one loud burst, a lady peering through her opera glass bubbled, "Splendid!" She believed McDowell was proving what she had heard so many times: "I guess we will be in Richmond this time tomorrow." The bellicose senator-soldier Jim Lane led Wilson and Senator Ben Wade of Ohio to a closer position where reporters were gathered, so they could actually see some of the fight. The Union attack seemed to be succeeding, driving in the Rebel left flank until it struck a new defensive line anchored on Jackson's brigade. There the Rebels held and Jackson won the name of "Stonewall" that would last long beyond his lifetime. His stand enabled the Confederates to mount a counterattack, forcing McDowell's troops to withdraw, at first slowly, then in panic.[17]

That break set off the most colorful stampede of the war. Henry Villard had just arrived, looking for McDowell, when a staff officer shouted, "You won't find him. All is chaos in front. The battle is lost.... Get back to Centreville!" Congressman Alfred Ely of New York wandered too far forward and was captured by the Rebels, then nearly executed by a raging South Carolina colonel who was stopped by calmer subordinates. The most fortunate civilians, those who had stayed close to their horses and buggies, pushed through roads choked with the baggage wagons of retreating regiments, to reach Washington ahead of the broken army. It was McDowell's green soldiers who had lost control, not all of them, but thousands, throwing away their weapons and fleeing cross-country, ignoring pleas to halt and regroup. Wilson's carriage was lost in the crush, and as he puffed to the rear with the crowd, he saw a familiar captain and exploded. "Cowards!" he yelled as he ran. "Why don't they turn and beat back the scoundrels?" Russell, coming late to the scene, described what he encountered: "Infantry soldiers on mules and draught horses, with the harness clinging to their heels ... ambulances crowded with unwounded soldiers; wagons swarming with men who threw out the contents onto the road to make room, grinding through a screaming, shouting mass of men on foot...." Captain James B. Fry of McDowell's staff wrote that "no power on earth could have stopped them short of the camps they had left less than a week before.... most of them were sovereigns in uniform, not soldiers."[18]

In the capital, Lincoln had gone to church that Sunday morning, assured by Scott that the campaign was proceeding as planned. Soon afterward, he started getting copies of contradictory telegrams from the front. As the sound of guns rumbled along the western horizon, he walked at midafternoon to Scott's office and woke the general from a nap to discuss what was happening. Scott said not to worry, the reports were mostly meaningless hearsay. Then he went back to sleep. More telegrams came, repeating that McDowell was driving the Confederates and wanted reinforcements to push on. When Scott awoke and said these reports of success were reliable, Lincoln called for his carriage and went for a drive about town. Before he returned, Seward arrived at the White House with the real news: the battle was lost; Scott must save the capital. Lincoln came back half an hour later, heard this without changing expression and walked to army headquarters to confirm it. The cabinet met in emergency session in Scott's office, interrupted by a telegram reporting that Secretary Cameron's brother, a Pennsylvania colonel, had been killed. Cameron soldiered on, issuing orders to rush all available troops to McDowell, putting Baltimore on alert and calling on the states to send all organized regiments to Washington immediately. And the president approved orders for a promising major general named George B. McClellan to report promptly to the capital.[19]

Lincoln did not go to his bed that night. Outside in the streets, the civilians who had ridden out to see McDowell trounce the Confederates were returning with wild personal accounts that made the fiasco seem even worse than it was. Then, toward dawn, the soldiers started streaming in, "baffled, humiliated." There was neither sight nor sound of the flags and bands with which they had marched away. Rarely was there as much as a regiment together. Along the Avenue, civilians watched from sidewalks and windows as the city became "all over motley with these defeated soldiers—queer-looking objects, strange eyes and faces, drench'd (the steady rain drizzles on all day) and fearfully worn, hungry, haggard, blister'd in the feet." Many citizens brought out food for them, setting up tables with bread and soup along the sidewalk. Exhausted troops dropped to sleep on walks, in doorways and vacant lots.[20]

Louisa Meigs had sat at her window until 4 A.M., waiting. "Oh what a night it was," she wrote. "I spent it in prayer, in supplications and in tears, agonizing tears for the safety of my dear absent ones, and grief for our national loss and disaster filled my mind." When her husband returned from across the river, he knew nothing about what had happened to their son John. Four hours later, "a horseman came galloping to the door. It was John, black with dust & smoke." He threw himself down by the sleeping general and groaned, "Father, the army is completely routed." Mrs. Meigs wrote to her mother that "our beloved country, with all its national greatness, seems on the verge of shipwreck."[21]

If indeed that was true, most of the country did not know it at the time, because only half of the news had been allowed past Washington. Gobright of the Associated Press told how his assistant rode back from the front that afternoon when McDowell seemed to be winning, and reached the capital too excited to write his own account of what had happened. Gobright took dictation, and when the long report was finished late in the evening, "Everything looked beautiful; we had conquered the Rebels and won a splendid battle." After filing their copy by telegraph, the two set out to find others more recently returned from Manassas, and at Brown's Hotel heard how seeming triumph had turned into defeat. They rushed to the telegraph office and sent a stream of dispatches to correct the record. Then, on Monday morning, when out-of-town papers arrived, the surprised journalists found out that the censor had been at work. He had allowed the first good news to go out by wire, but had stopped the later accounts. At the White House, it might seem to be "merely a question of hours rather than days when Beauregard would lead the Southern army into Washington." But farther north, patriots were celebrating the war's first glorious victory, not knowing yet that it had turned into a debacle. The *New York Times*'s man with the army had prudently reported that "the result is not certain at the moment I write," but the paper's page-one headline said, "Crushing Rebellion ... Greatest Battle Ever Fought on This Continent ... The Rebels Routed and Driven Behind Manassas Lines."

When Gobright realized what had happened, he nimbly found a way to get the real story out. By happenstance, he had handed a copy of the later accurate report Sunday night to the editor of Washington's *National Republican,* which ran it on Monday morning. Because news already published could not be censored, he clipped that article as printed and wired it off to his other clients, and so the rest of the Union learned, belatedly, the truth about the Battle of Bull Run.[22]

Some of the demoralized soldiers who straggled back to Washington brought with them fantastic tales of "shocking barbarities" by the Rebels, accusing them of using wounded Federals for target practice and mutilating them with knives and bayonets. Crowds gathered around these storytellers, and fears of the Confederate menace to helpless Washington grew as the wild tales were passed along. A *Times* correspondent reported the capital's "awfully distressing" mood: "The greatest alarm exists throughout the city, especially among the female portion of the population." Some officials who had boasted of how the Rebels would be easily defeated now made hasty arrangements to send their families away to safety. But not everyone was depressed, or scared. "Our city is filled with secessionists," wrote Louisa Meigs. "Many of them are delighted at the result of the late battle, and feel a hatred for our soldiers." Any Rebel sympathizers who were truly vindictive might have rejoiced at the sight of the wagonloads of wounded that followed the disorganized troops into Washington.[23]

At the time, the casualties from Bull Run seemed horrendous. Later, after other famous battles, they would prove relatively light: 418 Union troops killed, 1,011 wounded and 1,216 missing, compared to 387 Confederates killed, 1,582 wounded and only 12 missing. Because the Rebels chased the disorganized Federals and occupied the ground after the fighting, they took many more prisoners. But even Bull Run's casualties strained the medical resources of the capital. When war began, the city had only one established hospital, the Washington Infirmary, a three-story brick building on E Street, behind the courthouse on Judiciary Square. Other smaller hospitals were in use in Georgetown and Alexandria. The infirmary had been built in 1804 as a jail, and housed drunks, vagrants, felons, and free and slave African-Americans for forty years before being taken over by the medical department of Columbian College (later George Washington University).[24]

The surgeon in charge there was Dr. W. J. H. White, but the dominant presence was a woman, Dorothea Dix, who had won renown before the war crusading for reform of mental asylums at home and abroad. She was already a familiar figure in Washington, respected as the driving force in establishing the Government Hospital for the Insane, known today as St. Elizabeth's, east of the Anacostia River. On her way to Washington in April, she had passed through Baltimore just three hours after the Sixth Massachusetts battled its way between stations. This experience hastened her on her primary mission, to create an organized nurse corps to deal with what lay ahead. Arriving in the capital, she went at once to the infirmary to help the wounded men of the Sixth. Then she pressed her campaign. She was a fragile but determined woman who did not hesitate to hurt feelings and upset bureaucracies to get her way. She soon cajoled Secretary Cameron into appointing her to superintend the female nurses who would work with the army. Dix made it clear that she would not consider young and attractive women for such work: candidates must be matronly, at least thirty years old, plain-looking and plainly dressed. They would be paid forty cents a day plus food and housing. These strict standards began to give way when the hundreds of wounded and sick men from

Bull Run overran the infirmary, and the army had to requisition the first of many churches, schools and public buildings for use as hospitals. Dix set up an emergency ward in a stable on Twelfth Street.[25]

As the battle casualties came in wagons and ambulances, Union soldiers guarded a few Rebel prisoners slogging through the streets. Some onlookers cursed and stoned the captives, but Confederate sympathizers made bold by the Southern victory shouted encouragement from the sidewalks. The prisoners were marched to the Old Capitol, a brick structure at First and A streets Northeast, on the corner where the Supreme Court Building would later stand. The Old Capitol got that name from the five years when Congress sat there after the British burned the Capitol in 1814. Later it had been a school and a fashionable boardinghouse, where Calhoun had died and many a political coup had been plotted. Now it was a Federal military prison, soon to be famous for its collection of inmates, some notorious and some innocent, many of whom would write about their experiences.

Security there was remarkably loose in the early months of war. Eustace C. Fitz, mayor of Chelsea, Massachusetts, who came down to see how his hometown boys were faring, visited the Old Capitol and got past the guard by "pleading the dignity of my office." He talked freely with the Rebel prisoners, and seemed surprised to find that "many of them were men of intelligence" who nevertheless clung to their Southern views. While he was there, "Some ladies indicated that their sympathies were 'secesh' by bringing bouquets." Those ladies also brought cakes and other delicacies to the Confederates, and occasionally transported messages undetected by the guards.[26]

A fter Bull Run, the Northern public wanted revenge; in an upsurge of anger, volunteers flocked to recruiting offices. Lincoln wanted answers: Why had a plan that seemed so sure of success resulted in such a licking? Who could take charge to see that it did not happen again?

The president wanted a man who thought big, and no one thought bigger than Major General George Brinton McClellan. Five days after Bull Run, McClellan reported to General Scott and Lincoln. He was "the young Napoleon," the man of the hour, called to save the capital and the Union, a mission he was supremely confident of fulfilling. As army officer and railroad executive, he had never experienced failure. His campaign against minor opposition to secure the Ohio River, western Virginia and the vital Baltimore & Ohio Rail Road had been the brightest spot on the military map in the early weeks of the war. Now, fifteen years after graduation from West Point, he was appointed to command the Department of the Potomac, including all the forces around Washington. Within hours of his arriving in town, the president invited him to a cabinet meeting to which he did not invite Scott, which angered the old general. McClellan wrote to his wife that "by some strange operation of magic I seem to have become the power of the land." He did not consider that inappropriate.[27]

McClellan might be the key to future military success, but he had no answer to the army's recent failure. Surely what had happened at Bull Run could not have been a simple matter of generalship, training and luck; there must have been more to it, something sinister, unseen on the field. McClellan had brought with him just the man to find out whether this was true. As commander of the Department of the Ohio, he had employed Allan Pinkerton, the Chicago detective who had escorted Lincoln on his clandestine arrival in Washington. Now McClellan assigned Pinkerton to create a secret service in the capital under his command. After Bull Run, with suspicions running high, the detective was ordered to give special priority to watching Rose Greenhow.

The widow had not been prudent. In addition to openly expressing her enthusiasm for Jeff Davis and the Confederacy, she carelessly let it be known that she could send letters through the lines to the South. But before such indiscretions brought detectives staking out her house on Sixteenth Street, she had played an offstage part in the first important battle of the war. She was in New York, sending a relative off by steamboat to California, when the news of Bull Run broke, and she returned to Washington the next morning as defeated Union troops were stumbling in from the front. But before leaving Washington, she had dispatched at least two secret messages to advise Beauregard of McDowell's intentions.[28]

On July 9, she had sent a beauteous eighteen-year-old named Betty Duval into Virginia. Duval left the capital on a market cart, then switched to a horse at the home of a friend across the river. She reached Confederate lines at Fairfax Court House, controlled by South Carolinians under Brigadier General Milledge L. Bonham. Brought before him, she shook out her long dark hair and produced from it a black silk packet with a message inside, addressed to "Thomas John Rayford." That was the pseudonym used by Greenhow's erstwhile admirer Thomas Jordan for communicating across the lines. Bonham forwarded the message to Colonel Jordan at Beauregard's headquar-

ters at Manassas. It warned that McDowell was about to march in that
direction. Upon reading it, Beauregard began preparations to meet the
attack.[29]

A week later, Greenhow sent another warning by a courier named
George Donellan, a former Interior Department clerk. Donellan had
volunteered at Beauregard's headquarters for the mission, and crossed
the Potomac below Alexandria with a scrap of paper saying in Jordan's
cipher, "Trust bearer." In Washington, he showed this to Greenhow,
"the one person in all that city who could extract meaning from it."
According to Beauregard, Donellan had breakfast at her home while
she encoded one sentence: "Order issued for McDowell to march
upon Manassas to-night." With this message, Donellan set off into
southern Maryland in a buggy provided by friends, and returned to
Virginia by a clandestine Confederate ferry service across the
Potomac. A cavalry courier brought the message to the general by
9 P.M. He promptly sent warnings to his outlying units and asked again
that General Johnston's command in the Valley come to reinforce him
at Manassas. That set in motion the troop movements that produced
Confederate victory on July 21.[30]

Some modern researchers have questioned both the timing and
specificity of Greenhow's dispatches before the battle, and there is no
doubt that she romanticized her role when she wrote her memoirs in
mid-war. But Beauregard, Jordan and Jefferson Davis all made clear
that she had played a valuable part in what happened at Bull Run.
Beauregard wrote after the war, "Happily, through the foresight of
Colonel Thomas Jordan . . . arrangements were made which enabled
me to receive regularly, from private persons at the Federal capital,
most accurate information, of which politicians high in council, as well
as War Department clerks, were the unconscious ducts." His key "private person" he identified as a lady who lived "within easy rifle range
of the White House." Jordan named Greenhow when he confidentially
credited her with "the one great success of saving General Bonham
from a disastrous surprise on the 17th of July," the day McDowell's
army moved through Fairfax Court House. And Greenhow quoted
President Davis as saying to her later in Richmond, "But for you, there
would have been no battle of Bull Run."[31]

Success inspired Greenhow to keep sending reports, but did not
make her more discreet. The week after the army's return from Bull

Run, she wrote that "McClellan is busy night and day but the panick is great and the attack is hourly expected." As if she, too, expected the Rebels to march on the capital at any time, she wrote the following week that "we" were organizing to cut telegraph lines and spike Federal cannon when the Confederates approached. In a series of messages, she described troop strength and warned of hidden artillery batteries. She also confirmed unequivocally that much of her information came from Henry Wilson. She told Jordan that the senator was about to join McClellan's staff, which would give her "greater access to the secrets of the Cabinet and the War Office."* And while Greenhow and friends were watching McClellan's preparations, McClellan's detective was watching her.[32]

Pinkerton later described his comic adventures on the night when he got what he considered clear evidence of Greenhow's shenanigans. In the midst of a rainstorm, he took off his boots outside her home and climbed onto the shoulders of two of his agents to look into her parlor. As he peered through the slats of her window blinds, someone approached the front door, so he slid down and hid with his colleagues under the stoop. When the visitor was admitted inside, Pinkerton climbed up again and recognized him as a captain assigned to the provost marshal. Greenhow joined the captain in the parlor and the two talked closely, examining a map that he produced from an inside pocket. Then, according to Pinkerton, they disappeared for more than an hour before returning to the parlor arm in arm, and the captain departed with "something that sounded very much like a kiss." He walked off into the storm with Pinkerton following him in stocking feet. The captain broke into a run and turned abruptly into a building near Fifteenth and Pennsylvania. From it four soldiers emerged, surrounding the detective with bayonets pointing at his chest. Pinkerton tried to explain who he was, but they arrested him. The captain interrogated him, and because the soaked, mud-coated Pinkerton would not cooperate, he was thrown into a guardhouse cell to spend the night among drunks.

The next morning, the captain took him before Assistant Secretary Scott, and when Scott called Pinkerton in for a private conversation,

---

*Wilson, a peacetime brigadier in the Massachusetts militia, went home between congressional sessions to organize the state's Twenty-second Infantry Regiment, with himself as colonel. That fall, he volunteered as an aide to McClellan; according to the *Boston Journal* correspondent Benjamin Perley Poore, he gave up field service after a thirty-mile horseback inspection of outlying forts put him in bed for a week. (Benjamin Perley Poore, *Perley's Reminiscences of Sixty Years in the National Metropolis*, 2:332)

the two men laughed aloud at the "sorry spectacle" presented by the detective. After Pinkerton told what had happened, Scott arrested the captain and ordered the agent to arrest Greenhow if he detected her trying to send information to the enemy.[33]

That did not take long. On August 23, Greenhow returned from a morning stroll to find Pinkerton and his men waiting at her corner. The detective said he had come to arrest her, and she demanded to see his warrant. He had none but said he had verbal orders from both War and State departments. If this illegal confrontation had taken place indoors, she said, she would have killed him. A detective told her, "That would have been wrong, as we only obey orders, and both have families." Pinkerton's agents surrounded the building and began to search every room, keeping her prisoner in her own home. They tried to stay hidden from the street, so that Greenhow's friends would arrive suspecting nothing, and could be held for questioning. By her account, she had left nothing suspicious about the house except what was secreted in the library. While her guards were helping themselves to her stock of brandy that night, she sneaked into the library and removed these incriminating papers, concealing some of them in the shoe of a friend, Lily Mackall, who had called and been detained.[34]

But Greenhow's indiscretion, not to say arrogance, did her in. According to Pinkerton, his men found plentiful correspondence, "much of it highly treasonable . . . no small part of which was torn up recently as it appeared, some of the latter being thrown into the stove, but not burned." His agents pieced these scraps together into all the evidence he needed. Pinkerton wrote that Greenhow's home was "a focal center where treason found a resting place and where traitors were supplied with every needed care . . . by the untiring energies of this very remarkable woman." Always prone to exaggerate his enemies in order to magnify his triumphs, he wrote that Greenhow "possessed an almost superhuman power, all of which she has most wickedly used to destroy the Government. . . . She has used her almost irresistible seductive powers to win to her aid persons who were holding responsible places of honor and of profit under the Government. . . . She had her secret and insidious agents in all parts of this city and scattered over a large extent of country. . . . She had alphabets, numbers, ciphers and various other not mentioned ways of holding intercourse with traitors. . . ."[35]

As his men stood guard, Pinkerton turned Greenhow's home into a jail for suspected spies. Soon his agents brought in Mrs. Bettie H.

Hasler, who had been one of Greenhow's couriers, and the next day Eugenia Phillips, wife of lawyer and former Alabama congressman Philip Phillips, with her sister and two daughters. Mrs. Phillips, Greenhow and Mackall had been among the first to take food to the Rebel prisoners in the Old Capitol, delivering their gifts while showering the guards with defiant language. Secessionist women had delighted in sassing the authorities, assuming correctly until then that their gender protected them from official action.[36]

But Pinkerton's roundup of suspects was not limited to the ladies. At about ten-thirty in the evening after Greenhow was arrested, one William J. Walker appeared at her door with a companion named Frank Rennehan. They were quickly arrested, and when questioned gave "evasive, indefinite and contradictory" answers, which was enough for Assistant Secretary Scott to order them held in the Old Capitol. When friends attested to Walker's loyalty, Pinkerton declared it "a melancholy fact that hundreds of men who before this rebellion were above reproach, who were ornaments to society and high perhaps in public station, are now acting the traitor's part. . . . this is a time when if ever the line of demarcation between loyalty and disloyalty should be so clearly marked as to admit of very little doubt."[37]

Lincoln himself believed that Southern sentiments "pervaded all departments of the government and nearly all communities of people," and in that spirit, Congress passed a bill requiring everyone in government office to take or retake an oath of loyalty. In early July, the president authorized Scott to declare martial law in the capital, and a separate act created a federally controlled police force for the District. It made the mayors of Washington and Georgetown ex-officio members of the Metropolitan Police Board, therefore requiring them to take the oath. Mayor Henry Addison of Georgetown willingly did so, but Mayor Berret of Washington refused. He contended that because he was legally elected, he did not need to swear his loyalty. This did not persuade Lincoln or his officials, who had been uncomfortable since arriving in a city whose mayor never denied his Southern sentiments. Early on August 24, the provost marshal picked up Berret and clapped him briefly in the Old Capitol before shipping him off to prison at Fort Lafayette, in New York Harbor. A month later, Berret would be released after changing his mind, taking the oath and resigning his office. The city's aldermen had already elected their chairman, Richard Wallach, who had been narrowly defeated by Berret in the previous year's election, to succeed him as mayor. They apparently considered the fact that Wallach's brother was editor of the pro-Union *Evening Star* to outweigh his other brother's defection to Confederate service.[38]

Out of all the fright and confusion following Bull Run, with citizens unsure about which neighbor would be hauled in next by detectives, a new, calming influence began to take hold in the capital. The source was the thirty-five-year-old McClellan, who brought a vigor and talent for organization and training that was acutely needed by the defeated army as well as the thousands of incoming troops. Although McClellan had spent the immediate prewar years as vice president of the Illinois Central Railroad, his contemporaries still considered him a brilliant student of war, based largely on the report he had written after spending a year observing the armies of Europe. That reputation had been polished by his campaign in western Virginia, the success that brought him to Washington. He seemed meant for command: smart, stocky, of middle height, his dark hair and mustache glossy with health, his practiced pose pleading for reproduction in bronze and marble. He made such a contrast with old General Scott, whose glory years were so far in the past, who was so wheezy that he spent most of his time horizontal. When McClellan was not at his desk studying and planning, he was riding out among the troops, being seen, asking what they needed, winning their confidence. He gave them a new self-image, lifting morale that had plunged after Bull Run. Well before he formally succeeded Scott that fall, McClellan was general-in-chief in the minds of army, public and press. Thus it was to him that they turned when they became impatient again to march on to Richmond.

CHAPTER EIGHT

We Walk in a Fevered Dream

The vivandière of the Philadelphia Zouaves seemed at first glance to be an unusually fine-looking boy. But on closer inspection, he turned out to be Miss Virginia Hall, "a bright blonde, having a clear blue eye, and her hair cut short like a lad's, and parted on the side." By definition, a vivandière is a female sutler, one who sells refreshments and personal items to soldiers behind the lines. In Civil War practice, a vivandière was more of a regimental mascot, a usually legitimate camp follower who ran errands, tended the sick and boosted morale. When Miss Hall came to Washington with the Philadelphia troops that fall, she clearly dazzled the correspondent of the *New York Times*. "Her nose is slightly retrousse," he wrote, "her mouth well formed, and when she converses, even dentists might go mad at the display of so fine a set of teeth." He described her colorful outfit, from blue liberty cap to tan gaiters, including her short sword and small revolver, and unnecessarily added that "she impresses those who form her acquaintance very favorably."[1]

Virginia Hall was one of hundreds of women, young and older, who came to Washington in the early months of war, some with spouses, others seeking spouses; some to work for the government, others to freelance; some to care for the troops officially in hospitals, others to comfort them in private quarters where business was booming. There was a spirit of adventure abroad that defied the homebound, multi-skirted cliché of nineteenth-century womanhood. Miss Hall, though she may have driven dentists mad, reached her peak of renown on the day she was so enthusiastically introduced to the readers of the *Times*. The fame of another conspicuous arrival that spring, a "perfectly bewitching" horsewoman who called herself Agnes Leclercq, would last much longer.

"Of all the accomplished, witty, fascinating, and sharp women ever known in Washington, Miss Leclercq was the bright and particular star. Sprightly, bold, and brilliant, one quality outshone all others—her audacity was simply consummate." So wrote Noah Brooks, of the *Sacramento Union*. When the newspapers announced that "His Serene Highness, Prince Salm-Salm, of Prussia," had arrived in the capital, offered his services to the Union, and been invited to dine with secretaries Cameron and Seward, Miss Leclercq took notice.

At first, there was talk that the prince was a pretender, merely a German barber out to see how far his accent and manners would take him. Such a gamble would not have been unusual in Washington in 1861; indeed, Miss Leclercq's own background was misty, her very name believed by some to be "notoriously a stage disguise." Brooks wrote that she had been brought as a child from the streets of Paris to Philadelphia by the wife of an American diplomat. After the lady died, the well-educated but unmanageable girl allegedly left her adopted home and later followed her passion for horses to join a circus. When her ambition to ride in the show ring fell short, she became a tightrope walker, traveling the country with a troupe that folded. She spent the next two years moving between New York and Havana, inspiring "rumors of husbands, and of married respectability, but nothing of this sort was tangible or ever crystalized into fixed fact." But in fixed fact, she was not a Parisian foundling and circus performer, she was Agnes Elizabeth Winona Leclercq Joy, a Puritan girl from Vermont. She was only seventeen when she came to the capital with her sister, whose husband was an army captain, soon after the war began. From there on, much of what Brooks and other admirers said about her was true.[2]

She was an immediate sensation, "a sight to see." She loved the splendor of military couture; riding the Avenue and Lafayette Park, she wore a gilt-buttoned, gold-braided habit with captain's shoulder straps, and reportedly was followed by a mounted black groom in proper livery. Later she promoted her uniform to that of a general, but no general-in-fact was heard to object to such impertinence from "the dashing and fascinating beauty who had the hearts of half the men in Washington, and the bitter hatred and ill will of nearly every woman in that thronged city."

The Prussian minister vouched for Felix Salm-Salm's nobility, adding that he had been decorated for his services as a cavalry officer in the Schleswig-Holstein War. Thus the prince joined an array of blue-blooded European soldiers of fortune who came to further their careers in U.S. uniform. He was appointed aide to Brigadier General Louis Blenker, a distinguished Bavarian immigrant, one of the regimental officers who had performed creditably at Bull Run. As soon as the prince donned Union blue, he was targeted by Agnes Leclercq, and soon the glamorous horsewoman had added the title of Princess Salm-Salm to her other embellishments.[3]

With her title, her looks, her high spirits and her own ties in Washington (her mother was one of the Vermont Willards), Agnes enlivened every party except those hosted by the city's haughtiest dowagers. On one occasion at General Daniel E. Sickles's headquarters, she surprised and embarrassed President Lincoln by planting a sudden kiss on his cheek; she explained later that she had done it on a bet, and won a box of gloves for her boldness. She delighted in visiting such outlying camps, a favorite civilian recreation, especially among young and hopeful women who had suitable chaperones. Inevitably rivalry sprang up among them, especially when one magnetic and flirtatious visitor encountered another. In those qualities, Agnes more than held her own, but in self-regard she was no match for another regal beauty who considered herself by right the social superior of even the president's wife.[4]

This was Catherine Jane Chase—"Kate," the twenty-one-year-old daughter of Secretary of the Treasury Salmon P. Chase. She had been her father's greatest pride and sincerest idolator since her mother's death when she was five. After his third wife died, Kate had acted as his hostess when he was governor of Ohio, senator and cabinet secretary. They shared a driving ambition: he to be president of the United States, she to be first lady in his White House. The brilliant German immigrant, politician and later general Carl Schurz once came calling at Governor Chase's home in Columbus, and long remembered Kate's appearance at the breakfast table. He described her audacious little nose, her long dark lashes, and saw even then "something imperial in the pose of her head." He was impressed by how confidently she held her own in talk of practical politics, then considered a male province. After Salmon Chase's adamant opposition to slavery helped prevent him from getting the Republican nomination for president in 1860, his daughter seemed to consider the Lincolns impostors in a White House where she and her father morally belonged. Although Chase ranked second to the secretary of state by protocol, Seward's wife was seldom present on the social scene. Thus young Kate Chase came to see herself as first lady of the cabinet and, not satisfied with that, challenged Mary Lincoln in the very White House as the leading lady of Washington politics.[5]

At the first state dinner of the new administration, Mrs. Lincoln nervously fluttered her fan as she greeted guests. She made a special point of courtesy to Kate when she arrived on her father's arm, and told her, "I shall be glad to see you any time, Miss Chase."

Kate, half Mary's age, stood tall and replied: "Mrs. Lincoln, I shall be glad to have *you* call on *me* at any time." That left the first lady speechless.[6]

Mary Lincoln's social footing was still uncertain; she was already suspect among many Northerners because her brothers were in the Confederate army. She was struggling to establish herself, to camouflage her plainness with elaborate gowns, which provoked one correspondent privately to call her "the laughing stock of the town" with her "damnable airs." At the same time, she was striving to make the worn and seedy White House a mansion worthy of herself and a great nation. Within weeks after she moved in, these efforts had led her into trouble.[7]

On shopping expeditions to Philadelphia and New York, she bought French fashions for herself and luxurious furniture, carpets, drapes, wallpaper and china, quickly overrunning the congressional allotments of $6,000 a year for White House maintenance plus $20,000 for one-time redecoration. In desperation, she approved the sale of second-hand furniture from the mansion and then manure from the stables, which brought a dime a wagonload. John Watt, the head White House gardener, who did much more than oversee the grounds, volunteered to show her how to falsify accounts to cover up her spending sprees. He went with her on some of her shopping trips, and sometimes the temporary commissioner of public buildings, William S. Wood, accompanied her, stopping as she did at the Astor Hotel in New York. This inspired gossip that Mrs. Lincoln was romantically involved with one of her husband's appointees.[8]

Both Watt and Wood were eventually replaced, the latter by B. B. French, to whom Mrs. Lincoln gave a "ladylike reception." She impressed him as "evidently a smart, intelligent woman, & likes to have her own way pretty much." After thus befriending French, in late autumn Mary begged him to explain to the president that her over-spending was unavoidable, and that he should seek a supplemental appropriation.[9]

Lincoln was furious. He said "it would stink in the land" to admit that more than $20,000 had been spent on the mansion "when the poor freezing soldiers could not have blankets." The White House was fine as it was, he said, better than any house they had ever lived in. He insisted that he would pay for the overruns out of his own pocket. But eventually French had to ask Congress, quietly, for more money.[10]

Lincoln tried to avoid such household distractions, often telling complainants that domestic help and Mary's extravagances were beyond his responsibility. He had enough problems in the wider world. In St. Louis, the irrepressible explorer John Charles Frémont, "Pathfinder of the Rockies," erstwhile governor of California and 1856 Republican candidate for president, was in over his head as a major general commanding the newly created Department of the West. He had passed out contracts to shady operators, which was bad enough but hardly unique in those early months of war. Worse, for Lincoln's political purposes, was that Frémont had taken for himself the role of liberator. At the end of August, he proclaimed martial law in Missouri and, without consulting Washington, declared that all slaves of rebellious owners there were free. This enraged the president, who was still trying to hold the border slave states in the Union. Frémont ignored Lincoln's polite suggestion that he withdraw his action, and his tempestuous wife, Jessie, hastened to the White House on the general's behalf. The president heard her stonily, and she went away frustrated. Then he gave Frémont a direct order to cancel the proclamation. After sending Secretary Cameron and others to assess Frémont's generalship, he removed him from command. The whole affair further angered radical antislavery Republicans, who thought Lincoln was far too solicitous of border-state opinion. It stirred talk that Secretary Chase might resign in protest, and inspired yet another congressional investigation.[11]

Martial law could produce serious political problems like that brought on by Frémont, as well as slapstick efforts by soldiers trying to enforce General McClellan's campaign to clean up the capital. One night early in August, Lieutenant Richard Brindley of the Second U.S. Infantry was assigned to patrol duty under the provost marshal,

Colonel Andrew Porter. Brindley asked to see a stray soldier's pass, and when the soldier could not produce it, Brindley arrested him. The man broke away and fled along the Avenue. In the dark, he did not see a cow sleeping in the street. He ran onto her back, and she rose and tumbled him into "a very pretty somersault." Brindley caught up and smote him on the head with the flat of his sword. The prisoner ran off, but Brindley overtook him ("perhaps owing to my experience running from Bull Run," he wrote) and whacked him again. Finally reinforcements arrived and the man, a deserter, was taken away.

That same busy night, Brindley arrested Colonel Porter's orderly, and Porter sent him to rout a squad of rowdy officers from Willard's bar. "Washington is a different place since the martial law has been enforced," he wrote. "Before that the streets were crowded with volunteers and their officers drinking and getting drunk together." Porter's force of regulars put a stop to that, but only temporarily.[12]

Enforcing martial law on errant soldiers might be done with the flat of the sword, but when civilians were involved, constitutional confrontations were inevitable. Lincoln had said in his July 4 message to Congress that he had "no choice" but to invoke war powers, which included the denial of habeas corpus, and that he did it with "deepest regret." Thus, Rose Greenhow and other suspects were arrested and held without trial, but not without legal challenges. The president exerted his war power even more bluntly in Maryland, where he had earlier defied Chief Justice Taney's writ in the Merryman case. He was still worried that secessionists might swing the state into the Confederacy, and some around him believed the Rebels were trying to block the Potomac below Washington with heavy guns firing from Virginia so that gray troops could cross into Maryland as an "army of liberation." Lincoln was determined that the state's General Assembly would not meet in special session as scheduled at Frederick on September 17. On his orders, Major General John A. Dix, commanding in Baltimore, arrested Mayor Brown, more than a dozen legislators and the editors of two local newspapers friendly to the South. Marshal George P. Kane, formerly the city's police chief, was already in prison. Soldiers arrested more members and employees of the legislature when they arrived in Frederick, preventing the Assembly from mounting a quorum.[13]

By that fall, some attorneys were so persistent in defense of those arbitrarily arrested that the administration considered the lawyers themselves to be disloyal citizens. A well-connected correspondent wrote that "the Government will not in any way recognize the employment of counsel to procure the release of persons arrested and imprisoned for political offences." The secretary of state would investigate and decide on each case without argument by counsel. He would hold anyone found guilty "even though a hundred lawyers plead his case," and would not allow the innocent "to be subjected to the expense of feeing professional advocates who can do them no possible service." Lawyers would not be permitted to interview prisoners of state; only close family members could visit. These drastic assertions of wartime authority would be cited as precedent by some later chief executives, using Lincoln's name to justify their own arrogation of power in times of lesser national crisis.

But the Lincoln administration was ready to go still further. "Some lawyers," wrote the correspondent, "under the guise of doing a professional duty, are endeavoring to intimidate the officers and so embarrass the action of the Government, and ultimately to give encouragement to the rebels.... the Government has determined to treat all such intermeddlers as traitors, and to arrest and confine them where they will be incapable of further mischief."[14]

The obvious source of these threats was William Seward. Although his early attempt to set himself up as prime minister had been rejected by Lincoln, informally the secretary of state was still asserting himself as if the president had agreed. Just as the presidential proclamation of martial law arrogated authority from the judicial and legislative branches, within the executive branch Seward grabbed power from the other cabinet secretaries, ignoring them as if they were second-level paper-pushers. His secret maneuvering about Forts Sumter and Pickens in April had been an early and blatant example. Since then, Seward's congenial personality, quick mind and vast store of salty anecdotes had drawn Lincoln on many evenings to relax at his home on Lafayette Square. The two spent uncounted hours together driving about town, talking strategy. Far more consequential political and military thinking was done between them than in sessions of the whole cabinet. Seward did not think those formal cabinet meetings were necessary, and inevitably dominated them. Even on public occasions, he flaunted his intimacy with Lincoln, sometimes addressing him so casually that it further annoyed his already resentful colleagues. Attorney General Bates was unhappy when Seward sent orders directly to district attorneys and marshals working for the Justice Department. He led a successful effort to reinstate regular cabinet meetings, twice a week, but that did little to diminish Seward's influence. And in fact, despite all the hours Seward spent with the president, his counsel did not always prevail. Lincoln listened, then made his own decisions. Although Seward issued many of the orders that imposed martial law, that crackdown was Lincoln's doing, and rightly remains part of his legacy.[15]

The First Amendment took a severe beating in the president's campaign against disloyalty. Arresting citizens who talked and editors who wrote too freely was just the beginning; soon the government was shutting down newspapers that it deemed helpful to the enemy. John A. Kasson, first assistant postmaster general, took pleasure in doing this by denying mail privileges to errant journals as minor as the *Planters' Advocate,* of Marlboro, Maryland, while the government reached beyond the Mississippi to arrest the editor of the boldly anti-administration *Dubuque Herald,* who was held for three months at the Old Capitol, but never charged.[16]

Kasson, a New England Republican transplanted to Iowa, had come to Washington that spring with his bright and restless wife, Caroline. They took a suite at the Rugby House, on the northeast corner of Fourteenth and K streets, later the site of the Hamilton Hotel. While John tried to reorganize a Post Office Department thrown into confusion by the withdrawal of Southern states, thirty-year-old Cara busied herself writing long descriptive letters to the *Iowa State Register* in Des Moines. Signing herself "Miriam," she sometimes seemed to giggle over the curiosities of wartime Washington, but at moody moments she disclosed the religious and increasingly radical fervor that guided her life. After Bull Run, she had voiced the emotions of the Union. "We walk in a fevered dream, and bow to God's mysterious decree," she wrote. But "We shall rally! We shall conquer!"[17]

Cara disdained the many officers "glaring in tinsel on the streets" of the capital while others were dying in battle. She was full of contradictions. Though she made the rounds with her husband at evening entertainments and joined the hundreds strolling the Avenue, she became "heart sick and weary with the glare of gay crowds." Though she felt that "the better acquainted one becomes with the great men of Washington, the more their seeming greatness proves a myth," she also concluded that "we have a long-headed president; he takes time to move but his foot tells when he puts it down."[18]

She was not alone in the way her moods swung with events. In early September, there had been brief exultation in Washington at news that an expedition ordered by Ben Butler had captured two forts and several hundred Confederates guarding Hatteras Inlet on the Outer Banks of North Carolina. But there was the Rebel army still a few miles beyond the Potomac, there were Rebel cannon blocking river traffic between Washington and the sea, there was Jeff Davis orating undisturbed in the Rebel capital. Just as public and politicians had pushed General Scott to march on to Richmond in July, when the leaves began to turn, pressure rose again for McClellan to do something. Almost daily he was seen with his gaudy retinue of staff and guards, trotting out to review the well-equipped, increasingly well-drilled divisions on the outskirts of the city. Lincoln sometimes accompanied him, looking hopelessly rustic as he shared the soldiers' cheers with the magnificently uniformed commander. But while the army and its general preened, the sunny days of early fall were slipping by. Horace Greeley was editorially chanting "on to Richmond" again, and congressional Republicans were demanding action. Senator Zachariah Chandler of Michigan maintained that McClellan's inertia was the fault of a "timid, vacillating and inefficient" administration. Lincoln felt the pressure; he told McClellan not to move until he was ready, but added that he could not ignore what the eager Radicals were saying. The president had still to learn that McClellan would never be psychologically able to admit that he was ready.[19]

Unwilling to commit his main army against the Confederates dug in around Manassas, McClellan sent a smaller force to feel out the Rebels farther west, toward Leesburg. These Federals crossed from Maryland near Poolesville on October 21, only to be thrown back into the Potomac at Ball's Bluff. There were more than 800 casualties, among them Lincoln's close friend, Senator Edward D. Baker, who died commanding a brigade. Though not a major defeat, it was an ignominious debut for McClellan as general of the Army of the Potomac. Someone other than McClellan, someone on the scene, had to be blamed. The ax would fall on Major General Charles P. Stone, who as a colonel had so efficiently organized Washington's militia the previous winter. Early in 1862, Stone would be arrested and held six months without being charged. No official explanation was ever offered.

If the setback at Ball's Bluff in any way diminished McClellan's self-esteem, he hid it successfully. As the president grieved over the loss of

Baker, McClellan told him, "There is no loss too great to be repaired. If I should get knocked on the head Mr. President you will put another man immediately in my shoes." That was as modest as he got. After Ball's Bluff, the leading Radicals—whom John Hay in his diary called "the Jacobin club"—started to push again for action, and the president defended McClellan against their complaints. He manifested his support on November 1, when the old soldier Winfield Scott finally retired. Lincoln immediately named McClellan to succeed him as general-in-chief of the entire Union army.[20]

Even before he wore that title, McClellan did not usually deign to confer with Lincoln at the White House; instead, the president had called on him at his quarters, a few doors from Seward at the northeast corner of Lafayette Park. "The poor President!" wrote the British correspondent Russell. Lincoln was trying to learn weapons, maps, strategy, logistics, "all the technical details of the art of slaying. He runs from one house to another, armed with plans, mss, reports, recommendations, sometimes good humored, never angry, occasionally dejected, and always a little fussy." More than once, McClellan made clear that he considered his own time and rest more important than the president's. Less than two weeks after his appointment as general-in-chief, two nights after a torchlight parade and red, white and blue fireworks display in McClellan's honor, Lincoln and Hay went to see him and were informed that he was at a wedding but would soon return. After they had sat waiting an hour, the general came in, was told they were there, and went upstairs without acknowledging them. Half an hour later, they sent a servant to remind him that they were still waiting, and the answer came back that the general had gone to bed. Hay called it "a portent of evil to come. . . . unparalleled insolence of epaulettes." But Lincoln told Hay "it was better at this time not to be making points of etiquette and personal dignity." He stopped going to McClellan's house and exposing himself to such insults, but he did not know that behind his back the general was even more insulting. In conversation with other officers and especially in letters to his wife, McClellan had called Lincoln "an idiot" and "a well meaning baboon."[21]

Neither did the nation know this contemptuous side of the general-in-chief. A newly arrived soldier-correspondent to New York's *Jewish Messenger* wrote in praise of Lincoln that he was straightforward, honest, patriotic and morally courageous. But he went on: "Although in the eye of the law, the President is the chief of the nation, yet virtually at the present moment the real power of the common-wealth rests with the son of a Philadelphia surgeon, George B. McClellan, on whose sword . . . depends the triumph of our govern-ment, and in whom the hopes of this nation are concentrated, with the confident expectation that they will not be disappointed." Closely examining McClellan's portraits, the writer perceived great energy, perseverance, firmness and courage. But the general, he warned, would never show the kind of genius that "by bold and dashing move-ments overruns the enemy, and renders his troops a terror to the foe, but his success will consist in ingenious combinations, and in the wise application of well tested rules." By pure coincidence, phrenology, the then-fashionable study of bumps and dimples on face and skull, could produce the same conclusions about McClellan that professional sol-diers and politicians would reach after watching him for months.[22]

The general-in-chief was not to be hurried; he was devising his ingenious combinations and planning to apply well-tested rules, but at some unspecified time in the future. As he dithered, the capital's atten-tion turned suddenly to the high seas, where the Union warship *San Jacinto*, acting without orders from Washington, intercepted the British mail steamer *Trent* on November 8 and arrested the Confeder-ate ministers James M. Mason and John Slidell. Having run the block-ade to Havana, they were on their way to represent their government in Britain and France. Although this set off great celebration in the North, the British were furious at the affront to their neutral flag; Washington worried at the prospect of unwanted war with the world's mightiest naval power. Diplomatic messages rocked to and fro across the Atlantic while autumn slid toward muddy, paralyzing winter, and the weather provided McClellan further excuse for inaction.

The newspapers, meanwhile, were giving the government good rea-son to tighten censorship by reporting the gathering of an expedition at Annapolis, detailing how many regiments, cannon, horses and tons of provisions were aboard which ships. But most of the army, confi-dent that it was going nowhere soon, was settling in for the winter in forts and camps around the capital. Dorothea Dix issued an appeal for warm clothing for the troops, and let it be known that the quilts sent by so many home folks were too heavy to carry. She said that ladies preparing bundles for their soldiers should equip each man with two pairs of yarn socks, two pairs of flannel drawers, two flannel shirts, a pair of very stout shoes and a blanket, plus a comforter to protect the throat and two pairs of yarn mittens. As the seasons changed, Cara Kasson thought Washington was "more and more like a great fair." Circuses, concerts and the theaters were thronged with soldiers and civilians. On the Avenue, an entrepreneur had set up a telescope and was charging "five cents to look at the stars, ten cents to look at the moon!" Cara believed such frivolity was out of order—it was "no time to expend money in dress or extravagance, for the sick soldiery, and the poor, will claim every care this coming season of suffering." But no one could fairly criticize the daily excursions of citizens to visit the outlying camps, which boosted the morale of both soldiers and civilians.[23]

In late November, forty-two-year-old Julia Ward Howe and her husband came to town with Massachusetts Governor John Andrew and the Unitarian clergyman James Freeman Clarke. Julia was by then an established poet. She also helped publish an antislavery paper in Boston with her husband, Samuel Gridley Howe, who had helped finance John Brown's failed insurrection at Harpers Ferry in 1859. After they checked in at Willard's, she looked across Fourteenth Street to Newspaper Row and was depressed by the "ghastly advertisement" of an agency that embalmed and sent home the remains of soldiers. With Governor Andrew and Clarke, Julia called on Lincoln, and she later remembered how he told them he had "heerd" a good story. But on leaving the White House, Clarke said sadly, "We have seen it in his face: hopeless honesty; that is all." At that time, Julia wrote, with the war dragging on, few had faith in their president: "The most charitable held that he meant well."[24]

The visitors' spirits lifted when they were invited across the river to witness a review of Massachusetts troops. As the regiments strutted past, somebody reported a sudden movement by nearby Rebels, so the soldiers broke off in mid-parade and scattered to their posts. Driving back to Washington, the little group of Yankee tourists was surrounded and slowed by friendly troops on the road. The visitors started singing army songs, one of them the hymnlike "John Brown's body lies a-mouldering in the ground; His soul is marching on." Soldiers alongside thanked them for the music as they rumbled past. Turning to Julia, Clarke said, "Mrs. Howe, why don't you write some good words for that stirring tune?" She said she had wanted to do just that, but somehow had never found the inspiration.

That night, Julia slept soundly until near dawn. As she lay half awake, she could feel the tramp, tramp, tramping cadence of the soldiers she had seen. Long lines of verse began to twine through her mind. Fearing that she would fall back asleep and forget them, she rose, found a pen and scrawled the words hastily, hardly looking at the paper. She had learned to write that way when she woke in the night with an idea but did not want to arouse her infant child by lighting a lamp. Having written, she went back to sleep, pleased about the verses that had come to her in the morning half-light. When she woke again, she had to decipher her scribbles before they lost their meaning.

Julia perfected those words and offered them to the *Atlantic Monthly,* which published them in February 1862. Although they were admired, in the depths of wartime winter they were not widely noticed at first. But soon the lyrics were picked up by soldiers, who sang the hymn from camp to camp, and a Methodist preacher named Charles C. McCabe helped popularize it across the North. McCabe became chaplain of the 122nd Ohio, was captured at Winchester and held at Libby Prison in Richmond. He related how gloomy he and his fellow captives had been when a Rebel officer told them of a major Union defeat. But a black porter in the prison whispered to them that the Union, not the South, had won a great victory. At this the captives began to cheer, and McCabe (later known as "the singing bishop of Methodism") led them as they made the walls of the warehouse prison resound with "The Battle Hymn of the Republic."[25]

For the last three years of the war, and for generations afterward, the words that came to Julia on that November morning at Willard's Hotel would inspire Americans in times of trouble:

> *Mine eyes have seen the glory of the coming of*
> *the Lord,*
> *He is trampling out the vintage where the*
> *grapes of wrath are stored;*
> *He hath loosed the fateful lightning of His*
> *terrible swift sword;*
> *His truth is marching on.*

Chapter Nine

The Instrument of Divine Providence

I n a stretch of what the *Evening Star* called "really juicy" November weather, the flooding Potomac washed downstream the uniformed corpses of Federal soldiers who had died weeks earlier in the battle at Ball's Bluff, thirty-four miles above Washington. On a single day, 18 otherwise unidentifiable bodies were fished out along the riverbank between Chain Bridge and the Long Bridge at Fourteenth Street. The rains sent city sewers overflowing into streets near the river and canal. When Michael Downey of Limerick Alley went to the river to pick up driftwood for his fireplace, his little son fell in and was swept away by the current.[1]

Gloom and sickness closed in with the weather. Thousands of civilians from far corners of the North jammed into the hotels and boardinghouses of the capital, strangers commonly sleeping two to a bed because rooms were so scarce. Soldiers, many of them farm boys who had never been exposed to the seething germs of crowds and cities, bunked together in sodden camps on the surrounding hills. Smallpox and typhoid fever found them there. Each day, the papers printed a list of those who had died at the Washington Infirmary and in the makeshift hospitals that dotted the city, in buildings such as the E Street Baptist Church and the Union Hotel in Georgetown. Smallpox cases were sent at first to what had been a private home on First Street, northeast of the Capitol. Later they went to the more spacious Hospital for Eruptive Diseases, in and around the mansion of the Kalorama estate, overlooking Rock Creek near today's Twenty-third and S streets.[2]

Doctors and nurses of the day little understood what caused disease and infection,* or how futile their efforts were to treat them. Official Washington seemed almost as helpless against the thoroughly understood danger of fire. In November, a blaze quickly destroyed the Washington Infirmary, which had been the city's only hospital when war began. Police and volunteers carried about a hundred ailing soldiers and a few civilians through flames and smoke to safety. All the patients except one aged woman survived and were taken to a nearby schoolhouse that was already in use as a hospital, as well as to City Hall, Trinity Church and private homes. But as in the Willard's Hotel fire the previous spring, no thanks were due the city firemen; no alarm had sounded for an hour after the blaze was discovered by the Sisters of Charity in their quarters above, and no engine arrived for another hour. (Months later, firefighting was no better organized. A citizen signing himself "Active Fireman" wrote to the *Star* urging the District to coordinate competing companies under a single chief who would supervise the scene of major fires and investigate suspicious blazes, since "the majority of fires that occur are caused by incendiarism.")[3]

At Columbian College, a middle-aged nurse named Rebecca Pomroy wrote to friends back home in Massachusetts, thanking them for the crackers, fruit, clothes and writing material they had sent for her patients. Rebecca had arrived on October 1 to help care for sick and wounded soldiers in the college newly commandeered as a hospital, out Fourteenth Street in the Mount Pleasant neighborhood. Promptly thereafter, she oversaw a thorough scrubbing and whitewashing of her ward. She was one of ten nurses at the hospital, plus a secretary-treasurer, a cook and a steward. At first she was responsible for only twenty-five patients, among them three with typhoid fever and three with bullet wounds. She was motherly toward them all. "Take us all together, we are a happy family," she wrote to her hometown paper, the *Chelsea Telegraph and Pioneer.*

One autumn day, 17,000 soldiers paraded past Columbian Hospital, accompanied by Lincoln and McClellan, en route to a grand

---

*Crowding and disease worsened as the capital's population grew, approximately doubling in the first three years of war. In late 1861, Mayor Wallach asked the City Council to finance speedy evacuation of smallpox patients, and destruction of clothing and furniture where they had lived. Vaccination was ordered, and 2,280 inoculations were administered free to those unable to pay. Another epidemic swept the District in January 1864, when a total of 1,483 cases was reported—766 in Washington, 165 in Georgetown, 500 in the Kalorama Hospital and 52 in the almshouse. (Medical Society of the District of Columbia, "Report on the Sanatory Condition of the Cities of Washington and Georgetown," March 1864)

review. Pomroy sat her patients up in bed to watch and listen as regimental band succeeded band, one spirited march swelling, then merging with the next before it fell away. Many inmates "were bolstered up, and it seemed to put new life in them," she said. One man who had lost his left arm and three fingers on his right hand was eager to go back to his regiment, thankful that he still had one finger and a thumb to fire his musket. But later Rebecca told of a seventeen-year-old boy who was without relative or friend. "How assiduously was that boy watched!" she said, yet "typhoid fever, with its stiff mouth, black and crusted, hurried him to his narrow home." Early in December, she got ten minutes' notice to make room for twenty-six soldiers of the Eleventh Maine, who had measles. Four of them soon died, one boy whispering as he weakened, "What will my poor mother say when I am laid away from her?" Like most of the men whose remains were not forwarded to their relatives, he was buried at the Soldiers' Home, in the rural northern reaches of the District, with a wooden slab marking his grave.[4]

Lincoln felt the suffering around him, though he could not know how trifling the losses to date would be compared to the tens of thousands of dead and wounded yet to come, or how soon personal sadness would blanket the White House itself. He tried to look away when he could; he used humor to distract himself as well as some purposeful callers who sat, listened to his stories and left his office without ever finding an opening to say why they had come. Someone seeking a job that Lincoln was not prepared to give him might have to sit while the president propped his feet on his desk and read aloud the latest long column by "Orpheus C. Kerr," the pen name of Robert Henry Newell. In the *New York Sunday Mercury,* Kerr told of an imagined sojourn with prideful Union escorts to a battle site across the river: "Upon reaching the scene of strife, my boy, we discovered that the ten western Calvarymen [*sic*] had routed the rebels, killing four regiments, which were also carried away. On our side nobody was killed or wounded. In fact, two of our men, who went into the fight sick with the measles, were entirely cured." The president ended his reading with an outburst of laughter and pumped the baffled supplicant's hand as the next visitor was ushered in.[5]

Mary Lincoln did what she could to ease her husband's cares. There was the Sunday when she and the president received perhaps fifty persons, including Secretaries Seward, Cameron, Smith and Welles, as well as Generals Meigs and Fitz-John Porter, Commander John A. Dahlgren from the Navy Yard and assorted less lofty friends. Mrs. Lincoln's admirer B. B. French, commissioner of public buildings, whose job somehow included introducing guests to the presidential couple at White House levees, was himself a guest that evening. On his arm was Mary Ellen Brady, his housekeeper, who had become "like a gleam of the brightest sunshine" to him since his wife's death in May. Contrary to the sneers with which so many eventual friends described Lincoln early in his administration, French liked him for his seeming simplicity: "He is Old Abe, & nothing else, place him where you will. Everybody that knows him loves him . . . he is one of the best men who ever lived." Eager to please the Lincolns, French wrote in his diary as if he thought they might read it. Mary, he maintained, "looked remarkably well & would be taken for a young lady at a short distance. . . . say what they may about her, I will defend her." All of that evening's guests were there by about nine-thirty, but the entertainment did not begin until nearly eleven o'clock—Monsieur Herrmann, "the Great Prestidigitateur," who had made a sensation in New York earlier in the fall. He "astonished" French, an apparent connoisseur of the art, with "some of the best slight [*sic*] of hand performances I ever saw, and I have seen a great many. . . ."[6]

Herrmann had just opened at the Washington Theatre, at Eleventh and C streets. He was only one of the attractions drawing crowds as soldiers, speculators and returning congressmen sought diversion in the nighttime capital. Show business was booming, beckoning entrepreneurs and performers. Carlotta Patti, "the celebrated cantatrice," was in concert at the former Tenth Street Baptist Church. Canterbury Hall, on Louisiana Avenue behind the National Hotel, was advertising "50 star artists 50" plus a corps de ballet. Thomas King was featuring "Don Santiago Gibbonoise, the boneless man," at his new circus in a hastily built structure on the site of the old National Theater on E Street, which had burned down twice and collapsed once in its earlier incarnations. The Metropolitan Opera Troupe was trying to lift local musical taste at Odd Fellows Hall near the Navy Yard. Elsewhere a boulevardier could take in the long-running Campbell Minstrels, a "favorite company of Ethiopian serenaders"; the eccentric comedian Ben Rogers; or the "spirited, vivacious, black-haired" Susan Denin, singing "blood stirring Union songs" as Fanny Bombshell in *Our Volunteers* (she also played Lucretia Borgia). Occasionally the president appeared without fanfare in a theater box reserved for him, and often his sons Willie and Tad were seen happy together at the more frivolous entertainments.[7]

Lincoln was obliged by custom to greet the new session of Congress with a message summing up the situation of the moment and describing what he wanted from the legislature. In those days, the State of the Union document was not an address read in person to a joint session; that tradition would begin with Woodrow Wilson in 1913. Lincoln's was delivered to the Capitol on December 3 by a clerk, and was rare among his state papers because it lacked the coherence and eloquence that characterized most of his major writings. It was essentially a collection of status reports from his cabinet, with a few of what seemed throwaway suggestions of his own: establishment of an Agriculture Department, for example, and recognition of the black republics of Haiti and Liberia.

But there were signs that his thoughts were coming into focus on the most fundamental issue in American history, the underlying cause of the war itself. Over the years, Lincoln had left no doubt that he despised slavery, but his opinions on what to do about it had always seemed tailored to the politics of the moment. Once he had admitted, "If all earthly power were given me, I should not know what to do, as to the existing institution," and the truth of that seemed borne out by the way his later remarks varied with the times. Running for the Senate in Illinois, he had said, "I believe this government cannot endure permanently half slave and half free." But he made clear then, and said in the first minute of his inaugural address in March, that "I have no purpose, directly or indirectly, to interfere with the institution of slavery in the States where it exists." Now, nine months later, pressed by Radicals to make abolition a stated aim of the war, he still proceeded cautiously. But he did proceed.[8]

In November, George Bancroft, the acclaimed historian, former cabinet secretary and U.S. minister abroad, had written to Lincoln that fate had given the president a role in "times which will be remembered as long as human events find a record." "Civil war," Bancroft said, "is the instrument of Divine Providence to root out social slavery; posterity will not be satisfied with the result, unless the consequences of the war shall effect an increase of free States. This is the universal expectation of men of all parties."

Lincoln took this seriously because Bancroft was the premier interpreter of American history and a Democrat, not one of the Republican Radicals who harried him daily on the subject of slavery. He replied that the issue was one "with which I must deal in all due caution, and with the best judgment I can bring to it." Then in his message to Congress, he repeated that "the Union must be preserved; and hence, all indispensable means must be used." But, he said, "We should not be in haste to determine that Radical and extreme measures [i.e., straightforward abolition], which may reach the loyal as well the disloyal, are indispensable." He expressed the hope that some states would voluntarily end slavery if their owners were compensated for their loss. He noted that the war had already freed many slaves and would probably free many more, and that he would consider anything Congress sent him about freeing the slaves of disloyal owners. And once again, as he had for years past, he fell back on the idea of voluntary colonization of freed slaves, in some "place or places in a climate congenial to them." A later biographer has properly described the colonization movement as a "fantasy" that Lincoln endorsed as an unconscious way of avoiding hard thought about more realistic means. Even during the crisis over Fort Sumter, he had found time to talk with representatives of an outfit called the Chiriqui Improvement Company about colonizing ex-slaves in that potential coal region in the Isthmus of Panama.[9]

Colonization would never solve the problem, but in Lincoln's seemingly negative remarks about abolition, there were hints of concrete steps ahead. He was not going to act in haste, but he was going to use "all indispensable means" to save the Union, and if "Radical and extreme" steps became necessary, he would take them. He broached the possibility of the government's paying owners for liberated slaves—indeed, days before his message, he had quietly proposed a trial run of gradual emancipation in the little state of Delaware, compensated by the Federal government. The plan was narrowly defeated in the Delaware legislature, but the concept survived: in the U.S. Senate, Henry Wilson resurrected his proposal to end slavery in the District of Columbia, with the Treasury to pay owners $300 per slave.[10]

Lincoln's message to Congress was written with less than his usual care because he was worrying over the *Trent* affair, which he belatedly realized was a serious diplomatic crisis that could lead to war with

Britain. The Confederate diplomats Mason and Slidell, forcibly taken off the British mail packet, were in prison at Fort Warren in Boston Harbor. France had assured Britain that she would back her in any resulting hostilities with the United States. The mood of celebration that had greeted the first news of the Union coup on the high seas had evaporated by the time Lord Lyons, the British ambassador in Washington, presented a formal demand that the United States apologize and release the two captives. On Christmas Day, Lincoln called a cabinet meeting at which Seward maintained that the only way to avoid a second war was to back down. Lincoln prudently agreed with him.[11]

It was not a merry Christmas season. The international embarrassment of retreating before the British ultimatum dampened any attempt at official gaiety. General McClellan was sick with typhoid fever, so he surely would not surprise the world by taking the offensive anytime soon. When Lincoln went to the general's home, he was not allowed to see him. But the president's boys had "quite a noisey day" on Christmas, shooting firecrackers and pistols with the three sons of a Patent Office examiner, Horatio Nelson Taft. Even the Tafts' usually bookish and retiring sixteen-year-old daughter, Julia, got into the spirit of the day, cranking off a few rounds from her own pistol. The Taft and Lincoln boys were almost daily companions, playing, eating, sometimes sleeping together at the White House or the Tafts' home near Franklin Square. Julia escorted her brothers back and forth, and became friends with the daughterless Mary Lincoln, who enjoyed her talent at the piano.[12]

Just before the holiday, a riot broke out when a policeman named Nichols sought to stop a noisy postmidnight frolic in the Swampoodle neighborhood, along North Capitol Street. The revelers were unhappy that he had ordered their fiddler to finish one set and go home. Five nearby officers came to help Nichols, but then the lights went out, the policeman's club and pistol were stolen, and a soldier was shot before citizens named Minogean, Hogan, O'Day, Saunders, Quinlan, O'Keefe, Burns, Judson and Noonan were arrested for rioting and lesser offenses. Journalists had fun reporting this celebration, but could not conceal their horror when they described what happened on the day after Christmas, when one of the army's huge horse corrals caught fire.[13]

Thousands of animals were sheltered in ten long pine sheds covering a city block at Twenty-first and D streets, just east of the Naval

Observatory, on ground where the State Department Building would later be erected. When the blaze was discovered between 6 and 7 P.M., the captain in charge of the cavalry and artillery horses ordered them cut loose. But hundreds of wagon horses were still confined, and suffered worst. A thousand panicked animals stampeded through the city, one great herd fleeing eastward along Massachusetts Avenue. Some of the seriously burned horses were shot by soldiers and civilians in the crowd of spectators that quickly assembled. Army regulars rushed to fight the fire, control the crowd and try to save the tons of feed left on the lot. For days afterward, they were rounding up wandering animals. Angered at one more devastating fire and fearful of others to come, the editor of the *Star* demanded to know when the government was going to buy at least two steam fire engines; at the time, it had none.[14]

A hint of burned and decaying horseflesh still hung in the air over the west end of Washington on bright, sunny New Year's Day, when the Lincolns went through the motions of holiday festivity at the traditional White House reception. The diplomatic corps, Supreme Court and officers of the army and navy began to arrive at 11 A.M., after which the public poured through the receiving line. Commissioner French was delighted that Lord Lyons was welcomed "with peculiar distinction" so soon after settlement of the *Trent* affair, and the affable diplomat seemed especially pleased to be there. The atmosphere at the mansion was still more elegant a week later, when French proudly introduced the first lady he called "the American queen" to her guests. Mrs. Lincoln wore a silk-and-pearl headdress with ornaments and a wrought lace shawl "valued at $2,500!" he wrote. Cara Kasson told of how "the crimson and gold tapestry, the golden cables and tassels overhang pale weary faces, sparkling, laughing faces, and shrewd, treacherous ones alike."[15]

Amid all Mrs. Lincoln's expensive frippery, the president stood "gaunt and care-worn," shaking hands and being polite while his mind was on McClellan, Secretary of War Cameron, and the Radicals who had just dragged him into one of the most embarrassing incidents of his administration. On the evening of January 3, he had been invited to hear Horace Greeley, editor of the *New York Tribune,* speak at the Smithsonian Institution. At first, Smithsonian director Joseph Henry had denied such abolitionists use of the hall for a series of lectures because of the Institution's rule against political activity there. Nominally neutral, Henry was antiabolitionist, scornful of what he privately called the "peculiar doctrines" of "an avalanche of strong minded women and weak minded men... from the north." In response, the abolitionists organized themselves as the Washington Lecture Association, promising to have a variety of speakers, and successfully lobbied Republicans to pressure Henry into letting them use the auditorium. They began their series of lectures in mid-December, timed to attract the newly returned congressmen who were their main target. They loaded their schedule with celebrity abolitionists from Massachusetts and New York—Oliver Wendell Holmes, James Russell Lowell and Cornelius Felton from Harvard, Ralph Waldo Emerson from Concord, the Reverend Henry Ward Beecher from Brooklyn. But Greeley's platform as editor of the *Tribune* made him perhaps the best-known antislavery spokesman in the nation.[16]

More than a thousand persons in the auditorium that evening saw Lincoln, Secretary Chase and ten congressmen seated onstage behind Greeley, as if to endorse whatever he said. The bald, bespectacled editor may have pleased eleven of those twelve, but not the president. He asserted that General Frémont had been right in trying to free slaves belonging to Rebels in his territory, and every time he mentioned Frémont, partisans in the crowd jeered the president who had overruled the general. Greeley looked directly at Lincoln as he declared that freeing the slaves should be the war's sole purpose. Much of the audience roared its approval, but Lincoln sat silent and frustrated, hiding his feelings.

After Greeley's defiant lecture, the most noted of the Smithsonian series was by Wendell Phillips of Boston, who astonished his audience by saying that the black revolutionary Toussaint L'Ouverture of Haiti had been a greater champion of liberty than even George Washington. The most provocative lecturer might have been the great abolitionist Frederick Douglass, if he had been allowed to appear. But this was not to be: when the sponsors proposed that Douglass close the season's program, Henry flatly refused to permit a black man to speak in his hall.[17]

Between their speeches at the Smithsonian, the visiting abolitionists were welcomed at the Capitol, where the Congregational Reverend George B. Cheever of New York criticized the president in a sermon before the House of Representatives. To a certain extent, Cheever was preaching to the choir—the Republican Radicals who were now exerting their influence in the newly formed Joint Committee on the Conduct of the War. Originally created in December to investigate the defeat at Ball's Bluff, the committee was chaired by Senator Wade and dominated by Radicals from both houses. They promptly made it a partisan weapon, cross-examining generals about battlefield decisions, praising commanders who agreed with their politics and harassing those who did not.

One night in that first week of the new year, Wade brought his committee colleagues to see the president and laid out their case against the Democrat McClellan, who had defied their questioning. They even suggested that the general had not taken the offensive because he secretly hoped to bring about peace on Southern terms and so elevate himself to the White House. The next day, Lincoln summoned Quartermaster General Meigs and asked, "What shall I do?" Meigs suggested that the president bypass McClellan and talk strategy directly with his division commanders. Later, in conference with Generals McDowell and William B. Franklin, the president said that "if something was not soon done, the bottom would be out of the whole affair; and if General McClellan did not want to use the army, he would like to borrow it. . . ." At another presidential session with cabinet and army officers, the supposedly bedridden McClellan made a surprise appearance. He refused to disclose his plans there, but later confided to Lincoln that he wanted to take his army down the Potomac and the Chesapeake, to go at Richmond via either the Rappahannock or the James River. The president and the Joint Committee much preferred the direct approach, overland from Washington.[18]

But for the time being, winter mud ruled, among the armies and on the streets of the capital. Street urchins earned tips by clearing the crosswalks ahead of ladies wearing long skirts and gentlemen with polished boots, though few of the well-dressed walked door-to-door when they could ride above the mire. Three young daughters of Henry Sherman, a Treasury clerk from Connecticut who lived at Fourteenth and K streets, enjoyed watching a new horsecar line until they saw the animals struggling and suffering in the mud. "The horses would flounder in it," wrote Anna, the oldest girl, "and the men who were at work would beat them with picks and shovels, and the drivers with the whips, then the cars would get jerked off the track, and it would almost make us cry (I don't know but that we did sometimes) to see the poor beasts. It would seem as if they were expected to do more than horse flesh could do, and finally the men would have to get crow-bars and logs to pry the cars up on the tracks again and the passengers would have to get out, and find their way to the side walk on planks, and great pieces of stone, stuck in the mud at long intervals, to wait for the car to get righted."[19]

Nobody would march "on to Richmond" until the weather eased, though troops were stirring along the farther margins of the Confederacy. More immediate problems demanded the president's attention, close at hand.

For months, Lincoln and most of Washington had known of scandalously venal doings at the War Department. Endless opportunities for graft arose as the army multiplied thirtyfold in 1861, and few chances were missed. Simon Cameron was rewarding his political friends with jobs and contracts, and they in turn were taking care of their friends lower on the ladder. To them, it did not much matter whether the blankets and provisions they bought for the government were rotten. Favoritism ruled. The president complained privately that besides being "utterly ignorant" and "obnoxious," Cameron was incapable of handling his job, a position that would have strained even a brilliant administrator under such urgent pressure. Lincoln dropped hints that he would be happier with someone else at the War Department, but Cameron ignored them. Eventually, Cameron angered him with a lesser version of General Frémont's impolitic abolition venture out west. Knowing that the president's patience with him was growing thin, Cameron tried to solidify his backing among Radicals by issuing an annual report that supported what they were urging in Congress—freeing the slaves of "rebellious" citizens and using them as military labor. Without consulting the White House, he did this just as Lincoln was advising the cautious approach. The president ordered the Post Office to chase down mailed copies of Cameron's report, but both the original and a revised version got out. Lincoln had had enough. The new year was only ten days old when he informed Cameron that he was nominating him as minister to faraway St. Petersburg. The *New York Herald* opined that Cameron's departure from the cabinet was as beneficial to the Union as a great victory on the battlefield.[20]

Apparently unknown to the president, former Attorney General Edwin Stanton, who was then a legal adviser to the War Department, had approved and probably provided the language in Cameron's report that so angered Lincoln. There were those who suspected that this was done to provoke Lincoln into firing Cameron and appointing Stanton in his place; Stanton was that kind of cunning. Surprisingly the president did just that, despite the fact that his new secretary of war had been backbiting him, sometimes referring to him as "the original gorilla," since the morning Lincoln arrived in Washington. Indeed, Stanton's disdain for Lincoln reached back to 1855, when the two attorneys were on the same side in a patent suit brought by Cyrus McCormick, inventor of the reaper. "Why did you bring that damned long-armed ape here?" Stanton asked the leader of their legal team. He completely ignored the rough-cut lawyer from Springfield for the rest of the trial. But when Seward, his cabinet rival Chase and congressional Radicals led by Wade all supported Stanton for secretary of war, Lincoln took the chance of bringing him into the cabinet, and the Senate confirmed the nomination within forty-eight hours. Still the ruthless schemer, Stanton promptly supported the Joint Committee's campaign to replace McClellan, who had also endorsed him for the cabinet. But in time, the schemer would become more valuable to the Union war effort than any civilian except Lincoln himself.[21]

While the president, the secretary of war and the general-in-chief were talking about what to do across the Potomac, a little-noticed general out west was more comfortable fighting than talking. Ulysses S. Grant had left the army after his distinguished record in the Mexican War was tarnished by a drinking problem. When he sought command of a regiment after Fort Sumter, Washington had at first ignored him, then made him colonel of the Twenty-first Illinois. With the help of his governor and his congressman, Lincoln's friend Elihu Washburne, he was soon promoted to brigadier general. His only notable excursion since then had been an embarrassing near-disaster at Belmont, Missouri, in November. Now he had his chance to redeem his reputation, by leading a thrust into the western Confederacy along the Cumberland and Tennessee rivers rather than down the heavily defended Mississippi.

Grant, among others, had urged this strategy for weeks, but it is not clear who originated it. The most determined claimant for credit was neither a general nor a politician, but a woman, the indefatigable Anna Ella Carroll. By her energetic lobbying after Lincoln's election, she had helped keep Maryland in the Union, and in her prolific pamphleteering, she had spelled out a legal justification for the president's assumption of extraordinary war powers. After John Breckinridge left the Senate for the South in July, she had "pulverized" his secessionist farewell address so thoroughly that she became a darling of the Republican Radicals. But her busy mind, trained in the law, ranged far afield. According to Representative Albert Gallatin Riddle of Ohio, Carroll had shown a conspicuous "aptitude (genius we would call it in a man) for affairs, and for schemes and plans of campaign." In his memoirs, Riddle wrote that Assistant Secretary of War Thomas Scott had suggested sending her to St. Louis to consider how Union forces should advance down the Mississippi. She went and, after consulting experienced river pilots, submitted a paper on November 30 urging that Union forces take the Tennessee River route instead.[22]

Ben Wade, Carroll's champion when she later sought compensation for her war services, wrote that the Joint Committee on the Conduct of the War had been "in the deepest despair" when Assistant Secretary Scott informed him of Carroll's plan. Wade said he took it to Lincoln, who thought it was feasible, but worried that no general would risk it because it came from a civilian. Military men, the president said, were "extremely jealous of all outside interference." Wade wrote that one reason he had supported Stanton for secretary of war was that Stanton agreed to push Carroll's plan. Stanton joined the cabinet, Lincoln approved the Tennessee expedition, and in late January, Grant got orders to proceed. As Riddle told it, Carroll never got the credit due her because "*she was a woman,* and that fact would discredit all the generals and professionals in the army, and '*the good of the service*' required that she should be suppressed, and suppressed she was."[*23]

While Grant set out to prove his generalship by doing the unexpected, at the White House, Mary Lincoln had decided to proclaim her social standing the same way. Instead of the series of expensive state dinners hosted by presidents past, she would have a grand evening party—by invitation only, unlike the semiweekly receptions

---

*Carroll enthusiasts have alleged that in Francis Carpenter's famous painting of Lincoln reading the Emancipation Proclamation to his cabinet, the single empty chair symbolized Carroll's important place in wartime councils. In 1871, Carroll appealed to Congress for compensation for her services. Riddle wrote that she "sat daily in the galleries, a short, stout, middle-aged maiden lady, intently listening through an ear trumpet" to inconclusive discussion of her record. Although committees of both houses supported her claim, it dragged on through later sessions and was still unsettled when she died in 1893. (Albert G. Riddle, *Recollections of War Times,* pp. 190–191)

attended by crowds of the general public. She asked 500 or more guests to come on February 5, and annoyed perhaps as many more by not inviting them. Some thought that lavish entertainment at such a time was in bad taste—Wade declined the invitation, asking "Are the President and Mrs. Lincoln aware there is a Civil War?" Socially, the party was a great success, lasting till near daybreak. But privately, that night and the weeks that followed were among the most painful periods in Mary and Abe Lincoln's life together.[24]

As the Marine Band played, New York caterers laid out a splendid supper and guests mingled in the East Room, the president and first lady repeatedly slipped upstairs to sit with eleven-year-old Willie, who was in bed with a high temperature. He had typhoid fever.* Just days earlier, Willie and eight-year-old Tad had been having a joyous time with a gift pony and their friends the Taft boys. They laughingly scampered away from their patient tutor, preferring to organize a minstrel show in the White House attic. Willie sometimes walked importantly along the queue of favor-seekers waiting in the corridors, asking what each man wanted, as if he were screening them for his father. Now both boys were sick, and each day Willie's condition worsened.[25]

The day after Mary's fabulous party, U.S. Grant captured Fort Henry on the Tennessee River. Two days after that, a Union amphibious force under Ambrose E. Burnside took Roanoke Island, on the North Carolina coast, and four days after that captured the town of Edenton. Another four days later, Grant became a national hero when he took Fort Donelson on the Cumberland after informing the Rebel commander that "no terms except unconditional and immediate surrender can be accepted." It was a signal victory, the Union's first deep penetration of the Confederacy. But even this salutary news brought little cheer to the White House.

On February 20, Willie Lincoln died. Lizzie Keckley, who had been attending him, washed and dressed the boy's body. The president, she

---

*Running water was piped into the White House beginning in 1833, from a spring in Franklin Square at Fourteenth and K streets. By 1862 the mansion had also tapped into the new water line that served major government buildings as far distant as the Navy Yard in southeast Washington. Although most Washingtonians still got household water from neighborhood pumps, wells and backyard cisterns, some householders who could pay for a connection to this line had done so. But this supply still came untreated from the Potomac, a source already dangerous before thousands of soldiers, horses, mules and cattle swarmed its banks after war began. Water from above Great Falls did not arrive by the aqueduct until December 5, 1863.

said, looked into Willie's face and moaned: "My poor boy, he was too good for this earth. God has called him home. I know that he is much better off in heaven, but then we loved him so. It is hard, hard to have him die!" As Keckley watched him sob, she thought that there was "a grandeur as well as a simplicity about the picture that will never fade.... I really believe that I shall carry it with me across the dark, mysterious river of death." For days, according to Keckley, the president would interrupt work to shut himself in his room, to cry alone. But Mary Lincoln's anguish was beyond control; it threw her into convulsions, until the day her husband led her gently to a window and said, "Mother, do you see that large white building on the hill yonder?" He was gesturing toward the Government Hospital for the Insane, across the Anacostia River. "Try and control your grief," Lincoln told her, "or it will drive you mad, and we may have to send you there." Mary stayed in bed for three weeks, unable to attend Willie's funeral or take care of Tad, and for a long period after she emerged, she swathed herself in black.[26]

Meanwhile, the unfamiliar reports of progress by the army had put the capital in a mood to mount a mass celebration on Washington's birthday. A great crowd assembled at the Capitol, where one official counted forty-two generals and commodores on the House floor, along with legislators, cabinet and diplomats, listening to Senate clerk John W. Forney read Washington's Farewell Address. But the Lincolns stayed home, and the planned illumination of public buildings was canceled. At the Post Office, plumbers and painters had prepared gaslights and a thousand candles for the windows before the celebration was called off. Willie, the president's effervescent, promising favorite son, was buried in Oak Hill Cemetery just north of Georgetown. Tad, the affectionate, "tricksy little sprite" who could never quite fill his place, was still sick.[27]

Early on February 22, superintendent of nurses Dorothea Dix rode up in a carriage to Columbian Hospital to summon a nurse for special duty. Rebecca Pomroy was chosen. She resisted, but could not match wills with the redoubtable Dix. In ten minutes, she was off to the White House to care for Tad Lincoln. There she was instructed by the two attending physicians, Stone and Hall, before being introduced to Mr. and Mrs. Lincoln, who made her feel "very comfortable." Then she went into the sickroom where Tad lay feverish, occasionally crying that he could never speak to Willie again. "It was indeed a house of mourning," Pomroy wrote. After three days, she returned to Columbian, only to be called back to Tad's side for another three days. By then it seemed sure that he would survive.

Pomroy left without realizing how much more time she would spend with the Lincolns at the White House. Before she departed, she visited the conservatory, where the president had asked the gardener to cut a collection of flowers for the patients on her winter-dreary ward. She took them back to Columbian, to resume her mothering of soldiers like the two boys from the Fourth Vermont who arrived looking like "live skeletons." They were brought in covered with bedsores; "their bones had come through the skin, and when they were asleep they looked like dead." Pomroy could not understand why many soldiers were so afraid of hospitals that they would rather die than be sent to one, "such are the prejudices." Sometimes those fears were well founded: One of the skeletal boys pleaded with her to write to his father to come and take him home. "Poor fellow!" wrote Pomroy. "His letter was sent, but before the news reached his father, he was laid in the 'Soldier's Home.' "[28]

The news kept seesawing, good after bad. In a rainstorm in Richmond, Jefferson Davis was inaugurated for a six-year term as president of the Confederacy and admitted that "the tide for the moment is against us" in the war. Outside Washington, the Army of the Potomac was still stationary. But by the end of February, in a move made possible by Grant's earlier success, Union troops took Nashville without a fight. Secretary Stanton put all telegraph lines under War Department control, the better to censor what appeared in the newspapers.[29]

If one thing was clear in the mixture of sad and glad tidings brought by the press, it was that the nation faced a longer, more costly war than the politicians had expected on the morning when Lincoln sneaked into Washington before his inauguration. Then, there was still hope that war could be prevented, and even after the guns opened on Fort Sumter, there were fantasies on both sides that it could be over quickly. When the fear that the capital would be seized by the Confederates subsided, the persistent demand of "On to Richmond" rose, and now it was fading into realism. Yet on the first anniversary of Lincoln's inauguration, Federal armies held a protective zone of northern Virginia, plus Harpers Ferry, Fortress Monroe and most of mountainous western Virginia. They had moved onto the North Carolina coast, threatening Richmond from below, and onto the South Carolina coast, threatening Charleston and Savannah. On the Gulf Coast, they were threatening Mobile and New Orleans. They had cut deep into Missouri, Kentucky and Tennessee. Although the Army of the Potomac was not moving yet, it was well trained and, at least in the ranks below general-in-chief, it was ready to march.

CHAPTER TEN

The Whole World Moving Toward Richmond

Sarah Tracy could only imagine what was happening each day in the war that surrounded her little island of neutrality at Mount Vernon. When the faraway rumble of the guns at Bull Run reached the historic mansion by the Potomac, she had little doubt that a major battle was going on, but since then she had had to guess at the meaning of the martial sounds that drifted in, night and day. Cavalrymen chased each other back and forth across outlying farms, and she wondered whether they would keep coming, to tear up the little plots of vegetables and flowers that she cherished. In the quiet darkness of an early March morning, a rattle of musketry woke Miss Tracy. Later visiting soldiers told her about the encounter at nearby Pohick Church, where George Washington and George Mason had worshiped: Pennsylvania troops had laid an ambush for Rebel scouts, only to be ambushed themselves.[1]

Such particulars were not Tracy's business, and she was not supposed to have an opinion about them. A refined, educated upstate New Yorker, she had been hired almost three years earlier as secretary to Ann Pamela Cunningham, the woman who had rescued George Washington's home and made it a national shrine. The deteriorating mansion had been owned by the first president's grandnephew, John Augustine Washington III, when Cunningham organized the Mount Vernon Ladies' Association, which raised funds to buy and maintain the property. After fighting began, the disabled Cunningham remained at her South Carolina home, leaving Tracy with a bachelor friend of John Washington, an old-family Virginian named Upton Herbert, plus a few workers to protect the Washington estate from war and vandalism.

Within three days of Fort Sumter's fall, the *New York Herald* printed a false story alleging that Southerners had stolen Washington's body from its tomb at Mount Vernon. Tracy vigorously denied it, declaring that "the public, the owners of this noble possession, need fear no molestation of this *one national spot* belonging alike to North and South. Over it there can be no dispute!" She was underlining what Cunningham had written earlier, that "we need not have anything to do with politics—ought not to have. No sectional division should affect our position." This stance of neutrality was intended to protect the estate throughout the war. But rumors persisted. When Tracy heard that Union troops would be billeted at Mount Vernon, she went to the capital and protested to General Scott. "God bless the Ladies!" he exclaimed, and guaranteed that no troops would be stationed there "under any plea whatsoever."[2]

Union soldiers did come, but as tourists, sometimes in groups too big for Tracy's peace of mind, and occasionally bearing arms despite her rule against it. Fairfax County was then the seat of war, with great encampments of both armies, and between them farmland alive with spies and mounted patrols. Most young men of the county's deep-rooted Virginia families went south when war began, but the sons of Quakers who had bought farms near Mount Vernon went north rather than join the Confederate army. Women and servants left behind had to contend with foraging troops who raided their larders, crops and fences. A Union cavalryman recalled how sad he was to see that "within a single month war had made desolate what it had taken a century to beautify and perfect." Another Yankee told how "blackened ruins of dwellings" lined the roads of Fairfax, and a dead horse lay inside a deserted home. But both sides were guilty: a Confederate soldier admitted that his own comrades had torn down houses and fences to build winter quarters. He concluded that the county was "ruined for at least fifty years."[3]

Because the army would not give the dedicated Virginian Upton Herbert a pass, Miss Tracy often had to travel the nine miles to Alexandria to get supplies and mail, facing down Union soldiers at roadblocks along the way. McClellan failed to renew the pass that Scott had given her, so she took to the woods to avoid army barricades en route to Washington, where she appealed successfully to Lincoln himself. McClellan said the refusal had been a subordinate's mistake; in apology, he sent a boatload of provisions to Mount Vernon.

When Union authorities tried to confiscate the $200,000 that John

Washington had received for his property, Tracy helped keep the money out of government hands. Washington had joined the Confederate army, where he became a colonel and aide to Robert E. Lee, and was killed in western Virginia in September 1861. Before departing, he had deposited the funds at the Burke & Herbert Bank in Alexandria, where Upton Herbert's brother Arthur was a partner. Employees there pleaded ignorance when the Yankees arrived. Then John W. Burke took the funds from the safe and hid them from soldiers who came to search his home. Fearing that they would be found, Burke asked Tracy to slip them across the river to the capital. Hiding the funds in the bottom of a basket of eggs, she brazened her way to Riggs Bank, on the Avenue at Fifteenth Street, and plunked her basket on the desk of George Riggs, treasurer of the Mount Vernon Ladies' Association. He paid her for the eggs and rented her a safe-deposit box, and there she left the funds, across the street from the State Department.[4]

Amid these intrigues in the early months of war, Prince Napoleon of France suddenly appeared at Mount Vernon with his entourage, and Tracy entertained them as regally as she could manage. But most of the callers were not so celebrated. Private Thomas F. Walter and his comrade James Gordon of the Ninety-first Pennsylvania sneaked away from their company stationed in Alexandria to see the historic home of the first president. Arriving on foot, they found the manor house open and seemingly deserted. They walked through, but said "there was little of value to be seen." Spying cherry trees drooping low with fruit, they ate their fill and talked about "truthful George and his immortal little hatchet." Then, curiosity satisfied, they trudged back to Alexandria and got a mere reprimand for being absent without permission. When respectful soldiers from the Fifth Michigan came to visit Mount Vernon, they left behind a lieutenant who had fallen ill, in a feverish delirium. Army wagons came to fetch him, but Tracy "insisted that if forty ambulances came, he should not be moved." She had been what she called "doctress" to the estate's staff and visitors for months. After four days under her care, the lieutenant was strong enough to leave, and tried to thank her. She asked that if he ever found a comrade suffering, he would think of her and try to help. In tears, he told her, "So help me God, I will."[5]

All these minicrises and excitements intruded upon Mount Vernon from the land side; for months the broad Potomac was nearly empty of the marine traffic that had steamed and tacked past before the war, to and from Alexandria, Washington and Georgetown. The river between Virginia and Maryland became the line between Union and Confederacy—in fact, because Maryland historically owned the whole Potomac, that dividing line ran by the foot of Mount Vernon's lawn. Confederate guns sited at critical points along the river had nearly choked traffic despite sporadic efforts by Federal gunboats to break through. And at Hampton Roads, between Norfolk and Old Point Comfort, a frightening new weapon suddenly endangered Union access to Chesapeake Bay and the Potomac. The Confederates had raised the scuttled Union steamer *Merrimack,* plated her with iron, added ten heavy guns, renamed her the CSS *Virginia,* and sent her out against the Federal fleet. In her first sortie, she sank and drove aground several U.S. warships.

That battle threw some in Washington, particularly Stanton, into near-panic. According to Welles, the army secretary was afraid the Rebel ironclad "would destroy every vessel in the service . . . lay every city on the coast under contribution . . . come up the Potomac and disperse Congress, destroy the Capitol and public buildings," and perhaps demolish New York and New Orleans too. Welles tried to calm Stanton, assuring him that his fears were overwrought. On the night after the *Merrimack*'s opening victory, Welles's confidence was proven true. The Union navy's more advanced ironclad, commissioned only two weeks earlier, steamed into the Roads after a stormy trip from New York. She was the USS *Monitor,* a brainchild of the Swedish-born John Ericsson, who had invented the screw propeller. The next day, the two slow, clumsy men-o'-war pounded each other in the world's first battle between ironclads. It ended in a draw, but neutralized the Confederate threat to close the Chesapeake.[6]

Shortly before this historic collision, Miss Tracy and the workers at Mount Vernon could have seen a brightly lacquered balloon soaring to the west, in the direction of Pohick Church. In the basket dangling beneath it, Thaddeus Lowe was peering down, counting Confederate campfires toward Fairfax Station and Occoquan Creek. After winning Lincoln's approval, he had convinced skeptical generals that his aeronautical corps could be useful. On board the SS *George Washington Parke Custis,* which had taken tourists back and forth from Washington to Mount Vernon in prewar days, Lowe had set up his gas-generating equipment and moored one of his balloons, operating what must have been history's first aircraft carrier. Farther down the river, another of his balloons went aloft above Budd's Ferry. Seeing it from his own station on high gave Lowe the idea of passing visual signals from one aircraft to another, relaying their findings back toward the capital. A day later, Colonel Hiram G. Berry ascended and spotted the enemy pulling away from the Occoquan, the first evidence that the Confederates were withdrawing from the Manassas line they had held for more than six months.[7]

The long hiatus of war in the East was about to end.

To Anne Frobel, what she saw on the morning of St. Patrick's Day seemed to be "the whole world moving toward Richmond."

For months, she and her sister Elizabeth had struggled to fend off Yankee foragers at their home at Wilton Hill, overlooking Alexandria. That morning, Anne, a tall and formidable lady, came to town and gasped when she looked out across the river. Before her, from Washington City to Fort Washington, "as far as we could see was one solid mass of white canvass. You could only get a glimpse of the water here and there so thickly were the vessels—boats, steamers, little and big, of all sizes and shapes—crowded-crowded-packed together. I never saw, or could have imagined such a sight." Memorable though it was, the sight left her with "a sinking heart-sickness" to realize where such an "immence, immence army" was heading. Among the thousands of troops waiting on the waterfront, she came upon John Sedgwick's brigade, which had camped around her home, now ready to embark. Before suddenly departing their camp, the soldiers had burned great stacks of blankets and provisions, then marched off, bound south carrying only their muskets and haversacks.[8]

The Army of the Potomac was moving at last, in a steady stream of vessels bearing soldiers who crowded the rails as they slid past Mount Vernon, waving at Miss Tracy and her workers. McClellan had persuaded most of his generals and thus the president that rather than attacking the Confederates around Manassas, he could outflank them by moving down the Potomac and the Chesapeake Bay. Instead of fighting his way overland, he would take his army into the Rappahannock River to land at Urbanna, halfway to the Confederate capital. But as soon as this plan was agreed on, General Johnston withdrew his Rebel army from around Manassas, back into defenses along the Rappahannock. When he pulled away, the Federals followed carefully, moving their headquarters to Fairfax Court House. There, McClellan held a council of war with his generals and decided under the new circumstances to scrap the Urbanna plan. Instead he would sail down the bay to Fortress Monroe, then get at Richmond by marching up the peninsula between the York and James rivers. Though Lincoln approved this, he insisted that enough force be left behind to defend Washington.[9]

Because the Confederate withdrawal came so promptly after the Union high command agreed on McClellan's Urbanna plan, it raised suspicions that Federal strategic intentions had again been given away by Rebel spies. But Johnston's postwar narrative of the move makes no mention of secret intelligence, and the defiant agent who had warned of the advance to Bull Run was securely behind bars in Washington.

For five months, Rose Greenhow had been held captive in her home on Lafayette Square. Pinkerton and the provost marshal had turned the house into a prison, known about town as "Fort Greenhow," crowded with guards as well as other women arrested on suspicion of disloyalty. They kept Greenhow's eight-year-old daughter shut in with her mother. On Christmas Day, they had made a gesture of generosity by allowing Greenhow's niece, Stephen Douglas's widow, to bring in a cake for little Rose, and giving the child permission to play at the homes of friends. These tight restrictions obviously seemed necessary to the chief detective, who was so impressed by Greenhow's "almost irresistible seductive powers" that he feared she would find ways to continue her spying even when held prisoner. Indeed, by her own account, she did manage to slip letters in and out. The most noticed was addressed to Secretary Seward, demanding that the government formally charge her or let her go, and including a long harangue about the injustice of the Union's cause and conduct. It somehow made its way into the *Richmond Whig,* from which it was reprinted by the *New York Herald.*

This did not soften the hearts of Greenhow's keepers. In January, they moved her and her "female traitor" companions from Sixteenth Street to Old Capitol Prison, where the Greenhows had their own room but slept on hard straw mattresses infested with vermin. According to Greenhow, she told little Rose, "My darling, you must show yourself superior to those Yankees, and not pine"—to which her daughter said, "O mamma, never fear, I hate them too much. I intend to dance and sing 'Jeff Davis is coming' just to scare them." Soon the girl fell ill with measles, and after Greenhow refused the services of a physician who had annoyed her earlier, she accepted help from Jeff Davis's former doctor, Thomas Miller, himself the object of close scrutiny by Pinkerton's men.[10]

Greenhow was mightily offended by the presence of hundreds of black vagrants temporarily housed above and below her second-floor room, which was on the prison's northeast corner, away from the Capitol. She said the sounds and smells were "too revolting" to describe. In that mood, she would have been still more offended if she could have heard what her erstwhile confidant, Senator Henry Wilson, was doing in Congress as winter turned to spring.[11]

The army bakers and regiments of Zouaves were gone from the Capitol, and the squads of vendors selling apples, nuts and lager beer were back in business in the corridors. Here was a stand offering maps and guidebooks, there another selling Indian beads and moccasins. Senators and congressmen still drank their brandy and bourbon in private hideaways and did their most serious business in private committee rooms, off-limits to the public. But now that spy fever and the fear of invasion had receded, the halls and galleries were open to all comers. A British journalist, Edward Dicey, new to Washington but familiar with the speaker's gallery of Parliament, was amazed at the varieties of mankind watching the proceedings of Congress. "Irish workmen, with ragged coats, will be sitting next to Broadway swells, in the most elaborate of morning costume; and by the side of officers, in the brightest of uniforms, you will see common soldiers, in their gray serge coats, with the roughest of beards and the muddiest of boots." He advised that fastidious spectators could find choicer company in the ladies' gallery. On the House floor, Dicey said, there seemed "a want of life about the whole concern." The seats were spaced far apart since the departure of Southern legislators, and the scene was "like a lecture room where the class is paying no attention." Some of the members sprawled over their desks and some dozed, while most were reading, writing or chatting quietly. The Senate was just as sleepy. "It seems impossible that with such an audience any actor could work himself into a passion," Dicey said, and "harder still to imagine that bludgeons and fire arms could ever have been wielded amongst men so sober and respectable looking."[12]

The clubs and pistols were stowed away, but if Dicey had timed his visit a little differently, he would have seen that passion was still on call.

Egged on by the antislavery lecturers at the Smithsonian, congressional Radicals raised the temper of their oratory in the early months of 1862. Lincoln, often compassionate when soldiers appealed court-martial verdicts, held firm when asked to commute the death sentence of a Maine ship captain named Nathaniel Gordon, who had been overtaken at sea while attempting to bring nearly 900 slaves to the United States. The president refused to stop the execution but gave the slaver an extra two weeks to prepare himself. "In granting this respite," he wrote, "it becomes my painful duty to admonish the prisoner that, relinquishing all expectation of pardon by human authority, he refer himself alone to the mercy of the common God and Father of all men."[13]

Steeled by this experience, heeding the rising demands from Congress and public, and encouraged by reports from his armies on the move, the president decided that the time had come for a careful half step toward abolition. Although his trial balloon of compensated emancipation had failed in Delaware, he hoped that a broader proposal might tempt the other border states. On the morning of March 6, he called in Senator Charles Sumner of Massachusetts and read to him a draft bill that would allow individual states to choose emancipation, paid for by Federal funds, and give freed slaves the option of transplanting abroad. Sumner, a determined abolitionist, had long stood against gradual measures, but when presented with this concrete move, he was eager to support it. Within hours, his colleague Wilson took the lead in pushing a District of Columbia emancipation bill through Congress.[14]

He told how free blacks in the District had improved themselves in schools, churches, business and charitable organizations, despite the brutal "black code" that still restricted their lives. It was wrong, he said, for them to pay taxes to support public schools that their children could not attend because of their color. The debate wore on for days, drawing a group of "decent-looking and intelligent-appearing colored men" to the Capitol to listen. This displeased some senators, among them the sharp-tongued Garret Davis of Kentucky, who had been elected to fill John Breckinridge's seat. "I suppose in a few months they will be crowding white ladies out of the galleries!" he snarled in the midst of a particularly bitter speech against the bill. In the House, Ohio's increasingly shrill Peace Democrat Clement Vallandigham led the opposition against supporters headed by Pennsylvania's sarcastic, uncompromising Thaddeus Stevens.[15]

Wilson was strongly backed by the *National Republican,* Washington voice of the Northern Radicals, which reported that local free blacks owned some $500,000 in property, and no black public employee had ever been convicted of a crime. It asserted that many contrabands were ready to take up arms for the Union. Horace Greeley in New York was overjoyed by Lincoln's proposal, thanking the Almighty that the president whom his paper had so often lashed had turned into "so wise a ruler." In Washington, however, the *Evening Star* complained that the bill was aimed at "enforcing negro equality upon white men" and would cost too much. Like the *National Intelligencer,* the *Star* reflected majority opinion in the District.

White Washingtonians, afraid that emancipation would bring a greater flood of jobless African-Americans into the capital, inundated Congress and the newspapers with letters and petitions. The *Republican* admitted that even before the bill became law "the number of free negroes in this District [is increasing] to a degree which is pronounced alarming by many persons, and which has even attracted the attention of the City Fathers...." The mayor and the board of aldermen appealed to the Senate, saying the people of the District opposed abolition at such a critical time. The *Republican* suggested ending the B&O Rail Road's rule that kept blacks off its cars from Washington unless they had papers proving they were not runaway slaves, a change that would open an escape valve northward for those who fled to the District.[16]

But local opinion did not dictate what happened in the nation's capital. The District of Columbia was the one place where the Federal government could abolish slavery without voters' involvement. On April 6, the Senate approved the compensated emancipation bill for the District by a margin of 29 to 14. Five days later, the House passed it, 93 to 29. Even then, the way was not clear. Lincoln hoped the border states would voluntarily adopt compensated emancipation, thus casting themselves fully with the Union, and perhaps even encouraging breakaway states to follow. But so far, none of those border states—Maryland, Delaware, Kentucky, Missouri—had rushed to embrace the legislation. Some supporters of the bill were concerned that the president might withhold his signature, not wanting the capital, forced by Congress, to go first. As Lincoln considered whether and when to sign, he looked again at his maps of the war.

After months of inaction, troops were moving both in Tidewater and beyond the Appalachians. McClellan, demoted from general-in-chief so he could concentrate on the move toward Richmond, had brought his massive army ashore on the Peninsula and then quickly bogged down before Yorktown. But out west, U. S. Grant was heard from again. Although surprised by Confederate General Albert Sidney Johnston at Shiloh Church, the stubborn Grant had hung on and prevailed after Johnston was fatally wounded. The fight near the Tennessee-Alabama border was the bloodiest of the war to date, and the Federals lost more men than the Rebels. But news of Grant's success brought cheer to Washingtonians like Horatio Taft. "Our armies everywhere victorious, more prisoners, guns and munitions than our troops know what to do with," he wrote in his diary. "The City is in wild excitement over the news. A Salute of 100 guns ordered by the Sec'y of War. The great 'Anaconda' is drawing in his coils tighter and tighter around the rebels. . . . I think they are a race of bombaster cowards and events are proving it every day. We have had one Bull Run. They have a 'Bully Run' every time they meet our troops."[17]

Lincoln had to be more realistic. Some had said he should withhold any move toward abolition until the Union had won an important victory, and that the border states were waiting for such a moment to agree on compensated emancipation. But the president could see it the opposite way as well: if military success came first, those undecided might say that acting against slavery was not necessary to win the war and save the Union.[18]

Soon after Congress passed the District of Columbia bill, Sumner came back to the White House and put the issue to Lincoln face-to-face, in personal terms. "Do you know who at this moment is the largest slaveholder in this country?" he asked. "It is Abraham Lincoln, for he holds all of the 3,000 slaves of the District, which is more than any other person in the country holds." After Sumner came Bishop Daniel A. Payne of the African Methodist Episcopal Church, whom the president received warmly but noncommittally. The bishop recalled that as Lincoln left Springfield he had asked citizens to pray for him. "From that moment," he said, "we the colored citizens of the republic have been praying. . . ."[19]

For five days, despite rising pleas from both sides, Lincoln withheld his decision. Then, on April 16, 1862, he signed the bill that forever abolished slavery in the capital of the United States.

As on so many matters, the president's thinking on this had

evolved under the pressure of war. Twenty-five years earlier, as a young Illinois legislator, he had said he believed Congress could end slavery in the capital, but only at the request of Washington's citizens. When he proposed such a step as a congressman in 1849, it included that proviso. But now, on signing the bill, he wrote: "I have never doubted the constitutional authority of Congress to abolish slavery in this District. I have ever desired to see the national capital freed from the institution in some satisfactory way. Hence there has never been in my mind any question upon the subject, except the one of expediency, arising in view of all the circumstances." It was a remarkably frank admission, to say publicly that pure expediency had held him back on such a fundamental question. But now, whatever the explanation, he had done it, and brought joy to African-Americans and friends of liberty across the North.[20]

The city's black leaders, aware of their new responsibility, tried to restrain the celebration, but that was impossible. In black neighborhoods, spirited minstrel songs vied with reverent spirituals. One African-American wrote, "Should I not feel glad to see so much rejoicing around me? Were I a drinker I would get on a jolly spree today, but as a Christian, I can but kneel in prayer and bless God." On the following Sunday, born-free and newly liberated blacks lifted prayers of thanksgiving at the capital's seventeen colored churches. As preachers sermonized, some worshipers could not hold back, cutting loose with shouts of jubilation. In a joint meeting at the Colored (later Fifteenth Street) Presbyterian Church, their leaders thanked God, Lincoln and Congress, and resolved that "by our industry, energy, moral deportment and character, we will prove ourselves worthy of the confidence reposed in us in making us free men.... as in the past we have as a people been orderly and law-abiding, so in the future we will strive with might and main to be in every way worthy of the glorious privilege which has now been conferred upon us."[21]

CHAPTER ELEVEN

This Sudden & Radical Revolution

The day after Lincoln signed the local emancipation bill, the District of Columbia's largest slaveholder, George Washington Young, rode out to give the life-changing news to his workmen and their families. His Sixth Street in-law, John Carroll Brent, went with him to his Giesboro plantation, near the southern tip of the District. They crossed the Anacostia River by the Navy Yard Bridge and rode past the Hospital for the Insane, talking about what the emancipation law would mean to themselves, their bondsmen and their city. When Young stood before his sixty-nine men, women and children and told them they were now free, both master and ex-slaves were wrenched with emotion. After witnessing this moment, Brent wrote in his diary that it "severed the relations, always kind & patriarchal on the part of the owners, which have existed for their mutual benefit between the parties for almost half a century. This sudden & radical revolution . . . is productive of more consequences than mere pecuniary loss & inconvenience. For the severing, so abruptly, of ties like these is accompanied in a case like this, with pain & distress on the part of the humane & religious owner, which no language can describe."

Brent was a forty-seven-year-old lawyer, a product of the Catholic family that had given Washington its first mayor, Robert Brent, and the Carrolls who had once owned the land where the Capitol stands. His sympathy with Young and his former slaves was at least equaled by his contempt for the "abolition party" politicians who had brought on such drastic change. "It is barely possible that those who are responsible for this outrage, gilded with the delusive promise of inadequate compensation, may live to acknowledge & repent the fatal error or premeditated wrong," he wrote. "But it is, in my humble opinion, more than probable that the deluded, ignorant creatures who are thus made the scapegoats of fanatics & politicians will before long discover to their astonishment & dismay that they have 'got from the frying pan into the fire.' . . ."[1]

The first sentence of the District of Columbia Emancipation Act freed local slaves at the moment the president inscribed his "A. Lincoln." But carrying out the rest of the law would take time. Up to a million dollars was appropriated to pay loyal owners for loss of their slave property, and $100,000 to settle District ex-slaves who were willing to move to Haiti, Liberia, or "such other country beyond the limits of the United States as the President may determine." Despite Lincoln's years of lip service to colonization, the idea still stirred little interest among freedmen, who were as deeply rooted in America as their white countrymen. "Though debarred from the rights of citizenship, our hearts nevertheless cling to the land of our birth," a free black said. "We do not want to be exiled beyond the ocean to look for a home when there is land enough on the American continent. We are colored Americans and we want a home on the American soil. We now number as many souls as won the freedom of the white race of Americans from British rule."[2]

The former owners of those freedmen were greatly interested in the other major section of the law; they were eager to be paid for their financial loss. Lincoln promptly nominated three commissioners to carry out this provision. They were former Ohio congressman Samuel F. Vinton; Daniel R. Goodloe, a North Carolina–born Unionist who had edited the abolitionist *National Era* and corresponded for the *New York Times;* and, surprising to many, Washington's former mayor James G. Berret. The president nominated Berret as a goodwill gesture, trying to make up for having him arrested and removed from office nine months earlier; he already had offered to make the ex-mayor a colonel, with a safe staff job. But Berret was not to be assuaged, and declined both offers. Then, before the commission was fairly into its work, Vinton died. Lincoln named former Postmaster General Horatio King and Treasury official John M. Brodhead to take their places, and Georgetown lawyer William R. Woodward as clerk of the commission. Twelve days after the act was signed, the members announced that they would hear requests for compensation during regular hours at City Hall. They gave loyal former owners ninety days to present written statements specifically describing each freed slave.[3]

Thus the City Hall of Washington became the scene of the only compensated emancipation in American history, and of spirited disputes over the claimed value of individual slaves and the loyalty of their erstwhile owners.*

George Washington Young received more than $38,000 for his sixty-nine slaves, an average of about $550 each, ranging from $1,200 down to nothing at all. Altogether, the District's former owners submitted 966 petitions for payment, of which the commission accepted 909. It awarded compensation for 2,989 slaves but refused to pay for 111, because either the loyalty of the owners or their clear title to the slaves was disputed. The slave trade had been banned in Washington for more than a decade, so the commissioners had no handy reference for independent valuation of individuals. Rather than accept the owners' estimates, they called in a Baltimore slave-dealer named B. M. Campbell for expert advice. Because values in Maryland had fluctuated since the war began, they based payments on prewar prices, adjusted to bring the overall average to $300 and keep the total within the allotted $1 million. The next-largest slaveholder after Young claimed compensation for thirty-three men, women and children. Most of those applying were city people who had owned two or three house servants; the longer lists were mainly from those who operated farms in the rural District, outside Washington and Georgetown. A few petitions came from institutions such as the Sisters of Visitation, who had employed twelve slaves at their convent in Georgetown. For twenty-five cents, each ex-slave could receive a certificate proving that he or she was a free person by act of Congress.+

Day after day, the three conscientious commissioners sat as a loyalty court, often deciding on narrow grounds whether a petitioner or family had given aid or comfort to the Confederacy. There was the case of Mary Throckmorton: her husband had left to join the Confederates, but her son was an officer in the Union army, and because she presented "highly respectable" witnesses to her own loyalty, her claim

---

*The original City Hall at Judiciary Square, on Indiana Avenue between Fourth and Fifth streets, is the oldest surviving municipal building in Washington. Designed by George Hadfield, who also was an early architect of the Capitol, its central section was completed in 1820, and its east and west wings in 1826 and 1849. Before the war, it had served as a courthouse and at times as a slave market. In the first weeks after Sumter, it was fortified, like the Capitol and Treasury buildings, against feared Confederate invasion. Later it became a Civil War hospital. In 2003, after use as a courthouse annex, it was badly deteriorated and under repair. Before it stands the first public monument to Abraham Lincoln, erected in 1867. (Randall Bond Truett, ed., *Washington, D.C.,* p. 299)

was honored. But Sarah A. Abbott and Susan W. Harris were denied payment, because their husbands had gone south and there were no ameliorating circumstances. Smith Minor of Virginia had moved to the District with his slaves after the war started, but before leaving the Old Dominion, he had voted for secession. Minor admitted this, but maintained that he had been strongly influenced by friends. The commissioners, noting that others in Minor's precinct had voted against secession even though threatened with violence, refused to pay him. They also had to decide whether to compensate owners whose slaves had absconded before Lincoln signed the law on April 16; some of those runaways had returned in order to get their treasured certificates of freedom. Case by sticky case, the commissioners proceeded through petitions, witnesses and affidavits, so busy that the original mid-July deadline was extended by a month. Meanwhile, complicated questions of ownership were brought before the U.S. District Court.[5]

Predictably, hundreds of bondsmen had fled from Maryland and Virginia to seek freedom in the District. Most of these, if caught, saw their hopes crushed by the law: although the capital had become free territory, the U.S. court still helped loyal slave-state owners reclaim their human property. Dennis Duvall of Prince George's County named twenty men, women and children, from thirty-eight-year-old Lucy Jackson to nine-week-old Laura Spriggs, who he said had escaped into the capital. The court ordered the District marshal to "deliver the said fugitives now in his custody to the said claimant," authorizing "such reasonable force and restraint as may be necessary to take and remove said slaves back to the state of Maryland...." Duvall was one of many owners whose economic standing was upheld despite the new order of things, but others found their world turned upside down. Thomas A. Wethers, in Stafford, Virginia, sent a pleading letter that summer to his former slave, Washington Childs, who apparently had bought his freedom from Wethers for $200 yet unpaid. "I am sorry to write to let you know that my health is no better," Wethers said. He asked Childs to settle part of the debt by bringing him a barrel of sugar, sacks of coffee, two bolts of cotton and a pound of black tea. "Now Washington attend this as I stand now in need of money & grocery. I know you can't think hard of this if you knew my circumstance & you will be at liberty for life." He signed it, "Your friend," and to a P.S., he added "Most respectfully." Whether Childs responded by venturing fifty miles from the District back into Virginia is unstated, but doubtful.[6]

On the night of May 8, by the light of the spring moon, Abraham Lincoln secretly approached the shore of Confederate Virginia, close to the great naval base at Norfolk. A few miles away, around a bend in the coastline, the ironclad *Merrimack* lay waiting, still a menace to Union vessels operating in Hampton Roads. For all Lincoln knew, gray-clad troops might have been aiming at his little boating party from behind the beach. That the president of the United States was making such a risky, unnecessary venture into enemy territory, two hundred miles down the Potomac and the Chesapeake from the White House, says much about the course of the war by mid-spring of 1862, and even more about how Lincoln played the role of commander-in-chief.

The Potomac River was open, from Washington to Chesapeake Bay. After the Confederates withdrew behind the Rappahannock, the Yankees discovered that many of the dangerous-looking artillery pieces that had scared ship captains on the Potomac were merely "Quaker guns," logs charred or painted black and mounted in conspicuous earthworks. McClellan's great army had sailed down to Fortress Monroe unmolested, and many of those embarked expected the general's master plan to bring quick success. Dr. Charles S. Tripler, medical director of the Army of the Potomac, took "an extra and brand new wig with him to wear at the glorious entry into Richmond." The army moved a few miles up the Peninsula between the York and James rivers until it met resistance at Yorktown.[7]

There McClellan sat, insisting that he was outnumbered, lamenting that he was not fully supported. This provoked Lincoln to write one of the most plainspoken messages in his frustrating experience with the Young Napoleon. "Your dispatches complaining that you are not properly sustained, while they do not offend me, do pain me very much," said the president. "There is a curious mystery about the number of troops now with you." War Department figures showed that McClellan had 108,000 (against the Confederates' 60,000), but he maintained that he had only 85,000. Clearly implying that McClellan's career was at stake, Lincoln said, "Let me tell you that it is indispensable to you that you strike a blow.... The country will not fail to note—is noting now—that the present hesitation to move upon an intrenched enemy is but the story of Manassas repeated." He tried to conclude on a friendly note, saying, "I have never written to you or spoken to you in greater kindness of feeling than now," but "you must act."[8]

Only after the Confederates withdrew from Yorktown, more than three weeks after that letter of March 9, did McClellan's army edge forward. The next night, Lincoln set out down the Potomac with Secretaries Chase and Stanton and Brigadier General Egbert L. Viele of New York. They slipped away from the Navy Yard in great secrecy, with Chase playing host aboard the former luxury yacht *Miami,* which had been armed as a Treasury Department revenue cutter. Slowed by thick weather, they anchored overnight and eased downstream the next day, giving the president plenty of time between strategy talks to tell stories and recite Shakespeare. Showing off on deck, he lifted an ax and held it at arm's length by the end of its handle for several minutes, a feat that brawny crewmen tried and failed to match. Late on May 5, the group reached Fortress Monroe at the tip of the Peninsula, overlooking Hampton Roads. Around it lay a multitude of Union steamers, tugboats, sloops, barges, gunboats and all kinds of smaller craft; "towering above them all was the [3,360-ton] *Vanderbilt,* that leviathan of ocean steamers, a million-dollar gift by the owner [Cornelius Vanderbilt] to the government."[9]

Commodore Louis M. Goldsborough, chief of the North Atlantic blockading squadron, told the president and the two cabinet officers that the dreaded *Merrimack* (few used its Confederate name, *Virginia*) was slowing McClellan's advance. By blocking the mouth of the James River, it was preventing the Union fleet from moving upstream to guard the army's flank. Goldsborough had a scheme to lure the Rebel warship out to face the *Monitor,* then ram her with the *Vanderbilt,* specially reinforced for the purpose. The next day, the presidential party boated out to watch this action from the Rip Raps, fortified rocks in the Roads between Fortress Monroe and Willoughby Spit. Coast artillery roared on both sides. When the *Monitor* approached, the *Merrimack* slid slowly out of the Elizabeth River like a half-submerged prehistoric monster. But she refused to come farther; she sat where she was, defending Norfolk.

Their plan frustrated, Lincoln, Chase and Stanton urged Brigadier General John E. Wool and the commodore to move troops across under heavy artillery cover and take Norfolk from the rear. The army and navy made a gesture that way the following day but then backed off, still afraid of the *Merrimack.* When Viele suggested a landing site farther around toward Cape Henry, beyond the ironclad's reach, a colonel said the water there was too shallow. But Chase wanted to see for himself. He discovered not only that the approach was deep enough, but, according to Viele, what the colonel reported as a "large body of men" on shore consisted of two women, one of them waving a white flag, plus a child and a dog.

When Lincoln heard this, he could not resist taking his own look. Whether he actually stepped ashore was left a matter of dispute between Chase and Viele. The cabinet secretary, who had some political motive for making himself look bolder than the president, implied in his diary that Lincoln stayed just offshore in their tugboat while the rest of the party inspected the beach. But Viele wrote later that the president went ashore and walked up and down, demonstrating that the site was undefended. "How little the Confederacy dreamed what a visitor it had that night to the 'sacred soil'!" he said. The next day, five thousand Federals, accompanied by Chase, landed at Ocean View and despite confusion over who was in charge of what, moved toward Norfolk. On the way, they met Mayor W. W. Lamb, riding out to surrender the city while Confederate soldiers and sailors set fire to the navy base and everything of military value. Sometime after midnight, on the morning of May 11, a thunderous blast shook Norfolk and all about: it was the magazine of the *Merrimack* exploding as she was scuttled by her crew. "Thus," wrote Viele, "this most formidable engine of destruction that had so long been a terror, not only to Hampton Roads, but to the Atlantic coast, went to her doom, a tragic and glorious finale to the trip of the *Miami*." And thus the president of the United States played his own personal, chancy role in opening Hampton Roads and the James River to the Union fleet, encouraging McClellan to take up the march "on to Richmond."[10]

Four days after the *Merrimack* settled to the bottom, Federal gunboats forced their way up the James to seven miles below the Confederate capital, where they were stopped in a raging battle with Rebel gunners at Drewry's Bluff. Within three weeks, McClellan and 100,000 Union troops were at the doorstep of Richmond, where Joe Johnston's defenders made a stand at Fair Oaks, or Seven Pines, as the Southerners called it. Thudding artillery barrages rattled Jeff Davis's windows on Shockoe Hill; fair-weather politicians fled Richmond for the hinterlands; local newspapers argued for burning the city, the industrial heart and political symbol of Confederate independence, rather than surrendering it to the accursed Yankees.

With the war seemingly transported away from Washington, optimism rose in the hotels and saloons along Pennsylvania Avenue, from Lincoln's White House to the Capitol. While the president was at Fortress Monroe, Buildings Commissioner French wrote that "McClellan seems to be doing his whole duty now. He is making the Rebels skip down on the Peninsula . . . I think now, the rebellion is on its last legs. McClellan has been shamefully abused, but I have never lost faith in him. I have believed him, ever since Scott retired, the master spirit of the War. . . ." Thus encouraged, French went during May to see *The Barber of Seville* at Grover's Theater, took a pleasure ride with friends out to St. Elizabeth's Hospital and ordered repair of the Long Bridge after a locomotive broke through its wooden planking, preventing the draw from opening. On June 1, he joined Secretary of the Interior Caleb Smith and Capitol architect Thomas Walter on a jaunt to Clark Mills's sculpture studio and foundry in the District near Bladensburg. There they inspected and accepted the bronze statue of Freedom that Mills had cast from the plaster model brought from Italy.[11]

Slave workers, skilled and unskilled, were an essential element in Mills's latest success, as they had been in building the Capitol, the White House and every other local project since Washington was founded. When the fragile full-scale model of Freedom was to be removed from the old House Chamber for casting, the Italian artisan who had joined its parts and invisibly sealed its seams refused to disconnect them unless he got a major raise in pay and a long-term contract. He maintained that no one else could do it without damage. But Philip Reid, a mulatto slave for whose work Mills was paid $1.25 a day, devised an ingenious way to take the model apart: he attached an iron ring atop the head and lifted the whole thing with block and tackle just enough to slightly separate the five parts and allow access to the bolts inside. Reid, whom Mills had bought for $1,200 many years earlier in Charleston, South Carolina, became a free man before the statue was cast and returned to the Capitol. When Mills applied that summer for compensation for Reid and ten other slaves under the District emancipation law, he described him as short, forty-two years old, "not prepossessing in appearance, but smart in mind," and worth $1,500.[12]

Bringing the bronze statue to the Capitol was a signal step for

Walter, back at work after nearly a year officially removed from the great project of his life. During those months, he had made more than a dozen trips from Philadelphia to Washington to lobby Congress and the administration for resumption of work on the dome and wings of the Capitol. He, Secretary Smith and building contractors warned that the building was being damaged by the elements while work was halted. They argued that the War Department was so busy elsewhere that the project should be placed under the Interior Department. On April 30, days after Congress approved this transfer, Walter got permission to pick up where he had left off—free at last of interference by his archrival, General Meigs. Although construction had been officially suspended, the contractor had kept working to prevent the loss of tens of thousands of dollars' worth of material stacked on the Capitol grounds. On his repeated trips to Washington, the architect had slipped into his office to worry over his drawings of the dome and climbed up and down the scaffolding to look for potential problems.[13]

Professionally, Walter was elated to be on the job again, but his personal life was a microcosm of the crosscurrents that confounded and pained American families on both sides of the war. In the year since stopping work at the Capitol, since watching political debate turn into bloody war, he had completely reversed his attitude toward slavery and politics. Weeks after Fort Sumter, he had still been writing about "this unholy, fratricidal war," and complaining about those who belabored "the nigger question." But a summer later, his son Horace was in the Union army and in trouble with the law. Another son, Robert, was about to join the army. A third son, Thomas, who lived in Norfolk, was forsaken by his father because he supported the Southern cause. And Walter's son-in-law, Martin Harmstead, was a chaplain with a Union regiment at the front.

Twenty-six-year-old Horace, who had exhausted his father's patience by constantly asking for money, left his regiment and in late winter was back in Philadelphia. There he burglarized a jewelry store, after which his lawyers wrote Walter asking payment for their services. Walter, who had repeatedly told Horace that he had sent him his last dollar, gave in again, this time telling him, "Don't stay a single hour after you receive this, be off to your camp instantly." He did not believe Horace's excuse that his corps was being disbanded—"I tell you that you will be wanted until the end of the war. . . . I don't want to hear from you again until you are back with your regiment. . . ." Robert Walter, thirty, would become an officer in the Sixty-fifth Indiana Regiment, and by all reports a model soldier, apparently taking to heart his father's advice to avoid liquor, gambling and bad language.[14]

For some reason, Walter had feared that twenty-eight-year-old Thomas was killed or missing in combat on the Confederate side when the Rebels pulled away from Manassas that spring. But by summer, Thomas was again living safely as a photographer in Union-occupied Norfolk and taking sides with his Southern neighbors. This was perhaps the sharpest disappointment of all to his now fiercely Unionist father.

Walter was incensed that, in a letter, Thomas had referred to the Confederates as "our troops" and said "the Yankees were allowed to take possession" of Norfolk. He told his son that "The demons of the south call *all* the north 'Yankee,' by way of derision. Do you do so? I am a *Yankee,* in this sense, and so are you, and so are we all." Walter said the Rebels had become "thieves, and murderers, and have attempted to tear to pieces the government handed down to us by our fathers. They are banditti, traitorous hordes let loose on society, demons in human form, and they must be swept away, root and branch, and the country purged of the foul stain they have put upon it." Southerners, he wrote, "have shown themselves unworthy, as well as incapable of being the masters of black men—the black men are their superiors in as much as their hearts are not half so black as the hearts of the wretches who are fighting against us."

He urged his son to "repent of any defection you may have felt toward the North. Do so at once and *heartily* take the full *oath of allegiance* to the United States government, and repudiate forever this severance you have made between yourself and your family. If you do this we will let by-gones be by-gones, and we will consider you again as in the *Union*—family as well as national." In his letter, Walter enclosed family photographs, saying that Thomas could pick out his own likeness—and "of the rest I can say there is not one traitor there."[15]

As if these domestic tribulations were not distressing enough, Walter returned to Washington to find his church family ripped apart by the war. Even after a year of official crackdowns on citizens suspected of disloyalty, churchgoers in the District disagreed so publicly that schisms appeared in nearly every denomination. Perhaps because Southern sympathizers thought that in a religious setting they were beyond the reach of martial law, they continued to speak out openly—and at least one was doing more than speaking.

When the academic year ended at Thomas Conrad's Georgetown Institute that June, the commencement exercises held in the Dumbarton Methodist Church next door were full of Confederate conviction, and some of the graduating scholars even wore secession badges. Conrad hired the U.S. Marine Band, "the President's Own," for the occasion, and ordered it not to play any "national tunes," but to conclude the proceedings with "Dixie." The band's director announced that he would follow directions but did not want anyone to doubt that he was a loyal Unionist. This disclaimer brought moans of dissent from many fan-fluttering ladies present, but when the band rendered the Rebels' favorite song, their moans turned to loud applause. Police on hand walked away, saying they could not provide protection for such a display. The *Star* reported that some of those police thought the person who organized it should be arrested, though they made no motion to do so.[16]

But Conrad's apparent clerical immunity was about to run out. That provocative commencement exercise brought closer government scrutiny, and in early August, the Georgetown provost guard arrested the young reverend on charges of "communicating with the enemy" and "attempting to send his scholars as recruits to the rebel army." Several of his students were also brought in for "insolently" protesting when their headmaster was arrested, but they were soon released. By Conrad's own account, he and Southern friends had plotted earlier to assassinate General Scott, considered by them a traitor to Virginia. But when Conrad sent a message to Richmond about this scheme, Confederate authorities forbade it. Conrad thereupon tossed the old musket he had primed for the assassination into a well behind a building on the Avenue. He was held in the Old Capitol until officials paroled him to make room for seemingly more dangerous secessionists. Even then, for six weeks before he was sent south, he was allowed to roam loose in the city with eyes and ears open. Then he was deported to Fortress Monroe, en route to Richmond. But he would return, quietly, many times before the war was over.[17]

The government had gentler ways than jail and deportation to respond to spoken dissent—or unspoken support—from the pulpit. The bishop of the Episcopal diocese was William R. Whittingham, a forceful and unwavering Unionist. At the Episcopal Church of the Ascension, where Southern feeling ran high, the Reverend William Pinckney was nominally loyal but down deep a states'-rights Marylander. The Reverends Syle of Trinity Church, Hall of Epiphany Church and Morsell of Christ Church, near the Navy Yard, felt much the same way. The predictable collision between Whittingham and the ministers came in March 1862, when the bishop issued a prayer to be used in District churches in thanks for recent Union successes on the battlefield. Pinckney, maintaining that the bishop had overstepped his authority, refused to say the prayer at his church. So did Syle and Morsell. Hall told the bishop that he should not publish such controversial prayers without first consulting the ministers of the diocese. Promptly thereafter, the provost marshal advised Pinckney, Syle and Morsell that the government was taking over their churches for military hospitals. When their parishioners arrived for services, they found soldiers and workmen busy with saws and hammers.

Pinckney and his congregation, ousted from their church, protested in vain. But thanks to Washington's wealthiest pro-Southerner, they found a home: the capital's "patron saint," the sixty-three-year-old banker, philanthropist and former militia colonel W. W. Corcoran, offered the congregation temporary use of one of his buildings on H Street. Corcoran's only daughter, Louise, had married Louisiana Congressman George Eustis, who became secretary to John Slidell, one of the Confederate diplomats captured at sea in the *Trent* affair. Corcoran himself shipped more than a million dollars in gold to England and then followed it across the Atlantic. Rather than stay in wartime Washington, he exiled himself to the continent until peace returned.*[18]

According to Walter, the partisan split at his Baptist church reached the point at which "they have been knocking one another down in the aisles, calling each other 'liars' and 'blackguards' &c &c until the penny papers served them up under the caption of 'rare sport.' " At least thirty-one members, about a third of the congregation, withdrew from the church on E Street near Sixth and set up separately

---

*When the government moved to take Corcoran's home on Lafayette Square, the French minister stepped in, saying he had leased the building. But in time, the government did occupy another property, the Corcoran Gallery on the Avenue at Seventeenth Street, which was still under construction. Quartermaster General Meigs put the gallery to use as a warehouse for army blankets and clothing. In 1870, the government paid Corcoran for its use of that building, later renamed the Renwick Gallery. The present Corcoran Gallery of Art on Seventeenth between E Street and New York Avenue opened in 1897, nine years after Corcoran's death. (*Dictionary of American Biography*, 2:440)

as a "Mission School" in Temperance Hall. But soon thereafter, that hall was sold to become "a theater above and a lager-beer saloon below." Eventually, Amos Kendall, another of the capital's leading philanthropists, took the initiative to provide a place for the Baptists who had left E Street. Kendall, the former editor and postmaster general, had made much of his fortune as business agent for Samuel F. B. Morse, inventor of the telegraph. He proposed that if the congregants would build a $100,000 church and name it Calvary, he would put up the first $60,000. He did, and they raised the rest, founding what became Washington's foremost Baptist church.[19]

This feuding left Walter, the Sunday school teacher and architect who had overseen the rebuilding of the E Street church in 1860, dissatisfied with both those who departed and those who stayed. After the schism, he feared that E Street would have to be sold for debt; it, too, was temporarily taken by the government for a hospital. "The whole affair is in disrepute, both parties are to be avoided," he wrote. He considered moving to the First Presbyterian Church, whose pastor, Byron Sunderland, was a serious abolitionist. "All I have against him is, he sprinkles babies," Walter told a Baptist preacher who would appreciate his point. "That is quite too large a dose for me, notwithstanding it is upon the homeopathic principle. The truth is, we don't know exactly what to do."[20]

But Walter did know what to do about his work at the Capitol: he threw himself into it with a determination that had hardened during his year away. He wanted to complete the job during Lincoln's presidency: "No honor is too great for this administration, and if I can add a ray of glory, in the way of art, to the brilliancy that will surround it in the history that is to hand it down to future times, I will sacrifice any thing in reason to do it," he wrote to his son in Norfolk.[21]

One of the sacrifices he had to make was leaving the pleasant Philadelphia suburb of Germantown, where he was building a new home, to rejoin the thousands of others enduring summertime in Washington at war. He had rented a spacious house, but it was infested with vermin and pestered by "graceless scamps" who threw rocks through the windows the first few nights. He had to build a seven-foot fence to stop neighbors from dumping their filth in the side yard. "The bugs were busy, but they don't sing, and I gave their bites a dose of hartshorn during the night, which gave me a chance to sleep," he reported to his wife, who was coming to join him with their two youngest children.[22]

Three hundred yards from Walter's office, beyond the marble columns and the iron girders waiting to be lifted into place on the great dome, six soldiers escorted three women and a young girl out of Old Capitol Prison. A carriage awaited them, surrounded by a mounted guard with sabers drawn, an escort suitable for a minor head of state. One of the women stopped before she set foot in the carriage, and haughtily addressed the lieutenant commanding the guard: "Sir, ere I advance further, I ask you, not as Lincoln's officer, but as a man of honour and a gentleman, are your orders ... to conduct me to a Northern prison, or to some point in the Confederacy?" Only when the lieutenant assured her that she was bound for Dixie did she step aboard. On May 31, after nearly ten months as a prisoner, Rose Greenhow was on her way to freedom.[23]

For much of that time, Union authorities had sought a way to be rid of the defiant Greenhow's presence in the crowded prison overseen by Superintendent William P. Wood. After Stanton became secretary of war, jurisdiction over political prisoners passed from Seward to the War Department, and a two-man committee was appointed to look into the cases of such prisoners. As of mid-March, at least 110 were confined at Old Capitol, most of them arrested in outlying Virginia and Maryland. The "dangerous, skillful spy" Greenhow was at the top of the list. Eighteen others were officially described as spies, and most of the others were held on similar suspicions, such as "communicating with the rebels." Twenty-seven were simply called "prisoners of state," six were suspected of "assassination of U.S. pickets" and one was held with "no evidence." By the end of March, the commission had examined and released more than eighty of these on parole of honor or oath of allegiance to the Union. It found that the twenty-seven described as "prisoners of state" had been jailed for merely "furnishing aid to the insurgents by contributions to support the families of those absent serving in the rebel army." But prisoners considered hard cases were held off the list of those to be set free.[24]

For two of those hard cases, whether they were on that list or not turned out to be a matter or life and death: within weeks, they were shot and killed by guards. The first to go was Jesse B. Wharton, who had been a classmate of a future actor named John Wilkes Booth at St. Timothy's Hall, a military academy in Catonsville, Maryland, and had been court-martialed in the prewar U.S. Army. He was arrested before

Christmas on the Potomac above Washington and held as an armed spy. According to one Union guard, Wharton cursed a sentinel from a prison window and dared him to shoot. The corporal of the guard ordered the sentinel to fire if the prisoner did it again, and that is what happened on April 1. (In Greenhow's Confederate version, Wharton was innocently singing by the window when he was shot without warning.) Both guard and corporal, of Company C, Ninety-first Pennsylvania, were arrested and spent weeks in the Central Guardhouse downtown.[25]

The other victim was twenty-year-old Henry A. Steuart, who had been chased down in St. Mary's County while running a wagonload of medical and military supplies on the Rebels' clandestine route through southern Maryland. Steuart was a Confederate cavalryman who had fought at Manassas before becoming an agent and making a series of smuggling runs south from Baltimore and across the Potomac. One of his communications to Judah Benjamin, then Confederate secretary of war, had mentioned that he could be contacted safely through a certain person at the *Baltimore Sun*.

In the Old Capitol, Steuart joined a St. Mary's County man named Rudolph Watkins and an accused spy named William J. Rasin in a plan to escape. They colluded with friends outside, receiving tiny messages wadded in gift cigars. By patiently grinding away at night, they turned a table knife into a rough saw. They intended to cut through the wooden bars on their cell window, then lower themselves to the ground with a rope woven from fibers of an old doormat. In mid-plot, Superintendent Wood looked in and asked why they had curtained their window. The quick-thinking Watkins said, "O, that's our pantry, Colonel. The curtain keeps the flies off the preserves." When the night to escape came, the three cut cards to decide who would go first. Rasin won and swung himself out; the improvised rope broke and his comrades heard him hit the ground below. They quickly put the sawn bars back and got into bed. But no one sounded the alarm until next morning, when a strong wind blew out the hastily replaced bars and brought guards running. Steuart and Watkins learned that Rasin had not been recaptured, but had landed on his feet without attracting attention from sentinels who were busy chatting with a girl in the dark. He strode past and they saluted him, thinking he was one of their officers. After hiding in the city, he made his way to the Confederate army.

Wood conducted a detailed search to discover who else was

involved in Rasin's escape, but found nothing and could not prevent Steuart's trying again. Steuart grew recklessly desperate, creeping about the prison at night with socks over his boots to keep quiet while he approached guards, trying to bribe one into letting him slip past. One night, Watkins saw Steuart openly count out $50, tie the money in a roll and slip it into his pocket. One of his cellmates said, "Harry, are you going to trust that devil with your life?" Steuart brushed him away; he had made a deal with a guard who said he would allow him to pass after he dropped from the window. Watkins wrote that on the night of May 11, he heard someone whisper outside, "Come on; it will soon be too late." Steuart climbed up to the window, and Watkins heard a guard shout, "Halt!" A rifle ball crashed into Steuart's leg, splintering his right knee. Soldiers came and applied a tourniquet, and later that morning the leg was amputated. But medical help came too late; he had lost too much blood. In the dead man's pocket, they found the $50 with a note saying, "This is the money I promised you." Steuart's relatives had to wrangle with prison authorities over his body before taking it to Baltimore for burial in Greenmount Cemetery.[26]

No guard would have dared to shoot Rose Greenhow, despite her defiance. She was missing from the commission's list of prisoners to be released in March because she had quibbled over the conditions imposed. She wrote to the commission to protest her proposed "ban-ishment" to the South and refused to promise not to return. However, she said, "I will bind myself . . . not to blow up the President's house, equip a fleet, break open the treasury, or do any other small act which you may suppose comes within my limited powers to perform." Her sarcasm got her nowhere. When Congressman Alfred Ely, who had been kindly treated as a prisoner in Richmond, came to offer help, he told her that she was being detained because General McClellan feared that she knew too much. Greenhow eventually gave in, asking to be sent south. But another month passed and McClellan was on the outskirts of Richmond before she was allowed to step out of the Old Capitol into the late May evening.

With chin high, she proceeded amid her military escort to the B&O station, en route to Baltimore. All the way, she disdainfully treated the two women released with her, Mrs. C. V. Baxley and Augusta Morris, as social inferiors. In Baltimore, Stanton's chief detective, Lafayette C. Baker, had her name erased from the register at the Gilmer House, so that no one would know she was there. But by the next afternoon, word was out and a crowd of well-wishers waved handkerchiefs as she boarded a boat for Fortress Monroe. Early on June 2, the captain provided a festive luncheon with iced champagne, and the irrepressible Greenhow "had the pleasure of proposing the health of President Davis and the success of the Confederate cause under the bristling guns of the enemy." In Hampton Roads, the prisoners waited aboard another boat while its captain got directions from the commander of what Greenhow called that "low black thing," the *Monitor.* Then he delivered them up the James River to City Point, Petersburg and Richmond.

There, at the Ballard House on the evening of June 4, Jefferson Davis came to call. According to Greenhow, he told her, "But for you there would have been no battle of Bull Run." Celebrated as a heroine in the embattled capital of the Confederacy, she called that tribute "the proudest moment of my whole life."[27]

CHAPTER TWELVE

The Magnitude of the Moment

W hile Richmond toasted Rose Greenhow, McClellan's divisions sat a few miles away astride the swampy Chickahominy River, sweating in the heat and swatting mosquitoes. Now the Union general faced a new Confederate commander, Robert E. Lee, who had taken over after Joe Johnston was wounded in the costly collision at Seven Pines. That gave McClellan yet another reason to ponder and procrastinate, which further raised Lincoln's temperature in the sultry days of early June.

To escape the oppressive miasma of downtown Washington, the president and Mrs. Lincoln started spending nights in the woodsy upland of the Soldiers' Home. She had wanted to start using it as a retreat the previous summer, but the crisis atmosphere after Bull Run kept the family at the White House. Now the main Rebel army was on the defensive a hundred miles south, and Mary was slowly emerging from her grief over Willie's death. At first as an experiment, the Lincolns set up summer housekeeping in an "elegant, but not at all extravagant" fourteen-room stone cottage originally built for banker George W. Riggs. It was one of four houses around the main building of the Soldiers' Home, which was still under construction. Originally called the U.S. Military Asylum, the home had been founded in 1851, financed with $100,000 of the tribute that Winfield Scott exacted from Mexico City when he captured it in 1847. Senator Jefferson Davis, another hero of the Mexican War, had pushed the enabling bill through Congress. Just east of the cluster of buildings lay the military cemetery, soon to be outgrown because of casualties of the war in Virginia.[1]

Heading out after work at the White House, the president usually rode from Lafayette Square along Vermont Avenue to Seventh Street, following it gently uphill into the country. After about three shady miles, he turned right on Rock Creek Church Road, past W. W. Corcoran's Harewood estate, to the Soldiers' Home grounds at what would later be Upshur Street. Sometimes in those first weeks of commuting, he rode an easy-gaited gray horse, but more often he boarded a well-traveled open carriage and rattled along without an escort. Now and then his venturesome son Tad, recovered from his struggle with typhoid fever, kept up alongside on his pony. Later in the summer, the president sensibly agreed to a cavalry guard on the way and the protection of an infantry detail while he was in residence. On a typical morning, he was up, dressed, had a light breakfast and was back at the White House by eight o'clock.[2]

By retreating to the country most nights, Lincoln was escaping more than the oppressive air of the urban bottomland. The persistent favor-seekers who plagued him at the White House did not respect official business hours, and the hubbub of cavalry squadrons, regimental bands and droves of lowing cattle kept on into the night. At the Soldiers' Home, he could get away from those tribulations, but he could not leave behind the weight of his office. Many evenings he spent reading Shakespeare or his favorite humorists aloud to John Hay or whoever was willing to listen. But often legislators and cabinet members pursued him with problems that could not wait, hoping to get his attention without daytime distractions. As he rode back and forth to the country, he had perhaps an hour and a half each day to think alone.

City or country, behind his desk fending off politicians or on his horse in quiet contemplation, Lincoln could not escape the war. Not only was he worrying over what to do about McClellan, who was showing no sign of movement outside Richmond; now the Confederate general Stonewall Jackson was bedeviling Union armies closer to Washington. From late April to late June, Jackson won five battles in the Shenandoah Valley, completely outmarching and outfighting Union generals Nathaniel Banks, John Frémont and James Shields. Hoping to catch Jackson, Lincoln diverted McDowell's army in that direction rather than sending it to strengthen McClellan. Lee then pulled Jackson south to join in the Seven Days battles, a series of heavy counterattacks against McClellan that made by far the bloodiest week of the war to date. In the last of those fights, on July 1 at Malvern Hill, the South lost some 5,000 men, hundreds of them cut down by massed Union artillery. McClellan could have followed up by retaking the offensive. But he professed to believe the absurd overestimates of Lee's strength fed to him by his intelligence chief, Pinkerton. Asserting that he was still outnumbered two to one, he withdrew from Malvern Hill to Harrison's Landing on the James River, huddling his army under the protection of Federal gunboats.

Back from the Peninsula came streams of wounded and sick soldiers, quickly overflowing the existing and makeshift hospitals that had dealt with earlier, lesser battles. That summer, at least twenty-two emergency hospitals were created in Washington, thirteen of them in churches, plus several more in Georgetown, Alexandria and the outlying District. The immediate impact of the Seven Days struck home in July, when the government hastily opened eighteen of these new hospitals. Groggy soldiers just off boats from Virginia might wake to find themselves in Caspari's Hotel on Capitol Hill, the Jewish synagogue on Eighth Street, Odd Fellows Hall or the *National Era* building that had been Republican campaign headquarters. In Richmond, the Confederates were struggling to care for even more casualties from the battles on the outskirts, but their heavy losses were palliated by the fact of strategic success; their new hero Lee had driven McClellan away from their capital. There was no such solace for Lincoln and the thousands of Union soldiers' kinfolk who dreaded what they would find as they searched the long casualty lists printed in agate type by Northern newspapers.[3]

Even before the worst of the fighting on the Peninsula, the nurse and later author Katharine Wormeley told of the fear, the confusion, "the sounds, the screams of men" as mangled soldiers were loaded aboard vessels in the James River for shipment to Washington. "Imagine a great river or Sound steamer fitted on every deck, every berth and every square inch of room covered with wounded men," she wrote to her mother—"even the stairs and gangways and guards filled with those who are less badly wounded; and then imagine fifty well men, on every kind of errand, rushing to and fro over them, every touch bringing agony to the poor fellows, while stretcher after stretcher came along, hoping to find an empty place, and then imagine what it was to keep calm ourselves. . . ." Nurses trying to function in this chaos were "bitterly asking why a Government so lavish and perfect in its other arrangements should leave its wounded almost literally to take care of themselves...."[4]

Harrowing as medical conditions were, they were better than they had been when the army came stumbling back from Bull Run almost a year earlier. Wormeley was laboring not for the government but for the U.S. Sanitary Commission, a civilian project started in 1861 initially to investigate and advise commanders on protecting the health of their troops under wartime conditions. Before mid-1862, with the landscape architect Frederick Law Olmsted managing operations, the commission was sending medical help and supplies to the field, trying to bring order and compassion to the grim aftermath of combat. There were other, independent civilian efforts to help: Clara Barton, a Patent Office employee from Massachusetts, had pitched in when she saw the battered Sixth Massachusetts Regiment arrive from Baltimore before full-scale war began. After Bull Run, she wrote to readers of the *Worcester Spy* asking for contributions for the troops, and when supplies poured in, she set up her own agency to distribute them. But all the paid and volunteer help that the Union could muster, in the field, on ships and in hospitals, could not adequately deal with the thousands of casualties from the Peninsula.[5]

Railroad cars arriving in Washington from the North were filled with wives and parents who came looking for loved ones, eager to soothe the living and provide for the dead. The undertaking business boomed. "Dr. Hutton & Co." ran a display ad extolling "THE BEAUTIFUL ART OF EMBALMING THE DEAD." On E Street between Eleventh and Twelfth, amid the hotels, theaters and restaurants of downtown Washington, they set up "to convince the public that their method of Embalming exceeds any thing of like nature in the world.... Bodies Embalmed by us NEVER TURN BLACK! But retain their natural color and appearance; indeed the method having the power of preserving bodies, with all their parts, internal and external, WITHOUT ANY MUTILATION OR EXTRACTION, And so as to admit of contemplation of the person Embalmed, with the countenance of one asleep.... So convinced are we of the efficacy of the processes which we employ, that we shall always be ready at the request of authorities or friends to exhume those bodies which we may embalm, at any expressed period of time, knowing that each and every body exhumed will prove an enduring monument of our skill...."[6]

There was no such thing as air-conditioning, or enough ice to serve such enterprises. The smell of death hung over whole neighborhoods, making the noxious air of summertime Washington even more oppressive. Few could imagine that worse lay ahead.

One night while the Army of the Potomac lay at Harrison's Landing, Quartermaster General Meigs and another officer arrived at the Soldiers' Home after the president had gone to bed. In great agitation, Meigs woke Lincoln and urged the immediate withdrawal of the army from the Peninsula. Overreacting to one of McClellan's defeatist telegrams, he wanted to evacuate the troops on transports, destroy the army's supplies and kill all its horses, because they could not be saved. The president was less excitable; he heard Meigs out and went back to sleep. Later, telling John Hay of this episode, he lamented, "I who am not a specially brave man have had to sustain the sinking courage of these professional fighters in critical times."[7]

During the last seven days of June, Lincoln sat for hours on a sofa at Stanton's office, waiting for telegrams from McClellan. When they came, the president realized that the retreat to the James had ruined his own latest plan for a coordinated offensive. At Stanton's urging, he had brought to Washington Major General John Pope, who had performed ably in Mississippi, and given him command of the new Army of Virginia. Combining McDowell's forces with those in the Shenandoah Valley, Pope would move overland against the Confederate capital while McClellan renewed his attack up the Peninsula. Instead, McClellan pulled back and bombarded Washington with telegrams pleading for more troops. On the road to Malvern Hill, he wrote to Washington, "I have seen too many dead and wounded comrades to feel otherwise than that the government has not sustained this army. If you do not do so now the game is lost." His words were addressed to Stanton, but he knew that they would be seen immediately by Lincoln. However, the last lines of his message reached neither the secretary nor the president. "If I save this army now, I tell you plainly that I owe no thanks to you or any other persons in Washington," wrote McClellan. "You have done your best to sacrifice this army." Those sentences so offended the telegraph officer at the War Department that he deleted them, unwilling to place them before Stanton; only months later did they become known.[8]

Lincoln wanted to see for himself the condition of the army and its commander. A week after Malvern Hill, he arrived at Harrison's Landing aboard the steamer *Ariel.* He inspected the Union lines and asked McClellan's five corps commanders whether they thought the army should be withdrawn or stay facing Richmond. They voted three to two to stay. Before Lincoln departed, McClellan presented him a remarkable letter that dealt with political more than military strategy, advising against emancipation and urging appointment of a commander-in-chief of the army.

When the president returned to Washington, he did re-create the post of general-in-chief, but rather than returning it to McClellan, he gave it to forty-seven-year-old Major General Henry W. Halleck. The gruff, touchy Halleck had been known as "Old Brains" in the prewar army, where he studied and wrote on military science. He was a competent administrator, but had been less than brilliant as a field commander in the West. Nevertheless, Lincoln agreed to back off from his own involvement in the details of strategy, and let Halleck plan and direct operations—an arrangement that would last about two months. He dispatched Halleck to confer with McClellan, who still maintained that he was vastly outnumbered. After further testy exchanges about how many reinforcements Washington could send, McClellan said he could not resume the attack unless he got what he asked. At that, Lincoln decided that the Army of the Potomac must be brought back to northern Virginia; almost two bloody years would pass before it got so close to Richmond again. Historians have said correctly that the best decision would have been to keep the army on the Peninsula under a more aggressive commander—John Pope, for example. But Lincoln was not ready yet to replace McClellan.[9]

On Sunday, July 13, the president invited secretaries Seward and Welles to ride with him into the countryside, to the funeral of one of Edwin Stanton's children. Like Lincoln, Stanton had found a rural retreat several miles outside the capital. Seward, not expecting the trip in the president's carriage to become a policy conference, brought along his daughter-in-law. But Lincoln trusted her discretion; she had overheard him in many a nighttime conversation at Seward's home on Lafayette Square. On the way to Stanton's, the president disclosed his latest thinking on the subject that lay beneath all the politics and strategy: leaning forward as the carriage rumbled along the stony road, he asked Seward and Welles what they thought of emancipating the slaves by proclamation if the Confederates persisted in the struggle.

"He dwelt earnestly on the gravity, importance and delicacy of the moment," Welles wrote in his diary. The president said "he had given it much thought and had about come to the conclusion that it was a military necessity absolutely essential for the salvation of the Union, that we must free the slaves or be ourselves subdued...." Welles was surprised, because every time the matter had arisen previously, Lincoln had been "prompt and emphatic" in saying that slavery was an issue for the states rather than the Federal government, and the cabinet had agreed with him. His practice while mulling a decision was to argue both sides. When a delegation of Quakers came on June 20 urging him to proclaim emancipation, he had questioned whether a proclamation could abolish slavery. He admitted that he might be God's chosen instrument to make that happen, but said God's way might be different from theirs. Now, three weeks later, Welles said, "the reverses before Richmond, and the formidable power and dimensions of the insurrection ... impelled the Administration to adopt extraordinary measures to preserve the national existence." Though slaves were not soldiers, their labor supported the Confederate army directly and indirectly. Seward and Welles agreed that the question was so important that they needed time to think on it more deeply, but if emancipation was considered in military terms, it might be "expedient and necessary."[10]

Although this carriage conversation was kept confidential, Lincoln had discussed emancipation with a few others close to him; his aides in the White House certainly knew that change was under way. On signing the Second Confiscation Act, which seized the property of Rebels and freed their slaves as "captives of war," he still emphasized that Congress had no right to interfere with slavery in the states. That, he told his Illinois friend Orville Browning, was strictly within the war powers of the president. As he spoke, he was quietly preparing to exercise that power. "Things had gone from bad to worse" in the war, he said later. "I felt that we had reached the end of our rope on the plan of operations we had been pursuing, that we had about played our last card, and must change our tactics, or lose the game."[11]

William Stoddard described how the president looked south from his office window as he worked over "a paper stronger than an army with banners, which he will send across the river.... A first draft of it is lying now in one of the drawers of this writing-desk, but no other living soul is aware of it...." Hay had closely followed the evolution of Lincoln's thinking. To a lady friend, he wrote: "The President has been, out of pure devotion to what he considered the best interests of humanity, the bulwark of the institution he abhors, for a year. But he will not conserve slavery much longer. When next he speaks in relation to this defiant and ungrateful villainy it will be with no uncertain sound. Even now he speaks more boldly and sternly to slaveholders than to the world."[12]

On July 22, two days after Hay wrote that letter, Lincoln summoned his cabinet members to the White House. From his pocket, he drew a few folded pages, the draft he had secretly written and rewritten for weeks. He told them that he was not asking their advice on whether to take this step; he was firmly resolved to do it. Then he began to read. At first, they did not realize what it was about, but then the portent of it set in. Seward and Welles were not surprised, but the others—Chase, Stanton, Bates, Smith and Blair—heard the president in astonishment. All of them appreciated what Welles would call the "magnitude and consequences" of the moment.[13]

Lincoln's draft document promised a bill to support compensated emancipation in any state, loyal or seceded. Then it concluded: ". . . as a fit and necessary military measure . . . I, as Commander-in-Chief of the Army and Navy of the United States, do order and declare that on the first day of January, in the year of our Lord one thousand eight hundred and sixty-three, all persons held as slaves within any State or States wherein the constitutional authority of the United States shall not then be practically recognized, submitted to, and maintained, shall then, thenceforward, and forever, be free."

In fewer than five hundred words, Lincoln had devised a way to take the most meaningful step toward freedom since the Declaration of Independence, yet avoid the two major obstacles that had restrained him. By using his war power to declare emancipation a military necessity, he would sidestep the constitutional issue raised by congressional action against slavery, and by limiting his proclamation to states defying Federal authority, he would not disturb the property of slave-owners in the border states so vital to the Union cause. At the same time, though knowing that this was unlikely, he would give rebellious states a way to preserve slavery by returning to the Union.

Blair opposed the proclamation because he thought it would cost the Republicans the fall elections. Chase feared that it would hurt the government's financial position. Smith, a confirmed antiabolitionist, simply did not like it. Seward, ever the political tactician, said he did not oppose it, but that issuing it when the war was going so badly would be untimely, would seem an act of desperation. For the moment, Lincoln was noncommittal on the timing. Warning that their talk had been confidential, he put the draft back in his pocket and turned again to prosecution of the war.[14]

Major General John Pope arrived in Washington by railroad, but seemed to belong on a white horse. Big, handsome, confident and martial, he impressed soldiers and civilians on sight as a general who meant business. Without their asking, he told them so: On taking command of the new Army of Virginia, he composed an address to his troops. "I have come to you from the West, where we have always seen the backs of our enemies," he said, "from an army whose business it has been to seek the adversary, and beat him where he was found . . . whose policy has been attack and not defense." He went on that way, telling veteran soldiers to "dismiss from your minds" certain phrases about defensive measures and lines of retreat, "which I am sorry to find so much in vogue amongst you." This was hardly inspiring to men who had spent months trying to keep up with Stonewall Jackson. But they would not have to listen to Pope's bombast for long.[15]

On his first advance, Pope ran into Jackson on August 9 at Cedar Mountain, near Culpeper. The Federals were driving the Rebels back until Confederate Major General A. P. Hill turned the tide with a furious counterattack. Lee, seeing that McClellan's army was withdrawing by boat from the Peninsula, brought James Longstreet's corps from Richmond to join Jackson, hoping to combine against Pope before reinforcements arrived. In one of his boldest strokes, Lee outmaneuvered the larger Union army. Near the end of August, he sent Longstreet looping to the west, then back through Thoroughfare Gap in Bull Run Mountain. Pope, between Jackson and Longstreet, had a chance to crush one Rebel corps at a time. But Jackson, though outnumbered three to one, held off his attacks while Longstreet swung onto the Union flank. Together, they drove the Federals back toward Washington.

Pope's defeat in this Second Bull Run campaign cost him some 16,000 casualties, five times as many as McDowell lost in the first conflict there, and sent another surge of wounded men into Washington. Two thousand cots were laid and filled with suffering soldiers in the Capitol building; Georgetown College was commandeered as a hospital. So was Lydia Scutter English's Georgetown Female Seminary, at today's Thirtieth and N streets, for which the army paid Miss English $300 a month. But Secretary Stanton was unsuccessful in trying to take over the Convent of the Visitation, at Thirty-fifth and P. He dropped that effort after Winfield Scott, whose daughter had studied, become a nun and been buried there, declared that the government should not move into "a place sacred by the grave of my child."*[16]

After another disaster at Bull Run, Union spirits drooped, in and out of the army.

Lincoln removed the protesting Pope, assigning him to the Department of the Northwest, never to face Lee and Jackson again. To the chagrin of the "disturbed and desponding" cabinet, especially Stanton and Chase, he returned command of the army to George McClellan. He explained to Welles that McClellan was the most popular general among the troops, and he needed him to reorganize the demoralized army. McClellan agreed with that, but thought in bigger terms: to his wife, he wrote, "Again I have been called upon to save the country." The appointment hardly promised the military success that the president wanted before announcing his emancipation plan to the nation and the world, but Lincoln was desperate.[17]

The public knew nothing of that plan, a secret still held closely within his inner circle. Thus as the army fought, withdrew, fought and reorganized yet again, pressure kept building for Lincoln to do for the rest of the country's slaves what had been done for those in the capital. While concealing his intentions, waiting for the right moment to disclose them, he had to sympathize with the Republicans demanding action.

On August 14, for the first time in history, the president received a delegation of black Americans at the White House. Anticipating what would follow his proclamation, he presented to them his case for colonizing freed slaves. "Your race is suffering, in my judgment, the great-

---

*Britannia Peter Kennon, the pro-Southern great-granddaughter of Martha Washington, first cousin of Mrs. Robert E. Lee and owner of Georgetown's grandest mansion, Tudor Place, went to greater lengths to fend off the Federals. She had rented the estate and was sitting out the war in Richmond when she heard in 1863 that the government might turn Tudor Place into a hospital. Hurrying north by flag-of-truce boat, she quickly turned the mansion into a boardinghouse for Union officers, which effectively made it unavailable for hospital use. At about this time, Mrs. Kennon heard that two cousins who had joined the Confederate army, William Orton Williams and Walter Gibson Peter, had been hanged as spies at Franklin, Tennessee. (Mary Mitchell, "An Intimate Journey Through Georgetown," pp. 94–95)

est wrong inflicted on any people," he said. "But even when you cease to be slaves, you are yet far removed from being placed on an equality with the white race. ... The aspiration of men is to enjoy equality with the best when free, but on this broad continent not a single man of your race is made the equal of a single man of ours." He told of slavery's "general evil effect on the white race" as well—"without the institution of slavery, and the colored race as a basis, the war would not have an existence. It is better for us both, therefore, to be separated." He acknowledged that the free black men before him might be so comfortable that they had no interest in a new life somewhere else. But this, he said, was selfish of them. They should take the lead, set an example for the uneducated mass of slaves soon to be free, by being willing to resettle in Liberia or Central America—"the particular place I have in view is to be a great highway from the Atlantic or Caribbean Sea to the Pacific Ocean. ..."[18]

A few days after these black leaders departed the White House unconvinced, Horace Greeley lashed Lincoln in his *New York Tribune* for fighting the war without acting against the evil that caused it. In response, the president explained his position in a way that hinted at what lay ahead. His paramount goal was to save the Union, he said: "If I could save the Union without freeing any slave I would do it, and if I could do it by freeing *all* the slaves I would do it; and if I could save it by freeing some and leaving others alone I would also do that. What I do about slavery and the colored race, I do because I believe it helps to save the Union; and what I forbear, I forbear because I do *not* believe it would help to save the Union." In saying this, he added, "I intend no modification of my oft-expressed *personal* wish that all men everywhere could be free." Knowing that reaction for and against what he had in mind would be vigorous, he tried to rationalize his move in advance, without disclosing what it would be. Nicolay and Hay believed that his effort "to keep up an appearance of indecision ... only brought upon him a greater flood of importunities. During no part of his administration were his acts and words so persistently misconstrued as in this interim by men who gave his words the color and meaning of their own eager desires and expectations."[19]

Dissembling did not satisfy abolitionists like Charles Sumner, Henry Wilson and Thaddeus Stevens, or earnest churchmen like those who implored him to commit to emancipation. On September 13, he told a delegation of Chicago ministers that for months he had heard from clergy on both sides of the issue, each side purporting to represent divine will. He said, "It is my earnest desire to know the will of Providence in this matter. And if I can learn what it is, I will do it." He did not want to issue "a document that the whole world will see must be inoperative, like the Pope's bull against the comet." And suppose a proclamation should somehow free the slaves, "what should we do with them? They eat, and that is all. . . ." He conceded that "slavery is the root of the rebellion, or at least its *sine qua non*." But once again, he told them, "I view this matter as a practical war measure, to be decided on according to the advantages or disadvantages it may offer to the suppression of the rebellion." The moment he waited for was only four days away.[20]

On Saturday evening, September 6, 20,000 soldiers cheered as they trooped by McClellan's house on H Street, accompanied by sixty cannon. This was a departure from the familiar tradition of soldiers cheering the president as they marched along Pennsylvania Avenue past the White House. They were heading west toward Frederick, responding to news that Lee had crossed the Potomac above Washington, invading Maryland and aiming at Pennsylvania. As McClellan moved cautiously to meet Lee, Lincoln and the capital were in an anxious depression. The president still could not understand why the army consistently reported fewer than half as many troops on hand as were on the payroll. He had been told that in Virginia some soldiers let themselves be captured so that they might get discharged when returned on parole after pledging not to reenter the war. Henry Wilson was whispering that certain dissatisfied generals were plotting a coup and establishment of a military government. Reports of a bloody Sioux uprising in Minnesota stirred demands for army protection there and in other states from which soldiers had been sent to fight the Confederates. "The War Department is bewildered, knows but little, does nothing, proposes nothing," wrote Welles.[21]

Many of Lee's ragged Confederates were barefooted, but their morale was high as they crossed the Potomac and marched into Frederick. There Lee issued a proclamation of his own, expressing sympathy for the way Maryland had been treated as a "conquered province" by the Federal government. The Army of Northern Virginia came to aid Marylanders in "throwing off this foreign yoke," he said, "to assist you with the power of its arms in regaining the rights of which you have been despoiled." Inviting them to come over to the Rebel side, he said "the Southern people will rejoice to welcome you to your natural position among them," though "they will only welcome you when you come of your own free will." But in Frederick, there was no rallying to the Southern cause. A few friends showed themselves, but more loyal Unionists flew the Stars and Stripes from their windows, or held their noses as Lee's well-behaved troops marched past. Western Maryland was a hilly land of small farms and few slaves, settled largely by German families from Pennsylvania—a world away from the low plantation country of southern Maryland, across the Potomac from Lee's birthplace.[22]

Counting on McClellan's normal slowness, Lee devised a complex plan to divide his forces. He would loop Jackson's corps back to protect his rear by capturing Harpers Ferry before rejoining the rest of the army at Hagerstown. From there, they would march north up the Cumberland Valley into Pennsylvania. By doing so, Lee could at least feed and reshoe his army and cut Union rail links to the West, and at most capture Harrisburg, Philadelphia, Baltimore or even Washington, conceivably ending the war. Fear of his coming threw some state officials into near panic; Pennsylvania shipped its archives from Harrisburg to safety in New York. All was going according to Lee's plan when a copy of his Special Orders No. 191, outlining these moves, was found by Union soldiers in a field outside Frederick, wrapped around three cigars. This information promptly reached McClellan, inspiring him to move faster, though still with his ingrained caution. While Union troops attacked Rebels holding the passes of South Mountain, Jackson captured Harpers Ferry and 12,000 Federal soldiers, the biggest bag of prisoners taken by the Confederates in the whole war. Lee discovered that the lost order had been found by Union troops, so with his army still divided and the Federals pressing, he decided to stand and fight around the village of Sharpsburg.

On September 17, along Antietam Creek, McClellan threw a series of powerful assaults against the outnumbered Confederates, who held despite heavy casualties. In late afternoon, the Federals were about to drive in Lee's right flank when once again A. P. Hill saved the day for the Rebels, arriving in the nick of time after a forced march from Harpers Ferry. The Federals lost some 12,500 of their 75,000 troops on hand, while the Confederates lost about 10,500 of their 40,000, making that Wednesday the most costly single day of the war. Lincoln, anxious to know what had happened, did not find out until three days later. McClellan told his wife, "Our victory was complete." But objectively speaking, the battle was a tactical draw, and the president was unhappy that the general had let the battered Confederate army pull back to Virginia unmolested. However, McClellan's men had ended Lee's thrust into the North, and for Lincoln, that was victory enough to go ahead with the most important political step of his presidency.[23]

On Monday morning, September 22, a State Department messenger made the rounds of other cabinet secretaries, summoning them to meet the president at noon. After a few minutes of casual talk, Lincoln announced that "Artemus Ward," the cracker-barrel humorist whose real name was Charles Farrar Browne, had sent him his new book. As if he had nothing more urgent to discuss, the president read to the cabinet one of Ward's wilder excursions, titled "High-handed Outrage at Utica."

"In the Faul of 1856," it began, "I showed my show in Utiky, a trooly grate sitty in the State of New York. The people gave me a cordual recepshun. The press was loud in her prases. 1 day as I was givin a descripshun of my Beests and Snails in my usual flowry stile what was my skorn & disgust to see a big burly feller walk up to the cage containin my wax figgers of the Lord's Last Supper, and cease Judas Iscarrot by the feet and drag him out on the ground." The offender pounded the wax figure, raging that such a "pussylanermus cuss" as Judas was not welcome in "Utiky." "I sood him," Ward wrote, and "the joory brawt in a verdick of Arson in the 3rd degree."[24]

By then Lincoln's close associates were used to his habit of mixing attempts at humor with matters of high state; they realized that he wanted to relax the tension inevitable when great issues were before them. The dignified Chase wrote in his diary that Lincoln read Ward's piece aloud, and "seemed to enjoy it very much; the heads also (except Stanton), of course."

Then, wrote Chase, the president "took a graver tone." He said he had been waiting since July for the moment to move on emancipation, and "I think the time has come now. I wish it was a better time. I wish we were in a better condition . . . ," but "the rebel army is now driven out, and I am going to fulfill that promise." By Welles's account, Lincoln credited the Almighty for guiding his decision. The president said he had vowed to himself that "if God gave us victory in the approaching battle he would consider it an indication of Divine will," and now "God had decided the question in favor of the slaves." The document he presented was essentially the same as the cabinet had seen in July, proclaiming that as of January 1, 1863, all slaves in rebellious territory would be free. As before, Lincoln said his decision was made, but he would be glad to hear opinions on how to phrase the decree. In a long discussion, Seward made several suggestions, which Lincoln accepted. Blair strongly supported the proclamation in principle, but still thought it would drive away the border states, and asked if he could attach a memorandum of his reservations. Lincoln accepted that, too, though on second thought Blair withheld his memo.

From the White House Seward took the much-edited and -debated document to his department, where the language was formally inscribed and the great seal was stamped upon it. That afternoon, Lincoln signed it, and on Monday morning it was published in papers across the North. The next evening, a group of well-wishers came to serenade the president, and called on him for a speech. He said he was not sure why they had come, but assumed it was because of the proclamation.

"What I did, I did after a very full deliberation, and under a very heavy and solemn sense of responsibility," he told them. "I can only trust in God I have made no mistake."[25]

CHAPTER THIRTEEN

We Cannot Escape History

B attle, disease and McClellan demanded more and more bodies for a war with no foreseeable end. After the Union army's heavy losses in the Peninsula campaign, Lincoln had called for another 300,000 troops. That inspired the New York abolitionist and financier James Sloan Gibbons, a major backer of the American Anti-Slavery Society, to write a song intended to spur enlistments. It was set to music composed by the once supremely popular Stephen Foster, who was by then a down-and-out alcoholic in Manhattan.

> *We are coming, Father Abraham, three hundred thousand more,*
> *From Mississippi's winding stream and from New England's shore;*
> *We leave our ploughs and workshops, our wives and children dear,*
> *With hearts too full for utterance, with but a silent tear;*
> *We dare not look behind us, but steadfastly before:*
> *We are coming, Father Abraham, three hundred thousand more. . . .*[1]

But Lincoln could not count on patriotic songs to strengthen the army; lest his appeal for more troops fall short, he ordered governors to draft men from the state militia if they could not fill their quotas with volunteers. This provoked resistance, even riots in parts of Indiana and Wisconsin, causing Stanton to hold off on the draft. In other places, like the Mohawk Valley, men rallied to the colors. There they joined the new 153rd New York Volunteers, who left the village of Fonda in mid-October, arrived in Washington on the twenty-second and immediately crossed the river for guard duty in Alexandria.

In all outward aspects, the 153rd was like hundreds of other regiments that flowed through the capital on their way to and from the Peninsula, Bull Run and Antietam. But in one particular, this outfit was different. In Captain George H. McLaughlin's Company G, there was a Private Lyons Wakeman, of Afton, New York, twenty-one years old, five feet tall, with blue eyes and brown hair, who gave his occupation as boatman. At Alexandria, Wakeman did routine picket duty, not standing out and not complaining. He blended in with bigger, rougher volunteers when the regiment was rousted out in the middle of the night to block the roads against imagined raids by Confederate cavalry. Until he was alone in his tent, with time to write to his family, he seemed just another soldier.[2]

Wakeman's letters home were naïvely eloquent, partly because their spelling was so imaginative. "My Dear Father and Mother and sister and Brothers one in all," one began, telling how he had left Afton for Binghamton, where "I work half a mount for 4$ in mony," and then signed on for $20 to make four trips on a coal barge on the Chenango Canal. At "Canghira" (Canajoharie), he "saw some solgers thay wanted I shud inlest and so I did I got 100 and 52 $ in mony I inlest for 3 years or soons dischard . . . if you want to save inthing to remember me by keep that spoted calf and if I ever return I want yow to let me haver. . . . Father you nednent be a feard to wright . . . to me for I can reaid all you can wright I spose you thought that I wood hef to git somebody to reaid it for me but I reaid it all my self." The letter was signed, "Rosetta Wakeman."[3]

In the privacy of the tent, the young private was a woman, Sarah Rosetta Wakeman, masquerading successfully as a man in a fraternity where solitude was rare, where discovery and danger were far closer than in civilian life.

Rosetta was by no means the only woman playing that role in the Civil War. On both sides, there were hundreds who marched and fought beside their comrades in arms—a few who became well known to history, but many more who slogged on doing the humble duty of infantry privates. Medical examinations on enlistment were less than perfunctory, some woman volunteers were mannish in voice and stature, and the ill-fitting uniforms of common troops made it easy to camouflage what lay beneath. But other woman soldiers were as petite as Rosetta and pretended to be beardless boys. No doubt some were discovered and their secret kept by friends who either respected them as soldiers or cherished them as bunkmates, or both. Some had enlisted to stay with their husbands or sweethearts, some for patriotism and some, like Wakeman, for adventure. "I can tell yow what maid me live home," she wrote, "it was becaus I had got tiard of stay in that neighbourhood. I new that I cood help yow more to leave home then to stay thare with yow." Some, also like Wakeman, signed up to collect the bounty paid to volunteers. ("I was agun to send it home but finly lent it to the first lutenant and sargent they promist to pay me when we got our monts pay. We not got it yet.") Some female volunteers were prostitutes, quietly selling sex where demand was highest, until they were discovered and discharged. But among soldiers, the presence of women in uniform was not in itself a scandal. Wakeman often wrote of visiting male friends in other regiments, being recognized and carrying on normal conversations.[4]

In those letters to her family, she described the daily routines of army life and her hopes for the future but seldom mentioned the issues that had torn the nation apart. As if to assure her parents that she had not abandoned her gender, she often signed her real name in elaborate oversize script before sealing the envelope to protect her secret on its way back to Afton. Her fears came through only when she denied having them. When the 153rd got new Enfield rifles and marching orders, she wrote that "I feel perfickly happy if I go in to batel I shall be all wright. It is what I have wish for a good while. I hope that god will spair my life I beleve he will. I dont dread it a tall." And if she was afraid that other soldiers might take advantage of her sex, she covered that with bravado, too. "I dont want yow to morn a bought me for i can take car of my self and I know my bisness as well as other folks know them for me. I will dress as I am a mite for all eny one else and if thay dont let me A lone they will be sorry for it."[*5]

There is no other suggestion in Rosetta's letters that she might have been harassed, or that her relations with her Company G comrades ever became amorous. In and around the capital, as well as other major cities and military camps, there were myriad opportunities for soldiers to vent their libido, which they did so carelessly, or ignorantly,

---

*"Private Lyons Wakeman" stayed with the 153rd when it moved across the river in July 1863 for provost duty in Washington. Afterward she started signing her letters "Edwin R. Wakeman," apparently in fear that they would be read by strangers. In February 1864, the regiment traveled to Louisiana, and she saw action in the Union's unsuccessful Red River campaign. That spring, she became ill with chronic diarrhea, and died on June 19, 1864, in a New Orleans military hospital. Official records suggest that her true identity was never discovered. (Wakeman papers, Library of Congress)

that venereal disease became a serious problem for the army. Prostitution was well established in Washington long before 1861, catering to the steady flow of political, military and business transients. "Even our greatest statesmen have 'departed,'" wrote one correspondent. "It was not an uncommon thing for a Southern solon to bring a good-looking quadroon here, as he would bring a favorite horse or dog." But this went on with a certain amount of discretion; once war and its thousands of healthy young soldiers came, sexual commerce flourished in the open. The Avenue was decorated by "the most unblushing cyprians, who are estimated to number 15,000...." Freelancing women, white, black and mulatto, beckoned troops picketing or idling around the edges of outlying camps. Streetwalkers worked in the alleys and parks of the city, and some entrepreneurs of a higher esthetic class set up in respectable neighborhoods. But the hotbed of vice in the wartime capital was within a few minutes' stroll of the White House, the Treasury and Willard's Hotel.[6]

By the autumn of 1862, the provost marshal reported that there were 450 officially registered bawdy houses in Washington. The wild estimate that there were 15,000 prostitutes in and about the city challenged the *Star* to defend its community; it soberly figured that only about 5,000 did business in Washington proper, plus 2,500 more in Alexandria and Georgetown. Still later, police counted 2,313 white and 1,543 colored professionals in the capital, asserting that since the war started, "New York, Boston, Philadelphia, Baltimore and some of the western cities dumped this aggregation of unclean birds on the community."[7]

No one would ever know exactly how many there really were. Although they were sprinkled about the city, the densest concentration was in the bars and brothels south of Pennsylvania Avenue, from Fifteenth Street east toward the Center Market, embracing the area later known as the Federal Triangle. Police and newspapers called it "Hooker's Division," because Brigadier General Joseph Hooker had herded many of those businesswomen into the neighborhood so he could better control the off-duty doings of men in his command when they were stationed nearby in 1861. (It was mere coincidence that such women were referred to as "hookers"; that slang term originated before the general came on the scene.) The red-light district extended to houses on the mall south of the canal, an area then called "the Island."

Statistics can only hint at life and love in such popular establishments as the Haystack, the Blue Goose, Fort Sumter, the Cottage by the Sea and Madame Russell's Bake Oven. When the provost marshal registered them later in the war, he graded them by quality, as if he were publishing a guide for lonely visitors. Twenty-one places on one list, those the *Star* called the "upper-ten style of houses," were rated first-class. They included the two biggest enterprises, Mary Hall's with eighteen women and Maggie Walters's with fourteen. The trash dump outside Mary Hall's three-story house showed how, besides employing the most talented strumpets, she earned her high standing and income. Sifting through the detritus, late-twentieth-century archaeologists discovered terrapin shells, bones from the choicest cuts of beef, and corks and foil seals from Piper-Heidsieck champagne. Miss Hall, her staff and guests lived high; the horses of ranking officers were commonly tethered outside such houses overnight. But ill-paid privates and corporals had appetites, too: the provost marshal's ratings of eighty-four bawdy houses ran from first class down to fourth class, and even beyond. It is not romantic to imagine conditions in the nine houses, like Josephine Webster's twelve-girl enterprise on Fighting Alley, which were graded "low" (one step below fourth class), and the thirteen, like Julia Fleet's Fox Hospital, which ranked "very low."[8]

While Mary Hall's girls may have been the classiest prostitutes south of the Avenue, the city's more refined courtesans did not have to endure being ogled and picked out of the lineup at bordellos. They were more likely to be friends of lobbyists, who introduced them to venal quartermasters and well-placed politicians in expensive suites at the better hotels. George Alfred Townsend ("Gath" of the *New York Herald* and *World*) told of a voluptuous but questionably refined lady nicknamed "Comanche," after a famous ironclad vessel built on the West Coast. She was hired to smooth payment of a shipbuilder's claim against the government for some $200,000, her fee to be "a fair compensation based upon her influence." She had "only one manner of accommodation which was pretty sure to make an obligation," and to exercise it she took rooms at the National, where she reportedly made herself available to the chairmen of the Ways and Means and Military Affairs committees. It was not an easy campaign; it took her a year, after which the full claim was paid, and she presented to her lobbyist employer a bill for a reasonable 10 percent. He gave her a take-it-or-leave-it packet of only $4,000, which merely paid her hotel bills. When she raged, her duplicitous handler dared her to sue. Unlike him, the free-spending Jim Fisk was a man of his word, and chose a speedier class of administrative assistance. He hired a personable actress named Lottie Hough in 1862 to help him get passes through Union lines. Miss Hough's methods are not recorded, but the project did not take a year; Fisk promptly got the passes, which were critical to his large-scale speculation in cotton.[9]

As the Union navy's blockade of the South slowly took effect, the Confederate government pushed planters to shift from the cash crop of cotton to grow more food for the Rebel army. Cotton production dropped, and the price per pound in the North doubled, tripled and kept rising. Rebel fire-eaters' prewar boasts that King Cotton would quickly bring the Union to terms was so much bombast, but by 1862, northern mills were running short while thousands of bales sat rotting in warehouses in Dixie. Trading with the enemy was a crime, usually involving bribery, smuggling and other transgressions for which petty offenders were routinely prosecuted. Nevertheless, illegal cotton trade across the lines flourished. This amazed Brigadier General A. P. Hovey, serving with U. S. Grant's army in the West. "War and commerce with the same people!" he wrote. "What a Utopian dream!" In early 1863, Charles A. Dana, Secretary Stanton's liaison at Grant's headquarters, wrote from Memphis that "the mania for sudden fortunes made in cotton...has to an alarming extent corrupted and demoralized the army. Every colonel, captain or quartermaster is in secret partnership with some operator in cotton...."[10]

In time, rather than ordering a serious effort to stop this illicit trade, Lincoln took a relaxed view of it. Stoddard thought the president was "careless of moneymaking himself, [but] true to his Western training, could see no harm in a good 'speculation,' provided it was an honest one, and not at the expense of the country." In fact, it was useful to the Union war effort, and eventually the government issued a limited number of permits to trade in cotton. Late in the war, Lincoln would actually approve swapping food to feed Robert E. Lee's besieged army for cotton to feed northern mills, until Grant halted the exchange because he was trying to starve Lee out.[11]

Jim Fisk was much too ambitious to wait for official sanction; he could not pass up the chance to make immense profits without the blessing of the law. He took risky trips to make cotton deals in the Mississippi Valley, and employed a woman "admirably adapted to the purpose" among his agents crisscrossing the western lines of the war. He even sent his father, the former Yankee peddler, to help get "the forbidden fruit" back safely to the North. This he lived to regret, for the older man suffered a sunstroke that damaged his brain, and as a result spent much of his remaining life in a Massachusetts asylum. One of Fisk's biographers wrote that Jim had bought as much as $800,000 in cotton in a single day, keeping the New England mills of Jordan, Marsh & Company humming to fill war contracts. Although still in his twenties, Fisk never donned a uniform himself. But he professed his sympathy with troops in the field, reasoning that it made no sense for them to go without decent clothing just because of a silly law. For him, the same logic applied to an entrepreneur's chance to make a fortune.[12]

Neither cotton nor courtesans were first among Lincoln's concerns that fall. Nothing and no one vexed him as much as his ongoing worry over what to do about McClellan. He had visited the general after the battle at Antietam, where they exchanged outwardly sincere compliments. McClellan, despite his own reservations, had issued an order urging his troops to support the president's emancipation decree. His advice was not persuasive; Northern troops had not volunteered to fight to end slavery, and many puzzled over how the president's idea could possibly work. Lieutenant George Whitman of the Fifty-first New York could not understand why "Uncle Abe has issued a proclamation declaring the slaves free in all the States that are in rebellion.... one thing is certain, he has got to lick the south before he can free the niggers, and unless he drives ahead and convinces the south, before the first of January, that we are bound to lick them ... I don't think the proclamation will do much good."[13]

Considering McClellan's well-known opinion that slavery should not be an issue in the war, he was hardly being candid when he advised his troops to accept the proclamation. It was yet another reason for him to be dissatisfied with his president, but he did not need another reason to balk at Lincoln's orders; he was being his usual cautious self. Although he knew Lee's force was badly damaged, McClellan moved the Union army with groaning slowness back across the Potomac into Virginia. Lincoln wrote to ask him, "Are you not overcautious when you assume that you cannot do what the enemy is constantly doing?" When McClellan said his horses were exhausted, Lincoln replied, "Will you pardon me for asking what the horses of your army have done since the battle of Antietam that fatigue anything?" John Nicolay grumbled privately that the president put up with

McClellan's "whims and complaints and shortcomings as a mother would indulge her baby," but Lincoln's patience had finally run out; he was waiting for the right moment to be rid of McClellan at last.[14]

That moment came after the November 4 election. Weary of war, of continuing casualty lists, Northern voters gave Democrats substantial gains in state offices and Congress. Though Lincoln's Republicans held on to control of Congress, opposition was especially strong in New York, New Jersey, Illinois and Wisconsin. The day after the election, the president relieved McClellan from command and named the modest, so far uncontroversial Major General Ambrose Burnside to replace him. It took two days for the order to reach McClellan, camped in a snowstorm in Fauquier County. Lincoln had instructed the courier, a staff general, to offer command to Burnside before going to McClellan. Burnside at first declined, saying he was not competent to run a great army and was devoted to McClellan. But the staff officer said that if he refused, the job would go to Joe Hooker, whom Burnside could not stand. After much cogitation and consultation, Burnside changed his mind. Late that night, the two men took the order to McClellan. He knew it was coming and had told a fellow general that he would be replaced. Now he accepted it gracefully, pledging full cooperation. But his troops resented it mightily.[15]

Francis A. Donaldson, an officer with the 118th Pennsylvania, the Corn Exchange Regiment, told his brother that when he heard the news, he "sat down and cried, and in my dire distress cared no longer to continue in the service. . . . I tell you frankly, that if [McClellan] had placed himself at the head of the army and instead of marching on to Richmond turned against Washington, all would have followed, and instead of 'hanging Jeff Davis to a sour apple tree' . . . it would be down with Stanton, down with the whole dishonorable crew who dare to dictate such humiliating orders to the most skillful soldier of modern times." On November 10, when McClellan rode past his army to say farewell, "whole regiments broke and flocked around him, and with tears and entreaties besought him not to leave them, but to say the word and they would soon settle matters in Washington. Indeed it was thought at one time that there would be a mutiny, but by a word he calmed the tumult and ordered the men back to their colors and their duty."[16]

At last, but only for the time being, Lincoln was rid of McClellan. Burnside, personally so different from his predecessor, knew what he had to do, which was precisely what McClellan had not done—move with dispatch against the enemy. As predictable cries of joy and rage erupted across the North in reaction to the sacking of McClellan, the new commander started his army east toward Fredericksburg. Lincoln went down the Potomac to confer with him at Belle Plain, where Burnside resisted the president's idea of a three-pronged offensive. He vowed instead to go at Lee head-on. But first he had to wait for pontoon boats to use in bridging the Rappahannock River. Lincoln was glad to hear straight talk from the solid, bewhiskered Burnside instead of McClellan's endless excuses, but he hoped Burnside's concern about the pontoons did not foretell another long delay. He was relieved yet anxious as he turned back to a political scene roiled by the emancipation proclamation, the election and the departure of the Young Napoleon.

John Pope, sent away after defeat at Second Bull Run, left Washington angry at Lincoln for not defending him against those who blamed him for the debacle. Arriving at his new Northwest command, Pope turned his fury against 1,250 Dakota Sioux captured after an Indian uprising that had killed more than 350 Minnesota settlers in late summer and early fall. The massacre was brought on by a long string of grievances, capped by the government's failure to pay on time for land the Indians had given up by treaty. Pope vowed to treat the hungry Sioux as "maniacs or wild beasts," and shortly after the November election, a military commission sentenced 303 captured Sioux to death. Lincoln tried to avoid the duty of approving the sentences, and finally ruled that only 39 Indians who had committed the worst crimes should be hanged. The biggest massacre of whites by Indians in United States history would thus be followed by the biggest mass execution. Both the Indians and the settlers were unhappy with the president's ruling.

These were grave and consequential matters that would return to trouble Lincoln. But they were distractions from the greater issues of national survival and slavery that lay before him as he prepared for the return of Congress in December. In a season of stalemate and despondency, he had to describe the state of the Union in terms that would encourage the lawmakers and the nation to carry on. Through November, he cut short visiting hours and tried to minimize office routine in order to labor over his message. On December 1, Nicolay hand-carried it to the Capitol. There John W. Forney, secretary of the Senate, declaimed it on the opening day of the third and last session of the lame-duck Thirty-seventh Congress.

Neither Republicans nor Democrats heard anything inspirational as Forney read on through foreign relations, budgetary needs, mail delivery and Indian affairs. Although Lincoln had announced that emancipation was coming, he still felt the need to justify what he had done, and brought half-listening legislators to attention by proposing to carve his action in stone by amending the Constitution. He wanted to authorize payments to any state abolishing slavery by the year 1900, to loyal owners of slaves freed by the war, and to support colonization of willing freedmen. Even the abolitionists listening realized that such amendments were politically impossible in the short run. But in closing, the president fell back once again on his deep reserve of almost biblical eloquence to summon the Union to its task.[17]

"The dogmas of the quiet past are inadequate to the stormy present," he wrote.

> The occasion is piled high with difficulty, and we must rise with the occasion. As our case is new, so we must think anew and act anew. We must disenthrall ourselves, and then we shall save our country.
>
> Fellow-citizens, we cannot escape history. We of this Congress and this administration will be remembered in spite of ourselves. No personal significance or insignificance can spare one or another of us. The fiery trial through which we pass will light us down, in honor or dishonor, to the latest generation. We say we are for the Union. The world will not forget that we say this. We know how to save the Union. The world knows we do know how to save it. We—even we here—hold the power and bear the responsibility. In giving freedom to the slave, we assure freedom to the free—honorable alike in what we give and what we preserve. We shall nobly save or meanly lose the last, best hope of earth. Other means may succeed; this could not fail. The way is plain, peaceful, generous, just—a way which, if followed, the world will forever applaud, and God must forever bless.[18]

Historically true and uplifting as his words were, neither rhetoric nor political determination could substitute for victories in the field. Facing Fredericksburg, Burnside awaited his pontoons, giving Lee's outnumbered army time to dig in on the ridge behind the town. At last, on

December 11, a month and four days after taking command, Burnside sent the first Union regiments across the river and into Fredericksburg. Resisted mainly by Mississippi sharpshooters, Federal forces built up strength on the south side the next day, preparing for a grand assault on December 13. On that bitterly cold morning, Burnside threw wave after wave of infantry against the waiting Rebels, who repulsed every attack in desperate fighting. Looking on from the hill behind, Lee mused, "It is well that war is so terrible—we should grow too fond of it." Burnside, appalled at seeing his gallant army shredded, had to be restrained by his generals from personally leading a final charge. It was another disaster: some 12,700 Union casualties, more than at bloody Antietam, compared to about 5,300 suffered by the Confederates.[19]

Some of the wounded lay in freezing weather alongside the dead, blanketing the battlefield in Union blue until two days later, when Burnside sent out a flag of truce to recover his casualties. Thousands of the maimed were treated and operated on in commandeered homes and crowded tents on the Union side of the Rappahannock. Thousands more were taken on tracks of the Richmond, Fredericksburg & Potomac Railroad to the mouth of Aquia Creek, and from there up the Potomac to the capital.

Georgetown's Union Hotel, at Bridge and Washington (M and Thirtieth) streets, was one of several converted into hospitals. At dawn, a woman's voice rang out down its halls: "They've come! They've come! Hurry up, ladies—you're wanted!"

A nurse named Louisa May Alcott, there only three days, asked groggily, "Who . . . the rebels?"

The answer lay in forty ambulances lining up toward the door. Alcott assumed at first that such rough wagons must be market carts; then the sight of their cargo stirred in her "a most unpatriotic wish that I was safe at home again." That thought vanished when a six-year-old contraband came running with orders from the head nurse to "fly round right away. They's comin' in, I tell yer, heaps on 'em—one was took out dead, and I see him. . . ."

Alcott's post was in the former ballroom, where soldiers lay on forty cots or huddled around the stove—"ragged, gaunt and pale, mud to the knees, with bloody bandages untouched since put on days before; many bundled up in blankets, coats being lost or useless; and all wearing that disheartened look which proclaimed defeat, more plainly than any telegram of the Burnside blunder."

After surviving "the vilest odors that ever assaulted the human nose," Alcott was embarrassed at being ordered to disrobe wounded soldiers and wash them. "If she had requested me to shave them all, or dance a hornpipe on the stove funnel, I should have been less staggered," she wrote. But she pressed on, winning appreciation from an old Irishman as she pulled off his filthy shoes: "May your bed above be aisy darlin', for the day's work ye are doon!—Woosh! there ye are, and bedad, it's hard tellin' which is the dirtiest, the fut or the shoe." She told of caring for a man who had lost one leg and was sure to lose a shattered arm. "Lord!" he said. "What a scramble there'll be for arms and legs, when we old boys come out of our graves, on the Judgment Day; wonder if we'll get our own again?" Within a month, Alcott would go back to Massachusetts, ill with typhoid fever. Later she would write of the real characters in Washington hospitals with as much feeling as she described fictional New Englanders in *Little Women* and more than a score of other books.[20]

On December 16, the *New York Herald* listed First Lieutenant G. W. Whitmore of the Fifty-first New York among the casualties at Fredericksburg. But there was no Lieutenant Whitmore in the Fifty-first, and a hard-luck family on Portland Avenue in Brooklyn feared that the injured officer's proper name was George Washington Whitman instead. The following day, the *Times* confirmed that suspicion. Without waiting to learn more, the lieutenant's forty-three-year-old brother Walter left for Washington to find him.

Walt took the ferry to New Jersey, then a train to Philadelphia, where his pocket was picked while he changed cars, leaving him broke when he arrived in the capital. For two days, he wandered through the hospitals of Washington, searching vainly for his brother, then trying to wangle a military pass to go to Virginia. Finally, on December 19, he got aboard the boat to Aquia Creek and made his way to the camp of Brigadier General Edward Ferrero's brigade. He told his mother that "one of the first things that met my eyes in camp was a heap of feet, arms, legs &c, under a tree in front of a hospital." That was the historic Lacy mansion, overlooking Fredericksburg across the river. Clara Barton was there, struggling to care for more casualties than she could possibly handle. Whitman was delighted to find his brother, who had been promoted to captain, and to see that his wound was not serious—a shell fragment had gashed a hole through his cheek. Walt spent nine days at the front, sharing a tent with George and three other soldiers, taking notes on camp hardships and trying to comfort wounded men shivering in the cold. "I do not see that I do much good to these wounded and dying, but I cannot leave them," he wrote. When he returned to Washington, he had seen so much of needy, suffering soldiers that he could not put the war behind.[21]

Walt Whitman was an established and scandalous poet long before the war began. He had worked for newspapers for more than twenty years and produced three increasingly provocative editions of his magnum opus, *Leaves of Grass* (one reviewer of it advised him to commit suicide). In 1861, he had written a poem to spur enlistment in New York. But for several years, he had been in a slump, drifting, in a raffish bohemian existence that seemed to lead nowhere. Now he had found the great humanitarian cause of his life, as a freelance nurse in the teeming hospitals of the wartime capital. Years later, he would tell a biographer that "the war saved me: what I saw in the war set me up for all time."[22]

But first he had to have a place to live, and a way to support himself in his after-hours volunteerism. In his first brief stop in Washington, before going to the battlefield, Whitman had encountered two friends who helped him on his way. Charles W. Eldridge, a Boston publisher who had gone bankrupt after bringing out the third edition of *Leaves of Grass*, was now a clerk in the office of the army paymaster. William D. O'Connor, who had written a passionate antislavery novel titled *Harrington*, also published by Eldridge, had a job at the Lighthouse Board. The vigorous, blue-eyed O'Connor and his wife, Nelly, would become Whitman's close friends; the poet moved into what he called a "werry little bedroom" in the apartment house where they lived, on L Street near Fourteenth. Then he wrote to Ralph Waldo Emerson, the reigning sage of the nation's intellectual establishment, asking him for letters of recommendation to Seward, Chase and Sumner. Emerson was slow responding, and meanwhile Whitman started as a part-time copyist in the army paymaster's office where Eldridge worked. From there, on the fifth floor of the Corcoran Building at Fifteenth and F streets, later the site of the Washington Hotel, he had a broad view across the city he would adopt as his own.[23]

Whitman was dismayed in the mornings by routine army inefficiency at his office, and anguished during his afternoons and evenings by the travails of soldiers in overcrowded hospitals. To his sister-in-law, he described how soldiers climbed the stairs to the paymaster, many seeking a final payment before heading home, only to be turned away again and again. "The scenes of disappointment were quite affecting. Here they wait in Washington, perhaps week after week, wretched and heart-sick—this is the greatest place of delays and puttings-off, and no finding the clue to any thing . . . the crowds on the walk and corner of poor, sick, pale, tattered soldiers are awful. . . ."[24]

The next evening, he completed that letter with his first description of his hospital sojourns in the city. Two casualties from George Whitman's regiment had asked Walt to visit them in the recently built, nine-hundred-bed Campbell Hospital, on Boundary Street between Fifth and Sixth streets. Among a hundred patients in a long whitewashed shed, he found one who had been lying without attention since his arrival from Fredericksburg. Whitman sent for a doctor, who said the youth was suffering from diarrhea and bronchitis, but would recover. The soldier "seemed to have entirely given up, and lost heart—he had not a cent of money—not a friend or acquaintance." Whitman wrote a letter home for him, and left him a little change, at which the soldier "was overcome and began to cry."

"Then there were many, many others," wrote the poet, and there were—dozens and hundreds of despondent victims of the war who would appreciate his gentle friendship before the mayhem was over.[25]

Even in hard times, especially when war news was discouraging, Radical politicians could be counted on to make things worse for Lincoln.

Three days after the debacle at Fredericksburg, Senate Republicans held a secret caucus instigated by Chase, Stanton and friends. They formed a cabal against Chase's great rival Seward, recycling familiar complaints that he was soft on the Confederacy and slavery. About Lincoln, they said what they had been saying to each other for months; Wade charged him with promoting generals who did not believe in "the policy of the government," by which he meant the Radical agenda. Eventually all but one of them, Preston King, agreed on a drastic resolution that did not mention Seward's name but was clearly aimed at him. It called for reorganizing the cabinet and the military hierarchy to meet Radical political standards, and for all major presidential decisions and appointments to be made jointly with the revised cabinet. King, who had been Seward's New York colleague in the Senate, slipped away and went to warn the secretary at his home on Lafayette Square. Seward took the news calmly. Brandishing his usual cigar, he said the Radicals were "thirsty for a victim." He thought fast; writing out a one-sentence resignation from office, he sent it to the White House by King and his own son, Assistant Secretary Frederick Seward.[26]

Lincoln was taken by surprise. As he walked across the Avenue to talk to Seward, he thought out one of the most skillful infighting triumphs in presidential history. He did not accept Seward's resignation, but kept it. When the senators came with their resolution, he let them vent their feelings for three hours, then the following day asked them to return—without telling them he was also asking the cabinet, minus Seward. He was gloomy, not sure his scheme would work; he told Orville Browning that "they wish to get rid of me, and I am sometimes half disposed to gratify them." When Browning dissuaded him, he said, "We are now on the brink of destruction. It appears to me the Almighty is against us, and I can hardly see a ray of hope."

When he brought the two sides face-to-face, Lincoln invited the senators to state their case. Then he invited the reluctant Chase, senior cabinet member present, to respond. The pompous Ohioan did verbal somersaults to avoid saying to the president the things he had said so often to others. Chase was deeply embarrassed, and the senators resentful that he had flinched at the moment of truth. He saw no alternative afterward to offering Lincoln his own resignation, which was just what the president wanted. But when Stanton offered his resignation as well, the president brushed him aside. He pocketed Chase's letter, along with Seward's. Now he could accept either, both or neither, whenever he chose; no question remained of who was in charge. "This relieves me," he said. "The case is clear, the trouble is ended." Though Seward and Chase would never become friends with each other, thenceforth they cooperated as never before. With their resignations in his desk, Lincoln could focus on the great blow for liberty that he had promised months before.[27]

The president still was not satisfied that his emancipation edict was as clear and politically nuanced as possible. On December 30, he gave the cabinet a last chance to offer any suggestions short of fundamental change in the proclamation. Some of their minor revisions he accepted, others he rejected. Chase, for example, believed it would cause trouble for the proclamation to draw lines within states, but Lincoln kept language to exclude certain parishes of Louisiana and counties of Virginia then under Federal control. He also specified that freed slaves would be welcomed for garrison duty in the Union army. On New Year's Eve, he began to copy the entire edited document, even then making fine corrections as he wrote, and leaving temporary blank spaces to await the latest reports on exactly which territory was held by the Union. He was still writing at eleven o'clock the next morning, when guests began to arrive for the mass reception held at the White House each New Year's Day.

By tradition, that reception lasted three hours, the president standing welcoming diplomats, ranking officials and then the general public. Lincoln left the document unfinished in his office and went to shake hands in the Blue Room, seemingly unconcerned that he was postponing vital work for purely social duty. "Vast as were its consequences, the [proclamation] itself was only the simplest and briefest formality," wrote Nicolay and Hay. "It could in no wise be made exceptional or dramatic." The "mental conflict and the moral victory" had been in July, when he laid his draft before the cabinet, and in September, when he announced to the world that the proclamation was coming.

After Lincoln had greeted the last of several thousand well-wishers, his right hand was so cramped that he could hardly wield a pen. Nobody organized a ceremony to witness the final strokes as he appended his name to "one of the greatest and most beneficent military decrees of history." Fewer than a dozen persons looked on, those who happened to be nearby and came in out of curiosity.

The president's personal secretaries, heartfelt supporters of what he had done, wrote that "in the light of history we can see that by this edict Mr. Lincoln gave slavery its vital thrust, its mortal wound. It was the word of decision, the judgment without appeal, the sentence of doom. But for the execution of the sentence, for the accomplishment of this result, he had yet many weary months to hope and to wait...."[28]

Perhaps to Nicolay and Hay, who had followed the evolution of his thinking about slavery in public and private, the signing of the Emancipation Proclamation was anticlimactic and could not be made "exceptional or dramatic." But among the city's free blacks, and the recent slaves housed in the contraband camp at Twelfth and Q streets, there was exultation.

The Reverend Henry M. Turner, pastor of Israel Bethel Church, rushed to join the crowd around a printing office where the proclamation was being set in type. He grabbed the first sheet out the door, but it was ripped away, and the second was torn apart by other eager hands. Making away with the third, he raced panting down the Avenue to his church. When he got there, he was too breathless to read it to the waiting crowd. He handed it to a colleague, who pronounced it with great deliberation. Around them "men squealed, women fainted, dogs barked, white and colored people shook hands, songs were sung," Turner wrote. Hundreds, black and white, paraded before the White House, where the president came to a window and took a modest bow. "Rumor said that the very thought of being set at liberty and having no more auction blocks, no more separation of parents and children, was so heart gladdening that scores of colored people literally fell dead with joy," Turner wrote. "Nothing like it will ever be seen again in this life."[29]

At the contraband camp, one old man shouted, "I'm a free man now! Jesus Christ has made me free!" The crowd there sang hymn after hymn of thanks and promise. An ex-slave from Virginia told how he had worked so long for nothing, and now could keep what he earned, could educate his children. "But brethren," he warned, "don't be too free. The lazy man can't go to heaven." A revered character called "John the Baptist" took center stage, preaching as the day wore on. At seven o'clock there was an organized gathering at which the superintendent of freedmen, the Reverend Danforth B. Nichols, former head of the Chicago Reform School, solemnly read the proclamation, enunciating it word by word. Like the ex-slave from Virginia, Nichols counseled caution, explaining that the decree did not apply everywhere, not even in surrounding Maryland. But no such details mattered; nothing anyone said could possibly dampen the celebration.[30]

Abraham and "Tad" Lincoln
(National Archives)

Detective Allen Pinkerton (above)
and bodyguard Ward Hill Lamon,
who escorted Lincoln secretly
into Washington (Pinkerton,
Patriot Publishing Co.; Lamon,
Library of Congress)

Lincoln's first inaugural procession,
moving along Pennsylvania Avenue
toward the looming Capitol
(National Archives)

New York troops arriving at
Baltimore & Ohio Railroad station,
at New Jersey Avenue and C Street
(Leslie's Illustrated)

Mary Lincoln in a gown made by her seamstress and confidante Elizabeth Keckley (Lincoln, Library of Congress; Keckley, Lincoln Museum)

Montgomery C. Meigs, engineer
and quartermaster general
(Library of Congress)

Thomas U. Walter, architect of the
Capitol (National Archives)

The sluggish Washington canal
cut past the unfinished Capitol.
(National Archives)

William H. Seward, Secretary
of State (National Archives)

Henry M. Stanton, Secretary
of War (Library of Congress)

Gideon Welles, Secretary of the
Navy (National Archives)

Salmon P. Chase, Secretary of the
Treasury (National Archives)

U.S. troops after freeing inmates of
slave pen in Alexandria (Library of Congress)

Federal soldiers occupying Lee mansion
at Arlington (Library of Congress)

Rose O'Neal Greenhow and daughter
in prison (Library of Congress)

Senator Henry Wilson, Greenhow's
admirer (National Archives)

Old Capitol Prison (Library of Congress)

Lt. Gen. Winfield Scott
(National Archives)

Maj. Gen. George B.
McClellan
(National Archives)

District of Columbia
volunteers being
sworn in outside War
Department
(Harper's Weekly)

War casualties and
soldiers' relatives at
office of U. S. Christian
Commission (Library
of Congress)

Cattle and slaughter
pens covered grounds
of the Washington
Monument.
(Library of Congress)

Newly laid Washington & Alexandria
Railroad tracks ran past Capitol Hill.
(Library of Congress)

Guards check passes of troops boarding
crude ferry from Mason's Island to
Georgetown. (Library of Congress)

Dorothea Dix, superintendent of
nurses (Library of Congress)

Walt Whitman, poet and war nurse
(National Archives)

Mary Walker, physician and
feminist (National Archives)

John Hay, presidential secretary and
diarist (National Archives)

"Her Ladyship," Thomas Crawford's bronze
statue of Freedom, ready to stand tall at the
crown of the Capitol (Architect of the Capitol)

Antonia Ford as rebel spy
and as Mrs. Joseph C. Willard
(Library of Congress)

Sojourner Truth, voice of the
downtrodden (Library of Congress)

Jane Grey Swisshelm, journalist
and crusader (Minnesota Historical
Society)

Troops of Company E, Fourth U.S.
Colored Infantry at Fort Lincoln
(Library of Congress)

Cannoneers of Company F, Third
Massachusetts Heavy Artillery
at Fort Stevens, site of only battle
within District of Columbia
(Library of Congress)

John Wilkes Booth
(Library of Congress)

The fatal shot. To the
president's right, sit Mary
Lincoln, Henry Rathbone,
and Clara Harris.
(Harper's Weekly)

The Grand Review. The massed
armies of the Union in their two-day
victory parade along the Avenue
(Library of Congress)

CHAPTER FOURTEEN

What Will the Country Say?

Within days of arriving in Washington, Noah Brooks, the correspondent of the *Sacramento Union,* thought he understood why the North kept suffering defeats like those at Bull Run and Fredericksburg: While the South had a tradition of obeying an autocratic leader, the Federal army seemed to be cursed by a "reckless disregard of authority." From general down to private, Brooks believed, Northern soldiers were undisciplined rugged individuals. The situation reminded him of the New England militia company whose young captain ordered "Present arms"—to which one independent soldier replied, "Shan't do it!" The best response the captain could muster was "Wal, tain't no matter."[1]

Since Brooks had not yet been with the army in the field, he may have gotten that impression from watching two long-running military sideshows that occupied the capital in the depressing weeks after Fredericksburg. For sixty-seven days, a court of inquiry investigated General McDowell, at his own request, and he successfully defended himself against criticism of his actions before and during Second Bull Run. For forty-five days, a court-martial tried Major General Fitz-John Porter, very much against his own wishes. He was charged by General Pope with disobedience and misconduct in the same campaign, and cashiered from the army after eighteen years as an officer.*

Brooks was a shipbuilder's son from Maine who signed his pieces

---

*Porter kept fighting to clear his name, and eventually a board of generals found in his favor in 1879. President Chester A. Arthur remanded his sentence three years later. Reappointed colonel in 1886, Porter then retired from the service and pursued a career in public works, later becoming police and fire commissioner of New York.

"Castine," for his hometown on Penobscot Bay. He had met Lincoln during the 1856 presidential and 1858 senatorial campaigns, when the ambitious Republican was stumping across Illinois and Brooks was writing for the *Dixon Telegraph*. The correspondent was struck by Lincoln's appearance when he saw him in Washington four years later, at services at New York Avenue Presbyterian Church. The former "happy-faced Springfield lawyer" had become "grizzled, his gait more stooping, his countenance sallow, and there is a sunken, deathly look about the large, cavernous eyes, which is saddening to those who see there the marks of care and anxiety such as no President of the United States has ever before known." When the president heard that Brooks was in Washington, he asked him to the White House. They quickly bonded, and the thirty-two-year-old journalist became Lincoln's best friend in the press, a confidant perhaps as trusted as the White House aides Nicolay and Hay.[2]

In his get-acquainted meandering about Washington, Brooks was amused by the local use of paper "shinplasters" for change rather than the solid money he was used to in the goldfields of California. "It is not much to give a hotel porter a bit of green paper for merely looking at your trunks, but your green paper is current funds, redeemable in postage stamps at the rate of five ten-cent stamps per square of paper. Funny, isn't it?" At the Capitol, he read character in the looks of men like Henry Wilson—"rosy, portly, and with a dash of military on his waistcoat"—and Wilson's Massachusetts colleague Charles Sumner, who with his tousled gray hair and long, strong nose was "a model of forensic elegance, scholarly culture and precision." Brooks also picked up a false rumor that Montgomery Meigs would be fired as quartermaster general because he was responsible for the delay in providing pontoon boats that led in turn to disaster at Fredericksburg. Wherever Brooks looked, that defeat dominated the mood of the city; he felt the very air "heavy with the dolor of the hour."[3]

No one was more humbled by the latest reversal than the already humble general who had been defeated. On New Year's Day, Burnside sent a message to Lincoln saying that his troops lacked faith in the army's high command, specifically including himself, and it would be best for the nation if he stepped aside. Four days later, he sent a formal retirement letter, meant to avoid embarrassing Lincoln if he wanted to change commanders. But Lincoln urged him to try again, so on January 19, Burnside started the Army of the Potomac up the left bank of the Rappahannock, intending to cross above Fredericksburg and outflank Lee. Then the rains came and the offensive bogged down in Virginia loam. Horses and mules, trying to pull guns and wagons out of the deepening morass, dropped dead of exhaustion. Burnside's army became a demoralized crowd as it tried to march back to its old camps, collapsing at the end of another fiasco, known to history as the "Mud March." Burnside, furious at his subordinates, issued an order removing two generals and dismissing Hooker from the army. He personally followed this order to Washington, telling the president that if it was not approved, he would resign. At last, Lincoln had had enough of yet another commander; he accepted Burnside's resignation and reluctantly named Hooker to replace him. With that appointment, the president included one of the strangest messages ever addressed to a man who was being promoted rather than fired.

He and most of political and military Washington knew that Hooker had been conniving for months against whoever was in command above him, most recently Burnside. The vain, sometimes bibulous Hooker had gotten Lincoln's attention after First Bull Run, when he told the president that he was "a damned sight better general than you, sir, had on that field." He proved himself physically brave on the Peninsula, winning the nickname of "Fighting Joe," then rose to corps command and was wounded in the foot at Antietam. He spent that fall recovering at the Government Hospital for the Insane, part of which had been set aside for army casualties. There he further ingratiated himself with Radicals pressing for someone politically suitable to take charge of the army. He told Chase that if he had been commander on the Peninsula and at Antietam, those would have been great Union victories. After Fredericksburg, he wrote to Charles Nichols, the hospital superintendent, "Thank God I was not committed to [Burnside's plan of attack] by word or act." Although he cautioned Nichols that this was strictly private, he said much the same thing when he later testified against Burnside before the Radical-dominated Joint Committee on Conduct of the War.[4]

Lincoln made clear to Hooker that he was aware of his backbiting and self-promotion, and wanted no more of it. In his letter, he told the general, "You are ambitious, which, within reasonable bounds, does good rather than harm." But during Burnside's command, "you have taken counsel of your ambition, and thwarted him as much as you could, in which you did a great wrong to the country, and to a most meritorious and honorable brother officer." Not only that, but Lincoln had heard Hooker's talk about the need for a dictator. "Of course it was not *for* this, but in spite of it, that I have given you the command. Only those generals who gain successes can set up dictators. What I now ask of you is military success, and I will risk the dictatorship." He hoped the dissension Hooker had fueled would not turn against him; "Neither you, nor Napoleon ... could get any good out of an army while such a spirit prevails in it."

Lincoln ended this extraordinary message by wishing Hooker well: "And now, beware of rashness. Beware of rashness, but with energy, and sleepless vigilance, go forward, and give us victories."[5]

While some fellow generals were unhappy about Hooker's promotion, Radicals were delighted. Nichols's friend Edward P. Vollum, an army medical inspector, wrote: "Some time ago I prophesied ... that the result of the first battle in which the Army of the Potomac was engaged after Hooker had command of it would illuminate every loyal house in the country, and my confidence now is so great that I tell my friends to get their candles ready for the joyful occasion."[6]

Hooker had what he wanted; now he had to back up his boasting.

In those bleak winter weeks after Fredericksburg, the marriage of Lavinia Warren and Charles Sherwood Stratton brought a welcome momentary diversion to Washington. The happy couple was better known as General and Mrs. Tom Thumb, sometime star attractions of P. T. Barnum's New York museum and traveling extravaganza. Having long ago met Queen Victoria at Buckingham Palace and imitated Napoleon for the amusement of the duke of Wellington, Tom was amiably confident when he and his bride came to see Lincoln at the White House three days after their wedding in New York.

At three feet, four inches, he was exactly a yard shorter than the president, and the "plump but symmetrical" Mrs. Thumb was just as petite. The newspaper correspondent Sara Jane Clarke Lippincott, who wrote as "Grace Greenwood," witnessed this spectacle in the East Room. Wearing their wedding trappings, the miniature couple advanced with "pigeon-like stateliness" toward the president and looked respectfully "up, up, to his kindly face. It was pleasant to see their tall host bend, and bend, to take their little hands in his great palm, holding Madame's with especial chariness, as if it were a robin's egg, and he were fearful of breaking it." Though bending, Lincoln did not talk down to them, presenting them with all dignity to Mrs. Lincoln. There was "nothing to reveal to that shrewd little pair his keen sense of the incongruity of the scene." Before leaving town, the celebrated couple had been "feted and joked at, dangled and danced in Washington, by everybody who is anybody, from a high public functionary down to the hotel boys."[7]

Lincoln called Mrs. Lippincott "Grace Greenwood the Patriot," in appreciation of her fund-raising lectures and visits to soldiers' hospitals. Then forty-two years old, she had published nine prewar books of poetry and travel, and edited or contributed to more than a dozen newspapers and magazines. She was an antislavery reformer who pressed for women's rights and prison reform, and became one of the first women to be a regular newspaper correspondent in the capital.

But Grace Greenwood was neither the first correspondent nor the most fervent advocate. Jane Grey Swisshelm was ahead of her. When Greenwood was depicting the lighter, more pleasant side of Washington, Swisshelm went to the other extreme, writing that "slavery dies hard, if dying it is; and I doubt if the spirit of the Institution was ever more rampant in the Capital than it is today."

Those words sounded as if she were quoting a Radical New England politician in the weeks before secession, but Swisshelm was writing nearly two years after Jeff Davis left for Dixie and more than a month after Abraham Lincoln signed the Emancipation Proclamation. She had been angry for years about the status of women and slaves, and now she was angrier about the murder of Minnesota civilians by Sioux Indians. She was a veteran hell-raiser; in 1850 she had come from Pittsburgh, where she edited an abolitionist newspaper, to be a Washington correspondent for Horace Greeley's *New York Tribune*. She became the first woman to sit in the Senate press gallery, an honor quickly withdrawn after her first dispatch, which described Daniel Webster as a sot who had fathered illegitimate mulatto children. Advised against publishing the letter, she went ahead, saying, "Let God take care of the consequences." She had broken the press gallery's unwritten rule that journalists did not report the private weaknesses of politicians. Although she wrote the Webster attack for her Pittsburgh paper, it was widely reprinted, with the author identified as a *Tribune* correspondent. Greeley, embarrassed, fired her. Back in Pittsburgh, Swisshelm sold her paper and moved to Minnesota, where she started another—and after it was closed by a libel suit, yet another. She was writing for this one, the *St. Cloud Democrat,* when she came to Washington in the winter of 1862–63 to protest what she considered Lincoln's easy treatment of the Indians arrested after the previous summer's massacre.[8]

She wanted to raise political consciousness about the murders by lecturing, but her fiery reputation had preceded her, so she could not find a hall. She believed that the abolition lectures at the Smithsonian the previous winter had stirred such a fuss that "every hall and church in the city is closed and hermetically sealed against every lecturer suspected of any opposition to the peculiar institution."[9]

But Swisshelm was not easily defeated. Mary Clemmer Ames wrote that to see her "clear, frosty-blue eyes" and hear her determined voice was to "feel sure that she could take a ship across the ocean; that she could command a brigade; govern a state, and have superfluous power left for infinitesimal purposes." So Swisshelm did find a hall, thanks to the Reverend Byron Sunderland, chaplain of the Senate, who invited her to use his First Presbyterian Church. She spoke there for "two mortal hours," asserting that the Indians were enemies of the Union, effectively aiding the Confederacy. "If justice is not done, [Minnesota] will go to shooting Indians whenever these government pets get out from under Uncle Samuel's wing," she declared. "Our people will hunt them, shoot them, set traps for them, put out poisoned bait for them. . . . Every Minnesota man, who has a soul and can get a rifle, will go to shooting Indians; and he who hesitates will be black-balled by every Minnesota woman and posted as coward in every Minnesota home." Having spoken, Swisshelm took a War Department clerkship in order to stay on in Washington and dare the government to meet her expectations.[10]

"Washington is the great crucible which transmutes all gold to foil," she wrote. The congressmen who rushed to save the nation when war began, full of patriotic ardor, "have learned to wilt, and cower, and trim, and turn, to suit the malarious atmosphere of this slavery-cursed soil, until their disgusted constituents have become hopeless. . . ." Compromise was not in her vocabulary.[11]

Perhaps Swisshelm, calloused by the battles she had fought, was entitled to be cynical. Others arrived in Washington wide-eyed with idealism and refused to be disillusioned by what they found. Elida Rumsey was eighteen when she came from Tarrytown, New York, hoping to become a nurse in an army hospital. When Dorothea Dix predictably turned her away because she was too young and attractive, Rumsey began taking flowers and other comforts to the soldier patients. She had a beautiful voice and gladly obliged when they asked her to sing for them. She stirred ovations with "The Star-Spangled Banner," rendered as she stood on a captured Confederate flag, with Old Glory waving overhead. Soon an older Navy Yard clerk, John Fowle of Massachusetts, fell in love with her and joined in her volunteer works. They led prayer meetings for Nurse Pomroy and her wards at Columbian Hospital, and brought wagonloads of books and magazines to patients. This inspired the idea of a soldiers' reading room, to help keep idle troops out of trouble. In late 1862, they opened their first little library in a rented room on Fifth Street, near City Hall. Within weeks, it became so popular that they decided to expand—and Rumsey had become so popular that she largely financed the expansion with a concert tour.

On March 1, 1863, in the hall of the House of Representatives, Elida Rumsey and John Fowle became man and wife. Some said they were married there at the president's suggestion; though Mr. and Mrs. Lincoln could not attend, they sent a carriageload of flowers from the White House nursery. The chamber was full of well-wishers, among them a soldier in the gallery who shouted down when an army chaplain completed the ceremony, "Won't the bride sing 'The Star-Spangled Banner'?" Elida never had to be asked twice. The flag was unfurled, and in a plain drab poplin dress and her white bonnet adorned with red, white and blue flowers, she hit the high notes "with never more fervor in her beautiful voice." Later that day, on a corner of Judiciary Square, the newlyweds dedicated the 1,700-square-foot soldiers' reading room, stocked with books, stationery, stamps, free coffee and a melodeon.[12]

Joseph Clapp Willard, the genial and increasingly prosperous co-owner of the capital's premier hotel, had decided that he should be in uniform. His brother, Henry, was fully capable of caring for the free-spending travelers and lobbyists who ate, drank and slept under their roof. Henry's sense of humor helped him manage under stressful conditions. When one of the hotel's constant small fires broke out on a top floor, a guest smelled smoke and rushed to find Henry in the inner office. "Mr. Willard," he shouted, "the hotel is on fire! Where is it? Where is it?" Henry calmly summoned a bellboy and instructed him: "John, will you take the gentleman upstairs and show him the fire?"[13]

Whether Joseph Willard was driven to enlist by patriotism or was uncomfortable at standing by while others fought is uncertain. He did not have to go into the army; he was forty-one years old, there was no national draft yet, and even if there were, he could easily have hired a substitute to go in his place. Once in, he did not have to work his muddy way up through the ranks, but got himself appointed captain in April 1862. Three days later, he was assigned as aide to General McDowell and left Henry in charge of the hotel. That summer, he was promoted to major and commended by McDowell for his staff work at Second Bull Run; returning the favor, he testified on McDowell's behalf at the military court of inquiry.[14]

In the field, Willard was looked after by his longtime servant Jim, although Jim was not eager to go along if Willard was ordered far away. "I do not feel so well when I think I must take a stranger with me," Willard wrote to his mother, "but you know in wartime one must expect to suffer . . . if I do I will try and not complain."[15]

But Willard would never be sent far away from Washington. When Major General Heintzelman replaced McDowell in command of Washington and environs, Willard stayed on as his aide, which kept him much of the time within a day's ride of the capital. The main armies were dug in for the winter miles south along the Rappahannock, but on the road, lone riders like Willard had to look out for fast-moving Confederate raiders who kept the war alive behind the lines in Heintzelman's territory. Just before New Year's Day, the cavalier Confederate Jeb Stuart's raiders struck at Burke Station, a Fairfax County stop on the Orange & Alexandria Railroad, only fifteen miles southwest of the White House. From there, Stuart sent an impudent telegram thumbing his nose at Quartermaster General Meigs, complaining of the poor quality of the Union mules his Rebel troopers had been stealing lately. Stuart had surprised the station at Burke during a five-day expedition on which he led some 1,800 cavalrymen with a battery of horse artillery on a rampage deep into and safely out of Union-held territory. No one went about war with more jollity than Stuart, whose personal dash rubbed off on his men, and none of his men was more restless and reckless than "the Gray Ghost," a lean lieutenant named John Singleton Mosby.

Mosby had become a Stuart favorite by scouting the way when the Rebel cavalry first rode around McClellan's army outside Richmond. That winter, he prevailed on Stuart to cut him loose to operate with a handful of horsemen in the Virginia counties west of Washington, which soon became known as "Mosby's Confederacy." The Federal cavalry could not catch Mosby because his band was so small, fast and unpredictable, growing from a handful to only a few dozen riders that winter. Joe Hooker complimented Mosby and jeered his own cavalry by noting that for a while Union sentinels were taking up planks in Chain Bridge at night, afraid the daring raider might dash into Washington and kidnap the president. Between raids, Mosby's men did not cluster in camp but scattered into friendly farmhouses until summoned again. They were able to melt so successfully into the countryside because they had dedicated collaborators in the women left behind by Confederate soldiers.[16]

Thomas R. Lounsbury, a Yale-educated New Yorker and future professor of English, met some of these women when he was stationed with his Union brigade in western Fairfax. He saw there a "bloody debatable land . . . rapidly returning to the abandonment and waste from which the labor of successive generations had rescued it. . . . like all historic ground, [it] had become so at the price of tears and blood. . . . Ruined forts, in all cases made of earth . . . were scattered over the country; while rifle-pits half full of water stretched for miles in all directions." Despite this desolation, the women Lounsbury encountered were full of fight; their standard response to any Yankee comment about how poorly Confederate soldiers were uniformed was that men didn't need to dress up to slaughter hogs. These Rebel women were "bright, lively, intelligent brunettes, agreeable as girls, the world over, generally are. One of the most attractive of them, mentally, physically, and pecuniarily, professed herself exceedingly anxious to become a martyr to the cause of southern rights," wrote Lounsbury.[17]

More than one high-spirited Virginia girl felt that way, among them Laura Ratcliffe, who is said to have sheltered Mosby's men in her house at Frying Pan (later Herndon) in Fairfax, and smuggled information to both Stuart and Mosby. But Lounsbury clearly had in mind Antonia Ford, the flirtatious daughter of Edward R. Ford, a well-to-do merchant in the village of Fairfax Court House.

By the age of twenty-four, Antonia had played cat-and-mouse with many a suitor, in person and by mail. The week after war began, a future Confederate horse artilleryman named Louis C. Helm had complained at length that she made his life "unendurable" by withholding the answer he wanted to hear. "After all the affection and love that I have lavished upon you, you plainly tell me . . . that you had not forgotten Doct Griggsby," he moaned. That fall, another fluttery swain told her, "I infer . . . that you are not averse to a correspondence with me. . . . I embrace this idea most eagerly for I have long regarded you with much favor although our acquaintance has been brief and my opportunities to cultivate this friendship you tender me, few and hurried. The very first time indeed that [I] beheld your beautiful countenance and through it received a glimpse of the noble sold that animates it my poor heart has been strangely agitated by conflicting emotions of delightful hope and dispairing fear. . . . Pray write me forthwith and correct me *painful* though it be, if I have fallen into error. Till then I shall be most anxious and ever after be either the *happiest* or most *miserable* of mortals as your sovereign will determines. . . ."[18]

Antonia brushed off such lovelorn gentlemen after her brother Charles, a cadet at Virginia Military Institute, went away to war. She concentrated her charms on men in gray uniform, gallants who returned her interest and gladly accepted the gossip she gathered moving about the countryside. While the Confederates still held the country behind Alexandria, the future cavalry General Thomas Lafayette Rosser had invited her to Munson's Hill, close enough to peer through a spyglass at the skeleton of the Capitol dome. Her information was so valuable—or her personality so winning—that in October 1861, Stuart made her an honorary lieutenant and aide-de-camp on his staff. By an order stamped with his ring seal, he decreed that "she will be obeyed, respected and admired. . . ." Antonia treasured the appointment, honorary though it was, and took it seriously.[19]

But then suddenly her Confederate admirers were gone; after months of skirmishing back and forth through Fairfax Court House, the Yankees moved in to stay. Some of their officers, including Major Joseph Willard, roomed and dined at the Fords' house, one of the most imposing in town. Antonia focused her provocative wit on them, smiling as warmly on officers in blue as she had on the departed Confederates. When they talked among themselves, she listened carefully, and passed along what seemed interesting. Before Second Bull Run, she overheard something about Union intentions that she considered so urgently important that she enlisted her aunt, Mrs. Augustus Brower, to ride with her twenty miles at night through a rainstorm to deliver it to Stuart's headquarters. The kind of intelligence that Antonia picked up was particularly useful to Mosby in the raids and ambushes that bedeviled the Yankees that winter, but whether she figured in his most famous escapade of all is still uncertain.[20]

Late on March 8, Mosby departed from near Aldie with 29 men, including a Union sergeant named James F. Ames who had deserted to the Rebel side to protest the Emancipation Proclamation. On earlier outings, Mosby had tested him for trustworthiness. Now Ames guided the raiders between Federal pickets, winding twenty-five snow-streaked miles through the night to Fairfax Court House. There, Mosby hoped to swoop into Union cavalry headquarters and snatch Colonel Percy Wyndham, who had noisily promised to bring him in. Each of the fast-moving raiders carried two pistols rather than the usual cavalry sabers and carbines. After getting separated in the darkness, they rejoined to reach the village after midnight and spread out on assigned missions, some to the Federal stables, some seeking specific officers. Ames discovered that their main target, Wyndham, was away that night. But a more prestigious officer, Brigadier General Edwin H. Stoughton, was there. Indeed, he had entertained his visiting mother and sister all evening at the Ford house, where they were staying, and now he was dead asleep nearby.

With a handful of men, Mosby found the general and roused him with a slap on the backside. When the indignant Stoughton asked, "Have you got Mosby?" the raider answered, "No, Mosby's got you." He took the general away as a prisoner, and as his men slipped past the final Union picket posts at dawn, Stoughton was amazed that so few Confederates had done so much. Mosby turned over his prisoners at Culpeper, where Stuart declared that the Fairfax raid was "a feat unparalleled in the war." But Lincoln's reaction became more famous: informed that Mosby had got away with fifty-eight horses and a brigadier general, he said that was too bad—he could always make another brigadier, but he couldn't make horses.[21]

Six days afterward, the *New York Times* printed a letter purportedly written before the raid to a man in Vermont by a Union officer stationed at Fairfax Court House. It said, "There is a woman in the town (Fairfax) by the name of Ford, not married, who has been of great service to Gen. Stuart in giving information &c—so much that Stuart has conferred on her the rank of major in the rebel army. She belongs to his staff. Why our people do not send her beyond the lines is another question. I understand that she and Stoughton are very intimate. If he gets picked up some night he may thank her for it. Her father lives here, and is known to harbor and give all the aid to the rebs, and this in the little hole of Fairfax, under the nose of the provost marshal, who is always full of bad whiskey. . . ." Thus, Antonia was an item of intense curiosity among the Federals in her neighborhood even before Mosby rode in. When he rode away with his captive general, she became a prime suspect for detectives who were sure he could not have succeeded without help from some secret informant.[22]

Obviously, Antonia had not read that published letter when a woman calling herself Frankie Abel arrived at the Ford home, dressed in faded calico, saying she was a loyal Confederate on her way to New Orleans. She won Antonia's confidence by telling of her own exploits for the Southern cause. Antonia, now gullible after playing her double game with Union officers so skillfully, proudly brought out from beneath her mattress the commission that Stuart had given her. "Frankie," who was working for chief Federal Detective Lafayette C. Baker, had seen all she needed to see.

On March 13, shortly after Baker's agent left the Ford household, government authorities arrested Antonia and her father. Taken to headquarters at Centreville, Antonia was held there for three days before being transferred to Washington. Her military escort was none other than Major Joe Willard, who felt the full force of Antonia's magnetism on the way to Old Capitol Prison. The turn of the key locking her away marked the start of one of the capital's most desperate clandestine love affairs.[23]

Jane Swisshelm's cry for revenge against the Indians reminded Washingtonians, surrounded by war, that life and strife went on in ways that had nothing to do with secession and slavery. Amid tramping regiments and overflowing hospitals, Congress passed a series of important measures in 1862–63 that would speed the westward growth of the postwar nation. The Homestead Act granted plots of public land to families who settled and worked on them for five years, a step that would encourage migration and boost crop production and exports. The Morrill Land Grant Act approved the sale of 17 million acres of public land to loyal states to endow the agricultural colleges that would become great state universities. The Pacific Railway Act authorized the Union Pacific to build westward from Nebraska to meet the Central Pacific, coming east from California, bridging the continent. It doubled the land grants given the rail companies to meet expenses, and inspired lobbyists to launch one of the greediest feeding frenzies in the history of the republic. Yet carrying out all of these notable measures, as well as the Emancipation Proclamation, eventually depended on winning the war. To a delegation of abolitionists complaining that the proclamation was not being properly respected by the army in the field, Lincoln said that the masses were mainly unhappy over the lack of military success: "Defeat and failure in the field make everything seem wrong."[24]

In the winter of 1863, desertions from the Army of the Potomac were running at 200 a day, week after week. Saloons in Washington and railroad cars headed north were crowded with both officers and men absent from their regiments without leave. Thousands of troops did not answer roll call in the muddy, snow-covered camps along the Rappahannock. In battle after battle, the Union side had outnumbered the Confederates yet left the field in defeat. Lincoln had fired four generals and was gambling on still another in Hooker. "Fighting Joe" was trying to stop desertion, lifting morale by regularizing furloughs and ordering that fresh bread and vegetables be served to his troops. He wanted replacements, and more, for the spring offensive. Voluntary enlistments had slumped. New blood was needed.

For months, Lincoln had resisted the recruitment of freed slaves as combat soldiers. Although the Second Confiscation Act in mid-1862 and then the Emancipation Proclamation approved enlisting African-Americans, those measures nominally restricted them to support and garrison duty. But rising pressure from Radical leaders like Charles Sumner, appeals by black spokesmen like Frederick Douglass and the generals' demand for more manpower changed the president's mind. When Vice President Hamlin introduced him to his son and a group of young white officers who had volunteered to command black soldiers in combat, Lincoln was moved to say, "I suppose the time has come."[25]

With Stanton's quiet approval, Union officers in New Orleans, on the South Carolina coast and in Kansas had already been enlisting blacks since late 1862. Now the president urged generals and military governors to go all-out to sign up freed slaves. On May 22, a War Department bureau was created to handle their organization, and the scattered black regiments already in being were redesignated U.S. Colored Troops. Lincoln forecast that "the bare sight of fifty thousand armed and drilled black soldiers on the banks of the Mississippi would end the rebellion at once." He was wrong about that, but eminently right in believing that black soldiers would play an important part in prosecuting the war. Within weeks, the First Regiment, U.S. Colored

Troops, was recruited in Washington and training on Analostan (Mason's, later Theodore Roosevelt) Island, which was close to the Virginia shore and linked by crude ferry with Georgetown. Later the regiment was sent to duty in occupied Norfolk and Portsmouth, Virginia.[26]

But black troops would not be enough, nor was the 1862 order for governors to fill out their state recruiting quotas by drafting men from militia units. On the day slaves were freed in the District of Columbia, the Confederate Congress had passed the first law in American history for conscription of troops. Northern opinion and the U.S. Congress took almost eleven months to follow suit. The Union draft law, passed over Democratic resistance on March 3, 1863, fell far short of the ideal of fairness. "Let the conscription be just as Heaven, and inexorable as death," one editorialist had said. "Let it spare neither high nor low, rich nor poor, but reach all alike." The Federal law exempted fewer categories of potential draftees than the one passed in Richmond; with specific exceptions, it covered males between the ages of twenty and thirty-five, plus single men up to forty-five. But it had an egregious flaw that mocked the concept of equality. Anyone could avoid service by hiring a substitute: the rich could buy their way out, but the poor must go. A system so rankly unjust was bound to cause resentment, and trouble was not long in coming.[27]

It took Noah Brooks a while to accept ways of business in the wartime capital that did not make sense to him. One such peculiarity moved him to write a dispatch that ran under the heading "Treason in Washington." He was offended by the fact that many of those who had defected to the South, such as Raphael Semmes, captain of the feared Confederate high seas raider *Alabama,* were still accumulating rent money for their real estate in Washington. But the government was in the process of confiscating a sizable list of those properties. In time, Brooks would cover weightier events that taught him the true meaning of treason.[28]

Somehow he perceived near the end of winter that "the political aspect just now is particularly bright and cheerful." He did not cite any major military success, and the minor improvements he listed would prove ephemeral. Yet he felt that for the first time in many months there was confidence in "the immediate crushing of the rebellion, the termination of the war." Even in Washington—"the veriest nursery of faithlessness and unbelief—even here, the public sentiment is wonderfully changed, and men who have croaked dolefully through the long fogs of winter are coming out of the clouds with a cheerful chirp. . . ."[29]

That such a high flight of fancy was inspired by anything more tangible than the approach of spring seems questionable, but it was true that the tone of the news from the Rappahannock had changed. Hooker had fed, drilled and reorganized the Army of the Potomac, lifting its morale out of the mud where Burnside had left it. He was inordinately proud of what he had done; watching his troops parade past, he said: "I have the finest army the sun ever shone on. I can march this army to New Orleans. My plans are perfect, and when I start to carry them out, may God have mercy on General Lee, for I will have none."[30]

On Saturday, April 4, Brooks went along when Lincoln, his wife and son Tad boarded the steamer *Carrie Martin* and headed down the Potomac to visit the army. Wet, swirling snow forced the vessel to put into a cove overnight, and it reached Aquia Creek on Easter morning. From that jammed supply port, they rode a flag-bedecked railcar to Falmouth Station. In the next five days, the president reviewed the army in four grand parades, visited tent hospitals, and went down by the Rappahannock close enough to see Rebels wave from the other side. When he conferred with Hooker about his plan to take the offensive, the general kept telling what he would do "after we have taken Richmond." Lincoln was glad to hear positive talk after Burnside's confessions of inadequacy, but he was uneasy at so much of it. He told Brooks later, "That is the most depressing thing about Hooker. It seems to me that he is overconfident."[31]

Back in Washington, Brooks and the city were disgusted at the exposure of one "Joliffe, a shyster of the police courts," who had found a profitable way to defraud the relatives of dead soldiers. This swindler bought lists of the deceased from hospital clerks for $1 a name and filled in counterfeit forms with their particulars. He mailed these to the bereaved families, offering for a fee to forward the bodies of their loved ones. On being paid, sometimes he simply sent nothing, other times he sent the illegally acquired body of some other soldier. He was caught by Detective Baker after sending home a red-haired body in place of a black-haired soldier. "I have heard of the height of meanness being that of stealing the coppers from the dead mother's eyes," Brooks wrote, "but an offender guilty of that crime would be a worthy member of society compared with this speculator in sacred affections and dead men's bones—the maw worm, Joliffe."

The correspondent, still getting used to the outrages that flour-ished alongside the noble sacrifices of war, was honestly dismayed. But in that dispatch as in others he filed in late April, he was filling space, marking time. He told his California readers about a new presi-dential portrait, about a slice of the Prince of Wales's wedding cake sent through diplomatic channels to Mrs. Lincoln, about the scientific marvels at the Naval Observatory. (Citizens checked their timepieces when the observatory dropped a black ball from atop a pole each day at precisely noon.) Brooks reported these sidelights while "public expectation [was] feverish with anxiety" waiting for news that Hooker had attacked the Confederates. He sneered at a writer for the *New York Tribune,* "determined to relieve the bursting ignorance of the waiting public even at the expense of the truth," who reported that the Union army had successfully flanked Lee at Fredericksburg. But that was not wholly imaginary, it was just premature. Hooker had sent a major cav-alry expedition to cross higher up the Rappahannock, but it was frus-trated by a rainstorm and came back unsuccessful.[32]

The real thing did not begin until April 27, when Hooker marched most of his army toward Kelly's Ford north of Fredericksburg. Then, before dawn on the twenty-ninth, he sent infantry in pontoon boats against the Rebel positions that had repulsed Burnside in December. This direct crossing at Fredericksburg was secondary, meant to dis-tract Lee from the massive upriver swing onto his flank—and that much of the battle plan worked as perfectly as any maneuver in the entire war. On April 30, Hooker arrived with 70,000 men at Chancel-lorsville, a crossroads west of Fredericksburg. There he announced that the past three days' operations had "determined that our enemy must ingloriously fly, or come out from behind his defenses and give us battle on our own ground, where certain destruction awaits him."[33]

But Hooker did not fully understand either his enemy or himself. Lee, when he realized what had happened, sent Stonewall Jackson to confront the major Union force—and Hooker, when he realized that he had lost the element of surprise, pulled back onto the defensive rather than continue his advance. Lee then boldly split his much smaller army three ways. Leaving one division behind Fredericksburg, he sent Jackson on a sweeping march around Hooker's west flank while he kept the Federals busy on the opposite side. On May 2, Jack-son's corps roared out of the Wilderness to smash the Union flank. That evening Jackson, scouting ahead in the darkness, was acciden-tally shot by his own men; he would die eight days later. Stuart took over from him, and together with Lee drove the Federals back across the river. "Fighting Joe" Hooker had lost his nerve when he realized that at last he was face-to-face with the vaunted Lee, and in full command of the army without anyone above to blame if things went wrong. Chancellorsville was the most spectacular victory of Lee's career, and the bloodiest battle of the war to date—some 17,287 Union casualties versus 12,826 for the Confederates.

The first word of what had happened arrived in Washington by telegram at the War Department near midafternoon on May 6. Brooks and another presidential friend, Dr. Anson G. Henry, were at the White House when Lincoln got the news.

"Had a thunderbolt fallen upon the President he could not have been more overwhelmed," Brooks wrote. "One newly risen from the dead could not have looked more ghostlike.... Clasping his hands behind his back, he walked up and down the room, saying, 'My God! My God! What will the country say? What will the country say?' "

Within the hour, Lincoln and Halleck departed by special steamer from the Navy Yard to see Hooker. By evening, wild rumors spread through downtown. McClellanites and secessionists rejoiced. To escape Stanton's tight censorship of the local telegraph, out-of-town journalists took the train to file their stories from Baltimore or Philadelphia.[34]

Walt Whitman was at the foot of Sixth Street, trying to help, when casualties began coming in that night. Two boatloads of wounded were dimly visible by torchlight, men lying helpless in the rain on the wharf and nearby streets. Some were on soaking blankets and quilts, their wounds bound by bloody rags. Only a few attendants were there, and a few volunteers. "The wounded are getting to be common," wrote Whitman; "people grow callous." Ambulances came, and there were groans and occasional screams of pain as men were lifted aboard to go to hospitals. More and still more casualties were expected— "Quite often they arrive at the rate of 1,000 a day." Whitman visited and comforted them at Armory Square, Patent Office, Judiciary Square and Campbell hospitals, and his capacious heart was moved by every one. He was overwhelmed by love and pity, even for a column of Confederate prisoners herded along the Avenue: "Poor fellows, many of them mere lads—it brought the tears, they seemed our own flesh and blood...."[35]

CHAPTER FIFTEEN

I Will Now Take the Music

Feverish patients waking at night in the Patent Office must have wondered whether they were in heaven or in hell, lying among weird weapons and inexplicable machines that seemed to hang above them, dancing in reflected gaslight. Of all the Washington churches, colleges, hotels and public spaces commandeered by the government, no other place for a hospital was so otherworldly. Whitman found it "strange, solemn, and with all its features of suffering and death, a sort of fascinating sight.... crowded with models in miniature of every kind of utensil, machine or invention it ever entered into the mind of man to conceive.... a curious scene, especially at night when lit up. The glass cases, the beds, the forms lying there, the gallery above... the suffering, and the fortitude...."[1]

But in full light, the inventors' contraptions were less remarkable than the sight of an assertive five-foot-tall figure wearing trousers partly covered by a long coat, and sometimes a "girlish-looking straw hat, decked off with an ostrich feather." This was Dr. Mary Edwards Walker, who had been campaigning for women's right to wear sensible clothes for half her thirty-two years and now was asserting her right as a woman physician to help heal ailing soldiers. Although she had earned her certificate from Syracuse Medical College, her presence at the Patent Office hospital was opposed by male surgeons, the War Department and Dorothea Dix, who were not yet persuaded that a woman should or could play such a role. Dr. J. N. Green, in charge of the hospital, put her to work as his administrative assistant, but Surgeon General Clement A. Finley would not accept her as an official army surgeon. Nevertheless, Walker stayed as a volunteer, and was disgusted by Dix's "sham modesty" when the visiting director of nurses coldly looked away from exposed patients rather than pulling up their blankets.[2]

Walker persevered, and interfered, by mounting a quiet campaign against what she considered unnecessary amputations. Because infection and often gangrene were taken for granted with severe gunshot wounds, amputation was a routine procedure, and piles of severed limbs were common sights outside aid stations near the front. The hospitals had no separate operating rooms; surgery was performed there in the ward, among other patients. Nor were there X-rays; doctors trying to locate a bullet manipulated a slender, unsterilized silver probe, thus pushing more bacteria deep into the wound. Sponges used to clean away blood and pus were simply washed with water before being used again. Surgeon W. W. Keen recalled that "in our ignorance of bacteriology we did not know that they harbored multitudes of germs which infected every wound in which they were used." Another army doctor wrote that for abdominal wounds the standard treatment was "expectancy with folded hands." Under such conditions, it was not hard for Walker to persuade some Patent Office patients to refuse to submit to amputation—a breach of medical manners that saved some limbs but may have cost some lives.[3]

Outside the hospital, Walker organized the Women's Relief Association, eventually using her own house to care for war wives and children left destitute on the streets of the capital. She also kept writing and lecturing to liberate her sex from the dirt-sweeping skirts and other sartorial encumbrances that most women thought obligatory in polite society. But she did not give up her effort to become a commissioned army surgeon, although the president himself once turned her down. Conceivably he had heard of her writing in *Sibyl*, a women's magazine, that "no man is capable of fathoming a woman's mind. A woman reasons by telegraph, and his stage-coach reasoning cannot keep pace with hers." As if to prove herself deserving, Walker decided to go to the front and take her chances as soldiers did.*[4]

*In late 1863, Walker went to Tennessee, where she tended casualties of the battle of Chickamauga and was named to replace a deceased regimental surgeon but rejected by the army's medical staff. Crossing the lines to care for soldiers and needy civilians, she was captured and sent to Richmond's Castle Thunder Prison. After four months, she was exchanged in time to campaign for Lincoln's reelection. After the war, President Andrew Johnson awarded her the Medal of Honor. It was rescinded in 1917, along with many other medals awarded for Civil War service. Defiantly, she continued to wear it until her death two years later. (Charles McCool Snyder, *Dr. Mary Walker*, pp. 41–54)

Walker was not present on a particular day when Mr. and Mrs. Lincoln came to the Patent Office to thank and comfort wounded soldiers. The Lincolns found themselves following a well-dressed woman who was passing out religious tracts to patients. A badly injured soldier picked up the pamphlet she had left, took a look and chuckled aloud. The president gently admonished him; after all, the lady meant well. "Well, Mr. President, how can I help laughing a little bit?" asked the soldier. "She has given me a tract on *The Sin of Dancing,* and both my legs are shot off."[5]

Lincoln had been interested in the Patent Office since he was a congressman. Once, traveling between Washington and Illinois, he had been on a steamboat that ran aground on river shoals. Back in Illinois, he whittled out a model of an idea that had occurred to him as a youth, when he worked on a boat plying the Ohio and Mississippi rivers to New Orleans. His invention was a vessel with bellows low on each side of the hull, to be inflated when needed to float the craft over sandbars. He brought the model to Washington and in 1849 got himself Patent No. 6469, for "Buoying Vessels Over Shoals." The full-scale boat was never built, for the weight of the apparatus would probably have made it more rather than less likely to run aground. But the model was still in the Patent Office in 1861, stored away out of sight until the new president came to town, when it was brought forth on public display.[6]

The great Greek Revival building that fills two blocks between Seventh and Ninth, F and G streets has since become the National Portrait Gallery and the Museum of American Art. In Lincoln's time it was truly "the nation's curiosity shop," a combination of Patent Office, historical museum, national archive, temporary hospital and more. Besides the mechanical marvels in more than half a mile of glass cases on the third floor, there were uniforms, furniture, china, camp equipment, swords, canes and bric-a-brac of the Washington family, taken from the Lee mansion at Arlington.* There were Japanese imperial costumes and body armor, a Ben Franklin printing press, a 450-square-foot carpet given to Martin Van Buren by the imam of Muscat, and there were state papers—treaties with Turkey, Persia and Russia.

*When Mary Custis Lee left Arlington, she locked most of the Washington memorabilia in the mansion's cellar. Union soldiers started to loot the building but were halted by Selina Gray, the slave woman whom Mrs. Lee had left in charge. General McDowell then had the artifacts removed to the Patent Office for safekeeping. (Karen Byrne, "The Remarkable Legacy of Selina Gray" [Cultural Resource Management, U.S. Department of the Interior, no. 4, 1998])

There was also the Agriculture Department, officially created in 1862, still functioning where the farm commissioner had sat before, still dispensing seeds, planning to add its own museum of birds, beasts and insects of concern to the farmer. Wandering freely through this hodge-podge were off-duty soldiers fascinated by the ingenuity of patent-seekers, lawyers tracking applications, relatives looking for wounded loved ones, doctors and nurses trying vainly to ward off infectious diseases and the general public.[7]

The war caught the Patent Office still unfinished, just as it had interrupted other grand structures that would eventually define the capital for generations to come. George Augustus Sala, writing for the *London Telegraph,* conceded that the Post Office, Patent Office and Treasury buildings were "magnificent in proportions and design," but the city was "not quite begun yet. We are still at the soup and fish, and have not got to the first entrée. Never was there so interminable an overture." Washington resembled "an eel in a sand-basket, delicious when fried or stewed, but repulsive to the sight before it is skinned and cooked." Someday it would be "uproariously splendid," but not yet—"It is in the District of Columbia and the State of the Future."[8]

Toward the west end of the Mall, the stub of the Washington Monument stood as it had since 1855, when seven years' work was stopped by a lack of funds and a dispute over its records. The original plan for an elaborate pavilion about its base, immortalizing lesser heroes of the republic, had been abandoned for economic rather than esthetic reasons. Public adulation of the father of his country had refocused on the equestrian statue dedicated on his birthday in 1860, in Washington Circle west of the White House. Meanwhile the monument was roofed with wood, and stone slabs to ornament its interior walls waited within a collection of temporary sheds.

An unidentified soldier, writing for the *Jewish Messenger* of New York, was fascinated by the origins and artistry of these slabs, gifts to the young nation from the Emperor of China, the King of Greece, the Sultan of Turkey, the Governor and Commune of the Island of Poras and Nancy, the Grand Sire of Tuscarora Tribe No. 5, the Odd Fellows and various other foreign potentates and domestic fraternities, fire companies, temperance societies, Sunday school classes, dramatic clubs and daguerreotypists. He noted the irony of the inscriptions on stones sent by Louisiana and Tennessee, praising the sanctity of the Federal Union. On some of the acreage around the monument, troops drilled and ordnance officers, occasionally accompanied by the president, tested small arms. On what is now the Ellipse, thousands of army cattle grazed, and the stench of a slaughterhouse polluted the air.[9]

If the abbreviated monument and its surroundings spoke of frustration and wartime degradation, the mood had lifted at the other end of the Mall, beyond the Smithsonian, Armory Square Hospital, the gas works and the Botanical Garden. Thomas Walter, so long unhappy at the bureaucratic interference that had delayed his work on the Capitol, was actually optimistic for a while. He had begun the year in depression; returning to the E Street Baptist Church when the casualties departed, he found that "the hospital odor was so horrid" that he would not return soon—"it will require years to get entirely clear of the scent." But by March, he had resumed his place teaching Bible class there, and was saying privately that he intended to erect the statue of Freedom atop the Capitol dome on July 4. The rest of his team was less committed, however; on April 3, he wrote to Charles Fowler, of the Brooklyn firm Janes, Fowler, Kirtland & Company, which was providing the cast iron of the dome for 7 cents a pound installed. "The season is wearing away," said Walter, "things are moving very very very slowly—where is that great gang of men that we were to have on the ceiling 'right away'?" He suggested that Fowler, living in luxury in New York, was forgetting "us poor fellows here, who are daily struggling to get ready to put Freedom above every thing else, where we think it ought to be—*and where I wish it was.* Remember, it *must* go there on the 4th of July, and that is but 13 weeks off." A week later, the dome was fifty-two feet short of its peak, and he was still short of ironworkers. By April 20, Walter realized that "our 4th of July frolic is no go," and his outlook plunged again. But on Independence Day, there would be other reasons to celebrate.[10]

Night and day, alone as often as not, Lincoln walked back and forth between the White House and the War Department telegraph office, hoping to read bulletins of progress. Whenever anything encouraging came in, it was soon followed by the opposite. Too often, the prevailing condition was as Whitelaw Reid described it in a Washington dispatch to the *Cincinnati Gazette.* Beneath the heading of "The Situation on the Mississippi," it said in toto: "Nobody here understands the situation on the Mississippi." Then something understandable happened. In mid-May, General Grant pushed across the Big Black River and moved on Vicksburg, key to control of the Mississippi. But two head-on Federal assaults there in the following week were thrown back, and the action settled into a siege. Black troops joined a Union attack on Port Hudson, farther down the Mississippi, with the same result.[11]

Once when the president drooped back from the telegraph office, he found Elizabeth Keckley fitting Mrs. Lincoln for a dress, and Mary asked, "Any news?"

"Yes, plenty of news," he said, "but no good news. It is dark, dark everywhere."

Keckley wrote that he brought down his Bible then and read silently. After about fifteen minutes, his "dejected look was gone, and the countenance was lighted up with new resolution and hope." She got a look at the open Bible, and saw that he had been reading the book of Job: "Gird up thy loins now like a man: I will demand of thee, and declare thou unto me."[12]

Some of Keckley's anecdotes seem too convenient, fit too neatly into her story, but they accurately reflect life in the Lincoln household. According to Mary Lincoln, the president was "not a technical Christian"; he did not accept the dogma and ritual of organized religion. He went occasionally with Mary to the New York Avenue Presbyterian Church and less often to others in the capital. But increasingly he turned to the Bible, for solace and assurance as well as the language that so strongly influenced his own prose. He was aging himself rapidly, worrying over decisions great and small, only to see events unfold as if someone higher were in charge. Trying to explain the progress of his thinking on abolition, he would write that "I claim not to have controlled events, but confess plainly that events have controlled me." Yet John Hay thought it would be "absurd" to describe Lincoln's humility before events as modesty. It was his "intellectual arrogance and unconscious assumption of superiority" that proud men like Chase and Sumner could never forgive, Hay wrote. Lincoln believed that no man could have predicted the course of the war: "God alone can claim it." In this, his outlook resembled that of the more demonstratively devout Robert E. Lee, who also had a fully developed ego but whose reports of Confederate victory or defeat often concluded that God's will had been done.[13]

Mary Lincoln could not be so accepting of fate; the early death of two sons had grieved her so long and deeply that she felt she was somehow picked out for special travails. After Willie died, the consolations of churchmen did not ease her suffering. She listened to the

staunchly religious nurse Rebecca Pomroy, who had become an intimate friend. But months later she still blamed herself for Willie's
death, believing she was punished for hosting frivolous entertainment
when he lay critically ill. She canceled the Marine Band's bright Saturday afternoon concerts on the White House lawn. For more than a
year, she dressed in black mourning.[14]

In her desperation, Mary reached beyond friends and religion.
Keckley encouraged her, telling her how, after her own son died in
battle, she had communicated with his spirit through a medium who
could reach across the boundary of life. This was not a superstition
restricted to slaves and servants; prominent Boston intellectuals, European royalty, men as hardheaded as Dan Sickles and Gideon Welles
had sought to contact the dear departed in séances presided over by
mediums who claimed the magic touch. Spiritualism was an international fad of the mid-nineteenth century, its practitioners holding forth
in places as unexotic as Mary's hometown of Lexington, Kentucky,
and now in the White House itself.[15]

The president's wife abandoned all skepticism, consulting and
believing in the famous medium Nettie Colburn and a reputedly gifted
Georgetown couple named Laurie. Some of these séances in darkened
rooms allegedly put her in touch with Willie; others failed to reach
him but disclosed that all the president's cabinet members were disloyal, or that General Lee was about to execute some new strategic
coup. Mary was also fascinated by a suave faker who called himself
Lord Colchester, pretending to be the illegimate son of an English
noble. He interpreted mysterious scrapes and taps in the darkness to
be messages from beyond, so impressing Mary that she invited him to
perform his wonders for her at the Soldiers' Home and then in the
White House. She asked Noah Brooks to be there, but he declined.

The curious Brooks did, however, attend a Colchester séance at
the home of another Washington believer. In the midst of the
medium's hocus-pocus, the correspondent reached into the darkness
and grabbed a hand that was thumping a bell on a drumhead. He
shouted, "Strike a light!" but before someone could, he was whacked
on the head with the drum. When at last a friend struck a match,
Brooks was revealed with a bloody face, clutching the arm of Colchester. In the excitement, the magician slipped away, and the
unhappy host announced that he was so insulted he would not reap-
pear. Soon afterward, Brooks was surprised to be summoned by Mary
Lincoln. She showed him a note from Colchester asking her to get

him a War Department pass and hinting at blackmail if she did not. They arranged for the villain to come to the mansion, where Brooks confronted him as "a swindler and a humbug." He ordered him to get out of the White House and the city at once, warning that if he was still present the next day, he would be sent to Old Capitol Prison. Colchester left town as advised. Yet, though one charlatan was exposed, the needy Mrs. Lincoln clung to her belief in communication with the hereafter. She was sure that she reached her dead sons Willie and Eddie, and not only through spiritualists: In her mind, they appeared to her at night without the help of experts. For years after their departure, she still thought so.[16]

Mary's vulnerable psyche was under intense strain during the mid-war years, some of it because of her Confederate relatives. Her burden as White House hostess and grieving mother was heavier because of gossip that she was disloyal, even a Rebel spy. Her family, the Todds of Kentucky, was split down the middle by the war. Her brother, George Rogers Clark Todd, was a surgeon in a Confederate hospital. One of her half brothers had been killed fighting for the South, and two more would die that way within months. Her sister's husband, Confederate Brigadier General Benjamin H. Helm, would be killed in September at Chattanooga. Deeply committed as she was to her husband and his cause, there was no way she could deny her family, or disprove the baseless rumors that she was helping the enemy.[17]

In her communications with the beyond, Mary sometimes had premonitions of some greater tragedy to come. She worried out loud about her husband's movements in a city still infested with Confederate sympathizers. The president, in the way of a seasoned soldier, seemed to shrug off questions about his own personal safety. When war started, there were no guards around the White House. Though he often received crackpot threats in the mail, he ignored them. He did not like the cavalry detachment that rode with him to and from the Soldiers' Home because it made such a clatter. Only in 1863 did a select Ohio company called the Union Light Guard take over security, escorting him to the country and posting sentries at the White House gates, while a company of Pennsylvania infantry guarded the south side of the mansion. But at least outwardly, Lincoln seemed fatalistic about the possibility that anyone might attack him.[18]

As he headed to the War Department yet again, Mary said, "Father, you should not go out alone. You know you are surrounded by danger."

"All imagination," he said. "What does anyone want to harm me for? Don't worry about me, mother, as if I were a little child, for no one is going to molest me."[19]

Conspicuous among the young men about Washington who were not fighting and suffering in the army was the acrobatically fit, devilishly handsome twenty-four-year-old actor John Wilkes Booth, who opened on April 11 at Grover's Theater, playing *Richard III.* Son of the great tragedian Junius Brutus Booth and professional rival of his older brother Edwin, he was billed as "The Pride of the American People— A Star of the First Magnitude." Young Booth was proudly conscious that he had been named for John Wilkes, an eighteenth-century English radical who was in constant trouble for his defiance of tyranny. His theatrical career had taken him to all the nation's major cities, from Boston to New Orleans; he was a particular favorite in Baltimore, near his homeplace in Harford County, Maryland, and in prewar Richmond. Now Booth had decided to stop traveling and settle in Washington, where the population of high-rolling transients and fun-starved soldiers filled theaters every night.

One of the capital's most devoted playgoers was the president of the United States. In the first weeks of 1863, he had gone to see, among other theatrical outings, E. L. Davenport in *Hamlet* and the blackface minstrel and Irish comedian Barney Williams at Grover's, half a block from Willard's Hotel, and James H. Hackett in *Henry IV* at the Washington Theatre, at Eleventh and C streets. On the evening when Booth opened at Grover's, Lincoln was watching Mrs. John Wood in *Pocahontas* at the Washington Theatre. He thus missed the dramatic debut of the season: The papers reviewed Booth's performance with near ecstasy. The dashing actor's "youth, originality, and superior genius have not only made him popular but established him in the hearts of Washington people as a great favorite," said the *National Republican.*[20]

If that reviewer had known what Booth was thinking offstage, he could hardly have found words strong enough to condemn him. In 1859, Booth had donned the uniform of the famed Richmond Grays militia company long enough to go to Harpers Ferry and witness the hanging of the insurrectionist John Brown. When Lincoln was elected, Booth had been in Montgomery, Alabama, surrounded by militant secessionists damning the "gorilla" from Illinois. In the days after South

Carolina seceded, he was in Philadelphia, and apparently while there he wrote a long, histrionic speech with heavy Shakespearean overtones, for what purpose is not clear. "I will not fight for disunion," he wrote. "But I will fight with all my heart and soul, even if theres not a man to back me, for equal rights and justice to the South." As if he were delivering the speech in public, with his temper rising at every line, he wrote that "the fire now raging in the nations heart. . . . is a fire lighted and fanned by Northern fanaticism. A fire which naught but blood & justice can extinguish." Later, Booth was upset by the way Lincoln clamped martial law on Maryland to hold it in the Union. With each battle, each month of the war, the fire burned hotter inside him.[21]

Lincoln surely went out to the theater more often than any other president. Facing the nation's most desperate trial, he wisely tried to divert himself for a few hours whenever he could. Shakespeare was his favorite, but he could be wheedled into accompanying Mary to performances he would not have bothered with on his own. It is not certain when he first saw John Wilkes Booth on stage in Washington, but later in 1863, he and Mrs. Lincoln went with Nicolay, Hay and a lady friend to Ford's Theater, on Tenth Street, to watch him as the leading villain in *The Marble Heart*. Twice, as Booth uttered threatening lines, he seemed to gesture toward the presidential box. When he did this a third time, the lady friend said to Lincoln, "He looks as if he meant that for you."

"Well," said the president, "he does look pretty sharp at me, doesn't he?"[22]

In the weeks after Chancellorsville, General Lee kept Lincoln, Stanton, Halleck, Hooker and all their lieutenants guessing what he might do after his smashing victory along the Rappahannock. The only certainty was that he would do something, take the initiative, despite the fact that he had lost his strong right arm in Jackson, plus a greater proportion of his army than the defeated Hooker. In the defenses of Washington, there was a renewed bustle of digging and artillery practice. Across the Potomac around Alexandria, troops were blocking every road with brush and barriers, and now and then residents heard of a civilian accidentally killed by gunners drilling. Cameron, the vacated Alexandria home of Samuel Cooper, the Confederate army's senior general, was demolished to make way for yet another fort on the hills above the town.

The troops manning the ring of forts about Washington were mostly heavy artillerymen, living comfortably by comparison with infantry in the field. They did not have to march and get shot at and sleep in the rain, but neither did they loaf their days away; one described his regiment's pride at the end of a year constructing "miles of abatis, intrenchments, breast works of all kinds, forts, bastions, block houses, stockades, chevaux De Frize, bridges, log huts, corduroy roads, streets, walks, Demilunes, mortelloes ... under the greatest engineers of the country." But when the war was being fought fifty or a hundred miles distant and off-duty temptations were so close in Alexandria and Washington, the discipline of those outfits sometimes slipped.[23]

In the Second Connecticut Heavy Artillery, things began to change the moment Lieutenant Colonel Elisha Kellogg took command. Kellogg was a bronzed veteran of the Peninsula campaign, a strapping ex-sailor who reputedly had knocked down a man in a foreign port for insulting the American flag. When he arrived, some of the artillerymen were drilling as casually as usual. Suddenly he shouted "like a tiger" at a soldier named Burns: "Take that pipe out of your mouth, Sir, and attend to your drill!" In his fright, Burns threw the pipe so far away he never found it.[24]

Kellogg's drive to bring the Heavies into shape was chronicled by Sergeant Michael Kelly, an Irish immigrant who had helped recruit troops for the regiment in Connecticut. In his diary, Kelly told how the wives of some men he approached drove him away, once with a big meat knife, once with a broom; two other women splashed his face with cow manure and "barnyard stuff." He had to take verbal abuse from family defenders who called recruiters "Lincoln's hirelings," "black republicans" and "nigerheads."[25]

Sergeant Kelly was impressed by the way his colonel dealt with soldiers caught drunk. By Kellogg's order, about a hundred empty bottles were tied about one offender's body and he was forced to keep marching back and forth before his comrades with bottles ringing. Other soldiers who had gone to town without passes were sentenced to march with heavy rails on their shoulders. When a chronic troublemaker named Michael Curley came back to the fort drunk, his captain ordered him spread-eagled on a cannon wheel, his arms and legs tethered tight, while he was splashed with six buckets of water and left wet for an hour, plagued by biting flies. Curley was a slow learner; for his next offense, he was spread facedown on the ground, tied "so tight until you would hear the bones crack almost," soaked for two hours, then locked in the guardhouse on bread and water for two weeks. Soldiers were arrested for crimes as minor as laughing in ranks or scratching their head on parade. Kellogg was tough on his company commanders, too; when they made a mistake in drill, he called one captain an old woman, another a turkey-cock, and told another he could keep drilling his company "from hell to breakfast."[26]

While Michael Curley seems to have borne a grudge against Kellogg, most of the colonel's troops came to admire him. A squad formed a "bums' club" and took up a collection to buy him a rocking chair and a box of good cigars. Kelly got away with knocking the colonel's hat off in a good-natured snowball fight. And eleven months after Kellogg's arrival, the sergeant wrote: "Everything is growing easier and better. It is astonishing what a difference when each one, officer to private, does his duty.... Colonel Kellogg leave[s] no stone unturned to raise the Regt. to a high degree of discipline." The Heavies would show their discipline to the Rebels a year later at a hellhole called Cold Harbor,* but in the meantime they still went through endlessly repeated artillery drill, interspersed with occasional firing to adjust the targeting of their cannon.[27]

On Wilton Hill beyond Alexandria, Anne Frobel had never gotten used to hearing the boom of artillery without warning. There had been so much of it lately that she was nervous as she walked to a neighbor's home on the afternoon of June 8 to get some strawberries. On arrival, she was "startled by a most violent thundering explosion, followed by another, in quick succession, the earth shook and trembled, and the old house we were in seemed to move." A shell burst close by, and blue smoke streamed past. Frobel was afraid the house was falling. She ran toward the door, shouting and pushing others to leave. Outside, she looked toward Fort Lyon, half a mile south of Hunting Creek, at the moment it "went up with a tremendous shock.... my idea of a large volcano indeed it looked just like the pictures of Vesuvius during an eruption.... Every thing flew up into the air, an immense column of smoke and dust burst up from the center and seemed to stand still for a moment, and the sun reflected through

---

*The Second Connecticut Heavy Artillery and many other units from the defenses of Washington were converted to infantry duty in U. S. Grant's 1864 Overland campaign from the Wilderness to the James River. In the regiment's first serious combat, Colonel Kellogg was killed and his command ripped to pieces as they charged Confederate lines at Cold Harbor.

it made it look like flames." Logs, plants, iron, stones and dirt came rattling down, and then there was silence—"the stillness of death seemed there."[28]

Only after minutes went by did soldiers from a nearby camp venture carefully into the ruins of Fort Lyon. For days, they retrieved remnants of the twenty-eight men who died because of sloppy handling of ammunition stored in the "bombproof" fort. Lincoln and Stanton came to inspect the ruins on June 10, and the president made clear his impatience with the carelessness that had cost soldiers' lives. But the president and secretary of war could not stay long at the scene of such a minor tragedy. They had a more urgent, larger concern: Lee was on the move.

From his lines near Fredericksburg, Lee was marching his army west and north toward Culpeper. Screened by Jeb Stuart's cavalry, he was heading in the direction of the Shenandoah Valley, his favorite route into Maryland. On the broad fields along the Rappahannock, Stuart halted to put on an impressive review of his regiments, still unmatched by Union horsemen in any major action. But since a resounding clash at Kelly's Ford on St. Patrick's Day, Hooker's reorganized cavalry brigades had been itching for a full-scale test. Before dawn on June 9, they got it, surprising Stuart at Brandy Station and charging back and forth across the fields. When the day was over, the Federals had suffered almost twice as many casualties as the Rebels and withdrawn across the Rappahannock. But in the nation's biggest cavalry battle ever, the Yankee riders had shown they could stand up to Stuart's cocky troopers in head-on combat. The lesson would be crucial in the days ahead.

Now Hooker knew that Lee was on the march, but he and Lincoln disagreed on what to do about it. The general wanted to cross the Rappahannock and attack Lee's rear guard at Fredericksburg, but Lincoln warned against it: "I would not take any risk of being entangled upon the river like an ox jumped half over a fence, and liable to be torn by dogs front and rear, without a fair chance to gore one way or kick the other," he wrote. As Lee proceeded, Hooker next proposed that when the Rebels went north he should march south and take Richmond. Lincoln pointed out that Lee's army, not Richmond, was his main objective. Meanwhile the Confederates crossed the Potomac again, and Washington was all aflutter again.[29]

One day that spring, a fifteen-year-old Pennsylvanian named Brainard Warner had arrived in Washington alone, wondering how he was going to support himself. With the self-confidence of a boy who would later become one of the capital's leading bankers and real estate developers, he approached a respectable-looking man outside the Patent Office and asked if he knew where he could find a job. The man said no, but the boy would not be brushed away. He spotted the church newspaper the man was carrying, the *New York Observer,* and told him his father had subscribed to that paper for over twenty years.

"Your father's a Presbyterian?" asked the man.

"Yes," said the boy.

"Do you intend to follow the training you got at home?"

"Yes."

"Give me your name and address."

Twelve days later, young Warner was fifth clerk at Judiciary Square Hospital, earning $18 a month plus $3 for clothes. On his own in the capital, he was diligent in writing to his parents near Mifflintown. He marveled at the huge trains of supplies en route to the army, but based on the casualties he was seeing and conversations with the wounded, he doubted that unlimited matériel could end the war. That will take help from foreign troops, he wrote. "The rebels fight a good deal like Indians, I am told ... when they charge they come on with such a terrible yell, so loud, so long, so deep, that it requires a man of strong nerve to stand up to them." A visit from three "fine noble looking" Confederate officers looking for wounded Rebels reinforced this feeling. "I have some doubt about us conquering in this war," said Brainard. "The rebels, although they are dirty and ragged, have spirit enough to turn a river from its course."

As Lee moved on to Pennsylvania, Stuart was ranging east of the Confederates' main body, swiping at Fairfax Court House before crossing the Potomac and capturing 125 Union supply wagons on the road to Rockville. Excitement swept seemingly unprotected Washington. But Thomas Walter, busy at the Capitol, was scornful: "A good deal of noise is being made about the invasion of Penna., but I wonder if there is much in it," he wrote. "A few tatterdemalions are no doubt about Chambersburg stealing sheep &c, and our military authorities ought to be ashamed ever again to look in the glass, if they let them slip. The rascals ought to be caught and hired out to Barnum." Rumor said the president, who better understood the situation, had a boat waiting at the Navy Yard, ready to make an escape downriver. An officer came to enroll male nurses for duty with the civilian guards posted at vital points in the capital. Young Warner and the hospital's baggage master went outside and tried some shots with an eighteen-inch Colt revolver. "I could not hold one out straight with one hand," the boy admitted. "However, as the rebels are in Pennsylvania, I thought I had better practice a little."[30]

Lincoln was upbeat, believing that Lee's long line of communications gave Hooker a live chance to cut off and defeat the Confederate army. But Hooker balked at following orders. His repeated disagreements with Lincoln, combined with his refusal to respect the president's intermediary, General-in-Chief Halleck, finally meant he had to go. As the Union army moved north behind Lee, battle could come at any time. Lee's widely scattered divisions reached east of York, west of Chambersburg and as far north as Carlisle. Facing this challenging situation, on June 28, Lincoln ordered Major General George G. Meade to take command in Hooker's place. The message reached the glum, short-tempered Meade in camp near Frederick. He was neither excited nor reluctant; he told the courier that Major General John Reynolds would have been a better choice, but he would follow orders. Halleck's message reminded Meade that while moving against Lee, he was still to cover Washington and Baltimore. Three days later, elements of the two armies bumped into each other at the farm town of Gettysburg, seat of Franklin County, Pennsylvania.

On the morning of the Fourth of July, young Brainard Warner and friends got up at five o'clock and went out to fire sixty rounds of blank cartridges they had collected to herald the holiday. Outside the hospital wards, all Washington seemed determined to celebrate, regardless of events, as if cheers and music could lift the Union to victory. Reports from General Meade about the first two days of fighting at Gettysburg had been optimistic, but neither Warner nor the rest of the revelers up at dawn knew what had happened since. Organizers of the day proceeded with plans for the Marine Band to lead a parade up the Avenue, followed by various Masons, Odd Fellows, temperance societies, four regiments from the surrounding forts, and band after band. Not until all this holiday-making was under way did word spread that there was something tangible, indeed momentous, to celebrate.[31]

Lincoln, unable to sleep, had been at the telegraph office at midnight, hoping for news from Gettysburg. It came first not in a dispatch from Meade to the War Department, but in a personal telegram to Gideon Welles from a journalist friend named Byington. The operator showed the wire to the president. "Who is Byington?" asked Lincoln. "Ask the secretary of the Navy," said the operator. Welles told Lincoln that Byington, at the front for the *New York Tribune,* was reliable. But his message was vague, saying only that a great battle was fought and the Union army was winning, but it was not over. Hours later, Meade's first report still did not claim victory. About ten o'clock, the news was more conclusive: Lee had been defeated and apparently was retreating.[32]

From the War Department, Lincoln issued a statement announcing the "great success" and crediting God as much as the army. "On this day," he wrote, "He whose will, not ours, should ever be done, [should] be everywhere remembered and reverenced with profound gratitude." But even victory at Gettysburg was not enough to ease the concern that kept him hovering about the telegraph office. As far as he knew when he issued that statement, the struggle for Vicksburg and control of the Mississippi was unresolved. He had to wait three more days for news from Grant that Confederate general John C. Pemberton had surrendered his sick and hungry 29,000-man garrison on July 4.[33]

When word came, Washington rejoiced. Lee defeated! Vicksburg captured! Back-to-back, the most important Union victories of the war so far! Cannon at the Navy Yard fired a hundred-gun salute. Citizens crowded outside the White House to serenade the president. In welcoming them, Lincoln again thanked Almighty God before noting how many great events had marked American history on Independence Days past. He said that on this Fourth, "the cohorts of those who opposed the Declaration that all men are created equal turned tail and ran. Gentlemen, this is a glorious theme, and the occasion for a speech, but I am not prepared to make one worthy of the occasion." He praised the officers and men who had fought with such determination, but would not name any because he might forget one. "Having said this much, I will now take the music."[34]

Others could not restrain themselves, and let go the long-held pressure that built up waiting for success. B. B. French put his joy in writing: "Richmond must soon go, and then poor Jeff will be driven to his wits end. My guess is that the Rebs will soon find themselves a set of poor miserable wretches, and they will cry to come back into our glorious Union! I see national glory in the future such as the past has never seen. Slavery forever abolished! The South populated and thriving under Free labor & Free rule!...Industry, Wealth, Happiness, Virtue, all marching hand in hand, and millions of voices raising their thanks to God for his goodness in doing good to all...."[35]

The major flaw in French's golden vision was the word "soon."

CHAPTER SIXTEEN

From These Honored Dead

Elizabeth Keckley felt deeply pained by the gulf between urban African-Americans like herself and the thousands of "poor dusky children of slavery" who fled into Washington after the Emancipation Proclamation.[1]

She was among the literate blacks who celebrated the first anniversary of emancipation in the District at the Reverend John F. Cook's comfortably upholstered Fifteenth Street Presbyterian Church. So was William Slade, a White House steward who had become Lincoln's trusted private messenger. With inspired eloquence, a procession of speakers encouraged black pride as they looked ahead to vistas opened by emancipation. William E. Matthews, a fiery seventeen-year-old orator from Baltimore, said they should celebrate the birthdays of black heroes such as Hannibal of Carthage, Toussaint L'Ouverture of Haiti and Benjamin Banneker, astronomer and surveyor of Washington itself. J. Willis Menard, a Creole poet from Illinois who had become the first black clerk at the Interior Department, gestured to the gold leaves on the collar of Major Alexander T. Augusta, the first black man commissioned as an army surgeon. Menard had been assigned to investigate Belize as a possible site for colonization of ex-slaves, but he said he would give up such ideas if he could see the epaulettes of a major general on a black man's shoulders. Then he read his poem "One Year Ago Today," praising God for answering his people's prayers for freedom. The gathering concluded with a heartfelt rendition of "John Brown's Body"; whether they sang its original words or the version written by Julia Ward Howe is unrecorded.[2]

As those free black citizens exhorted and sang, four blocks away hundreds of untaught escapees from slavery, still loosely called "contrabands," crowded into Camp Barker, a barracks on Twelfth Street near what is now Logan Circle. After local emancipation, the first former slaves reaching the District were kept off the streets in quarters at the Old Capitol. Later they were housed nearby in Duff Green's Row of townhouses, also called Carroll Prison, until more prison space was needed. Then they were moved to Camp Barker, a complex that had been McClellan's Barracks, a block of offices and stables expanded with tents. It was a miserable place next to a swampy excavation, and its inhabitants were harassed by Maryland slave-owners trying to recover missing bondsmen. "Many good friends reached forth kind hands" to help the freedmen, wrote Keckley. They included Major Augusta, who urged that the swamp be filled and city water be provided for the camp. But because "the North is not warm and impulsive," Keckley said, "the bright joyous dream of freedom to the slave faded"—any kind word for the luckless seemed to be answered with two that were unkind.

One evening as she walked past a festive garden party held to raise funds for suffering soldiers, she decided that "well-to-do colored people" should do something similar to help suffering blacks. She brought this up at church, and within two weeks the Contraband Relief Society was organized, with Keckley as president. When she told Mrs. Lincoln of her project, the first lady quickly contributed $200. Then when the two women traveled together to New York and Boston, Keckley called on abolitionists like Wendell Phillips and black spokesmen like Frederick Douglass, who not only contributed, but lectured on behalf of her society. She saw opportunity in all directions, cajoling the dining-room waiters at New York's Metropolitan Hotel into taking up a collection.[3]

Keckley was far from alone in her striving. At the same time, the National Freedmen's Relief Association came into being, along with major efforts by Quakers and other church and nonreligious groups in individual states. And belatedly the Federal government took its first steps to relieve conditions at Camp Barker by moving those ex-slaves out of Washington. In early May 1863, Superintendent Nichols and Lieutenant Colonel Elias M. Greene, chief quartermaster of the Department of Washington, moved to create Freedman's Village on the former Custis-Lee plantation at Arlington. There, Greene wrote, they would enjoy "the salutary effects of good pure country air and a return to their former healthy avocations as field hands under much happier auspices than heretofore. . . ." By midsummer, the vanguard of several thousand freed slaves was installed in tents about half a mile south of the mansion at Arlington. This delighted strong Unionists who thought it appropriate that the plantation of the South's leading general, land that soldiers had already stripped of trees and upturned for fortifications, would now be home to former slaves. But most of the freedmen balked at moving, suspicious that decamping to any plantation would be a step back toward serfdom. Able-bodied men among them would rather work on the streets and as scavengers at 40 cents a shift. Not until December 1863 would the village be formally dedicated and about 1,500 ex-slaves transported across the river to new barracks-style quarters.[4]

Ten days after President Lincoln got the news of Gettysburg, he sat and wrote a letter, composing it as carefully as he did his best-remembered addresses. He was angry. After the national exhilaration set off by victory in Pennsylvania and on the Mississippi, General Meade had let the battered Confederate army get away across the Potomac, back to Virginia. The July 4 dream of a quick conclusion to the war was gone. Lincoln had urged Meade to follow and crush Lee's command, and when Meade did not, Halleck had telegraphed the general that the president was disappointed. Meade thought Halleck was suggesting that he should resign and wired back offering to do so. Now, in responding, Lincoln told Meade that he was reluctant to cause him the slightest pain, but "I do not believe you appreciate the magnitude of the disaster involved in Lee's escape." Rather than ending the war, this meant that it would be "prolonged indefinitely." "Your golden opportunity is gone," he wrote, "and I am immeasurably distressed because of it."[5]

If Lincoln had sent that message, Meade surely would have quit. But Lincoln did not send it. Meade had, after all, won the greatest battle of the war. In doing so, his own army had been damaged as badly as Lee's, in raw numbers though not in percentages. Besides, Meade had been in command for little more than two weeks. Lincoln had already changed commanders of the army in the East six times in two years. If this one departed, who would succeed him? After pouring his frustration into the letter he had written, Lincoln put it away unsigned and turned his attention to another war raging at his back, in the heart of the Union.

To fill the ranks depleted by the campaigns of spring and summer, plus the disbanding of 130 regiments at the end of their enlistments, in early July the War Department issued its first call for draftees. Roars of protest rose within hours. In some places still resentful of the Emancipation Proclamation, the summons to join a war to end slavery set off violence. New York was a hotbed of political resistance. Governor Horatio Seymour complained that Democratic districts were assigned unfairly high quotas. Mayor Fernando Wood maintained that anyone who opposed the war on the basis of "conscientious disbelief" in its "humanity, necessity or eventual success" should be exempt. Laborers, especially the Irish, were already fearful that freed slaves would come north and take their jobs. They were angry that wealthier men could avoid service by hiring a substitute or paying a commutation fee of $300—about a year's wages for an unskilled worker. On July 13, their accumulated grievances exploded into class and race warfare. Riots and arson spread across Manhattan. For three days, armed mobs rampaged through the streets, demolishing conscription offices, burning homes and Protestant churches, terrorizing black neighborhoods, and murdering innocent citizens. Before the revolt was crushed by a mixed force of police, local troops and hastily summoned regiments who had fought at Gettysburg, more than 105 persons were killed in the worst domestic riots in the nation's history.[6]

To dampen the crisis in New York, the War Department halted conscription there, but only temporarily. When Governor Seymour asked Lincoln to suspend the draft because it was illegal, the president refused. In principle, he said, he did not object to a court test of the law's constitutionality, but the Union could not waste time waiting for a decision. The government had demonstrated that it would use force to put down insurrection, and he left no doubt that the draft would be enforced, however unfair the rules might be.[7]

The unfairness endemic in wars sits heaviest on those already afflicted—with poverty, disease, ignorance and oppression. Thousands of black men had not waited to be drafted, but volunteered and were now fully engaged in the war, dying for their freedom. At Fort Wagner, South Carolina, the black Fifty-fourth Massachusetts led an assault in July that cost them more than a quarter of their number, including their white colonel. To such soldiers, it seemed especially unfair that they would be paid barely more than half what white privates got—$7 net a month, versus $13 for whites. They were commanded by white officers, and Jeff Davis had vowed that, if captured, Union officers commanding black troops would be charged with inciting servile insurrection, a capital crime in Southern states. Some captured black soldiers had been slaughtered in cold blood. Facing these facts, black leaders recruiting for colored regiments looked for help. In early August, the best known of those leaders, Frederick Douglass, decided to take his recruiting problems to the White House.

Douglass had been born a slave in Talbot County on Maryland's Eastern Shore and, after fighting back against a cruel master, was sent to be a house servant in Baltimore. Jailed after one failed escape attempt, in 1838 he tried again, succeeded and fled north. There he became a thunderous antislavery orator, wrote his autobiography, paid his former master for his freedom and started an abolitionist newspaper, the *North Star.* Well before the war, his had become the most powerful black voice in the nation. Thus, when he called on ranking members of the Republican establishment for entrée to President Lincoln, they were quick to respond.

Senator Samuel C. Pomeroy, the sleek, hard-line Radical from Kansas, escorted Douglass into the president's cluttered workroom. Lincoln, looking tired and solemn, was in a low chair, his legs stretched out among scattered documents. He rose and welcomed Douglass so openly that his visitor "felt myself in the presence of an honest man—one whom I could love." However warmly affected, Douglass did not soften his message. He told Lincoln that recruiting was hard because black soldiers were not fairly paid. If captured, they should be treated the same as any other prisoners; if the Confederates showed no mercy to colored troops, Union officers should retaliate in kind. And when black soldiers distinguished themselves in battle, they should be recognized and promoted the same as their white comrades in arms. Lincoln listened sympathetically but gave Douglass less than full satisfaction. Black men had a greater motive to enlist, he said, and for them to serve at all was a great advance in their status. Douglass related that the president said "they ought to be willing to enter the service upon any conditions." Paying them less was a way to ease them into service over continuing resentment among many Northerners, but eventually they would get equal pay. As for retaliation, Lincoln considered it "a terrible remedy.... the thought of hanging men for a crime perpetrated by others was revolting to his feelings." Once retaliation began, there was no telling where it might end.[8]

Douglass could not agree, but left the White House impressed by what he saw as Lincoln's "tender heart ... his humane spirit." He did not get that impression of the man he called on next, Edwin Stanton. Stanton's manner announced that "politeness was not one of his weaknesses." But after Douglass presented his case, the secretary's "contempt and suspicion, and brusqueness" disappeared. Again, Douglass was unsatisfied, yet he left persuaded that "the true course to the black man's freedom and citizenship was over the battlefield," so he determined to go on recruiting. Stanton promised to make him an assistant adjutant general with officer's status, but the commission never came. Meanwhile, Douglass's three sons were all serving, two in Massachusetts regiments and one recruiting in the Mississippi Valley.[9]

The victories of summer moved Lincoln to declare August 6 a day of thanksgiving. Government offices, shops and saloons in the capital were closed; churches were open, sermons were preached, steeple bells were rung. The news that John Mosby's raiders had struck at Fairfax Court House again, capturing a Union wagon train, did not arrive soon enough to mar the day in Washington. When it did arrive, it must have given Antonia Ford a moment of pleasure and perhaps strengthened her plea of innocence; from her room in Old Capitol Prison, she could hardly have tipped off the Confederates about this raid.

With the influence of her smitten friend, Joseph Willard, Antonia had made herself comfortable in captivity. She sent home a list of items she needed, which included tea, sugar, needle, thread, all the bows and plumes off her velvet bonnet and approximately enough clothes for a season at White Sulphur Springs. She had plenty of time to read, so asked for Victor Hugo's *Les Misérables,* a sensation of the period, especially in the South, plus an up-to-date history of the war. Any thought that prison life had dulled her spirit was quashed by her request for the music to "Maryland, My Maryland," "The Bonnie Blue Flag" and "Dixie," all songs of Confederate defiance.[10]

Antonia must have maintained her appearance and personality, for a male prisoner wrote and slipped a mushy poem to her, dated Easter Monday, 1863. Whether she was able to socialize with yet another inmate of the Old Capitol, a proud genuine Rebel spy named Belle Boyd, is unlikely. Boyd was irrepressible in her war against the Yankees. In 1861, at age eighteen, she had shot a Union soldier who abused her mother at their home in Martinsburg, Virginia. She was not arrested then, but was caught a year later after becoming an eager informant for Confederate cavalry brigadier Turner Ashby during the Shenandoah Valley campaign. Briefly held in Baltimore, she was released with a lecture from General Dix. Then, at her uncle's hotel in Front Royal, she eavesdropped on Union officers and rode to report their plans to Stonewall Jackson's scouts. But love betrayed her; she made the mistake of entrusting a note for Jackson to a beau she thought was a paroled Rebel soldier. He was in fact a Union scout who had wooed her to win her confidence. Belle was arrested again and this time taken to Old Capitol. After a month, she was exchanged, and resumed her adventures until being picked up yet again in August 1863.* On arriving at Old Capitol, she told the superintendent, William P. Wood: "Sir, if it is a crime to love the South, its cause and its president, then I am a criminal. I am in your power, do with me as you please. But I fear you not. I would rather lie down in prison and die than leave it owing allegiance to a government such as yours. . . ."[11]

Brusque though he was, Superintendent Wood did not rely on fear to control his captives. A forty-three-year-old skilled craftsman who had been a private in the Mexican War, he was strangely indulgent toward many of his prisoners. As a model-maker, he had been used as a witness by Edwin Stanton in the McCormick reaper case, and at Old Capitol he was paid a cavalry colonel's salary by Stanton's personal order. Born in Alexandria, Wood loudly proclaimed his opposition to slavery and his loyalty to the Union, yet he once told a Rebel captive that if Lee should take Washington, he would willingly manage the same prison for "Mars' Jeff" Davis. He buried some of the Confederates who died in his prison at Congressional Cemetery, to lie with distinguished statesmen of the early republic. On one occasion, he took a dozen prisoners along for one of these burials, though that was against regulations, and after the service left them to stroll in the fresh air, saying, "I know you will not get me into any trouble." An ex-captive told of a Sunday when the superintendent allowed Union and Confederate chaplains to conduct separate services in the prison. The irreverent

---

*This time, Boyd spent seven months at Old Capitol. She was glad to be exchanged again for a Union officer held by the Confederates. Later, bearing dispatches from Richmond, she boarded a blockade runner headed to England. The vessel was intercepted at sea by a Federal gunship. En route to captivity, she charmed the young Union officer in charge, Samuel W. Hardinge, who was himself arrested and sent to Old Capitol. They were later married.

Wood shouted down the halls, "All ye who want to hear the Lord God preached according to Jeff Davis, go down to the yard, and all ye who want to hear the Lord God preached according to Lincoln, go down to Number 16!"[12]

Antonia Ford specified that the long list of luxuries she had requested be packed in a trunk and addressed to Wood at "Carroll Prison." That was the annex where female prisoners were now kept, a row of townhouses alongside the Old Capitol that had sheltered contrabands earlier in the war. By regulation, prisoners could receive visits and packages only from relatives, but this rule was often stretched by friends pretending to be close kin. Wood won good will among his charges by handling (and inspecting) unofficial mail for them to and from the South. Whether this illegal communication was lubricated by money is impossible to know, though bribery was rampant in wartime prisons North and South. But Wood's cultivation of some prisoners and forwarding of illicit mail had other motives, specifically intelligence; he wrote later that he furnished Stanton with reliable information from his inmates. He also had undertaken a venturesome intelligence mission of his own in 1862—accompanying prisoners to Richmond for exchange, he tried unsuccessfully to bring back three Union spies arrested and jailed there.[13]

Since Miss Ford was being held on suspicion of espionage, Wood surely was reading her letters, but he must have found in them more titillation than information. One of her missives included a long poem addressed to her mother, just before Antonia was deported to the Confederacy as Rose Greenhow and Belle Boyd had been. "Do not have the 'blues,' " she wrote, "But hope now for the best / This cannot last so very long / And then 'twill seem a jest." It lasted longer than she expected. In May, she was taken to Fortress Monroe with a shipment of other women prisoners. Among them were at least two alleged "notorious prostitutes," who were sent back when the Confederate exchange officer complained that on landing at City Point they had "descended to a depth of infamy that I hardly thought could be reached by the sex." After making her way home, Ford was arrested again and returned to the Old Capitol.[14]

Antonia, unlike Greenhow and Boyd, did not brag in prison about her services to the Confederacy. Early in her captivity, she had advertised her passion for the South with "Dixie" and "The Bonnie Blue Flag." But outside the Old Capitol, friends on both sides of the lines were trying to prove her innocent of spying. Jeb Stuart wrote to John

Mosby asking for exculpatory evidence, "so that I can insist upon her unconditional release." In August, Stuart's aide, the Virginia novelist John Esten Cooke, wrote sarcastically in Richmond's *Southern Illustrated News* about Antonia's honorary commission from Stuart. He recalled the mood in camp when he introduced Stuart to Ford—"O gay vanished hours that come back with the sight of that document!... Who could ever have imagined that... this mere billet doux... would in these days become the ground of a grave accusation against the maiden who smiled as she received it! It was only a jest... I do assure you, only meant to produce a good-humored laughter from a young lady." The Yankees "can't catch our partisans," Cooke wrote, "but they arrest our young ladies. They cannot crush the men, and they make war on the women of the South! O 'nation of shopkeepers,' how thoroughly you are acting out your real character!"*[15]

Meanwhile, Union Major Willard was exerting all his influence to free the woman for whom he had fallen so completely. As staff aide to General Heintzelman, Willard was well placed to make the case that Antonia was innocent. Eventually he prevailed on Heintzelman to release her, but only after she apparently took the oath of loyalty to the Union on September 16, 1863. One wonders whether she literally did so, since the officer who witnessed and signed the document was Major Willard himself. Two days later, Heintzelman ordered that she be permitted to go home, "there to remain subject to orders from these Head Quarters—excepting under instructions from Head Quarters Department of Washington she will in no wise be molested or interfered with by any military authority."[16]

Willard conducted Antonia home to Fairfax, as he had escorted her to prison after her first arrest. Her gratitude to him quickened their romance; he became so ardent that before the end of the year she was fending off his pleas to join in a "private marriage." Because he was still a Union officer, a public wedding with a suspected spy was out of the question. On a stormy winter night, she sat at her window and wrote, firmly but teasingly, "Major, you have placed me under so many obligations, I shall never be able to extricate myself, but will be obliged to pay you... 'with a vengeance.' Do you remember how that is?... You

*Half a century later, John Mosby would also deny that Miss Ford had been involved in his March 1863 raid on Fairfax Court House. He was already closely familiar with the village, he said. The allegation that she helped him was "a pure fable.... Antonia was as innocent as Abraham Lincoln." (John S. Mosby to Maude Merchant, 9 Dec. 1914, Willard Family papers, LC)

know I *love* you, but ... [my] parents and relatives would be mortified to death; acquaintances would disown me; it would be illegal, and above all it would be *wrong*. ... I would make you 'the luckiest man in the world' if I could without compromising myself. ... You ask for my 'heart and hand.' The heart is yours already. When *your* hand is free and you can claim mine before the world, *then that also is yours*." Destiny had thrown them together, she said—"Now, Major, let's be hopeful, and expect 'Destiny' ... to work out something joyful for us." She ended that letter by gently scolding him for not coming to Fairfax lately. Soon she would be warning him not to risk riding out to see her because he might be caught on the road by her friend John Mosby.[17]

Weather, stubborn foremen, bossy bureaucrats, the very force of gravity seemed to conspire against Thomas Walter's goal of hoisting the statue of Freedom to crown the Capitol. In May, a workman had fallen through the roof of the building's new library, one of two killed before the project was done. John P. Usher of Indiana, who had replaced Caleb Smith as secretary of the interior, suddenly ordered that the artist Constantino Brumidi halt his work on the historical frieze for the inside of the dome. "I suppose [Usher] will remove his interdict when he learns more about it," Walter wrote. But Usher was not concerned as an art critic; he was curious about Brumidi's contract, and once he was satisfied, the artist resumed painting. This did nothing to hurry the ironworkers, still shorthanded as they creaked along. Frustrated in his effort to top off the dome on July 4, Walter had shifted his target date to the return of Congress in early December. But he was unable to transmit his own sense of urgency to the ironworkers' foreman, John Cuddy. Besides that, he was worried that the wooden supports of the dome were showing signs of age, a potential problem he blamed on the earlier delays caused by Meigs.[18]

Walter's anxiety was heightened by the continuing complications of his life in two places, with a family fractured by the war. He still turned his back on two of his sons, one an army deserter and criminal, the other a Confederate sympathizer in Norfolk; a third was now with his Indiana regiment fighting in Kentucky. In Germantown, Walter's new home was being completed, with murals by Brumidi, who had painted there when work at the Capitol was shut down. In Washington, the architect had moved again, into another house full of bugs and smells. There, in "the dirtiest hole I ever lived in," at the corner of Fifth and E streets, he and his wife had to put up with their landlord, the eccentric Dr. Leonard D. Gale.[19]

Gale had been a professor of science at New York University when he became a vital collaborator in Samuel F. B. Morse's perfection of the telegraph. Like Joseph Henry of the Smithsonian, another early participant, he had been pushed aside by Morse after the historic first message, "What hath God wrought!" was sent in 1844 between the Supreme Court Chamber in the Capitol and Mt. Clare Station in Baltimore. Since then, Gale had published a textbook of "Natural Philosophy," which covered "Mechanics, Hydrostatics, Hydraulics, Pneumatics, Acoustics, Optics, Electricity, Magnetism, Galvanism, and Astronomy," all for 62½ cents a copy. Now, sixty-three years old, he was reduced to puttering in the cellar of the house he shared with Walter.[20]

Gale "gets things in shocking confusion," said the precise and orderly architect. "The smell from the laboratory this morning was worse than ever. I tried to get him to smell it but he said that it was no go; his excuse was that he has been uncorking and recorking various drugs, and chemical solvents, which may have permitted the escape of . . . gases which, coming in contact with atmospheric air, combined respectively with the oxygen, the hydrogen, and the azole, exercising an acidifying principle, and resulting in effluvia not always agreeable to all olfactories—in other words, he made a horrid stink in the library and the parlor that I am going to have stopped if I have to send the villainous compounds out on the commons and have them buried."[21]

The professor who had helped to revolutionize world communication was experimenting on a new way to roast coffee, or perhaps to synthesize it. If his scientific ingenuity had been turned loose at the Capitol, he might have contributed to progress there; Walter only now, years into the work, had the idea of installing a speaking tube from the dome to the engine room below to coordinate movements of the tall building crane. "I wonder we have not thought of it before," he admitted. Privately, but not officially, he said in late October that he then hoped to have the statue of Freedom atop the dome in two weeks.[22]

Even in this turmoil at home and on the job, Walter took time to help a longtime White House guard and messenger, Louis Burgdorf, who he said had lost six children to scarlet fever. They were buried in three graves, two in each, and Burgdorf wanted to have three head- and foot-stones as markers. But locally, gravestones would cost $35 a set, which Burgdorf could not afford. He turned to Walter, apparently because the architect presided over the most conspicuous pile of loose marble and granite in the capital, and Walter wrote to a friend in Philadelphia asking him to provide the stones for much less. In wartime Washington, the law of supply and demand meant that gravestones, like coffee, came at a premium.[23]

John Hay, intelligent and playful, worldly beyond his years, did much to keep Lincoln from sinking into depression on days when even Union victories were followed by long newspaper lists of the dead and missing. They spent so much time together that Lincoln's style of storytelling humor rubbed off on the college-educated Hay, a future secretary of state. After the president spent an hour test-firing the excellent Spencer breechloading carbine, Hay told of a rustic who witnessed the weapon's kick and advised that "it wouldnt do; too much powder: a good piece of audience should not rekyle: if it did at all, it should rekyle a little forrid." One Sunday evening, Lincoln went with Hay to the Naval Observatory, where they took a look at the stars, and later went out to the Soldiers' Home, where the president read aloud to him from Shakespeare's *Henry VI* and *Richard III* until Hay started nodding and was sent off to bed. In his diary, Hay often referred to the president as "the Tycoon," but later edited that nickname out when he realized that others might read it. He privately delighted to mock the more mockable callers at the White House. There was the delegation of temperance advocates that entered the mansion "looking blue & thin in the keen autumnal air," eyed by Hay's half-tight coachman with "an air of complacent contempt and mild wonder." A trio of "blue-skinned damsels" symbolizing "Love, Purity & Fidelity in Red, White & Blue gowns" made a speech at the president, blaming alcohol for the Union's military defeats. But Lincoln "could not see it, as the rebels drink more & worse whiskey than we do." Thus, wrote Hay, the delegation "filed off drearily to a collation of cold water & green apples, & then home to mulligrubs."[24]

Hay was such a social creature that the White House could not contain him. Though some of his free evenings were spent admiring the bare-legged showgirls at the Canterbury Music Hall, his socializing also seined up useful town talk for the president. He enjoyed squiring the capital's nicer young ladies, downing oysters at Harvey's

Restaurant at Eleventh and C streets, and tippling with politicians and newspapermen, two trades often embodied in one person.

Benjamin Perley Poore of the *Boston Journal,* W. W. Worden of the *New York Times, Baltimore Sun* and *Cincinnati Enquirer,* and John W. Forney, publisher of the *Washington Chronicle* and *Philadelphia Press,* exemplified the hybrid class that reported on politics while holding political jobs. Before the war, news was scarce between congressional sessions. Thus many Washington correspondents, paid by the column inch, took government positions to support themselves during the legislature's absence. Although the war provided news year round, the custom remained common among established correspondents, who exercised seniority and enjoyed access superior to the dozens of newcomers who flocked to the capital after fighting began.

The forty-six-year-old Forney was no ordinary correspondent. He had been around newspapers since he was a teenager in Pennsylvania. While owning and editing the *Philadelphia Pennsylvanian,* he had held the political job of surveyor of the port of Philadelphia. When the Democrats lost, he came to Washington, where he wrote for the *Daily Union* while serving as clerk of the House of Representatives. He quit that role to run for the Senate and campaign for James Buchanan; though Buchanan won, Forney lost. Back in Philadelphia, he started the *Press,* split with Buchanan and opportunely became a Republican. In appreciation, Lincoln helped him become secretary of the Senate. Forney's was the voice that recited Washington's Farewell Address on the general's birthday, and read Lincoln's State of the Union messages to the two houses jointly assembled. While serving the Senate, he started the *Washington Sunday Chronicle,* and in 1862, urged by Lincoln, he made the *Chronicle* a daily—loyal to the president, supported by government advertisements and distributed by the thousands to troops in the East. All the while, Forney was sending Washington commentary to his Philadelphia paper, unapologetically supporting his patron and president.

Politics and journalism worked hand in glove; the later ideal of an independent press was hardly conceived. With few exceptions, newspapers were tied to party or faction, and everything they printed was assumed to reflect the prejudices of their publishers. When the *New York Tribune* ran an especially heated editorial, readers asked each other, "Did you see what Greeley said today?" In the same way, the *New York Herald* was identified with James Gordon Bennett, the *Times* with Henry J.

Raymond, the *Evening Post* with William Cullen Bryant and two of the most influential Democratic papers, the *World* and the *Journal of Commerce,* with their editors, Manton Marble and William C. Prime.

Washington editors were not as flamboyant, and their papers were not as sharply differentiated as those in Manhattan. Noah Brooks appraised Forney's Washington journal: "The *Chronicle's* chief duty is to act as the Greek chorus upon all possible occasions, wait for the announcement of intentions or opinions, and then applaud the act as the height of wisdom, skill, and ability." The moderate *Intelligencer,* founded in 1800 and carried on by Joseph Gales and his partner W. W. Seaton, who survived past the war, had become "an ancient fossil whose faultfinding has become a chronic malady and whose high-toned conservatism is so very high-toned as to be above the intelligent comprehension of simple-minded loyalists." The *National Republican,* edited by Simon P. Hanscom, was "thoroughly loyal, liberal, and gossipy, but not very reliable." The *Congressional Globe,* started in 1830 by Francis P. Blair, had phased out of political opinion and become the official recorder of legislative proceedings. By far the liveliest paper in Washington was the *Evening Star,* edited by the mayor's brother W. Douglas Wallach. Every day, it covered murders, fires, lectures and politics with an institutional curiosity that would be much appreciated by future historians.[25]

Forney's newspaper may not have impressed Brooks, but its fidelity to Lincoln and its omnipresence in the Army of the Potomac was increasingly valuable as political opposition took shape a year ahead of the 1864 election. After Republican losses in the 1862 congressional contests, the president worried over the outcome of off-year voting in sixteen states, including gubernatorial elections in two of the biggest, Ohio and Pennsylvania. In Ohio, the Democrats had nominated in absentia the most defiant Copperhead of them all, Clement Vallandigham, who was for immediate peace, letting the South and slavery go their own way. Vallandigham had been arrested in May by General Burnside, then commanding the Department of the Ohio, for making treasonable speeches. He was imprisoned briefly until Lincoln ordered him deported to the South. From there, he ran the blockade to Bermuda and made his way to Canada. He stayed in Windsor, Ontario, while his supporters campaigned for him for governor of Ohio. In Pennsylvania, one of Lincoln's staunchest backers, Governor Andrew Curtin, was challenged by a popular state Supreme Court judge. The president used all the levers of his office, providing railroad passes for government clerks from those states to go home to vote, and authorizing leave for Pennsylvania regiments to cast their ballots. On election day, he sat up past midnight at the telegraph office, waiting for returns. When they came, he was elated: Curtin was safe, Vallandigham was overwhelmingly repudiated and the other fourteen states had gone Republican.[26]

Forney was glad to take credit for the role of his Washington and Philadelphia papers, and the victory gave a lift to his personal propagandizing on Lincoln's behalf. To evenings at his apartment on Capitol Hill, he invited great men not only of politics, but of the arts and sciences. The photographer Mathew Brady, the actors Joe Jefferson and Edwin Forrest and the portraitist Charles Loring Elliott were among the eminences who drank deep and talked long. Young John Hay was there the night when Forrest sobbed through a poem about "The Idiot Boy" and General Dan Sickles, standing with the crutches he flaunted after losing a leg at Gettysburg, roared that the nation would come out of this war stronger and purer, with discord eliminated.*[27]

For nearly two years, Washington society had been fascinated by the polite courtship of Salmon Chase's daughter Kate by Rhode Island's former governor, then regimental commander, now United States Senator William Sprague IV. She was more strong, sober, smart and calculating than Sprague, but he was much, much richer. He had inherited an array of textile mills established by his grandfather and, though worth a rumored $25 million, had come close to great scandal by trying to enrich himself further in a wartime scheme to buy cotton from Confederate Texas. Luckily for him, the scheme failed because Secretary Chase refused to approve it. But Chase, who would need financial backing for his relentless presidential ambitions, eagerly approved Sprague's attentions to Kate. After some cool intervals, the young couple announced their engagement in the spring of 1863, with the marriage scheduled for the fall. During the courtship, Kate had

---

*After the Army created its medical museum in August 1862, it sent collectors to the field to bring back body parts and missiles for study. Soldiers who had lost limbs or comrades often objected to this grisly educational effort. One man demanded the return of his arm, but a curator told him that since his term of enlistment had not ended, all of him was still government property; he could not reclaim his arm until its term was up. Sickles felt differently: Specimen No. 1335, an amputated leg crushed by a twelve-pound shot at Gettysburg, arrived at the museum in its own little coffin, on which was tacked a visiting card saying, "with the compliments of Major General D.E.S, United States Volunteers." (John H. Brinton, *Journal of the American Medical Society,* 28 Mar. 1896)

often been seen with parasol and bonnet, visiting outlying military camps to cheer the troops, when she was not busy with her expensive social schedule. Even after the engagement was on record, she was often seen about town without her fiancé, sometimes with John Hay, who except for lack of money would have been a much fitter match for such a woman.[28]

One wonders how open Hay and the Chases could have been in the hours they spent together, each knowing what the other knew. The young man was the president's aide and intimate friend, the young woman was the first lady's most resented social rival, and her father was the unannounced but leading Republican candidate to replace the president in the election now barely a year away. In late October, Hay spent one evening at the Chases', and the following evening took the future Mrs. Sprague to the theater to see *The Pearl of Savoy*. He was astonished that the play "made the statuesque Kate cry like a baby." In November, the morning after joining President and Mrs. Lincoln to see Booth in *The Marble Heart*, he organized a boat trip to Mount Vernon for Kate's bridesmaids.

Chase had to sell a farm in Ohio to help pay for the wedding extravaganza. The president, but not Mrs. Lincoln, was among the Who's Who of social, political and military life who saw the five-foot-six multimillionaire and the tall, cool beauty become husband and wife. Hay was in the crowd, too, as the Marine Band played the new composition, the "Kate Chase Wedding March." He was still so friendly with Kate that he stepped into her bridal chamber to say goodnight. He found her more relaxed than before; she "seemed to think she had arrived." Whitelaw Reid, the "Agate" of the *Cincinnati Gazette*, was moved to report the event in poetry: "Deck, O flowers, this bride so rare / Come with beauty, blush and scent / Roses twine her silken hair / Queen of all the continent."[29]

After midsummer, Federal armies in the West had moved on Knoxville, Chattanooga and Little Rock, and lost a close, bloody battle at Chickamauga. Elsewhere the war was nearly static as summer became fall, unexciting except to those in the line of fire. Union batteries were pounding Confederate-held Fort Sumter into rubble. Generals Meade and Lee were back in Virginia, nudging their armies into position along the Rapidan River. During this lull, Lincoln had issued public statements rebutting critics of his military and political decisions, had sadly informed the vacationing Tad that his goat Nanny had somehow disappeared from the White House grounds, and had written a fan letter to the Shakespearean actor James Hackett: "I think nothing equals *Macbeth*. It is wonderful." To restive Unionists meeting back home in Springfield, he had written and published a letter justifying the war, the draft, the Proclamation and the use of black soldiers. He was optimistic: "The signs look better. The Father of Waters again goes unvexed to the sea.... Peace does not appear so distant as it did." And when peace comes, "there will be some black men who can remember that with silent tongue, and clenched teeth, and steady eye, and well-poised bayonet, they have helped mankind on to this great consummation, while I fear there will be some white ones unable to forget that with malignant heart and deceitful speech they strove to hinder it."³⁰

Like so much of his writing, that letter was telling, cadenced, almost poetic in places. But he was not satisfied with writing letters and proclamations. He wanted somehow to help his countrymen understand the historic magnitude of this struggle without having to frame his message as a legal or political case. He kept turning over what he had said to the celebrating crowd that came to serenade him when news of Gettysburg and Vicksburg arrived. Speaking for less than three minutes, he had referred three times to the Declaration of Independence's assertion that "all men are created equal." This, he said then, "is a glorious theme, and the occasion for a speech, but I am not prepared to make one worthy of the occasion." He pondered advice from friends such as the Boston businessman John Murray Forbes, who urged him to "teach your great audience of *plain people* that the war is not North against South but *the People against the Aristocrats.*" By November 2, when Lincoln was invited to make "a few appropriate remarks" at the dedication of the soldiers' cemetery at Gettysburg, this theme had matured in his mind.³¹

He would not be the featured speaker at Gettysburg: that role would fall to former Senator and Secretary of State Edward Everett, long known for his elaborate oratory. Nevertheless, the president worked hard over drafts of his own remarks. When his four-car special train left Washington for Gettysburg on November 18, he had on paper only about half of what he wanted to say the next day. He folded his notes into the stovepipe hat that often served as his briefcase, hoping to complete the text along the way. But he was unable to concentrate on the train, surrounded as he was by cabinet secretaries, admirals, politicians and diplomats. Besides that, little Tad was sick again, and Mary had pleaded with her husband not to go.

At Gettysburg, Lincoln was the guest of the banker David Wills at his mansion on the public square. Seward stayed next door, while others in the party scattered to find lodgings about town. When the inevitable bands and serenaders appeared outside begging for a speech, the president demurred. But Seward obliged them, speaking so indistinctly that Hay, staying around the corner, could not understand him. Whether the fault was Seward's or Hay's is not certain, because Hay and Nicolay had fallen in with John Forney, who had been partaking of local hospitality since before they arrived. After a few more drinks and some songs, they decided that Forney should make a speech, and summoned a band to serenade him. Forney chastised the celebrators for giving him more applause than they had the president. He told them that to Lincoln "you owe your country—you owe your name as American citizens," and then talked on until he ran down. After that, Hay wrote, "We sang John Brown and went home." Meanwhile, Lincoln had completed a smooth copy of his own speech, which he tried out on Seward before they both retired for the night.[32]

The next morning, military bands played dirges as they led the procession to the cemetery, where an estimated 15,000 men, women and children stood waiting. When Lincoln stepped onto the packed platform, looking out across an arc of crude wooden stakes marking soldiers' graves, he was hard to distinguish from far back in the crowd. The Reverend Thomas H. Stockton, chaplain of the Senate, delivered the invocation, and then the august Everett spoke for two hours, without a text. Each of them made the emotional and patriotic best of his opportunity. B. B. French, who sat among the speakers, wrote that Everett rendered "one of the greatest, most eloquent, elegant, and appropriate orations to which I ever listened. . . . I think [it] could not be surpassed by mortal man. . . . Mr. Everett was listened to with breathless silence by all that immense crowd, and he had his audience in tears many times during his masterly effort."

As for the president, said French, he dedicated the cemetery with "a few brief, but most appropriate words." Lincoln's young friend Hay gave those words less than a sentence in his diary, saying that the president "in a firm free way, with more grace than is his wont said his half dozen lines of consecration and the music wailed and we went home through crowded and cheering streets." All the details were in the papers, Hay said. And they were: The *New York Times,* for example, printed Everett's speech verbatim, which took approximately 185 column inches, more than a full broadsheet page of tiny hand-set type. It also printed the president's, which took less than four inches.[33]

From his first phrase, "Four score and seven years ago," Lincoln needed just two minutes to deliver the 272 words about which many million words have since been written. He was right, about his own words and public reaction at that moment, when he said the world would little note what was said there. But he had never been more wrong than when he said the world would not long remember. His words would be engraved in the walls of the great temple that memorializes him in Washington. Scholarly treatises would be written parsing his ten sentences. A Pulitzer Prize would be won for speculations on their stylistic roots and classical influences. Yet they were so simple and so moving that generations of schoolchildren would memorize them. Uncounted Americans would feel an epiphany as they heard Lincoln's words, would first grasp the meaning of their country as they recited his vow that "this nation, under God, shall have a new birth of freedom, and that government of the people, by the people, for the people, shall not perish from the earth."

CHAPTER SEVENTEEN

Her Ladyship Looks Placid
and Beautiful

Ashrieking gale tore along the Potomac at the end of November, driving vessels ashore and scattering tents in the outlying camps. At the White House, the president had lain ill since returning from Gettysburg. Confined with varioloid, a milder form of smallpox, he was "quite unwell" on the last Thursday of the month, the day he had designated as the nation's first official Thanksgiving. His sense of humor was feebler than usual, too: he told a visitor that "since he had been President he had always had a crowd of people asking him to give them something, but that *now he has something he can give them all*."[1]

The dangerously high wind halted work on the Capitol dome, where architect Walter was driving his crew to have the statue of Freedom in place before Congress reconvened. With the framework erected to the base of the statue, in early November he was still imploring the iron contractor to send the next sections "without a moment's delay." Three weeks later, he could report with relief that workmen had raised the heaviest piece of iron into place "without starting a joint or springing a timber." Encouraged, he had taken a chance of public embarrassment by notifying officials to be ready to celebrate at noon on December 2, the moment he had set for attaching the final section of the statue. But then he had to wait for the weather to ease, not daring to risk the loss of more lives.[2]

For Walter, to see Freedom on high would push weeks and months of travail and frustration into the background where they belonged. Not that he would forget the nervous year when his role was officially halted and the iron framework rose without his oversight; nor would he ever fully forgive the trespasses of his nemesis Meigs, whom he still considered to be an "unprincipled, unscrupulous, vindictive scamp." Inflation had forced cost overruns so that work had to be stopped repeatedly while he beseeched Congress for new appropriations. For months, troops had occupied and dirtied the building, and hundreds of casualties from battles in Virginia had lined the rotunda and corridors. The new secretary of the interior, John P. Usher, had asserted himself by interfering in the details of Walter's work, replacing his employees without bothering to ask him and harassing the artist Brumidi.[3]

But none of these broader problems had brought the architect to such a pitch of anxiety as the high wind, the below-freezing tempera-tures and the deliberate pace of workmen in the final days before his self-imposed deadline. On December 1, he told his wife that "I am all excitement today. The crowning of the statue is advertised in all the papers, and it seemed earlier in the day that it would be impossible to get ready, on account of the wind and the extreme cold." Charles Fowler, the iron contractor, had been there but left town—"they say that he was afraid of an accident, and consequently slipped away," said Walter. "Had I been in his place I would have stayed at all hazzards—I don't think him overstocked with courage." Tension mounted, but as he wrote, the weather began to moderate, and the last section of the bronze figure was slowly lifted to the platform at its base. After dinner, Walter met Major General Christopher C. Augur, commander of the Department of Washington, to go over the army's role in the planned celebration. The general was willing to "burn as much saltpeter on the occasion as we may desire," Walter wrote. The architect was refusing to talk to reporters, saying strangely, under the circumstances, that "I want as little fuss as possible."[4]

Instead he stirred a joyous fuss just after noon the next day, when the head of Freedom was finally lifted into place, with the Stars and Stripes flying above. As an immense crowd on Capitol Hill cheered, cannon boomed, answered by thirty-five forts around the capital. "Her ladyship looks placid and beautiful," Walter wrote to his wife, "much better than I expected." Congratulations showered upon him as the guns thundered their salute. The dome, the statue and the flag were visible for miles—from outlying camps like those at Tenallytown; from Alexandria, unhappy in its role as a huge Union supply base; from hos-pitals on both sides of the river; from Freedman's Village at Arlington, where the statue of Freedom meant something vastly different from what Jefferson Davis was thinking when he decreed that it must not wear a liberty cap.[5]

Few onlookers exulted more extravagantly than a recently resigned army colonel named Nathan W. Daniels, just arrived from Louisiana. The statue "crowns the summit of The Capitol of America," he wrote in his diary. "It was an eventful day in the history of This Republic. As I looked out of my window upon the magnificent structure, I saw the workmen tear away the slim scaffolding that enshrouded the image in a gossamer web and [let] the beautiful statue of Freedom soar free and unfettered to the gaze of the admiring and enthusiastic multitude below. . . . It was a most beautiful sight to behold and is an emblem that I trust no recreant hand may ere defile or traitor heart overthrow— May the Golden rays of God given sunlight that have ushered her into existence enveloping her in a cloud of Eternal glory be an omen that the duration of her life shall be as boundless and eternal as the noble souls who had the heart to dream of her reality and the hand to vitalize the dream."[6]

Even while it was was still under construction, the gleaming white* dome of the Capitol had become a national icon. It decorated the pages of soldiers' letters home and was carved into the nameplate of the popular New York weekly *Frank Leslie's Illustrated Newspaper,* symbolizing to millions the Union's determination to prevail and survive. In 1863, the Washington Monument was more of a joke than a statement of national self-respect, and there was as yet no copper goddess lifting a lamp of welcome in New York harbor. Walter looked up at the statue with justified pride. But the dome and the rest of the Capitol project were still not done. The connecting corridors and the eastern porticoes where legislators' carriages would arrive were unfinished, and Brumidi could not begin work on his great *Apotheosis of Washington* within the eye of the inner dome until the shell was complete. The architect still had months to go, perhaps years, before he could retire to his new home at Germantown.[7]

Added to the success of raising Freedom, there was good news, for a change, within Walter's war-strained family. His son Thomas, the Confederate sympathizer living in Norfolk, turned up on Christmas

---

*Walter paid the painting contractor James Galway 15 (later 25) cents a pound for paint and $1.75 (later $2.25 to $2.50) a day for each workman. Ten men labored full-time for two years applying four coats of paint to both sides and all edges of each iron panel, using a total of 5,000 pounds of paint. (James Goode, "Architecture, Politics and Conflict," p. 281)

Eve in Baltimore. From there, he wrote to his father, apparently suggesting that he would like to visit him. Walter answered this "mysterious" letter by saying that "We have been compelled by your course to consider you as forever lost, but if you have any misgivings as to . . . the rebellious south, we would do any thing in the world to promote such misgivings." If Thomas would take the oath of allegiance to the Union, "we shall welcome you again to the bosom of your family," he said. But "we hold no intercourse with secessionists, nor do I suppose that one has ever been in our house, nor do we intend that any one shall ever come under our roof." Thomas made clear in response that he was ready to change his stance, but then postponed visiting Washington because his wife in Norfolk was ill. Walter, writing that "we feel now that you are again one with us," expressed regret and asked for a photograph of her, with her name and vita to be inscribed in the family Bible.[8]

Like the Capitol itself, the freedom symbolized by the statue was still an unfinished work. There were still many, and not only in the South, who believed in the kind of freedom that Davis had in mind when he approved the figure's final design—the freedom of men to own other men, and of states to withdraw from the Union. And there were stern abolitionists and Unionists, even in Lincoln's own political circle, who still thought that this president was not the man to prosecute the war for freedom and the peace to follow. After the state-level victories over the Democrats in November, Lincoln was most concerned about contending factions in his own party as he drew up his message to the new session of Congress. Confined to his sickroom, he in effect pasted together reports from the cabinet for most of his message. Then he delivered a proclamation distinctly his own. He offered amnesty to all Confederates who would take the oath of allegiance, except for high-ranking civil and military officials. They would retain all property rights, "except as to slaves." To begin political reconstruction, he would recognize any state government supported by at least 10 percent of its 1860 voters who would take the oath, which meant accepting emancipation. He pledged not to return any person to slavery, and was determined that the Southern politicians who had fomented secession should not return to Congress.[9]

The president's message brought public praise from conservatives and many Radical Republicans, including some legislators and editors who had been his leading critics. "I have never seen such an effect produced by a public document," wrote Hay. "Men acted as if the Millenium had come." John Forney said the nation had been waiting for "the bold word," and now it had come—"I shall speak in my two papers tomorrow in a way to make these Presidential aspirants squirm." Peace Democrats were not pleased, of course, and the message did not quell the ambitions of those presidential aspirants—including Salmon Portland Chase, the only cabinet member who had objected to it.[10]

On two consecutive days in early January, Lincoln commuted the death sentences issued to two young army deserters and, before the end of the month, suspended at least fourteen more. Weary of the grim duty imposed by his office, he explained that he did it "because I am trying to evade the butchering business lately." The dank days at the turn of the year deepened the mud and the mood of the capital. Jane Swisshelm, seeming to hold her nose as she wrote, told her Minnesota readers of the dead horses buried around the city, barely covered with dirt. The street around the White House and War Department "has the gutter heaped up full of black, rotten mud, a foot deep and worth fifty cents a cart load for manure," she wrote. "It appears to be a matter of national pride that the President is to have more mud, and blacker mud, and filthier mud in front of his door than any other man can afford.... the statue of Washington stands on one side and that of Jackson on the other, guarding this national mud, even as great and honored names are used to sanction and sanctify the moral slough which has nearly engulphed the Government."[11]

Except for raids and skirmishes, the armies were at a winter standstill as a cold wave froze the roads into deep, hard ruts. To many in Washington, it seemed that the war was in a rut, too. Amid what Noah Brooks called the "gab, gab, gab" of Congress, a naïve senator sought to empower Lincoln to enroll another hundred thousand recruits, who would be assigned to take Richmond before their ninety-day enlistments ran out. The sub rosa political maneuvering always at work beneath the public discourse was turning into a network of crisscrossing conspiracies. The sour, gray capital was in a mood for something fresh and uncynical. And so on January 16, nearly 2,500 politicians and citizens jammed into the House Chamber to hear the twenty-one-year-old oratorical phenomenon named Anna Elizabeth Dickinson.

Dickinson had been stumping for women and against slavery and liquor since she was fifteen. A year earlier than that, she had first attracted attention by writing an article for William Lloyd Garrison's abolitionist newspaper the *Liberator*. She had had a job in the U.S. Mint in Philadelphia until she made a speech asserting that the battle of Ball's Bluff had been lost not by incompetence but by treason on the part of the commanding general, George McClellan. Since then, she had made her living and a vivid reputation by speaking up and down the Northeast.[12]

Now Vice President Hamlin and Speaker Schuyler Colfax invited her to appear in the Capitol, where Hamlin introduced her as a new Joan of Arc and her dramatic performance raised $1,000 for the Freedmen's Relief Society. Forney's *Chronicle* covered her with "rhapsodic laudation," according to Brooks, who was there. But Brooks's *Sacramento Union* readers got a less admiring review. Dickinson was "a nice girl, smart, witty . . . and possessing in an eminent degree the gift of gab," he reported. He described her black silk dress, long train and red velvet furbelows, and conceded that "her figure is graceful and full . . . her face is open, sunny and bright." But of what she said, Brooks disclosed little. He predicted that "she will flash out her brief and splendid career and then subside into the destiny of all women and be heard of no more."

Brooks obviously was what later feminists would call a male chauvinist, and as such he may have dismissed the substance of Dickinson's speech as just another example of a woman unable to make up her mind. She had started out excoriating all who disagreed with her furiously radical views, asserting that Lincoln's gradual approach to emancipation made him "an Ass . . . for the Slave Power to ride." But then the president and Mrs. Lincoln appeared in the hall, taking places of honor directly in front of her, and suddenly the crowd was amazed to hear her endorsing him for reelection. Yet, within two months, Dickinson was back in Washington at Grover's Theater, where she "raked the Lincoln administraton fore and aft." In a private audience with the president, she interrupted when he started to ease the tension with a story. "I didn't come to hear stories. I can read better ones in the papers any day," she said. As for his reconstruction policy, she told him point-blank that it was "all wrong; as radically bad as it can be." By that time, Dickinson was lavishing her rhetorical affection on John Charles Frémont.[13]

Shifting of support from one Republican to another was often strictly business: desperate job-seekers preferred whoever offered the best chance at a political appointment, and some speakers spoke for the faction that offered the most generous honoraria. But except for devoted Lincolnites, the various factions had one thing in common: dissatisfaction with the sitting president. The normal heaping of blame on an incumbent for whatever goes wrong became heavier in wartime. Every day Lincoln had to wrestle with matters as sweeping as the survival of the nation, and as personal as those deserters sentenced to death. With every appointment, from cabinet secretary to rural postmaster, he made enemies as well as friends. On the cutting issues of defeating and then reconstructing the South, opposition within the Republican Party was just as serious as that from the Democrats. Yet all his potential rivals assumed he would run again. Bennett's *New York Herald* quoted the Reverend Henry Ward Beecher, who said nothing was definite except " 'the great central facts'—that President Lincoln is prepared to serve another term, and that Mr. Secretary Chase expects to supersede him."[14]

But it was not quite that simple. No president since Jackson had served a second term, and while Lincoln had allies in every state and had confided to friends that he would run if nominated, he had made no public commitment. As for the secretary of the treasury, Chase certainly believed he was more qualified than Lincoln to be president, indeed that he should have been chosen in 1860. As head of a department where he could reward backers with jobs and contracts, and with his political roots in Ohio, he seemingly had a stronger base than any other Republican challenger. Lincoln himself said that Chase was "about one and a half times bigger than any other man that I ever knew." But Frémont, the Republican Party's first presidential nominee in 1856, was more radical than Chase, and angrier at Lincoln. Smacked down by the president in 1861 after independently trying to free slaves in his military department, then fired after his unsuccessful generalship against Stonewall Jackson, he was strong among abolitionists like the German-Americans of St. Louis. And the old Democrat Ben Butler, decisive though often wrong, had won Republican admirers with his forceful opposition to slavery and his heavy-handed occupation of Baltimore and New Orleans.[15]

Lincoln was banking on the concept of a National Union Party, embracing conservative Republicans, War Democrats and other loose voters whatever their label, to outweigh the Republican Radicals and then defeat the Democratic candidate in the coming fall. By now, it was obvious that General McClellan would be that Democrat. After being fired by Lincoln, he had gravitated to New York, with its powerful Democratic machine and oceans of tappable cash. His Napoleonic poses, disrespect to Lincoln and arrogance toward other generals had long illustrated his grandiose opinion of himself. His 1862 letter from the Peninsula, instructing Lincoln that the war's aims should not include emancipation, had laid his beliefs on the record. Since leaving Washington, he had basked in Democratic praise but withheld partisan commitment until writing a letter in support of Pennsylvania Governor Curtin's opponent in the fall. If the nation sought a man on horseback to ride to its rescue, McClellan already had one foot in the stirrup.

All the talk about political maneuvers and military strategy was only a distraction to Major Joe Willard. As he slept alone that winter, it was hard for him to think of anything but how to bring his beloved Antonia to his side. She had told him, "Remember, Major, the obstacle is with you, not me." That obstacle was the uniform he wore; she would not marry him as long as he was a Union officer. Now, after months of struggle between his heart and his duty, his heart prevailed. In dark February, he rode out to Fairfax Court House and told Antonia he had made up his mind to resign his commission. She inquired about a marriage license, but no one there could issue one, and she would not consider being wed without one. Warning him not to risk riding the Little River Turnpike again, she said she would come to Washington. But her father objected to the idea of her going to him and insisted that he come to get her. Amid these negotiations over who would travel where, the Fords got a false report that Antonia's brother Charles had been killed in action with Stuart's horse artillery, a development that did not make her father any warmer toward his Yankee prospective son-in-law.* But Antonia wrote that a neighbor had spoken of the major fondly, that "None of them consider you an enemy." Willard apparently reminded her that although he was shedding his uniform, he was not shedding his loyalty to the government. "My dear Major," she assured him, "no one has ever accused you of being any-

---

*A few months later, on May 31, 1864, First Lieutenant Charles E. Ford, of McGregor's battery, Stuart's horse artillery, was killed near Ashland in Hanover County. He was temporarily buried there, and his body was later removed to Hollywood Cemetery in Richmond. (Box I-171, Willard Family papers)

thing but the *most decided* unionist.... but I love you none the less for it. With all my heart do I believe in *one* union—do you know what it is?"[16]

This teasing relationship was almost over. Willard's resignation was effective March 1. Nine days later, he risked the ride to Fairfax, and the next day Mr. and Mrs. Ford, Antonia and Willard set out up the pike to Washington. Just as Antonia had feared, one of Mosby's riders stepped out of the bushes and halted them. "Who goes there?" he asked. "Ford of Fairfax," said her father, "taking my daughter to Washington to see a doctor." He did not explain who else was in the back of the carriage, and the sentry let them pass. Later that day, at the Metropolitan Hotel on Pennsylvania Avenue, the Reverend Phineas D. Gurley pronounced Joseph and Antonia man and wife. They departed on a wedding trip to Philadelphia, where the groom sent a polite note to his new mother-in-law, to which the bride appended a longer postscript suggestively describing their wedding night. She did not go to the hotel dining room for supper, she said, but had tea sent up "and fooled over that until it was ridiculous, but the Major went ahead to undress as if I was a statue." He later told her "he was so free on purpose because he was determined to break down all restraint and put me at my ease by being so himself. He succeeded much better than I supposed could be the case.... I do not promise to drink any more champagne...."[17]

Both groom and bride were concerned over how their North-South merger impressed others. Joseph apparently had asked an esteemed Washingtonian, Benjamin Ogle Tayloe, how the marriage would play in social circles. "I shall 'not think less' of you for marrying a poor but intelligent and more than all a *respectable* Virginian," the old gentleman assured him. Antonia told her mother-in-law, "I do very much wish to know what the people say of me," but she had not lost any of her mischievousness. When a friend asked why she had married a Union man, Antonia answered, "I knew I could not revenge myself on the nation, but was fully capable of tormenting one Yankee to death so took the Major."[18]

Despite Lincoln's commitment to emancipation and the growing involvement of black troops in the war, Radicals were unsatisfied. They accused him of being too easy on defeated Confederates, insufficiently harsh in plans for postwar reconstruction. Some were working openly, others secretly, to replace him in the White House. In late January, for example, Nathan Daniels, who had commanded a regiment of black and Creole soldiers in Louisiana, was invited to join what he called "the Strong Band." It was an undercover lodge of Radicals whose purpose was "to introduce into every department of government the most rigid system of [reconstruction] and reform compatible with a vigorous and successful prosecution of the war," and to put into office only such "true and loyal patriots as have the ability to drive it, and the firmness & will to enforce all measures necessary to accomplish these ends." Its candidate would be Chase or Butler, "whichever is the most available."[19]

These Radical intrigues burst into the open on George Washington's birthday, when a sensational document bearing Pomeroy's name appeared in the *National Intelligencer.* By then the hard-line Kansan had become a recognized leader of anti-Lincoln cabals, and he was bold enough to acknowledge the widely distributed circular, which denounced the president and boosted Chase to replace him. The first reason it cited for changing presidents was that "even were the election of Mr. Lincoln desirable, it is practically impossible against the union of influences which will oppose him." But the Pomeroy circular itself triggered responses that effectively ended any chance that a Republican other than Lincoln could win the party's nomination. Northeastern Radicals like Sumner and Wilson of Massachusetts had never joined the maneuvering against the president. Legislators in Pennsylvania had already declared for him. Within three days after the circular became public, Republicans in the Ohio legislature caucused and endorsed him, undermining Chase's home base. The same thing happened in Rhode Island, which Chase had considered secure because of his son-in-law's money and influence. Indiana's state convention went on record for the president. Chase wrote to Lincoln denying any knowledge of the circular, and soon afterward wrote to Ohio friends asking that "no further consideration be given to my name." Nicolay and Hay maintained that Chase's candidacy "never could have been said to exist except in the imagination of Mr. Chase and a narrow circle of adherents." But Chase would still make trouble for the president, and the likes of Pomeroy did not yet concede that further efforts against the president were futile.[20]

Led by Radicals Wade of Ohio and Chandler of Michigan, the Committee on the Conduct of the War was chipping away at Lincoln by persecuting his generals. That winter they were investigating

George Meade, bringing in rival officers like Dan Sickles and Abner Doubleday to criticize his generalship before and after his victory at Gettysburg. They contrasted him with "Fighting Joe" Hooker, who had courted and been courted by Chase. They attributed the army's misfortunes to "McClellanism" and "copperheadism" in its leaders, and by extension faulted Lincoln for appointing and retaining politically unreliable generals.

In early March, Wade, Chandler and new Congressman Benjamin F. Loan of Missouri asked for an appointment at the White House. It was a gray day, and Lincoln was not inclined to be gracious toward men who had spent many months carping at his leadership. Moreover, he had just learned of another Union failure, the disastrous end of an expedition to free the Federal prisoners in Richmond. An earlier effort by Ben Butler's troops from Fortress Monroe had turned back, but after hearing descriptions of how the captives at Belle Isle and Libby prisons were suffering, Lincoln had approved a mass cavalry raid against Richmond. It was led by Brigadier General Judson Kilpatrick and Colonel Ulrich Dahlgren, son of the president's friend, Rear Admiral John A. Dahlgren, former commandant of the Washington Navy Yard. Kilpatrick's raid broke up against Richmond's defenses, and Dahlgren was killed as he rode away. On his body, the Confederates found orders indicating that he had intended to dash in and kill Jeff Davis and the Rebel hierarchy. Although Union officials disputed the authenticity of those papers, the orders were real enough to plant the idea of assassination in the minds of some vengeful Southerners.

Lincoln was thus in no mood to hear advice, let alone threats, from the Radical committeemen. They told him, however, that it was their duty "on behalf of the army and the country to demand the removal of General Meade." They maintained that they were not promoting any particular successor, but said they would be satisfied with Hooker. Uncautiously, they added that if the president did not act promptly they would publish the committee testimony against Meade, along with appropriate comments. Lincoln, holding his temper in check, refused their demand. He himself had come close to firing Meade after Gettysburg, and had prodded him, unsuccessfully, to take the offensive during this fall and winter. But he was not about to let these Radicals dictate his decisions. In any case, he had already reached his own solution to the problem of army command.[21]

On the morning of February 29, a magnificent presentation sword went on display in the office of the Speaker of the House. Its pommel was ornamented with fourteen impressive diamonds, and along its gold scabbard were inscribed the names of twenty-seven battles, from Palo Alto in Mexico to Lookout Mountain in Tennessee, where Ulysses S. Grant had fought. The elaborate sword was a gift to the general from the grateful citizens of Jo Daviess County, Illinois. In a nearby committee room hung a full-length portrait of him, field glasses in hand, standing by a demolished Rebel cannon. Although Grant was still out west, the way east was being paved for him at the Capitol. There Congress re-created the rank of lieutenant general, an honor that had been held only by George Washington and Winfield Scott (the latter belatedly breveted for his exploits in Mexico). Everyone involved knew who would wear the newly authorized third star.[22]

After the Radical committeemen had departed the White House unsatisfied, Lincoln called Grant to Washington. It was not an impromptu decision; since at least December, he had considered bringing him east to give the army a jolt of new energy and determination. But politics shadowed every military promotion. If Democrats were counting on the proven loser McClellan as their candidate, why shouldn't Republicans look to Grant, the winner at Shiloh, Vicksburg and Chattanooga? The examples of Washington and Andrew Jackson were conspicuous in history, and in fact there was rising interest in Grant within both parties. Before putting him in a position to take credit for any ensuing victories, Lincoln wanted to be sure he had no presidential ambitions. The president had already heard of two letters in which Grant assured friends that he had no desire for political office, but before acting, he sought out yet another friend of the general, who showed him a letter confirming Grant's apolitical stance.[23]

Late on the afternoon of March 8, 1864, Grant and his son stepped off the train at Washington's B&O station. No one was there to greet him, and when he arrived at Willard's, tired and disheveled, the clerk did not recognize him. Thousands of officers, hundreds of generals had checked in there in the past three years, and this one was less imposing than the typical rear-area quartermaster. Of less than average height, wearing a close-cut reddish brown beard and ordinary uniform, he "doesn't put on any airs whatever," Noah Brooks wrote later.

When Grant came down to dinner at the hotel, he was not noticed until someone looked twice, and then murmurs ran about the dining room. An admirer who could not contain himself stepped onto a chair and called for three cheers, which were rendered with gusto and the pounding of tables. Surprised and seemingly chagrined, Grant stood, modestly bowed and sat to finish his meal. When he was done, Congressman James K. Moorhead of Pennsylvania introduced him to each of the citizens clamoring to shake his hand.

From Willard's, Grant went to the White House, where one of the regular levees was already in swing. An immense turnout was there because word had spread that he was coming. About nine-thirty, he arrived and was greeted by Lincoln. The two great Illinoisans, the most dominant figures in saving the Union, had never met before, and they had no time to get acquainted before Seward took Grant by the hand and led him to meet Mary Lincoln, and then into the crowded East Room. What followed seemed to Gideon Welles "rowdy and unseemly"—people cheered and thronged about Grant, who was pressed by a host of crinolined ladies. Men mounted tables to get a better look; Grant had to stand on a sofa to escape the crush. Only when Lincoln drew him away did the excitement subside and gossip resume about exactly how he would play his new role.[24]

In the Blue Room, the president told Grant and Stanton that he would present the general's new commission the next day. He said he would make a short speech from text, and suggested that Grant, unaccustomed to such occasions, do the same. He asked him to make two points: something to mollify jealousy among other generals, and something to make the Army of the Potomac feel good. As he handed Grant the commission the following afternoon, Lincoln told him, "As the country herein trusts you, so, under God, it will sustain you," and assured him that he heartily concurred. Grant, reading briefly from a half-page of notes, did not find words to make the points Lincoln had mentioned. Whether the president was surprised by this, considered it a flash of independence, is not recorded. A day later, Stanton announced that Halleck had been relieved as general-in-chief at his own request, and would become chief of staff instead. U. S. Grant would thenceforth command all the armies of the United States.[25]

Without waiting for more formalities, Grant took the Orange & Alexandria Railroad to Brandy Station, to meet and assess the commander of the Army of the Potomac. Meade wisely told him that if the new general-in-chief wanted someone else, perhaps Sherman, to command that army, he was ready to step aside. This impressed Grant favorably, but what he said next had the opposite effect on Meade. The new supreme commander would not make his headquarters in a Washington office; instead he would make his headquarters in the field, right there alongside Meade. In this, he would heed the advice of Sherman, his chief lieutenant in the West, who had warned him about the snake pit of politics that would surround him in the capital. Grant would be effectively breathing down Meade's neck when the winter mud dried and the Army of the Potomac was ready to move again.[26]

A new war was about to begin.

CHAPTER EIGHTEEN

And Now May God Sustain You

T hen the sun rose up from a bed of vapors, and seemed fairly to dissolve with tenderness and warmth. For an hour or two the air was perfectly motionless, and full of low, humming, awakening sounds. The naked trees had a rapt, expectant look. From some unreclaimed common near by came the first strain of the song sparrow; so homely, because so old and familiar, yet so inexpressibly pleasing. Presently a full chorus of voices arose, tender, musical, half suppressed, but full of genuine hilarity and joy."[1]

This is what John Burroughs, a twenty-six-year-old schoolteacher recently arrived from New Jersey, saw in springtime Washington: not the mud and corruption bemoaned by Jane Swisshelm and ladies with skirts that swept the earth, but wonders that long preceded the coming of bureaucrats and crinolines. Before the war, he had begun writing poetry and nature essays. Dazzled by Walt Whitman's *Leaves of Grass,* he had gone to New York to meet the poet, and had not found him but mingled with his coterie there. Now, at the urging of his friend Elijah Allen, another aspiring writer, he had come to Washington hoping to meet Whitman as well as find a better-paying job. While looking for work, Burroughs slept on a cot in the storeroom of Allen's army-navy supply store. For weeks, he was frustrated at job-seeking, and to eat he took temporary work for the quartermaster general, burying black soldiers at segregated mass grave sites on the outskirts of the capital. He wore a bandana over his face, trying to mask the smell of wagonloads of bodies that had been days in transit from the front. Sometimes he had to step aside to be sick, then return to the task. He worked at this for more than three weeks, for which he was paid $1.65 a day. When he could take it no longer, he quit and was out of work for another month before finding a clerkship at the Treasury Department.[2]

But in his other mission, to find and know Whitman, Burroughs succeeded soon after arriving in Washington. Allen, who had introduced him to Whitman's poetry before the war, introduced him to the poet in late 1863. Whitman had cadged a knapsack from Allen's store to carry books and treats on his hospital rounds, and he often stopped in. There, Burroughs finally encountered him, and began a companionship that would inspire his work for the rest of his life. "The first and last impression which [Whitman's] personal presence always made on one was of a nature wonderfully gentle, tender, and benignant," he wrote. "His culture, his intellect, was completely suffused and dominated by his humanity." Whitman was above six feet tall; his voice was "a tender baritone. . . . He always had the look of a man who had just taken a bath. . . . His physiology was undoubtedly remarkable, unique. . . . If that is not the face of a poet, then it is the face of a god."

As their friendship deepened, the two men took walks through the woods about the capital, and Burroughs sometimes accompanied the poet on his rounds in the hospitals. "I have been much with Walt," he wrote to a friend. "Have even slept with him. I love him very much. . . ." Again he wrote, "He loves everybody and everything. I saw a soldier the other day stop on the street and kiss him. He kisses me as if I were a girl." These words did not necessarily mean what they would have if written generations later: in crowded wartime Washington, strangers often slept in the same bed, and in 1864, kissing girls was usually a chaste and gallant venture. However, Burroughs seemed puzzled by Whitman's attentions: "I occasionally see something in [his eyes], as he bends upon me that almost makes me draw back. I cannot explain it. . . . It is as if the earth looked at me—dumb, yearning, relentless, immodest, inhuman."[3]

By that time, more than a year after coming to Washington, Whitman had warmed many a soldier's heart with his kindness but alarmed some of those beside whom he worked, and others to whom he appealed for funds to help the ailing. "There comes that odious Walt Whitman again to talk evil and unbelief to my boys," wrote a nurse at Armory Square Hospital. "I think I would rather see the Evil One himself." Nurse Amanda Akin complained of Walt's "peculiar interest in our soldier boys," especially Erastus Haskell, a young carpenter from upstate New York who died of smallpox. Whitman wrote to Haskell's family, "So farewell, dear boy . . . you did not lay here & die among strangers without having one at hand who loved you dearly, & to whom you gave your dying kiss." A friend in Boston informed the poet that "There is a prejudice agst you here among the 'fine' ladies and gentlemen of the transcendental School. It is believed that you are not afraid of your reproductive organs."[4]

Whitman was unashamed of his homosexuality, but expressed it less in erotic overtures than as an all-encompassing love of everyman. In the hospitals, he offered his hands-on gentleness to hundreds of patients, but became more closely attached to a series of favorites, like the Maryland soldier Lewis Kirk Brown, whose leg had been amputated. After Brown had gone home, Whitman wrote to him as "my darling," and in one letter told of a poor woman who had come to visit her husband in Judiciary Square Hospital. At 3 A.M., she had given birth to a child that fell five feet into a latrine and thence into the sewer beneath the building. The hospital chaplain roused workmen, who dug into the sewer outside and found the baby lying safe on its back in two inches of water. Whitman often began and ended such descriptions of Washington life with personal endearments; he told his friend "Lewy" how he wished that they and some other man could live together—"I should like it so much. But it is probably a dream. . . . Well my darling I have scribbled you off something to show you where I am. So good bye Lewy, good bye my dear son & comrade. . . ." We do not know whether Lewy understood those words as anything more than straight fatherly affection.[5]

Burroughs brought his wife Ursula to Washington and moved out of Allen's store, eventually to a small brick house near the Capitol, where the Russell Senate Office Building would later stand. He had to persuade "Sulie" to come; she had been sickly, staying with her parents, and complained that John's "scribbling" was a waste of time. But now she tended their vegetable garden and their chickens and cow, which brought in a few dollars to supplement his pay as a Treasury clerk. Whitman often came to eat Sunday breakfast and talk. For a while William and Ellen O'Connor, who had befriended the poet when he arrived in Washington, moved in upstairs from Burroughs. Their noisy bohemian life upset Sulie; William was a flagrant womanizer, and Ellen had an unrequited infatuation with Whitman.

Gradually, the Burroughses replaced the O'Connors as the poet's closest friends. Walt and John sat on the Capitol steps and hiked in the hills surrounding the city, picnicking and philosophizing. Whitman was working on the book of war poetry that he called *Drum-Taps,* and at the same time the prose sketches that he would later publish as *Memoranda During the War.* While he focused on the soldiers in hospitals and afield, Burroughs was describing the wider, eternal context of the war. Since discovering John James Audubon's *Birds of North America* in the library at West Point, near where he taught at Highland Falls, he had aspired to be an Audubon of prose. Out of his rambles about Washington came the essays in the first of his many nature books, *Wake-Robin.*[6]

"The national capital is situated in such a vast spread of wild, wooded, or semi-cultivated country, and is in itself so open and spacious, that an unusual number of birds find their way into it in the course of the season," he wrote. From trees near the White House, and early one April morning from his own pear tree, he heard the soft secret tones of the veery and noted the "liquid bubble and cadence" of the ruby-crowned kinglet. He was fascinated by the towering columns of vultures that often soared above. Near the Smithsonian, his ear detected "a burst of bobolink melody from some mysterious source. . . . a strange remoteness and fascination about it." Along Rock Creek, he found a profusion of spring flowers—hepatica, anemone, saxifrage, arbutus, houstonia, bloodroot, spring beauty, violets, vetch, corydalis, potentilla. The creek valley, mostly outside the city limits, had "an abundance of all the elements that make up not only pleasing, but wild and rugged, scenery. There is, perhaps, not another city in the Union that has on its very threshold so much natural beauty and grandeur, such as men seek for in remote forests and mountains." With "a few touches of art," it could become "a park unequaled by anything in the world."[7]

At work at the Treasury Department, Burroughs sat on a high stool, recording millions of dollars in banknotes as they moved in and out of an iron vault in the building's northeast corner. Elsewhere in the vast Treasury, hundreds of women worked in the Bureau of Printing and Engraving, where paper currency was produced. This was a departure from the past, when banknotes were printed by New York firms and mass employment of women, especially at night, was unheard of. But counterfeiting had become a problem, so the superintendent of the bureau, Spencer M. Clark, worked with Dr. Stuart Gwynn of Massachusetts to develop a grade of banknote paper that was difficult to copy. The outside contractors were angered by the resulting loss of business, and some said they instigated the spicy scandal that distracted the capital that spring.[8]

Early in 1864, there was rising talk of irregularity in Treasury business and immorality among the men and women who worked there. One New Yorker who wrote to Lincoln began by accusing Secretary Chase of speculation in stocks, gold and cotton. But he said the "astounding" offenses of Chase and his special friends were "comparatively nothing" beside what Clark was doing. "The Treasury has been converted into the most extensive Whorehouse in the nation.... drunkenness, seduction, adultery and abortion [are] carried on in your Treasury building.... at least 30 members of Congress have their women in Clark's department...." Thomas Walter was happy to believe the worst, telling his wife that "some 20" women had sworn that they could not get or keep their jobs without "yielding to the embraces of the said gentleman" Clark. He heard talk that between forty and fifty of the Treasury women were "about to increase the population." "It is a perfect Sodom," he concluded.[9]

To investigate these charges, Chase borrowed the War Department detective Lafayette Baker. True to form, Baker found outrages right and left, and arrested Gwynn, charging him with trying to swindle the Treasury. Soon afterward, a special congressional committee headed by former general and future President James A. Garfield began its inquiry. It heard a long parade of witnesses, including two clerks, Ella Jackson and Jennie Germon, who swore that they had sexual encounters with Clark outside the office. Chase suspended Clark, but thereafter reinstated him and got Gwynn out of jail when it developed that Baker had coerced the women to testify.*[10]

Eventually the Garfield committee also split over whether the charges were true, but most readers preferred to believe the minority report, which echoed the gossip that had occupied the capital. It alleged an "atrocious.... mass of immorality and profligacy.... These women seem to have been selected, in the Printing Bureau, for their youth and personal attractions." It cited letters arranging for woman employees to dress as men for rendezvous at Canterbury Hall, where

---

*The zealous Baker was known to use extralegal methods and was suspected of shakedowns that enriched him during his career as detective and provost marshal. After the war, he justified his "deceptions and misstatements" as "honorable means of securing victory over the foe. The work of detectives is simply deception reduced to a science or profession...." (Jacob Mogelever, *Death to Traitors*, p. 91)

showgirls danced naughtily and "assignations are made." The committee minority asserted that "neither the laws of God nor of man, the
institution of the Sabbath, nor common decencies of life seem to have
been respected by Clark in his conduct with these women," and said
his bureau was "converted into a place for debauchery and drinking,
the very recital of which is impossible without violating decency."[11]

Spring had advanced, then retreated several times before finally
bringing the violets and warblers that so delighted John Burroughs.
On the first Wednesday in April, Buildings Commissioner French
slogged through mixed rain and snow to a White House reception.
There he met Baltimore city councillors who had come to visit the
Deaf, Dumb & Blind Institution, later Gallaudet College, established in
the District by Amos Kendall. One of the lady guests rendered an
updated version of the song written to boost army recruiting in 1862,
making it "We are coming, Father Abraham / *Five* hundred thousand
more," and all present joined in the chorus.[12]

French found the president looking happy that day, and Mrs. Lincoln "uncommonly cheerful." She had endured a hard two years; after
her son Willie's death threw her into convulsions of grief, one of her
brothers and two of her half brothers, all Rebels, had died in battle.
When her half sister Emilie Todd Helm's husband was killed, the stubbornly Confederate Emilie was brought to the White House and
stayed long enough to stir more malicious gossip about Mary's alleged
disloyalty. While fighting raged at Gettysburg, Mrs. Lincoln had a
serious accident en route from the Soldiers' Home. Apparently someone hoping to hurt the president had unscrewed bolts holding the carriage seat, which fell with her and panicked the horses. She struck her
head on a rock, suffering a wound that became infected. After that, she
had even more of her chronic headaches, as well as more dreams and
spiritualist forebodings of harm coming to her husband. Now in April,
she escorted French to the White House library to show him a display
of wax fruit made by a black woman admirer. French said it was the
first time Mary had entered that room since Willie died, and as she did
her "uncommonly cheerful" mien disappeared. He saw that "the tears
came into her eyes, & my very soul pitied her. Alas, alas! what are all
the honors of this world when offset against such an affliction as that
poor woman has undergone!"[13]

It may have been politics that made the president appear happy to

French that day. His nomination for reelection was by no means assured, but his friends in the states were busily undercutting his rivals. Chase was still in the cabinet, and still ambitious despite his letter withdrawing his name from contention. Lincoln considered Chase less of a threat at Treasury than if he had accepted his offered resignation and set him loose to campaign. Frémont's extreme Radical backers scheduled a convention in Cleveland at the end of May. That was a week before the Lincoln Republicans, under the banner of the National Union Party, would convene in Baltimore. Worldly observers suspected that Frémont would turn out to be a stalking horse for Chase, who would step in at the last moment. As for Butler, he was still in uniform, but highly available.

With the Radicals so far from coalescing behind one challenger, Lincoln understood that the only thing that stood between him and renomination was some serious setback on the battlefield. Soon the April sun would dry the roads of the Old Dominion, and the plebeian Illinois soldier to whom Lincoln had entrusted the fate of his administration would meet the aristocratic General Lee.

Again and again, the South had fought off Union offensives, in part because interior rail lines enabled its generals to shift troops quickly from one threatened front to another. Grant meant to take advantage of the North's increasing superiority in men and materials to end that frustrating pattern. He would move against the Confederacy on five fronts at once, thrusting into Georgia and toward the Alabama coast while sending three separate forces deeper into Virginia. He with Meade would attack Lee, starting along the Rapidan where the Army of the Potomac and the Army of Northern Virginia had faced each other since the Gettysburg campaign. The whole nation understood that Grant would take on Lee directly because his was the most important Confederate army, defending the prize city of Richmond. But Rebel leaders were also concerned about an uncommitted Union force concentrating at Annapolis. It was Ambrose Burnside's Ninth Corps, 22,000 troops who could be sent on a diversionary mission or suddenly strike somewhere down the Atlantic Coast. The Confederates needed to know what Burnside would do. To find out, they sent Thomas Conrad.

Since being arrested for his flamboyant secessionism and sent away from Washington in 1862, Conrad had been back repeatedly. While nominally serving as chaplain of Jeb Stuart's Third Virginia Cavalry, he often uniformed himself as a Union army chaplain on intelligence missions across the lines. By his own account, he had worked with undercover Confederate agents like Edward Norton, a mole in Lafayette Baker's Secret Service Office. On those visits to the capital, Conrad stayed at the allegedly haunted Van Ness mansion at Seventeenth Street near the river, then occupied by a sympathetic Colonel Thomas Green. Once before, Norton had warned Conrad that Baker was on his trail, and the spy narrowly got away when a woman acquaintance gave him $150 with which he bought a boat to escape down the river. He wrote that before the Peninsula campaign, he had sneaked away a copy of McClellan's order of battle that an ally had left on a desk for him to pick up at lunchtime in the War Department. President Davis had ordered him to set up a regular North-South communications link; he did so by enlisting three Washington and Maryland physicians to operate what became known as the "doctors' line" through southern Maryland. Caught by a Union patrol in that area, he was taken to the military prison at Point Lookout, in St. Mary's County at the mouth of the Potomac. He later told of escaping by pretending to have smallpox and being sent to the camp's lightly guarded hospital, from which he slipped away to cross the river.[14]

To find out what Burnside would do, Conrad entered Maryland this time via the Shenandoah Valley, wearing civilian clothes and a full beard to disguise himself from detectives who knew him earlier as a smooth-shaven suspect. In Washington, his previously reliable War Department informant could not help; Stanton had sealed off leaks from his office. After a fruitless night in the city, Conrad went to his hideout down the river, shaved off his beard and changed into his Union chaplain's uniform. In addition to discovering Burnside's intentions, he had a secondary mission. Two of his couriers were smuggling from Confederates in Baltimore a splendid gift uniform for Lee and a pair of gold spurs for Jeb Stuart. He needed to see that they got safely past Federal patrols and across the river with their bundle. At Charlotte Hall, in northern St. Mary's County, he met a Union cavalry sergeant in charge of patrols and paid him a $10 gold piece to let the couriers through. Returning to Washington, he got a forged pass from his War Department accomplice and took the train to Annapolis. There he ambled about Burnside's headquarters and along the waterfront, seeing and hearing enough to satisfy himself that no invasion of the South by sea was planned; Burnside's corps was going to reinforce

Grant. Conrad was condescendingly "amused" by his first view of black Union troops, who provided him "an inward jollification." Before departing for the Potomac, he talked with "some of these embryo Ethiopian Sons of Mars," men of Edward Ferrero's division of Burnside's Ninth Corps, and seemed surprised to find them proud of their soldierly qualities.[15]

Black pride glowed on thousands of faces at midday on April 26, when those troops marched through Washington on the way south. After plodding thirty-plus miles from Annapolis in two days of rain, Burnside's men reformed on the capital's outskirts, polished themselves and their equipment, and headed down New York Avenue. When the war was young, every column of troops had attracted attention and applause; by now, passing regiments were hardly noticed. But this was no ordinary column. It included seven regiments of U.S. Colored Troops, three of them recruited in Maryland. When the corps reached Fourteenth Street, it turned south and strutted past cheering crowds. It passed Willard's, where the president stood on a balcony with Burnside to review the parade, and when the black troops saw him there, they waved their hats and hurrahed the Great Emancipator. Watching on the opposite corner, Burroughs stood with Whitman, who had waited to see his recovered brother George march by with the Fifty-first New York. When Walt spotted George, he hurried alongside the column and so distracted him that he forgot to salute Lincoln. Walt thought the black soldiers "looked and marched very well," and that "it looked funny to see the President standing with his hat off to them just the same as the rest. . . ."[16]

The column took four or five hours to cross the Avenue, troops followed by ambulances followed by thousands of cattle, heading across the river to Virginia. The citizens along the curbs and the marching men felt a sense of purpose, of determination that had been missing from the capital for months. It spread from Grant—not from his public words, because he spoke none—and from the quiet seriousness of soldiers striding again toward Richmond. Urgent preparations were being made behind the front. The nurse Rebecca Pomroy told of orders for Columbian Hospital to be ready for a thousand incoming casualties. At nearby Carver Hospital, tents were being thrown up to take another 1,400." "Can we help at times feeling sad, as we see all this going on?' she asked. "Can we help crying out, 'How long, O

Lord! How long?' " But Whitman felt that with Grant in command it would not be long. To his mother, he wrote that "Grant is determined to bend everything to take Richmond . . . he is in earnest about it, his whole soul & all his thoughts night and day are upon it—he is probably the most in earnest of any man in command or in the government either. . . ."[17]

Nothing spoke more eloquently of this mix of hope and fear than the eager faces of the black soldiers marching south. Charles Carleton Coffin of the *Boston Journal,* one of the North's premier war correspondents, called the passing of the colored troops a "sublime spectacle." But as they continued across the Long Bridge to join Grant's army, their parading was over. They had never been in battle, wrote Coffin, and "till a year ago [they] never had a country . . . even now are not American citizens . . . are disfranchised—yet they are going out to fight for the flag!"[18]

On the last day of the month, Lincoln wrote to Grant:

> Not expecting to see you again before the spring campaign opens, I wish to express in this way my entire satisfaction with what you have done up to this time, so far as I understand it. The particulars of your plans I neither know nor seek to know. You are vigilant and self-reliant; and, pleased with this, I wish not to obtrude any constraints or restraints upon you. While I am very anxious that any great disasters or capture of our men in great numbers shall be avoided, I know these points are less likely to escape your attention than they would be mine. If there is anything wanting which is within my power to give, do not fail to let me know it. And now, with a brave army and a just cause, may God sustain you.[19]

It was a commission that he had entrusted to no other officer. He had inquired about and often intruded upon the plans of every previous commander. Now he had promised to let his general run the war. To go with the third star of a lieutenant general, he had awarded Grant the credit, or blame, for whatever happened.

That night, the president came chuckling into the office where Nicolay and Hay had stayed late. He wanted to show them a caricature in a book he had been reading. Hay wrote that he seemed "utterly unconscious that . . . with his short shirt hanging about his long legs & setting out behind like the tail feathers of an enormous ostrich [he] was infinitely funnier than anything in the book.... What a man it is! Occupied all day with matters of vast moment, deeply anxious about the fate of the greatest army of the world, with his own fame & future hanging on the events of the passing hour, yet he has such a wealth of simple bonhommie [*sic*] & good fellow ship that he gets out of bed & perambulates the house in his shirt to find us that we may share with him the fun...."[20]

In the darkness early on May 4, the Army of the Potomac began crossing the Rapidan River into the Spotsylvania County forest where Lee had outfought Hooker a year earlier. At the same time, Butler's army was loading aboard transports to steam up the James River and cut off Richmond from the south, and Sherman was beginning his advance from Chattanooga toward Atlanta. Grant's coordinated, all-fronts offensive was moving out on schedule. He hoped to hurry Meade's army across the Rapidan and through the tangled woods before Lee could react, but the Confederates caught his divisions there and for two days the armies struggled in the bloody battle of the Wilderness. Close to 18,000 Union troops were killed, wounded or missing, against fewer than half as many Confederate casualties. Earlier Union commanders would have withdrawn the army across the river after such a costly blow, but Grant made a resounding statement to Lee and the world: instead of pulling back, he gave orders to keep going, intending to get around the Confederate flank and push on south. From the Wilderness, Lee raced to block the Federals around Spotsylvania Court House, and there the armies seesawed in battle for almost two weeks. The Army of the Potomac lost almost as many men there as it had in the Wilderness, making a total of some 35,000 casualties in the first fifteen days of the campaign. Despite his losses, Grant swung south again, trying to get between Lee and Richmond.

Lincoln delighted to hear stories of his new commander's calm optimism, as when Meade commented to Grant that Lee seemed to want to make a Kilkenny cat fight of it, to which Grant said simply, "Our cat has the longest tail."* It did: He had called in reinforcements from all directions, far exceeding the meager numbers that Lee could

---

*An old Irish limerick goes thus: "There once were two cats from Kilkenny / Each thought there was one cat too many / They fought and they fit / And they scratched and they bit / Till excepting their nails / And the tips of their tails / Instead of two cats, there weren't any."

summon. He converted the defensive units in the forts around Washington into infantry regiments and ordered them to the front, replacing some of them with untrained hundred-day men from farther north. Marching south with the Second Connecticut Heavy Artillery, Michael Kelly wrote of "fields, green fields, dust, fields strewned with dying, hospitals, all ways to Fredericksburg, every bit of it, sidewalks, every floor, from cellar to attic, barn & shed a hospital." As after Bull Run, the Peninsula, Antietam and Gettysburg, the dead and wounded came flooding from those field hospitals back to Washington.[21]

During the Spotsylvania fighting, Georgeanna Woolsey, one of four dedicated New York sisters who volunteered as nurses, was on duty with the Sanitary Commission at Belle Plain, the Potomac River port above Fredericksburg. "The wounded arrived in ambulances, one train a day," she wrote, "but the trains are miles long, plunged in quagmires, jolted over corduroys, without food, fainting, filthy, frightfully wounded; arms gone to the shoulder, horrible wounds in face and head. I would rather a thousand times have a friend killed on the field than suffer in this way; it is worse than White House, Harrison's [both on the Peninsula], or Gettysburg.... Mules, stretchers, army wagons, prisoners, dead men, and officials all tumbled and jumbled on the dock, which falls in every little while and keeps the ambulances waiting for hours.... Hard work, dirt and death everywhere...."[22]

In the capital, Noah Brooks had written soon after the offensive began that "the city is pervaded with a feeling which can scarcely be called excitement, it is too intense.... People go about the streets with their hands full of 'extras' from the newspaper offices.... Every loyal heart is full of joy at the glorious tidings which continue to come up from the front, and citizens everywhere are congratulating each other upon the near prospect of an end of this wasteful and wicked war." Within days, Brooks's tone had changed: "All Washington is a great hospital.... Boatloads of unfortunate and maimed men are continually arriving.... The town is full of strangers from the North who have come in quest of friends and relatives who are in the hospitals or lying dead upon the battlefield....

"It is inexpressibly sad to see so much pain and waste of life occurring right in the midst of this buoyant and springing season when nature seems her gayest and most vigorous, and only man, dying man, is decaying, perishing, and painfully wasting," Brooks wrote. Late on May 25, he was there as 3,000 severely wounded landed at the Sixth Street wharf. "The long, ghastly procession of shattered wrecks; the groups of tearful, sympathetic spectators, the rigid shapes of those who are bulletined as 'since dead'; the smoothly flowing river and the solemn hush in foreground and on distant evening shores—all form a picture which must some day perpetuate for the nation the saddest sight of all this war...."[23]

And it was not over, not nearly over. From Spotsylvania, Grant slipped around Lee again, only to be confronted at the North Anna River, where his army escaped a tactical trap that the ailing Confederate commander failed to close upon it. Then, once again, the two armies slid south, fighting at Totopotomoy Creek and Bethesda Church, to dig in facing each other around an obscure crossroads named Cold Harbor. There, Grant ordered an all-out assault on Lee's lines, a final attempt to thrust by main force into the Confederate capital, less than ten miles away.

Some soldiers said it took only ten minutes, some twenty minutes, others an hour. In fact, it took most of the morning of June 3 for the Confederates to smash Grant's climactic attacks in the most lopsided major battle of the war. Grant, always the close-mouthed stoic in public, would confess to his staff that ordering the assault was the greatest military mistake he ever made. But word of it was slow in reaching Washington, and slower reaching the nation.

That Friday morning, while the fight was going on, Lincoln sent a message to a New York political meeting saying that "my previous high estimate of Gen. Grant has been maintained and heightened by what has occurred in the remarkable campaign he is now conducting...." At two o'clock that afternoon, Grant sent his first report of the morning's fight, asserting incorrectly that "our loss was not heavy, nor do I suppose the enemy to have lost heavily." But the news officially released to the public was not based directly on Grant's telegrams. Assistant Secretary of War Charles A. Dana, the former newspaper editor traveling with Grant, sent Stanton his own report of each day's events, and from these Stanton compiled his censored communiqués. He slowed the bad news from Cold Harbor so that it only trickled into print, thus cushioning its impact on the nation and on the delegates headed to Baltimore for the National Union Party convention.[24]

Before Brooks left for Baltimore, he quoted wise men in the capital as saying that if Grant's campaign was successful, he would be the next president, whereas if the campaign failed, neither Grant nor Lincoln could be elected. There was an undercurrent of talk for Grant as early-arriving politicians brandished cigars at Baltimore's Eutaw House and Barnum's City Hotel, and the usual grumbling by Radicals unhappy with the president. But by the time the mass of delegates pushed into the Front Street Theater, it was clear that there would be no contest for the presidential nomination. The only question was who would run for vice president with Lincoln. The president would give no hint of whom he preferred, whether the incumbent Hannibal Hamlin, another Republican or perhaps a War Democrat to spread the ticket. When the convention voted to seat a Tennessee delegation over the opposition of New England, it signaled that the number-two position would go to Andrew Johnson, the self-educated Tennessee Democratic tailor who had been congressman, governor, then senator before becoming the state's wartime military governor. After that, there was short work nominating Lincoln by acclamation. When the Ohio delegation came to the White House to celebrate by serenading the president, he responded by waving his hat as he led three cheers for Grant and his soldiers.[25]

That was the face of optimism that the president presented to the crowd outside. Inside, he was reading the newspapers, where the truth of Cold Harbor was becoming clear to the country in the columns of names of men killed, wounded and missing. The hospitals were overfull; Whitman wrote on June 7 of the "immense numbers" of casualties arriving, neglected and in terrible condition. "Many of the amputations have to be done over again," he said. "One new feature is that many of the poor afflicted young men are crazy, every ward has some in it that are wandering—they have suffered too much, & it is perhaps a privilege that they are out of their senses." A week later, Walt himself felt ill, and doctors told him not to come to the hospitals. He thought "hospital poison" might be causing his occasional faintness, headaches and stomachaches; as close as he had been to so many ailing soldiers, it seemed miraculous that he had not fallen sick before. Shaky, near collapse, he decided to go home to Brooklyn for a spell.[26]

The embalming parlors, like the hospitals, were crowded beyond capacity. Some restaurateurs complained that the odor of death and chemicals from nearby undertakers was ruining their business. Dr. Thomas Holmes, who had perfected the technique of embalming as a New York coroner in the 1850s, had become an army surgeon until he realized the profit potential in his art. Since then, he had practiced in downtown Washington, but now neither he nor his competitors could keep up with the flow of business, and in the summer heat the waiting bodies spread a noxious aroma across sections of the city. Holmes, falling behind as he tried to work through this backlog, was briefly arrested for causing a public nuisance. But it was not something he could control. The corpses kept coming.

As the hospitals and mortuaries were overfull, so was the military cemetery at the Soldiers' Home, where 8,000 had now been interred. In mid-May, as Quartermaster General Meigs rode through Arlington Plantation with the president, he had seen men collecting bodies from the temporary hospital there to be taken to the Soldiers' Home. The Arlington mansion and grounds had been bought by the government at a public auction in January for nonpayment of taxes by the Lee family. Now the property was available not only for temporary use, as for Freedman's Village, but for permanent government installations. Stopping the presidential carriage, Meigs ordered the workmen to bury the bodies where they were. The first soldier laid away there was Private William Christman of the Sixty-seventh Pennsylvania. Meigs urged the War Department to take two hundred acres of the estate as a resting place for fallen soldiers, and Stanton quickly agreed.

Apparently more than practicality was at work: Meigs despised Lee for his disloyalty and wanted to stake the place irrevocably for the Union. At the behest of staff officers working in the mansion, the earliest burials took place well away from the building. When Meigs returned and saw this, he angrily ordered that thenceforth graves would be dug as close as possible to what had been Lee's home. His son, Lieutenant John Rodgers Meigs, killed in action in the Shenandoah Valley late in 1864, would be among some 16,000 soldiers buried in Arlington Cemetery during and soon after the war, about 5,000 of them "known but to God." The general had his final revenge against Lee in 1892, when he was laid beneath his own conspicuous memorial not far from the mansion.[27]

CHAPTER NINETEEN

The Darkness That Settled Upon Us

T he sultry heat of mid-June deepened the miasma of death and suppurating wounds that had hung over the capital for weeks, making thousands of citizens desperate for a few hours of fresh air. To accommodate them, the Saddle and Harness Workers Association announced a grand suburban picnic, admission 50 cents for a man "with ladies," and the Hiawatha Boys countered with a picnic where "a good police force has been engaged to preserve strict order." Every such affair was advertised as "grand," including the season's first steamer excursion down the river to Glymont in Charles County, a $1 outing past Mount Vernon and the guard boats that protected the capital from waterborne threats. The armies of Grant and Lee were a hundred miles away, so the War Department had approved the day trip; no military passes were needed.

But most of Washington's war workers had neither a day nor a dollar to spare. At the Arsenal, by the Potomac near the mouth of the Anacostia, a few off-duty soldiers lolled at riverside on the quiet morning of Friday, June 17, watching boats ease past. A sentry paced at the gate, sweating in his woolen uniform. In a long one-story brick building, 104 women were busy assembling munitions for the army. They were "choking" rifle cartridges, tying the neck of powder charges with bits of string. Each worker had perhaps five hundred rounds on the table before her, pointing her way. Just outside this building, workmen had laid several large pans of signal shells to dry in the sun. Each black metal pan contained two to three hundred stars. As the sun climbed toward noon, those pans absorbed its heat.

At 11:50 A.M., "suddenly there was a great flash of light just outside of the building, and through the open windows...went a dart of flame that ran like a hissing serpent along the table where the girls were at work. In an instant there was a greater flash of light that seemed to fill the entire room, which was followed by a deafening explosion. The report came like an earthquake shock." Across southeast Washington, people looked up, wondering what had happened, until they saw a cloud of dense smoke billowing above the Arsenal. So many came running to help that the gate had to be closed to prevent mob chaos. One man grabbed a young woman whose clothes were in flames and threw her into the river. Other women ran from the blaze, their dresses afire until rescuers tore them off. Thirteen injured women managed to get onto a tugboat and were taken to the Sixth Street pier, then to Armory Square Hospital. The most horribly burned victims were caged in the wire of their hoop skirts. After the blaze was finally out, officials tried to piece together and count the remains of those who died. Seventeen bodies, most of them unrecognizable, were laid on the grass, some in boxes, on boards, in tin pans. A few could be identified by a shoe or a piece of jewelry. Bartholomew McCarthy and Honora Murphy recognized the corpse of Johanna Connor by a charred patch of dress that somehow had not burned away. Most of the victims were unmarried Irish girls, with names like Bridget Dunn, Lizzie Brahler, Julia McEwen, Bettie Brannagan, Kate Branahan, Emily Collins and Sallie McElfresh. Twenty-three died, seventeen at the site and six later from burns.*[1]

A coroner's jury found that the Arsenal superintendent, Thomas B. Brown, who had been a pyrotechnician there for twenty-one years, was guilty of placing the pans of combustible stars too close to the building where cartridges were assembled. When one was set off by the hot pan, the rest started shooting in all directions, exploding the loose powder in the workroom. Brown was rebuked for "culpable carelessness and negligence and reckless disregard for life." This was little solace for the victims' families, among more than a thousand persons who crowded the Arsenal grounds for a mass funeral that Sunday afternoon. Fifteen closed coffins were on a platform draped with the

---

*On the same Friday, officials received a letter from the Allegheny Arsenal near Pittsburgh, thanking the Washington employees for their $170 contribution to aid victims of a similar explosion there. The Washington explosion also resembled a worse disaster in Richmond that should have been a warning. On March 13, 1863, forty-five girls, some as young as ten years, were killed or mortally injured doing comparable work in the Confederate laboratory on Brown's Island in the James River. (*Star*, 20 Feb. 1904; *Richmond Examiner*, 15 Mar. 1863)

flag and black crepe—seven with identified bodies on one side, eight with unidentified on the other. The remaining victims were buried separately. Since most of the dead were Catholics, Father Bokel of St. Dominic's Church led the service, followed by the Reverend S. V. Leech of Gorsuch Chapel for the Protestant victims. "There were many exhibitions of hysteria and intense grief by families of victims, who begged to have the coffins opened that they might view the remains." Because of the condition of the bodies, "it was held inadvisable and unwise to do so."[2]

The shock and grief that followed the violent end of fewer than two dozen young, innocent civilians seemed to exceed Washington's response to the death of thousands of soldiers, even those who died close at hand. From the Arsenal, a procession of some 150 vehicles and marching citizens, led by the Findlay Hospital Band and the Sons of Temperance, moved up to Pennsylvania Avenue and then east to the Congressional Cemetery. The bells of St. Dominic's and the Columbia Fire Company tolled above the band's dirges. Lincoln and Stanton rode together as chief mourners, in a carriage with Stanton's son. Noah Brooks estimated that 25,000 persons, an unlikely number, crowded in and around the cemetery. Those close enough could see the fifteen coffins lowered into two long graves, and some relatives of the dead hanging over the pits, wailing the names of loved ones. Whatever the president and the secretary of war may have said to each other about the proceedings as they rode back toward the White House could hardly have been more depressing than their conversation about the current state of the war.[3]

On the day of the fire, Lincoln had returned from Philadelphia, where he spoke solemnly at the Great Central Sanitary Fair held to raise funds to help the soldiers. "War, at the best, is terrible," he said, "and this war of ours, in its magnitude and in its duration, is one of the most terrible. . . . it has carried mourning to almost every home, until it can almost be said that 'the heavens are hung in black.' " But he promised that "we are going through on this line if it takes three years more."[4]

A month earlier, Grant had briefly lifted Northern spirits after the terrible fight in the Wilderness by declaring that "I propose to fight it out on this line, if it takes all summer." Now the president had extended the vow of determination to three years, and if those thirty-six months were nearly as bloody as the past six weeks, even the Union's seemingly endless well of manpower must run dry. Grant, after being turned back at Cold Harbor, had shifted his army across the James River. There his dispirited troops had made a series of unsuccessful efforts to capture the vital rail center of Petersburg from a skimpy line of defenders. Now Lee had crossed to confront him, and the two major armies in Virginia were digging in for a siege. Grant was reluctant to admit that he would have to fight a war of attrition after failing to defeat Lee by maneuver or head-on assault. In the Shenandoah Valley, Confederates under Lieutenant General Jubal Early had stopped Major General David Hunter's thrust south and were marching toward the Potomac, while in Georgia, Confederate General Joseph E. Johnston was parrying Sherman's offensive thrusts as he fell back toward Atlanta. The only notable Union success was taking place across the Atlantic, where the USS *Kearsarge* finally ended the worldwide rampage of the Confederate raider *Alabama* in a circling sea battle off the French port of Cherbourg. But that morsel of good news would be eighteen days reaching Washington.[5]

On the Tuesday after the mass funeral at Congressional Cemetery, Lincoln and his son Tad headed down the Potomac, then up the James to visit Grant outside Petersburg. When Grant had notified him that the army had smoothly pulled away from Cold Harbor and crossed the James, Lincoln sent back an encouraging wire: "I begin to see it; you will succeed. God bless you all." But he wanted to see it firsthand. Arriving unheralded, he told Grant, "I don't expect I can do any good, and in fact I'm afraid I may do harm, but I'll put myself under your orders and if you find me doing anything wrong just send me [off] right away." He conferred aboard his steamboat with Grant, Meade and Butler, and made a point of calling on U.S. Colored Troops of the Eighteenth Corps, who cheered him as "Father Abraham." Hearing Grant's plans, he said he did not want to butt in, but "I do sincerely hope that all may be accomplished with as little bloodshed as possible." Bolstered by Grant's single-minded resolve, he returned to Washington seeming to feel better, a transitory mood that briefly prevailed over what was in the newspapers. Before the end of June, Sherman abandoned his customary flanking tactics and attacked Johnston head-on at Kennesaw Mountain, Georgia. The result was another bloody Union defeat.[6]

Brooks wrote that "those days will appear to be the darkest of the many dark days through which passed the friends and lovers of the

Federal Union." The early years of the war had been full of grief, he said, "but the darkness that settled upon us in the summer of 1864 was the more difficult to be endured because of its unexpectedness. The hopes so buoyantly entertained by our people when Grant opened his campaign in Virginia had been dashed. No joyful tidings came from the Army now; a deadly calm prevailed where so lately resounded the shouts of victory."[7]

In Washington, there were always political shenanigans to take minds momentarily off the casualty lists and the sight of wagons loaded with corpses. For months, this diversion had been supplied by supporters of Chase and other politicians who thought the president's war leadership was either too weak or too strong. Now that the Baltimore convention had renominated Lincoln, the Chase threat was close to nil, but Chase himself had not yet grasped this. Near the end of June, the secretary defied Lincoln over a major Treasury Department appointment and once again threatened to quit if he did not get his way. This time, the president shocked him by accepting his resignation. Lincoln first proposed former Ohio Governor David Tod to replace Chase, but Tod bowed out in the face of strong opposition. The president then nominated Maine Senator William Pitt Fessenden. He had not consulted the reluctant Fessenden, who wrote him a letter declining the job. Lincoln refused to read it, and Fessenden was speedily endorsed by the Senate.

While the Chase dispute was going on, Radical legislators led by Ben Wade of Ohio and Henry Winter Davis of Maryland produced a bill intended to take reconstruction policy out of the president's hands. Presented as the session neared its end, the measure would have stiffened requirements for seceded states to rejoin the Union, curtailed voting rights of former Rebel soldiers, and flatly decreed the end of slavery. Congress easily passed this frontal challenge to the president, but he would not give way. He disposed of the bill by pocket veto, letting it die unsigned when Congress adjourned on July 4. Coming after the president called Chase's bluff, his veto further offended the angriest Radicals, assuring that there would be no political peace of mind in the White House.[8]

As Congress left town, what seemed at first "a summer raid down the Shenandoah Valley" by the Confederates began to look like something more. Jubal Early's Army of the Valley kept coming north, bypassing

Harpers Ferry and crossing the Potomac farther up, at Shepherds-town. Then it pushed toward Hagerstown and Frederick, throwing a new fright into the citizens of Maryland. With the main Union army settling in below Richmond, worried state officials in Pennsylvania and New York called out 24,000 militiamen for home defense. This time their fears seemed justified.[9]

On July 6, Early sent cavalry brigadier John McCausland to capture Hagerstown and levy a $200,000 payment from its citizens to retaliate for the destruction left by Union General Hunter's troops in Virginia. Someone's faulty handwriting caused McCausland to demand just $20,000, plus 1,500 suits, shirts, and pairs of shoes, socks and drawers for his troops. He got the cash, but not all the clothing, despite his threats to burn the town. As the Rebel force moved toward Frederick, it lost stragglers who fanned out rustling cattle and horses and sweeping through orchards in the green, unravaged countryside. A patched-together Union force of volunteers and irregulars under Union Major General Lew Wallace did its best to slow the invaders as they flowed through the gaps in South and Catoctin mountains. Marching into Frederick, Early's men again demanded $200,000 ransom, plus tons of flour, sugar, coffee, salt and bacon. The city fathers argued that this was ten times what was levied against Hagerstown, but with Confederate troops standing ready to torch the place, they gave in and Early got what he demanded.[10]

Since before Early crossed the Potomac, citizens and officials on the Northern side had been unsure what to make of his expedition. As if the war were a thousand miles away, a party of Treasury employees set out on a pleasure trip to Harpers Ferry aboard the C&O Canal packet *Flying Cloud*. As they sat for dinner, shots whizzed about them. A few men jumped off to try to open the next lock in the canal, but were driven away by more shots. At this, the whole company abandoned ship and headed for the hills to watch Rebels burn the packet behind them. The next day the captain and three passengers remained missing. Because the Federals still held Harpers Ferry and Maryland Heights, the tendency at first was to minimize Early's approach as "simply a plundering expedition and nothing more." It was that, but it was more.[11]

Lee had sent Early north to threaten Washington and Baltimore, hoping to divert strength from Grant's force south of Richmond. He might menace Washington long enough to convince foreign powers that there was still reason to recognize the Confederate government.

Some of Early's officers imagined themselves dashing in to kidnap Lincoln and hold him for political ransom. As always when the lean, footsore Rebels moved into undisturbed farmland and towns, they hoped to gather food, horses and shoes. But this excursion had another potential purpose, outlined in a message sent by Lee after Early's army was well on its way. Lee thought that one of Early's cavalry brigadiers, the Marylander Bradley T. Johnson, might be able to lead his horsemen between Baltimore and Washington and then dash some eighty miles south to the prison camp at Point Lookout, which was known to be lightly guarded by U.S. Colored Troops. Coordinating with a landing force brought up the Chesapeake by the Confederate navy, Johnson would free more than 15,000 captured Rebels, arm them and march back to join Early in besieging Washington. The idea was so iffy that Early apparently tucked it far back in his mind as he pushed north, then east.[12]

Northern estimates of Early's strength ran from 5,000 to 30,000 troops and beyond. In fact, he had crossed the Potomac with fewer than 20,000. Not until after that crossing did Federal authorities decide that he might be doing more than plundering, and even then they did not say so publicly. On July 6, Grant had at last reacted by ordering Major General Horatio Wright's veteran Sixth Corps to hurry north from the Petersburg front, and one of its divisions debarked at Baltimore the next day. Another day later, Secretary Welles wrote that the president was concerned but "enjoined to silence, while Halleck is in a perfect maze, bewildered, without intelligent decision or self-reliance, and Stanton is wisely ignorant." By July 9, the *New York Times*'s man in Baltimore reported, "It may without exaggeration be said today that we are having something of an excitement." The governor and the mayor proclaimed an emergency, calling citizens to arms, saying "Come in your Leagues, come in your militia companies—but come in crowds, and come quickly."[13]

That Saturday, General Wallace made a stand along the narrow Monocacy River, southeast of Frederick, with his own assorted troops and the first Sixth Corps regiments arriving from Baltimore. He positioned his skimpy force to resist Early's advance along either the National Road toward Baltimore or the Georgetown Pike toward the capital. There on the Monocacy, some forty miles from Washington and Baltimore, he fought one of the most important minor battles of the war.

It was an unequal contest. Early dispatched a cavalry force to men-

ace Baltimore while he turned his main body toward Wallace and
Washington. He was still planning his attack when the impetuous
McCausland led his horsemen across the Monocacy against Wallace's
left flank. The Rebel infantry followed up, brigade by brigade, driving
the defenders back along both key roads. Wallace ordered his troops
to burn the covered bridge where the Georgetown Pike crossed the
river, and wood smoke from that fire blended with powder smoke
from the guns, blanketing the battlefield. By late afternoon, the fight
was over and Wallace withdrew toward Baltimore. He had lost nearly
2,000 casualties, against about 750 in the Rebel ranks. But his outnumbered men had resisted stoutly, delaying Early's advance for a full day.

The War Department, hoping to prevent panic, still withheld information of Early's advance as he pushed his troops toward Washington. On Sunday morning, July 10, Welles was in his office reading his
mail when a clerk came in and said Rebel pickets were on the outskirts
of Georgetown. When another man brought the same information,
Welles sent a messenger to Stanton's department next door to find out
the facts. "They were ignorant," he wrote, "had heard street rumors,
but they were unworthy of notice—[they] ridiculed my inquiry." Early's
main force was not yet near Georgetown, but by midafternoon it had
reached Rockville, barely twenty miles from the White House.[14]

That evening, John Hay called at Horatio Wright's home, where
the general's wife and daughter were awaiting his arrival with the rest
of the Sixth Corps. Returning to his quarters, Hay found that an official had "stampeded the servants" by leaving a message urging that the
president should have a gunboat ready to take him away because the
Confederates were within five miles. Hay, considering that there had
been "the usual flight of rumors but no special excitement," went to
bed. (Unknown to him, Gustavus Fox, assistant navy secretary, had
ordered the ordnance boat *Baltimore* to stand by for the president in
case the Rebels broke into the capital.) Just after midnight, young
Robert Lincoln arrived and told Hay that Stanton had sent a carriage
and guard detail to bring the president and family in from the exposed
Soldiers' Home because of approaching Confederates. This annoyed
the president, as did the standby boat when he heard about it.[15]

Most Washingtonians had been so confident that Grant would deal
with any threat that few believed the alarming rumors printed, then
denied, then printed again in extra editions of the newspapers. But
some die-hard secessionists not only believed the rumors; they were
ready to greet the Rebels marching in. "Not a few of them boasted that

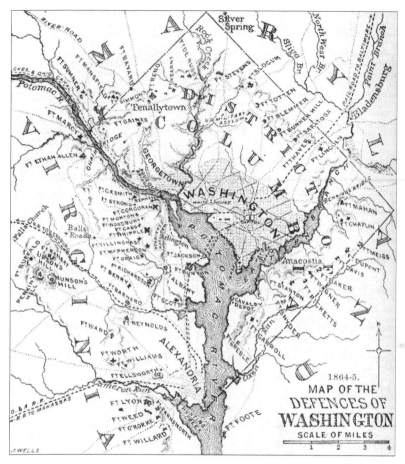

1864-5.
MAP OF THE
DEFENCES OF
WASHINGTON
SCALE OF MILES

in so many days ... the public buildings would lie a mass of ruins," wrote Jane Swisshelm. As late as breakfast on July 11, two army men at Willard's told Treasury official Lucius Chittenden that Washington was in no more danger than Boston. But a third officer, a general of the Invalid Corps, sat quiet. After breakfast, he invited Chittenden to ride with him out beyond Georgetown. They were stopped at a picket line just past Tenallytown, where the River Road branched west from Georgetown Pike. Across a broad valley, they saw a bustling army camp. Chittenden, assuming it was a friendly force, asked whose corps that might be. "We think it's Early's," said the officer, "but don't certainly know. It might be Breckinridge's." Shocked, Chittenden declined the officer's invitation to continue around the circuit of the city's defensive forts.[16]

By then, country people were streaming in from Frederick and upper Montgomery counties on wagons piled with household valuables, cattle stringing behind. Contraband women with infants in their arms and toddlers about their knees asked Swisshelm, "What do you tink Missus? Will de Yankees be able to keep dem out?" The devoted abolitionist Swisshelm knew the city was unprepared, but told them that "the wheels of God's Providence could not turn backward. He had delivered these poor oppressed out of the hand of the oppressor and he would not again give them to the spoiler."[17]

To make good that promise, every available hand was needed. The Pennsylvania Bucktails who guarded the White House left their usual post and marched to the front. Meigs ordered out his quartermaster clerks, the fit and the unfit. Officers turned out 1,800 men from the convalescent camp, and another 3,200 of the Invalid Corps from the city's hospitals. Ordinary civilians were recruited into a Loyal League militia. A unit of U.S. Colored Troops marched up Twelfth Street with wives and children trailing alongside, and black men in the Swampoodle neighborhood were dragooned into service as teamsters. Almost a thousand marines and mechanics from the Navy Yard dropped their tools and formed into companies. All were heading into the defensive perimeter left thinly stretched when Grant swept the previous occupants into the Army of the Potomac for his march toward Richmond. Thirty-seven miles of trenches and earthworks surrounded Washington, including sixty-eight forts and nearly a thousand artillery pieces. But they were manned mostly by part-timers and hundred-day soldiers, many of them National Guardsmen from Ohio, untrained on the heavy artillery bristling from the forts. They needed all the help they could get.[18]

Grant, declining Lincoln's suggestion that he bring most of his army to Washington to try to bag Early, assured the president that the Sixth Corps plus smaller elements he was sending would hold off the Confederates. Then General Hunter, returning from West Virginia after his defeat in the Valley, could cut off Early's retreat and most of the Rebels would never make it back across the Potomac. But even the Sixth Corps could not cover the entire northwestern quadrant of the District, where Early's outriders appeared on July 10. The Confederate general set up headquarters at Silver Spring, the homestead of Francis P. Blair. Confederate soldiers ransacked the house, but John Breckinridge, commanding one of Early's corps, intervened to protect it from destruction because of his prewar respect for old man Blair. Before departing, the troops would take their vengeance by burning the nearby house of Francis Blair's son, the postmaster general.[19]

At 3:30 A.M. on July 11, a hot and hazy Monday, Early's infantry divisions started in from near Rockville while his cavalry and skirmishers were already feeling the capital's defenses, seeking a weak spot. Approaching by the Georgetown Pike, they turned away from heavily gunned Fort Reno and its complex of outlying positions around Tenallytown. They shifted eastward, past Fort De Russy, and tried Seventh Street Road, the main north-south route into the capital. It was defended by Fort Stevens, about a mile inside the District line. Viewed from the city, this strongpoint was near the middle of the northern defensive perimeter, with Forts Reno and De Russy to its left beyond Rock Creek and Forts Slocum and Totten to its right. Trenches and separate gun pits were dug to connect and protect the belt of forts about the capital, but most of those were unoccupied.

Fort Stevens, originally named Fort Massachusetts by troops who helped build it, had been enlarged and renamed to honor Brigadier General Isaac I. Stevens, killed in action at Chantilly in 1862. It was an irregularly shaped eleven-gun bastion of packed earth and timber, with two ammunition magazines and a "bombproof" shelter for its crew. In an arc covering two to three miles from northwest to northeast, the gradual slope had been largely cleared to construct the fort and open fields of fire. Despite the pleas of residents, soldiers preparing the defenses did not hesitate to demolish houses, barns, and even a church when they were in the way. Elizabeth Thomas, a free black woman who lived close by Fort Stevens, related how she stood crying, holding her six-month-old baby, as German-American troops razed her modest home. By one account, Lincoln told her as she wept that "it is hard but you shall reap a great reward."[20]

As the Confederates pushed close, the defenders in the fort opened fire. Any chance of a surprise attack was gone. Early himself rode near enough to conclude wrongly that the position was heavily defended, when in fact it was held then by green troops praying for the arrival of veterans. At first, the Rebels tried to gauge the strength of the garrison with small arms and a few scattered artillery rounds. Soon bullets were singing in both directions and the Federals let go with their heavy guns, trying to keep Early's skirmishers at a respectful distance.

Apparently the Confederates did not recognize the conspicuously tall, dark-bearded civilian who stood on the parapet of the fort until a nearby soldier "roughly ordered him to get down or he would have his head knocked off." It was Lincoln, who had asserted his presidential right to inspect the front when bullets were flying.

The danger was real. Rebel sharpshooters, clustered in scattered houses and barns, were picking off gunners at the fort. The Federals turned converging cannon fire on them from Forts Stevens, De Russy, Slocum and Totten, demolishing the buildings, sending the snipers scurrying away and pushing Early's skirmish line back to extreme rifle range. Lincoln was not the only civilian who came out to distract the nervous soldiers, most of them under fire for the first time. Thousands of men, women and children streamed north to see the show, reminding some of the festive crowd that went out expecting to see the Rebels defeated at Bull Run more than three years earlier. Eventually a cordon of guards was formed to turn spectators back from the front, so eager citizens climbed hills, trees and fences trying to get a view of the fight. Then, after 7 P.M., the first dusty infantrymen of the Sixth Corps started moving into the trenches strung between the forts.[21]

That evening, Lincoln was "in very good feather," according to Hay, although disturbing news had arrived in the afternoon about Rebel cavalry rampaging north of Baltimore. Raiders led by Major Harry Gilmor had burned Governor Augustus Bradford's home in retaliation for the Yankees' burning former Virginia Governor John Letcher's place in Lexington. They cut rail and telegraph lines, set a train ablaze and ran it onto the Gunpowder River bridge, breaking communications with Philadelphia and the North for the first time since early 1861. Among the passengers on one of two intercepted trains, they captured Major General William B. Franklin, who got away that night as his exhausted guards slept.[22]

But the president focused on what was near at hand, and showed more concern about bagging Early's force than about the safety of the capital. He was confusingly overstaffed with generals: Chief of Staff Halleck was the senior officer in town, but Christopher C. Augur commanded the District of Washington and Alexander M. McCook was in charge of the northern defenses. Abner Doubleday was recruiting new militia, while George C. Thomas and the grocer-brigadier Peter F. Bacon were summoning the existing District militia companies to duty for sixty days. Meigs manned a fraction of the perimeter with his quartermaster clerks and hospital convalescents, and other officers were directing their own sectors. Behind them came Wright and the generals and colonels commanding his divisions and brigades. With Lincoln and Stanton contributing their civilian suggestions, this mélange of egos had a hard time deciding whether to go on the attack against Early or merely strengthen the line facing him.[23]

On the morning of July 12, Bradley Johnson with the main Confederate cavalry force rode between Baltimore and Washington, cutting the tracks of the B&O's Washington branch and telegraph wires at Beltsville. From there, he turned toward Upper Marlboro, on the road to Point Lookout. But before he was well started, a messenger from Early caught up, canceling the raid on the prison camp. Johnson had previously informed Early of an intercepted telegram that said two Union corps, not just Wright's command, were on their way to Washington. Early conferred with his generals: Breckinridge, Robert E. Rodes, John B. Gordon and Stephen D. Ramseur were all spirited soldiers, dedicated to offensive warfare. If they intended to march into the city, they had better do it quickly, before major Union reinforcements arrived.

Early issued orders for a dawn attack. Then, at first light, he rode to the front again. This time, he lifted his binoculars to see thick lines of blue uniforms along the ramparts of the fort and in the rifle pits protecting it. All those reported reinforcements must have moved in during the night. He concluded that even if he succeeded in ramming through such a force, his army would be destroyed. Reluctantly, he called off his planned attack and sent a courier to inform Johnson.* He would put on a a daylong demonstration of strength before the Federal lines, pretending to form for an assault. Then, when night came, he would pull away from Washington.[24]

In fact, less than two-thirds of Wright's corps and a handful of men from the Nineteenth Corps, the latter diverted on their way from New Orleans to Grant's army, were in place when Early decided not to attack. But other regiments were close behind, including the Second Connecticut Heavy Artillery, which had marched away from the capital's defenses less than two months earlier as an oversized contingent of cannoneers. Now the regiment, which had lost its colonel and many men assaulting Lee's lines at Cold Harbor, returned as battle-seasoned

---

*Two fast steamboats with some 800 troops had been organized to move into Chesapeake Bay from Wilmington, N.C., to carry out the naval part of the Point Lookout scheme. But word of the plan got out in Richmond and among the troops around Petersburg, where Ben Butler heard of it from a Rebel deserter as early as July 7. The Federals increased their naval patrols off Point Lookout, and on July 10, Jefferson Davis decided to abandon the whole idea. (Benjamin F. Cooling, *Jubal Early's Raid,* p. 173)

infantry. A private in Company B told how the troops jammed aboard the transport *Rebecca Clyde* at City Point near Petersburg and enjoyed the fresh-air voyage down the James, then up the Chesapeake and the Potomac to Washington. When they passed their old base outside Alexandria, they put out all flags, the band played and the troops cheered, wishing they could move back into the relatively luxurious life of heavy artillerymen.[25]

Lucius Chittenden, who had escorted his wife to Baltimore to catch the last train north before the rails were cut, was astonished to hear applause as he returned to Washington. Under the circumstances, he said, "I should not have been more surprised by an outburst of cheers from a funeral procession." He hurried to see haggard but determined Sixth Corps troops marching out Seventh Street, paced by the beat of a single drum at the head of each regiment. Residents rushed out from the curbs, bringing food and buckets of water. It was hard for men of the Second Connecticut Heavy to follow orders to stay in line and not look right or left. Writing to his hometown newspaper, the regiment's correspondent said, "The inhabitants seemed almost overjoyed to see the fighting 6th corps" as it marched to the outskirts near midday on July 12.[26]

No inhabitant was more pleased than Lincoln, who rode out to Fort Stevens again, accompanied by Stanton. So did dozens of bureaucrats like Chittenden, who had no official reason to get passes to the front but went to satisfy plain curiosity. What Early's men were doing looked more serious than a mere demonstration. Until a rainstorm crashed down about 2 P.M., cannon boomed and riflemen skirmished within three hundred yards of the fort. Confederate divisions were arrayed in the distance, positioned to advance astride Seventh Street Road, with cavalry spread for miles to both flanks. After the storm, the fighting resumed, thundering loudest between five and seven o'clock. A battery of Maine artillery, with Sixth Corps infantry, drove the Confederates from a conspicuous house overlooking Rock Creek, and a single sharpshooter from the Seventy-sixth New York reportedly silenced half a dozen Rebel snipers.

Unwisely, Lincoln mounted the parapet again. His tall form, made taller by his stovepipe hat, was a clear target for marksmen firing from trees and houses north of the fort. As he peered out toward the invaders, a Rebel bullet struck down a Pennsylvania surgeon standing beside him.

Chittenden wrote that a young artillery colonel, distressed by the president's stubborn insistence on exposing himself to fire, asked what he should do. Chittenden told him he should order the president either to move or be moved. After debating whether he would face court-martial for addressing his commander-in-chief that way, the colonel steeled himself and said, "I will. I may as well die for one thing as another. If he were shot, I should hold myself responsible." Approaching Lincoln politely, he said, "Mr. President, you are standing within range of five hundred rifles. Please come down to a safer place. If you do not, it will be my duty to call a file of men, and make you."

Lincoln looked down at him and said, "You would do quite right, my boy." He stepped out of the line of fire, admitting that "you are in command of this fort. I should be the last man to set an example of disobedience." The colonel showed him to a safer spot from which he could see many New York soldiers cut down as their brigade moved into the trenches and drove Confederate skirmishers away from the fort.*[27]

Lincoln was and still is the only American president to face enemy fire while in office. While he and thousands of soldiers risked being killed at Fort Stevens, life proceeded as usual at theaters four miles away downtown. At the Canterbury, proprietor George Lea presented a "Mammoth Combination of vocalists, dancers, comedians, Negro delineators &c.," including "Miss Naomi Porter with her great challenge jig" and that "great sensation Drama, 'Bushwhackers of the Potomac.'" Outside, according to Nathan Daniels, preparations were being made on every street to confront advancing Rebels. "If Washington is captured," he wrote, "'twill be after every street is taken one by one, and then it will not be worth the holding.... We must take to half rations and the trenches as this is the death struggle of Rebellion and will be a fierce one."[28]

The defenders of Washington expected Early to make his elaborately advertised attack on the morning of July 13, and they were

---

*Whether the soldier addressed the president as a "damned fool," and whether he was Wright's staff officer, Lieutenant Colonel Oliver Wendell Holmes, Jr., as some accounts have it, is unproven. Others, including Elizabeth Thomas, have also claimed the honor of telling the president what to do. While most accounts tell of Lincoln being warned down off the works once, John Hay wrote in his diary that it happened twice, on both July 11 and 12. Because Hay's diary entries were contemporaneous (he mentioned that he could see columns of smoke north of the White House as he wrote), they are probably more reliable than later recollections. (John Hay, *Inside Lincoln's White House*, pp. 221–222; Benjamin F. Cooling, *Jubal Early's Raid*, p. 143; L. E. Chittenden, *Recollections*, pp. 415–416)

finally ready for him. But Early knew that, and when the Union troops looked out from their forts and rifle pits into the gray dawn, the Rebels had disappeared. According to Michael Kelly of the Second Connecticut Heavy, "Jubal Early saw the G—d d—n 6 Corps red cross & left the scene," and that is just what had happened. Moving onto ground the Confederates had occupied, the Federals found a letter said to have been lost by a Captain Wat Drew of the Twenty-second Virginia Cavalry, a Washingtonian who had gone south. He told his mother in the capital that "it seems hard that here I am within sight of my home and cannot get there. It seems like a pleasant dream to be in such a familiar place." His horse had been shot from under him, he said, but he had been untouched in battle. "I wonder how you all look. I would give worlds to see you again . . . but I guess we will have to wait till a kind Providence grants our prayer. I fixed up nicely to come to W. & it will be a sore disappointment to me. . . ." Perhaps he had brought along a fresh uniform for his planned visit home.[29]

One of Early's soldiers from the District, Henry Loughborough, was luckier than Captain Drew, for he slipped away from his command long enough to have supper with his parents. They lived at Grasslands, an estate that included the later sites of American University and the Department of Homeland Security. Henry's father, Hamilton Loughborough, was an unrepentant Southern sympathizer, and two of his sisters had been arrested for trying to smuggle fine dresses to friends in Virginia.[30]

Henry Loughborough sneaked back to his company in time to rejoin Early's ranks as the Confederates marched west away from Washington, moving faster in retreat than they had when advancing. They had started pulling out at sunset July 12, and before dawn their last cavalry pickets trotted away from the battlefield. All night long, the Rebel columns passed Silver Spring, then Rockville, on their way to Poolesville and the nearby Potomac River crossings. The Federals were unsure where Early was heading, and short of cavalry to find out. When Union horsemen caught up with McCausland's rearguard at Rockville, the Rebel riders turned and drove them back through town. There was confusion over who was in command until Grant ordered Wright to take over the pursuit of Early's force. By then the Confederates had a long head start.

On July 13 and 14, Early's expedition got away unmolested, crossing the Potomac at White's Ford above Poolesville with some two thousand cattle, hundreds of fresh horses and a contingent of Maryland recruits. But they left behind many of the 1,500-plus casualties they had suffered since arriving in Maryland, including a ragged sharpshooter whose body Chittenden examined where it fell facing Fort Stevens. He said the Rebel's rifle and cartridge box were "the only things about him which did not indicate extreme destitution." His shoes were in pieces, held together by twine; his straw hat had lost much of its crown and brim; his hair was matted with grime, and his whole dusty being was "the color of the red Virginia clay." In his haversack was a jackknife, a plug of tobacco, a tin cup, an ounce of salt and about two quarts of cracked corn ground upon the cob, "the provender which the Western farmer feeds to his cattle." That was the Confederate soldier's complete inventory.[31]

In thirty-two days since leaving the Richmond front, Early's Rebels had marched well over four hundred miles in midsummer heat, fighting and winning four battles and a series of skirmishes. But they recrossed into Virginia without entering Washington, freeing the prisoners at Point Lookout or accomplishing their main mission of easing Grant's hold on Petersburg and Richmond. There were many reasons why, but the key was the July 9 battle on the Monocacy River, where Union troops were defeated but delayed the Rebels for a day. That enabled the Sixth Corps to reach the Washington defenses before Early gathered his men for a full-scale attack, and that in turn convinced him that he should not try it. History has never properly acknowledged the importance of Lew Wallace's stand at Monocacy.

Solomon Brown, the first black employee of the Smithsonian, had dug a pit within its walls to bury valuables in case the Rebels got that far. Writing to the Institution's assistant secretary, Spencer Baird, he said that "many have been much frightened at the annual visit of the Rebels to their friends at Maryland." They had knocked at Washington's door, but when it was not opened, "they being a set of high bread gentlemen concluded not to come in." He was contemptuous of the "great number Brave fighting men that came out from their hiding Places and Paraded through streets in serch of arms to meet the Rebels. But they was mustered out to return to they several dens I.E. the drinking Saloons, gambling halls and after hour places . . . it was Imposable for decently disposed persons to pass certin localities with out be interfered with by this brave men who wanted to fight when the Rebel had gone." This rowdiness went on despite the provost mar-

shal's decree that no intoxicants be sold along either Seventh or Fourteenth streets north of F, an order meant to prevent reinforcing troops
from straggling on their way into the lines.[32]

The Rebels had departed, and hundreds of mobilized clerks,
mechanics and convalescents were proudly cheerful as they marched
back from the lines. But Lincoln was unhappy that the Confederates
had once again gotten away, as they had after Antietam and Gettysburg. The fact that so many enemy troops had come so close did not
dissuade the president from returning to the Soldiers' Home as soon
as they were gone. As at Fort Stevens, others seemed more concerned
about his safety than he was. "The old fellow evinces no fear," wrote
Daniels, "although he is in great danger from enemies abroad and
more particularly from the dastard secesh, who lurking as citizens in
the rear, will not hesitate even at assassination to accomplish their
plans." As Lincoln started to ride past the battlefield to the Soldiers'
Home, he told Hay drily, "Wright telegraphs that he thinks the enemy
are all across the Potomac but that he has halted & sent out an infantry
reconnaissance, for fear he might come across the rebels & catch some
of them." Hay noted that "The Chief is evidently disgusted."[33]

If "the Chief" had looked beyond Virginia to the deeper South, he
might have felt less frustrated. Sherman had pushed to the outskirts
of Atlanta, causing Jeff Davis to replace the cautious General Johnston with the impetuous John Bell Hood. For Lincoln, the Union
advance was good news, and the Confederate change of command
led promptly to better news. Three days after taking over, Hood
ordered a fierce but unsuccessful counterattack at Peachtree Creek
that cost the Confederates almost 5,000 men. Two days later, in the
opening battle of Atlanta, they lost nearly 10,000 more. The Rebels
could not replace such numbers, but the Federals could: Lincoln called
for another half million volunteers, who would more than make up
for Sherman's battles and Grant's severe losses on the way toward
Richmond.

Outside Petersburg, coal miners in the Forty-eighth Pennsylvania
had spent more than a month digging a tunnel to plant a massive powder charge under Confederate lines. At 4:45 A.M. on July 30, they set off
an explosion that blew a broad thirty-foot-deep crater in the Rebel
defenses. Blue infantry charged into the gap, but the Confederates rallied and massacred the attackers, many of them black troops. The

Union side lost about 4,000 men, against some 1,500 Rebel casualties. More than that, Lincoln and Grant lost their gamble that a sudden *coup de main* could crush Lee and end the war before the coming election. And while this was going on at Petersburg, Early turned on his pursuers in the Valley, defeating the Federals at Kernstown and sending his cavalry raiding across the Potomac once again. McCausland's horse brigade reached Chambersburg, Pennsylvania, where he demanded $500,000 in currency or $100,000 in gold as reparations for Yankee destruction in Virginia. This time the residents could not raise the ransom, so McCausland set the town afire.

In Washington, rage over this Rebel arson joined broad disappointment over how the war was being managed. Welles feared that Grant was "less able than he is credited." He remembered Admiral Porter's saying "there was something wanting in Grant, which Sherman could always supply, and vice versa, as regards Sherman, but that the two together made a very perfect general officer and they ought never to be separated." Considering the mass casualties of the past two months, followed by the Petersburg mine fiasco, Welles suspected that Grant without Sherman was not up to his job. "A blight and sadness comes over me like a dark shadow when I dwell on the subject," he wrote. "A nation's destiny almost has been committed to this man, and if it is an improper committal, where are we?"[34]

Senators Ben Wade and Winter Davis were still angry that Lincoln had pocketed their reconstruction bill, and furious about how he later explained his veto. Perhaps they also sensed that he was politically weakened by the midsummer military setbacks. In early August they tried to make his life more miserable by issuing an ill-tempered manifesto that was published by Greeley's *Tribune*. It accused the president of "dictatorial usurpation" of power and demanded that he "confine himself to his executive duties—to obey and execute, not make the laws—to suppress by arms armed rebellion, and leave political reorganization to Congress." This time they overshot; most Republicans, including their fellow Radicals, disapproved and said so. Lincoln himself pretended to brush away their harangue with a story of a friend who bought his son a microscope. The eager boy went about focusing his instrument on items in the household until one evening at dinner, when his father started to take a bite of cheese. The boy warned him not to, that it was "full of wrigglers." The old gentleman took a big chunk and said, "My son, let 'em *wriggle*. I can stand it if they can."[35]

So the president let Wade and Davis wriggle, but their tactical blunder did not end the Radicals' machinations against him. They were convinced that he could not win in November, and were talking of holding another convention in September to replace him with a more aggressive candidate, someone like Butler or Chase. In the mood that dominated the White House at that moment, Lincoln was not sure he could win, either. After the wholesale battle losses of spring and summer, no end to the war was in sight. He was hearing ominous predictions from political friends that not only New York, but Pennsylvania, perhaps Indiana and even his home state of Illinois might go against him. He wrote to a friend, "You think I don't know I am going to be beaten, but *I do* and unless some great change takes place, *badly beaten*."[36]

On August 23, the president sat and wrote two remarkable sentences: "This morning, as for some days past, it seems exceedingly probable that this administration will not be reelected. Then it will be my duty to so cooperate with the President-elect as to save the Union between the election and the inauguration, as he will have secured his election on such ground that he cannot possibly save it afterward." At the next cabinet meeting, he produced this sheet of paper, folded so that his written words could not be seen, and asked each member to sign it. He expected the Democrats, about to convene in Chicago, to nominate McClellan, and he expected him to run and win on a platform promising peace. As August ended, he believed he was entering the last six months of his presidency.[37]

CHAPTER TWENTY

A Wild, Visionary Longing

ATLANTA

Fall of the Rebel Stronghold
SHERMAN ENTERS THE CITY

A THUNDERBOLT FOR COPPERHEADS

War Department,
Washington, Sept. 2, 6 P.M.
This Department has received intelligence this evening that General Sherman's advance entered Atlanta about
noon today. The particulars are not
yet received, but telegraphic communication during the night with Atlanta
direct is expected.[1]

The summer of despair was over.

Three newsbreaks, all long expected, came just days apart to lift Northern spirits and mislead many Unionists into thinking that victory was imminent. On August 23, Union troops captured Fort Morgan off Mobile after Rear Admiral David G. Farragut, shouting "Damn the torpedoes!" had cleared the bay. That left Wilmington, North Carolina, as the only important seaport under Confederate control. Then on September 2, Sherman took the vital rail hub of Atlanta in the greatest Union victory since Gettysburg, grasping a symbolic prize second only to Richmond itself.

A jubilant Lincoln ordered every arsenal and navy yard to fire a hundred-gun salute to celebrate Farragut's success, and repeated the order two days later to honor Sherman's march into Atlanta. Grant, on his own initiative, saluted his comrade Sherman by commanding all his batteries at Petersburg to fire live rounds at the enemy "within an hour, amidst great rejoicing."[2]

The third welcome development took place between these feats of arms, on August 30, and this one did not inspire a presidential proclamation of thanks. But in retrospect it might well have, for eventually it was as important to the Union cause as Atlanta, Mobile or any other recent military achievement. The event was the Democrats' nomination of McClellan at their convention in Chicago—and especially what they said in the process.

By adopting a peace platform that shrugged at slavery, the Democrats had framed the overriding question of the election campaign and all but assured Lincoln's survival in office. When Gideon Welles read the platform, he reduced it to its essence, writing in his diary that the platform was "unpatriotic, almost treasonable to the Union. The issue is made up. It is whether a war shall be made against Lincoln to get peace with Jeff Davis. Those who met at Chicago prefer hostility to Lincoln rather than to Davis." The news from Atlanta "will not be gratifying to the zealous partisans who have just committed the mistake of sending out a peace platform, and declared the war a failure." Their partisanship is "a terrible spirit, which in its excess leads men to rejoice in the calamities of their country and to mourn its triumphs."[3]

McClellan was slow to realize what Welles had grasped so quickly. Only after drafting and discarding a series of letters accepting the convention's nomination and its platform did he finally give in to influential War Democrats and disavow the party's peace plank. It charged the administration with "failure to restore the Union by the experiment of war," and demanded that "immediate efforts be made for the cessation of hostilities." McClellan explained that he could not face his former troops if he said that they had fought and sacrificed in vain. But if the Confederates wanted to negotiate, he would do so in "a spirit of conciliation and compromise." His only condition would be restoring the Union—"we ask no more." Though that letter was meant to appease his War Democrat backers, it angered the Peace Democrats like Vallandigham who had dominated the convention, and did McClellan no good at all among the rest of the electorate. He began the campaign as he had ended his military career, wavering in the face of hard decisions.[4]

With the spring of horrendous casualties and the summer of

depressing defeats behind, the president had taken on a different image for the fall campaign. Now he stood tall as the commander-in-chief of victorious armies, a role reinforced when Grant sent the pugnacious Major General Philip H. Sheridan to deal with Early in the Shenandoah Valley. Sheridan, described by one of his soldiers as "a quick, fiery, active, live, go-ahead, bony little man," was given more troops and ordered to pursue Early "to the death." He immediately took the offensive, and despite occasional setbacks, he would never relinquish it. With the political lines so clearly drawn and military fortunes on the upswing, the Radical effort to organize a rump convention to replace Lincoln as the Republican candidate dwindled away. Senator Chandler of Michigan took it on himself to bring other hard-liners into the Lincoln camp, and the president helped him by finally firing Postmaster General Blair, whose presence in the cabinet had long displeased the Radicals. He sent Blair off with a friendly note, and the loyal Blair proceeded to stump for him in Maryland. The issue of reconstruction, which had divided Republicans for and against the president, was put aside for the sake of harmony. Even Anna Dickinson, who had stormed about the North denouncing the president, decided to support the Union ticket, although she insisted she was opposing McClellan, not approving Lincoln. Within the month, Frémont withdrew his name from contention, leaving voters a straight choice between Lincoln and McClellan.[5]

Confederates watched these political shifts just as carefully as loyal Republicans, and knew that the boost in Lincoln's reelection prospects was a clear blow to Southern hopes in the war. Desperate men thought of desperate measures. Thomas Conrad, who had made repeated undercover visits to Washington to carry away Union secrets, could see how Confederate manpower was dwindling. "The flower of the South, almost to the last man, had already been under arms for years and what help there was for the situation must come from within," he wrote. "One shrewd move, a skillful capture of somebody high in Federal authority, and the advantage gained might equalize the struggle. Why was it not possible to capture Lincoln himself, take him into Confederate lines and hold the Northern president as a hostage for peace?"

According to Conrad, he got the idea in camp from South Carolina officers in Wade Hampton's cavalry command, but they were not the first Rebels to think of it. After Gettysburg, Mosby had suggested it, only to be squelched by President Davis. Conrad wrote that when he brought it up over a year later, it went no further than Confederate Secretary of War James Seddon, who opposed it at first but then gave his quiet approval as long as no violence was involved. Conrad enlisted his former Dickinson College roommate, Daniel Mountjoy Cloud, another Virginia cavalryman detached for spy work in and out of Washington. Slipping into the capital, they brought into their plot Edward Norton, Conrad's collaborator inside the Federal Secret Service.

To study Lincoln's daily habits, Conrad lazed about Lafayette Square, watching as the president came and went to the Soldiers' Home, nearby Federal offices and occasionally the theaters downtown. Days passed as he and his accomplices argued over where to ambush their prey, and whether to take him across the Potomac above or below Washington. They decided that Conrad and Norton would track the president's carriage on horseback as it left town for the night, and capture him at pistol point when he reached a clump of woods near the Soldiers' Home. Cloud would follow, driving a carriage in which he would take the bound and gagged president east, then south, bypassing the closely guarded Navy Yard Bridge across the Anacostia. Conrad and Norton would stay behind, holding the president's driver so he could not sound the alarm. At a prearranged spot on the Potomac, Cloud would signal accomplices on the Virginia side to come and get the prisoner for delivery to Richmond.

The plotters scheduled their surprise for a Saturday afternoon. That Friday, Conrad and Cloud were watching from Lafayette Square, summoning up nerve for their escapade, when Lincoln's carriage rumbled out of the White House grounds surrounded by a squad of Union cavalry. A Saturday morning newspaper reported that authorities had learned of a plot to kidnap the president, and so increased the armed guard riding with him. Incredulous that anyone could have discovered their plans, Conrad and his collaborators abandoned the effort. He wrote that he did not find out until years later that it was Mosby's men who had ruined his plot. A half dozen of them had come to Washington, intending to capture Lincoln and hold him in the Van Ness mansion overnight before taking him across the river. "But the blandishments of John Barleycorn were more than those thirsty warriors in butternut could withstand," Conrad wrote. At the bar of Brown's Hotel, one of them had let their secret slip, and word quickly reached Norton's boss, Lafayette Baker. In addition to his plainclothes force, the detective chief commanded "Baker's Rangers," the First District of Columbia Cavalry, organized expressly to combat Mosby and his ilk.

Afterward, Conrad was glad his scheme had been thwarted. "Even had we succeeded in capturing Mr. Lincoln or any two or three members of his cabinet, a child could conclude in the light of subsequent events that the move would have accomplished no tangible good to the Confederacy," he wrote. "The scheme was nothing more than a wild, visionary longing 'to do something,' anything which had about it a ray of promise. . . ."[6]

But there were others, wilder and more visionary, whose plotting was not so easily discouraged.

When McClellan wrote that restoring the Union would be his only condition in seeking peace with the Confederates, he affirmed that as far as he and like-thinking Democrats were concerned, slavery could continue undisturbed. In this, they were ignoring reality, because by then the breakdown of slavery was impossible to reverse—as Swisshelm had written, "the wheels of God's Providence could not turn backward." Federal troops were liberating slaves as they marched across wide swaths of the Deep South. Tens of thousands of former bondsmen were uniformed soldiers of the Union. More thousands had refuged into Washington and Alexandria, and despite overcrowding, disease and frequent abuse by resentful ruffians, they were not going back.[7]

However, at Freedman's Village at Arlington and smaller such clusters about the capital, families had to be on guard against slave-owners who tried to snatch former slaves back into bondage as well as recruiters who tried to dragoon youths into the army. In June, after Rebel sympathizers were disfranchised in Maryland, a state constitutional convention had voted by a two-to-one margin to abolish slavery there. But the new Declaration of Rights would not be ratified by voters for another four months. Until then, some planters close to Washington tried to make up for the earlier loss of slave labor by kidnapping freedmen and taking them back across the river to Maryland. When this happened to several young men at Freedman's Village, their mothers raised such a commotion that the officer in charge of the village locked the women in the guardhouse for disturbing the peace.[8]

This miscarriage of justice drew the wrath of the tall, imposing black evangelist and civil rights crusader, sixty-nine-year-old Sojourner Truth. Born Isabella Van Wagener, she had started life as a slave belonging to a Dutch family in upstate New York; her abolitionist fire was lit when she fought to reclaim her own son after he was illegally sold away. At Arlington, she persuaded the authorities to free the distraught mothers, and organized a defense against further raids by slavers. She asked trusted nearby soldiers to form a posse, and the next time kidnappers came, they were caught. She also instructed the mothers who had lost children to take legal action to get them back. The Marylanders, offended by such effrontery from a grandmotherly black woman, threatened to have her arrested. She told them that if they tried, she would make the whole United States "rock like a cradle."[9]

Sojourner Truth made things rock wherever she went. After arriving in Washington early that fall, she spent three weeks with Jane Swisshelm. It is easy to imagine how these two battlers must have reinforced each other's will to fight injustice. Swisshelm had just recovered from a debilitating illness contracted as a volunteer nurse. While waiting for a government job, she had visited an outlying fort and found an ailing soldier who needed a bed. In her effort to help him, she had a predictable clash with the domineering Miss Dix. "Her tall, angular person, very red face, and totally unsympathetic manner chilled me," wrote Swisshelm. When Swisshelm sought a bed for the soldier, Dix told her she was too busy to bother that Saturday, and never worked on Sunday. "Emergencies were things of which she had no conception," said Swisshelm. "Everything in her world moved by rule...." Soon, Swisshelm maneuvered her way into Campbell Hospital, which had taken pride in being the only one staffed entirely by males. She began by bringing lemonade to patients, then helping comfort them on their cots, then dressing wounds without being asked. She was accepted as the hospital's only female nurse and moved in, but still gave the staff a false name lest they reject her as the woman who had made heated political speeches and written to the newspapers about hospital conditions.

When a dying and delusional young German-American patient reached out to Swisshelm calling "*Mutter, mutter!*" she was amazed to be ordered by the presiding surgeon, "No sympathy! No sympathy!" So instead of soothing the soldier, she told him firmly, "Be a man and a soldier!"

Remorsefully, she wrote later that "he had asked me for bread; I gave him a stone. No wonder he dashed it back in my face. With a fierce cry he said: 'I hev been a man and a sojer long enough!' "

Eventually, Swisshelm was fired from Campbell because once she was there, Dix wanted to install more woman nurses, and the surgeon in charge refused. After a spell as a War Department clerk, Swisshelm had gone to Fredericksburg over Dix's protests to help care for casualties of Grant's overland campaign. Defying bureaucratic protocols day and night, she labored there until returning to Washington deeply fatigued. She asked help from Mrs. Lincoln and Stanton in organizing a society of nurses independent of Dix, but before she could press her effort, she fell ill. Doctors decided that she "had been inoculated with gangrene while dressing wounds," and she went to recover with friends in Pennsylvania.[10]

When Swisshelm came back, there was Sojourner Truth, who told about her audience with the president, arranged by Elizabeth Keckley at the behest of Truth's friend, the outspoken white abolitionist and feminist Lucy Colman. According to Truth, she had arrived at the White House to find a dozen others waiting, among them two black women. She was impressed to see that Lincoln "showed as much kindness and consideration to the colored persons as to the whites—if there was any difference, more." When her turn came, he rose and bowed as she entered. She told him that when he took office, she had been afraid he would be like Daniel thrown into the lion's den—"if the lions did not tear you into pieces, I knew that it would be God that had saved you." When she said he was the best president ever, he gave credit in a way to the Rebels for his role in ending slavery. Washington or other early presidents might have done the same under similar circumstances, he said. Pointing toward Virginia, he told her that "if the people over the river had behaved themselves, I could not have done what I have done; but they did not, which gave me the opportunity to do these things." When she told him that before he ran for president she had never heard of him, he smiled and said, "I had heard of you many times before that."

The president showed her an elaborately decorated Bible presented to him by the "the loyal colored people of Baltimore." On its cover was a gold plate depicting a slave with his shackles falling away, stretching out his hands to Lincoln in gratitude. Beneath it was a scroll with one word: "Emancipation."* Truth said it had cost its donors $5,800. Lincoln then autographed for her a copy of the autobiography she had dictated fifteen years earlier. But she had not come merely to exchange compliments; she wanted a commission to look after the welfare of suffering ex-slaves, and though it took time, she got it.[11]

Lucy Colman, who accompanied Truth at the White House, was the militant, free-thinking matron of the National Colored Orphan Asylum, where she had struggled to banish lice and harsh treatment. She also worked with Truth at Freedman's Village. Much later, she wrote a contradictory version of that meeting with the president, asserting that he had kept them waiting more than three hours, was not courteous, and called Truth "Aunty, as he would his washer-woman." Colman quoted him as saying, "I'm not an Abolitionist; I wouldn't free the slaves if I could save the Union in any other way— I'm obliged to do it." Since the meeting with Lincoln came two years after he issued the Emancipation Proclamation and made the end of slavery an inseparable part of his war aims, Colman's version seems less plausible than Truth's. While it is true that Truth had every reason to dignify her own image by writing that Lincoln treated her courte-ously, he had no reason for treating her otherwise. Earlier, he had received Frederick Douglass with cordiality, and more recently had granted Douglass's appeal to discharge his seriously ill son Charles from the army.[12]

While staying with Swisshelm, Truth lectured twice at the Rev-erend Henry Highland Garnet's Fifteenth Street Presbyterian Church to raise funds for ex-slaves. Then she spent a week among the over-flow of contrabands housed on Mason's Island and spoke there to cel-ebrate emancipation in Maryland. But her greatest concern was Freedman's Village at Arlington, by then home to thousands, and she worked there more than a year as an agent of the National Freedman's Relief Association. "I think I can be useful and will stay," she wrote. And she was useful, encouraging illiterate men and women to stand up for their rights, a concept few of them had encountered before. By then the village had grown into a small town of about fifty two-story

*This design may have inspired the Emancipation Monument in Lincoln Square on East Capitol Street, which features a bronze statue of Lincoln standing with one hand on the Emancipation Proclamation and the other on the shoulder of a crouching slave whose shackles have been broken. The statue was executed by Boston sculptor Thomas Ball and paid for by voluntary contributions of former slaves. Frederick Douglass spoke at its unveiling in 1876, which was attended by President Grant and his cabinet. (Randall Bond Truett, ed., *Washington, D.C.*, p. 388)

frame buildings, and the American Tract Society operated a school in the village's chapel. Hundreds of the men worked on outlying farms abandoned by secessionists and managed by the government. Other hundreds were employed by the army's quartermaster and engineer departments, and on double shifts as scavengers cleaning the streets and privies of Washington. Most of the village's residents had been illiterate field hands, and dozens of Yankee women volunteered to teach them to read and write.[13]

John Rapier, Jr., a newly appointed black doctor at the Village, admired one of these schoolteachers, Harriet Carter, who had come down from Massachusetts. "Do not imagine Miss Carter to be an old and homely one who has sighed for someone to love her and has taken up this occupation, perhaps as a penance for saying 'no' when she should have said 'yes,' " wrote Rapier. She was twenty-four, pretty, and "as full of learning as an Episcopal minister." Rapier told his uncle that the most eventful day of his life occurred when he got his first $100 check, made out to him as "Acting Assistant Surgeon, Rank 1st Lieutenant, U.S.A." He was proud to find that when a black officer walked into military offices he was saluted "as promptly as if your blood was a Howard or Plantagenet instead of Pompey or Coffee's." He had not intended to wear his uniform, but after this he changed his mind, vowing to appear "in full dress—gold lace, pointed hat, straps and all."[14]

Sojourner Truth was as eloquent in speech as John Rapier was on paper, but she could not read and write, so busied herself teaching women the rudiments of housekeeping. "They all seem to think a great deal of me, and want to learn the way we live in the North," she recalled.[15]

When Congress created the Freedmen's Bureau in early 1865, the village and other such contraband settlements became the government's first major venture into social welfare. Although Freedman's Village was intended as a temporary home and bridge to self-sufficiency, among many residents it fostered such a culture of dependency that the project was still in operation decades after the war.*

---

*The war brought a sharp and lasting increase in Washington's African-American population. From 1860 to 1870, the capital's white population increased by 40.6 percent, from 50,139 to 73,731, which suggests that most of the thousands of soldiers, government workers and opportunists who flocked to the city during the war went home after Appomattox. But the capital's colored (black and mulatto) population went up in the decade by 222.24 percent, from 10,983 to 35,392. Most of these citizens were former slaves who had no desire to return to the South. (Eighth and Ninth U.S. Censuses)

Before Sojourner Truth left Washington, she confronted discrimination on the capital's streetcar system with her usual boldness. When war began, privately operated omnibuses and rickety, ubiquitous hacks were the only public transportation. The omnibuses were horse-drawn cars that rumbled over cobblestones and rutted dirt streets, often blocking other traffic as they halted to pick up passengers. In 1862, Congress incorporated the Washington & Georgetown Railroad Company, which began streetcar service between the Navy Yard and Georgetown, mostly along Pennsylvania Avenue. Soon a competing line ran along F Street to the B&O station. These streetcars were horse-drawn, too, but along iron rails that demanded constant maintenance. It took a while for old-time Washingtonians to realize that streetcars would not swing over to the curb in response to a waving hand or lady's parasol. Drivers had to ride out front exposed to the elements because the owners thought a windshield would be unsafely blurred by rain and mud.[16]

Until early 1865, these streetcars were racially segregated. On the old omnibuses, black riders were allowed to sit on the roof; when streetcars began, blacks had to stand out front in the weather with the driver. With the arrival of so many freedmen, the company responded to public pressure and provided two cars with signs saying, "Colored Persons May Ride in This Car," but this created as many problems as it solved. Occasionally a self-important white person who had waited for a ride would step into one of these designated cars, see that it was occupied by blacks and demand that it be cleared.[17]

Truth started to board one of the nondesignated cars with Josephine Griffing, the white general agent of the National Freedmen's Relief Association of the District of Columbia. She was dragged several yards when the car started without waiting for her. The two women complained to the company and got the conductor fired. On another occasion, a driver passed Truth by, and she stopped the next car by stepping on the tracks and shouting "I want to ride! I want to ride!" This time she got aboard, and refused to stand out front. Later, with another white companion, the Michigan abolitionist and underground railroad agent Laura Haviland, Truth boarded a car only to be told to leave. When she refused, the angry conductor tried to wrestle her off and injured her arm. He asked Haviland, "Does she belong to you?"

"She does not belong to me, but she belongs to humanity," Haviland declared.

Again, the two women got the offender fired, and Truth had this one charged with assault and battery. "Before the trial was ended, the inside of the cars looked like pepper and salt," she said.[18]

The campaign of resistance to streetcar segregation succeeded after Major A. T. Augusta boarded a car in his army surgeon's uniform on a nasty winter day, on his way to be an important witness at a court-martial. Told he would have to ride out front because he was black, he refused and walked, thus arriving late at the trial. This so inconvenienced government officials that at last Congress stepped in and forbade further discrimination by the company.[19]

If this country gets ultimately through [the fall political campaign], I shall set it down as the most wonderful miracle in the whole history of events," wrote Francis Lieber. Never before or since has any country held a free national election amid civil war, and by that September the Democrats were going all-out to make further history by ousting a president in mid-war. Hanging above the streetcar tracks, stretching across the Avenue, great banners proclaiming the names of George McClellan and his vice presidential running mate George Pendleton demonstrated how New York financiers had come through after the candidate bowed to their demands on the party platform: the out party seemed to have money to burn. In September, it drew an immense crowd to a rally at Washington's City Hall, with speakers holding forth from each of the building's three porticoes at once, followed by a torchlight parade and fireworks that lasted till near midnight. In October, the party stepped up its campaign pace, organizing a flag-raising at Massachusetts Avenue and Seventh Street with banners, bonfires and cannon salutes, and another when they draped the biggest banner of all across the Avenue near Tenth Street. The rhetoric at these rallies may have been overoptimistic, but it resonated among youngsters whose families still wished the war would go away and leave things as they were. At recess one day in mid-October, students at Columbian College took a straw vote among themselves, and McClellan defeated Lincoln 46 to 12.[20]

But there were bigger test votes that October, elections for lesser offices in states that would be crucial in November. Already, Maine and Vermont had voted for governor and Congress, and given Union candidates healthy margins. Republicans cheered, but Maine and Vermont were no surprise. The most serious of the bellwether contests, in Pennsylvania, Ohio and Indiana, were chancier for the president. On the night of their election day, October 11, Lincoln and Hay walked over to the War Department to wait for incoming telegrams. They were locked out; Stanton had turned the key and taken it with him upstairs. When a messenger spotted Lincoln in the cold moonlight, he led them through the Navy Department and into Stanton's territory by a side door.[21]

The president had heard encouraging news earlier from supporters in Pennsylvania, but later reports came trickling in from one city or congressional district at a time. After a series of dispatches, there was a lull with the overall returns still out. As the little group waited, listening for the telegraph key to start clicking again, Lincoln eased the suspense by pulling out the latest essay by the acidic humorist whom Hay called "the saint & martyr Petroleum V." This was David Ross Locke, an Ohio newspaperman who wrote as Petroleum V. Nasby, a rural Northern preacher of Southern sentiment. Lincoln enjoyed his works as much as he did the concoctions of Artemus Ward. According to Noah Brooks, the president had fully memorized Nasby's famous satire of citizens protesting the flood of ex-slaves into the border North. Exhorting fellow citizens of "Wingert's Corners, Ohio" to political action, the Reverend Nasby called on them to: "Arowse to wunst! Rally agin Conway! Rally agin Sweet! Rally agin Hegler! Rally agin Hegler's family! Rally agin the porter at the Reed House! Rally agin the cook at the Crook House! Rally agin the nigger widder in Vance's addishun! Rally agin Missis Umstid! Rally agin Missis Umstid's childern by her first husband! Rally agin Missis Umstid's childern by her sekund husband! Rally agin all the rest of Missis Umstid's childern! Rally agin the nigger that kum yesterday! Rally agin the saddle-kulurd gal that yoost a be hear! Ameriky fer white men!"[22]

According to Charles Sumner, Lincoln wanted to tell Locke that "for the genius to write these things I would gladly give up my office." Nasby's witticisms disconcerted some dignitaries who heard Lincoln recite them at unlikely wartime moments, but for those moments they took him away from the heaviest burdens ever borne by any president. As it turned out, on that October night at the telegraph office, the burdens were briefly lightened by the incoming news. All three of the big key states went Republican, though the count in Pennsylvania was uncomfortably close. In response, the Lincoln-Johnson Club of Washington got up a massive display of confidence that stretched out of sight along the Avenue.[23]

"Nothing so fine has ever been seen in this city, and seldom, perhaps, has it been outdone elsewhere," wrote Brooks, who could not restrain his enthusiasm for Lincoln and the Union. The procession must have been two miles long, alight with torches and banners. Red, green and blue Roman candles lent a lurid glow to the smoke of fireworks as the parade passed, "creeping like a living thing and winding its slow length around the White House." Workers at the Navy Yard had built a miniature monitor, with revolving turret spouting fireworks, that threatened spectators as it passed on its float.

Hoots and insults rained back from plenteous McClellan fans along the curbs, who called the marchers "Lincoln hirelings." Their cries turned mean when one of the paraders' torches ignited a low-hanging McClellan-Pendleton banner outside Democratic headquarters on the Avenue. The Democrats held a special meeting to pass angry resolutions accusing the Unionists of intentionally setting fire to their banner. The Lincoln Club replied that although the McClellan fans "used exceedingly vile, insulting, and taunting remarks toward those composing the procession, and particularly toward soldiers, even going so far as to hurl stones and other missiles into the line," the club regretted the incident and condemned it if it was intentional.[24]

By accusing the curbside McClellanites of taunting soldiers in the procession, the Republicans no doubt meant to inspire other servicemen to take revenge by voting for Lincoln. Indeed, the soldiers in the Lincoln-Johnson parade were not able-bodied marching men but convalescents, many in ambulances bearing signs saying BALLOTS AND BULLETS and WE CAN VOTE AS WELL AS FIGHT. The military vote had already boosted the Union Party in the October elections, and made the crucial difference in ratifying the new Maryland constitution.* Although there were concerns that McClellan's earlier popularity among his troops would be a serious problem for Lincoln, the Democratic candidate was unable to escape his party's platform. He sat above the fray, not deigning to campaign actively but writing to old

---

*Ballots cast locally in Maryland would have rejected the new constitution abolishing slavery by 29,536 to 27,541. But soldier votes favored the change by a margin of more than sixteen to one, making the final count 30,174 for the constitution and 29,699 against. (Benjamin P. Thomas and Harold M. Hyman, *Stanton*, p. 331)

army friends, asking them to canvass on his behalf. On Lincoln's side, soldiers did their part in different ways. Sheridan campaigned on horseback, defeating Early at Cedar Creek in the Valley and proceeding on his mission to devastate the breadbasket of Virginia. And Grant, though on active duty, entered the election by writing a letter that left no doubt of his presidential preference. It was sent privately, but soon made public by its recipient, Lincoln's friend Elihu Washburne. The Rebels were wearing down, said Grant. They could only try to hold out through the election, hoping that the peace candidate would win. If the North stood true to itself, the war would soon be over.[25]

Lincoln, like McClellan, pretended to stay above politics. But he involved himself as intimately as the Union Party's official manager, Henry J. Raymond, who was still editor of the *New York Times*. The president got into campaign details, suggesting speakers for this or that occasion, manipulating the levers of patronage wherever they might help. He voiced no qualms about dunning Federal jobholders for 10 percent of their pay to help finance the campaign. Washburne said that Lincoln was "as good a politician as he is a President, and if there was no other way to get those votes he would go around with a carpet bag and collect them himself."[26]

When the ancient Chief Justice Taney died in mid-October, the president had another chance to demonstrate his political adroitness. Salmon Chase, still sulking after his departure from Treasury and hoping that there might be another convention to nominate him instead of the president, had been reluctant to fall in line when other Radicals were endorsing Lincoln. But when Taney's health began to fail and prospects for another convention faded, Chase began to compliment the president in public. Then when Taney died, Chase's friends flooded the White House with claims that he deserved to be chief justice. Lincoln coolly waited. He was reminded how Chase in office had held himself superior to the president, had often worked against him in the cabinet. Fervent appeals came in touting friendlier qualified men, including Stanton, Attorney General Bates and ex–Postmaster General Blair. Chase wrote warm notes to the president, who ignored them. Then Chase wrote to Sumner, knowing his words would be passed on. He said he would accept if called to the bench, and added that he was now sure the next president would be Lincoln, "from whom the world would expect great things." Still Lincoln waited. At last, Chase swallowed his pride and set out to stump for the president in essential states of the Midwest. Lincoln, understanding that no matter whom he chose, it would make some supporters unhappy, still waited, until weeks after the election.[27]

Stanton realized that the soldier vote could be the deciding factor in the November election and was determined to mobilize it to reelect Lincoln. He commissioned a brigadier general to write a scathing review of McClellan's Peninsula generalship for the newspapers. When the Democratic New York legislature arranged for the state's troops to vote in the field, then have their ballots sent home for counting, Stanton refused at first to tell state agents where those regiments were located. Then he pressed ranking officers to help Republican agents and obstruct Democrats. When he learned that Democratic Governor Horatio Seymour was going to use the state's National Guard as poll-watchers, he countered by having Grant send Ben Butler to New York with a contingent from his Army of the James.[28]

Though not campaigning openly, Lincoln used public opportunities to explain himself when the setting was right. He was deeply gratified by Maryland's move to emancipation, and said so twice to celebrators who called on him for a speech. The first was a crowd of Maryland loyalists who came to the capital with bands and banners. A few days later, the black citizens of Washington sang and exulted at church before advancing on the White House bearing torches and banners left over from earlier Unionist demonstrations. Brought out by their cheers, Lincoln told them, "It is not secret that I have wished, and still do wish, mankind everywhere to be free." He was especially moved by the fact that in Maryland, "by the action of her own citizens, the soil is made forever free." He felt no sense of triumph over those who had opposed the change, but he believed that "it will result in good to the white race as well as to those who have been made free." In closing, he hoped that "you, colored people, who have been emancipated, will use this great boon which has been given you to improve yourselves, both morally and intellectually." The crowd hurrahed into the night, having heard the eminently political president say something to appeal to or at least assuage everyone concerned.[29]

On November 7, the day before the election, the trains out of Washington were packed. "Once more the invincible Army of the Potomac is in motion," Brooks wrote, "but this time the movement is not toward the city of Richmond but directly toward the heart of the rebellion by way of the ballot box." To avoid shenanigans or delays in transporting soldiers' ballots from the field to be counted at home, Stanton cleared the way for thousands of New York, Pennsylvania and Maryland troops to go home and vote. Convalescents and walking wounded from the hospitals in and about the capital took up their crutches and headed homeward. So did trainloads of civilian government employees. "Washington is deserted," Brooks said, "and its dirty dullness is heightened by an unceasing fall of rain which has deluged the streets for the past twenty-four hours."[30]

The next morning, as the rest of the country voted, the capital barely stirred. John B. Wiltberger, who lived near Rock Creek Church, complained to police that somebody's cow had wandered onto his premises, and the schooner *Francisco* docked at the foot of Eleventh Street with a cargo of Prince Albert and Jackson White potatoes from Maine. At the White House, hardly anyone came or went. "Everybody . . . not at home voting seems ashamed of it and stays away from the President," said Hay. The weather seemed foreboding; Lincoln put on a confident front but admitted that he was anxious. He presided over a cabinet meeting attended by only two members, Welles and Bates, who slogged away after having transacted no business. From New York, Butler reported that his show of force was working; he sent a telegram saying, "quietest city ever seen." A Baltimore supporter sent a "rose-colored estimate" of prospects there, based on the morning's voting. The worried president told a story about Tad's pet turkey. Little more news came in during the long gray afternoon.[31]

At about 7 P.M., Lincoln and Hay splashed through the soaking rain to the War Department. As they entered, someone handed the president a telegram from Forney in Philadelphia, another from Baltimore, another from Boston, all optimistic. Thomas T. Eckert, head of the telegraph office, came in covered with mud after slipping in the street, which triggered a homely recollection from Lincoln. Each time a fresh report clicked in, it reminded the president of something or somebody. Welles, other officials and generals arrived to wait for news. The telegraph was working spasmodically because of the widespread rain, but glad tidings came in spurts from Indiana, even from Pennsylvania. Lincoln sent someone with the news to Mary, explaining that she was more anxious than he was. Butler reported what seemed an impossibly large victory under way in New York. Near midnight, the president's mood was lifting. He sat and shoveled down fried oysters, part of a hearty supper provided by Eckert.

The realization that he had won did not burst upon him with some decisive telegram; it sank in steadily and he welcomed it calmly. The final tally would show that he had drawn 55 percent of the popular vote—2,203,831 votes to McClellan's 1,797,019, so distributed that the president's margin in electoral votes would be 212 to 21. Of soldiers who voted in the field, 119,754 or 78 percent went for Lincoln, against McClellan's 34,291. If the thousands of troops who went home to vote split the same way, their support probably provided the president's winning margin in half a dozen important states. All of those around Lincoln that night understood that his reelection meant the war would go on and many more thousands would die, but it also meant the nation would be united once again, and slaves forever free. There in the telegraph office, the moment was too serious to be celebrated with cheers and backslapping. After midnight, the president's friends came one by one to shake his hand in solemn congratulation, and at about two o'clock a messenger splashed in saying that a gathering of Pennsylvanians was serenading the White House, thinking he was there. So he went home and delivered to them what Brooks called "one of the happiest and noblest little speeches of his life."

He said he believed that "the consequences of this day's work . . . will be to the lasting advantage, if not to the very salvation, of the country." Whatever the final outcome, he would not change it, for all who had labored for the Union did so "for the best interests of the country and the world, not only for the present, but for all future ages." He ended by saying, "If I know my heart, my gratitude is free from any taint of personal triumph. I do not impugn the motives of any one opposed to me. It is no pleasure to me to triumph over any one, but I give thanks to the Almighty for this evidence of the people's resolution to stand by free government and the rights of humanity."[32]

Though the president would not gloat over his triumph, he could not restrain the public celebration. After the results were published, a spontaneous crowd pushed around the White House with bands and banners. When Lincoln appeared, he had to wait long minutes before the cheering subsided. He told them that holding an election in mid–civil war proved that a free nation could survive the gravest emergency. "We cannot have free government without elections," he said, "and if the rebellion could force us to forgo or postpone a national election, it might fairly claim to have already conquered and ruined us." He urged all factions not to hold grudges, but to reunite to save the country. As he later told Hay, "I am in favor of short statutes of limitations in politics."

The crowd cheered again, and cannon roared and rattled the White House windows. Tad rushed from one window to another, putting up his own illuminations, having a fine time in his boyish ignorance of what still lay ahead.[33]

The Judgments of the Lord

W hen Lincoln finally went to bed that early morning after the election, his friend and self-appointed bodyguard, U.S. Marshal Ward Hill Lamon, took a slug of whiskey, rolled up in his cloak and stretched across the entrance to the president's room. There he passed the remainder of the night "in that attitude of touching and dumb fidelity, with a small arsenal of pistols & bowie knives around him."[1]

Lamon feared for the president's life. But that had been true every day since February 1861, when the president-elect arrived incognito under Lamon's protective eye. Lamon worried more after the 1864 election reduced to near zero the likelihood of Southern success by any orthodox means, in battle or negotiations. Lincoln took warnings more seriously than he had earlier in the war but still did not let the presence or absence of bodyguards restrict his coming and going. For almost four years, he had heard so many threats that it was hard for him to take them seriously. "His mail was infested with brutal and vulgar menace," wrote Nicolay and Hay. It was "mostly anonymous, the proper expression of vile and cowardly minds." When a threat seemed credible, it was investigated, but none had yet proven to be real. The president told his secretaries that the Rebels should have no motive to kill him, since Vice President Hamlin was well known to feel more harshly toward the South. Any time an assassin was willing to sacrifice his own life to murder him, that could happen; the only way Lincoln could guarantee against it was "to shut himself up in an iron box, in which condition he could scarcely perform the duties of the president."[2]

But not all the threats were mere words. John Nichols, one of the troops assigned to guard Lincoln's retreat at the Soldiers' Home, recalled that one night he heard a rifle shot, then Lincoln came galloping toward him bareheaded, riding alone. According to Nichols, he and other soldiers found the president's stovepipe hat near the gate, with a bullet hole through the crown. Lincoln blamed the shot on some careless hunter and ordered the soldiers not to talk about it. Following the election, new rumors of plots abounded, and Lincoln objected but consented when the city's chief of police, William B. Webb, assigned a four-man detail of plainclothesmen to take turns guarding him at the White House and on his excursions about the neighborhood.[3]

Lamon, obsessed with his friend's well-being, wrote to Lincoln in near despair. "You are in danger," he said, adding that if the president did not take his warnings seriously, he should accept his resignation. That very night, "as you have on several previous occasions, you went unattended to the theatre. When I say unattended, I mean that you went alone with Charles Sumner and a foreign minister, neither of whom could defend himself against an assault from any able-bodied woman in this city. . . . your life is sought after, and will be taken unless you and your friends are cautious for you have many enemies within our lines. . . . God knows that I am unselfish in this matter; and I do think that I have played low comedy long enough. . . ."[4]

Curiously, the only individual about whom Lincoln voiced wariness was the very opposite of a fanatical Confederate. Count Adam Gurowski was not a Rebel; he was a Radical in Civil War terms, but he had been an insurrectionist in his native Poland and carried an aura of conspiracy about him for the rest of his days. Several times imprisoned and once condemned to death in Europe, he had come to America in 1849 and served as a translator in the State Department. He had been a prolific author, writing memoirs and books on European politics and slavery before publishing the first installment of his Civil War diary in 1862. It was scathingly critical of Lincoln's administration and cost Gurowski his government job. But he was still omnipresent in the capital, and Lincoln simply did not trust him. "Gurowski is the only man who has given me a serious thought of a personal nature," he told Lamon. "I have sometimes thought he might try to take my life. It would be just like him to do such a thing." But Gurowski at fifty-nine was a man of words; others, younger, were committed to action.[5]

Mary Surratt had been a widow for two years when she moved

from Prince George's County into Washington, hoping to make a living by taking in boarders. The Surratts were Southern sympathizers who had been modestly prosperous in the country, running a crossroads tavern that became a post office, community forum and polling place. When war began, it also became a stop on the secret Confederate communications line through southern Maryland. But after Mary's husband, John, died, she had a hard time keeping up the tavern. In October 1864, she rented her Surrattsville property and moved thirteen miles into the city, to a townhouse owned by the family on H Street near Sixth. Almost immediately that house became a rendezvous for clandestine Confederates, including the headstrong actor John Wilkes Booth.

Booth's fury toward Lincoln and the Union cause burned hotter as the war turned in favor of the North. By the autumn of 1864, his stage schedule had slacked off and he had speculated unsuccessfully in the oil fields of western Pennsylvania. He had other matters on his mind. For months, he had used his show-business travels as cover to smuggle embargoed quinine onward to the South. Then in late July, at the Parker House in Boston, he met undercover agents from the busy Confederate political and intelligence organization in Canada. It is still uncertain whether they or Booth proposed kidnapping and holding Lincoln as a hostage for Southern independence, or for the release of Confederate prisoners. But within weeks, he began to recruit a small band of men to do what Thomas Conrad was simultaneously and independently planning. Booth started in Baltimore with two boyhood friends, Michael O'Laughlin and Samuel B. Arnold, both former Confederate soldiers. Then early in the fall he went to Montreal, and returned to Washington by November 9 with $1,500, which he deposited in a bank. Soon afterward, he was prowling southern Maryland, ostensibly looking for real estate, but actually laying an escape route to Virginia. Those explorations brought Mary Surratt's son John into Booth's secret circle.[6]

John H. Surratt, Jr., was an eighteen-year-old student, training to be a priest, when war began. He left the seminary and returned home, soon becoming a busy courier on the Confederate communications line from Baltimore south across the Potomac to Richmond. He said later that when he met Booth, the actor persistently questioned him about different roads through that neighborhood, and he refused to cooperate until the kidnapping plan was explained to him. He was "amazed—thunderstruck" by the audacity of it, but after thinking it

over, he joined the adventure. By then, Booth's intense personal magnetism had drawn in at least four other henchmen, with a specific role
intended for each.[7]

Lewis T. Powell, alias Paine, was a big, strong youth from Florida
who had fought as a Confederate until being wounded and taken prisoner at Gettysburg. He had escaped and headed south, briefly joining
Mosby's raiders before slipping back across the Potomac to Baltimore,
where he was enlisted by Booth. One of Powell's brothers had died
and another was disabled in the Confederate army, so he was motivated to continue his war by joining Booth. Prussian-born George
Atzerodt, a carriage repairman by trade, was enlisted because he knew
the creeks and hiding places along the Potomac south of Washington.
He had served as a boatman for Rebel agents running the river blockade in the dark from inlets near Port Tobacco, in Charles County.
Another recruit was Edman Spangler, who was well known to Booth
as a carpenter at Ford's Theater on Tenth Street, five blocks from the
Surratt house. David Herold, a druggist's assistant, was brought in for
his familiarity with potential escape routes; he seems to have been the
least intelligent and capable of the group. One other man, a New York
actor, was approached by Booth but turned him down. Booth warned
him that his coconspirators had sworn a solemn oath to kill anyone
who betrayed their plot.[8]

On November 25, Booth was at Manhattan's Winter Garden Theater to appear with his brothers Junius and Edwin in *Julius Caesar.* It
was a major theatrical event, the only time the three appeared on stage
together, a benefit performance to raise funds for the statue of Shakespeare that still stands in Central Park. On that occasion, John played
Marc Antony, and it was Edwin who played the assassin Brutus. But
their theatrical success was overshadowed in the next day's newspapers, because even as the brothers were emoting on stage, Confederate
saboteurs made a spectacular attempt to set New York on fire. This
was another venture mounted by the Rebel organization in Canada.
The Booth brothers' joint performance was momentarily interrupted
in mid-act by an alarm at a neighboring hotel. The play resumed while
city firemen battled outbreaks started by Rebel agents using an incen-
diary phosphorus-and-turpentine mixture called "Greek fire" in ten
hotels, two theaters and P. T. Barnum's Great American Museum,
which was featuring "The Tallest, Shortest and Fattest Specimens of
Humanity Ever Seen." The effort to burn Manhattan failed, but it was
another show of Confederate bravado as the war entered its fourth

winter. With *Julius Caesar* over, Booth said goodbye to his brothers and left for Washington, planning his turn on a grander stage.[9]

Thomas Walter's E Street Baptist Church had weathered the months when its congregation split over secession and its building was taken over for a war hospital, and now it was functioning again. Walter, a demanding critic of ministerial talent, considered the new pastor, E. H. Gray, to be "the most intellectual preacher that I ever sat under—no clap traps, no nonsense of any kind." Inside, the lingering odors of disease and infection had thinned away. But at the Capitol, Walter still had to wrestle with labor problems. Stonecutters struck over demands for wages of $4 a day; their original contract was twelve years old, made in "gold times," and wartime inflation had multiplied living costs. The ironworkers' "ignorant but honest" foreman, John Cuddy, insisted that he could manage only a handful of men, while Walter believed that dozens were needed to complete the dome inside and out. The architect threatened to leave if work was not speeded up, saying he could not face another session of Congress unless the ceiling of the Rotunda was finished and the artist Brumidi was at work there.[10]

Somehow, by the end of November, that got done. Noah Brooks wrote that Congress would return to "find the building greatly beautified and purified since the adjournment." From the mess of paint and lumber, "the noble pile is emerging in pristine beauty," he said, noting that the chief attraction would be the completed interior of the dome over which Walter had worried for so long. But each such success for the architect only led to another phase sure to be accompanied by more trouble from foremen, contractors and bureaucrats. The church on E Street was Walter's sanctuary from this nagging pressure, and now his letters gave little sign that he knew or cared about the politics that would have stirred him earlier in the war, such as the appointment of a new chief justice.[11]

Exactly four weeks after the election, Lincoln finally nominated Chase to head the Supreme Court. According to Secretary Welles, the president had said "he would rather have swallowed his buckhorn chair" than do it. He explained in private that the presence of former Treasury Secretary Chase at the court would reassure government bondholders that their investments were protected. At the same time, the record of Radical Republican Chase would confirm the administration's commitment to emancipation. The president might have added that he hoped elevating Chase to the court would keep him out of day-to-day politics. Senator Sumner had assured Lincoln that this would be so, but Welles could not believe it. "My own convictions are that, if he lives, Chase will be a candidate and his restless and ambitious mind is already at work," he wrote. "It is his nature." Senate action on Chase's nomination was delayed when the Judiciary Committee took four days, which was then considered a long time, to confirm Lincoln's little-known Kentucky friend, James Speed, as attorney general in place of retiring Edward Bates. But then Chase's appointment whisked through without even going to committee. Kate Sprague, "gorgeous in millinery," ornamented the Capitol's crowded Supreme Court room as her father was sworn in, pledging to "administer equal and exact justice to the poor and to the rich."[12]

On the same day when Lincoln nominated Chase, he sent the annual presidential message to the lame-duck session of the Thirty-eighth Congress. He began solemnly: "The war continues." But unlike his previous State of the Union reports, this one went upward from there. He intended it to be read in Richmond: "Our arms have steadily advanced," he said, and the election showed that the people were solidly behind the Union cause. Despite heavy losses, the North had more men and matériel than when the war began. The nation's resources, he said, "are unexhausted, and, as we believe, inexhaustible." Facing this, the South could have peace any time merely by laying down its arms and submitting to national authority. But there would be no compromise on slavery. Indeed, he called on Congress to reconsider a constitutional amendment abolishing it. The Senate had supported the resolution in the previous session, but Democrats had prevented the necessary two-thirds approval in the House. Since then the election had boosted Republican strength there; it was only a matter of time before the amendment was cleared and sent to the states. Thus, asked Lincoln, why not "the sooner the better"?[13]

If the president had written his message a few days later, he could have been even more optimistic. While Chase was taking the oath of his new office, the capital welcomed news that Sherman had reached the Atlantic Ocean at the end of his march across Georgia. After living for weeks off the Rebel land, his army started taking on supplies from the Union fleet near Savannah. In Tennessee, Major General George H. Thomas, after delays that nearly got him sacked by Grant, at last opened his attack against Hood's army at Nashville. In two days of fighting, he won the last major battle in the West, capturing some

4,500 Confederates and driving Hood's defeated army into flight. While General Lee had to tell Jeff Davis that he could not spare troops to help against Sherman in Georgia, Lincoln demonstrated the North's seemingly bottomless resources by ordering up another 300,000 volunteers. And then, on Sunday, December 25, a telegram arrived from Sherman to the president: I BEG TO PRESENT TO YOU, AS A CHRISTMAS GIFT, THE CITY OF SAVANNAH, WITH 150 HEAVY GUNS AND PLENTY OF AMMUNITION, AND ALSO ABOUT 25,000 BALES OF COTTON.[14]

The capital was observing Christmas with eggnog and fireworks, "somewhat in the style of a Fourth of July up North," when the news from Sherman came, and it took another day to organize a proper celebration for such an important victory. Then a three-hundred-gun salute roared from cannon along Vermont Avenue, near enough to Welles's home for him to grumble that sixty would have been enough. By this time, Washington householders had learned to open their window sashes halfway from top and bottom and leave all their doors ajar to minimize concussion damage from such salutes. Young Anna Sherman wrote of watching the guns fire at Franklin Square on one occasion, when "it seemed as if the doors, the windows, the walls even, must fall around our ears," but because of the family's precautions, not a thing was broken.[15]

After nearly four years, White House receptions had become routine to the Lincolns and their high-ranking guests, but there was a different feeling about the one on Monday, January 2, 1865, as if those present had made a long, hard climb together and could see that the road ahead was all downhill. The daughters of Treasury clerk Henry Sherman were now nine, eleven and fifteen years old, and their father decided they were ready to attend such a levee, an experience they could share someday with their grandchildren. When the Sherman sisters went through the receiving line, the president shook the hands of Anna and Ellen as cordially as if he were greeting the wives of ranking diplomats. But when he saw the youngest, the doll-like Ada, he "stooped clear down and gave her a kiss," a token she cherished all her life. An estimated 4,000 citizens pushed into the mansion, packed so thickly that some had to exit through a floor-level window in the East Room and down a long plank ramp to the ground. The girls were impressed to see field soldiers with muddy boots mixed among fashionably dressed ladies. But they were most fascinated by their contemporary, Tad Lincoln, and his impish handling of a social situation that puzzled him only briefly. Tad had eaten an orange, and then found no place to discard the peel. After a moment's contemplation, a solution struck him, and he edged toward a door between reception rooms. Standing with eyes downward and hands behind his back, he flicked the peel into the corner behind the open door so quickly that no one except the watching girls saw him. They thought this was "very cute" and laughed about it for years afterward.[16]

Northerners were still arriving in Washington and writing home about it as if it were a primitive outpost beyond the seas. A correspondent to the *Chelsea Telegraph & Pioneer* in Massachusetts found local citizens peculiar "and their conversational powers limited." He maintained that they never said yes, but "I reckon," or "deed it is," or "they merely snore out through their nose a kind of a 'ha hum.' " By 1865, the influx of soldiers, merchandisers, clerks and kinfolk from the rest of the Union had given the city a rich mixture of regional accents and dialects, but this New England Yankee attributed all such peculiarities to Washington's nearness to Dixie. Like thousands of his predecessors, he was impressed by the mud, and the "two or three hundred bootblacks laying around loose," asking passersby if they wanted a shine. He wrote that fifty or sixty broken-down horses were put to death every day in the city, with hundreds more turned out to pasture or sold cheap. All of these decrepit animals were branded with the initials "I.C.," meaning "inspected, condemned" by the government. And as the winter deepened, the correspondent noted the growing stream of Rebel deserters who had "once more come under the protective folds of the brave old flag."[17]

Those gray-clad Southerners who crossed the lines and were sent to Washington were only a fraction of the thousands who were leaving the Confederate army and heading home from the war. For months, they had been hungry, pinned down in their sodden trenches around Petersburg. Blockade runners could supply them no more; in mid-January, a combined Union army-navy expedition closed the port of Wilmington, North Carolina, by capturing outlying Fort Fisher. Lee reported that hundreds of his once high-spirited troops were departing every night. Hoping to end the suffering, old Francis Preston Blair nagged Lincoln into letting him go to Richmond to see whether Jeff Davis was ready to talk. Davis sent him back with word that he was willing to discuss "peace between the two countries." Lincoln answered that he would allow talks affecting "the people of our one common country." Despite this fundamental difference, the two sides went ahead with a conference at Hampton Roads between Seward and a three-man Confederate commission headed by Vice President Alexander H. Stephens. The talks were getting nowhere when Lincoln suddenly decided to join them personally. On February 3, in the salon of the Union steamer *Indian Queen*, he laid down his three firm conditions: restoring the Union, ending slavery, and complete surrender by Confederate forces. On other points, he was ready to be generous. He said the Confederates should realize their hopeless situation and agree to save the lives of more thousands of men. But Davis was immovable (a little later, Stephens would say he was "demented"), and Southern independence was not negotiable. So the talks failed, and Davis tried with "intemperate and wrathful utterance" to rouse his demoralized citizens to fight on.[18]

Any Southern hope that the North might have bargained over slavery had been erased by Congress on January 31, the day Lincoln sent Seward to the Hampton Roads conference. The House, which had failed earlier to approve the constitutional amendment abolishing slavery, ended a long debate by voting on January 31 to join the Senate in backing the historic resolution. The margin was close, and the amendment still had to be ratified by three-fourths of the states. Lincoln used all his powers of public persuasion and private deal-making to help the resolution's sponsor, James M. Ashley of Ohio, squeeze out the necessary two-thirds in the House.

When word swept Washington that the final vote was scheduled for three o'clock, the House galleries filled and Supreme Court justices, cabinet secretaries and other dignitaries crowded around the members at their desks. One by one, members who had opposed the amendment in the previous session stood to explain why they had changed their minds. But others swore to their proslavery principles, and bitterly chastised the colleagues who had abandoned them. The hall fell quiet when the yeas and nays were ordered to move the previous question, to end discussion and bring up the resolution for a vote. That motion passed, but only by 112 to 57, which would not be enough to endorse the amendment. Suspense gripped the crowd as the clerk then called the roll on the amendment itself. Reporters in the gallery above checked off the members' replies on their tally sheets. The outcome was uncertain until applause greeted one, then two more previous opponents who voted aye. Their votes were decisive, and when that became clear, a few more members switched to be on the winning side.

There was a moment of silence when the speaker announced the final count of 119 in favor, 56 opposed and 8 not voting; all present seemed to hold their breath as they realized the gravity of what had happened. Then came "a burst, a storm of cheers, the like of which no Congress of the United States ever saw," wrote Brooks. "Strong men embraced each other with tears. The galleries and spaces stood bristling with cheering crowds; the air was stirred with a cloud of women's handkerchiefs waving and floating. Hands were shaken, and cheer after cheer, burst after burst followed, and full five minutes elapsed before enough silence returned" for someone to move adjournment, and the defeated Copperheads slunk away.

"The final blow at the crime of slavery has been struck, but a few more events will follow in natural sequence," Brooks wrote. Then "we may truly say that no rood of soil beneath our flag holds a slave."*[19]

Coming almost three years after slavery ended in the District of Columbia and two years after the Emancipation Proclamation, approval of the Thirteenth Amendment set off an explosion of emotion among the capital's African-Americans. No longer was the promise of freedom a disputed wartime weapon wielded by the president. To black citizens, ratification by the states was moot. As far as they were concerned, their freedom was now an irreversible reality, and they set out to exercise it.

The day after the House voted, Senator Sumner appeared before the Supreme Court and asked that John S. Rock, a lawyer from Massachusetts, be admitted to practice there. Chief Justice Chase said, "Let the gentleman nominated be admitted." Out from the wings stepped Rock, a handsome, well-dressed black man, to take the oath of office standing before the disgusted clerk, a proslavery leftover from Chief Justice Taney's time. Brooks called it "a practical reversal of the Dred Scott decision," and it was promptly followed by another unprecedented event at the Capitol.[20]

On Lincoln's fifty-sixth birthday, Sunday, February 12, a black man spoke publicly for the first time in the chamber of the House of Representatives. Slave labor had helped build the Capitol, but since 1827

---

*The Thirteenth Amendment was finally declared in effect by Secretary Seward on December 18, 1865, a week after Oregon became the twenty-seventh state to ratify it.

black persons had been officially banned from both legislative chambers. Now Henry Highland Garnet entered with the choir from his Fifteenth Street Church and made his way on crutches to the speaker's rostrum. Forty-nine years old, Garnet was an established leader of the free black abolitionist movement. He had been born a slave in Kent County, on Maryland's Eastern Shore, and as a child fled north with his family. Between escaping slave catchers and doing farmwork to support himself, he managed to get an excellent education. After one of his legs was injured and amputated, he turned to the ministry. Soon he emerged as a forceful antislavery spokesman, supporting colonization and urging political action instead of the moral suasion practiced by Frederick Douglass. When war began, he recruited black troops and served as chaplain for those enlisted in New York. All this made him a target of the draft rioters in 1863, who missed him only because his daughter had chopped the brass nameplate off his door. Now he stood erect where no man of his race had ever stood before.[21]

When the blended voices of his choir had set the tone of the occasion with "All Hail the Power of Jesus' Name," Garnet spoke to the quiet, solemn gathering. He based his "fearless and timely" sermon on Matthew 23:4—"For they bind heavy burdens and grievous to be borne, and lay them on men's shoulders, but they themselves will not move them with one of their fingers." Lois Bryan Adams, writing for the *Detroit Advertiser and Tribune,* said that Garnet's eloquence repeatedly "thrilled the vast audience with an intensity of feeling which only the sacredness of the day prevented from breaking into loud applause." Slavery, said Garnet, "is the highly concentrated essence of all conceivable wickedness—theft, robbery, pollution, incest, cruelty, coldblooded murder, blasphemy, and the defiance of the law of God...." He appealed to the lawmakers to extend black freedom from simple emancipation to full citizenship. "Emancipate," he said. "Enfranchise. Educate, and give the blessings of the Gospel to every American citizen."[22]

In midwinter Walt Whitman, recovered and recently returned from New York, started a comfortable new job arranged by his friend William O'Connor. It was in the Interior Department's Bureau of Indian Affairs, in the basement of the Patent Office, a building now busy with painted chieftains from the West instead of suffering soldiers. One raw night, Whitman left John Burroughs's house on Capitol

Hill, throwing a blanket over his shoulders as he stepped into the storm. When he boarded a streetcar headed down the Avenue, he was the only passenger. "He seemed like an old sea-captain" to the conductor, who came in out of the weather to sit beside him. "Something in me made me do it and something in him drew me that way," the young man said years later. He was Peter Doyle, twenty-one, a red-haired, blue-eyed ex-Confederate soldier born in Ireland. "We were familiar at once," he recalled. "I put my hand on his knee—we understood." Whitman, instead of getting off at the stop nearest his latest home on M Street, stayed and rode back with him. "From that time on we were the biggest sort of friends," Doyle said.[23]

It was love at first sight. The gray-bearded poet, old enough to be Doyle's father, was smitten by the boyish, flirtatious streetcar conductor. His friends the O'Connors could see it in his face, and Whitman gloried in it. "Love, love, love!" he said. "Love is better than all." Many days he rode the cars back and forth from the Navy Yard to Georgetown just to sit out front with Pete; the pair became a familiar sight to others along the Avenue. Doyle shared with Whitman his memories of coming to America at the age of eight, settling in Alexandria and then Richmond, where his father was a blacksmith before the war in the great Tredegar Iron Works. Pete had served as a Rebel artilleryman, was wounded and survived Confederate hospitals before being arrested crossing into Union lines and held briefly in Old Capitol Prison. But he and Walt talked little; another passenger said theirs was "the most taciturn mutual admiration society ... perhaps because the young Apollo was as uninformed as he was handsome." Sometimes at the Georgetown end of the streetcar line, they stopped in the saloon of the Union Hotel, no longer used as a hospital. Whitman often spoke to Doyle of his world, of Shakespeare and planets and birds, but sometimes his friend nodded off in mid-lecture, his head on Walt's shoulder. We do not know just how intimate Whitman became with other men such as Burroughs and the soldiers whom he nursed so tenderly, but there was never any doubt about the love between Walt and Pete.[24]

Whitman's new job officially occupied him from nine to four, but he had plenty of time to meander with Doyle and visit ailing soldiers. About twenty of the temporary hospitals in commandeered quarters had been closed, and during static winter warfare there were many fewer casualties. As Whitman comforted patients, including Confederates, he hoped that somewhere in Dixie a Rebel was being as kind to his brother George, who had been captured in a battle outside Petersburg. General Grant, after refusing for months to exchange prisoners, had lifted this ban, and Walt hoped his brother would be among the first captives sent north. When George did not appear among two batches of returned prisoners, Walt went to Annapolis hoping to find out something from those who had returned. He was distraught by what he saw: many of those the Confederates sent from Richmond were sick, deteriorated living skeletons. "Probably no more appalling sight was ever seen on this earth," he said.* The Confederates had scant medicine and food for prisoners, their own troops and the civilians jammed into their capital city. Though Walt's brother was somewhere in Annapolis, he could not find him. He did not learn that George had been released until days later, when he got a letter from his mother in Brooklyn, saying he had come home. He was thin but well, considering how seriously ill he had been in prison.[25]

In desperation, the Confederate Congress had finally made Lee general-in-chief of all Southern armies, but there was little left to command beyond the increasingly demoralized force confronting Grant's army around Richmond and Petersburg. By early February, Grant had stretched Lee's defenses so thin that the Confederates were holding thirty-seven miles of line with little more than a thousand famished troops per mile, and every day there were fewer: Lee reported an "alarming" number of desertions from his dwindling army. In Georgia, Sherman had paused to rest and resupply his army after taking Savannah, and begun his march into South Carolina. On February 17, he took Columbia, capital of the state that had started the bloodshed, and that night much of the city burned to the ground. The next day, the Federals moved into Charleston. That, combined with George Washington's birthday, set off another celebration in the capital and inspired B. B. French to write, "Thank God the hotbed of Treason is

---

*David Bachrach, a Baltimore photographer, wrote that he had been sent by the government to Annapolis with orders to photograph "only the worst cases—men in the last stages of horrible disease" among the returned prisoners. Although Bachrach was a firm Union supporter, he refused when summoned after the war to testify against Henry Wirz, the commandant of the notorious Andersonville, Georgia, prison camp. He protested that "the idea that his work was to help to swear away a man's life was too much." Wirz was nevertheless convicted of inhuman treatment of prisoners and hanged in November 1865 at the Washington Penitentiary, the only Civil War participant to be executed for war crimes. (Richard D. Steuart, "Truth Is Mighty," p. 266)

humbled.... I hope there will not be left one stone upon another of that city where treason was hatched & grew up into a crowing & strutting cock...it will crow no more!" Four days later, Sherman's men reached Wilmington, North Carolina, and as March began, Sheridan's cavalry cleared the Shenandoah Valley of Rebel resistance by scattering the remnants of Early's force at Waynesboro. At that point Lee, with Davis's approval, secretly wrote to Grant suggesting that they meet to seek "a satisfactory adjustment of the present unhappy difficulties." Grant, on Lincoln's instructions, said he had no authority to enter such talks. He and the president knew that they held all the cards.[26]

Indeed, Lincoln had understood this when he returned a month earlier from the Hampton Roads conference. Nevertheless, he then wrote a remarkable proposal to pay the slave states to end slavery and come peaceably back into the Union. He estimated that the war was costing $4 million a day and might last another hundred days, consuming another $400 million and an uncertain number of lives. He was willing to pay that amount to stop the war, save the lives and reunite the country with minimum suspicion and estrangement. But this extraordinary gesture was too generous for his cabinet, which unanimously opposed the idea, so he withdrew it and never brought it up again.[27]

Lincoln was still motivated by compassion as he labored over the speech he would deliver at his second inauguration on March 4. He meant to address himself to both North and South. He did not have to lay out the situation confronting the nation, as he had four years earlier. He needed to express the Union's determination to grind on if the South insisted on continuing the war. But he wanted to spread his arms wide to embrace the nation as one when the bloodshed was over. He sought words to combine the two traits that characterized his presidency: determination and compassion.

With his speech drafted, Lincoln sat past midnight on March 3 in the President's Room off the Senate Chamber, signing or rejecting bills sent him in the tumultuous last hours of the Thirty-eighth Congress. As on all occasions of high drama or historic importance, the Capitol was crowded with officials and their families, journalists, and fancy-gowned society matrons, now multiplied by a horde of strangers in town for the inauguration. By late evening, the clerk and the members had trouble hearing and being heard above the confusion. The speaker banged and bawled for order, and messengers fought their way from chamber to chamber. Brooks wrote that "bills that were reckoned as dead were somehow galvanized into life and lived as laws, while many a healthy child of legislation was nipped untimely and died for want of breath."[28]

It was a chaos typical of last nights of session in many a lawmaking body across the land, but more so. Ellen Mills, visiting from New York, had many illusions shattered as she looked on from the gallery. She wrote that House members were much less dignified than senators: "They behave disgracefully, putting their legs on the desks, their hands in their pockets, roaming about, spitting &c. One was smoking and one combing his hair." However, the *New York Times* found it notable that no personal quarrels erupted, "nor were there any prominent or noisy manifestations of drunkenness as heretofore." After midnight the hubbub diminished, and some members who had stood guard to prevent legislative snakes from slipping through began to nap at their desks. Toward dawn, "with the suddenness of a thunder-bolt, burst one of the most angry and crashing storms of rain and hail ever heard. It beat like a deluge on the heavy glass roof of the hall, and the wind literally howl'd and roar'd," wrote Whitman. "The slumberers awaked with fear . . . and the little pages began to cry." Some of the few members remaining ran panicked into the corridors. Then, bowing to the elements, they recessed until later in the morning.[29]

The storm turned the city's streets and sidewalks into a mucky paste up to ten inches deep. Through this morass horses and men plodded to form a splendid inaugural parade, including that model ironclad gunboat with revolving turret and miniature cannon that fired blanks on its way along the Avenue. The local typographical society had a hand press mounted on a wagon, printing and distributing broadsides as it proceeded. The Washington and Philadelphia fire departments strutted with civic bodies and fraternal lodges of all stripes. But the notable difference between this inaugural parade and the one in 1861 was the presence of black marchers where there had been none. African-American civic associations and a battalion of black soldiers testified to what had happened in those four years. Nicolay and Hay wrote that "Imaginative beholders, who were prone to draw augury and comfort from symbols, could rejoice that the great bronze statue of Freedom now crowned the dome of the Capitol, and that her guardianship was justified by the fact that the Thirteenth Amendment virtually blotted slavery from the Constitution."[30]

Although Mrs. Lincoln's carriage led what Whitman called "this

absurd procession," the president was not in it. He went to the Capitol
at a smart trot in his own barouche, arriving ahead of time to sign last-
minute bills. The vice president–elect, Andrew Johnson, was welcomed to a nearby anteroom by his predecessor, Hannibal Hamlin.
Johnson had been ill and was exhausted by the long trip from Tennessee. According to Benjamin Perley Poore of the *Boston Journal,*
Johnson told Hamlin that he was sick and tired, and needed a drink.
When a bottle of brandy arrived from the Senate restaurant, he gulped
down about two-thirds of a tumbler. The sergeant-at-arms called the
group into the packed Senate Chamber for the vice presidential oath-
taking. Johnson excused himself, walked back and drank as much
again. Then, after Hamlin made brief and appropriate remarks, Johnson embarked on a "rambling and strange harangue" that contrasted
his own impoverished beginning with that of the generals, admirals,
politicians and diplomats assembled. He was qualified to do so: while
Lincoln had little formal schooling, Johnson had none at all. He
orated, red-faced and semicoherent, until John Forney, in his role as
secretary of the Senate, tried and failed to stop him. Referring to each
of the cabinet officers, Johnson forgot Welles's name, saying, "And you
too, Mr.——." Leaning, he asked one of the officials, "What's the name
of the secretary of the Navy?" and then rambled on. Attorney General
Speed whispered to Welles, "The man is certainly deranged," and
Welles told Stanton that Johnson was either drunk or crazy. Seward
was more generous, suggesting that Johnson was merely overcome
with emotion on returning to the Senate under such circumstances.
Apparently it was not chronic alcoholism or lunacy, but a single day's
combination of fatigue and brandy that ruined Johnson's debut before
the broader world.[31]

Lincoln came in during this fiasco and endured it with head bowed
in silence. He watched as Johnson, still muttering asides, was sworn in.
Then the newly elected senators were inducted, and the president led
the chosen hundreds who had witnessed this out onto the East Front
of the Capitol. They closed in behind him as he moved onto the inaugural stand, and Mrs. Lincoln had to squeeze through as if she were
any ordinary celebrity's spouse. Miss Mills recalled being packed so
tightly in the crowd that she could neither see nor hear, but did "have
the consciousness of being present." Before the president, a multitude
of well-wishers spread far toward the Old Capitol Prison to his left and
his old boardinghouse farther to the right. Closer at hand, within easy
pistol range, stood six men who wished him ill. John Wilkes Booth

was on a platform looking over the president's left shoulder, jammed in with distinguished spectators. He had a preferred spot because he came as the guest of his secret fiancée, Lucy Hale, daughter of former New Hampshire Senator John P. Hale. Directly below the president, no more than twelve feet beneath the speaker's platform, stood Booth's recruits: Lewis Powell, wearing a broad-brimmed hat; black-bearded George Atzerodt; David Herold, John Surratt and Ned Spangler.[32]

The president stepped toward the rostrum, holding his brief speech, which had been set in type and run off on a proof sheet. When the crowd recognized him, it let out a great roar, and the sun broke through the clouds that had hung over the capital all morning. As the *Star*'s man wrote, it "brighten[ed] with its beams the snow-white dome and upturned faces of the throng, a well accepted omen of the better days just dawning on the country." From the moment Lincoln spoke his first words, "Fellow-countrymen," he had the full attention of the thousands. His voice was more tenor than baritone, yet it conveyed the full weight of the occasion.[33]

When he had stood there in 1861, he said, all had dreaded war and were trying to avert it. Once it started, neither North nor South had expected it to be of such magnitude and duration. Both sides prayed to the same God for success, he noted, each invoking His aid against the other. Lincoln did not need to specify the South when he said, "It may seem strange that any men should dare to ask a just God's assistance in wringing their bread from the sweat of other men's faces; but let us judge not, that we be not judged.... The Almighty has His own purposes....

"Fondly do we hope—fervently do we pray—that this mighty scourge of war may speedily pass away. Yet, if God wills that it continue until all the wealth piled by the bondsman's two hundred and fifty years of unrequited toil shall be sunk, and until every drop of blood drawn with the lash shall be paid by another drawn with the sword, as was said three thousand years ago, so still it must be said, 'The judgments of the Lord are true, and righteous altogether.' "

To this grim vow, Lincoln added the suggestion of forgiveness, in words that would live long after him:

"With malice toward none; with charity for all; with firmness in the right, as God gives us to see the right, let us strive on to finish the work we are in; to bind up the nation's wounds; to care for him who shall have borne the battle, and for his widow, and his orphan—to do all

which may achieve and cherish a just and lasting peace among ourselves, and with all nations."[34]

Lincoln's friend Noah Brooks, like generations of Americans since
that day, was moved by "the beautiful solemnity, the tender sympathy,
of these inspired utterances." After a moment of quiet, there were tears
as well as applause among the thousands who stood in the mud listening. Then the president turned toward Chief Justice Chase. He placed
his hand upon an open Bible held by the clerk of the high court and
repeated the oath after Chase. Closing with "So help me God," he
leaned and kissed the Bible as artillery boomed, and the crowd
cheered and cheered.[35]

Afterward, Chase gave the Bible to Mrs. Lincoln. He had marked
the passage where the president's lips touched the page. It was Isaiah
5:27–28:

> None shall be weary nor stumble among them; none shall slum-
> ber nor sleep; neither shall the girdle of their loins be loosed, nor
> the latchet of their shoes be broken:
>> Whose arrows are sharp, and all their bows bent, their horses'
> hoofs shall be counted like flint, their wheels like a whirlwind.[36]

The muddy hoofs of the four gray horses that drew Lincoln's open
carriage struck no sparks as he and Tad rode amid the inaugural
parade, reversing its way back down the Avenue. Mrs. Lincoln followed in another carriage, and their son Robert in another. The president could not help but notice the float titled "Temple of Liberty,"
bedecked in red, white and blue. "Within this temple, as one of its pillars, stands a black man," wrote Lois Adams. "He is at the rear end of
the edifice, but the tallest man in it, and the only one standing."[37]

Let 'Em Up Easy

Y ou folks needn't have a fight with Old Bob Lee. Just hold on and worry him, as you are doing now, and he ain't going to have anything to fight with."

The Confederate who said that was one of the hundred, sometimes two hundred, who were arriving in Washington at about 4 P.M. every day on the "deserters' transport" from the James River. Many more were abandoning Lee's army and going home from the war rather than into Northern lines. Those reaching the Union capital took the oath of allegiance and were sent to work on farms, in factories or soldiering on the western frontier. But before assignment, they were free to wander about Washington in the remains of their gray uniforms, making small talk as casually as if they were Treasury clerks, sharing plugs of tobacco with disabled Yankees who had been their mortal enemies a few days before. There were so many of them that Brooks thought it "a grave question if we are not in danger of an organized conspiracy from this formidable element in the midst of our loyal country." But they were dangerous no more. They might say they had abandoned Lee because, in Brooks's words, they were "tired of fighting for rich men's niggers." But what drove most of them was hunger, and the knowledge that a Confederacy that could not feed its soldiers could not hold out much longer. In Lee's thin brigades, "Desertion became too common to punish," wrote Nicolay and Hay. "If men were to be shot for deserting, it would have been a question whether there were soldiers enough to shoot them."[1]

Whitman was full of sympathy for these long-haired, ragged men, some with pieces of old carpet, blankets or bags tied as capes about their shoulders. He talked with them for hours, extracting their life stories. John Wormley, recently of the Ninth Alabama, told him how much he wanted clean underclothes and a chance to wash, and Whitman "had the very great pleasure of helping him to accomplish all these wholesome designs." The poet was more in tune with these straightforward ex-Rebels than with the lofty Union brass whom he joined at the White House to congratulate Lincoln on his inauguration.[2]

B. B. French considered it his duty to calculate how many hands the president shook on such occasions. That evening, he figured that Lincoln stood in his claw-hammer coat and white gloves from eight o'clock till nearly midnight, greeting well-wishers "at the rate of 100 every four minutes—with about 5,000 persons! Over, rather than under, for I counted the 100 several times, and when they came the thickest he was not over 3 minutes, never over 5." Ellen Mills, less experienced at estimating crowds, thought there were 15,000 to 20,000 at the reception, though "evidently the elite for the most part had staid away." She retreated from the East Room, where the gowns of fancy-dressed ladies were crumpled in the crush, to watch Mrs. Lincoln, who "declined to shake hands with Tom, Dick & Harry, Jenny, Sally and the baby." She did not note how or whether the first lady greeted Frederick Douglass, or the other black citizens who were welcomed at a White House reception for the first time. Dozens of carriages lined up outside, the occupants waiting as much as two hours to make their way to the North Portico; some gave up and went home.

Mary Lincoln's mind may have been elsewhere as she greeted or cold-shouldered the familiar and foreign well-wishers blurring past. Her lost sons were never far away. The day after the inauguration, she sat with Nathan Daniels and a few others in the Green Room while the Andersons, a couple of New York spiritualists, pretended to "give some very fine descriptions of friends in the spirit world of all parties present." They told of seeing Willie, awaiting her with a vase of flowers. She wanted desperately to believe them; when they described the vase, she said it was one that had been in the boy's room when he died.[3]

The next evening, at the Inaugural Ball in the great hall of the Patent Office, there was more fashion but less decorum than at the White House reception. "Such a display of laces, jewelry, silks, feathers, gold lace, and things was never seen, no, not since the war began," said Brooks. Some in the crowd were only pretending to celebrate, for among them was John Wilkes Booth, escorting the plump and personable Lucy Hale. The senator's daughter had also been courted by both John Hay and Robert Lincoln but preferred the rakish actor, who could devote time to her since he had been absent from the stage for months. Booth wrote to his mother in Maryland that he intended to marry Lucy. But his attention to her may have been based less on her feminine charms than on her closeness to two members of the inner White House circle, for he also kept frequent company with Ella Turner, a prostitute at a brothel on Ohio Avenue in Hooker's Division.[4]

After all the government grandees at the inaugural ball had supped and departed, barriers were lowered for the hungry rest, who "rushed in, pushed the tables from their places, snatched off whole turkeys... smashed crockery and glassware, spilled oyster and terrapin on each other's heads, ruined costly dresses, tore lace furbelows, made the floor sticky with food," and, according to Brooks, "behaved in the almost invariably shameful manner of a ball-going crowd."[5]

From these festive heights, the capital returned to the ceaseless business of bureaucracy. As the new presidential term began, Treasury Secretary Fessenden resigned, and Lincoln named Hugh McCulloch, comptroller of the currency, to replace him. Three days later, Interior Secretary Usher also resigned, and Lincoln nominated Senator James F. Harlan of Iowa in his stead. This left the president with only Seward at State and Welles at Navy from his original cabinet.

Notwithstanding the triumphant atmosphere surrounding the inauguration, there was still a war to win. Sherman drove into North Carolina from the south, while another Union force pushed into the state from the coast. Grant stretched Lee's lines west of Petersburg, trying to cut off his last remaining railroad connections to the Deep South. Lee warned John Breckinridge, who had become Confederate secretary of war, that unless his men and horses could be fed, "the army cannot be kept together, and our present lines must be abandoned." In its desperation, the Confederate Congress turned to what had long been beyond open discussion in Richmond. For months, Lee had seen the enlistment of black soldiers as the only source of fresh manpower left to the South. On March 8, after long, emotional debate, the Confederate Senate agreed by a single vote. The following week, the House sent the measure to Davis, who signed it immediately. By implication but not by law, slaves could then win their freedom by fighting for the Confederacy. But Virginia Senator R. M. T. Hunter asked his colleagues, if slavery is abandoned, "who is to answer for the hundreds of thousands of men who have been slain" to preserve it?

Nine days after Congress approved, three companies of black soldiers in gray were drilling smartly in Richmond's Capitol Square. That was as close as they would get to combat.[6]

By the age of thirty-five, John Thomson Ford was a veteran impresario whose enterprises were surrounded by intrigues on- and offstage. He had started as manager of a minstrel troupe, then had taken over the Holliday Street Theater in his native Baltimore. In prewar politics, he leaned southward, and served for two years as Baltimore's acting mayor. He also branched out to share in operating the Old Marshall Theater in Richmond, where John Wilkes Booth had thrilled local belles. Then in 1861, with business booming in Washington, Ford bought the Tenth Street Baptist Church and rented it briefly to George Christy as the venue for Christy's famous minstrels. Inspired by Christy's great success, he took over the building, remodeled and ran it as Ford's Atheneum until it was gutted by fire a few months later. He rebuilt and reopened it in 1863, this time as Ford's Theater. There, in a two-week period that November, Booth appeared twelve times, starring in nine different plays, including the performance of *The Marble Heart* when he glared and pointed toward Lincoln in the presidential box.*[7]

Long before 1865, Ford and Booth had become friends, and the actor moved casually in and out of Ford's Theater as if he owned it. Thus it was easy for him to learn that Lincoln would not be occupying the theater's state box on the evening of March 15, and to reserve it for two friends. They were John Surratt and Lewis Powell; Booth wanted to familiarize them with the theater and that box, which looked down on the end of the stage. To make their attendance at the play *Jane Shore* seem innocent, they took along two young girls who were staying at Mrs. Surratt's boardinghouse. Booth stopped in briefly to see them during the performance. Afterward, he and his six conspirators met in a private room at Gautier's Restaurant on the Avenue to discuss how to go about kidnapping Lincoln from the theater. They talked, drank and argued until five in the morning before disbanding without agreement on a detailed plan. But little more than thirty hours later, an unexpected opportunity arose, and Booth mobilized his team.

*The other plays in which Booth appeared in those two weeks were *Richard III* (three times), *The Apostate*, *The Robbers* (twice), *A Lady of Lyons*, *The Merchant of Venice*, *Hamlet*, *Romeo and Juliet* and *Money*.

At about noon on St. Patrick's Day, he learned that Lincoln was going to a matinee performance of *Still Waters Run Deep,* arranged to entertain the soldier patients at Campbell Hospital. Booth quickly sent David Herold into the country to stow two Spencer carbines, two shotguns and other small arms at the Surratt tavern. Booth, Surratt, Atzerodt, Powell, Arnold and O'Laughlin would stop and subdue Lincoln and his driver as he returned from the hospital, out Seventh Street beyond the city limits. From there, they would take the president in his carriage through southern Maryland and across the Potomac. Herold would meet them en route with the weapons. But when the group assembled at a restaurant near the hospital, Booth rode ahead only to find out that Lincoln was not coming after all.[8]

Instead of attending the play at the hospital, the president went to the National Hotel, which happened to be where Booth was staying, to pay tribute to men of the 140th Indiana. He told them of the Rebels' decision to enlist black soldiers, which meant to him that they were near the end of their rope. Standing on a hotel balcony, he said that "if [the Negro] shall now fight to keep himself a slave, it will be a far better argument why [he] should remain a slave than any I have before heard.... Whenever [I] hear anyone arguing for slavery I feel a strong impulse to see it tried on him personally."[9]

Frustrated and angry at Lincoln's change of plans, Booth returned to the National and his henchmen scattered. The next day, the papers announced that "the celebrated young American tragedian has kindly volunteered his valuable services" to play the role of the villain Duke Pescara in a benefit performance of Richard Lalor Sheil's *The Apostate* at Ford's. It was Booth's next-to-last appearance on stage.[10]

Washington on the verge of victory impressed a newcomer from abroad as a place of focused and confident power, completely different from the divided, fearful capital into which the president-elect had crept four years earlier. The Marquis Adolphe de Chambrun, a lawyer and journalist who came as an observer for the French foreign minister, had been in Washington barely two weeks when he wrote that the political class seemed naïvely proud of what the United States was achieving. This attitude was understandable, he said, because the "terrible duel now being fought to the death" made the Revolutionary War seem "child's play"; American pride was "legitimate and justified by the sacrifices everyone has made." Perhaps Chambrun himself was naïve: He obviously had yet to meet, or recognize, the voracious minority who had not sacrificed but grossly profited in those four years. He believed that everyone gladly paid their taxes and willingly complied with the military draft simply because "it is necessary."[11]

Chambrun wrote at length to his wife in Paris, who was a granddaughter of the Marquis de Lafayette. He described the usual travails of transient life in Washington, and items of etiquette that seemed peculiar to one reared in Continental society. At a Kate Sprague party, food was placed on a narrow sideboard too crowded for women in expansive skirts, so gentlemen served themselves and their ladies, "all naturally on the same plate after the custom of the country." Chambrun helped two women thus, but "my appetite was not tempted by this way of serving supper." With his own title and his Lafayette connection, he was received everywhere. Invited to one of Mrs. Lincoln's levees, he was surprised to find the president greeting guests. "It is plain that this man has suffered deeply," he said, discerning what others have seen in the photographs of Lincoln taken in those last weeks of war. "It cannot be said that he is awkward; his simplicity is too great for that. He has no pretense to having worldly ways and is unused to society, but there is nothing shocking in this, quite the contrary. The elevation of his mind is eloquent; his heroic sentiments are so apparent that one thinks of nothing else.... As President of a mighty nation, he remains just the same as he must have appeared while felling trees in Illinois. But I must add that he dominates everyone present and maintains his exalted position without the slightest effort."

The Frenchman had spent much time with Charles Sumner and found him charming but adamant, unforgiving of his enemies. Such harshness convinced Chambrun that when Richmond fell, "we will witness a war of extermination. The defeated soldiers are going to be nothing but objects of pity; even the rights of belligerents will be denied them; they are just insurgents!" He felt that "this epilogue to the great tragic drama would be...a wretched ending." Still he was uncertain: he feared that this would be the outcome if the Sumners decided the fate of the South, but he also predicted that Sumner's influence would wane on the day the war ended.

The test lay just ahead, but not as close as he expected. "The hour of decision has struck," he wrote on March 24. "Two days more and the evacuation of Richmond will be an accomplished fact."[12]

Chambrun must have heard the same gossip that Welles heard to explain why Lincoln had left Washington the previous day for the

Petersburg front. The president went "partly to get rid of the throng [of office-seekers] that is pressing upon him," Welles wrote, "though there are speculations of a different character." In fact, Lincoln had quickly accepted an invitation from Grant to visit him at City Point, and set out aboard the *River Queen* with Mary, Tad and a small party of attendants and bodyguards. He was glad to break his onerous office routine; Welles thought Lincoln took upon himself too many trivial matters, "often causing derangement and irregularity. The more he yields, the greater the pressure upon him. It has now become such that he is compelled to flee."

"Besides," said Welles, "he wishes the War terminated, and, to this end, that severe terms shall not be exacted of the Rebels."

And besides that, the president was eager to see his son Captain Robert Lincoln, who had spent most of the war at Harvard but had recently been made a captain on Grant's staff at his father's request.[13]

Both Grant and Lee expected a decisive burst of action as soon as the roads were dry enough for their armies to move. Lee knew that Grant would try to cut his final connections to the South; Grant expected Lee to make a last-minute attack against the Union lines before trying to escape the Union noose. Both commanders were correct.

At about 4 A.M. on March 25, Confederate skirmishers crept through the blackness toward Fort Stedman, one of the closest strongpoints in Grant's noose about Petersburg. So many Rebel deserters had sneaked over during the preceding nights that at first Union pickets assumed this was just another gaggle of weary Confederates ready to quit in exchange for a good meal. But behind them came a determined assault, by which Lee hoped to alarm Grant and force him to shorten his lines. Success might give the Confederates time and room to get away to the southwest and unite with Joe Johnston's army, which was falling back before Sherman in North Carolina. Lee's troops took Fort Stedman and nearby fortifications, turning Union guns around against the defenders. They held the works for several hours before the Federals recovered and drove them out, capturing hundreds of attackers. Young Robert Lincoln had the pleasure of informing his father at City Point that "there was a little rumpus up the line this morning, ending about where it began."[14]

The "little rumpus" was Lee's last offensive effort. It was bold and desperate, and it failed. Grant asked the president to ride with him to the front, and Lincoln was curious to see and talk with some of the Rebels captured that morning. He seemed to put his petty Washington duties out of mind, now and then offering selections from his immense archive of stories appropriate for whatever occasion. Later he went with Grant to review Major General E. O. C. Ord's troops on the north side of the James River. Mrs. Lincoln and Mrs. Grant followed in an ambulance slowed by shin-deep mud, and when they caught up, they found the review already started. Mary, accustomed to taking honors with her husband on such occasions, was infuriated to see the president riding along the ranks, accompanied by the comely Mrs. Ord. At her first opportunity, Mary tongue-lashed the younger woman, and kept up her jealous tirade through the evening. Then, ashamed, she stayed in her riverboat cabin most of the time until April 1, when she returned to Washington without her husband.[15]

On the evening of March 27, Sherman arrived from North Carolina by boat to confer with Grant, and entertained his old comrade and his staff with the story of his march through the South, "a grand epic related with Homeric power." Then he went to meet Lincoln in the cabin of the *River Queen,* and the next day the president conferred there with the two generals and David Dixon Porter, now a rear admiral. Grant told them that he intended to move at once to cut off Lee's escape routes. All understood that the end was near, and Lincoln made clear that when it came, he intended to be generous toward the defeated South. On March 29, Grant left the president at City Point as he moved his headquarters toward the front to set out on his last campaign. He sent Sheridan, who had returned from the Shenandoah Valley, to turn the western end of Lee's line. Three days later, Sheridan did it, smashing George Pickett's Rebel division at Five Forks. He sent a collection of captured Confederate flags to Grant, who forwarded them to the president. When Lincoln unfurled them, his deeply lined face broke into an exultant smile. "This means victory!" he shouted. "This is victory!"[16]

The next day, Grant ordered an all-out attack along the entire Petersburg line, and Lee sent word to Jeff Davis that Richmond must be evacuated. That night, the Confederate president and cabinet got away on the railroad to Danville. On April 3, Major General Godfrey Weitzel's troops marched without resistance into the burning Rebel capital, and he sent a dispatch saying, "We took Richmond at 8:15 this morning."[17]

Praise God, from whom all blessings flow!"

The usually stern Stanton was shouting as he stepped out of the War Department telegraph office. Amid deafening cheers, the crowd waiting for news joined him in singing the Doxology and the "Old Hundred," then the "Star-Spangled Banner" and "Yankee Doodle." Weitzel's telegram from Richmond had reached the War Department before it caught up with Grant, who was moving with the army in pursuit of Lee. The news spread across Washington as if by electricity; in what seemed minutes, the newspapers were out with extra editions. Government offices and most shops closed for the day. Up and down the streets, friends and strangers were laughing, singing, shouting, crying, embracing. Lois Adams told her readers in Detroit that "people seem to have gone mad with joy." Patriotic banners and bunting hung from private windows and draped public buildings.

The crowds called notable personages out of home, office and hotel for speeches. Stanton was one of the few orators who could be heard above the uproar. He thanked God, the president, the generals and their troops, and asked that Providence "teach us how to be humble in the midst of triumph; how to be just in our hour of victory, and to help us secure the foundations of this republic, soaked as they have been in blood, so that it shall live forever and ever." This time he ordered an *eight*-hundred-gun salute that shook the city, three hundred booms for the fall of Petersburg, five hundred for Richmond. Each succeeding celebration, after Atlanta, election night, Savannah and Charleston, had been more tumultuous than the ones before. After almost four years of frustration and bloodshed driven by cries of "On to Richmond," this one was the wildest.[18]

But all was not jubilation. Andrew Johnson emerged from the War Department speaking for those who thought the war demanded vengeance against those who had started it. The new vice president seemed perfectly sober when he declared, "I would arrest them, I would try them, I would convict them, I would *hang* them." He was not shouting, he was deeply serious. "Leniency for the masses," he said, but "*halters* for the leaders." He was unaware that Lincoln at City Point had suggested that he would be glad if the Confederate leaders escaped abroad rather than drag the country through their prosecution and punishment.

Jane Swisshelm heard Johnson, and disagreed with him. At that moment, she felt that "there was room enough in the world for [the Rebels] and us, and that they were no longer foes worthy of pursuit." She had just been talking with an old black woman who wept and thanked God that Richmond had not been burned. Unknown to this ex-slave, Union soldiers were then fighting fires that had spread over downtown Richmond from tobacco warehouses torched by departing Confederates. But she told Swisshelm she was glad the Confederate capital's "precious souls" were not lost.

"But Aunty," said Swisshelm, "they are rebel souls!"

As Swisshelm wrote it, the woman said, "I knows dat, Ma'am, but hell am too bad for cat or dog. I don't want nobody to go dar, an' I tank my Jesus dat Richmond isn't burned."

Swisshelm apparently was softened by this exchange; she stopped Johnson and told him he had been too harsh. "Let there be no hanging," she said. Disfranchising Rebel leaders would be enough. Johnson did not yield. He told her, "Mrs. Swisshelm, a very good way to disfranchise them is to break their necks!"

By the time she reported the day to her readers in Minnesota, Swisshelm had reclaimed her usual antipathy toward the Confederacy. "It is so long since I have lived South that my convictions of the irredeemable depravity of the people have been wearing out.... The nation can never be safe while these, her implacable and wily foes, are above the ground." Among the rejoicing throngs, there were many celebrators who agreed with her. And behind shuttered windows, refusing to cheer or to decorate their doorways, there were others who thought that vengeance was owed in the other direction.[19]

But Lincoln, as if no one could possibly wish him harm, went by tugboat and barge from City Point up the James to enter Richmond the day after the Confederate army evacuated it. Flames were still flickering in the ruins as he strode about the fallen capital, surrounded by black Richmonders shouting "Glory, Hallelujah!" and praising "Massa Linkum." He inspected the White House of the Confederacy and sat at Davis's desk. Touring the city with General Weitzel, he passed Libby Prison and remembered the many emaciated Union soldiers sent north from there. Yet when Weitzel asked him how the defeated Confederates should be treated, he said, "If I were in your place, I'd let 'em up easy—let 'em up easy."[20]

Mary Lincoln, chastened, returned on April 6 to have her own look at captured Richmond. She brought along the Marquis de Chambrun, Senator Sumner, Attorney General Speed and James Harlan, the newly designated interior secretary. But the most deeply appreciative member of her entourage must have been her best friend, Elizabeth Keckley, who had been born a slave at Dinwiddie Court House, near Petersburg. Keckley sat in Virginia's historic Capitol, and when they visited Petersburg, she found a few old friends. Mrs. Lincoln particularly wanted to see Richmond's infamous prisons, then holding some 900 captured Rebel soldiers. Most of them stood respectfully when she came in; a few dared to hiss or whistle.[21]

While his wife was in Richmond, Lincoln heard from Stanton that Seward had been seriously hurt in a carriage accident and the president should hurry back to Washington. Then word came that Seward's condition was less dire than first feared, so Lincoln stayed in Virginia. He wanted to be there when the whole thing was over.[22]

Grant's troops were racing to get ahead of Lee, to head him off before he could join Johnston. At Sayler's Creek, they caught up and cut away nearly half of the Confederate force, capturing six generals, including one of Lee's sons. But the remaining Rebels kept going, and the end point was uncertain, so on April 8 the presidential party left City Point for Washington. As the sidewheeler chuffed slowly up the bay and the Potomac, Lincoln avoided debating reconstruction with Sumner by falling back on Shakespeare, reading aloud somber lines from *Macbeth*. Chambrun noted how dramatically he dwelt on Macbeth's torment, pausing to point out how the Bard imagined a murderer's mind "when, the dark deed achieved, its perpetrator already envies his victim's calm sleep." As the *River Queen* passed Mount Vernon, Chambrun told the president that in the future his home at Springfield would be honored along with Washington's in Virginia. "Springfield," mused Lincoln. "How happy I shall be four years hence to return there in peace and tranquility!"

Back in Washington near sundown on that Palm Sunday, April 9, Chambrun accompanied the Lincolns in their carriage to the White House. Looking about, Mary said the city was "full of enemies."

The president winced and gestured as if to brush away her comment. "Enemies," he said. "Never again must we repeat that word."[23]

The telegram Washington had waited and prayed for came that night, four years minus three days after the first guns were fired at Fort Sumter.

Grant had finally cut off Lee's retreat at the village of Appomattox

Court House, seventy-five miles west-southwest of Richmond. Lee tried to break through and found himself surrounded. At the brick home of Wilmer McLean, who had left Manassas to get away from the war, he surrendered the storied Army of Northern Virginia to Grant. The Union commander was generous, as Lincoln had said he should be: he allowed the remnants of Lee's force to be paroled and go home, taking their horses for spring plowing. When word of the surrender reached Jeff Davis at his temporary capital at Danville, he fled south, still talking of fighting on. There were no such delusions when Washingtonians awoke to the same news the next morning.

A five-hundred-gun salute shook every window at daybreak, and everyone knew what it meant. As if the cannon were claps of thunder, a heavy rain commenced at dawn. People rushed into the streets, ignoring the downpour. "The tumult of excitements so intense, so rapidly succeeding each other during the past ten days, has almost bewildered our senses," wrote Lois Adams. "The rains have opened the leaf and blossom buds, as the good tidings of great joy have opened the hearts of the people, and beauty and incense, rejoicing and thanksgiving fill the land."[24]

Steam fire engines bedecked with flags shrieked their whistles: every band in town was strutting and tootling in the muddy streets; soldiers and civilians linked arms and splashed along, singing "Rally Round the Flag" and "Yankee Doodle." Government departments did not even attempt to open for business. In from the Navy Yard rolled an impromptu battery of six howitzers, towed by sailors and mechanics who fired them at intervals. A crowd surged outside the White House, singing "The Star-Spangled Banner." They kept singing, calling the president out for a speech. When Tad stuck his head out a window, a great cheer went up, and another when he waved a captured Rebel flag. Then Lincoln appeared, and hundreds of hats flew into the air. After the roar subsided, he told the crowd that he would save his formal remarks for a planned celebration the next day. Pointing to the band, he said the Confederates had claimed the tune of "Dixie" as their own, but now the Union had fairly captured it. In fact, he joked, he had requested an opinion from the attorney general, who ruled that the song was now Federal property, so he asked the band to play it. "Dixie" had never been rendered with more spirit, not even by the Rebels. Before bowing back inside, the president led three cheers for Grant and his army and three more for the navy. Then the crowd wandered away, still singing, still rejoicing.[25]

When the masses returned the next day to the north lawn of the White House, Brooks thought "there was something terrible about the enthusiasm with which the beloved Chief Magistrate was received." The president stood calm in a window until the applause tapered off. Then, rather than the commemoration expected by the festive capital, he offered a reasoned treatise on reconstruction. The subject was "fraught with great difficulty," so he had written his remarks carefully. On the debated point of whether the seceded states should be considered legally in or out of the Union, he said the best way to bring them back was simply to bypass that question. The new Louisiana constitution, which he supported in general, would give the state legislature power to enfranchise blacks, and open public schools to both races. Lincoln was more restrained; he said he was ready for the right to vote to be conferred on "very intelligent" blacks and those who served as Union soldiers. But to suggest even limited black citizenship was infuriating to some of those in the crowd, including John Wilkes Booth and Lewis Powell. As the two walked off across Lafayette Square, Booth told his accomplice, "That is the last speech he will ever make."[26]

Night fell and the city glowed with torches and gaslight. Government buildings bore huge illuminations with triumphant slogans. The Post Office mounted a transparency showing a Pony Express rider, with the words "Behold I bring you good tidings of great joy." The Treasury, still strictly business, depicted a $50, 7 percent, thirty-year bond. The names of Grant, Sherman, Sheridan, Thomas and Farragut were everywhere (but not the long-ignored George Meade, still commander of the Army of the Potomac). A circle of fireworks about the statue of Jackson cast Lafayette Park in dancing multicolored patterns. Noah Brooks viewed all this from Arlington Heights, from which "no object was more remarkable than the Capitol, gemmed with thousands of lights, and the dome, apparently floating in air, outlined by the diminishing curves of the rows of lights which pierced the rounded sides." The Arlington mansion, once Lee's home, "glowed with Union fires, while the people who were once his slaves sang a Song of Jubelo on the lawn, the strains stirring the peaceful shades where the soldiers of the Union, slain by rebel arms, lie tranquilly sleeping near by.

"We live in strange times," Brooks concluded.[27]

In a city where free African-Americans had been oppressed and runaway slaves jailed in the past, it was strange indeed to see colored guards marching columns of Rebel prisoners through the streets. Lois Adams sneered at McClellanite editorialists who complained that what she called "captured traitors" were subjected to such indignity. The prisoners themselves showed no obvious irritation at this reversal of fortune, she wrote, and "Why should they?" She thought they had been cared for by black men all their lives, so deserved to be humiliated. The Marquis de Chambrun believed that if the words "The earth cries out and asks for blood" were ever true, this was the time and place. But he was impressed that "forgive and forget" seemed to be the popular watchword in post-Appomattox Washington. No insults were cast at the passing groups of prisoners—"The population seems to avoid looking at them, as though not wishing to hurt the feelings of these misled creatures." A week after Richmond fell, it was being fed and supplied entirely by Yankee quartermasters. Chambrun could hardly believe how quickly the attitude of the North had changed; he heard "peace, pardon and clemency" everywhere. By Mrs. Lincoln's invitation, he had been at the White House when the president spoke, and in private conversation afterward heard him declare "his firm resolution to stand for clemency against all opposition."[28]

On Good Friday, April 14, "The sermons all day were full of gladness.... The country from morning till evening was filled with a solemn joy." At Fort Sumter in Charleston harbor, Union warships and captured Rebel guns fired a grand salute as Brigadier General Robert Anderson raised the same United States flag that he had been forced to lower four years earlier. The nation's most famous abolitionist preacher, Henry Ward Beecher, spoke there in the cradle of rebellion with what Nicolay and Hay called "an earnest, sincere and unboastful spirit of nationality ... with a feeling of brotherhood to the South ... a speech as brave, as gentle, and as magnanimous as the occasion demanded." In Washington, the exultation of the first days after Lee's surrender eased into a calm mood of peace and gratitude, and concern for what still lay ahead.[29]

General Grant and Captain Robert Lincoln arrived from Virginia that morning, and at breakfast the youth gave his father a firsthand description of what had happened at Appomattox. For two hours, the president endured a series of conferences with legislators and petitioners before the regular Friday meeting of his cabinet. There, Grant met members appointed since he was last at the White House, including new Postmaster General William Dennison. When they congratulated the victorious general, he reminded them that the war was not over; he was unsure what was happening between Sherman and Johnston in North Carolina. But Lincoln told him he had experienced a dream the previous night that suggested all would be well. It was like others he had had before great events: he was aboard a ship headed for a dark, unknown shore. He had dreamed this before Antietam, Stone's River, Gettysburg and Vicksburg, he said. The literal Grant noted that Stone's River had not been a victory. Never mind, said Lincoln; Sherman will prevail.[30]

The general stayed for the cabinet meeting, where he may have made mental notes about the difference between give-and-take politics and crisp military decision-making. Stanton arrived late. Immediately after Appomattox, he had told Lincoln he wanted to resign, but the president had told him: "You cannot go. Reconstruction is more difficult and dangerous than construction or destruction. You have been our main reliance; you must help us through the final act." Stanton complied, and to the meeting brought his own plan for reconstruction of the South, beginning under martial law. Among other things, it would have made Virginia and North Carolina a single administrative district. Welles and Dennison objected to this, because since 1861 western Virginia had had a rump Unionist government, headed by Francis Pierpont, which should still be recognized. The president agreed with them, but also agreed in general with Stanton's plan. He said he was glad this discussion was taking place while Congress was away; he hoped a lenient reconstruction program could be in operation before meddling legislators returned in December.[31]

But the particulars of the conversation were less important than the dominant mood. Stanton wrote later that Lincoln was "more cheerful and happy than I had ever seen," and "manifested in marked degree the kindness and humanity of his disposition, and the tender and forgiving spirit that so eminently distinguished him." The president made clear that he wanted no more shedding of blood, no vindictiveness toward the South's leaders. Welles agreed. "No one need expect he would take any part in hanging or killing these men, even the worst of them," he wrote in his diary. " 'Frighten them out of the country, open the gates, let down the bars, scare them off,' said [Lincoln], throwing up his hands as if scaring sheep. 'Enough lives have been sacrificed; we must extinguish our resentments if we expect harmony and union.' "[32]

Too busy for a midday meal, Lincoln ate an apple as he sifted through more office routine with a vim and efficiency that seemed markedly improved since Appomattox. In midafternoon he set out on a carriage ride with Mary, visiting the Navy Yard to inspect the battle-scarred monitor *Montauk*. As they eased about the city, Mary was delighted by his bright mood. He talked of going home to Springfield, or perhaps Chicago, and opening a law office. The war was ending at last, he said, and thenceforth both of them must be more cheerful, because between the war and the death of their cherished Willie, "we have both been very miserable."[33]

The president and Mrs. Lincoln had decided earlier to go to Ford's Theater that evening, to see Laura Keene in the popular comedy *Our American Cousin*. Mary had invited General and Mrs. Grant to go with them, and they had accepted. Their plans were made early enough to be disclosed in the afternoon newspapers, and the general was sure to be lionized on his first public appearance since his great victory. Perhaps because of this, and perhaps because his wife still resented Mrs. Lincoln's jealous behavior at City Point, the Grants changed their minds and left late in the afternoon to visit their children in New Jersey. Since the president had complained of being "worn out with the incessant toils of the day," Mary then suggested canceling their theater plans. But those toils would still beset him if they stayed home, so he wanted to go out, and in any case did not want to disappoint citizens who expected to see him and Grant at the theater. Ford had announced that a new patriotic song, "Honor to Our Soldiers," with words by H. B. Phillips and music by Professor W. Withers, Jr., would be sung by the entire cast in honor of the general.[34]

Then, to replace the Grants, the Lincolns asked a series of others, including their son Robert, the Stantons, Brooks, Speaker Schuyler Colfax and Thomas T. Eckert, the chief of the telegraph office. Partly because Mary had been so snappish and erratic of late, the president and his lady were turned down by a dozen before a stylish young couple from across Lafayette Park accepted their invitation. Major Henry R. Rathbone was engaged to his stepsister, Clara Harris, who had become close to the first lady during White House visits with her father, Senator Ira Harris of New York. Henry and Clara had grown up together; after his father and her mother died, the surviving parents married each other. Twenty-seven-year-old Henry, assigned to the provost marshal general's office, had rented quarters on Jackson Place, on the west side of the park. The genteel life of a well-to-do staff officer in Washington was remote from the horrors he had witnessed as a captain in the Twelfth U.S. Infantry at Antietam, Fredericksburg and the Crater outside Petersburg.

Early on Friday evening, White House doorkeeper Alphonso Dunn took Tad to Grover's Theater on E Street, where the boy was eager to see *Aladdin*, plus "a grand illumination and pyrotechnic display," plus a recitation of several topical poems, including "Sherman's March to the Sea." The president was delayed by appointments with Colfax and former Congressman George Ashmun of Massachusetts, so Mrs. Lincoln sent coachman Ned Burke and footman Charles Forbes in her carriage to fetch Henry and Clara from the the Harrises' home. Before departing, the president chatted with one of his plain-clothes guards, William H. Crook, as Crook was going off duty. Crook later related how Lincoln told him that for three straight nights he had dreamed of being assassinated. He urged the president not to go out and then volunteered to accompany him to the theater, but Lincoln sent him home. The policeman recalled that instead of saying "Good night," as usual, Lincoln told him, "Goodbye, Crook."

The carriage returned with Henry and Clara to pick up the Lincolns at the north portico of the mansion. Unescorted, they proceeded to Ford's Theater on Tenth Street, where they arrived without incident at about eight-thirty.[35]

Now He Belongs to the Ages

By that Friday in mid-April, both soldiers and civilians in Washington wanted to believe that for them the war was over. Even as they awaited news from Sherman, they were beginning to wonder what to do with the rest of their days. The military draft was halted, the embargo on trade with the South was lifted. Speculators who had profited in war were eager to expand their fortunes in peace, clamoring to get at the cotton that had been sitting baled in the warehouses of Dixie. But for millions of Americans whose lives had been forever changed by the past four years, their concerns were more modest, more familial.

Antonia Ford Willard, so recently a daring secret informant for Confederate cavalrymen, was thoroughly domesticated and large with child. Her husband, whom she still called "the Major," was busy playing host at his hotel to generals, politicians and grafters, and was jealously protective of Antonia and their unborn son. Even late in the war, when fighting was far removed, he forbade Antonia's going to Fairfax to see her family. "The M. dont want me to be out of the house even when he is in it & wont consent for me to leave after dark at all," she wrote to her mother. Soon her maternal confinement would begin, with the birth on May 1 of Joseph Edward Willard, her adored "Jodie," who would grow up to be a distinguished Virginia politician and diplomat.*[1]

*Joseph C. and Antonia Willard had two other children, who died in infancy: Charles, who lived less than five months in 1867, and Archie, born five days before Antonia died on February 14, 1871, at the age of thirty-two.

Thomas Walter, who had moved yet again to another downtown boardinghouse, was lonely and still unhappy. He had returned from Germantown without his wife, on a suffocating railcar where "there must have been 20 stinking pipes and segars going at once, and it rained too hard to keep the windows up." He was pleased that the divided congregation of E Street Baptist was talking about reuniting, but the pastor he liked most intended to leave "the moment he can hear of something to do elsewhere . . . such seems to be the general feeling in Washington." Walter was also thinking beyond his work at the Capitol, knowing that whatever he undertook next, it would be a comedown from creating the shining symbol of the nation's ideals and endurance.[2]

Adolphe de Chambrun wrote a letter to his wife in Paris that afternoon, and stopped briefly in the quietness of church, where he always felt her presence closer than in the bustle of the streets. Outside, he fell in with Charles Sumner, who told him of Lincoln's insistence at the cabinet meeting on "clemency and pardon on the part of the victors." After listening to the disapproving Sumner, Chambrun perceived "a storm brewing" against the president because of his magnanimous reconstruction views. That evening, the Frenchman was "trying to imagine what might be the results" of Lincoln's forgiveness toward the South.[3]

B. B. French returned aboard the elderly steamship *Baltimore* from Richmond, where he had gone with the Committee on the Conduct of the War and a happy band of semiofficial tourists. They inspected the home of "Autocrat Jeff" Davis, Libby Prison and the Confederate political jail called Castle Thunder. From the Virginia Capitol, they saw that Richmond was "a heap of smoking ruins," and appreciated "the vandalism—the revenge—the wickedness that the flying Chivalry had left behind them." The visitors had planned to go on to Charleston, but Senator Wade felt ill, so they headed back up the Potomac, stopping briefly at Point Lookout, which still held 18,000 Rebel prisoners. As they reached Washington, French told his wife that he believed "Providence had ordered that the party should not go to Charleston for some especial reason that we could not understand."[4]

Walt Whitman's friend Pete Doyle was at loose ends in Washington because Walt was on leave from the Bureau of Indian Affairs. The poet was in Brooklyn, caring for his still recovering brother George and arranging for publication of *Drum-Taps,* his book of war poetry. That work, he wrote, would "express in a poem . . . the pending action of this Time & Land we swim in. . . ." Thus it was "unprecedentedly sad (as these days are, are they not?)—but it also has the blast of the trumpet, & the drum pounds & whirrs in it. . . ." On these spring evenings while Walt was gone, Doyle was lonely after his shift on the streetcar line. When he heard that the Lincolns and the Grants would be at Ford's Theater that night, he decided to go, too.[5]

John Wilkes Booth, who had been waiting, seething and plotting for months, determined his future when he found out on Friday morning that the Lincolns were coming to Ford's. The wild dream of kidnapping the president had evaporated—Richmond was gone, so where would they take him, to whom? The whole scheme of capturing and holding him for political ransom had always been fantastic; now it was nonexistent. But with the president so lightly guarded, revenge was still possible. Booth, after the ignominy of Appomattox, saw it as his sacred mission. Thousands of weary Confederate soldiers who had fought through the war might be willing, even glad, to give up and go home, but to the brilliant swordsman whose duels had all been on stage, surrender was unthinkable. He imagined that he might yet become the greatest hero of the South that he loved.

Early that morning, Booth met his fiancée, Lucy Hale, and then had his hair trimmed at a barber shop on E Street. It was when he went to Ford's Theater at about eleven o'clock to pick up his mail that he learned of the Lincolns' plans for the evening. That sent him whirling about downtown Washington. Three of his would-be kidnapping accomplices were unavailable—John Surratt was in Elmira, New York, scouting a possible raid to free Confederate prisoners there, and Samuel Arnold and Michael O'Laughlin had backed away when Booth spoke of assassination. That left George Atzerodt, Lewis Powell and David Herold. Booth had instructed Atzerodt to take a room at the Kirkwood House, where Vice President Johnson lived. At James Pumphrey's livery stable on C Street behind the National Hotel, the actor hired a small, fast bay mare, saying he would come for her in the afternoon. Then he met Powell at the Herndon House, where he laid out his plan to behead the Federal government, hoping blindly to cause enough confusion for the North to let the South go. He assigned Powell to murder Seward, the first minister of the cabinet, who was in bed after the serious carriage accident earlier in the month. Herold would guide Powell through the nighttime streets of Washington. Meanwhile, Atzerodt would kill Johnson, the constitutional successor to the president. At the same time, about 10:15 P.M., Booth himself would play the starring role of presidential assassin.

Near midafternoon, he went to Mary Surratt's townhouse and dispatched her to Surrattsville to tell the tavernkeeper, John Lloyd, to have the cached weapons ready that night. Then he went to the Kirkwood seeking Atzerodt, who was not there. Returning to the National, Booth sat in the hotel office and wrote a long letter that he sealed and took with him. Outside again, he ran into his actor friend John Matthews, whom he had tried and failed to enlist in his kidnapping plot. He gave the letter to Matthews, asking him to deliver it by hand to the *National Intelligencer* the next day because it was too important to send through the mail. On the Avenue, Booth passed the Grants, whom he expected to be at Ford's that evening, in their carriage on their way to the rail station. He reversed course to look again to be sure it was them. Mrs. Grant told the general that that was the same strange man who had made her uneasy earlier by glaring at her in the dining room at Willard's. Heading back to Ford's, Booth found Atzerodt and gave him orders to kill the vice president at the appointed hour. Atzerodt was reluctant, saying he had signed on to kidnap the president, not to murder him. But Booth threatened and cajoled him into agreeing to do his part.

At Ford's, the actor invited the carpenter Ned Spangler and three other stagehands for a drink at the next-door Star Saloon. Returning to the theater, he went upstairs alone to a narrow hallway running off the dress circle, behind the presidential box. Stepping inside the box, he fixed a wooden bar that he would use to jam the door against entry from the corridor, and drilled a small hole in the door. Then he went back to his room at the National, dressed himself in black suit and black hat, armed himself with a little single-shot .44-caliber derringer, and hid a long hunting knife in his pants leg. Apparently he had one more meeting with his accomplices to go over plans: after their simultaneous actions, they would rush to the Navy Yard Bridge across the Anacostia and flee together to Surrattsville. At about nine-thirty, Booth rode to a stable he had used in the alley behind Ford's and asked Spangler to take care of his horse. Spangler busied himself in the theater and got another stagehand to hold the horse. In the tavern next to the theater, Booth asked for a bottle of whiskey and a glass of water. A garrulous drinker, recognizing him, told him bluntly that he would never equal his father as an actor. To this Booth said, "When I leave the stage I will be the most famous man in America."[6]

President and Mrs. Lincoln, with Henry Rathbone and Clara Harris, arrived at Ford's Theater after *Our American Cousin* had begun. Some of the spectators on the sidewalk, expecting to see General Grant, mistook Major Rathbone for the general-in-chief. Laura Keene, the star of the play, knew the play backward and forward; she had introduced it at her own theater in New York and performed her role hundreds of times. She was onstage when the president entered his box, and when she looked up and saw him moving to his chair, she interrupted the dialogue by smoothly curtsying and ad-libbing a line in his direction. The audience of some 1,700 then rose and applauded as the orchestra played "Hail to the Chief." Lincoln made a modest bow, he and his guests took their seats and the play resumed.

Their box was draped for the occasion with red, white and blue flags and had been doubled in size by removing a partition that separated two compartments. When Lincoln's party entered, city policeman John Parker, recently assigned as a presidential guard, closed the door behind them and went to find a place where he could see the performance. He apparently left the Lincolns' footman, Charles Forbes, on a chair near the stairs.* In the enlarged box, the president sat in a cushioned rocking chair at the left as he faced the stage. Mrs. Lincoln was seated to his right, and Clara beyond her. Rathbone sat on a sofa slightly behind and farther right, looking between the two women. They were about twelve feet above the right end of the stage, as viewed from the audience; there were smaller boxes below.[7]

Booth took a last drink at the tavern and entered the theater shortly after ten o'clock. Unnoticed, he made his way to the stairs leading to the president's compartment and showed his calling card to Forbes, who let him pass. Then he peeped through the hole he had drilled in the door, saw who was sitting where and stepped quietly into the box behind the president.

The Lincolns seemed happier together and more relaxed than they

---

*On this and other details of what happened on April 14, the testimony of witnesses before, during and after the conspiracy trial differs substantially. This is particularly true of what Booth did that day, and in what exact sequence. The author has omitted many vivid but less plausible anecdotes that have grown up around the assassination.

had been in many months. Mary rested her hand on the president's knee through much of the play, leaning toward him to comment on what was happening onstage. At about ten-fifteen, she whispered to him as she held his hand, asking what Henry and Clara would think of their little show of affection. Just then the actor Harry Hawk uttered the line "Don't know the manners of good society, eh? Well, I guess I know enough to turn you inside out, you sockdolagizing old man-trap!" That set off a burst of laughter, in the midst of which Booth fired his pocket pistol from about two feet behind the president's head.

Because of the noisy laughter, many in the theater either did not hear the shot or thought it had something to do with the play. Rathbone leaped to grab Booth, who dropped his empty derringer, switched his knife to his right hand and deeply slashed the major's arm. Vaulting over the railing of the box, Booth leaped down onto the stage, shouting "*Sic semper tyrannis!*"—Virginia's motto, "Thus ever to tyrants." As he did so, his spur caught a flag draped around the box, throwing him off balance and causing him to break the small bone of his lower left leg when he landed. Limping, he strode across the stage brandishing his knife, shouting "Revenge for the South!" and got away to the alley in the rear before most spectators grasped what had happened.

Then there was chaos. Mrs. Lincoln screamed, "Oh, my God, have I given my husband to die?" Many in the audience recognized the murderer and cried, "Booth! Booth!" and then "Hang him! Hang him!" as men rushed to the stage. But they were too late. Booth knocked aside the man holding his horse, mounted and raced through the dark streets toward the Navy Yard Bridge.

Meanwhile, three hundred yards from the White House, Lewis Powell rang the doorbell of Seward's house on the east side of Lafayette Square. He told the servant who answered that he brought a prescription from the ailing Seward's doctor, which had to be delivered in person. When the servant resisted, the hulking Powell forced his way upstairs. Frederick Seward, who had been acting as secretary of state while his father was disabled, tried to block him. Powell put a pistol to Frederick's head, but it misfired and he beat him senseless with it, fracturing his skull. Crashing into the room where the elder Seward lay in bed, he cut his way past Seward's daughter and a soldier nurse named George Robinson and plunged a knife repeatedly at the secretary's head and throat. Seward suffered a gash in his right cheek and two stab wounds in the throat; his life was saved by his iron neck brace and by his rolling off the bed to the floor. Robinson grabbed Powell from behind, and the assassin stabbed him. Seward's other son, Augustus, came onto the hellish scene in his nightshirt and momentarily could not tell what was happening; he thought someone had gone mad. He clutched at Powell, who knifed his way out of the room, slashing another attendant as he fled. Mounting his horse outside the door, Powell rode out Vermont Avenue into the night. David Herold, who had been waiting there to lead him to their rendezvous with Booth, had fled when he heard screams from inside the house. Later he would meet Booth on the road, but without him Powell got lost and hid out in the city.

Thus two of the three intended assassins believed that they had carried out their missions. But Atzerodt could not force himself to try to kill Johnson. While his colleagues acted, he sat at the bar in the Kirkwood, drinking. But he could not drink enough to nerve himself to murder.[8]

At Ford's, Pete Doyle heard the pistol shot but "had no idea what it was, what it meant—it was sort of muffled." Then he saw Mrs. Lincoln lean out of the box and cry, "The President is shot!" Everyone in the audience could hear Clara Harris screaming "Water! Water!" and someone else shouting for a doctor. Charles A. Leale, an army surgeon who had been seated farther around the dress circle, was the first person admitted to the presidential box. Mary gained control of herself to say "Oh doctor, what can you do for my husband?" and ask Leale to take charge. He started to examine the president and discovered a smear of blood on his left shoulder. Thinking Lincoln had been stabbed there, he asked someone to cut away the president's coat and shirt, but found no wound. Then as he inspected Lincoln's body, his fingers felt a spot behind the left ear. The bullet had pierced the skull there and penetrated the brain. When those crowded around demanded information, Leale had to say that the wound was mortal. Laura Keene came up from the stage and begged to hold the president's head, which Leale permitted.[9]

Another army surgeon, Charles Sabin Taft, was lifted up from below into the box. He found Lincoln unconscious on the floor with Mary wailing above him and Leale ministering to him along with another doctor, Albert F. A. King. Someone had called a carriage to take the president to the White House, but the surgeons decided to move him to someplace closer where he could lie on a bed. The three of them lifted his head and shoulders and others held his body, carrying him downstairs and through the excited crowd on Tenth Street. They took him across the street, into the small back room of a brick row house owned by a tailor named W. P. Peterson. There they had to stretch him diagonally on a bed that was too short for his long frame.

So many people jammed into the room that the provost guard of the theater cleared it of all but the surgeons. Later, Stanton arrived and ordered General Meigs to take control at the site. Doyle lingered in the theater until a soldier yelled at him, "Get out of here! We're going to burn this damned building down!" The cast of the play was closeted in the dressing rooms, forbidden to leave, told that all were under arrest. Among them was John Matthews, who suddenly remembered Booth's letter in his coat pocket. He took it from its envelope, read it twice and realized that it could implicate him in the assassination plot, get him "no doubt lynched on the spot." At the first opportunity, he burned it.[10]

A steward brought medicine to Peterson's house from Lincoln Hospital, east of the Capitol. One of the doctors placed a spoonful of diluted brandy in the president's lips, but he had trouble swallowing. His breathing was labored, his pulse rate as low as forty-four. His pupils did not respond to light; the left was barely a pinpoint, and the right, behind which the bullet had lodged, was widely dilated. The doctors removed his clothes and applied mustard plasters from his neck to his toes. There was no response. Occasionally the president emitted a deep sigh. Robert Lincoln arrived and collapsed in sobs as he leaned over his father. Then he turned away and put his head on the shoulder of Charles Sumner, who tried to comfort him. About twenty-five minutes after the president was brought to Peterson's, Surgeon General Joseph K. Barnes and the Lincolns' family physician, Robert King Stone, came and took charge. Army surgeon Taft tried to administer another spoonful of brandy, with no success. Mrs. Lincoln, keeping vigil in the crowded front room with Clara, came back occasionally to sit close and whisper to her husband.

The president's wound bled little, and even this oozing stopped as dawn approached. His breathing became rattly, stopping for as long as a minute before resuming with great effort. Mrs. Lincoln came into the room again and saw Taft with his hand on Lincoln's chest and his eyes on Barnes's watch, while the surgeon general held a finger to the patient's carotid artery. She fell in a faint before being brought to and helped to the bedside. "Love," she moaned, "live but for one moment to speak to me once—to speak to our children!" Cabinet secretaries, the Reverend Gurley and other dignitaries surrounded the bed, watching silently, wanting to be able to tell their grandchildren that they were there at the end. More than once, Lincoln's breathing halted, they looked at their watches for long seconds, and then came another tortured sigh. Finally, at twenty-one minutes and fifty-five seconds past seven o'clock on the morning of April 15, the president drew his last breath. For another fifteen seconds, his great heart refused to quit.[11]

"Now he belongs to the ages," said Stanton. He pulled down the window shades as one of the surgeons gently placed silver dollars upon the president's eyes. Then they left the body alone and posted a guard at the door of the room. Gurley delivered a long prayer that was hard to hear above the weeping of men and women alike. Stanton and the other cabinet members present met in the rear parlor of the house and signed a message informing Vice President Johnson that "the government devolved on him." Mrs. Lincoln's wails could be heard up and down the street, where hundreds had gathered. Robert led her out to her carriage, and as she departed, she looked across at Ford's Theater and moaned, "Oh, that dreadful house! That dreadful house!"

At seven-thirty, first one, then all of the city's church bells began to toll the news that the president was dead. Soon a hearse came to take his body to the White House, led by army officers walking bareheaded in the rain and escorted by the soldiers who had guarded the mansion. Dr. Taft wrote that as the sad procession moved along the muddy streets, "terrible execrations and mutterings" came from a few citizens among the mourners who removed their hats at the curbs. Disparaging remarks about Lincoln and muttered praise for Jeff Davis were quickly squelched by the surrounding throng. At the mansion, the surgeons conducted a postmortem examination, during which Mrs. Lincoln sent a servant to ask for a lock of her husband's hair. Stone clipped a blood-matted lock for her. Without speaking, Taft held out his hand, and Stone clipped another for him, then one for each of the doctors present.[12]

As soon as the president's distraught widow reached the White House, she sent for Elizabeth Keckley, but the messenger went three times to the wrong address and did not find her. When Keckley heard from a neighbor that "the entire cabinet had been assassinated," she said, "I felt as if the blood had been frozen in my veins, and that my

lungs must collapse for want of air." She and her landlord, Walker
Lewis, went through Lafayette Park to the White House but found it
surrounded by guards. She fretted through the night, accurately imag-
ining Mrs. Lincoln "wild with grief." When the first lady could not
locate Keckley, she summoned Gideon Welles's wife, who spent the
night with her despite having been ill for the past week. After breakfast, Secretary Welles and Attorney General Speed went to the White
House and encountered Tad. "Oh, Mr. Welles," the boy pleaded, "who
killed my father?" Both of the men, who had held their composure
through the death watch at Peterson's, broke down in tears.

At about 11 A.M., Keckley relieved Mrs. Welles at Mary Lincoln's
side. She took a few minutes to gaze on the dead president's face as he
lay surrounded by cabinet secretaries and generals. She was pained by
remembering how Willie Lincoln's body had lain in the same room
and how much sadness had clouded the Lincolns' years in that house.
Returning to Mrs. Lincoln, she found her in "a new paroxysm of grief,"
with Robert bending over her and Tad crouched at the foot of the bed.
When his mother let go a shriek of anguish, Tad said, "Don't cry so,
Mama! Don't cry, or you will make me cry, too! You will break my
heart."[13]

Never had a nation fallen so swiftly from elation to despair. "It
seemed as if everybody was in tears," wrote Noah Brooks. People
thronged the streets, asking strangers exactly what had happened to
whom. Flags that had flown high in triumph fell to half-staff, all shops
and government offices closed, and tiny hovels as well as grand official
edifices were draped in mourning. Some of the humblest shanties were
"grotesquely but touchingly" festooned with discarded scraps of crepe
patched together in strips. "Nature seemed to sympathize in the general lamentation," Brooks said. The cold gray rain swirled down, and
the wind moaned as it tugged at the sodden black bunting.

At about nine o'clock, Attorney General Speed called on Johnson
at the Kirkwood House with the message from the cabinet. Two hours
later, the cabinet minus Seward assembled with a few other dignitaries
in a parlor there, and Chief Justice Chase administered the oath of
office to the seventeenth president of the United States. Brooks spoke
for millions when he wrote that the assassination of a leader committed to leniency had "nerved the people to a demand that his successor
shall do a great deal of hanging" in retaliation. "Fearful retribution"

was coming, he said. "[T]he people, blind with rage, demand a blood sacrifice and will have it."[14]

Lincoln's body was moved into the East Room on April 17, resting there on a high catafalque beneath a canopy of black. An honor guard of two generals and ten other officers stood watch around the clock until the funeral two days later. Bleachers covered with black cloth were erected about the room to accommodate the hundreds of official mourners, who included delegates from the New York Chamber of Commerce, diplomats in gaudy costume and a plainly uniformed, tearful General Grant, but only six women. Robert Lincoln was there, but neither his mother nor Tad could face the ritual. Byron Sunderland, one of four clergymen present, delivered the funeral sermon. There was no music.

At 2 P.M. on soft, sunny April 19, the funeral cortege moved out of the White House grounds. Church bells tolled, military bands played dirges and cannon boomed in the city and the surrounding forts. Regiments of infantry, cavalry and artillery fell in to head the procession, followed by the elaborate hearse, politicians, foreign dignitaries, and at the end an assortment of black lodges and associations. Then as all began to move, there suddenly came marching the Twenty-second U.S. Colored Troops, just off the boat from Petersburg. Stepping in front of the column, the regiment took the lead past mourning citizens along the mile and a half up the Avenue to the Capitol.

There in the Rotunda, the coffin lay as many thousands came to pay their final tributes. Soldiers funneled them into the great room beneath Walter's dome in a double line that divided as it passed the catafalque. Brooks got permission to go alone up the stairs to the apex of the dome, and looking down from there, he said his own goodbye. His tears could be felt in what he wrote of his great friend—"A martyr to the national cause, his monument will be a nation saved, a race delivered, and his memory shall be cherished wherever Liberty hath a home ... 'to the last syllable of recorded time.' " The next evening, Lincoln's body was taken to the B&O station to start its slow journey to Springfield, past masses of grieving Americans, reversing the same circuitous route that he had taken on his way to Washington.[15]

Walt Whitman saw none of this. He had read of Lincoln's death at home in Brooklyn, and in his gloom he could not eat, but wandered morosely along Broadway in the same rainstorm that drenched Washington. When he returned to the capital, the latest secretary of the interior was purging his department of disloyal and inefficient employees, along with those whose conduct, habits or associations defied "the rules of decorum & propriety prescribed by a Christian Civilization." Unfortunately for Walt, the secretary had come upon a copy of *Leaves of Grass,* and so fired him. But Whitman quickly got another job, in the attorney general's office, that gave him time to write. Only after months of trying, through false starts and lesser efforts, would he find the words that will always bind him to the fallen president, the masterpiece that begins:[16]

> *When lilacs last in the dooryard bloom'd,*
> *And the great star early droop'd in the western*
> *sky in the night,*
> *I mourn'd, and yet shall mourn with*
> *ever-returning spring.*
>
> *Ever-returning spring, trinity sure*
> *to me you bring,*
> *Lilac blooming perennial and drooping*
> *star in the west,*
> *And thought of him I love.*

Out of Sorrow into Holy Memories

From Lafayette Park, the White House seemed a vast mausoleum draped in black. The whole capital had been in a daze, numb, "like a widow in the first desolation of her grief." Now, after the president's funeral, offices and businesses were opening again and military traffic was clattering along the Avenue. But Mary Lincoln was still there in the mansion, in bed, weeping, sometimes shrieking, even as servants and stray visitors downstairs were lifting away silver, china and souvenirs. She refused to see most of the many who called to console her. The new legal occupant of the White House was not among them; Andrew Johnson neither came nor wrote to offer sympathy. On the night of the assassination, he had hurried to the Peterson house but had been turned away, told that the mere sight of him after his boozy inaugural speech was so upsetting to Mrs. Lincoln that he must leave. He would not risk such treatment again. He was president now, doing the business of the nation in a small office in the Treasury Building, courteously waiting while the former first lady recovered. In due course, Mary would humble herself by writing to him seeking jobs for some of her friends and staff. But for almost six weeks, she stayed in the White House, resisting going back to Springfield, while the war dwindled to its end and detectives and soldiers tracked down her husband's murderer.[1]

Booth had galloped away from Ford's Theater and escaped Washington by persuading the guard at the Navy Yard Bridge, who had heard nothing of the assassination, to let him pass nearly two hours after the 9 P.M. curfew. Close after him came David Herold, who had fled from outside Seward's house on Lafayette Park. They left behind them a city wild with rumor; some citizens locked and barred their doors when they heard that the president and his whole cabinet had been murdered. The two fugitives reached the Surrattsville tavern about midnight, picking up a rifle and some whiskey to ease the pain of Booth's broken leg. Riding on into the night, they went to Dr. Samuel A. Mudd's home near Bryantown, where the doctor splinted Booth's leg and the actor slept, shaved off his mustache and tested hastily homemade crutches. Leaving Mudd's on Saturday afternoon, the conspirators got lost in Charles County swampland before paying a black farmer to guide them to a Rebel sympathizer named Samuel Cox. Cox passed them to Thomas A. Jones, a reliable link in the Rebel network, who supplied them with food and newspapers while they went to ground in the woods.

Booth now had a $175,000 price on his head—a $100,000 reward offered by the Federal government, plus $25,000 each by three states. While hiding without shelter, he wrote in his diary, trying to explain why he had committed the crime of the century. His rationale was much as he had elaborated it in the letter that Matthews burned. He could never repent what he had done, he said. He hated to kill, but "our country owed all our troubles to [Lincoln], and God simply made me the instrument of his punishment."

For six rainy days, Booth and Herold lay low until they were told that Federal troops searching nearby had moved on. When Jones brought newspapers, Booth read with disappointment that Confederates as well as Yankees deplored what he had done. The once staunchly secessionist *Richmond Whig,* the first newspaper to resume publishing in the Virginia capital, said, "The heaviest blow which has ever fallen upon the people of the South has descended." Such words hurt Booth, but he knew that he could not expect praise from a paper printed under the eyes of Grant's occupying army. He must get across the river, where surely he would be lauded by right-thinking Virginians.

On Friday, April 21, a week after the assassination, Jones led the fugitives through the night to a creek that flowed into the Potomac near his home at Huckleberry. Booth's swollen and infected leg tortured him at every move, so Jones and Herold carried him down the steep bank to where Jones's former slave had hidden a fourteen-foot rowboat. With one oar, one paddle and a simple compass, the fugitives climbed aboard. Jones gave them a bearing to Machodoc Creek in King George County, Virginia, then pushed them off toward the dark, two-mile-wide river, patrolled night and day by Union gunboats.[2]

While Booth and Herold were fleeing, Stanton was overseeing a furious search for the assassin. He ordered Lafayette Baker, on assignment in New York, to return immediately to "see if you can find the murderers of the President." Baker knew how. Booth's accomplices had been rounded up one by one, and the detective had experience at extracting information from prisoners. Lewis Powell, after attacking Seward, had gotten lost in the dark city and rode his borrowed one-eyed horse until it gave out near Lincoln Hospital. He hid in a cemetery until the night of April 17, when he unwisely went to Mary Surratt's house, carrying a pickax and pretending to be a workman. The house was full of policemen, who had closed in on Mrs. Surratt and now arrested him. When Powell was identified by the servant who had opened the door at Seward's, he was locked up aboard the monitor *Saugus,* moored off the Navy Yard. On the same day, Samuel Arnold was arrested at Fortress Monroe and Michael O'Laughlin gave himself up in Baltimore. Police thought at first that the man who tried to kill Seward was Atzerodt. Still drinking, Atzerodt had zigzagged about the city and then left a conspicuous trail through Georgetown and Rockville on his way to hide out at a cousin's house near Germantown, in Montgomery County. Despite near-comical clumsiness by the troops in pursuit, they arrested him on April 20 and imprisoned him with Powell on the *Saugus.*[3]

But the most wanted criminal in America was still at large, and Baker was tracking him. Early in the war, the detective chief had commanded a cavalry detachment looking for Rebel collaborators in southern Maryland. He was familiar with the roads and towns of Prince George's, Charles and St. Mary's counties, and with settlements like Chaptico, Leonardtown, T.B. and Port Tobacco. Now his troops combed the territory, questioning everyone, arresting those suspected of helping or merely knowing anything about the conspirators. The crews of Federal patrol craft on the Potomac scanned the river and its banks with binoculars, ready to stop and inspect anything coming or going. But they narrowly missed catching Booth and Herold, who almost blundered into a gunboat in the darkness.

The fugitives steered the southward course described by Jones until they came upon the USS *Juniper* near their destination on the Virginia shore. When another gunboat passed, heading up the river, and a wind arose from the south, they decided to turn back to Maryland. They put ashore in Nanjemoy Creek, well above where they had started. At Indiantown, a nearby farm run by another Southern sympathizer, John J. Hughes, they went into hiding again. Booth was in despair. He wrote of being "hunted like a dog ... chased by gunboats ... wet, cold, and starving. And why? For doing what Brutus was honored for, what made Tell a hero. And yet I, for striking down a greater tyrant than they ever knew, am looked upon as a common cutthroat." In his deluded state, he even imagined that he might return to Washington "and in a measure clear my name."

The next night, he and Herold set out again and this time made it to Virginia, where the Rebel network was still functioning in King George County. On landing, Booth sent Herold off to make contact with a widow Quesenberry, who passed them on to two other operatives, who passed them to another, who provided them with horses and passed them to Dr. Richard H. Stuart. They reached Stuart's home at dusk, and he fed them but refused further help, sending them to the cabin of a free black named William Lucas. Booth threatened Lucas and took over his cabin that night, and the next morning Lucas's son drove them to Port Conway, on the Rappahannock. There they encountered three disbanded Confederate officers, Willie Jett, Absalom R. Bainbridge and Mortimer B. Ruggles, who had been an intelligence operative with Thomas Conrad. The three were surprised when the haggard, black-whiskered Booth identified himself, but they were eager to help. They joined the fugitives on the crude ferry across the Rappahannock to Port Royal. One suggested seeking shelter for Booth and Herold at the farm of Richard Garrett, three miles into Caroline County. Garrett was willing to take in the crippled man, who identified himself as "James W. Boyd," while the others went to nearby Bowling Green to determine their next move.

That morning, April 24, Lafayette Baker was at the telegraph office when a message arrived from searchers reporting that two unidentified men had been seen crossing the Potomac near Port Tobacco eight days earlier. Baker, mistakenly assuming that these two were Booth and Herold, quickly dispatched Detectives Everton J. Conger and Luther Baker, with twenty-five troopers of the Sixteenth New York Cavalry under Lieutenant Edward P. Doherty, on board the steamboat *John S. Ide*. They headed down the river, landed at 10 P.M. at the former Union army supply base at Belle Plain and started banging on farmhouse doors along the roads south into King George. The next day at Port Conway, they questioned shad fishermen who said the men who crossed there matched photographs of Booth and Herold. It took the rest of the afternoon to pole the cavalrymen with their horses across, six at a time, on the scow that served as a ferry. As they set out toward Bowling Green, Ruggles and Bainbridge heard that they were coming and galloped to the Garrett farm to warn the fugitives. The searchers rode past Garrett's on their way to Bowling Green, where they found Jett at his sweetheart's home. The scared eighteen-year-old told them where to look.

It was 2 A.M. when Doherty and his men rode up to Garrett's gate. They approached the house quietly, but dogs started barking as they came close. The troopers dragged Richard Garrett out into the yard, promising to hang him if he did not say where the assassins had gone. He was trying to talk when his son John emerged from an outbuilding where he had been sleeping to be sure the fugitives did not steal the farm's horses. Young Garrett said the two were locked in the tobacco barn.

Soldiers surrounded the barn and sent John Garrett in to demand that Booth and Herold surrender. Booth refused, offering to fight it out at fifty paces. As officers tried to negotiate with him, cavalrymen piled brush against the barn. When Herold heard a warning that they were about to set it aflame, he gave himself up. Booth remained defiant. At about three o'clock, Conger lit the fire. Through gaps in the plank siding, they could see the silhouette of Booth standing with one crutch, surrounded by burning hay. He seemed to raise—or perhaps drop—his carbine. Sergeant Boston Corbett, a religious zealot who later went insane, aimed his pistol through a crack in the barn and, without orders, shot the assassin in the back of the neck.

Troopers dragged Booth into the yard and onto the farmhouse porch. A nearby doctor was summoned and said the wound was fatal. As Booth grew weaker, he gasped repeatedly, "Tell my mother I died for my country," and pleaded, "Kill me. Kill me." He died shortly after 7 A.M. on April 26, almost exactly eleven days after Lincoln breathed his last. Lieutenant Doherty sewed his body into a saddle blanket. Using a farm wagon, the cavalrymen took Booth's remains to Belle Plain and returned them to Washington on board the *John S. Ide*.[4]

A few hours after Booth's death, Confederate General Johnston met Union General Sherman at a farmhouse near Durham, North Carolina, and surrendered the last major Rebel army. Sherman, believing he was doing what Lincoln wanted, had made an earlier agreement with Johnston that would have covered all Rebel forces, recognized

Southern state governments and otherwise reached beyond local military matters. Washington overruled this so summarily that Sherman was infuriated with Stanton and Halleck. The revised surrender document signed April 26 included terms much like those allowed by Grant at Appomattox. Meanwhile, Jefferson Davis and what was left of his Confederate government were fleeing south from Charlotte, hoping to reach one of the two smaller Rebel armies that were still resisting in the deep South and beyond the Mississippi.

Neither the demise of the assassin nor the news from Sherman could lift the gloom over Washington. One of Booth's lady friends, presumably the trollop Ella Turner, was riding a capital streetcar when she heard of his fate. According to the newspapers, she responded as melodramatically as her lover might have done on stage, taking his photograph from her purse and kissing it repeatedly as she wept. Thousands of curious citizens went to the Navy Yard hoping to view the assassin's body, but all except official visitors were turned away while a postmortem proceeded aboard the vessel *Montauk*. At Willard's and along the Avenue, everyone seemed disappointed that the leading villain had not been taken alive, so they could watch his trial and hanging.[5]

Those dramas would come, but few among the general public would witness them. Despite the fact that both the conspirators and their victims were civilians, Stanton insisted that they be tried by a military commission of nine army officers. On May 2, President Johnson formally accused Davis and other Rebel leaders of inciting and planning Lincoln's murder, and offered a $100,000 reward for the arrest of the Confederate president. Although there is evidence that the Confederate civilian high command was involved in the earlier plan to kidnap Lincoln, there has been no proof that Davis endorsed the assassination. As May began, he was deep in South Carolina, and his entourage was peeling away as he fled on. He was finally captured near Irwinville, Georgia, on May 10, the date when Johnson officially proclaimed that armed resistance in the South was over.

Two days later, the eight defendants in the Lincoln assassination case pleaded not guilty as the military commission started taking testimony on the third floor of the Washington Penitentiary, close by the Arsenal. Soldiers guarded the surrounding streets, and journalists like Noah Brooks and Benjamin Perley Poore had to clear a series of security checkpoints, then be approved by staff officers to gain admission. Each of the male defendants was restrained by leg-irons connected by a one-foot chain, and all except Dr. Mudd wore handcuffs connected by a ten-inch iron rod; his were linked by a chain. Mary Surratt, veiled and wearing black, also wore leg-irons that clanked beneath her long dress. About twenty-five reporters were regularly present, and gave their readers word pictures of the defendants whose names by then were familiar across the country.

Mrs. Surratt fascinated them as she sat fanning herself, "rather buxom-looking . . . fleshy, placid, and about forty-five." Herold had "a low forehead . . . stooping figure, and a sottish expression [on his] vulgar face." Powell, alias Payne, was "the incarnation of a Roman gladiator, tall, muscular, defiant . . . with much of the animal and little of the intellectual." The "low, cunning" Atzerodt had "a decided lager-beer look," "the meanest face of the whole crowd." The descriptions of Arnold, O'Laughlin and Spangler were no more flattering, but Mudd was given credit for seeming more intellectual, and perhaps more innocent.[6]

For nearly seven weeks, the trial proceeded as Judge Advocate Joseph Holt examined witnesses, who were then cross-examined by the separate counsel for each defendant. Major General David Hunter, scourge of the Shenandoah Valley, sat as head of the commission, whose uniformed members squirmed impatiently in their seats as they listened. Days went by before any defense witness was presented. Brooks wrote that "but for the looks of the thing," the defendants "might as well be hanged forthwith."*

As the trial proceeded, the streets and hotels of Washington were filling in anticipation of a more public display, the last and greatest of Civil War celebrations, the most meaningful parade in the nation's history. In the days before May 23, trains from the North were expanded but still running hours late, overloaded with citizens coming to witness the passing of the armies, the symbolic end of the war to preserve the Union. It would be a two-day spectacle, with the Army of the Potomac parading down the Avenue first, and then the winners of the West, the armies of the Mississippi and the Tennessee. The crowds

---

*On June 30, the commission found Herold, Powell, Atzerodt and Surratt guilty and sentenced them to death. They were hanged at the Washington Penitentiary on July 7, 1865. Arnold, McLaughlin and Mudd were given life in prison at hard labor, while Spangler was sent to jail for six years. McLaughlin died at Fort Jefferson on the Dry Tortugas in 1867, and President Johnson pardoned the remaining three prisoners in 1869. John Surratt, who had fled to Canada, Europe and Egypt, was arrested in 1867 and returned to face a civilian court that failed to convict him. Lafayette Baker had Booth's body buried secretly by night in an unmarked grave beneath the prison floor.

were even bigger and more jubilant than those that had thronged Lincoln's inaugurations. The generals' orders to coordinate the final joint movements of more than 150,000 troops were more detailed than any they had issued on the eve of battle. Sheridan's cavalry corps, which would lead the way for the Army of the Potomac, crossed the river to apply its final spit and polish at Bladensburg the day before the parade. Taverns and offices were closed. The capital was festooned again with red, white and blue, replacing the black that had draped the city for more than a month. The nation was ready to end its mourning.

At 8:30 A.M. on May 23, the momentous pageant was assembling on Capitol Hill when Thomas Walter arrived in his office and shut himself in, ignoring the festivities, to spend the day working on a ventilation report. He found it "exceedingly annoying" that his staff was taking two days off with the rest of the government, and that Sherman and his family were staying at his boardinghouse and sitting up late talking with visiting generals. One morning he would actually find himself having breakfast beside Sherman but decline to speak to him. Despite war, landlords, cockroaches, labor shortages and bureaucratic harassment, Walter had succeeded in his most ambitious project. Within the week, he would resign to return to Pennsylvania to pursue his brilliant architectural career. But now he was depressed, unable to admit to himself that his determination to press on with the dome had helped lift the morale of the capital and the nation, that he deserved to share in the victory being celebrated around him.[7]

Beyond the gloom of Walter's office, the morning was sunny and recent rains had settled the dust; it was a perfect day for a parade. On schedule at nine o'clock, General Meade rode from Maryland Avenue past the Senate wing at the head of his army. He lifted his eyes to a banner strung across the Capitol that read "THE ONLY NATIONAL DEBT WE NEVER CAN PAY IS THE DEBT WE OWE TO THE VICTORIOUS SOLDIERS." Clustered on both sides of the Avenue were perhaps two thousand public schoolchildren, the girls in white dresses, singing in their treble voices "The Battle Cry of Freedom." As the soldiers started west along the Avenue, women flung flowers from the sidewalks and infantrymen laced bouquets about the barrels of their rifles. Celebrators crowded sidewalks and windows along the line of march to the White House.

There Johnson, Grant, ranking generals, the cabinet and their ladies sat and often stood to review the passing veterans. Grant understood better than the politicians what these men had been through at places like Bull Run, Antietam, Chancellorsville and Gettysburg—what he himself had put them through at the Wilderness, Spotsylvania, Cold Harbor and Petersburg. Their stained and shot-riddled flags told the story of the passing regiments. As their officers snapped eyes left toward the reviewing stand, Grant returned their gaze with the same respect they showed to the stars on his collar. But it was not all solemnity—past the Treasury came that great cavalryman and great showman, Brigadier General George Armstrong Custer, weighted down with flowers, yellow locks flowing, his steed seemingly getting away from him as he dashed ahead alongside the column. He lost his broadbrimmed hat before he brought the horse under control just in front of the presidential stand, then made a sweeping bow. For nearly six hours the procession filed past. Few of those reporting the parade noted that there were no black troops marching that day. Most of those watching felt, as the *New York Times*'s man wrote, that "it is the greatest epoch of their lives; with the soldiers it is the last act in the drama; with the nation it is the triumphant exhibition of the resources and valor which have saved it from disruption and placed it first upon the earth."[8]

No one appreciated the deeper significance of the spectacle more than William Seward, still an invalid, who was propped up to see the marchers from a window of General Augur's office. For four years, he had witnessed, at close hand, the internal struggles that beset the martyred president, the towering hero of all American history. Seward had had time, lying wounded, to contemplate what victory meant to the nation's future. He watched the army move past along the broad aorta of a city grown beyond the dusty, muddy capital that urban sophisticates had joked about before the war. Washington would be more than a meeting place for delegates from states with notions of their own sovereignty; Lincoln had made it the seat of a forceful central government. Henceforth the world would say that the United States *is,* not are, a power among nations—its name transformed by war into a singular noun.

The most impressive sights were yet to come along the Avenue. The next day, Sherman rode at the head of the troops who had gutted the Southland, fighting at Shiloh, Vicksburg, Corinth, Lookout Mountain, Nashville and Atlanta. To some eastern eyes, they seemed "tall, erect, broad-shouldered, stalwart men, the peasantry of the West—the best material in the world for armies." Between their divisions came a battalion of black pioneers, heads high, in work clothes with axes and shovels, keeping step and maintaining an even front as well as the sharpest regiments ahead and behind. There was close order, and occasionally there was controlled disorder: soldiers with pet eagles and raccoons; a pack mule train with black men and women riding disreputable animals and escorting roosters and a nanny goat.[9]

John Hay thought that "no such touching pageant was ever seen." There marched the survivors of battle after battle, and somewhere above them hovered the ghosts of the president and the hundreds of thousands of soldiers who did not survive—"the victors and the martyrs, out of the army into peace, out of our sorrow into holy memories. And with the sweet and thrilling sounds of all the bugles and the rising dust of the columns smitten into golden glory by the sun setting over Georgetown Heights, passed away the Heroic Age from Washington."[10]

The fortunate spectators at the south end of the Treasury, where the column turned into Fifteenth Street and a slight elevation opened a broad panorama down the Avenue, had the best view of the unforgettable cavalcade. From there they watched mile after mile of soldiers advancing toward them, shoulder-to-shoulder, men whose stride and solidarity symbolized Union. And soaring beyond the unending lines of blue, gleaming in the clear distance, Thomas Walter's dome atop the Capitol stood as it still stands, forever upholding the promise of Freedom.

NOTES

Prologue: *Freedom Triumphant*

1. Charles E. Fairman, *Art and Artists of the Capitol*, pp. 169, 171, 183.

Chapter One: *God Alone Can Avert the Storm*

1. *Washington Evening Star* (cited hereafter as *Star*), 29 Oct., 7 Nov. 1861.
2. *Star*, 7 Nov. 1860.
3. Andrew Harllee to John Harllee, 8 Nov. 1860, William Curry.
4. Thomas U. Walter (hereafter TUW) to J. D. King, 29 Nov. 1860; to Charles Fowler, 29 Dec. 1860.
5. TUW to J. D. King, 29 Nov. 1860; to Robert Walter, 15 Dec. 1860.
6. Hans L. Trefousse, *The Radical Republicans*, p. 118.
7. George W. Bagby, "Washington City," pp. 1–8.
8. Allen C. Clark, "Beau Hickman," p. 81.
9. Bagby, p. 8.
10. Sydney Greenbie and Marjorie Barstow Greenbie, *Anna Ella Carroll and Abraham Lincoln*, pp. 209–211; *Atlanta Confederacy*, n.d.
11. C. H. Hall, *Reminiscences of Epiphany*, p. 21.
12. Virginia Clay-Clopton, *A Belle of the Fifties*, pp. 135–136.
13. Mrs. Roger A. Pryor, *Reminiscences of Peace and War*, pp. 110–112.
14. *Star*, 14 Nov. 1860; Pryor, pp. 110–112.
15. Pryor, pp. 110–112.

Chapter Two: *The Sword of Damocles*

1. *Star*, 25, 26, 27 Dec. 1860.
2. Elizabeth Lindsay Lomax, *Leaves from an Old Washington Diary*, pp. 135–136.
3. *Star*, 27 December 1860.
4. Elizabeth Keckley, *Behind the Scenes*, pp. 63–69; *New York Evening Post*, 23 Apr. 1862.
5. Virginia Miller, "Dr. Thomas Miller and His Times," pp. 312, 314–317.
6. "Diary of a Public Man," pp. 131–132.
7. Maury Klein, *Days of Defiance*, p. 169.
8. Nancy Macomb to Montgomery C. Meigs, 2 Jan. 1861, Meigs papers.
9. Mrs. Roger A. Pryor, *Reminiscences*, pp. 113–115.
10. B. B. French, *Witness to the Young Republic*, p. 337.
11. Lafayette S. Foster to his wife, 22 Dec. 1860.
12. *Harrisburg Telegraph*, 22 Dec. 1860.
13. Nancy Macomb to Montgomery C. Meigs, 2 Jan. 1861, Meigs papers.
14. Virginia Clay-Clopton, *A Belle of the Fifties*, pp. 107–8.
15. Henry L. Dawes, "Washington the Winter Before the War," p. 161.
16. William Henry Trescot, "Narrative and Letter of William Henry Trescot," pp. 543–545.

17. Dawes, pp. 161–163.
18. George Lowell Austin, "The Conspiracy of 1860–61," p. 240.
19. Dawes, p. 163; Burton J. Hendrick, *Lincoln's War Cabinet,* pp. 236–237.
20. [Henry Wilson], "Edwin M. Stanton," p. 237.
21. Ibid., p. 236; Dawes, p. 162.
22. *Richmond Enquirer,* 26 Dec. 1860.
23. Charles P. Stone, "Washington on the Eve of the War," pp. 7–11.
24. *New York Times* and *Star,* 1 Jan. 1861.
25. *Southern Literary Messenger,* Jan. 1861, pp. 1–4; F. N. Boney, *John Letcher of Virginia,* p. 103.
26. *Star,* 1 Jan. 1861.
27. Lomax, p. 138.
28. Pryor, p. 115; *Star,* 1 Jan. 1861.
29. Stone, p. 11.
30. U.S. Congress, House of Representatives, 36th Cong., 2nd sess., Report no. 79.
31. *Jackson Mississippian,* 2 Feb. 1859; Benjamin Perley Poore, *Reminiscences,* 2:54.
32. *Star,* 11 Jan. 1861.
33. *Dictionary of American Biography* (hereafter *DAB*) 8:618; Klein, p. 227.
34. Stone, p. 12.
35. Ibid., p. 13; *Star,* 5, 14 Jan. 1861.
36. *Washington Constitution,* 12 Jan. 1861; *Star,* 15, 17 Jan. 1861.
37. Stone, pp. 14–17; James H. Whyte, "Divided Loyalties in Washington," p. 106.
38. Keckley, pp. 69–73.
39. Clay-Clopton, pp. 147–148.
40. Varina Davis, *Jefferson Davis,* 2:5–6.
41. Ibid.
42. L. E. Chittenden, *Recollections,* pp. 20, 33–35; *Star,* 10 Feb. 1861.
43. Dawes, p. 164.
44. Chittenden, pp. 38, 45.
45. Ibid., p. 42.

Chapter Three: *We Must Not Be Enemies*

1. Norma B. Cuthbert, *Lincoln and the Baltimore Plot, 1861,* pp. 9, 80–81; Allan Pinkerton, *Spy of the Rebellion,* pp. 96–97; Ward Hill Lamon, *Life of Abraham Lincoln,* p. 525.
2. Lamon, pp. 511–512.
3. Pinkerton, pp. 59–66; Cuthbert, p. 7; Lamon, pp. 512–517; Chittenden, *Recollections,* pp. 59–64.
4. Pinkerton, pp. 80–85; J. G. Nicolay and John Hay, "Abraham Lincoln: Lincoln's Inauguration," *Century* 35, no. 2 (Dec. 1887): 271; Lamon, pp. 520, 522–524.
5. Pinkerton, pp. 89–97; Lamon, pp. 521–525; Cuthbert, p. 81.
6. Lamon, p. 525.
7. Ibid., p. 526.
8. Ibid., p. 526; Henry Kellogg Willard, "Henry Augustus Willard," *Records of the Columbia Historical Society* (hereafter *CHS*) 20: 249–250.
9. Nathaniel Hawthorne, "Chiefly About War Matters."
10. Dean R. Montgomery, "Willard Hotels of Washington," *CHS* 46 (1966–68): 277–288; Willard, p. 246; Rose O'Neal Greenhow, *My Imprisonment,* pp. 74–76.

11. Willard, pp. 246–247; Montgomery, pp. 282–284; *Springfield Republican,* 14 Apr. 1862.

12. *Star,* 25 Feb. 1861.

13. Henry L. Dawes, "Washington the Winter Before the War," p. 165; Lamon, pp. 526–527; *New York Times,* 25 Feb. 1861; Nicolay and Hay, p. 272; "Diary of a Public Man," p. 260.

14. *Star,* 23 Feb. 1861; Miers, *Lincoln Day by Day,* 3:21–22; Nicolay and Hay, pp. 273–274.

15. Burton J. Hendrick, *Lincoln's War Cabinet,* pp. 114–115.

16. Francis P. Blair to Mrs. Norman B. Judd, 30 Jan. 1861, Blair papers, LC; Miers, 3:21–22; Nicolay and Hay, "Abraham Lincoln: The Call to Arms," *Century* 35, no. 5 (Mar. 1888): 722.

17. Chittenden, pp. 74–77.

18. Allen C. Clark, "Richard Wallach," *CHS* 21: 201–202.

19. Chittenden, pp. 77–78.

20. Clark, p. 202; *Star,* 23, 25 Feb. 1861.

21. Henry Villard, "Recollections of Lincoln," pp. 165–174.

22. William C. Allen, *The United States Capitol,* pp. 4–13.

23. *DAB* 10:39.

24. TUW to Mr. Anderson, 14 March 1854.

25. Henry L. Abbot, "Memoir of Montgomery C. Meigs, 1816–1892"; J. F. Meigs, *Memoir of Charles D. Meigs, M.D.,* cited in *DAB* 6:505.

26. James Moore Goode, "Architecture, Politics and Conflict," pp. 240–241.

27. TUW to Rev. J. B. Swain, 16 Nov. 1858.

28. Allen, *Capitol,* pp. 26–27; Allen, *Dome,* p. 49.

29. Russell F. Weigley, *Quartermaster General,* p. 88; Goode, p. 258.

30. TUW to Mr. Anderson, 4 Feb. 1861; to son Thomas, 15 Feb. 1861.

31. Dawes, pp. 166–167.

32. *Star,* 25 Feb. 1861.

33. *Star,* 27, 28 Feb. 1861.

34. *Springfield Republican,* 11 Apr. 1862.

35. Clark, pp. 204–205; L. A. Gobright, *Recollections,* p. 286.

36. "Diary of a Public Man," pt. 3, p. 375; Hendrick, p. 4.

37. Nicolay and Hay, "Abraham Lincoln: Seward and Chase," *Century* 37, no. 4 (Feb. 1889): 562.

38. Nicolay and Hay, "Abraham Lincoln: Lincoln's Inauguration," p. 283.

39. *Star,* 4 Mar. 1861; Clark, p. 205.

40. *Magazine of History,* 1929, p. 26.

41. *Star,* 4 Mar. 1861; Stone, pp. 24–25.

42. Lamon, p. 528; Gobright, pp. 287–288; *New York Times,* 5 Mar. 1861.

43. Charles Francis Adams, "Lincoln's First Inauguration," pp. 148–149; Gobright, p. 289; Daniel B. Carroll, "Henry Mercier in Washington," p. 76.

44. *New York Times,* 5 Mar. 1861; "Diary of a Public Man," pt. 3, p. 384.

45. *New York Times,* 5 Mar. 1861; Gobright, pp. 288–290.

Chapter Four: *Why Don't They Come?*

1. *New Orleans Crescent,* 12 Mar. 1861.

2. *Providence Press,* 13 Apr. 1861.

3. *Congressional Globe,* 36th Cong., 2nd sess., p. 1371; Mrs. D. Giraud Wright, *A Southern Girl in '61,* pp. 33–34.

4. Sara Pryor, *My Day: Reminiscences of a Long Life,* pp. 137–138.

5. William O. Stoddard, *Inside the White House in War Times,* pp. 3–4; William Howard Russell, "Recollections of the Civil War," p. 240.

6. Stoddard, pp. 4–6; Francis Fessenden, *Life and Public Services,* 1:127.

7. Stoddard, pp. 4–6; Noah Brooks, *Mr. Lincoln's Washington,* pp. 251–253.

8. *New York Times,* 8 Mar. 1861.

9. "Diary of a Public Man," pt. 3, pp. 387–388.

10. Elizabeth Keckley, *Behind the Scenes,* pp. 80–89.

11. Allen G. Clark, "Richard Wallach," pp. 205–206.

12. John Hay, *At Lincoln's Side,* pp. 135–136.

13. Charles Francis Adams, Jr., "Lincoln's First Inauguration," p. 151; O. O. Browning to Lincoln, 26 Mar. 1861, Lincoln papers, LC.

14. Martin J. Crawford to Robert Toombs, 6 Mar. 1861, cited in Klein, *Days of Defiance,* p. 325; Charles Francis Adams, *Autobiography,* p. 4.

15. Klein, pp. 325–334; Confederate commissioners to Toombs, 9 Mar. 1861, quoted in J. G. Nicolay and John Hay, "Abraham Lincoln: Premier or President?" *Century* 35, no. 4 (Feb. 1888): 600.

16. Klein, pp. 353–359.

17. Nicolay and Hay, pp. 615–616.

18. Gideon Welles, "Mr. Lincoln and Mr. Seward," pp. 687–690.

19. Louisa Meigs to Minerva Denison Rodgers, 8 Apr. 1861, Meigs papers, LC.

20. Porter, *Incidents and Anecdotes,* pp. 21–22; ORN 4:112 (U.S. Government Printing Office, *Official Records of the Union and Confederate Navies in the War of the Rebellion,* ser. 1, vol. 4, p. 112).

21. Daniel W. Crofts, *Reluctant Confederates,* p. 139.

22. Thomas, *Abraham Lincoln,* p. 252; John Minor Botts, *Great Rebellion,* pp. 194–196.

23. Russell, *Diary,* pp. 100–103.

24. Klein, pp. 387–409.

25. Pryor, *Reminiscences,* p. 121.

26. *New York Times,* 15 Apr. 1861.

27. Botts, *Great Rebellion,* p. 206; F. W. Boney, *John Letcher,* p. 112.

28. Douglas Southall Freeman, *R. E. Lee,* 1:431–438.

29. Francis S. Low to his son, 18 Apr. 1861; John Hay, *Inside Lincoln's White House,* p. 8.

30. Nicolay and Hay, "Abraham Lincoln: The National Uprising," *Century* 35, no. 6: 906; Hay, *Inside Lincoln's White House,* pp. 1, 9.

31. *New York Times,* 18, 19 Apr. 1861; TUW to Mr. Skirving, 18 Apr. 1861; to son Robert, 19 Apr. 1861.

32. *New York Tribune,* quoted in *Cincinnati Commercial,* 19 July 1861.

33. *OR,* I, 2, pt. 2:7. (U.S. War Department, *War of the Rebellion, Official Records,* ser. I, vol. 2, part 2, p. 7).

34. *OR,* I, 2, pt. 2: 7–10; Ernest Wardwell, "Military Waif," p. 430; *Cambridge* (Mass.) *Chronicle,* 27 Apr. 1861.

35. *New York Daily News,* 6 Dec. 1865.

36. *OR,* I, 2:7–10.

37. L. E. Chittenden, *Recollections of President Lincoln and His Administration,*

pp. 125-126; John Call Dalton, *John Call Dalton M.D., U.S.V.*, pp. 14-20; Andrew Carnegie, *Autobiography*, p. 95.

38. Marcus Benjamin, "The Military Situation in Washington in 1861," in *Washington During War Time*, pp. 19-20.

39. Ibid.

40. *Richmond Examiner*, 26 Apr. 1861; *OR*, I, 5: 24-25.

41. George Williamson Smith, "A Critical Moment for Washington," pp. 104-105; TUW to son Robert, 19 Apr. 1861; *Star*, 22 Apr. 1861.

42. Nicolay and Hay, "National Uprising," p. 922.

43. Hay, *Inside Lincoln's White House*, pp. 11-12.

44. Henry Villard, *Memoirs*, 1:170; Carnegie, *Autobiography*, pp. 95-96.

45. Freeman, *R. E. Lee*, 1:439-442.

46. George Williamson Smith, "Critical Moment," p. 104; Elizabeth Lindsay Lomax, *Leaves from an Old Washington Diary*, p. 150.

47. J. William Jones, *Life and Letters*, p. 438; Lee to Mary Custis Lee, 15 May 1861, quoted in Freeman, *R. E. Lee*, 1:444; Mary Custis Lee, "Reminiscences," p. 315; Edward C. Smith, "Keeper of the Keys," p. 16.

48. *Star* and *New York Times*, 25 Apr.-3 May, 1861.

49. Hay, *Inside Lincoln's White House*, p. 13.

Chapter Five: *The Performance of a Sacred Duty*

1. TUW to wife, 9 May 1861.

2. *New York Times*, 10 May 1861.

3. John Hay, *Inside Lincoln's White House*, pp. 20, 22.

4. TUW to daughter Olivia, 20 Apr. 1861; TUW, diary, 23 Apr.-1 May 1861.

5. TUW to wife, 3, 8 May 1861; TUW to M. E. Harmstead, 3 May 1861.

6. TUW to wife, 2, 8 May 1861; TUW, diary, 6, 7 May 1861.

7. TUW to wife, TUW, diary, 15 May 1861.

8. John G. B. Adams, *Reminiscences of the 19th Massachusetts Regiment*, n.p.

9. Mary Mitchell, *Divided Town*, pp. 40-42; T. A. Lambert, "Recollections of the Civil War," p. 284.

10. *OR*, I, 2:7-10.

11. Ibid., pp. 28-31.

12. Ibid.; Margaret Leech, *Reveille in Washington*, pp. 79-80.

13. Elizabeth Lindsey Lomax, *Leaves*, pp. 151-155.

14. James G. Barber, *Alexandria in the Civil War*, pp. 5-6.

15. *Star*, 24, 25 Apr. 1861; Barber, p. 9.

16. Barber, pp. 12-13.

17. *OR*, I, 2:40-41; *OR*, I, 3:681; Charles O. Paullin, "Alexandria County," pp. 112-113; William O. Stoddard, *Inside the White House*, p. 9.

18. *New York Times*, 27 May 1861.

19. *OR*, I, 4:478-481; OR, I, 2:40-41.

20. *New York Times*, 25 May 1861.

21. *OR*, I, 2:41; Jeff Stoek to Father, 3 June 1861; *New York Times*, 26-28 May 1861.

22. *New York Times*, 28 May 1861; Montgomery C. Meigs, diary, 25 May 1861.

23. *New York Times*, 30 May 1861.

24. Ex parte Merryman, 17 Fed. Cas. 144; James M. McPherson, *Battle Cry of Freedom*, pp. 287-288.

25. *New York Times,* 1 June 1861.
26. Ibid.

Chapter Six: *Thirsting for Deliverance*

1. *New York Times,* 1 June 1861; Julia Ward Howe, *Key to Uncle Tom's Cabin,* p. 42.
2. "Slavery and the Slave Trade in the District of Columbia." Printed Ephemera Collection, Rare Books Division, LC.
3. David Herbert Donald, *Lincoln,* pp. 134–137; Randall Bond Truett, *Washington, D.C.,* p. 51; Robert Reed, *Old Washington, D.C.,* p. 104; E. S. Abdy, *Journal,* 2: 96–98; Walter C. Clephane, "Local Aspect of Slavery," p. 237, 241.
4. Donald, pp. 136–137; Ida M. Tarbell, *Life of Abraham Lincoln,* 1:228.
5. Seventh and Eighth U.S. Census; James H. Whyte, "Divided Loyalties," p. 104.
6. *New York Times,* 30, 31 May 1861.
7. *Boston Journal,* n.d., reprinted in *New York Times,* 2 June 1861; *OR,* II, 1:752–754.
8. Daniel Drayton, *Personal Memoir,* pp. 24–41, 101–102; Howe, *Key to Uncle Tom's Cabin,* pp. 155–159.
9. Thomas Smallwood, *Narrative,* pp. 18–35; Hillary Russell, "Underground Railroad Activists," pp. 30–36.
10. William Still, *Underground Rail Road,* pp. 44, 413–414; Russell, p. 36.
11. Russell, pp. 36–37; Constance McLaughlin Green, *Secret City,* pp. 50–51.
12. *Star,* 12 June 1861.
13. William Howard Russell, "Recollections," p. 243.
14. Robert V. Bruce, *Lincoln and the Tools of War,* p. 85.
15. Bruce, pp. 35, 85–87; Ida M. Tarbell, 2:44–45; T. S. C. Lowe to Lincoln, 16 [18] June 1861, Lincoln papers, LC.
16. Bruce, pp. 23–27, 33–34; William O. Stoddard, *Inside the White House,* p. 22.
17. Stoddard, pp. 21–23.
18. *Star,* 6 June 1861; Bruce, pp. 118–121.
19. William Howard Russell, "Recollections," p. 243.
20. W. A. Swanberg, *Jim Fisk,* pp. 15–19; Marshall P. Stafford, *Life of James Fisk, Jr.,* pp. 22–24; Nathan Miller, *The Founding Finaglers,* pp. 181–183.
21. *OR,* III, 2:188–189; Miller, 182–183.
22. Fawn M. Brodie, *Thaddeus Stevens,* p. 148.
23. Burton J. Hendrick, *Lincoln's War Cabinet,* pp. 219–223.

Chapter Seven: *The Panick Is Great*

1. Christian Hines, *Early Recollections of Washington City,* cited in Junior League, *City of Washington,* p. 125; James Croggon, "Old Washington: Lafayette Square," *Star,* 19 Apr. 1913.
2. *Washington States,* 18 Feb. 1859.
3. Rose O'Neal Greenhow, *My Imprisonment,* pp. 59–60; Ishbel Ross, *Rebel Rose,* pp. 92–131.
4. William Howard Russell, "Recollections," p. 620.
5. Ross, pp. 75–81; Pierre G. T. Beauregard, "First Battle of Bull Run," p. 81.
6. James F. Whyte, "Divided Loyalties," pp. 110–114.
7. Eunice Tripler, *Eunice Tripler,* p. 143.
8. John Bakeless, *Spies of the Confederacy,* pp. 6, 65–66, 77.
9. Mary Mitchell, "An Intimate Journey," pp. 85, 91.

10. *New York Tribune,* 25 June 1861.

11. Russell, "Recollections," pp. 620–621.

12. Russell, *My Diary,* p. 199.

13. Bernard A. Weisberger, *Reporters for the Union,* p. 79; *Cincinnati Commercial,* 20 June, 13 July, 1861; *New York Tribune,* 13 July 1861.

14. Louisa Meigs to Dear Mother, 25 July 1861.

15. John J. Hennessy, "War-Watchers at Bull Run," pp. 40ff.

16. Russell, "Recollections," p. 625.

17. Joseph Mills Hanson, *Bull Run Remembers,* pp. 2–7; Hennessy, pp. 41ff.

18. Hennessy, pp. 41ff.; Eugene C. Tidball, "View from the Top," pp. 175–193; F. Lauriston Bullard, *Famous War Correspondents,* p. 56; James B. Fry, "McDowell's Advance to Bull Run," p. 192.

19. Nicolay and Hay, "Abraham Lincoln: The Advance—Bull Run, Fremont, Military Occupation," *Century* 36, no. 2 (June 1888): 287–288.

20. Ibid.; Walt Whitman, *Specimen Days,* pp. 26–27.

21. Louisa Meigs to Dear Mother, 28 July 1861.

22. L. A. Gobright, *Recollections,* pp. 316–317; W. H. Russell, "Recollections," p. 629; *New York Times,* 22 July 1861.

23. *New York Times,* 22, 23 July 1861; Louisa Meigs to Dear Mother, 28 July 1861.

24. Mark Mayo Boatner III, *Civil War Dictionary,* p. 101; John Wells Bulkley, "The War Hospitals," in Marcus Benjamin, *Washington During War Time,* p. 139.

25. Bulkley, p. 140; Alice P. Stein, "The North's Unsung Sisters of Mercy," n.p.; U.S. Congress, *Joint Select Committee to Investigate Charities,* 3:31–36.

26. Louisa Meigs to Dear Mother, 28 July 1861; Harold H. Burton and Thomas E. Waggaman, "Story of the Place," pp. 144–145; *Chelsea Telegraph and Pioneer,* 3 Aug. 1861; *New York Times,* 24 July 1861.

27. T. Harry Williams, *Lincoln and His Generals,* p. 24.

28. Greenhow, pp. 17–19.

29. James D. Horan, *Desperate Women,* p. 14; *OR,* I, 51, 2:688.

30. Beauregard, "First Battle of Bull Run," pp. 199–200.

31. Ibid., p. 197; *OR,* II, 2:565; Greenhow, p. 322.

32. National Archives, RG 59, entry 490, 516; RG 107, entry 68.

33. Allan Pinkerton, *Spy of the Rebellion,* pp. 254–267.

34. Greenhow, pp. 54–65.

35. "E. J. Allen" to Brig. Gen. Andrew Porter, *OR,* II, 2:566–569.

36. Ibid., p. 237.

37. Ibid., pp. 568–569.

38. Constance McLaughlin Green, *Washington,* 1:248–249.

Chapter Eight: *We Walk in a Fevered Dream*

1. *New York Times,* 22 Oct. 1861.

2. Noah Brooks, "Career of an American Princess," pp. 461–463.

3. Ibid., pp. 463–464.

4. Brooks, "Glimpses of Lincoln," p. 464.

5. Thomas Graham Belden and Marva Robins Belden, *So Fell the Angels,* pp. 18–24; Carl Schurz, *Reminiscences,* 2:169–170.

6. Mrs. Charles H. Walker, quoted in Belden, pp. 3–4.

7. Murat Halstead to Timothy C. Day, 8 June 1861, quoted in Donald, *Lincoln,* p. 324.

8. Jean H. Baker, *Mary Todd Lincoln*, pp. 184–185.
9. Benjamin Brown French, *Witness to the Young Republic*, p. 375.
10. Ibid., p. 382.
11. Hans L. Trefousse, *Radical Republicans*, pp. 176–177.
12. Richard Brindley to Dear Mother and Sisters, 3 Aug. 1861.
13. J. Thomas Scharf, *Chronicles of Baltimore*, pp. 616–618; *New York Times*, 14, 18 Sept. 1861.
14. *New York Times*, 23 Oct. 1861.
15. Burton J. Hendrick, *Lincoln's War Cabinet*, pp. 188–189.
16. *New York Times*, 26 Oct. 1861; Benjamin F. Gue, *History of Iowa*, 2:85.
17. Edward Younger, *John A. Kasson*, pp. 123, 126.
18. Ibid., p. 125.
19. Donald, p. 318.
20. John Hay, *Inside Lincoln's White House*, p. 27.
21. William Howard Russell, *My Diary*, p. 317; Hay, p. 32; Donald, pp. 319–320.
22. *Jewish Times*, "Sketches from the Seat of War," n.d.
23. *New York Times*, 26, 27 Oct. 1861; *Iowa State Register*, 27 Nov., 2 Dec. 1861.
24. Julia Ward Howe, "Reminiscences," pp. 705–706.
25. Laura E. Richards and Maud Howe Elliott, *Julia Ward Howe*, 1:187–189.

Chapter Nine: *The Instrument of Divine Providence*

1. *Star*, 4, 5, 7 Nov. 1861.
2. John Wells Bulkley, "The War Hospitals," in Marcus Benjamin, *Washington During War Time*, pp. 138–149; Richard B. Parker, "Neighbors of the Cosmos Club."
3. *Star*, 4 Nov. 1861, 28 July 1862.
4. *Chelsea Telegraph and Pioneer*, 15 Nov., 31 Dec. 1861.
5. *Star*, 7 Nov. 1861, reprinted from *New York Mercury*.
6. B. B. French, *Witness to the Young Republic*, pp. 381–384.
7. *Star*, 29 Oct., 6 Nov. 1861.
8. Donald, *Lincoln*, pp. 166–167.
9. Donald, p. 167; Nicolay and Hay, "Abraham Lincoln: First Plans for Emancipation," *Century* 37, no. 2 (Dec. 1888): 276–277; *Star*, 10 Mar. 1861.
10. Nicolay and Hay, "First Plans," pp. 277–278; Herbert Mitgang, *Washington, D.C.*, p. 180.
11. Donald, pp. 320–323.
12. Benjamin Thomas, *Abraham Lincoln*, p. 290; Horatio Nelson Taft, diary, 25 Dec. 1861.
13. *Star*, 23 Dec. 1861.
14. Ibid., 27 Dec. 1861.
15. French, p. 384; *Iowa State Register*, 29 Jan. 1862.
16. Michael F. Conlin, "The Smithsonian Abolition Lecture Controversy," pp. 309, 311.
17. Ibid., pp. 311, 313, 320; *Star*, 4 Jan. 1862.
18. Thomas, pp. 290–293; William Swinton, *Campaigns of the Army of the Potomac*, p. 80; Alexander S. Webb, *Peninsula*, pp. 17–18.
19. [Anna Sherman], "A Little Girl's Experience of the War."
20. Hendrick, *Lincoln's War Cabinet*, pp. 220–224, 235; Donald, p. 325; Thomas, pp. 293–294.

21. Hendrick, pp. 242, 257; William H. Herndon to Jesse W. Weik, 6 Jan. 1887.
22. Albert G. Riddle, *Recollections,* pp. 189–191; U.S. House of Representatives, 46th Cong., 3rd sess., Report 386.
23. Riddle, p. 191.
24. Jean H. Baker, *Mary Todd Lincoln,* pp. 205–207.
25. Baker, pp. 208–209; John Hay, "Life in the White House," p. 35.
26. Elizabeth Keckley, *Behind the Scenes,* pp. 102–104; Donald, p. 337.
27. Horatio Nelson Taft, diary, 20 Feb. 1862; John Hay, *At Lincoln's Side,* p. 111; Augustus Jordan to wife, 7 Aug. 1862.
28. *Chelsea Telegraph and Pioneer,* 23 Feb., 3 Mar. 1862.
29. *Richmond Enquirer,* extra edition, 22 Feb. 1862.

Chapter Ten: *The Whole World Moving Toward Richmond*

1. *OR,* I, 5:518–520.
2. Dorothy Troth Muir, *Presence of a Lady,* pp. 8–10, 25–27; David L. Ribblett, "Saviors of Mount Vernon," p. 22; James G. Barber, *Alexandria,* p. 17.
3. Noel G. Harrison, "Atop an Anvil," pp. 160–161.
4. Muir, pp. 47–51.
5. Ibid., pp. 39–41, 59–60; T. F. Walter, "Personal Recollections," p. 1.
6. Gideon Welles, *Diary,* 1:62–63.
7. *OR,* III, 3:270–271.
8. Anne S. Frobel, *Civil War Diary,* pp. 81–83.
9. Alexander S. Webb, *Peninsula,* pp. 17–32.
10. Rose O'Neal Greenhow, *My Imprisonment,* pp. 162, 167–168, 202, 216, 221–222, 243–244.
11. Ibid., 222.
12. Edward Dicey, *Spectator of America,* pp. 67–73.
13. Philip Van Doren Stern, *Life and Writings,* pp. 694–695.
14. Benjamin Quarles, *Negro in the Civil War,* p. 137.
15. Melvin R. Williams, "Blueprint for Change," pp. 371–374; Noah Brooks, *Washington, D.C.,* pp. 181–182.
16. *National Republican,* 13, 15, 27–29 Mar. 1862; Quarles, p. 138; Page Milburn, "Emancipation of Slaves," pp. 102–104; Walter C. Clephane, "Local Aspect of Slavery," p. 256.
17. Horatio Nelson Taft, diary, 9 Apr. 1862.
18. Donald, *Lincoln,* p. 347.
19. Quarles, pp. 138–139.
20. Milburn, p. 112.
21. Junior League of Washington, *City of Washington,* p. 222; *Star,* 28 Apr. 1862.

Chapter Eleven: *This Sudden & Radical Revolution*

1. John Carroll Brent, diary, 17 Apr. 1862; Page Milburn, "Emancipation of Slaves," p. 118.
2. *Star,* 30 Apr. 1862.
3. Milburn, pp. 117–118.
4. District of Columbia, Final Report of the Board of Commissioners for the Emancipation of Slaves.
5. Ibid.

6. U.S. Circuit Court for District of Columbia Records Relating to Slaves, Emancipation Papers Resulting from the Act of Congress, 12 July 1862 (supplement), Publication M433, Roll 3.

7. Eunice Tripler, *Some Notes,* p. 144.

8. *OR,* I, 12, pt. 1:230–231.

9. Egbert L. Viele, "A Trip With Lincoln, Chase and Stanton," pp. 813–818.

10. Ibid., pp. 818–822; OR, I, 11, pt. 1:634, pt. 3:162–163; Salmon P. Chase, *Papers,* 1:340–342.

11. B. B. French, *Witness to the Young Republic,* pp. 396–399.

12. S. D. Wyeth, *Federal City,* pp. 194–195; D.C., Final Report of the Board of Commissioners for the Emancipation of Slaves.

13. James Moore Goode, "Architecture, Politics, and Conflict," pp. 274–275; TUW, diary, 15, 28 May, 3 July, 14–15 Aug., 16 Sept., 5 Nov., 12 Dec. 1861; 2 Jan., 20 Feb., 6, 27 Mar., 16, 29, 30 Apr. 1862.

14. TUW to Horace, 21 Apr. 1862; TUW to Robert, 2 Aug. 1862.

15. TUW to Thomas Walter, 16 Aug. 1862.

16. *Star,* 28 June 1862.

17. Ibid., 4 Aug. 1862; Thomas N. Conrad, *Confederate Spy,* pp. 7–8.

18. Frederick S. Tyler, "100th Anniversary," pp. 73–75; James H. Whyte, "Divided Loyalties," pp. 117, 119; Lucille Warfield Wilkinson, "Early Baptists," p. 259; Constance McLaughlin Green, *Washington,* p. 272.

19. TUW to J. D. King, 4 June 1862; Wilkinson, p. 265.

20. TUW to Rev. J. D. King, 4 June 1862; TUW to Rev. Warren Randolph, 18 June 1862.

21. TUW to son Thomas, 16 Aug. 1862.

22. TUW to Dear Wife, 22, 25 July 1862.

23. Greenhow, *My Imprisonment,* pp. 314–315.

24. *OR,* II, 2:271–272, 277–279.

25. Asia Booth Clarke, *John Wilkes Booth,* pp. 55–56; *OR,* II, 2:271; Thomas F. Walter, "Personal Recollections," p. 2; Greenhow, p. 286.

26. Richard D. Steuart, "Henry A. Steuart—Rebel Spy," pp. 332–334.

27. Greenhow, pp. 282–286, 315–323.

Chapter Twelve: *The Magnitude of the Moment*

1. Matt Pinsker, "Lincoln's Wartime Retreat," pp. 12, 103; Randall Bond Truett, ed., *Washington, D.C.,* p. 314.

2. Pinsker, p. 10; Walt Whitman, *Specimen Days,* p. 59; John Hay to William H. Herndon, 5 Sept. 1866, in John Hay, *At Lincoln's Side,* p. 109.

3. U.S. Congress, Joint Select Committee to Investigate the Charities and Reformatory Institutions of the District of Columbia, pt. 3, pp. 32–36.

4. Katharine Wormeley to Dear Mother, 5 June 1862, in Wormeley, *Cruel Side of War,* pp. 102–106.

5. *DAB* 1:19.

6. *Star,* n.d.

7. John Hay, *Inside Lincoln's White House,* p. 191.

8. *OR,* I, 11, pt. 1:61; T. Harry Williams, *Lincoln and His Generals,* pp. 126–127.

9. Williams, pp. 135–145.

10. Gideon Welles, *Diary,* 1:70–71; Roy P. Basler, ed., *Collected Works,* 5:278–279.

11. Basler, 5:329; Browning, *Diary*, 1:555; Francis B. Carpenter, *Six Months at the White House*, pp. 20–22; David Herbert Donald, *Lincoln*, p. 364.
12. William O. Stoddard, *Inside the White House*, p. 86; John Hay, *At Lincoln's Side*, p. 23.
13. Donald, p. 366; Welles, *Diary*, 1:144–145.
14. Donald, pp. 365–366; Benjamin Thomas, *Abraham Lincoln*, pp. 333–334.
15. Mark Mayo Boatner III, *Civil War Dictionary*, pp. 101–105, 659–660.
16. Mary Mitchell, *Divided Town*, pp. 49–50, 92; *Star*, 2 July 1861, 2 June 1957.
17. Welles, 1:105, 113; George B. McClellan to Mrs. McClellan, 5 Sept. 1862, in Henry Steele Commager, ed., *Blue and Gray*, 1:201.
18. Philip Van Doren Stern, ed., *Life and Writings*, pp. 715–718.
19. Ibid., pp. 718–719; J. G. Nicolay and John Hay, "Abraham Lincoln: Announcement of Emancipation," *Century* 37, no. 3 (Jan. 1889): 440.
20. Stern, pp. 720–723.
21. D. H. Strother, "Personal Recollections," *Harper's Monthly* 36, no. 13:273; Welles, 1:111, 117, 118.
22. *OR*, I, 19, pt. 2:601–602.
23. McClellan to Mrs. McClellan, 20 Sept. 1862, 9 A.M., in Commager, 1:202.
24. *Artemus Ward: His Book*, pp. 34–35.
25. Nicolay and Hay, pp. 444–445.

Chapter Thirteen: *We Cannot Escape History*

1. Henry Steele Commager, ed., *Blue and Gray*, 1:564–565.
2. Compiled Military Service Record of Lyons Wakeman, 153rd N.Y. Infantry, RG 94, National Archives.
3. Rosetta Wakeman to family, 24 Nov. 1862.
4. DeAnne Blanton, "Woman Soldiers," n.p.; Lauren Cook Burgess, ed., *Uncommon Soldier*, pp. 1–5; Wakeman to father, 23 Dec. 1862; to parents, 5 June 1863; Mary Elizabeth Massey, *Bonnet Brigades*, p. 84.
5. Wakeman to parents, 5 June 1863.
6. *Philadelphia Sunday Dispatch*, 6 Dec. 1864.
7. U.S. War Department, Provost Marshal, Department of Washington, "Bawdy Houses"; David Rankin Barbee, "Washington Society in the 1860s."
8. Provost Marshal; Thomas P. Lowry, *Story the Soldiers Wouldn't Tell*, pp. 61–75; Smithsonian Institution, "Archaeological Investigations," 17 Dec., 1997.
9. George Alfred Townsend, *Washington Outside and Inside*, pp. 454–455; W. A. Swanberg, *Jim Fisk*, p. 18.
10. *OR*, I, 17, pt. 1:532; *OR*, I, 52, pt. 1:331.
11. William O. Stoddard, *Inside the White House*, pp. 195–196.
12. Swanberg, pp. 18–19; Marshall P. Stafford, *Life of James Fisk, Jr.*, p. 28.
13. George W. Whitman, *Civil War Letters*, p. 71.
14. Darius M. Couch, "Sumner's 'Right Grand Division,'" *Battles & Leaders* 3:105–106; Roy P. Basler, *Collected Works*, 5:474–479; John G. Nicolay to Theresa Bates, 9 Nov. 1862.
15. T. Harry Williams, *Lincoln and His Generals*, pp. 179–180; Couch, p. 104.
16. Francis A. Donaldson to Jacob Donaldson, 11 Nov. 1862, in J. Gregory Acken, ed., *Inside the Army of the Potomac*, pp. 162–164.
17. David Herbert Donald, *Lincoln*, pp. 392–398.

18. Philip Van Doren Stern, *Life and Writings*, pp. 736–746.

19. Douglas Southall Freeman, *R. E. Lee*, 2:455–465.

20. Louisa May Alcott, *Hospital Sketches*, pp. 27–32.

21. Walt Whitman to his mother, 29 Dec. 1862, in Whitman, "Walt Whitman in War-Time," pp. 840–841; Walt Whitman, *Specimen Days* p. 33.

22. Roy Morris, Jr., *Better Angel*, pp. 11, 26–27; Horace Traubel, *With Walt Whitman in Camden*, 6:194.

23. Morris, pp. 50, 73, 76, 83.

24. Whitman to Dear Sister (Mrs. Thomas Jefferson Whitman), 2 Jan. 1863, in "Walt Whitman in War-Time," pp. 841–842.

25. Ibid.

26. Burton J. Hendrick, *Lincoln's War Cabinet*, pp. 331–334.

27. Ibid., pp. 335–347.

28. J. G. Nicolay and John Hay, "Abraham Lincoln: The Edict of Freedom," *Century* 37, no. 5 (March 1889): 701–704.

29. Henry M. Turner, *The Negro in Slavery, War and Peace*, quoted in Dorothy Sterling, ed., *Speak Out in Thunder Tones*, pp. 315–317.

30. *Star*, 2 Jan. 1863.

Chapter Fourteen: *What Will the Country Say?*

1. Noah Brooks, *Mr. Lincoln's Washington*, pp. 38–39.

2. Noah Brooks, *Washington, D.C.*, pp. 4–10; Brooks, *Mr. Lincoln's Washington*, p. 29.

3. Brooks, *Mr. Lincoln's Washington*, p. 66; Brooks, *Washington, D.C.*, p. 33.

4. Walter H. Hebert, *Fighting Joe Hooker*, pp. 47–49; Joseph Hooker to Charles H. Nichols, 19 Dec. 1862.

5. Lincoln to Hooker, 26 Jan. 1863, in Philip Van Doren Stern, *Life and Writings*, pp. 749–750.

6. Edward P. Vollum to Charles H. Nichols, 27 Jan. 1863.

7. David C. Mearns, "View of Washington in 1863," *CHS* 1963–65, p. 217; *New York Times*, 9 Mar. 1863.

8. Donald A. Ritchie, *Press Gallery*, pp. 43–46; *DAB* 9:253–254.

9. Jane Grey Swisshelm, *St. Cloud Democrat*, 26 Feb. 1863, in *Crusader and Feminist*, pp. 170–172.

10. Ibid., pp. 181–184; *Leslie's Illustrated Newspaper*, 4 Apr. 1863, quoting *Springfield Republican*.

11. Swisshelm, pp. 181–184.

12. Marjorie Barstow Greenbie, *Lincoln's Daughters of Mercy*, pp. 175–177; John Lockwood, "The Union Army's Two-Person USO," *Washington Post*, 22 June 2003.

13. Henry Kellogg Willard, "Henry Augustus Willard," p. 248.

14. Joseph C. Willard to Edwin M. Stanton, 3 Apr. 1862. *OR*, I, 12, pt. 1:161–162, pt. 2:346; Brooks, *Mr. Lincoln's Washington*, pp. 33–34.

15. Willard to his mother, 10 Apr. 1863.

16. John S. Mosby, *Memoirs*, p. xi.

17. Thomas R. Lounsbury, "In the Defenses of Washington," pp. 386–387, 392–393, 403–404.

18. L[ouis] C. Helm to Antonia Ford, 21 Apr. 1861; A.J. [Allen Percy?] to Antonia Ford, 27 Nov. 1861.
19. T. Lafayette Rosser to Antonia Ford, 18 Sept. 1861; J. E. B. Stuart, "To All Whom It May Concern," 7 Oct. 1861, Willard Family papers.
20. Ben H. Miller, "Antonia Ford, Confederate Spy," *Baltimore Sun*, 1 Jan. 1932.
21. John S. Mosby, "A Bit of Partisan Service," *Battles and Leaders*, 3:148–151; Mosby, *Memoirs*, pp. 174–176; *Baltimore Sun*, 1 Jan. 1932.
22. *New York Times*, 14 Mar. 1863.
23. *Baltimore Sun*, 1 Jan. 1932.
24. David Herbert Donald, *Lincoln*, p. 429.
25. Ibid., p. 430.
26. Budge Weidman, "Fight for Equal Rights," pp. 91–94; Roy P. Basler, *Collected Works* 6:149–150.
27. *Leslie's Illustrated Newspaper*, 16 Aug. 1862.
28. Brooks, *Mr. Lincoln's Washington*, pp. 172–173.
29. Ibid., pp. 137, 139.
30. Warren W. Hassler, *Commanders of the Army of the Potomac*, p. 134.
31. Brooks, *Mr. Lincoln's Washington*, pp. 147–164; Brooks, *Washington, D.C.*, p. 56.
32. Brooks, *Mr. Lincoln's Washington*, pp. 164–165, 167; *New York Commercial Advertiser*, 7 Aug. 1861.
33. OR, I, 25, pt. 1:171.
34. Brooks, *Mr. Lincoln's Washington*, pp. 179–184.
35. Walt Whitman, *Specimen Days*, pp. 43–44; Walt Whitman to Dear Mother, 5 May 1863, in "Walt Whitman in War-Time," p. 843.

Chapter Fifteen: *I Will Now Take the Music*

1. Walt Whitman, *Specimen Days*, p. 39.
2. *New York Tribune*, quoted in *Oswego Times*, 19 June 1863; Charles McCool Snyder, *Dr. Mary Walker*, pp. 29–32, 51–52.
3. Snyder, pp. 32–33; W. W. Keen, "Study in Contrasts in Surgery"; John H. Brinton, *Journal of the American Medical Association* 26, no. 13 (28 Mar. 1896).
4. Snyder, p. 38.
5. Noah Brooks, *Washington, D.C., in Lincoln's Time*, p. 19.
6. Kenneth W. Dobyns, *Patent Office Pony*, p. 150.
7. Lois Bryan Adams, *Letter from Washington*, pp. 46–49.
8. David C. Mearns, "A View of Washington in 1863," p. 212.
9. "Sketches from the Seat of War," *Jewish Messenger*, n.d., 1862.
10. TUW to Charles Fowler, 3, 20 Apr.; to Henry Lyles, 9 Apr.; to W. Randolph, 9 Apr. 1863; William C. Allen, *United States Capitol*, p. 23.
11. *Cincinnati Commercial*, 26 Mar. 1863.
12. Elizabeth Keckley, *Behind the Scenes*, pp. 118–120.
13. David H. Donald, *Lincoln*, p. 514; Roy P. Basler, *Collected Works*, 7:281–282; John Hay to William H. Herndon, 5 Sept. 1866, in John Hay, *At Lincoln's Side*, p. 110.
14. Jean H. Baker, *Mary Todd Lincoln*, pp. 128, 235–237.
15. Ibid., 218–219.
16. Noah Brooks, *Washington, D.C.*, pp. 66–68.

17. Baker, 222–223.
18. Donald, p. 547.
19. Keckley, pp. 120–121.
20. "Lincoln and the Lively Arts," *Lincoln Lore* 1508 (Oct. 1863); Gene Smith, *American Gothic,* pp. 97–98; *National Republican,* 14 Apr. 1863.
21. John Rhodehamel and Louise Taper, eds., *Right or Wrong, God Judge Me,* pp. 27–44.
22. Katherine Helm, *True Story of Mary,* p. 243; Smith, p. 98.
23. Michael Kelly, diary, 31 Dec. 1863.
24. Ibid., 15 Aug. 1862.
25. Ibid., 5, 6, 8, 18 July 1862.
26. Ibid., 29 Aug., 12, 22 Oct., 13 Nov. 1862.
27. Ibid., 26 Dec. 1862, 20 Apr., 7, 8 July 1863.
28. Anne S. Frobel, *Civil War Diary,* pp. 194–196.
29. Donald, pp. 438–439.
30. TUW to Charles Fowler, 18 June 1863; Brainard H. Warner, "Extracts from Letters," pp. 311–315; Donald, p. 439.
31. Warner, pp. 315–316; Brooks, *Mr. Lincoln's Washington,* p. 194.
32. Gideon Welles, *Diary,* 1:357.
33. Donald, p. 446.
34. Philip Van Doren Stern, ed., *Life and Writings,* pp. 763–764.
35. B. B. French, *Witness to the Young Republic,* p. 426.

Chapter Sixteen: *From These Honored Dead*

1. Elizabeth Keckley, *Behind the Scenes,* p. 111.
2. Benjamin Quarles, *Negro in the Civil War,* pp. 233–235.
3. Keckley, pp. 110–113.
4. Bobbi Schildt, "Freedman's Village," pp. 10–11; Elias M. Greene to Maj. Gen. S. P. Heintzelman, 5 May 1863, U.S. War Department, Office of Quartermaster General, Cemetery file, RG 92, National Archives.
5. Philip Van Doren Stern, ed., *Life and Writings,* pp. 765–767.
6. James M. McPherson, *Battle Cry of Freedom,* pp. 600, 609–610; Noah Brooks, *Washington, D.C.,* p. 104.
7. Stern, pp. 768–769.
8. Frederick Douglass, *Life and Times,* pp. 351–353.
9. Ibid., pp. 354–355.
10. Antonia Ford, n.d., Willard Family Papers.
11. Patricia Rorie, "Belle Boyd"; Richard F. Snow, "Belle Boyd."
12. Curtis Carroll Davis, "The 'Old Capitol,' " p. 214; S. A. Ashe, "Unusual Experiences," p. 343.
13. Davis, pp. 220–222; *Washington Sunday Gazette,* 10 Jan. 1887.
14. Willard Family papers.
15. Antonia Ford, Willard Family papers; *OR,* II, 5:627–628; J. E. B. Stuart to John Mosby, n.d., Willard Family papers; *Southern Illustrated News,* 15 Aug. 1863.
16. Willard Family papers.
17. Antonia Ford to Joseph C. Willard, 31 Dec. 1863, Willard Family papers.
18. TUW to Charles Fowler, 4, 8 May, 23 June, 25 Aug. 1863.
19. TUW to Rev. J. D. King, 30 July 1863.
20. James P. Thompson, *Higher Arithmetic,* n.p.

21. TUW to Mrs. Walter, 29 Aug. 1863.
22. TUW to Mrs. Walter, 27 Aug. 1863; to R. Gardiner, 20 Oct. 1863.
23. TUW to John Baird, 5 Nov. 1863.
24. John Hay, *Inside Lincoln's White House,* pp. 75–76, 89.
25. Noah Brooks, *Washington, D.C.,* pp. 189–190; Fred A. Emery, "Washington Newspapers," pp. 46–52.
26. John C. Waugh, *Reelecting Lincoln,* pp. 14–17.
27. John W. Forney, *Anecdotes of Public Men,* 1:75–77; Hay, p. 186.
28. Thomas Belden and Marva Belden, *So Fell the Angels,* pp. 55–62.
29. Hay, pp. 97–98, 110–111; Belden, pp. 94–95; *Cincinnati Daily Gazette,* 20 Nov. 1863.
30. Stern, pp. 769–770, 775–780.
31. David Herbert Donald, *Lincoln,* pp. 459–461; Forbes to Lincoln, 8 Sept. 1863, Lincoln Papers.
32. Donald, pp. 462–463; Benjamin Thomas, *Abraham Lincoln,* p. 400; Hay, pp. 111–113.
33. B. B. French, *Witness to the Young Republic,* pp. 434–436; Hay, p. 113; *New York Times,* 20 Nov. 1863.

Chapter Seventeen: *Her Ladyship Looks Placid and Beautiful*

1. John Hay, *Inside Lincoln's White House,* p. 118; *Chicago Tribune,* 15 Dec. 1863.
2. TUW to Charles Fowler, 9 Nov.; to Mrs. Walter, 30 Nov. 1863.
3. TUW to G. W. Anderson, 29 Dec. 1863.
4. TUW to Mrs. Walter, 1 Dec. 1863.
5. Ibid., 2 Dec. 1863.
6. Nathan Daniels, diary, 2 Dec. 1863.
7. James Goode, "Architecture, Politics and Conflict," p. 276.
8. TUW to Thomas Walter, 25, 31 Dec. 1863.
9. David Herbert Donald, *Lincoln,* pp. 471–474; Philip Van Doren Stern, *Life and Writings,* pp. 790–793.
10. Hay, pp. 121–122.
11. Jane Grey Swisshelm, *Crusader and Feminist,* p. 269.
12. James Grant Wilson and John Fiske, eds., *Appleton's Cyclopedia.*
13. Noah Brooks, *Mr. Lincoln's Washington,* pp. 280–282; John C. Waugh, *Reelecting Lincoln,* pp. 101–105; James Harvey Young, "Anna Elizabeth Dickinson," p. 72.
14. *New York Herald,* 9 Nov. 1863.
15. Waugh, p. 34.
16. Antonia Ford to Joseph Willard, 22, 24, 29 Feb. 1864; Gussie Bragg to Belle Willard, 22 Aug. 1925, Willard Family papers.
17. Katherine Malone Willis to Mrs. Joseph E. Willard, 3 Apr. 1928; Joseph and Antonia Willard to Mrs. Willard, 19 Mar. 1864, Willard Family papers.
18. Benjamin Ogle Tayloe to Joseph C. Willard, 9 Mar. 1864; Antonia Willard to Mrs. Willard, 19 Mar. 1864; Sallie Ford to My Dearest Holly, 8 July 1924, Willard Family papers.
19. Nathan Daniels, diary, 23, 25, 28, 29 Jan. 1864.
20. J. G. Nicolay and John Hay, "Abraham Lincoln: The Pomeroy Circular," *Century* 38, no. 2 (June 1889): 281–283.
21. George G. Meade, *Life and Letters,* 2:172–173.
22. Brooks, *Mr. Lincoln's Washington,* pp. 288–289.

23. T. Harry Williams, *Lincoln and His Generals*, pp. 297–298.
24. Brooks, *Mr. Lincoln's Washington*, pp. 289–291; Gideon Welles, *Diary*, 1:538–539.
25. Williams, pp. 298–300.
26. Meade, 2:177–178.

Chapter Eighteen: *And Now May God Sustain You*

1. John Burroughs, *Wake-Robin*, pp. 140–141.
2. John Burroughs to Ursula Burroughs, 25 Oct., 6 Dec. 1863, quoted in Edward J. Renehan, Jr., *John Burroughs*, pp. 70–72.
3. Renehan, pp. 51, 57; Roy Morris, Jr., *Better Angel*, p. 150; Justin Kaplan, *Walt Whitman*, p. 307.
4. Martin G. Murray, "Traveling with the Wounded," pp. 72–73; Kaplan, p. 276.
5. Whitman to Lewis Kirk Brown, 1, 11 Aug. 1863.
6. Kaplan, pp. 277–78; Morris, pp. 164–165.
7. Burroughs, *Wake-Robin*, pp. 154–159.
8. Benny Bolin, "Spencer M. Clark," p. 77.
9. J. Henry Mullford to Lincoln, 27 Apr. 1864, reel 73, Lincoln papers, LC; TUW to wife, 6 May 1864.
10. John Ellis, *Sights and Secrets*, pp. 384–385.
11. Bolin, p. 77.
12. B. B. French, *Witness to the Young Republic*, p. 448.
13. David H. Donald, *Lincoln*, p. 448; French, pp. 448–449.
14. Thomas N. Conrad, *Confederate Spy*, pp. 12, 26–28, 30–34, 38, 48–50; George Alfred Townsend, *Washington, Outside and Inside*, p. 604.
15. Conrad, pp. 56–59.
16. Noah Andre Trudeau, *Like Men of War*, pp. 207–208; A. A. Humphreys, *Virginia Campaign of 1864 and 1865*, p. 408; Whitman to his mother, 26 Apr. 1864, in Walt Whitman, "Walt Whitman in War-Time," p. 847.
17. Rebecca Pomroy in *Chelsea Telegraph and Pioneer*, 9 Apr. 1864; Whitman to his mother, 19 Apr. 1864, in Whitman, "Walt Whitman in War-Time," p. 847.
18. Trudeau, pp. 208–209.
19. Philip Van Doren Stern, ed., *Life and Writings*, pp. 812–813.
20. Hay, *Inside Lincoln's White House*, p. 194.
21. Hay, p. 195; Michael Kelly, diary, 19 May 1864.
22. Georgeanna Woolsey to sister Jane, 13 May 1864, in Sylvia G. Dannett, ed., *Noble Women*, p. 286.
23. Noah Brooks, *Mr. Lincoln's Washington*, pp. 317, 320–323.
24. E. B. Long, *Civil War Day by Day*, p. 515; *OR*, I, 36, pt. 1:11.
25. Brooks, pp. 324, 335, 340.
26. Whitman to his mother, 1, 14 June 1864, in Whitman, "Walt Whitman in War-Time," p. 850.
27. David G. Miller, *Second Only to Grant*, p. 259; *OR*, I, 43, pt. 1, p. 30; Montgomery Meigs papers, container 45, reel 14, LC.

Chapter Nineteen: *The Darkness That Settled Upon Us*

1. *Star*, 18 June 1864, 20 Feb. 1904.
2. Ibid., 20 Feb. 1904.

3. Ibid.; Noah Brooks, *Mr. Lincoln's* Washington, p. 344.

4. Philip Van Doren Stern, ed., *Life and Writings,* pp. 816–818.

5. *New York Times,* 6 July 1864.

6. T. Harry Williams, *Lincoln and His Generals,* pp. 320–321; David Herbert Donald, *Lincoln,* pp. 515–516.

7. Brooks, *Washington, D.C.,* p. 157.

8. Hans L. Trefousse, *Radical Republicans,* pp. 287–289.

9. Gideon Welles, *Diary,* 2:68.

10. Benjamin Franklin Cooling, *Jubal Early's Raid on Washington, 1864,* pp. 41–51.

11. *National Intelligencer,* 7 July 1864.

12. Cooling, p. 41.

13. *New York Times,* 10 July 1864; Welles, 2:70.

14. Welles, 2:71.

15. Hay, *Inside Lincoln's White House,* pp. 221, 357 n. 224.

16. Jane Grey Swisshelm, *Crusader and Feminist,* p. 272; L. E. Chittenden, *Recollections,* pp. 405–406.

17. Swisshelm, pp. 243–244.

18. Brooks, *Mr. Lincoln's Washington,* pp. 353–356; Mary Henry, diary, 11 July 1864.

19. *OR,* I, 37, 2:260–263.

20. Cooling, p. 132; William Van Zandt Cox, "Defenses of Washington," p. 138.

21. *Star,* 12 July 1864.

22. Ibid.; Cooling, pp. 171–172.

23. Hay, p. 221; *OR,* I, 37, 2:212, 214, 260.

24. Cooling, pp. 171–172; Douglas Southall Freeman, *Lee's Lieutenants,* 3:565–566; Jubal A. Early, *War Memoirs,* p. 392.

25. *Winsted* (Conn.) *Herald,* 29 July 1864.

26. Ibid.; Chittenden, pp. 410–411; Michael Kelly, diary, 12 July 1864.

27. Hay, pp. 121–122; Cooling, p. 143; *Star,* extra edition, 13 July 1864; Chittenden, pp. 415–416.

28. *Star,* 13 July 1864; Nathan Daniels, diary, 12 July 1864.

29. Michael Kelly, diary, 12 July 1864; *Star,* 16 July 1864.

30. James H. Johnston, "A Mansion's History of Insecurity," *Washington Post,* 3 July 2003.

31. *OR,* I, 37, 1:250–254; Chittenden, p. 420.

32. Solomon Brown to Spencer Baird, 15 July 1864; *Star,* 12, 13 July 1864.

33. Nathan Daniels, diary, 13 July 1864; Hay, p. 223.

34. Welles, 2:92.

35. *New York Tribune,* 5 Aug. 1864; Trefousse, pp. 293–294.

36. Trefousse, pp. 294–295; Donald, pp. 528–529.

37. Stern, p. 823.

Chapter Twenty: *A Wild, Visionary Longing*

1. *New York Times,* 3 Sept. 1864.

2. *OR,* I, 38, 1:87.

3. Gideon Welles, *Diary,* 2:135.

4. *New York Times,* 10 Sept. 1864.

5. Michael Kelly, diary, 10 Aug. 1864; James M. McPherson, *Battle Cry of Freedom,* pp. 775–776; John C. Waugh, *Reelecting Lincoln,* pp. 305–306.

6. Thomas N. Conrad, *Confederate Spy,* pp. 68–75; Jacob Mogelever, *Death to Traitors,* pp. 215–216.
7. Jane Grey Swisshelm, *Crusader and Feminist,* p. 274.
8. Richard Walsh and William Lloyd Fox, eds., *Maryland: A History, 1634–1974,* p. 376; Bobbi Schildt, "Freedman's Village," p. 12.
9. Olive Gilbert, *Narrative of Sojourner Truth,* p. 177; Schildt, p. 12.
10. Jane Grey Swisshelm, *Half a Century,* pp. 239–244, 269–270, 354–355.
11. Gilbert, pp. 177–181.
12. Carole Gray, "I Love Lucy!"; Lucy N. Colman, *Reminiscences,* p. 67; Nell Irvin Painter, *Sojourner Truth,* pp. 206–207; William S. McFeely, *Frederick Douglass,* pp. 229–230.
13. Gilbert, pp. 177–179; Schildt, pp. 12–14.
14. John Rapier, Jr., to James P. Thomas, 19 Aug. 1864.
15. Gilbert, p. 179.
16. William Tindall, "Beginnings of Street Railways," pp. 26–27; Constance McLaughlin Green, *Washington,* 1:263.
17. Noah Brooks, *Washington, D.C.,* pp. 191–192.
18. Painter, pp. 210–211.
19. Brooks, *Washington, D.C.,* pp. 192–193; Green, *Secret City,* pp. 66–67; Keith E. Melder, "Angel of Mercy," pp. 252–253.
20. Francis Lieber, *Life and Letters,* p. 351; George Y. Coffin, diary, 17 Sept., 7, 14 Oct. 1864.
21. John Hay, *Inside Lincoln's White House,* p. 239.
22. Brooks, "Personal Reminiscences," pp. 563–564.
23. Charles Sumner, "Introduction to 'Petroleum V. Nasby,'" p. 15.
24. Brooks, *Mr. Lincoln's Washington,* pp. 379–381.
25. Ibid., pp. 380–381; Waugh, p. 325.
26. Waugh, pp. 326–329; Allen Thorndike Rice, ed., *Reminiscences of Abraham Lincoln,* p. 430.
27. Hay, p. 242; David Herbert Donald, *Lincoln,* p. 536.
28. Benjamin P. Thomas and Harold M. Hyman, *Stanton,* pp. 331–334.
29. Brooks, *Mr. Lincoln's Washington,* pp. 382–383.
30. Ibid., pp. 384–385.
31. *National Intelligencer,* 7, 9 Nov. 1864; Hay, p. 243.
32. Hay, pp. 243–246; Thomas and Hyman, p. 334; Brooks, *Mr. Lincoln's Washington,* pp. 385–387; Brooks, *Washington, D.C.,* pp. 195–198.
33. Brooks, *Mr. Lincoln's Washington,* pp. 387–388; Philip Van Doren Stern, *Life and Writings,* pp. 827–828; Hay, p. 249.

Chapter Twenty-one: *The Judgments of the Lord*

1. Hay, *Inside Lincoln's White House,* p. 246.
2. J. G. Nicolay and John Hay, "Abraham Lincoln: The Fourteenth of April," *Century* 39, no. 3 (Jan. 1890): 431–432.
3. Ibid.; *Cincinnati Enquirer,* 15 Aug. 1885, quoted in William A. Tidwell, *Come Retribution,* p. 237.
4. Ward Hill Lamon, *Recollections of Abraham Lincoln,* pp. 254–255.
5. *Appleton's Cyclopedia;* Lamon, p. 274.
6. Clara E. Laughlin, *Death of Lincoln,* p. 185; Tidwell, pp. 263–264.
7. *Star,* 7 Dec. 1870.

8. Gene Smith, *American Gothic*, pp. 111–112.

9. Smith, p. 106; Tidwell, p. 335; *New York Times*, 26 Nov. 1864.

10. TUW to [illegible] Jenner, 25 Aug. 1864; to Charles Fowler, 21, 28 June, 24 Aug. 1864; to Solomon Foot, 5 Aug. 1864.

11. Noah Brooks, *Mr. Lincoln's Washington*, pp. 390–391.

12. Gideon Welles, *Diary*, 2:196; Brooks, pp. 398–401.

13. Philip Van Doren Stern, *Life and Writings*, pp. 793–800.

14. E. B. Long, *Civil War Day by Day*, pp. 608–614.

15. Welles, 2:209; [Anna Sherman], "A Little Girl's Experience," pp. 21–22.

16. [Sherman], pp. 25–26; "Quad" to *Chelsea Telegraph and Pioneer*, 8 Jan. 1865.

17. "Quad," 8 Jan. 1865.

18. James M. McPherson, *Battle Cry of Freedom*, pp. 821–824; William C. Davis, *Jefferson Davis*, pp. 594–595; Nicolay and Hay, "Abraham Lincoln: The Second Inaugural," *Century* 39, no. 1 (Nov. 1889): 132–151.

19. Brooks, pp. 407–411.

20. Ibid., pp. 411–412.

21. W. M. Brewer, "Henry Highland Garnet," pp. 36–52.

22. Lois Bryan Adams, *Letter from Washington*, pp. 232–233; Constance McLaughlin Green, *Secret City*, p. 73; Martin B. Pasternak, *Rise Now and Fly to Arms*, pp. 120–121.

23. Martin G. Murray, "Pete the Great," pp. 12–13; Richard Bucke, ed., *Calamus*, p. 23.

24. Roy Morris, Jr., *Better Angel*, p. 211; Murray, p. 18; William Tindall, "Beginnings of Street Railways," pp. 49–50.

25. Morris, pp. 202–205.

26. Long, pp. 631–644; B. B. French, *Witness to the Young Republic*, p. 469.

27. Nicolay and Hay, "Abraham Lincoln: Second Inaugural," pp. 132–133.

28. Brooks, pp. 415–418.

29. Ellen Mills, diary, 3 Mar. 1865; *New York Times*, 6 Mar. 1865; Walt Whitman, *Specimen Days*, p. 98.

30. Benjamin Perley Poore, *Reminiscences*, 2:157–158; Nicolay and Hay, "Second Inaugural," p. 135.

31. Poore, p. 159; Brooks, p. 423; Welles, 2:252.

32. Mills, diary, 4 Mar. 1865; Asia Booth Clarke, *John Wilkes Booth*, p. 86.

33. *Star*, 4 Mar. 1865.

34. Stern, pp. 840–842.

35. Brooks, *Washington, D.C.*, p. 214.

36. Ibid.

37. Adams, pp. 243–244.

Chapter Twenty-two: *Let 'Em Up Easy*

1. Noah Brooks, *Mr. Lincoln's Washington*, pp. 393–394, 427–428; J. G. Nicolay and John Hay, "Abraham Lincoln: The Second Inaugural," *Century* 39, no. 1 (Nov. 1889): 138.

2. Walt Whitman, *Specimen Days*, pp. 90–92.

3. B. B. French, *Witness to the Young Republic*, p. 466; Ellen Mills, diary, 4 Mar. 1865; *New York Times*, 6 Mar. 1865; Nathan Daniels, diary, 5 Mar. 1865.

4. Noah Brooks, *Mr. Lincoln's Washington*, p. 427; Gene Smith, *American Gothic*, pp. 117–119, 133.

5. Brooks, p. 427.
6. E. B. Long, *Civil War Day by Day*, pp. 645–651; Ernest B. Furgurson, *Ashes of Glory*, pp. 308, 313.
7. *Appleton's Cyclopedia;* John P. King, "Brief History of the Handful of Theatre Buildings"; King, "Ford's Theatrical Venture"; King, "Lincoln and the Lively Arts."
8. Tidwell, *Come Retribution*, pp. 413–414.
9. Roy P. Basler, *Collected Works*, 8:360–362; Stanley Kimmel, *Mr. Lincoln's Washington*, p. 172.
10. *Star,* 18 Mar. 1865.
11. Adolphe de Chambrun, *Impressions of Lincoln*, p. 31.
12. Chambrun, pp. 21–28, 53.
13. Welles, *Diary,* 2:294; Horace Porter, *Campaigning with Grant*, p. 403.
14. Porter, pp. 403–405.
15. Jean Baker, *Mary Todd Lincoln*, pp. 240–241.
16. Porter, pp. 405–406, 418, 422–424, 452; Sylvanus Cadwallader, *Three Years with Grant*, pp. 306–307.
17. *OR,* I, 46, 2:509.
18. Lois Bryan Adams, *Letter from Washington*, pp. 251–252; Brooks, pp. 430–432.
19. Jane Grey Swisshelm, *Crusader and Feminist*, pp. 290–292.
20. David Dixon Porter, Private Journal No. 2; Godfrey Weitzel, *Richmond Occupied*, p. 56.
21. Chambrun, pp. 73–76.
22. David Herbert Donald, *Lincoln*, p. 577.
23. Chambrun, pp. 83–84.
24. Adams, pp. 253–254.
25. Ibid.; Brooks, pp. 436–438.
26. Brooks, p. 439; Philip Van Doren Stern, *Life and Writings*, pp. 846–851; Nicolay and Hay, "Abraham Lincoln: Fourteenth of April," *Century* 39, no. 3 (Jan. 1890): 430; Tidwell, p. 421.
27. *Star,* 12 Apr. 1865; Brooks, pp. 440–441.
28. Adams, pp. 254–255; Chambrun, pp. 91–93.
29. Nicolay and Hay, "Fourteenth of April," p. 430.
30. Ibid.; Donald, pp. 392–393.
31. Fletcher Pratt, *Stanton*, p. 411; Nicolay and Hay, "Fourteenth of April," p. 430.
32. Welles, *Diary,* 2:280–283; *OR,* I, 46, 3:785; Welles, "Lincoln and Johnson," *Galaxy* 13, no. 10 (Apr. 1872): 526; Nicolay and Hay, "Fourteenth of April," p. 430.
33. Philip B. Kunhardt, Jr., et al., *Lincoln*, p. 348; Donald, p. 593.
34. *Star,* 14 Apr. 1865; Kunhardt et al., p. 347.
35. Thomas Pendel, *Thirty-six Years*, pp. 39–40; Donald, pp. 594–595; Kunhardt et al., pp. 346–347.

Chapter Twenty-three: *Now He Belongs to the Ages*

1. Antonia Willard to her mother, n.d., Willard Family papers.
2. TUW to Mrs. Walter, 12, 13 Apr. 1865.
3. Adolphe de Chambrun, *Impressions of Lincoln*, p. 94.
4. B. B. French, *Witness to the Young Republic*, pp. 472–475.
5. Roy Morris, Jr., *Better Angel*, p. 217; Bucke, ed., *Calamus*, p. 25.

6. Nicolay and Hay, "Abraham Lincoln: Fourteenth of April," *Century* 39, no. 3 (Jan. 1890): 433; Gene Smith, *American Gothic,* pp. 138–145; William A. Tidwell, *Come Retribution,* p. 430; John Rhodehamel and Louise Taper, *Right or Wrong,* pp. 144–153.

7. Noah Brooks, *Mr. Lincoln's Washington,* pp. 443–444; Allen C. Clark, *Abraham Lincoln in the National Capital,* p. 109; Philip B. Kunhardt, Jr., et al., *Lincoln,* pp. 346–353.

8. Nicolay and Hay, pp. 433–436; David Herbert Donald, *Lincoln,* pp. 595–597; Kunhardt et al., pp. 346–353.

9. Bucke, p. 25; Barbara Hughett, ed., "A Statement from Lincoln's Deathbed Physician."

10. Bucke, p. 26; Charles Sabin Taft, "Abraham Lincoln's Last Hours," pp. 634–636.

11. Taft, p. 636.

12. Nicolay and Hay, p. 436; Taft, p. 636.

13. Keckley, *Behind the Scenes,* pp. 184–192; Welles, *Diary,* 2:288–290.

14. Brooks, *Washington, D.C.,* pp. 231–234; *New York Tribune,* 18 Apr. 1865; Brooks, *Mr. Lincoln's Washington,* pp. 450–452.

15. Brooks, *Washington, D.C.,* pp. 234–236; Brooks, *Mr. Lincoln's Washington,* p. 452.

16. Justin Kaplan, *Walt Whitman,* pp. 303–306.

Epilogue: *Out of Sorrow into Holy Memories*

1. Lois Bryan Adams, *Letter from Washington,* pp. 256, 259; [Anna Sherman], "A Little Girl's Experience," p. 27; Jean H. Baker, *Mary Todd Lincoln,* pp. 248–250.

2. William A. Tidwell, *Come Retribution,* pp. 444–451; Gene Smith, *American Gothic,* pp. 178–179, 182–186; Prentiss Ingraham, "Pursuit and Death," p. 443; Philip B. Kunhardt, Jr., et al., *Lincoln,* p. 367.

3. Tidwell, pp. 431, 433–438; *OR,* I, 46, 3:783.

4. Tidwell, pp. 454–477; Nicolay and Hay, "Abraham Lincoln: Fourteenth of April," *Century* 39, no. 3 (Jan. 1890): 437–439; Ingraham, pp. 446–449; *Philadelphia Weekly Times,* 14 Apr. 1877.

5. *New York Times,* 28 Apr. 1865.

6. Benjamin Perley Poore, *Reminiscences,* 2:163–186; Noah Brooks, *Mr. Lincoln's Washington,* pp. 466–471.

7. TUW to Mrs. Walter, 22, 24, 25 May 1865.

8. *New York Times,* 23, 24 May 1865.

9. Ibid., 25 May 1865.

10. John Hay, *At Lincoln's Side,* pp. 130–131.

SOURCES

For their patient cooperation, I am especially grateful to the staffs of the institutions below. I must also say, for the first time, that I am thankful for the Internet. As a printer's son and natural Luddite, with ingrained affection for the feel of the letter-press page, I was long a skeptic about anything so nebulous and cluttered as the World Wide Web. Bringing up the technological rear, I used the Internet for a sub-stantial part of the research on this book, and now concede that it is an invaluable tool if approached with guard up against misinformation. Among the most useful sites for U.S. history research are the Making of America collections put on line by Cornell University and the University of Michigan. For example, the War Depart-ment's entire 128-volume *Official Records* of the Civil War is there, searchable in sec-onds. Because John G. Nicolay and John Hay's forty-part life of Lincoln as it appeared in *Century* magazine from 1886 to 1890 is so easily accessible by computer, I have referred to it rather than the ten-volume printed version, which is hard to find and harder to pay for. This said, I never expect to find any other resource as reward-ing as the old-fashioned, eminently tangible card catalogue, still available, at the Library of Congress. And no computer will ever offer the personal interest in a researcher's quest that is given every day by librarians at archives such as these:

Alderman Library, University of Virginia, Charlottesville
Archives of American Art, Smithsonian Institution, Washington, D.C.
Bowdoin College Library, Brunswick, Me.
Connecticut Historical Society, Hartford
Curator's Office, Architect of the Capitol, Washington, D.C.
Duke University Library, Durham, N.C.
Gelman Library, George Washington University, Washington, D.C.
Historical Society of Pennsylvania, Philadelphia
Historical Society of Washington
Hornbake Library, University of Maryland, College Park
Kroch Library, Cornell University, Ithaca, N.Y.
Lauinger Library, Georgetown University, Washington, D.C.
Manuscript, Newspaper & Periodical, Local History & Genealogy, Geography
    & Map, Rare Book & Special Collections, and Prints & Photographs
    divisions, Library of Congress, Washington, D.C.
Maryland Historical Society, Baltimore
Massachusetts Historical Society, Boston
Moorland-Spingarn Collection, Howard University, Washington, D.C.
Mullen Library, Catholic University, Washington, D.C.
National Archives, Washington, D.C.
New-York Historical Society, New York City
Richmond National Battlefield Park, Richmond, Va.
Southern Historical Collection, University of North Carolina, Chapel Hill

State Historical Society of Iowa, Des Moines
U.S. Capitol Historical Society, Washington
Virginia Historical Society, Richmond
Waidner-Spahr Library, Dickinson College, Carlisle, Pa.
Washingtoniana Division, Martin Luther King Public Library, Washington, D.C.

MANUSCRIPTS

Adams, J. F. Alleyne. Diary, letters. Burt Green Wilder papers, Cornell University.
Babcock, John C. Letters. Babcock papers, Manuscript Division, Library of Congress (hereafter LC).
Bancroft, George. Letters. Bancroft papers, LC.
Bigelow, Jacob. Letters. Bigelow papers, Massachusetts Historical Society.
Brent, John Carroll. Diary. Historical Society of Washington.
Brindley, Richard. Letters. Richmond National Battlefield Park.
Brooks, Daniel, First U.S. Colored Troops. Compiled Military Service Record, Record Group 94, National Archives.
Brown, Francis H. Diary. Burt Green Wilder papers, Cornell University.
Brown, Solomon. Letters. Joseph Henry papers, Smithsonian Institution.
Carroll, Anna Ella. Letters. Carroll papers, Maryland Historical Society.
Coffin, George Y. Diary No. 1. Coffin papers, George Washington University.
Crockett, Richard, 19th Maine. Letter. Special Collections, Gelman Library, George Washington University.
Daniels, Nathan. Diary. Courtesy of C. P. Weaver (since donated to Manuscript Division, LC).
Documents on Reconstruction and Freedman's Village. Freedom and Southern Society Project, History Department, University of Maryland, College Park.
Dwight, William, Jr. Letters. Charles H. Nichols papers, LC.
Ford, Antonia. Letters. Willard Family papers, LC.
Foster, Lafayette S. Letters. Foster papers, Massachusetts Historical Society.
Fowle, Elida Rumsey. Letter. Burt Green Wilder papers, Cornell University.
Fowler, James H. Letters, memoirs. Burt Green Wilder papers, Cornell University.
French, Benjamin Brown. Letters. Brown papers, LC.
Hanna, Mark. Letters. Hanna-McCormick papers, LC.
Harllee, Andrew. Letter. William Curry Harllee MSS, Southern Historical Collection.
Hassler, Mary C. Diary. Simon Newcomb papers, LC.
Henry, Mary. Diary. Joseph Henry papers, Smithsonian Institution.
Herndon, William Henry, and Jesse William Weik. Letters. Herndon-Weik Collection, LC.
Hooker, Joseph. Letters. Charles H. Nichols papers, LC.
Jewett, Levi. Letters. Jewett papers, Connecticut Historical Society.
Jordan, Augustus. Letters. Jordan-Stabler papers, Virginia Historical Society.
Kelly, Michael. Diary. Connecticut Historical Society.
Lincoln, Abraham. Lincoln papers, LC.
Low, Francis S. Letters. Low papers, LC.
Meigs, Louisa Rodgers. Letters. Meigs papers, LC.
Meigs, Montgomery C. Journal. Meigs papers, LC.

Mills, Ellen. Diary. Low-Mills Family papers, LC.

Newcomb, Simon. Diary. Newcomb papers, LC.

Nicolay, John G. Letters. Nicolay papers, LC.

Olmsted, Frederick Law. Letters. Olmsted papers, LC.

Pickard, Alonzo. Letters. Pickard papers, LC.

Pinkerton, Allan. Letters. Pinkerton's National Detective Agency papers, LC.

Porter, David Dixon. Private Journal No. 2. Porter papers, LC.

Rapier, John, Jr. Letters. Rapier papers, Moorland-Spingarn Collection, Howard University.

[Sherman, Anna.] "A Little Girl's Experiences of the War." George Washington University.

Southworth, Mrs. E.D.E.N. Letters. Southworth papers, Duke University Library.

Stoek, Jeff. Letter. J. F. Stoek papers, Historical Society of Washington.

Taft, Horatio Nelson. Diary 1861–1865. LC.

Vedder, Timothy. Letters. Special Collections, Gelman Library, George Washington University.

Vollum, Edward P. Letter. Charles H. Nichols papers, LC.

Wakeman, Sarah Rosetta. Letters. LC.

Walker, Aldace F. Letter. Fort Ward Museum Library, Alexandria, Va.

Walter, Thomas U. Diary. Athenaeum of Philadelphia (copy in Archives of American Art, Smithsonian Institution).

———. Letters. Athenaeum of Philadelphia (copy in Curator's Office, Architect of the Capitol).

Whitman, Walt. Letters. Lewis Kirk Brown papers, LC.

Wigfall, Louis Trezevant. Family papers, LC.

Wilder, Burt Green. Letters, hospital records, memoir "A Washington Hospital." Wilder papers, Cornell University.

Willard, Joseph C. Letters. Willard Family papers, LC.

PUBLISHED FIRSTHAND AND CONTEMPORARY SOURCES

Abbott, Henry L. "Memoir of Montgomery C. Meigs, 1816–1892." *National Academy of Sciences Biographical Memoirs* 2:314–315.

Abdy, E. S. *Journal of a Residence and Tour in the United States of North America from April, 1833, to October, 1834.* 2 vols. London: J. Murray, 1835.

Acken, J. Gregory, ed. *Inside the Army of the Potomac.* Mechanicsville, Pa.: Stackpole, 1998.

Adams, Charles Francis. *Charles Francis Adams 1835–1915: An Autobiography.* Boston: Houghton Mifflin, 1916.

Adams, Charles Francis, Jr. "Lincoln's First Inauguration." *Massachusetts Historical Society Papers* 42:144–154.

Adams, John G. B. *Reminiscences of the 19th Massachusetts Regiment.* Boston: Wright, Potter Printing Co., 1899.

Adams, Lois Bryan. *Letter from Washington, 1863–1865.* Evelyn Leasher, ed. Detroit: Wayne State University, 1999.

Alcott, Louisa May. *Hospital Sketches.* Reprint. Bessie Z. Jones, ed. Cambridge: Belknap Press of Harvard University Press, 1960.

Ames, Mary Clemmer. *Ten Years in Washington: Life and Scenes in the National Capital, as a Woman Sees Them.* Hartford: A. D. Worthington, 1873.

Ashe, S. A. "Unusual Experiences as Soldier and Prisoner." *Confederate Veteran* 35 (1925):341–343.

Austin, George Lowell. "The Conspiracy of 1860–61." *Bay State Monthly* 3, no. 4 (Sept. 1885):233–244.

Bagby, George William. Correspondence to *New Orleans Crescent, Petersburg Virginia Index, Richmond Dispatch*. George W. Bagby papers, Virginia Historical Society.

——. "Washington City." *Atlantic Monthly* 7 (1861):1–8.

Baker, L[afayette] C. *History of the United States Secret Service*. Philadelphia: King & Baird, 1868.

Basler, Roy P., ed. *Collected Works of Abraham Lincoln*. Springfield: Abraham Lincoln Association, 1953.

Beauregard, Pierre G. T. "The Battle of Bull Run." *Century* 29, no. 1 (Nov. 1884):80–100.

——. "The First Battle of Bull Run." *Battles & Leaders of the Civil War* (hereafter *Battles & Leaders*) 1:196–227.

Benjamin, Charles F. "Recollections of Secretary Stanton, by a Clerk of the War Department." *Century* 33, no. 5 (Mar. 1887):758–768.

Berard, Augusta Blanche. "Arlington and Mount Vernon, 1856." Clayton Torrence, ed. *Virginia Magazine of History and Biography* 59 (1949):140ff.

Berret, James G. "Address of Ex-Mayor James G. Berret." *Records of the Columbia Historical Society* (hereafter *CHS*) 2:206ff.

Blackwell, S. E. "The Case of Miss Carroll." *Century* 41 (Aug. 1890):638–639.

Botts, John Minor. *The Great Rebellion: Its Secret History, Rise, Progress and Disastrous Failure*. New York: Harper, 1866.

Boynton, H. V. "The Press and Public Men." *Century* 42, no. 6 (Oct. 1891):854–862.

Briggs, Emily Edson. *The Olivia Letters: Being Some History of Washington City for Forty Years as Told by the Letters of a Newspaper Correspondent*. New York: Neale, 1906.

Brinton, John H. Address at closing exercises, Army Medical School. *Journal of the American Medical Association* 26, no. 13 (28 Mar. 1896).

Brock, R. A. *Virginia and Virginians: Eminent Virginians*. 2 vols. Reprint. Spartanburg, S.C.: Reprint Co., 1973.

Brooks, Noah. "The Career of an American Princess." *Overland Monthly and Out West Magazine* 5, no. 5 (Nov. 1870):461–469.

——. "Glimpses of Lincoln in War Time." *Century* 49, no. 3 (Jan. 1885):457–467.

——. *Mr. Lincoln's Washington: Selections from the Writings of Noah Brooks, Civil War Correspondent*. P. J. Staudenraus, ed. South Brunswick, N.J.: T. Yoseloff, 1967.

——. "Personal Reminiscences of Lincoln." *Scribner's Monthly* 15, no. 4 (Feb. 1878):561–569.

Browne, Charles F. *Artemus Ward: His Book*. London: Chatto & Windus, 1887.

Browning, Orville H. *The Diary of Orville Hickman Browning*. Theodore Calvin Pearse and James G. Randall, eds. 2 vols. Springfield: Illinois State Historical Library, 1927.

Bucke, Richard Maurice, ed. *Calamus: A Series of Letters Written During the Years 1868–1880 by Walt Whitman to a Young Friend (Peter Doyle)*. Boston: Small, Maynard, 1897.

Bullitt, Thomas W. "Lee and Scott: Paper Read at the Re-union of Morgan's Men at Lexington, Ky." *Southern Historical Society Papers* 14 (1886):442ff.

Burgess, Lauren Cook, ed. *An Uncommon Soldier: The Civil War Letters of Sara Rosetta Wakeman, Alias Private Lyons Wakeman.* New York: Oxford University, 1995.

Burroughs, John. *Wake-Robin.* Boston: Houghton Mifflin, 1904.

——. *Whitman: A Study.* Boston: Houghton Mifflin, 1904.

Butts, Joseph Tyler, ed. *A Gallant Captain of the Civil War, Being the Record of the Extraordinary Adventures of Frederick Otto Baron von Fritsch.* New York: F. Tennyson Neely, 1902.

Cadwallader, Sylvanus. *Three Years with Grant.* Benjamin F. Thomas, ed. New York: Knopf, 1955.

Carnegie, Andrew. *Autobiography of Andrew Carnegie.* Boston: Houghton Mifflin, 1920.

Carpenter, Francis B. *Six Months at the White House.* New York: Hurd & Houghton, 1866.

Chambrun, Marquis Adolphe de. *Impressions of Lincoln and the Civil War: A Foreigner's Account.* New York: Random House, 1952.

Chase, Salmon P. *Salmon P. Chase Papers,* vol. 1: *Journals, 1829-1872.* John Niven, ed. Kent, Ohio: Kent State University Press, 1993.

Chittenden, L. E. *Recollections of President Lincoln and His Administration.* New York: Harper & Brothers, 1891.

Clarke, Asia Booth. *John Wilkes Booth: A Sister's Memoir.* Terry Alford, ed. Jackson: University Press of Mississippi, 1996.

Clarke, James Freeman. *Diary and Correspondence.* Boston: Houghton Mifflin, 1891.

Clay-Clopton, Virginia. *A Belle of the Fifties: Memoirs of Mrs. Clay, of Alabama, Covering Social and Political Life in Washington and the South, 1853-66.* New York: Doubleday, Page, 1905.

Coleman, Evan J. "Gwin and Seward: A Secret Chapter in Antebellum History." *Overland Monthly* 18, no. 107 (Nov. 1891):465-471.

Colman, Lucy N. *Reminiscences.* Buffalo: H. L. Green, 1891.

Conrad, Thomas N. *A Confederate Spy.* New York, J. S. Ogilvie, c.1892.

——. *Rebel Scout: A Thrilling History of Scouting Life in the Southern Army.* Washington, D.C.: National Publishing, 1904.

Couch, Darius M. "Sumner's 'Right Grand Division.' " *Battles and Leaders* 3:105-120.

Cox, William Van Zandt. "The Defenses of Washington—General Early's Advance on the Capital and the Battle of Fort Stevens, July 11 and 12, 1864." *CHS* 4 (1901):135-165.

Cunningham, D., and W. Miller. "The 36th Ohio in Washington City." *Ohio at Antietam: Report of the Ohio Antietam Battlefield Commission,* 1904.

Dalton, John Call. *John Call Dalton, M.D., U.S.V.* Privately printed, 1892.

Dana, Charles A. *Recollections of the Civil War.* New York: D. Appleton, 1902.

Davis, George B. *War Paper: Some Reminiscences of the Early Days of the Army of the Potomac.* Washington, D.C.: District of Columbia Commandery, Military Order of the Loyal Legion of the United States, 1914.

Davis, Harriet Riddle. "Civil War Recollections of a Little Yankee." *CHS* 44-45:55-75.

Davis, Henry E. "Ninth and F Streets and Thereabout." *CHS* 5 (1902):238–258.

Davis, Varina. *Jefferson Davis*. 2 vols. New York: Belford, 1890.

Dawes, Henry L. "Washington the Winter Before the War." *Atlantic Monthly* 72, no. 430 (Aug. 1893):160–167.

"The Diary of a Public Man: Unpublished Passages of the Secret History of the American Civil War," pts. 2–4, *North American Review* 129, nos. 173–176 (Aug.–Nov. 1879).

Dicey, Edward. *Spectator of America*. Herbert Mitgang, ed. Athens: University of Georgia, 1989.

District of Columbia. *Records of the Board of Commissioners for the Emancipation of Slaves in the District of Columbia, 1862–63*. Microcopy 520, National Archives.

Drayton, Daniel. *Personal Memoir of Daniel Drayton, for Four Years and Four Months a Prisoner (for Charity's Sake) in Washington Jail, Including a Narrative of the Voyage and Capture of the Schooner Pearl*. Boston: Bela Marsh, 1854.

Douglass, Frederick. *Life and Times of Frederick Douglass, Written by Himself, His Early Life as a Slave, His Escape from Bondage, and His Complete History to the Present Time*. Hartford: Park Publishing, 1881.

Fiske, S. R. "Gentlemen of the Press." *Harper's Monthly* 26, no. 153 (Feb. 1863):361–367.

Forney, John W. *Anecdotes of Public Men*. 2 vols. New York: Harper & Brothers, 1873, 1881.

French, Benjamin Brown. *Witness to the Young Republic*. Reprint. Hanover: University Press of New England, 1989.

Fritsch, Frederick Otto Baron von. *A Gallant Captain of the Civil War*. Joseph Tyler Butts, ed. New York: F. Tennyson Neely, 1902.

Frobel, Anne S. *The Civil War Diary of Anne S. Frobel, of Wilton Hill in Virginia*. Reprint. McLean: EPM Publications, 1992.

Fry, James B. "McDowell's Advance to Bull Run." *Battles and Leaders* 1:167–193.

Gobright, L. A. *Recollections of Men and Things at Washington*. Philadelphia: Claxton, Remsen & Haffelfinger, 1869.

Goss, Warren Lee. "Recollections of a Private." *Century* 29, no. 1 (Nov. 1884):107–113.

Grant, U. S. *Personal Memoirs of U. S. Grant*. Vol. 2. New York: Charles L. Webster, 1885.

Greenhow, Rose O'Neal. *My Imprisonment and the First Year of Abolitionist Rule at Washington*. London: Richard Bentley, 1863.

Greenwood, Grace (Sara Jane Clarke Lippincott). *Records of Five Years*. Boston: Ticknor & Fields, 1867.

Hall, C. H. *Reminiscences of Epiphany*. Cambridge, Mass.: Riverside Press, 1873.

Hallock, Charles. "The Hidden Way to Dixie." *Confederate Veteran* 18 (1910):424–426.

[Hawthorne, Nathaniel]. "Chiefly About War Matters, by a Peaceable Man." *Atlantic Monthly* 10, no. 57 (July 1862):43–61.

Hay, John. *At Lincoln's Side: John Hay's Civil War Correspondence and Selected Writings*. Michael Burlingame, ed. Carbondale: Southern Illinois University, 2000.

——. *Inside Lincoln's White House: The Complete Civil War Diary of John Hay*. Michael Burlingame, ed. Carbondale: Southern Illinois University, 1997.

——. "Life in the White House in the Time of Lincoln." *Century* 41, no. 1 (Nov. 1890):33–37.

Holzer, Harold, ed. *Dear Mr. Lincoln: Letters to the President.* New York: Addison-Wesley, 1993.

Howe, Julia Ward. *The Key to Uncle Tom's Cabin.* Boston: John P. Jewett & Co., 1853.

———. "Reminiscences of Julia Ward Howe." *Atlantic Monthly* 83, no. 499 (May 1899):701–712.

Hughett, Barbara, ed. "A Statement from Lincoln's Deathbed Physician." *Lincoln Newsletter,* n.d.

Humphreys, A. A. *The Virginia Campaign of 1864 and 1865.* New York: Charles Scribner's Sons, 1883.

Hutton, C. M. "Sketches of Prison Life." *Confederate Veteran* 19 (1911):331–332.

Ingraham, Prentiss, ed. "Pursuit and Death of John Wilkes Booth." *Century* 39, no. 3 (Jan. 1890):443–449.

Johnson, Albert E. H. "Reminiscences of the Hon. Edwin M. Stanton, Secretary of War." *CHS* 13:69–97.

Johnson, Robert Underwood, and Clarence Clough Buel, eds. *Battles and Leaders of the Civil War.* 4 vols. Reprint. New York: Thomas Yoseloff, 1956.

Jones, J. William. *Life and Letters of Robert E. Lee.* New York: Neale, 1906.

Kasson, Mrs. John A. (Caroline). "An Iowa Woman in Washington, D.C., 1861–1865." *Iowa Journal of History* 52, no. 1 (Jan. 1954):61–90.

Keckley, Elizabeth. Reprint. *Behind the Scenes, or Thirty Years a Slave, and Four Years in the White House.* New York: Oxford University, 1988.

Keen, W. W. "A Study in the Contrasts in Surgery of the Civil War and of the Present Time." Reviewed in *New York Medical Journal,* n.d. Burt Green Wilder papers, Cornell University.

Lambert, T. A. "Recollections of the Civil War." *CHS* 2 (1899):272–292.

Lamon, Ward Hill. *The Life of Abraham Lincoln, from His Birth to His Inauguration as President.* Boston: J. R. Osgood, 1872.

———. *Recollections of Abraham Lincoln, 1847–1865.* Chicago: A. C. McClung, 1895.

Lee, Mary Custis. "Reminiscences of the War." Robert E. L. deButts, Jr., ed. *Virginia Magazine of History and Biography* 109, no. 3:301–325.

Lieber, Francis. *The Life and Letters of Francis Lieber.* Boston: J. R. Osgood, 1882.

Livermore, Mary A. *My Story of the War: A Woman's Narrative of Four Years Personal Experience.* Hartford: A. D. Worthington, 1889.

Lomax, Elizabeth Lindsay. *Leaves from an Old Washington Diary 1854–1863.* Reprint. New York: E. P. Dutton, 1943.

Lounsbury, Thomas R. "In the Defenses of Washington." *Yale Review* 2, no. 3 (Apr. 1913):385–411.

Meade, George G. *The Life and Letters of George Gordon Meade, Major-General United States Army.* George Meade, ed. 2 vols. New York: Scribner, 1913.

Medical Society of the District of Columbia. "Report on the Sanitary Condition of the Cities of Washington and Georgetown," Mar. 1864.

Miller, Virginia. "Dr. Thomas Miller and His Times." *CHS* 3 (1900):303–323.

Mitgang, Herbert, ed. *Washington, D.C. in Lincoln's Time: A Memoir of the Civil War Era by the Newspaperman Who Knew Lincoln Best, Noah Brooks.* Chicago: Quadrangle Books, 1870.

Mosby, John S. "A Bit of Partisan Service." *Battles and Leaders* 3:148–151.

———. *The Memoirs of Col. John S. Mosby.* Charles Wells Russell, ed. Boston: Little, Brown, 1917.

Nicolay, John G., and John Hay. "Abraham Lincoln: A History." 40 parts.
    Century, Nov. 1886–Feb. 1890.

Parris, Albion Keith. "Recollections of Our Neighbors in the First Ward in the
    Early Sixties." *CHS* 29–30:269–289.

Pendel, Thomas. *Thirty-six Years in the White House*. Washington, D.C.: Neale,
    1902.

Pinkerton, Allan. *The Spy of the Rebellion*. Hartford: M. A. Winter & Hatch, 1883.

Poore, Benjamin Perley. *Perley's Reminiscences of Sixty Years in the National
    Metropolis*. Vol. 2. Philadelphia: Hubbard Brothers, 1886.

——. "Washington News." *Harper's Monthly* 48 (Jan. 1874), pp. 225–236.

Porter, Horace. *Campaigning with Grant*. Reprint. New York: Mallard Press,
    1991.

Pryor, Mrs. Roger A. *Reminiscences of Peace and War*. New York: Macmillan,
    1904.

Pryor, Sara Agnes. *My Day: Reminiscences of a Long Life*. New York: Macmillan,
    1909.

Pyne, Charles M., et al. *War History of the National Rifles, Co. A, 3d Bn., District of
    Columbia Volunteers of 1861*. Wilmington, Del.: Ferris Bros., 1887.

Reiff, W. C. "A Federal Prison Guard." *Confederate Veteran* 19 (1911):526.

Rhodehamel, John, and Louise Taper, eds. *Right or Wrong, God Judge Me: The
    Writings of John Wilkes Booth*. Urbana: University of Illinois, 1997.

"Richmond and Washington During the War." *Cornhill Magazine* 37
    (1863):93–102.

Rice, Allen Thorndike, ed. *Reminiscences of Abraham Lincoln by Distinguished
    Men of His Time*. New York: North American Review, 1885.

Riddle, Albert G. *Recollections of War Times: Reminiscences of Men and Events at
    Washington, 1860–1865*. New York: Putnam, 1895.

Rives, Jeannie Tree. "Old-Time Places and People in Washington." *CHS* 3
    (1900):73–80.

Russell, William Howard. *My Diary North and South*. Fletcher Pratt, ed. New
    York: Harper, 1954.

——. "Recollections of the Civil War," pts. 4 and 5. *North American Review*, May,
    June 1898.

Salm-Salm, Princess Felix. *Ten Years of My Life*. London: Richard Bentley,
    1876.

Schurz, Carl. *The Reminiscences of Carl Schurz*. New York: McClure, 1907.

"Slavery and the Slave Trade in the District of Columbia." Printed Ephemera
    Collection, Rare Books Division, LC.

Smallwood, Thomas. *Narrative of Thomas Smallwood (Coloured Man): Giving an
    Account of His Birth—The Period He was Held in Slavery—His Release—and
    Removal to Canada, etc. Together with an Account of the Underground Railroad*.
    Toronto: By the author, 1851.

Smith, George Williamson. "A Critical Moment for Washington." *CHS* 21
    (1918):87–113.

Snethen, Worthington G. *Snethen's Black Code of the District of Columbia, in Force
    September 1, 1848*. New York: A. & F. Abolition Society, 1848.

Stanton, Henry M. "A Page of Political Correspondence: Unpublished Letters of
    Mr. Stanton to Mr. Buchanan." *North American Review* 129, no. 276 (Nov.
    1879):474–482.

Sterling, Dorothy, ed. *Speak Out in Thunder Tones: Letters and Other Writings by Black Northerners, 1787–1865*. Garden City, N.Y.: Doubleday, 1973.

Stern, Philip Van Doren, ed. *The Life and Writings of Abraham Lincoln*. New York: Modern Library, 1940.

Still, William. *The Underground Rail Road*. Philadelphia: People's Publishing Co., 1879.

Stoddard, William O. *Inside the White House in War Times: Memoirs and Reports of Lincoln's Secretary*. Michael Burlingame, ed. Lincoln: University of Nebraska, 2000.

Stone, Charles P. "Washington on the Eve of the War." *Battles and Leaders* 1:7–25.

Strother, David Hunter. "Personal Recollections of the War." *Harper's Monthly* 36, no. 13 (Aug. 1867):273–297.

——. " 'Porte Crayon' in the Tidewater." Cecil D. Eby, Jr., ed. *Virginia Magazine of History and Biography* 67 (1959):438ff.

Sumner, Charles. Introduction to "Petroleum V. Nasby" in *The Moral History of America's Life-Struggle*. Boston: I. N. Richardson, 1866.

Sunderland, Byron. "Washington as I First Knew It, 1852–1855." *CHS* 5 (1902):195–211.

Survivors' Association, District of Columbia Volunteers '61 to '65. *Memorial to the U.S. Senate and House of Representatives*, 18 Jan. 1902.

Swinton, William. *Campaigns of the Army of the Potomac*. Reprint. Secaucus, N.J.: Blue & Grey, 1988.

Swisshelm, Jane Grey (Cannon). *Crusader and Feminist: Letters of Jane Grey Swisshelm*. Arthur J. Larsen, ed. St. Paul: Minnesota Historical Society, 1934.

——. *Half a Century*. Chicago: Jansen, McClurg, 1880.

Taft, Charles Sabin. "Abraham Lincoln's Last Hours." *Century* 45, no. 4 (Feb. 1893):634–636.

Thompson, James P. *Higher Arithmetic*. New York: Newman & Ivison, 1853.

Townsend, George Alfred. *Campaigns of a Non-Combatant and His Romaunt Abroad During the War*. New York: Blelock, 1866.

——. *Washington, Outside and Inside*. Hartford: James Betts, 1873.

Traubel, Horace. *With Walt Whitman in Camden*. New York: D. Appleton, 1908.

Trescot, William Henry. "Narrative and Letter of William Henry Trescot, Concerning Negotiations Between South Carolina and President Buchanan in December, 1860." Gaillard Hunt, ed. *North American Historical Review* 13 (1908):543–545.

Tripler, Eunice. *Eunice Tripler: Some Notes of Her Personal Recollections*. New York: Grafton Press, 1910.

Truth, Sojourner. *Narrative of Sojourner Truth, a Bondswoman of Olden Time*. Battle Creek, Mich.: For the author, 1878.

U.S. Circuit Court for District of Columbia. Records relating to slaves, 1851–1863, Manumission Papers, 1857–1863. Publication 433, Roll 3, National Archives.

U.S. House of Representatives. 36th Cong., 2nd sess. Report no. 79. *Alleged Hostile Organization Against the Government Within the District of Columbia*. Washington, D.C.: Government Printing Office, 1861.

——. 38th Cong., 1st sess. (1863). *Emancipation in the District of Columbia*.

——. 40th Cong., 1st sess. (1867). House Report 7, Serial set 1314, *Impeachment of the President.*

U.S. Navy Department. *Official Records of the Union and Confederate Navies in the War of the Rebellion* (cited as *ORN*). Washington, D.C.: Government Printing Office, 1894–1922.

U.S. War Department, Provost Marshal, Department of Washington. "Bawdy Houses." 22nd Army Corps, 1864–1865, RG 393, vol. 298, National Archives.

——. Quartermaster General. Functions Cemeterial, 1929–1929, General Correspondence and Reports, National and Post Cemeteries, Arlington, 1865–c.1914.

——. "Rebel Property Seized in Washington City." Letter from the Secretary of War in Answer to Resolution of the House, of the 12th Instant . . . , Jan. 20, 1863.

——. *The War of the Rebellion: Official Records of the Union and Confederate Armies* (cited as OR). Washington: Government Printing Office, 1880–1901.

Viele, Egbert L. "A Trip with Lincoln, Chase and Stanton." *Scribner's Monthly* 16, no. 6 (Oct. 1878):813–822.

Villard, Henry. *Memoirs of Henry Villard, Journalist and Financier, 1835–1900.* 2 vols. Reprint. New York: Da Capo Press, 1969.

——. "Recollections of Lincoln." *Atlantic Monthly* 93, no. 556 (Feb. 1904): 165–174.

Walter, Thomas F. "Personal Recollections and Experiences of an Obscure Soldier." *Grand Army Scout and Soldiers' Mail* 3, no. 35 (9 Aug. 1884).

Wardwell, Ernest. "Military Waif: A Sidelight on the Baltimore Riot of 19 April 1861." Frank Towers, ed. *Maryland Historical Magazine* 89 (Winter 1994):427–446.

Warner, Brainard H. "Extracts from Letters of the Late Brainard H. Warner, Written from Washington in 1863." *CHS* 31:311–323.

"Washington City." *DeBow's Review* 24 (June 1858):502–508.

Webb, Alexander S. *The Peninsula: McClellan's Campaign of 1862.* New York: Scribner, 1882.

Weitzel, Godfrey. *Richmond Occupied.* Louis H. Manarin, ed. Richmond: Civil War Centennial Committee, 1965.

Welles, Gideon. *The Diary of Gideon Welles.* 3 vols. Boston: Houghton Mifflin, 1909.

——. "Fort Pickens: Facts in Relation to the Reinforcement of Fort Pickens, in the Spring of 1861." *Galaxy* 11, no. 1 (Jan. 1871):92–107.

——. "Mr. Lincoln and Mr. Seward." *Galaxy* 16, no. 5 (Nov. 1873):687–700.

Whitman, George W. *Civil War Letters of George Washington Whitman.* Jerome Loving, ed. Durham: Duke University Press, 1975.

Whitman, Walt. *Specimen Days in America.* Reprint. London: Oxford University, 1931.

——. "Walt Whitman in War-Time: Familiar Letters from the Capital." *Century* 46, no. 6 (Oct. 1893):840–851.

[Wilson, Henry.] "Edwin M. Stanton." *Atlantic Monthly* 25, no. 148 (Feb. 1870):234–246.

——. "Jeremiah S. Black and Edwin M. Stanton." *Atlantic Monthly* 26, no. 156 (Oct. 1870):463–475.

Windle, Mary Jane. *Life in Washington, and Life Here and There.* Philadelphia: J. B. Lippincott, 1859.

Wormeley, Katherine. *The Cruel Side of War.* Boston: Roberts Brothers, 1898.

Wright, Mrs. D. Giraud. *A Southern Girl in '61: The War-Time Memories of a Confederate Senator's Daughter.* New York: Doubleday, Page, 1905.

Wyeth, S. D. *Federal City.* Washington: Gibson Brothers, 1868.

SECONDARY SOURCES

Abell, Julie D., and Petar D. Glumac. "Beneath the MCI Center: Insights into Washington's Historic Water Supply." *Washington History* 9, no. 1 (Spring/Summer 1997):24–41.

Allen, William C. *The Dome of the United States Capitol: An Architectural History.* Washington, D.C.: Government Printing Office, 1992.

——. *The United States Capitol: A Brief Architectural History.* Washington, D.C.: Architect of the Capitol, 1990.

Ames, William E. "The National Intelligencer: Washington's Leading Political Newspaper." *CHS* 66–68:71–83.

Anthony, Carl Sferrazza. *First Ladies: The Saga of the Presidents' Wives and Their Power, 1789–1961.* New York: Morrow, 1990.

Arms, Florence. *Bright Morning.* Boston: Bruce Humphries, 1962.

Bakeless, John Edwin. *Spies of the Confederacy.* Philadelphia: Lippincott, 1970.

Baker, Jean H. *Mary Todd Lincoln: A Biography.* New York: Norton, 1987.

Barbee, David Rankin. "Washington Society in the 1860s." Barbee papers, Georgetown University.

Barber, James G. *Alexandria in the Civil War.* Lynchburg: H. E. Howard, 1988.

Belden, Thomas Graham, and Marva Robbins Belden. *So Fell the Angels.* Boston: Little, Brown, 1956.

Bell, Felicia. "Slave Labor and the Capitol: A Commentary." *The Capitol Dome,* special issue. Washington, D.C.: U.S. Capitol Historical Society, 2003.

Benjamin, Marcus, ed. *Washington During War Time: A Series of Papers Showing the Military, Political, and Social Phases During 1861 to 1865.* Washington, D.C.: National Tribune, 1901.

Billings, Elden E. "Early Women Journalists of Washington." *CHS* 66–68:84–97.

——. "Military Activities in Washington in 1861." *CHS* 60–62:123–133.

——. "Social and Economic Conditions in Washington During the Civil War." *CHS* 63–65:191–209.

Blackwell, Sarah Ellen. *A Military Genius: Life of Anna Ella Carroll, of Maryland.* 2 vols. Washington: Judd & Detweiler, 1891–1895.

Blanton, DeAnne. "Woman Soldiers of the Civil War," pt. 3. *Prologue* 25, no. 1 (Spring 1993).

Boatner, Mark Mayo III. *Civil War Dictionary.* New York: David McKay, 1959.

Bolin, Benny. "Spencer M. Clark: Cornerstone of the Bureau of Printing and Engraving." *Paper Money Whole,* no. 135.

Boney, F. N. *John Letcher of Virginia: The Story of Virginia's Civil War Governor.* University: University of Alabama Press, 1966.

Boyle, Regis Louise. *Mrs. E.D.E.N. Southworth, Novelist.* Washington, D.C.: Catholic University, 1939.

Brewer, W. M. "Henry Highland Garnet." *Journal of Negro History* 13 (Jan. 1928):36–52.

Brockett, L. P., and Mary C. Vaughan. *Woman's Work in the Civil War: A Record of Heroism, Patriotism and Patience.* Philadelphia: Zeigler, McCurdy & Co., 1867.

Brodie, Fawn M. *Thaddeus Stevens: Scourge of the South.* New York: Norton, 1959.

Bruce, Robert V. *Lincoln and the Tools of War.* Indianapolis: Bobbs-Merrill, 1956.

Bryan, Wilhelmus. *The History of the National Capital.* 2 vols. New York: Macmillan, 1916.

Bullard, F. Lauriston. *Famous War Correspondents.* Boston: Little, Brown, 1914.

Burton, Harold H., and Thomas E. Waggaman. "The Story of the Place: Where First and A Streets Formerly Met at What Is Now the Site of the Supreme Court Building." *CHS* 51–52:138–147.

Canby, Courtland, ed. *Lincoln and the Civil War: A Profile and a History.* New York: Braziller, 1960.

Carroll, Daniel. "Henry Mercier in Washington, 1860–1863." Ph.D. dissertation, University of Pennsylvania, 1968.

Cary, Francine Curro. *Urban Odyssey: A Multicultural History of Washington, D.C.* Washington, D.C.: Smithsonian Institution Press, 1996.

Chandler, Lucinda B. "Anna Ella Carroll: The Great Unrecognized Military Genius of the War of the Rebellion." *Godey's Magazine,* Sept. 1886, pp. 249–267.

Clark, Allen C. *Abraham Lincoln in the National Capital.* Washington: priv. pub., 1925.

——. "Beau Hickman (Robert S. Hickman)." *CHS* 40–41:79–98.

——. "Richard Wallach and the Times of His Mayoralty." *CHS* 21 (1918):195–245.

Clark-Lewis, Elizabeth, ed. *First Freed: Washington, D.C., in the Emancipation Era.* Washington, D.C.: A. P. Foundation, 1998.

Clephane, Walter C. "The Local Aspect of Slavery in the District of Columbia." *CHS* 3 (1900):224–256.

Cohen, Anthony M. "The Underground Railroad in Montgomery County." *The Montgomery County Story* 38, no. 1 (Feb. 1995):1–4.

Commager, Henry Steele, ed. *The Blue and the Gray.* 2 vols. Reprint. New York: New American Library, 1973.

Conlin, Michael F. "The Smithsonian Abolition Lecture Controversy: The Clash of Antislavery Politics with American Science in Wartime Washington." *Civil War History* 46, no. 4 (2000):301–323.

Conradis, Albert E. "The Battle of the Monocacy." *The Montgomery County Story* 1, no. 1 (Nov. 1957):1–5.

Cooke, Michael A. "Physical Environment and Sanitation in the District of Columbia 1860–1868." *CHS* 52:289–303.

Cooling, Benjamin F. "Defending Washington During the Civil War." *CHS* 71–72:314–317.

——. *Jubal Early's Raid on Washington, 1864.* Baltimore: Naval & Aeronautical, 1989.

Corrigan, Mary Beth. "Imaginary Cruelties? A History of the Slave Trade in Washington, D.C." *Washington History* 13, no. 2:5–27.

Coryell, Janet L. *Neither Heroine Nor Fool: Anna Ella Carroll of Maryland.* Kent, Ohio: Kent State University, 1990.

Cox, William V. "The Defenses of Washington: General Early's Advance on the Capital and the Battle of Fort Stevens, on July 11 and 12, 1864." *CHS* 4 (1901):135–165.

Crofts, Daniel W. *Reluctant Confederates: Upper South Unionists in the Secession Crisis.* Chapel Hill: University of North Carolina, 1989.

Curtis, William T. S. "Cabin John Bridge." *CHS* 2 (1899):293ff.

Cuthbert, Norma B. *Lincoln and the Baltimore Plot, 1861: From Pinkerton Records and Related Papers.* San Marino, Calif.: Huntington Library, 1949.

Dannett, Sylvia G., ed. *Noble Women of the North.* New York: Thomas Yoseloff, 1959.

Davis, Curtis Carroll. "The 'Old Capitol' and Its Keeper: How William P. Wood Ran a Civil War Prison." *CHS* 52:207–234.

Davis, William C. *Jefferson Davis: The Man and His Hour.* New York: HarperCollins, 1991.

Dickinson, William C., Dean A. Herrin and Donald R. Kennon, eds. *Montgomery C. Meigs and the Building of the Nation's Capital.* Athens: Ohio University, 2001.

Dobyns, Kenneth W. *The Patent Office Pony: A History of the Early Patent Office.* Spotsylvania, Va.: Sergeant Kirkland's Press, 1997.

Donald, David Herbert. *Lincoln.* New York: Random House, 1995.

Downing, Margaret Brent. "Literary Landmarks, Being a Brief Account of Celebrated Authors Who Have Lived in Washington, the Location of Their Homes, and What They Have Written." *CHS* 19 (1916):23–60.

Durkin, Joseph T. *Georgetown University: First in the Nation's Capital.* Garden City, N.Y.: Doubleday, 1964.

Ellis, John B. *The Sights and Secrets of the National Capital.* New York: United States Publishing Company, 1859.

Emery, Fred A. "Washington Newspapers." *CHS* 37–38:41–68.

Evans, Thomas R. "Tells Story of Flying Machine of Confederacy." Reprint from Richmond *News Leader,* Sept. 22, 1909. *Southern Historical Society Papers* 37:302–303.

Everly, Elaine C. "Freedmen's Bureau Records." *Prologue* 29, no. 2 (Summer 1997):95–104.

Fairman, Charles E. *Art and Artists of the Capitol of the United States of America.* Washington, D.C.: Government Printing Office, 1927.

Fessenden, Francis. *Life and Public Services of William Pitt Fessenden.* Boston: Houghton Mifflin, 1907.

Fitzsimons, Mrs. Neal. " 'Uncle Tom' in Montgomery County." 2 pts. *The Montgomery County Story* 18, nos. 1 and 2 (Feb., May 1975).

Fraser, Richard A. R. "How Did Lincoln Die?" *American Heritage* 6 (Feb.–Mar. 1995):63ff.

Freeman, Douglas Southall. *Lee's Lieutenants: A Study in Command.* 3 vols. New York: Scribner's, 1942–1944.

——. *R. E. Lee: A Biography.* 4 vols. New York: Scribner's. 1935.

Furgurson, Ernest B. *Ashes of Glory: Richmond at War.* New York: Knopf, 1996.

Gibbs, C. R. *Black, Copper and Bright: The District of Columbia's Black Civil War Regiment.* Silver Spring, Md.: Three Dimensional Publishing, n.d.

Gilbert, Olive. *Narrative of Sojourner Truth.* Boston: By the author, 1850.

Goode, James Moore. "Architecture, Politics and Conflict: Thomas Ustick Walter and the Enlargement of the United States Capitol, 1850–1865." Ph.D. dissertation, George Washington University, 1995.

Graf, Mercedes. "Women Physicians in the Civil War." *Prologue* 32, no. 2 (Summer 2000):87–98.

Gray, Carole. "I Love Lucy!" *American Atheist* 37, no. 2 (Spring 1997), n.p.

Green, Constance McLaughlin. *Secret City: A History of Race Relations in the Nation's Capital.* Princeton: Princeton University, 1967.

——. *Washington: Village and Capital, 1800–1878.* 2 vols. Princeton: Princeton University, 1962.

Greenbie, Marjorie Barstow. *Lincoln's Daughters of Mercy.* New York: Putnam, 1944.

Greenbie, Sydney, and Marjorie Barstow Greenbie. *Anna Ella Carroll and Abraham Lincoln: A Biography.* Manchester, Me.: University of Tampa Press in cooperation with Falmouth Publishing House, 1952.

Gue, Benjamin F. *History of Iowa.* 4 vols. New York: Century History Co., 1903.

Guelzo, Allen C. "A Reluctant Recruit to the Abolitionist Cause." *Washington Post,* 11 Feb. 2001.

Hall, Herbert A. "Lincoln & His Quartermaster General." *Quartermaster Review,* May–June 1950.

Hanson, Joseph Mills. *Bull Run Remembers.* Manassas, Va.: National Capitol Publishers, 1953.

Harrison, Noel G. "Atop an Anvil: The Civilians' War in Fairfax and Alexandria Counties, Apr. 1861–Apr. 1862." *Virginia Magazine of History & Biography* 106, no. 2 (Spring 1998):133–164.

Hassler, Warren W. *Commanders of the Army of the Potomac.* Baton Rouge: Louisiana State University, 1962.

Hebert, Walter H. *Fighting Joe Hooker.* Indianapolis: Bobbs-Merrill, 1944.

Helm, Katherine. *The True Story of Mary, Wife of Lincoln.* New York: Harper, 1928.

Hendrick, Burton J. *Lincoln's War Cabinet.* Boston: Little, Brown, 1946.

Hennessey, John J. "War Watchers at Bull Run." *Civil War Times,* Aug. 2001, pp. 41–47, 67–73.

Hickin, Patricia. "Yankees Come to Fairfax County." *Virginia Cavalcade* 26, no. 1 (Winter 1977):100–109.

Horan, James D. *Desperate Women.* New York: Putnam, 1952.

"A Jewish Soldier." "Sketches from the Seat of War." *Jewish Messenger,* Nov. 1861.

Junior League of Washington. *The City of Washington: An Illustrated History.* New York: Knopf, 1977.

Kane, Harnett T. *Spies for the Blue and Gray.* Garden City, N.Y.: Hanover House, 1954.

Kaplan, Justin. *Walt Whitman: A Life.* New York: Simon & Schuster, 1980.

Ketchum, Richard M., ed. *The American Heritage Picture History of the Civil War.* New York: American Heritage, 1960

Kimmel, Stanley. *Mr. Lincoln's Washington.* New York: Coward-McCann, 1957.

King, John P. Notes on Washington, D.C., Theatre Collection, 1800–1945. Special Collections Register, Historical Society of Washington.

Klein, Maury. *Days of Defiance: Sumter, Secession, and the Coming of the Civil War.* New York: Knopf, 1997.

Kunhardt, Philip B., Jr., Philip B. Kunhardt III and Peter B. Kunhardt. *Lincoln.* New York: Knopf, 1992.

Laughlin, Clara E. *The Death of Lincoln.* New York: Doubleday, 1909.

Lee, Richard M. *Mr. Lincoln's City: An Illustrated Guide to the Civil War Sites of Washington.* McLean, Va.: EPM Publications, 1981.

Leech, Margaret. *Reveille in Washington 1860–1865.* New York: Harper, 1941.

Leonard, Elizabeth D. *Yankee Women: Gender Battles in the Civil War.* New York: Norton, 1994.

Lessoff, Alan. *The Nation and Its City: Politics, Corruption and Progress in Washington, D.C., 1861–1902.* Lexington: University of Kentucky Press, 1994.

Life of Col. James Fisk, Jr. Chicago: J. W. Goodspeed, 1872.

"Lincoln and the Lively Arts." *Lincoln Lore* 1508 (Oct. 1963).

Long, E. B. *The Civil War Day by Day.* Garden City, N.Y.: Doubleday, 1971.

Lowry, Thomas P. *The Story the Soldiers Wouldn't Tell.* Mechanicsburg, Pa.: Stackpole, 1998.

Massey, Mary Elizabeth. *Bonnet Brigades.* New York: Knopf, 1966.

McFeely, William S. *Frederick Douglass.* New York: Norton, 1991.

McPherson, James M. *Battle Cry of Freedom: The Civil War Era.* New York: Oxford University Press, 1988.

Mearns, David C. "A View of Washington in 1863." *CHS* 63–65:210–220.

Melder, Keith E. "Angel of Mercy in Washington: Josephine Griffing and the Freedmen, 1865–1872." *CHS* 63–65:243–272.

———, with Melinda Young Stewart. *City of Magnificent Intentions: A History of Washington, District of Columbia.* Washington, D.C.: Intac, 1997.

———. "Slaves and Freedmen." *Wilson Quarterly* 13, no. 1 (1989):77–83.

Miers, Earl Schenck, ed. *Lincoln Day by Day.* Washington: U.S. Lincoln Sesquicentennial Commission, 1960.

Milburn, Page. "The Emancipation of Slaves in the District of Columbia." *CHS* 16 (1913):96–119.

Miller, David G. *Second Only to Grant: Quartermaster General Montgomery C. Meigs.* Shippensburg, Pa.: White Mane Press, 2000.

Miller, Nathan. *The Founding Finaglers and Other Scoundrels.* New York: David McKay, 1976.

Mitchell, Mary. *Divided Town.* Barre, Mass.: Barre Publishers, 1968.

———. "An Intimate Journey Through Georgetown in April 1863." *CHS* 60–62:84–102.

———. "I Held George Washington's Horse: Compensated Emancipation in the District of Columbia." *CHS* 63–64:230–240.

Mitchell, Pauline Gaskins. "Mt. Zion Church and Cemetery." *CHS* 51:103ff.

Mogelever, Jacob. *Death to Traitors: The Story of General Lafayette C. Baker, Lincoln's Forgotten Secret Service Chief.* New York: Doubleday, 1960.

Montgomery, Dean R. "The Willard Hotels of Washington, D.C., 1847–1968." *CHS* 66–68: 277–293.

Morison, Samuel Eliot. "The Peace Convention of February, 1861." *Massachusetts Historical Society Papers* 73:58–80.

Morris, Roy, Jr. *The Better Angel: Walt Whitman in the Civil War.* New York: Oxford University, 2000.

Muir, Dorothy Troth. *Presence of a Lady: Mount Vernon 1861–1868.* Reprint. Mt. Vernon, Va.: Mount Vernon Ladies Association, 1993.

Murray, Martin G. "Pete the Great: A Biography of Peter Doyle." *Walt Whitman Quarterly Review* 12 (Summer 1994).

———. "Traveling With the Wounded: Walt Whitman and Washington's Civil War Hospitals." *Washington History* 8 (1996–1997):58–73.

National Park Service. Special Resource Study Draft, "President Lincoln and Soldiers' Home National Monument." Washington, D.C.: U.S. Department of the Interior, 2002.

——. *Underground Railroad.* Washington, D.C.: Department of the Interior, 1998.

Painter, Nell Irvin. *Sojourner Truth: A Life, A Symbol.* New York: Norton, 1996.

Parker, Richard B. "Neighbors of the Cosmos Club." *Cosmos Journal,* 2001.

Pasternak, Martin B. *Rise Now and Fly to Arms: The Life of Henry Highland Garnet.* New York: Garland Publishing, 1995.

Paullin, Charles O. "Alexandria County in 1861." *CHS* 28 (1925):107–131.

Perry, Leslie J. "Lincoln's Home Life in Washington." *Harper's Monthly* 94, no. 561 (Feb. 1897):353–359.

Pinsker, Matthew. "Lincoln's Wartime Retreat." Seen in MS, published as *Lincoln's Sanctuary: Abraham Lincoln and the Soldiers' Home.* New York: Oxford University Press, 2003.

Powell, Frances J. "Statistical Profile of the Black Family in Washington, D.C., 1850–1880." *CHS* 52:269–288.

Pratt, Fletcher. *Stanton: Lincoln's Secretary of War.* New York: Norton, 1953.

Press, Donald E. "South of the Avenue: From Murder Bay to the Federal Triangle." *CHS* 51:51–70.

Quarles, Benjamin. *The Negro in the Civil War.* Boston: Little, Brown, 1953.

Reed, Robert. *Old Washington, D.C. in Early Photographs 1846–1932.* New York: Dover, 1980.

Renehan, Edward J., Jr. *John Burroughs: An American Naturalist.* Post Hills, Vt.: Chelsea Green Publishing, 1992.

Rhodes, James Ford. *History of the United States.* Vol. 5. New York: Macmillan, 1919.

Ribblett, David L. "Saviors of Mount Vernon." *Civil War* 21 (Dec. 1987):21–26.

Richards, Laura E., and Maud Howe Elliott. *Julia Ward Howe.* 2 vols. Boston: Houghton Mifflin, 1916.

Ricks, Mary Kay. "A Passage to Freedom." *Washington Post Magazine,* 17 Feb. 2002.

Ritchie, Donald A. *Press Gallery: Congress and the Washington Correspondents.* Cambridge: Harvard University Press, 1991.

Robertson, James I., Jr. "Old Capitol: Eminence to Infamy." *Maryland Historical Magazine* 65 (1970):394–412.

Rogers, J. A. *Africa's Gift to America: The Afro-Americans in the Making and Saving of the United States.* New York: Futuro Press, 1959.

Rollin, Frank A. *Life and Public Services of Martin R. Delany.* Boston: Lee & Shepard, 1883.

Rorie, Patricia. "Belle Boyd." *Blue & Gray Magazine,* (Aug.–Sept. 1984).

Rose, P. K. "The Civil War: Black American Contributions to Union Intelligence." *Studies in Intelligence* (Winter 1998–1999).

Ross, Ishbel. *Rebel Rose: Life of Rose O'Neal Greenhow, Confederate Spy.* New York: Harper, 1954.

Russell, Hilary. "Underground Railroad Activists in Washington, D.C." *Washington History* 13, no. 2:29–49.

Scharf, J. Thomas. *The Chronicles of Baltimore; Being a Complete History of "Baltimore Town" and Baltimore City.* Baltimore: Turnbull Brothers, 1874.

——. *History of Maryland, from the Earliest Period to the Present Day.* 3 vols. Reprint. Hatboro, Pa.: Tradition Press, 1967.

Schildt, Bobbi. "Freedman's Village." *Northern Virginia Heritage* (Feb. 1985).

"Slavery and the Slave Trade in the District of Columbia." *Negro History Bulletin* (Oct. 1950).

Smith, Edward C. "Keeper of the Keys." *Civil War* 31 (Dec. 1989):16–18.

Smith, Gene. *American Gothic: The Story of America's Legendary Theatrical Family—Junius, Edwin, and John Wilkes Booth.* New York: Simon & Schuster, 1992.

——. "The Booth Obsession." *Civil War Chronicles* 3, no. 3 (Winter 1994):40–53.

Smith, George Williamson. "A Critical Moment for Washington." *CHS* 21:87–113.

Smithsonian Institution. "Archaeological Investigations, National Museum of the American Indian Site, Washington, D.C." 17 (Dec. 1997).

Snow, Richard F. "Belle Boyd." In *The Civil War: The Best of American Heritage.* Stephen W. Sears, ed. Boston: Houghton Mifflin, 1991.

Snyder, Charles McCool. *Dr. Mary Walker: The Little Lady in Pants.* Reprint. New York: Arno Press, 1974.

Stafford, Marshall P. *A Life of James Fisk, Jr.: A Free & Accurate Narrative of His Career, His Great Enterprises, and His Assassination.* New York: Polhemus & Pearson, 1872.

Steers, Edward, Jr. "The Escape and Capture of George A. Atzerodt." *The Montgomery County Story* 26, no. 3 (Aug. 1983):62–72.

Stein, Alice P. "The North's Unsung Sisters of Mercy." *Civil War Magazine,* (Sept. 1999).

Steuart, Richard D. "Henry A. Steuart—Rebel Spy." *Confederate Veteran* 16 (1908):332–334.

——. "Truth Is Mighty." *Confederate Veteran* 24 (1916):266–267.

Swanberg, W. A. *Jim Fisk: The Career of an Improbable Rascal.* New York: Scribner, 1959.

Swift, Hildegarde Hoyt. *The Edge of April: A Biography of John Burroughs.* New York: Morrow, 1957.

Tapp, Bruce. *Over Lincoln's Shoulder: The Committee on the Conduct of the War.* Lawrence: University Press of Kansas, 1998.

Tarbell, Ida M. *The Life of Abraham Lincoln.* Vol. 2. New York: Lincoln Memorial Association, 1895.

Thomas, Benjamin P. *Abraham Lincoln.* New York: Knopf, 1952.

——, and Harold M. Hyman. *Stanton: The Life and Times of Lincoln's Secretary of War.* New York: Knopf, 1962.

Tidball, Eugene C. "The View from the Top of the Knoll: Captain John C. Tidball's Memoir of First Battle at Bull Run." *Civil War History* 44, no. 3 (Sept. 1998):175–193.

Tidwell, William A., with James O. Hall and David Winfrey Gaddy. *Come Retribution: The Confederate Secret Service and the Assassination of Abraham Lincoln.* Jackson: University of Mississippi Press, 1988.

Tindall, William. "Beginnings of Street Railways in the National Capital." *CHS* 21:24–60.

——. "Booth's Escape from Washington After the Assassination of Lincoln, His Subsequent Wanderings and His Final Capture." *CHS* 19 (1916):1–24.

Trefousse, Hans L. *The Radical Republicans.* New York: Knopf, 1969.

Trudeau, Noah André. *Like Men of War: Black Troops in the Civil War 1861–1865.* Boston: Little, Brown, 1998.

Truett, Randall Bond, ed. *Washington, D.C.: A Guide to the Nation's Capital.* Originally Compiled by the Federal Writers' Program of the Work Projects Administration. New York: Hastings House, 1968.

[Turner, Sarah] "Troops in the Capitol During the Civil War." Typescript monograph, Curator's Office, Architect of the Capitol.

Tyler, Frederick S. "100th Anniversary of Ascension Parish in the District of Columbia." *CHS* 46–47:73–75.

U.S. Congress, Joint Select Committee to Investigate the Charities and Reformatory Institutions of the District of Columbia. Part III—Historical Sketches. Washington, Government Printing Office, 1898.

U.S. Department of the Interior, National Park Service. "Ford's Theatrical Venture." N.d.

Walsh, Richard, and William Lloyd Fox, eds. *Maryland: A History, 1634–1974.* Baltimore: Maryland Historical Society, 1974.

Ward, Geoffrey C. *The Civil War: An Illustrated History.* New York: Knopf, 1990.

Waugh, John C. *Reelecting Lincoln: The Battle for the 1864 Presidency.* New York: Crown, 1997.

Weaver, C. P., ed. *Thank God My Regiment an African One: The Civil War Diary of Colonel Nathan W. Daniels.* Baton Rouge: Louisiana State University Press, 1998.

Weidman, Budge. "The Fight for Equal Rights: Black Soldiers in the Civil War: Preserving the Legacy of the United States Colored Troops." *Prologue* 29, no. 2 (Summer 1997):91–94.

Weigley, Russell F. *Quartermaster General of the Union Army: A Biography of M. C. Meigs.* New York: Columbia University Press, 1959.

Weisberger, Bernard A. *Reporters for the Union.* Boston: Little, Brown, 1953.

Whyte, James H. "Divided Loyalties in Washington During the Civil War." *CHS* 60–62:103–122.

Wilkinson, Lucille Warfield. "Early Baptists in Washington, D.C." *CHS* 29–30:211ff.

Willard, Henry Kellogg. "Henry Augustus Willard: His Life and Times." *CHS* 20 (1917):239–252.

Williams, Melvin R. "A Blueprint for Change: The Black Community in Washington, D.C., 1860–1870." *CHS* 71–72: 359–393.

Williams, T. Harry. *Lincoln and His Generals.* New York: Knopf, 1952.

Wilson, James Grant, and John Fiske, eds. *Appleton's Cyclopedia of American Biography.* New York: D. Appleton, 1887–1889.

Wojcik, Susan Brizzolara. "Thomas U. Walter and Iron in the United States Capitol: An Alliance of Architecture, Engineering, and Industry." Ph.D. dissertation, University of Delaware, 1999.

Wright, William C. *The Secession Movement in the Middle Atlantic States.* Rutherford, N.J.: Fairleigh Dickinson University Press, 1973.

Wyeth, S. D. *The Federal City.* Washington, D.C.: Gibson Brothers, 1865.

Young, Harvey. "Anna Elizabeth Dickinson and the Civil War: For and Against Lincoln." *Mississippi Valley Historical Review* 31 (June 1944).

Younger, Edward. *John A. Kasson: Politics and Diplomacy from Lincoln to McKinley.* Iowa City: State Historical Society of Iowa, 1955.

NEWSPAPERS

Atlanta Confederacy
Baltimore American
Baltimore Sun

Berkshire County (Mass.) *Eagle*
Boston Herald
Boston Journal
Cambridge (Mass.) *Chronicle*
Charlestown (Mass.) *Advertiser*
Chelsea (Mass.) *Telegraph and Pioneer*
Cincinnati Commercial
Cincinnati Gazette
Dedham (Mass.) *Gazette*
Harrisburg Telegraph
Harper's Weekly (New York)
Iowa State Register (Des Moines)
Jackson Mississippian
Jewish Times (New York)
Leslie's Illustrated Newspaper (New York)
National Tribune (Washington)
New Orleans Crescent
New York Commercial Advertiser
New York Daily News
New York Herald
New York Mercury
New York Times
New York Tribune
Oswego (N.Y.) *Times*
Philadelphia Inquirer
Philadelphia Sunday Dispatch
Philadelphia Weekly Times
Providence Press
Richmond Enquirer
Richmond Examiner
Richmond Whig
St. Cloud (Minn.) *Democrat*
Southern Illustrated News (Richmond)
Springfield (Mass.) *Republican*
Washington Congressional Globe
Washington Constitution
Washington Daily Chronicle
Washington Evening Star
Washington National Intelligencer
Washington National Republican
Washington Post
Washington States
Washington Sunday Chronicle
Washington Sunday Gazette
Winsted (Conn.) *Herald*

Index

Page numbers in *italics* refer to maps.

Printed in the United States
by Baker & Taylor Publisher Services